Managing and
Networking AutoCAD®

Kenneth W. Billing

New Riders Publishing, Carmel, Indiana

Managing and Networking AutoCAD®

By Kenneth W. Billing

Published by:
New Riders Publishing
11711 N. College Ave., Suite 140
Carmel, IN 46032 USA

Printed in the United States of America 1 2 3 4 5 6 7 8 9 0
Library of Congress Cataloging-in-Publication Data

Billing, Kenneth W., 1959-
      Managing and Networking AutoCAD / by Kenneth W. Billing.
         p. cm.
      Includes bibliographical references and index.
      ISBN 0-934035-85-7 : $29.95
         1. AutoCAD (Computer program)   2. Computer networks.   I. Title.
T835.B55 1991
620'.0042'02855369—dc20   91-2653
                                                          CIP

Publisher
David P. Ewing

Product Director
Rusty Gesner

Developmental Editor
Tim Huddleston

Editors
Rob Tidrow
Rich Limacher

Technical Editors
Robert L. Knight
William R. Valaski

Book Design and Production
William Hartman, Hartman Publishing

Proofreader
Susan Huddleston

Indexed by
Jill D. Bomaster
Susan VandeWalle

Composed in Bookman and American Typewriter by
William Hartman, Hartman Publishing

About the Author

Kenneth W. Billing has been consulting on AutoCAD networks, management, customization, AutoLISP programming, and presentation graphics since 1985. He is a former chairperson of the SPOCAD AutoCAD User Group at Gonzaga University and served as CAD manager for MW Consulting Engineers of Spokane, WA. There, he introduced a progressive AutoCAD implementation and one of the first AutoCAD/ Novell NetWare networks in the Northwest.

Mr. Billing holds an Associate of Specialized Technology degree in Computer-Aided Design from Miller Institute, and attended the college of architecture at Montana State University. He currently is Senior Project Editor and Technical Developer for New Riders Publishing, where he is responsible for maintaining the technical superiority and practicality of the New Riders line of computer books and disks.

New Riders Publishing extends special thanks to the following contributors to this book:

Steven Lee, who developed the section on Sun NFS for Chapter 7. Mr. Lee is Director of Technology for AVCOM Systems, Inc., Palo Alto, CA, and specializes in the integration of workstations and PCs into CAD/CAM and electronic design automation networks.

Randy Soultz, who contributed the material on LAN Manager for Chapter 7. Mr. Soultz is PC/LAN Administrator at Shambaugh and Son, Inc., Ft. Wayne, IN, a construction/engineering firm specializing in design/build projects.

Evan Yares, who developed the section on LANtastic for Chapter 7. Mr. Yares is a CAD integration consultant for Design Automation System, Inc., Phoenix, AZ. He also is a contributing editor for *CADalyst* magazine and a contributing technical editor for *PC Week* magazine.

Acknowledgments

A host of people have contributed in many ways to making this book what it is. Space permits me to acknowledge only a few of them here. To all those who are not mentioned individually, please accept my unwritten gratitude. You are remembered.

My thanks to Christopher Klompe, who recounted much of the CAD history of Boeing, which was used in Chapter 1. Also to the many others I interviewed who manage AutoCAD networks every day, especially those who completed the lengthy survey. You have helped further the industry's understanding of CAD management.

Many companies provided beta and released software that aided in the development of this book. I especially want to thank Novell, Inc. for supplying Advanced NetWare 2.15; Saber Software for Saber Menu System, Saber Meter, Saber Print Manager, and Saber Secure; and LAN Systems, Inc., for LANSpace. Special thanks go to Janet Florentin and the great folks at Cheyenne Software for their help in getting ARCserve to work with our changing network. Also, I salute Collette Bunton and Acer America Corp. for providing an Acer 1100/33 computer that performed flawlessly no matter what was thrown at it. I appreciate David Brown and Dean Warren at Nehalem Bay Software Inc. for giving us first glimpses, then a demo copy of Drawing Manager. Thanks also to Vincent Everts at Cyco International for AutoBASE; to Mark Reineck of Automation Software Consultants, Inc. for Net EDMS and Plotware; and to Dale Hays of ACS Telecom for AutoEDMS, which arrived too late to be included in this edition (what a time to get sick, Dale). Thanks to Bob Palioca and the people at KETIV Technologies, Inc. for support with many critical details. To all these companies, yours are the businesses that are genuinely serious about CAD and network productivity. I wish you continued success.

Several people volunteered the time to provide us with valuable feedback on this book during its early stages. I appreciate Manuel Pena of Standard Steel, Kristine Fallon of Computer Technology Management, Inc., and James Carrington of Autodesk, Inc. for their impressions and observations, and especially Carl Machover for his flattering words. Thanks also go out to all of the Autodesk staff and other forumites who share their knowledge and time on the ADESK forum of CompuServe. You know who you are. Your unselfish commitment to the promotion and development of AutoCAD is truly amazing.

At New Riders Publishing, I am indebted to Rusty Gesner for believing in this project and giving me the opportunity to write this book, to Tim Huddleston for the incessant queries that challenged me to dig a little deeper, and to everyone else at New Riders who lent their advice and suggestions for this experiment in eclectic computer books. Your support was crucial.

The people to whom I am the most grateful are my wife Patty, and my children Brian and Kristin. Their sacrifices over the last year and a half may never be fully repaid. I dedicate this book to your patience.

Above all, I thank God for creating within me a spirit that, strengthened by His love, was not bound by the circumstances and experiences of this life, but overcame them. Without Him, my ideas for this book would never have been born, nor I.

Trademark Acknowledgments

Warning and Disclaimer

Contents at a Glance

Table of Contents

Part One

Part Three

XV

11 System Maintenance and Development 331

Part Four

Appendixes

Foreword

As a CAD consultant, I often am asked by my clients to recommend a particular system. Over the years, I have made it a policy not to make such recommendations because I feel that the selection of a particular system is only one of the factors that contribute to that system's success in a given installation. In fact, I frequently tell my clients that while ten percent of their success depends on the selection of the system, 90 percent depends on their attention to detail in managing the system. After the system has been selected, the client needs to be committed to that system.

Therefore, it was a delight for me to read Ken Billing's book, *Managing and Networking AutoCAD*. There are few books that talk about what I consider to the most important issues of CAD/CAM; that is, how to organize the work and manage the installation, rather than the details of features and functions. Certainly, features and functions are important and one needs to be sure that the system acquired has adequate capabilities. In today's competitive world, however, most systems are adequate to meet most requirements, although there are specialized requirements whose performance is enhanced by unique features and functions.

This book's value is that it provides valuable information about operating a facility— data that is not readily available from other sources. The lack of this kind of information scars and bruises inexperienced CAD managers and is usually learned only after long years on the firing line. The material on CAD management, job requirements, system design and installation, and user relationships is invaluable. The book also discusses advanced technical issues, such as network operating systems and hardware features. Many of the concepts are applicable to other systems as well as to AutoCAD.

The material obviously reflects the conclusions of an experienced manager, and should prove invaluable for any systems manager and user. This book deserves a place on any CAD person's bookshelf.

Carl Machover
President
Machover Associates Corporation

Introduction

AutoCAD is a great drafting tool. You can design or draw practically anything with it. It has become such a good tool that thousands of companies around the world have adopted it as the basis for their design and drafting departments. At first, most of these companies had only a few AutoCAD workstations scattered among many drawing boards. Today, AutoCAD workstations threaten to make the drawing board totally obsolete.

For years, companies and individuals have been learning how to work with AutoCAD on stand-alone workstations. The emergence of the AutoCAD workgroup, however, has forced many AutoCAD users to re-evaluate the way they use and manage their AutoCAD systems. Many companies have only recently begun to understand the special care and organization that are required when AutoCAD is used in a group environment. Managers and end users face new and unfamiliar problems in managing this tool and the way they work with it.

Further, businesses encounter a major set of new problems when they attempt to operate AutoCAD on a networked computer system. Networking has become very popular with businesses and institutions as a way of managing information and resources. AutoCAD, however, requires unique approaches and solutions when integrated into a network.

Managing and Networking AutoCAD is a guide to AutoCAD workgroup organization and administration. It also is your handbook to networking AutoCAD for better productivity and efficiency.

1

Who Should Read This Book?

Although any intermediate- or advanced-level AutoCAD user will find many helpful solutions in this book, *Managing and Networking AutoCAD* is designed particularly as a tool for managers of small or medium-sized AutoCAD workgroups. You will learn ways to manage a growing workgroup's activities, control the use of program and data files, and maximize the productivity of shared data and peripherals. If your workgroup is networked, you will find special techniques that will help you configure AutoCAD and your network software for optimum performance. If you do not have a network, the text will show you the many advantages of networking and introduce you to networking concepts and several popular network operating systems. The text also examines various workstation hardware and operating system options, to help you make wise choices as your workgroups grows.

What Software Versions are Covered?

You can benefit from the information in *Managing and Networking AutoCAD* no matter what version of AutoCAD you use. The text does offer more instructions for use with AutoCAD Release 11 because it has more networking features than earlier releases.

You do not need a network, however, to benefit from this book. In fact, most of the techniques described in this book apply even if you use AutoCAD as a stand-alone program on a single PC.

If you do have a network, or if you are considering installing one, *Managing and Networking AutoCAD* includes configurations and tips for Novell NetWare, Microsoft LAN Manager, Artisoft Lantastic, and Sun NFS—the most popular networks among AutoCAD workgroups.

How This Book is Organized

AutoCAD management is a broad topic, encompassing many small interrelated subjects. Further, AutoCAD management can be measured in degrees. A one-man office obviously needs much less management than a multidiscipline, Fortune 500 firm located at multiple sites with hundreds of employees. Yet, above all these concerns remains the fundamental need for sound management practices. For these reasons, *Managing and Networking AutoCAD* is organized to give you complete coverage of AutoCAD management no matter what your circumstances. The text begins by emphasizing the basic need for one person who can take responsibility for managing the entire CAD department (one workstation or many), then progresses to sophisticated system development for large workgroups in specialized environments.

Along the way to better AutoCAD management and system growth, you will encounter the need to consider networking. Because networking is basically a tool for managing resources, however, rather than an end unto itself, this text includes networking within the overall discussion of AutoCAD management.

Managing and Networking AutoCAD is divided into four parts. Part One will help you better understand basic CAD management concepts, the CAD manager's role in the workgroup, and the basics of AutoCAD networking. Part Two covers topics concerning your AutoCAD system itself, including hardware, software, operating systems, networks and the contributions each component makes to AutoCAD performance and functionality. Part Three shows you how to manage a professional AutoCAD workgroup once the system is installed. Part Four helps you develop your AutoCAD system by installing custom AutoCAD applications and selecting the right hardware for your needs. The appendixes document the optional *Managing and Networking AutoCAD Disk*, list A/E/C layering guidelines, and provide you with a resource guide for more information on AutoCAD management and networking.

Part One: Looking at Your Needs

Chapter 1, "Perspectives on CAD Management," gives you a historical overview of CAD management in the past, AutoCAD management in the present, and possible issues the future may bring. You learn which problems to avoid and ways to prepare yourself and your system for future changes.

Chapter 2, "Requirements of a CAD Manager," shows you what it takes to be a good CAD manager. This chapter supplies a job description template that you can use when reviewing prospective CAD managers, and lists the skills a CAD manager needs to handle the job's responsibilities effectively. Through examples, the chapter illustrates a number of workgroup settings and the specific skills they may require of a CAD manager. You also learn to take advantage of your own strengths as a CAD manager or to recognize the right skills in others.

Chapter 3, "Introduction to Networking," helps you decide whether you can benefit from networking by examining some of the advantages and disadvantages of AutoCAD networks. The chapter examines the problems of using older versions of AutoCAD on a network, and looks at the future of network technology.

Part Two: Planning and Installing an AutoCAD Network

Chapter 4, "Comparing Operating Systems," examines the strengths and weaknesses of the various operating systems and hardware platforms that support AutoCAD. If you plan to expand or replace your current AutoCAD system, you can use this chapter to help you decide which operating system would be best for you and your level of computer knowledge.

Chapter 5, "Choosing a Network Operating System and Hardware," teaches you everything you need to select the right networking software and hardware. The chapter provides an overview of all the popular networking technologies and helps you pick the right components for the best fit with AutoCAD.

Chapter 6, "Designing and Installing the System," takes you through the administrative steps of selecting, buying, installing, and testing new equipment and systems. The chapter also provides valuable tips to help you select and work with a dealer.

Chapter 7, "Configuring Popular Networks for AutoCAD," outlines the steps needed to configure Novell NetWare, Microsoft LAN Manager, Sun Microsystem's Network File System, and Artisoft's LANtastic for best use with AutoCAD. The chapter shows you how to organize directory structures, set up network plotting, use network file attributes, and more.

Chapter 8, "Configuring AutoCAD for a Network," shows you how to install and configure any version of AutoCAD to take advantage of a network operating system. You learn the pros and cons of installing AutoCAD on a file server, how to make AutoCAD use network plotters, and how to tune AutoCAD's performance on a network. This chapter also shows you how to exploit the special network features of AutoCAD Release 11.

Part Three: Managing the AutoCAD Office

Chapter 9, "Network Management Techniques," discusses network-management issues for AutoCAD workgroups, including sneaker-net strategies for those without a formal network. The chapter shows you how to improve network control, performance, security, and user-friendliness.

Chapter 10, "AutoCAD Management Methods and Economics," shows you how to use other computer technologies to help you manage your system, and teaches you how to document and standardize procedures. The chapter also gives you an introduction to the economics of using AutoCAD in your business.

Chapter 11, "System Maintenance and Development," shows you how to keep your system healthy, avoid downtime, perform preventative maintenance, and schedule backups. You also learn how to get more than just drawings from your AutoCAD systems.

Chapter 12, "Managing AutoCAD Users," covers the human side of AutoCAD management. This chapter teaches you how to find, select, train, and evaluate skilled AutoCAD specialists.

Part Four: Expanding and Upgrading Your AutoCAD System

Chapter 13, "Custom AutoCAD Software," teaches you how to find AutoCAD applications that are well-supported, open-ended, and can meet your needs for many years to come. You also learn how to manage an in-house software development project using either your own people or an outside consultant.

Chapter 14, "Understanding AutoCAD Workstation Equipment," demystifies the performance claims made by hardware manufacturers. The chapter provides a detailed examination of every component of a fully equipped AutoCAD workstation. This chapter explains which features to look for whether you are shopping for that first personal computer or upgrading an entire company.

Appendixes

Appendix A, "The MN Disk Software," tells you how to install the utilities that are featured on the optional *Managing and Networking AutoCAD Disk*. The appendix briefly describes each program and provides an example of the program's display or dialogue, along with suggestions for its use with AutoCAD.

Appendix B, "The MN Disk Sample Forms," gives you full-page copies of the forms described in Chapter 9. These forms can be photocopied for your own use, or you can copy the text files from the *Managing and Networking AutoCAD Disk* and modify them to suit your own needs.

Appendix C, "A/E/C Layer Guidelines," provides complete listings of both the AIA CAD Layer Guidelines and the 16-Division CAD Layering Protocols. These two documents are widely used in architecture, engineering, and the construction trades to standardize layer names for drawing exchange. You can use one as your own layer standard. The 16-Division CAD Layering Protocols are also included as an ASCII text file on the MN Disk.

Appendix D, "A CAD Manager Resource Guide," lists recommended books, magazines, articles and reports, newsletters, trade shows and seminars, and professional associations for the progressive CAD manager. The appendix also features a comprehensive listing of AutoCAD user groups.

The *Managing and Networking AutoCAD Disk* (MN DISK)

This optional software disk can help you get a good start on managing your AutoCAD workgroup or network. It contains, on one high-density diskette, shareware and freeware programs collected from all over the country. The disk provides valuable software for AutoCAD and network performance testing, handy utilities for network configuration, troubleshooting and management, sample forms for various administration tasks, and examples of standards for documentation.

You do not need the disk to use this book; in fact, you do not even need a computer as you read along. You can read *Managing and Networking AutoCAD* any time, anywhere. The disk, however, can save you hours of frustration, typing, and waiting. The CAD manager's time is valuable, and is better spent on other pursuits than retyping forms and standards.

If you would like to order this collection of management tools, send in the order form in the back of this book, or call the New Riders Publishing order hotline at (800) 541-6789, and specify either 5 1/4-inch or 3 1/2-inch high-density diskette format.

Defining the Terms Used in This Book

Before going any further, you need to understand some of the terms that are commonly used in this text, and which can be interpreted in different ways.

The first is the acronym *CAD*. CAD can stand for "computer-aided drafting" or "computer-aided design." Some people use the term *CADD* to mean "computer-aided design and drafting." This book uses the acronym "CAD" to mean computer-aided drafting because it is usually used in the context of a computer-aided drafting department or workgroup. Also, you should be aware that not much true computer-aided design (that is the actual engineering of a design) is being done with AutoCAD at present. Whenever you see the term "CAD" in this text, you can safely assume that it can mean either computer-aided design or computer-aided drafting, whichever is more appropriate to the discussion.

Many people have strong feelings about the term *CAD operator*; in fact, many career AutoCAD professionals find the term degrading. The word "operator" carries with it connotations of a key-punch operator from days gone by. That job generally does not require the same level of skills that are required to be a good AutoCAD drafter. To many talented AutoCAD users, being called a CAD operator is like calling a desktop publisher a typist. Granted, there may be some literal AutoCAD operators out there. But AutoCAD drafters generally prefer a more dignified title. This book, therefore, uses the terms "AutoCAD user," "CAD drafter," or "CAD specialist."

Part One
Looking at Your Needs

Perspectives on CAD Management

Requirements of a CAD Manager

Introduction to Networking

Illustration courtsey of Autodesk, Inc. Sausalito, California

1

Perspectives on CAD Management

The management of technology has been a problem in every age. The Gutenberg press, television, and atomic power are just a few examples of technologies that have given rise to both tremendous benefits and tremendous responsibilities. Although this book does not submit that computer-aided design (CAD) should be considered on the same scale as the printing press or the nuclear reactor, these inventions are alike in that they all were created to serve mankind. These inventions, however, also have something else in common: their creators probably had little idea of the extent to which their creations would affect the lives of others in years to come.

Like many inventions, CAD has been welcomed with open arms by eager workers who—while trying hard to envision its potential usefulness—are unable to foresee its ramifications. As a result, many businesses have installed CAD systems with little more forethought than they would give to installing a new water cooler. These companies, however, should not bear the full blame for the misconceptions about CAD. After all, CAD has been touted by the media and vendors as a cure-all for a multitude of documentation maladies, and as a productivity godsend. Inevitably, the love affair with the new technology begins to fade, and these companies find themselves supporting a mismanaged, disorganized parasite.

These firms often discover (especially in the early stages of CAD implementation) that they are no more productive with CAD than without it. Or they find out that CAD technology is so costly that they cannot justify the expense of developing or operating a CAD system. What these companies often lack, however, and what is believed to be the key element of the successful management of CAD, is a competent CAD manager. By placing one qualified person in charge of administering the CAD equipment, software, manpower, and methods, companies can avoid wasting both money and time.

This book provides you with a clear picture of successful CAD management and the knowledge you need to apply it to your business. In this text, you will find useful strategies that will help you get the most out of your CAD system. Although this book focuses primarily on AutoCAD systems, the fundamental concepts apply to almost every drafting and design endeavor and to most types CAD systems.

CAD has brought many changes to the ways designers and drafters do their jobs. Remember that growth and progress seldom come without painful adjustments. This chapter discusses some of the major CAD management issues of the past, present, and future, and introduces the central character in the CAD management scenario: the CAD manager.

In the Beginning

In the spring of 1961, an MIT doctoral candidate named Ivan Sutherland began experimenting with man/machine communications through graphics on a TX-2 computer. The program he created and named Sketchpad was the grandfather of the CAD programs in popular use today, including AutoCAD. Using a light pen, Sutherland drew lines and arcs, and created subpictures (*blocks*). As he worked with Sketchpad, Sutherland helped develop many of the concepts that today's CAD users take for granted, including graphical database structures, rubberbanding, dragging, associativity, copying, and constraints.

By using Sketchpad on real-world and simulated projects, Sutherland discovered many of the now-familiar benefits of interactive computer graphics. Among other things, he found that he could easily change existing drawings, study mechanical linkages and other engineering problems, use CAD drawings as input to analysis and simulation programs, and create highly repetitive drawings. Today's AutoCAD users enjoy all these capabilities.

In the 1960s, Sutherland probably had no idea what a revolution his research would inspire. Further, he probably could not predict the hassles that this technology would create for the professionals who are trying to manage it today.

Sutherland later went on to become a founding partner of Evans & Sutherland, a computer graphics company that develops simulators for the Armed Forces and commercial aircraft manufacturers such as Boeing. His early work went on to become commercially viable products and ended up in the hands of design professionals working in government and in the aerospace and automotive industries. The first CAD managers evolved in these organizations, using huge, proprietary, turnkey systems that had only a fraction of the power that AutoCAD users have on their desktops today.

The Emergence of the CAD Manager

The early CAD manager was either an engineer who had considerable experience and education on mainframe equipment, or was a systems analyst who was trained to apply automation techniques to business problems. As a newcomer to this fledgling technology, the early CAD manager had two ways to solve CAD management problems. The first method was to apply proven answers to the problems; the second (and more difficult) method was to find new, untried solutions.

Consider, for example, the simple question of who should be trained to use the CAD system. For today's CAD manager, the answer is easy and not too expensive: send your most talented drafters through a local AutoCAD training course. But because early CAD programs required more training time than today's programs require, and because trainees could not simply attend a night course at the local community college, a vendor's representative often had to teach the program on-site. This meant high costs and valuable work time spent on training while production time was lost. Many trainees, therefore, had to be high-revenue producing designers to justify this expense to the company.

CAD training is just one of a multitude of issues faced by CAD managers in every discipline. Consider some of the other issues CAD managers deal with every day:

- Trying to live up to management's expectations
- Improving communications between the engineering and CAD departments concerning capabilities and capacities
- Helping drafters and designers who are only casual computer users overcome the complexity of the CAD system
- Scheduling workstation use for maximum efficiency
- Overcoming cyclic business trends and their negative effects on productivity and training
- Training CAD drafters in design and manufacturing
- Finding and keeping the most highly skilled CAD specialists
- Helping engineering and drafting "old-timers" accept and cooperate in the CAD design and drafting process
- Acquiring the authority to go along with the responsibilities of overseeing the CAD department, which may be a new department in the company

- Maintaining management interest, understanding, and support for CAD development
- Reconciling personality differences between CAD specialists
- Ensuring the security of the CAD database
- Keeping up with advances in CAD technology
- Finding new and productive uses for CAD within the company, aside from drafting and design
- Developing, documenting, and enforcing system procedures and standards
- Tracking drawing revisions and library development

Some companies that have tried to implement a CAD system failed because they never made up for the high cost of getting started with CAD. Further, they never made the adjustment to computer-aided drafting from manual methods. Other companies, however, adopted sound CAD management strategies and discovered that CAD revolutionized the way they did business.

A Typical Early CAD Management Case History: Boeing Commercial Airplane Co.

Boeing began using interactive graphics for design in the early 1970s. The company started with Gerber software running on desk-size, 16K Hewlett Packard 2100 computers connected to central file servers. These then-state-of-the-art computers acted as hosts for small, cursor-driven, monochrome Tektronix graphics terminals. When the systems began production work in 1974, the need for flexible data management became painfully obvious. Designers could not re-use valuable design databases, and no format translators were available. CAD vendors were woefully ignorant of their customers' needs. Companies with the resources to implement CAD in those days also had to commit to system development, and Boeing was no exception.

Boeing's CAD technicians researched interactive graphics fundamentals and performance, and developed translators of their own. They eventually licensed the CAD software source code themselves and developed it to meet their own specifications.

Like many companies, Boeing found that getting designers to accept CAD was like pushing a wet noodle—unless someone is pulling it from the other end, it goes nowhere. When CAD was presented to potential users, they often responded, "We don't need it. Who needs that?" System performance and reliability were low compared with today's CAD systems, and programs could model only limited types of geometry. Not until work began on large-scale projects, such as Boeing's 767 and 757 models, did anyone offer to grab the other end of the noodle. When designers realized the benefits of applying CAD to such large problems, they began to take an interest in data management. Training programs started soon thereafter, and CAD use grew to the point that Boeing designs are now totally digital.

Leaders at Boeing and other companies soon realized the value of training managers with practical design experience instead of allowing pure computer "gurus" to manage CAD users. User management involved groups of in-house CAD experts with scientific degrees in aeronautical engineering and extended education in mathematics or computer science. These experts were responsible for helping other users overcome the ongoing problems of applying CAD technology to practical needs.

AutoCAD Today: Some Important Lessons Learned

Early CAD technology earned both good and bad reputations. For companies such as Boeing, which persevered until the benefits were realized, CAD was The Wonder Tool. Other companies, however, could not succeed after switching from traditional methods to computer-based design and documentation. In the end, they either tried again until they got it right, or they went out of business entirely—succumbing to the competitive advantages of those who had succeeded. The biggest differences between those who succeeded and those who did not were vision and commitment.

To use AutoCAD successfully, an organization must develop a clear vision of AutoCAD's possibilities and applications; from that vision, the company can develop a plan. As the saying goes, "If you fail to plan, you plan to fail." Many organizations and individual users approach AutoCAD haphazardly, with little or no vision of its potential, without determining their expectations for the CAD system, and without considering it in relation to the goals of their business plan. Some organizations simply want to give AutoCAD a spin like some amusement park prize wheel. If it works out and they win, great. If not, they drop it and resume moving along the same old path. A commitment to CAD, however, means staying with the system until your goals are achieved. Not many CAD installations pay off in the short term. The big gains are realized only after years of developing the CAD system and fitting it into the business plan.

Boeing is just one of the many companies that had the vision and commitment to see CAD through. These firms looked ahead to a time when they would need CAD's power to tackle projects, such as a huge airliner, with precision and efficiency. They knew that they would need the advantages of CAD to remain competitive in the global marketplace. Boeing committed the resources necessary to obtain those long-range goals in spite of short-term costs and disappointments.

An Overview of CAD Management

The term "CAD management" means different things to different people. To AutoCAD users, it may mean file and plot management. To business executives, it means developing an implementation strategy. To most CAD product vendors, it means solving a software problem. To many dealers, who are not involved in the day-to-day operations of an AutoCAD workgroup and are not aware of the problems, let alone the solutions, CAD management is a big question mark.

Although PC-based CAD systems, and AutoCAD systems in particular, have been in popular use for some time, the issue of CAD management is fairly new to PC users. Until recently, AutoCAD users have been preoccupied with hardware revolutions, work-arounds, and making AutoCAD practical to use for professional projects. Now that most organizations have used AutoCAD for a few years and have answered the feasibility and productivity questions, the issues of CAD management need to be addressed.

CAD management is a broad issue that includes basic file management, high-level corporate strategy, and everything in between. Unless it is managed properly, your AutoCAD operation can easily become unreasonably costly and misguided. A poorly managed AutoCAD system often features ineffective hardware and software and inefficient personnel, and results in redundant, inconsistent, and unreliable drawing production.

Much of this book is about AutoCAD management. By applying the concepts offered in the following chapters, you can develop an efficient, organized, and profitable AutoCAD operation. As you will see, this book's main character is the CAD manager, who must implement the system and help its users solve their problems. Regardless of your company's size or mission, you should appoint a qualified person to act as CAD manager if your CAD effort is to succeed and grow. As mentioned earlier, CAD has changed the way drafters and designers work and think, but also has created a new set of challenges and problems. In nearly any CAD environment, the CAD manager plays a key role in meeting those special challenges and solving your company's unique CAD-related problems.

Who is the CAD Manager?

How do you know if you are a CAD manager? For this text's purposes, if you are responsible for implementing an AutoCAD system to solve drafting productivity problems, you are a CAD manager. If you are a business executive involved in organizing AutoCAD within your company, you are a CAD manager. If you are the administrator of a 50-workstation CAE/CAD/CAM/CIM (C4) network, you are a CAD manager. In short, if you think that CAD management may affect you, then you probably are a CAD manager or you are about to become one.

You do not need to hold the official title of CAD manager, however, to read this book. You may not even be thinking about becoming one. When this text addresses "you," it is with the understanding that you may or may not actually be a CAD manager.

No concrete industry-standard definition exists for the term "CAD manager." The CAD manager's role is being determined on the front lines of graphical computing every day. This book will help you define the CAD manager's role as it applies to your company, and select a qualified CAD manager, if necessary. Chapter 2 lists the many responsibilities that make up the CAD manager's job, and the qualifications that make an "ideal" CAD manager.

Perspective on the Future

Despite the fact that businesses and products are evolving at consistent rates, management methods are unlikely to change noticeably in response. Computer technology, on the other hand, continues to advance exponentially. These technological changes probably will have the greatest impact on AutoCAD managers and users in the way they do their jobs in the future (see fig. 1.1).

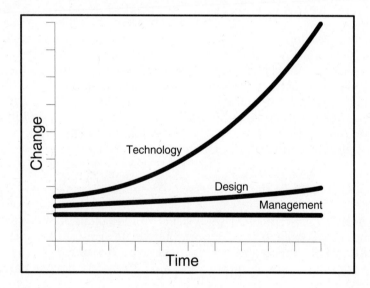

Figure 1.1:
Technology growth outpaces other job aspects.

These changes require additional training and sophistication for the AutoCAD user. The CAD manager of the future needs extra knowledge in order to evaluate the cutting-edge technologies and determine if they are appropriate for his company. He too will need to become more technically sophisticated if he is to keep up with them.

AutoCAD software is becoming more sophisticated and AutoCAD users will have to keep up with it. Updates keep adding more features and tools to the command sets, enabling users to do complex geometric construction and modeling with what began as basic drafting programs. Consider, for example, the repositioning of AutoSolid as an optional extension of AutoCAD Release 11, and amazing new programs such as 3D Studio.

The expanding use of automation in various industries is causing an increased exchange of graphical data between and within companies. The capability to exchange data will require CAD users to develop an ever-increasing mastery of translation programs and formats. More manufacturers are looking to computer-aided manufacturing (CAM) and computer-integrated manufacturing (CIM) to retain or regain competitive advantages over foreign manufacturers. CAD users in these situations need knowledge of both numerical control (NC) programming and basic robotics. Such technological advances will require that CAD users and managers get extra education in areas that previously were unrelated to drafting.

Autodesk programmers constantly are researching new and exciting technologies, but Autodesk also watches for interesting developments by other companies. These outside technologies sometimes can be licensed or purchased outright. If, after acquiring a new technology, Autodesk determines that the technology can be put to use in an Autodesk product, then Autodesk attempts to develop a business relationship with the vendor. Such was the case with AutoCAD 386, when Autodesk and Phar Lap came together. Other developments in the evolution of AutoCAD are probable in several areas of interest to Autodesk and its customers, including further improvements in solids modeling, surface modeling, and constraint management. Autodesk has shown its interest by licensing rights to outside technologies.

AutoCAD's solids modeling features may become enhanced by the integration of boundary-representation (B-rep) modelers. A B-rep modeler provides an integrated data structure that is equally adaptable to wireframe, surface, and solid models. AutoCAD presently supports these forms only in discrete, rudimentary fashions. Autodesk hopes that such a data structure will help its army of third-party developers create extremely sophisticated mechanical computer-aided engineering (CAE) applications with programming interfaces to a single multi-purpose database.

Autodesk also is investigating adding dimensional constraint management (DCM) technology to AutoCAD. A constraint manager enables an engineer to apply a variety of constraints to a model. When any element of the design is altered, the DCM automatically solves all the necessary equations to determine the effects of the change on the model (see fig. 1.2).

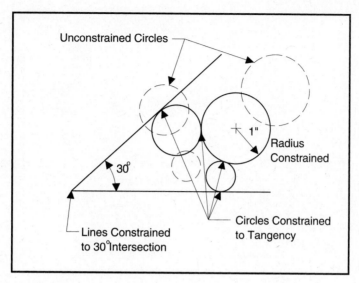

Figure 1.2:
New technology may enable AutoCAD to maintain dimensional constraints automatically.

With such a product integrated into AutoCAD, a designer would be free to explore design alternatives without much editing.

To improve surface modeling, Autodesk is researching non-uniform rational B-spline (NURBS) geometry to describe curves much more accurately than is possible using present methods. If this technology is added to AutoCAD, curved models could be made much more accurate than is possible now. This curve accuracy is valuable to CAM and CIM users who need to machine products directly from computer models. Even if this technology does not make it into AutoCAD, Autodesk could conceivably put NURBS in another high-end product as the company broadens its product line of CAD, engineering, and multimedia software (see fig. 1.3).

The makers of CAD programs, including Autodesk, are adding increasingly powerful programming and macro languages to their software. These additions enable the end user and third-party developers to create customized products in ways that appear and perform like processes native to the CAD program. The addition of the AutoCAD Development System (ADS) to AutoCAD Release 10 for OS/2 and most Release 11 platforms heralded a bright future for AutoCAD third-party developers. No longer restrained by memory restrictions, and now free to use languages that are more powerful than AutoLISP, developers soon will be offering astonishingly powerful applications for AutoCAD that will mean even more specialized training programs for and by CAD managers (see fig. 1.4).

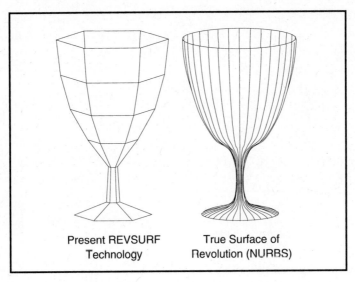

Present REVSURF
Technology

True Surface of
Revolution (NURBS)

Figure 1.3:

An example of NURBS geometry.

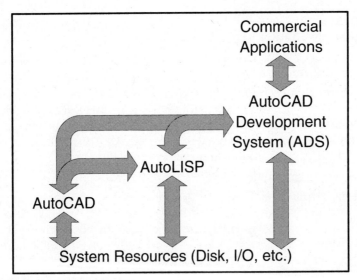

Commercial
Applications

AutoCAD
Development
System (ADS)

AutoLISP

AutoCAD

System Resources (Disk, I/O, etc.)

Figure 1.4:

ADS extends AutoLISP for greater power.

The future also will bring a continued departure from the manual methods of traditional graphic document production. AutoCAD drawings increasingly will be combined with other imaging systems, necessitating improvements in AutoCAD document storage, retrieval, and review. Compact disc-Read-only memory (CD-ROM), write-once-read-many (WORM) and rewritable optical storage technologies will play significant roles in making mass storage of drawings and quick retrieval possible.

Increasingly, CAD programs will be linked to design and engineering calculation programs such as finite element analysis (FEA), lessening the dependence on manual calculation and verification.

These changes and those brought by other emerging technological advances will provide AutoCAD users with many new options in the way they work. The CAD manager and the CAD user of the future will need to be flexible and teachable enough to adapt to these new technologies.

Summary

Emerging technology has changed not only the way drafters and designers work and think, but has created new challenges and responsibilities for its users. End users must master and keep current with CAD technology, and managers must find ways to keep CAD systems productive and cost-effective.

Early CAD users realized that their success depended on the adoption of sound CAD management practices. These included system development and maintenance, system and workgroup organization, and a commitment to training. Management learned that the CAD effort's success depended on planning, finding ways to fit CAD into the business, and developing the CAD system as a means to achieving long-term goals. From this early awareness emerged the CAD manager of today, whose role continues to evolve.

The CAD manager has come to embody business' answer to the question of technology management in product documentation. He is a natural outgrowth of the traditional drafting manager, yet CAD has completely rewritten his job description. Chapter 2 presents a template job description for the ideal CAD manager. It includes all the duties and traits that most organizations have come to expect from a CAD manager.

2

Requirements of a CAD Manager

You now should be formulating an image of the CAD manager's job and its importance. This chapter describes responsibilities that a CAD manager should perform and traits that can help him succeed. You can think of this information as the "ideal" job description and use it as the basis for the job description of your company's CAD manager.

Of course, not all the duties described here will apply to every company or every CAD manager. You should add to the list any duties that are unique or of special importance to your organization. No matter what set of responsibilities your company assigns to the CAD manager, however, every CAD manager should be aware of the job's potential scope and be prepared to take on new responsibilities when necessary.

As this chapter discusses each of the CAD manager's responsibilities, it attempts to identify key traits or skills that can help the CAD manager fulfill those responsibilities. Upper-level management should look for these traits and skills when hiring a CAD manager. Certainly, not everyone possesses all the qualifications described in this chapter, but many of these desirable qualities can be developed through education and experience. You will find some resources for developing these traits and skills near the end of this chapter; a more complete resource guide appears in Appendix D.

If you are a CAD manager, you can use this chapter as a checklist to see how your position compares with the one described here. Do not worry, however, if they do not

21

match up exactly. Each CAD department is different and yours may not need some of the services included in the job description. This chapter may describe tasks that someone else in your organization is handling. But if you find tasks described here that nobody is responsible for, take it as a warning that you may not be managing your system as well as you should be.

If you are a CAD manager's supervisor, you can use this chapter as a guide to help you direct his or her professional development in the areas that will do your company the most good. If you are searching for a CAD manager for your organization, you can use this chapter as a guide in developing a job description geared specifically to your company's needs.

A Portrait of Today's CAD Manager

Through the 1980s, CAD management matured into a real occupation. Today, CAD management is no longer a sideshow of the elite design professions, but has become a necessary part of any successful AutoCAD operation. Further, the title "CAD manager" now accurately describes the job; the CAD manager no longer needs to be called the "computer guy" or "CAD guru." CAD vendors, users, and the press now almost universally recognize the CAD manager as the person (or, in some cases, the persons) responsible for the daily operation and overall performance of an organization's CAD system. Business leaders are now beginning to understand the complexity and importance of the CAD manager's duties, and are according the CAD manager the appropriate recognition.

The typical CAD manager has been on the job for as little as a few weeks, or as long as PC CAD has been around. He may have little formal post-secondary education, or he might hold an advanced degree in one of a number of fields. Not surprisingly, most CAD managers come from a technical rather than managerial background, and have earned their position as a result of their own initiative with computers rather than formal training. The typical CAD manager is ambitious, and strives to improve his systems and himself. Many managers enjoy computer technology so much that they become interested in programming and other computer-related fields.

A CAD manager's life, however, is not all management. He typically has regular production duties to perform in addition to his system management chores. The CAD manager either has free reign to develop the AutoCAD system, or must fight the resistance and ignorance of people who want to maintain the status quo. Understandably, he struggles with the personnel management responsibilities of the job. As a result, most CAD managers have developed an informal, team-oriented management style, relying on implied authority, incentives, and earned respect rather than intimidation.

The typical CAD manager oversees the operations of three to six workstations, and usually is the primary source of technical support not only for the AutoCAD workgroup, but for the entire company's computing resources, as well. He relies on a dealer only when he needs to order new equipment or has a particularly difficult problem that cannot be handled in-house. (This point punctuates the continuing decline of the full-service computer dealership. Retailers are becoming more volume and discount oriented as customers become more educated, and are reducing their role as comprehensive, service-oriented vendors of turnkey systems.) Many CAD managers consider themselves to be expert in hardware, software, and systems analysis, and can integrate AutoCAD with other third-party applications as a total solution to design and documentation. Many CAD managers, however, consider themselves knowledgeable only to an average level in the areas of operating systems and networking.

The CAD manager also must find talented, AutoCAD-skilled drafters, and weed them out from AutoCAD "operators." Today's CAD manager knows the value of all those years on the table. When looking for new personnel, he is interested in someone who has industry experience, has had AutoCAD or other computer training, and has demonstrable manual drafting skills. When evaluating existing staff, the CAD manager looks for accuracy, speed, and volume in production. As drawing boards disappear, however, the CAD manager of the 21st century may have to adopt a new set of criteria for his drafters.

Today's CAD managers come from a variety of backgrounds and arrive in their position in a number of ways. A large corporation, for example, may hire a CAD manager through a personnel agency or through its own internal personnel department. Because CAD managers are not yet around in great numbers, competition for their services is fierce (see fig. 2.1). Such large-scale institutional searches often entice a CAD manager to leave a similar position at one company for better working conditions or better compensation at another company.

Figure 2.1:
Good CAD managers are in demand, even in the "Nowrhtwest."

Most CAD managers, however, get their job by working their way up through the company ranks. They develop their knowledge and skills and demonstrate hard work and commitment. In return, they are promoted to a supervisory or management position within the CAD department. If your company is looking for a CAD manager, you may not need to look out of house at all; the best-qualified candidate may already be working for you. A good candidate would have an understanding of your company's products or services, above-average manual or electronic drafting skills, and a thorough understanding of computers.

Skills Assessment for a CAD Manager

The CAD manager's job can be broken into three basic parts: drafting or designing, management, and computer technology and automation techniques. The CAD manager should already have the design and drafting skills. They are prerequisite to working with AutoCAD and are part of the foundation on which successful AutoCAD management is built. It is far beyond the scope of this book to teach them to you.

The management aspects of the CAD manager's job include managing the resources of the CAD department, such as hardware, software, time, money, and people. Throughout this book you will learn proven techniques for managing these resources. Entire books have been written that provide exhaustive coverage of each individual area of management, such as personnel management, in their purest context. This book, however, simply provides an overview of critical areas that require attention in the AutoCAD workgroup.

The well-rounded CAD manager can gain computer expertise in a couple of different ways. If your company is already using AutoCAD, then any in-house candidate is probably familiar with the system at least at a user level. With help from a competent dealer and through study, the new manager can master most technological concepts. In a new AutoCAD installation, the manager-to-be needs to learn about the new system not just from an end user's perspective; he also must learn about the system's underlying technology so that he can support the system. To attain this level of computer expertise, the new CAD manager must depend heavily on the dealer and take the extra initiative to learn about the system on his own.

Ideally, any CAD manager will be equally strong in each of these three areas (see fig. 2.2). If you operate in a highly specialized field, however, you may find it difficult or impossible to find a CAD manager with the right balance of skills. Many CAD managers start as CAD drafters and learn to become managers. They begin with the drafting and technical skills necessary and develop the management skills. A competent AutoCAD drafter or designer, for example, can learn the necessary management skills and become a successful CAD manager.

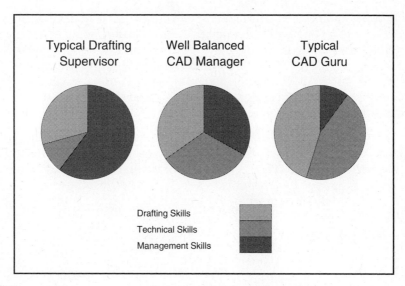

Figure 2.2:
Effective CAD management requires a balance of skills.

You may reasonably assume that a CAD manager could start out with any two of the three necessary skills. There is one case, however, that simply does not work well for most design companies. That is when the CAD manager has no drafting or design experience.

A traditional information systems manager (who has computer knowledge and a degree of management skill), for example, may be quite capable of managing a system's hardware and software. An AutoCAD system, however, is used by drafters and designers who have needs and problems related to their specific tasks. Companies too often make the mistake of hiring CAD managers who have no experience with design or drafting applications. CAD management requires expertise and understanding that extends far beyond traditional system management. The fastest way to stunt the acceptance and cooperation of AutoCAD users is to install a non-CAD user as their supervisor. If the manager cannot understand the AutoCAD users' specific needs and problems, then he may not be able to earn their respect.

A successful drafting supervisor, on the other hand, may be the best candidate for the job of new CAD manager. A good drafting supervisor already has the required drafting experience. Further, if he has supervised a drafting group for long, he has built a relationship with the drafters who will most likely be trained to occupy new AutoCAD seats. The drafting supervisor may be the most motivated to take on the task and have the most at stake, both personally and professionally. If he is an exceptional drafter and manager, the drafting supervisor may be able to learn CAD technology with the required emphasis on system maintenance and support.

Generally, if you combine the skills of a drafter with the skills of a computer technician, you will create a CAD user. Competent AutoCAD specialists are seldom without work today, and many can find more than enough work to keep themselves busy. A CAD "nut," however, probably would not find himself in a manual drafting environment. An AutoCAD-trained drafter may be able to serve as CAD manager under the supervision of a drafting supervisor, who could help the new CAD manager round out his management skills.

If your firm is searching for a CAD manager, remember that only you can determine which balance of skills the CAD manager must possess for your circumstances. Make an objective evaluation of the people in your organization. What balance of the three necessary skills does each person possess? Weigh each person's strengths and weaknesses, and determine what steps would be required to bring that person to the full definition of a CAD manager. Finally, you must determine the types of risks your company might take in attempting to develop this person as a CAD manager.

The process of developing a well-rounded CAD manager is much like training an already capable manual drafter in the use of AutoCAD. AutoCAD either allows a bad drafter to make mistakes more quickly or more often, or it helps a good drafter do good work at a faster pace. The computer is not going to add much more quality and accuracy than the drafter already produces by himself. It is easier and more cost-effective to take a good designer and teach him AutoCAD than to take a CAD specialist and teach him good design techniques. When you add another dimension to an individual's skill inventory, you make it possible to move a person into the position of CAD manager.

People who assume a role in CAD management by moving up within the company almost always do a commendable job. They are familiar with the company's goals and management style, the employees, and the equipment. One of the biggest challenges they have to overcome is receiving the cooperation of their former peers.

Job Description of a CAD Manager

As you can see, the CAD manager must be a jack-of-all-trades. The following sections examine the production, managerial, and technical aspects of the CAD manager's job, and break them into a series of specific duties. As mentioned earlier, not all of these duties may apply to the CAD manager at your company. If they did, you might need a superman to fill the position! As you read the following sections, look for the responsibilities that do apply—or that should apply—to your organization. Then think about the qualifications a CAD manager would need to handle those responsibilities as they apply specifically to your company.

You also should consider the type of support your company's CAD manager needs or will need. By providing adequate resources, such as time, support, and authority, upper management can reduce the CAD manager's level of frustration and ensure that the job gets done. If, for example, the CAD manager must train other AutoCAD users but is not given enough training time because of production demands, then the department suffers in the long run. The firm can solve this problem by giving the CAD manager the authority to delegate less important tasks to other staff members. This gives the CAD manager time to concentrate on larger tasks, such as training, so that the department does not fall behind.

Drafting and Design Responsibilities

If the CAD manager already uses AutoCAD, he probably will continue to perform the same drafting or design functions he did before becoming CAD manager, only now as a manager. In addition to his standard drawing chores, however, the CAD manager may take on other tasks, such as checking drawings, estimating drawing time, and setting standards. These are natural extensions of tasks the CAD manager already has been doing, but they now must be done on a larger scale.

If the CAD manager is making the switch from a lead drafter's or drafting supervisor's position in a manual environment, the drafting-related functions do not change; only the medium changes. Now instead of managing only paper drawings, the workgroup must maintain digital files as well. Drafters, for instance, often borrow graphics from catalogs by tracing or redrawing them. Converted to CAD, however, this function involves importing a file into AutoCAD from a scanned illustration in the catalog.

Management Responsibilities

The CAD manager's managerial responsibilities are often overlooked or undervalued by upper management or even by the system's users. Nevertheless, these duties make up a large part of the CAD manager's job description. The "ideal" CAD manager handles all the following activites, and a typical CAD manager will certainly be involved in most of them in some capacity:

- Designing and selecting the system
- Selecting and training new users
- Participating in preproduction planning
- Scheduling workflow
- Coordinating users
- Coordinating projects
- Tracking documents

The CAD manager may perform these management-related activities either alone or in partnership with other managers, supervisors, or end users. Note that most of these chores do not create tangible results that can be measured or visualized on a drawing board. Rather, the primary purpose of these activities is to protect the CAD department's interests.

Designing and Selecting the System

The CAD manager should be involved in the design, evaluation, selection, and procurement of the CAD system for several reasons. The CAD manager can play a critical role in helping the management team determine the merits of certain system features by adding a perspective that otherwise may not be considered. He may be able to contribute his knowledge of other installations with which he is familiar, or comment on performance implications as they relate to an existing system. In some cases, the CAD manager can play a major role in recommending part or all of the new system, especially if he is knowledgeable of AutoCAD systems. The CAD manager can test equipment and software, observe product demonstrations, provide AutoCAD expertise, and help in any other ways needed.

To participate effectively in the system design and selection process, the CAD manager must have an in-depth technical knowledge of AutoCAD, computer hardware and peripherals, operating systems, and (preferably) network systems. He also must have well-developed communications skills if he is to educate management about technical requirements and consult with dealers and vendors about system options.

If the CAD manager is allowed to participate in this process, he will be better prepared to teach users about the system's capabilities and management's expectations. The CAD manager also will be better able to support the system if he has contributed to its integration. The groundwork and research that went into the system's design and selection will help the CAD manager troubleshoot, expand, and upgrade the system later.

Selecting and Training New Users

Another of the CAD manager's basic duties is the hiring or replacing of CAD drafters. In this role, he is active in scouting, reviewing resumes, performing interviews, and hiring or recommending new employees. This role also may involve promoting and transferring existing employees.

If the CAD manager is an expert AutoCAD user himself, then he understands the skills and temperament a CAD specialist will need to succeed in the company. Only an experienced AutoCAD user, for example, can tell if an AutoCAD drawing has been drawn properly. This is an area in which the CAD manager must work extra hard if he is not familiar with AutoCAD. The AutoCAD-inexperienced CAD manager should rely on outside training sources and be careful when judging the AutoCAD skills of interviewees who may have more experience than he does. Chapter 11 discusses user selection and training in greater detail.

Good interpersonal skills are important to the CAD manager, especially during the interviewing process. Much is at stake in an interview, and much can be lost if the CAD manager is not able to communicate well. By adopting effective interviewing techniques, the CAD manager can select the right people for the drafting department. Interviewing is a science in itself; if your organization has a personnel or human resources department, then the CAD manager should go there for help in developing his interviewing skills.

The CAD manager should stay up to date on the status of the local employment market for CAD drafters. By keeping in touch with local CAD training schools, the CAD manager can find out what educational opportunities are being offered in his area and determine the quality of people trained at those institutions.

The CAD manager also is generally responsible for implementing an ongoing training program to keep the CAD department dynamic and efficient. Ideally, the manager places himself at the center of any such program, by organizing educational opportunities and teaching from his own experience, either in formal classes or through day-to-day interaction with the operators. If operators do not have the chance to discover and explore new techniques, CAD drafting can become a nearly mindless procession of sketches and plots. By encouraging the staff to discover and experiment, the CAD manager not only boosts morale, but also reaps benefits in increased productivity.

Just as he is best prepared to select qualified AutoCAD specialists, the CAD manager is best prepared to teach AutoCAD if he has experience in using, troubleshooting, upgrading, customizing, and programming AutoCAD. The CAD manager realistically cannot attain this level of expertise unless he spends time with AutoCAD and develops a good understanding of the program. Further, to be a good teacher, the CAD manager must have patience, good organization skills, good written and verbal communications skills, and good problem-solving skills.

Many CAD managers find that ongoing training can be as easy as having a weekly "brown bag session" at the office during a lunch hour. These informal sessions are like having your own in-house AutoCAD users group. The class can discuss a particular feature of AutoCAD, or the CAD manager may hold a question-and-answer forum about problems encountered during the week.

Participating in Preproduction Planning

All too often, a production department is thought of as a magic box, into which management pours materials and instructions. Out of this box, management expects a perfect product to appear. A more realistic approach, however, is to "dovetail" the production effort into the design and planning process. Ideally, to enable himself to communicate the company planners' expectations back to the production group, the CAD manager attends meetings in which his group's resources are committed. In turn, he conveys information about resource capability and availability to the planners during the decision-making process. The CAD manager also encourages everyone to consider the implications CAD may have on the project. By sitting in on meetings with project managers, the CAD manager gathers information about the project ahead of time so that he can prepare and organize his staff and resources. Preferably, this allocation of resources takes place as soon as the project is launched.

As explained earlier, the CAD manager must have a working knowledge of the design discipline(s) with which he will be dealing. Otherwise, he will not be able to recognize the important aspects of his projects. A CAD manager with a background in log home manufacturing, for example, probably would have a tough time adapting to a new position at an aerospace company.

The CAD manager's organizational skills come into play in the preproduction process. When he is armed with information about the quantity, complexity, and scheduling of working drawings, the CAD manager should be able to plan ahead to make sure the right resources are available when production must begin.

Scheduling Workflow

The model CAD manager anticipates, manages, and schedules the group's workflow. This means keeping project schedules updated and communicating with his staff to meet deadlines, thoroughly understanding the CAD system's capabilities, and knowing the abilities and limitations of each of the system's users. Most important, the manager must be able to mesh these factors so that the job is done efficiently. Drawing from this knowledge, the CAD manager can accurately predict how much time should be required to complete a given project.

Organizational skills continue to dominate the skill requirements for scheduling, yet experience also is important. These two qualifications can help a CAD manager, for example, determine how a project might be affected if a CAD specialist becomes ill and cannot return to work for several days or weeks. The CAD manager should know if the CAD department can handle the lost production by working some overtime (with its associated high costs). With his estimates and schedules, the CAD manager should be able to tell if certain circumstance might jeopardize the project deadline and affect subsequent projects. Problem-solving and decision-making skills are crucial if serious conflicts arise and sacrifices or compromises need to be made to prevent the deadline from slipping, possibly costing the company money and confidence of its clients or customers.

Note: Project management software can be a useful tool for resource management. These programs enable a manager to describe entire projects in terms of individual tasks. He then can use the software to assign both personnel and equipment resources to the tasks or set up various what-if scenarios for further study. Many programs also assign costs to resources and produce reports detailing the financial impact of various scheduling strategies. Schedules can be updated as conditions change, enabling the manager to make quick decisions about the amount of time, resources, and effort required to maintain deadlines. Project management programs are covered in Chapter 9.

Coordinating Users

The CAD manager coordinates tasks among the system's users and makes assignments according to the skills of each user. The CAD manager is the traffic controller that keeps everything organized so others can do what they do best. If one worker has strong 3D modeling skills, for example, that person logically should be assigned to work on complicated 3D modeling projects. This is not to say, however, that each AutoCAD user should be "pigeonholed" according to existing skill levels. Assigning work loads may mean making sure that one person works only on a certain type of drawing because of his or her aptitude for that kind of work. Or it may mean making sure that a person works on several types of drawings because he or she has a talent that can be used widely. The wise CAD manager, nevertheless, makes sure that every drafter has the opportunity to broaden his horizons by mastering new tasks. If the schedule allows enough time for training, the CAD manager should use that time to sharpen and test users' skills and allow them to pursue their own CAD interests.

The CAD manager also ensures that users working on different parts of a project are coordinating their efforts. If one drafter makes a change to a drawing that must be used by others, that drafter should notify the others of the change, especially if the change could adversely affect other parts of the project. To facilitate this coordination, the CAD manager might schedule regular progress meetings. These informal sessions can be very important to a project's success, especially if the meetings include workers who normally do not work together closely. The time spent away from production pays off in fewer errors and corrections.

Organization is crucial if tasks and personnel are to be coordinated effectively. Coordinating several CAD projects between multiple users to meet interdependent deadlines demands organization. Once information is organized, options can be deduced, and coordination decisions can be reached. Without the ability to organize information and resources, the CAD manager cannot make reasonable decisions about staff and resource coordination. In most business scenarios, upper management cannot be expected to make decisions about the daily application of technology. Within a proper political framework, the CAD manager is the primary decision-maker regarding the allocation of CAD system and user resources.

Coordinating Projects

The CAD manager is involved in coordination not only at the user level, but also may be active at the phase, departmental, office, and company levels as well. If your organization includes several divisions, each may have its own procedures and schedules. The CAD manager must work with the managers of other divisions to coordinate the activities of the various groups involved in the same projects. The coordination may include exchanging progress prints, arranging for joint representation at meetings about shared design problems, or matching up people with their counterparts in other departments to work out a problem together.

During the kick-off phase of a project, the CAD manager arranges meetings with the CAD managers of any other departments or companies involved. Then they can exchange layer lists, symbol libraries, and standards so that these conventions can be in place before the project begins. As early as possible, they determine how layers will be used, translations performed, files distributed, and plots made.

Tracking Documents

Just as in a manual drafting department, everyone in a CAD department needs to know where any particular drawing is stored. In hard-copy form, drawings are large, easily identified objects that do not become lost too often. Such is not the case in a CAD system. Disks and tape can contain hundreds of individual drawings, which are difficult to identify and easy to destroy.

The organized CAD manager sets up a system for tracking each electronic drawing's location. Such a system can exist in either hard copy or electronic form (or both) and includes labels that indicate when a document was released and revised, who worked on it, and what it contains. A simple paper system can be set up using drawing log forms that are updated when a new drawing is made or an existing drawing is updated. An electronic system can be used that automatically presents the user with forms on-screen to control drawing access and track revisions.

Whatever system is choosen, everyone must help maintain the system by remembering to check drawings in and out, and by not bypassing the tracking system for the sake of convenience. An electronic document-tracking system is by far the easiest to use, most secure, and the most flexible. The job of making sure the system is used consistently, however, rests with the CAD manager. The CAD manager should check periodically to make sure that the tracking forms are being used and kept up to date. Chapter 9 offers an example of a paper drawing-tracking system.

Technical Responsibilities

The most obvious part of the CAD manager's job involves the technical aspects of the position. This part of the CAD manager's job is divided so that he can ensure the CAD system's success. To do this, he manages the workgroup's hardware and software resources by performing the following functions:

- Expanding AutoCAD's usefulness to the company
- Documenting the system
- Performing backups
- Troubleshooting and periodic maintenance
- Overseeing data distribution
- Continuing education

The CAD manager's technical knowledge and problem-solving skills serve him best in these areas. Ideally, he should have training and experience in many facets of computer technology, from a board-level understanding of hardware, to knowledge of operating systems, to applications program savvy.

In performing these duties, the CAD manager becomes the in-house computer expert, at least where AutoCAD is concerned. He becomes responsible for appropriate and profitable application of technology wherever it can benefit the company.

Expanding AutoCAD's Usefulness to the Company

CAD technology has enabled many companies to enter new markets, bring products to market more swiftly, and explore new ideas more easily. The ideal CAD manager is not afraid to try new technical innovations and is a pivotal player in the company's realization of AutoCAD's benefits. Preferably, the CAD manager has demonstrated the ability to build and expand information systems. This can be almost any previous experience where the CAD manager exhibited vision enough to see an opportunity for expansion and the creativity to design an answer for it.

Whether starting with a new installation or working in a long-established and stable environment, the CAD manager should stay on the lookout for ways to further exploit the company's CAD investment. This involves the following three processes:

1. Identifying repetitive tasks that are likely candidates for automation
2. Expanding the use of AutoCAD data into areas other than drawing
3. Looking for useful technological advances

The following sections briefly examine each of these approaches to maximizing a system's usefulness.

Automating Manual Processes

When you choose a process for automation, you should look at the gains other departments or companies have realized by automating similar processes, if possible. If your company is considering generating bills of materials electronically, for example, find out how other companies like yours have benefitted by automating the process. As you examine the pros and cons of automating any process, try to answer the following questions:

- What increase in productivity can be achieved by letting AutoCAD perform the process instead of continuing to perform the process manually?
- How much can the company expect to pay for hardware, software, manhours, and support to automate the process?
- Will the anticipated gains be worth the costs?
- By automating the process in question (in this case, bills-of-materials creation), will the company take a step toward automation of another, larger process (such as inventory control)?

The CAD manager does not have to do all the work in automating a new process. The work may involve skills or resources that he does not have. He should, however, be as involved as possible according to his skills, but more important, the CAD manager should act as the catalyst and initiator of the change.

Finding New Uses for AutoCAD

Many companies are finding that they can use the data stored in their AutoCAD systems for purposes other than working drawings. You may be able to get more mileage out of your AutoCAD data by using it to create product documentation, marketing and presentation materials, or engineering analyses. Chapter 11 presents other ideas on reusing the information stored in AutoCAD databases.

Updating System Technology

The CAD manager also can maximize the system's performance by keeping up with technological developments in the CAD field. System vendors are continually creating new products that can make your existing investment work better, more quickly, or with less effort. Such enhancements may even give your CAD system new value. A new scanner, for example, may enable you to use paper drawings as input. Or, by installing an accelerator card in an obsolete computer, you can create an ideal training machine. Similarly, a laser printer may help out the data-processing staff as well as the CAD group, resulting in great-looking presentation graphics and check plots. Chapter 14 examines CAD hardware technology in greater detail.

By increasing the CAD system's usefulness within the company, the CAD manager diversifies AutoCAD's benefits and dilutes its single-purpose image. System maximization, however, requires a commitment from management to stand behind CAD. Management has to believe strongly in CAD to devote money, time, and resources to realize the system's long-term benefits.

Documenting the System

If you already oversee several PCs, you understand the need for adequate system documentation. If you have PCs in your company but do not manage them yourself, do you think anyone can tell you, on a moment's notice, how each workstation is configured, or how a certain software-related problem was solved several months ago?

System documentation involves more than just keeping inventory of a company's hardware. While documentation is a relatively simple process, it can save hours of downtime. If your system is properly documented, you should not need to waste time looking for misplaced manuals and your troubleshooting headaches should be less painful. The "big-system guys" document their systems, and so should the CAD manager. Appendix B shows you some easy ways to document your system with some sample forms.

Along with writing system documentation, CAD managers are often involved in creating training materials and preparing reports and system support correspondence. The CAD manager also may write requests for proposals to vendors, reports on system performance, personnel evaluation reports, budget requests, and other technical and business documents. A strong technical writing ability, written communications skills, and writing experience are valuable for all these tasks. The ability to communicate in writing results in a better understanding of the CAD manager's desires and achievements. By eliminating confusion, clear communication at any level saves the company both money and time.

Performing Backups

Most people agree that if any duty belongs to the CAD manager, that duty is the regular backing up of system and data files. Project data is the most valuable part of a CAD system. An architectural or engineering firm's primary products, after all, are drawings. For these companies, virtually all revenues are based on the delivery of accurate and complete drawings. Imagine, then, what would happen if a crash destroyed all the drawing files in your system. What might your company have to pay to reproduce one day's worth of drawings? When you consider the possibility of such a scenario, you begin to see that a system of regularly scheduled backups is vital to your company. Yet, for all the money it can save a firm, a backup and archiving system is relatively inexpensive.

To make complete and accurate backups, a CAD manager needs a thorough understanding of files of all types, file organization, file attributes, directory structures, operating system techniques, and backup media, hardware, and software. A wise man once said, "It's not a matter of *if* you will lose data, it's *when*." If you have difficulty making backups of your system's data, Chapter 10 offers some ideas for making backups easy to perform.

Troubleshooting and Periodic Maintenance

Sooner or later, things break down or go wrong—even in the best systems. Because he is responsible for the system, the CAD manager is responsible for its repair. This duty might include tasks such as replacing failed circuit boards in computers, making cables, or solving conflicting software interrupts.

If he is to deal with equipment and software that is logical by its very nature, the CAD manager must himself use sound logic and have problem-solving skills. A good CAD manager uses deductive reasoning and empirical analysis to troubleshoot problems. Of course, in order to recognize problems, the CAD manager must understand how computers operate, their common problems, and typical hazards. Training in basic to intermediate electronics and mechanical aptitude is especially helpful.

Many breakdowns can be prevented with proper preventative maintentance. The disk drives, for example, are the only moving parts in your computer system other than the power switch, fan, and possibly the lock. Floppy disk drives require periodic maintenance of their read/write heads even though the rest of the computer may require only an occasional internal and external cleaning. Hard disk drives need frequent optimization by defragmenting file clusters. The CAD manager should make sure that all hardware receives regular maintenance, to avoid data loss and downtime. Hardware maintenance is covered in step-by-step detail in Chapter 10.

In a computer network, troubleshooting and maintenance headaches are multiplied by the number of workstations, and then some. Network management requires exceptional judgment that enables the manager to differentiate between many possible causes of bottlenecks or breakdowns. A sharp CAD manager must isolate the most likely problems quickly because many users may be affected. He needs to know how to perform conclusive tests (depending on the problem) and see that the problem gets fixed, either by himself or by others.

Overseeing Data Distribution

Companies must often export, exchange, and import AutoCAD drawings when data must be shared across different CAD systems. This can happen, for example, when different design firms work on the same project with different software, or when different programs are used within the same firm. Neutral formats, such as DXF, DXB, and IGES, can be used to make the transfer. Sometimes both programs can use only one file format. Other times, several formats may be possible, yet only one may work best.

The CAD manager should know how to perform these digital acrobatics and oversee their use by others. Experience with drawing translators, familiarity with the different application programs being used, and an understanding of the various data formats can help. Because periodic exchanges may be required during the design process, the CAD manager also should be responsible for monitoring the use of any data changed by revisions. Chapter 10 discusses data exchange with other programs and shows examples of DXF, IGES, and HP-GL files.

Continuing Education

Much can happen in only one year to change CAD implementation strategies. If you look at any CAD magazine from a year ago, you will see how much CAD has changed. What was then state-of-the-art is perhaps now obsolete. Progressive companies expend a great deal of energy to keep current with CAD technology, but it pays off in the end. Your company should avoid the tendency to rely on today's technology far into the future, too. For these reasons, and to support his duties in the areas just discussed, the CAD manager must be committed to continuing his own education and keeping current with technological advances. If his computer knowledge is weak in any area, the CAD manager should seek to strengthen his skills in that area. Even with all his management responsibilities, the busy CAD manager must find time to maintain his proficiency with AutoCAD; it is far too easy to fall behind.

CAD managers can turn to many resources for information on AutoCAD, hardware, software, networking, management, and other topics. Here are just a few helpful resources:

- Autodesk supports a nationwide network of over 150 Authorized Training Centers (ATCs) that offer training on Autodesk products and other subjects. Most community colleges offer classes on management, programming, and business through adult continuing education programs.

- Consultants and user groups often hold professional seminars on management and technology. Many such organizations publish newsletters, and advertise their seminars in professional magazines and the business section of local newspapers.

- A number of annual conferences and expositions report on the state-of-the-art in CAD and computers. These conferences are routinely reviewed in CAD periodicals and many magazines publish schedules for these events.

- Professional organizations, such as the National Computer Graphics Association, the Association for Computing Machinery, and the Association for Systems Management, are devoted to the advancement of automation and computing in professional and educational settings.

- Local AutoCAD user groups share solutions and learn new topics. Your local AutoCAD dealer should have information on any user groups that meet in your area.

- Professional CAD journals such as *CADalyst*, *Cadence*, and *MicroCAD News* carry articles, reviews, and tutorials on CAD and CAD-related subjects.

- The Autodesk Forum of the CompuServe Information Service is a trove of information on topics related to AutoCAD. The forum also provides some of the fastest and most expert advice anywhere. If you already are a member of CompuServe, enter **GO ADESK** at any CompuServe prompt to get to the Autodesk Forum. If on-line communications is foreign or intimidating to you, get a copy of *Inside CompuServe*, published by New Riders Publishing.

You can find more information on many of these and other resources in Appendix D.

Summary

The "ideal" CAD manager is skilled in many areas, and faces a wide variety of responsibilities in his job. The tasks can be categorized as drafting or design duties, managerial activities, and technical responsibilites. Of course, not all CAD managers have such a far-reaching job description. Remember that it is not important (or even possible) that the CAD manager know everything. Sometimes simply knowing where to find the answers is enough. In many companies, especially smaller ones, many of these duties simply do not apply to the CAD manager. In larger companies, all these tasks must be carried out, but the CAD manager typically does not do them by himself. Instead, he shares the load with other managers and higher-level end users.

The next chapter presents an overview of AutoCAD networking to help you gain an appreciation of the requirements put on the CAD manager. As you learn about the nature of networks, you will see why an AutoCAD network is where the problems of CAD management can be magnified if not properly addressed. Be sure to read Chapter 3 if networking is new to you, if your company is considering purchasing a network system, or if you need to integrate AutoCAD into an existing network system.

3

Introduction to Networking

If you are one of several AutoCAD users working together in a workgroup, you may have already heard about networking and may be wondering if it is right for you. Even if your workgroup includes only two or three AutoCAD users, networking probably will become an issue at some point soon. Whenever two or more people begin using AutoCAD with the same data and peripherals, networking inevitably becomes an issue. This chapter's goal is to dispel your inhibitions about networking and to discuss the problems that arise once the decision is made to network.

This chapter introduces you to networking and its benefits, to help you decide if you should network your AutoCAD workgroup. The text poses some simple questions that can help you determine whether your company is a candidate for networking. The chapter also briefly discusses some of the problems that have arisen in networked AutoCAD workgroups in the past, and explains why networking has not been a popular option for design and drafting firms until the emergence of AutoCAD Release 11. You will then glimpse the future of networking, and learn how the networked AutoCAD workgroup can benefit from recent and anticipated technological advances.

If networking is new to you, you should read this chapter. The following sections introduce basic networking terms and concepts, and discuss many of the benefits and drawbacks of computing in a networked environment. You also will learn the kinds of demands a network will place on the applications programs you use in your daily work. You should find this information especially helpful if your company is considering installing a network, or if your AutoCAD workgroup must integrate into an existing network system. If you already have an AutoCAD network, you can skim this chapter for information that may be new to you, or skip to the next chapter, which discusses various operating systems and their behavior when used as the basis for AutoCAD or a network.

What is a Network?

In its simplest definition, the term "networking" refers to the interconnecting of computers so that they can share programs, data, and peripherals. This is done usually with some kind of wiring that connects the computers, either to each other or to a central computer called a *file server*. Computers can be interconnected by hard wiring, fiber-optic cable, or even by special infrared or radio frequency devices. Special software—called the *network operating system*—makes the programs, data, and peripherals available to the networked computers.

Most networks are confined to a single building or other small geographical area, hence the term "LAN," which stands for *local area network*. If a network is spread across a large city or several smaller ones, it is called a "MAN," for *metropolitan area network*. An interstate or international system is called a "WAN," for *wide area network*. This interconnection of computers and sharing of resources can happen across the hallway and involve just a few users, or around the globe, incorporating multiple companies.

When AutoCAD workstations are networked, they can share files that contain drawings, symbols, menus, and other data. They also can share printers, plotters, and other devices. Networking has been used in non-CAD information systems for years, but has been slow in working its way into PC-based CAD departments. Networked AutoCAD users experience many of the same problems experienced by networked word processor and database users, but a networked AutoCAD workgroup also has unique problems of its own. A network encourages (almost requires) standardization, consistency, and control of all its shared resources—issues with which AutoCAD users have been struggling for years.

Making the Decision To Network

If your operations are not organized or controlled before you network, you will wish that you had gotten them organized and under control after you start networking. Networking is a complex, technical, and unforgiving task to undertake and is not for the faint of heart. On the other hand, an AutoCAD network is extremely productive once installed. Centralized drawing storage, backup, and output make an AutoCAD network easier to control and administer than stand-alone workstations. Any changes in your data or in the tools you use to create it (such as block libraries, menus, macros, or AutoLISP programs) can be instantly distributed to the entire organization.

Before installing a network, you must make many decisions about the overall organization, structure, and resources of the workgroup. You must envision the network's effect on file sharing, security, and data integrity. At the same time, however, you must anticipate the demands the system will make on the workgroup, and particularly on the CAD manager or system manager. Network management extends well beyond backups and troubleshooting. It involves applying organization and structure to hardware and software technology so that the entire system appears and performs as a consistent, cohesive whole.

To help you understand how much networks are underestimated, consider the results of a recent *LAN Magazine* survey of major network installers. The survey yielded the following top five client misconceptions about LANs:

1. LANs are off-the-shelf, do-it-yourself beings.
2. LANs do not need to be managed.
3. LANs are toys; they cannot replace minicomputers.
4. LANs are a panacea.
5. LAN users and administrators do not need training.

Can you relate to any of these popular (but incorrect) notions about networks? If so, you need to make special preparations before deciding whether to install a network system. Specifically, you need to perform a basic assessment of your networking needs and expectations.

Performing a Needs Assessment

Because networking is such a big investment in money, time, and energy, you should make sure that a network will meet your needs before your organization installs one. The following questions can help you recognize whether you should install a network now or wait until your needs are more clearly defined.

To find out whether your company can benefit from a network, answer the following questions:

How many AutoCAD workstations do you have now?

If your company has only a few AutoCAD workstations and is not expected to grow appreciably in the near future, you may not need a network. Generally speaking, networks are more valuable to large workgroups than to small workgroups. Even so, an inexpensive, entry-level network could be helpful for standardizing single-symbol library files and sharing peripherals. Such a network is called *peer-to-peer* because it does not require a dedicated computer that acts as a file server; users can share only those resources that are installed on the networked computers. Server-based and peer-to-peer networks are discussed in more detail in Chapter 5.

If your firm now has more than three workstations and if the workstations are scattered around the company, you should investigate networking. Installations of a dozen or more workstations are almost impossible to manage effectively without a network.

How many workstations do you plan to have in the future?

If your AutoCAD workgroup is growing, you should network now, before a network is absolutely necessary just to maintain order. You can design and install a small network easily and fairly inexpensively now, and then expand it later. A large network takes more money, time, and energy to implement all at once. The longer you put off the decision to network, however, the more expensive and difficult the initial installation will be.

Do drawings need to be shared among users?

If each staff member works on different drawings and does a unique type of work, a network probably will offer your company few, if any, production benefits. Networking makes more sense, however, if you have staff members who need to work on the same drawings at the same time, as is the case at many multi-discipline design firms. A network will enable your staff to share drawings and other AutoCAD data. Further, the resources come from one source rather than many.

Are your present CAD management efforts ineffective now, even though you are well organized?

When several non-networked AutoCAD users work on the same drawing, problems can arise when different versions of the drawing reside in different workstations. Which one is most current? Did the change made by one drafter affect the work of another, and if so, did the second drafter actually receive a copy of the changed file? A network can help eliminate the problems of redundant data and misplaced revisions. The right software can help you keep track of drawing files, so that all users can easily determine who is currently working on a drawing, when a file was most recently updated, and the types of changes that were made to the file. A network can give you back the control you lost when workstations began springing up all over.

Do your users have to compete for the use of plotters or printers?

A single networked plotter can do the work of many and still seem as though it is the exclusive property of each user. By connecting the plotter to your network, you eliminate the need to move the plotter from one workstation to another whenever a plot is needed. A network also reduces the maze of serial cables and switch box connections that can make plotter-sharing a hassle. A network can save the money you otherwise would need to spend to purchase multiple plotters, printers, and modems.

Is data security a problem?

A network is the best solution to data security problems. A network's advanced security schemes control access to files. You also can select hardware that assists in protecting data security. If your system uses diskless workstations, for example, users cannot copy files to floppy disks.

Can your company justify the cost of a network?

If, after answering the above questions, you are confident that your company could benefit from a network, you need to weigh those benefits against the costs involved. In addition to the capital expenditure required for networking equipment, your company also must bear the overhead of network maintenance and expansion. Most networks are fairly trouble-free, however, if maintenance is scheduled properly over time.

Only you and upper management can decide if your company can justify the cost of a network based on your financial status. Few companies, however, ever regret networking. The network has become a standard part of computing in the business environment and most companies would be at a real loss without their network to improve productivity and efficiency.

Network Application Prerequisites

In order for any application program (not just AutoCAD) to integrate with the features of a network operating system and support multiple users, the program must have some basic network capabilities of its own. Single-user applications generally do not need or have such features; AutoCAD did not until Release 11. Unless a program has these features to make it more network-compatible, however, the network administrator must take extra steps and establish protection schemes when installing the program. Otherwise, users may "bump into each other" when several people are using the application at the same time. If an application is not "network aware," then it may think that it is dealing with one user when it actually is dealing with several users.

The following sections discuss the basic network capabilities that an application should have to be considered a network application. AutoCAD Release 11 supports networks in a generic fashion, not according to specific network types. This makes network considerations easier overall for the programmers at Autodesk, but it also means that you must make some compromises when implementing AutoCAD on any specific network.

In order to integrate successully with a network, an application must have the following features:

- File locking to prevent users from editing the same file at the same time
- File compatibility among different workstation platforms and application versions
- File-naming and routing facilities for network drive and directory structures
- Security over application configurations and cooperation with network operating system security features
- Output management features that recognize network output facilities

File Locking

Any network application must be able to *lock* a data file when the file is opened by a user. This *file-locking* capability is not needed in a single-user situation because only one person can use the application and data file at one time. On a network, however, file locking is critical. One of networking's primary advantages is that it enables several users to share one set of data files. If a network application did not have file-locking capabilities, the system could not stop one user from overwriting the changes made by another user when the two are working on the same file simultaneously. Generally, when one user of a network application opens a file for editing, the program "locks" the file to prevent other users from opening the file. The file remains locked until the first user closes it. The program then "unlocks" or releases the file so that it can be reopened by someone else. Only one person can edit the file at one time, and each person's edits are saved in the file (see fig. 3.1).

AutoCAD Release 11 implements a basic form of file locking. Before Release 11, AutoCAD did not feature a built-in file-locking facility. Release 11 does not actually lock a drawing file the way most other network or multi-user programs do, which is by maintaining the file's status (open or closed) as a part of the file itself. Instead, it creates a second file, called a *lock file*. AutoCAD checks for the presence of a lock file before it will open any drawing file. As long as only Release 11 workstations attempt to open an active file, AutoCAD will protect the file. Other versions of AutoCAD, however, do not recognize Release 11 lock files. Release 11 lock files are covered in Chapter 8.

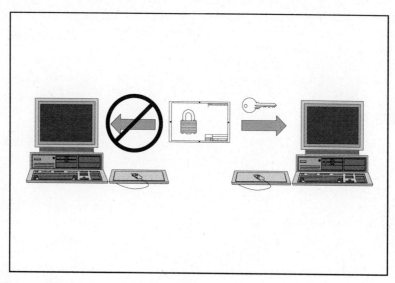

Figure 3.1:

File locking protects shared drawings.

True *multi-user* applications, however, are fundamentally different from single-user applications. A multi-user application is basically the same as a network application, except that it places the lock at the *record* level instead of the file level. Multi-user application files are made up of many individual pieces of data, called *records*, which can be accessed individually. Multi-user database programs commonly utilize this type of file structure. Network applications, further, allow the sequential sharing of a data file by many users. Each user is allowed, in turn, exclusive access to the entire file. A multi-user application allows *concurrent* access to the same file by many users, but exclusive access to make changes only in individual records.

Suppose, for example, that a retail business uses a multi-user database application. Within this system, a single database file might contain individual entries (records) for each item in the business' inventory, as well as entries for orders. Employees at each point of purchase must be able to access the database to find out if an item is in stock and to place or update an order. Conceivably, therefore, all employees could need access to the database at the same time. Orders would take too long if users were forced to wait until the file was inactive. When the database is accessed, the multi-user application locks only the records that currently are being changed. The remaining records are available for others to access.

Multi-user capability would be a powerful addition to AutoCAD. Several people could then work on a drawing simultaneously, each adding his own input, and changes would be reflected in near real-time on each user's screen. AutoCAD would need to consider each entity in a drawing file (which is essentially a database) as an individual file record. It would then need simply (simple to imagine, not to program) to lock each entity as it is selected for editing, rather than locking the entire file. The last person to leave the file would save all the last changes to disk. Perhaps an upcoming release of AutoCAD will include this feature if enough customers want it.

File Compatibility

Many organizations use several different computer platforms, each of which utilizes its own file structure. Files must be compatible, therefore, if they are to be shared by the same program across different platforms. If your company uses a network that includes different types of computers, each network application must be able to save its data the same way on each computer. Although the low-level file structure (that is, the manner in which the data is recorded on disk) may differ from one machine to the next, the file contents (that is, the order of the data) should remain the same. As long as the network operating system can reconcile the differences in file structure, the data should not need to be translated between different platforms for the same program. Many network operating systems support different computer platforms, so that different types of computers can be connected in the same network. These operating systems can reconcile the different file formats and store the data in a common format on the shared disk space.

Fortunately, AutoCAD has had complete file compatibility from the beginning. That is, AutoCAD uses the same file format for all platforms. This type of portability makes good sense from Autodesk's point of view, because it is easier to support one file format for all platforms than it is to support a different file format for each platform. This degree of compatibility might mean passing up some possible benefits of the file structure of some platforms, but it pays off by enabling all the network's users—regardless of their individual platforms—to access files without trouble or delay.

Temporary File Management

When two or more users are running the same application on a network, the routing and naming of temporary files become important from a management standpoint. Most major applications (single-user and otherwise, AutoCAD included) create temporary files to store intermediate data, swap unused data from RAM to disk, and reserve disk space for the finished file. Temporary files are usually given a descriptive name that identifies them to the program as being temporary. The program normally deletes such temporary files automatically when the data file is closed. The application may place its temporary files in one of four locations: in the directory where the application resides; in the directory where the data file resides; in the current directory; or in a user-configurable location. AutoCAD can use either of the two latter options. AutoCAD stores some temporary files in the drawing directory by default, and stores others in the current directory by default. The user can configure AutoCAD to store temporary files in a specific directory.

When several people are active on a network, each incidence of the same program (that is, each copy of the program running on different computers) must create its own temporary files—one set of files for each user. If the files are not given unique names to identify them with their respective owners, they may overwrite one another, or they may be read by the wrong incidence of the program. One of the most critical steps in setting up an AutoCAD network is assigning these names. By using a unique name for each person on the network as part of the temporary files' names, the application can keep the files separate. If the program is being run on a multitasking operating system, it also must be able to differentiate between possible multiple incidences of the program that are being run by the same person. Applications such as AutoCAD that run on multitasking operating systems usually handle this chore by including the files' time of creation as part their name. As long as each incidence of the program keeps track of its own set of temporary files, everything should run smoothly. AutoCAD's temporary files feature is discussed in detail in Chapter 8.

Finally, the application must be able to accept the logical drive designations used by network operating systems to identify the directories of the various hard disk volumes within the file server. These drive designations are considered logical because they do not each represent an actual hard disk. Rather, they represent specific directories on the high-capacity hard disks typically used in file servers. The drive letters make it easier to refer to these directories, which may have long path names. Most current applications, including AutoCAD, do not have problems with high logical drive letters (F: through Z:). Other applications, however, have difficulty using these high logical drive identifiers, or they insist that the drive letter be assigned to a physical drive installed in the workstation.

Security

Because a network places computing resources at the disposal of anyone with access to a networked workstation, most networks implement security features to control access to those resources. Thus, a network supervisor can make sensitive directories and files or critical devices off-limits to certain users. A proper network application should integrate with, or at least not interfere with, the network's own security system. AutoCAD leaves network security up to the network operating system. AutoCAD recognizes the general nature of attempted network security breaches and responds with meaningful rather than ambiguous error messages. If, for example, you try to edit a drawing for which you do not have the appropriate network security privileges, AutoCAD responds with the ? error message.

The netware application may even implement its own security system to prevent unauthorized use of its files. AutoCAD Release 11 can use a password to protect its network authorization file when it is installed for multiple users. Chapter 8 shows in more detail how this is done.

Network users and software vendors are becoming increasingly aware of the importance of controlling the number of users that can run networked programs. AutoCAD Release 11 uses a server authorization code to ensure that only the licensed number of users can execute the program simultaneously on a network. The problem of network security has become large enough, in fact, that third-party *metering* programs are now available to control single-user application use and network application access for those programs that have no protection of their own. A metering program tracks the number of times an application program has been executed on a network. This way, you can be sure not to violate the software licensing agreements you are bound to by your software vendor.

In addition, a metering program can prevent unauthorized usage of programs and data files by unauthorized users. If, for example, all the people who are supposed to be working with AutoCAD on your network are busy doing their jobs, a metering program can prevent additional users from casually using the program to intentionally or unintentionally modify files without authorization. A shareware metering program called XMETER is provided on the *Managing and Networking AutoCAD Disk.* See Appendix A for details.

Output Management

Hard-copy management is one of the biggest hassles of networking. Standard single-user applications do not recognize networked printers or plotters, of course, but neither do many so-called network programs. Network operating systems generally handle network printing by capturing printer output destined for the workstation's printer port. The output is then diverted to a temporary file on the file server where it is placed in a waiting line, or *queue*, to be printed. As far as the application is concerned, the data went to a printer and was printed. Each queued print job is then sent out in turn as a printer becomes available.

Better network applications, such as WordPerfect Network version, can recognize network print queues and pass print jobs directly to the plotter or printer, instead of requiring complicated work-arounds. WordPerfect also allows the user to select from among multiple printer configurations. AutoCAD Release 11, on the other hand, neither recognizes network print queues, nor allows multiple plotter or printer configurations.

Project Management

Networks enable users to share resources. When several people work on the same file, for example, you probably want to be able to tell who worked on the file most recently. Unfortunately, few network applications have built-in project management features. As a result, project management information often must be recorded by hand.

When a drawing is drawn by hand on a drafting board, for instance, major revisions are usually listed in a revision block within the drawing's title block. Although the user can do this chore manually with AutoCAD, or even automatically with AutoLISP, listing is such a fundamental process that it should be performed as a core part of AutoCAD.

To accomplish this electronic listing, in fact, would not be difficult. AutoCAD and your computer know almost all the necessary information to record a history of the drawing you are working on. AutoCAD, for example, knows who you are by your network name, what drawing you are working on, the present date and time, and whether the drawing has been edited or is a new drawing. The only thing AutoCAD does not know is how you would like to describe the changes you have made. Basic revision logging as an integral part of AutoCAD, therefore, would be a welcome feature to networked AutoCAD users. Each drawing history then could be saved in the drawing file as a permanent record when the drawing is edited by different drafters in an AutoCAD workgroup. This, in turn, would contribute to better and quicker drawing management.

As it stands now, however, network drawing management is provided only by third-party programs. Although most of these programs do a good job, they do it in incompatible, proprietary ways. A drawing's history, for example, cannot follow the drawing file as it is exchanged, archived, or reactivated unless the drawing management program's data follows along and others who may use the drawing also use the same management program. These kinds of drawing and project management solutions, however, are better than none at all.

Looking Back at AutoCAD Networks

Until the appearance of AutoCAD Release 11, AutoCAD was merely "networkable." That is, it did not have any features that took particular advantage of a network. Rather, the program simply stayed out of the way so that it did not conflict with a network's operation.

AutoCAD has been used in networks since PC local area networks came into use, but such systems have been neither easy nor elegant. They were undertaken primarily by the courageous and the wealthy: courageous CAD managers and technocrats who knew there must be a way to make it work, and wealthy corporations that could afford to try almost anything to make it work. Many of the missing prerequisites manifested themselves in these early AutoCAD networks, as well as in today's AutoCAD networks that are without Release 11's advantages.

Without file locking, for example, drawings stored on a network have to be downloaded (moved) to the workstation for editing so more than one user cannot edit the same file at the same time. Or, drawings are left on the network and users must be sure not to make changes to a drawing that someone else is already working on. Either way, file access is either clumsy or dangerous.

File compatibility, on the other hand, was assured with Release 10 of AutoCAD. Before Release 10, files that needed to be exchanged between different platforms had to be translated by DXF files as if they were going to a totally foreign system.

Although its plotting flexibility is improving continually, AutoCAD used to have few work-arounds for plot spooling and network plotting. Only in recent versions has AutoCAD had the capability to use device file names, such as LPT1 or PRN, to help make network plotting easier. Chapter 8 shows you how this works.

Before Release 11, the closest thing AutoCAD had to reference files was block redefinition and replacement. There was no easier way to allow a group of drafters to work on portions of a composite drawing and periodically update each other's files.

All this lack of suitability, however, is not because of negligence on Autodesk's part. AutoCAD was never intended to be used on a network before Release 11. So far, AutoCAD has been primarily a single-user product and has been ported to multi-user operating systems, such as XENIX and Sun OS. This move was undertaken largely to satisfy customers who wanted to take advantage of those operating systems' inherent networking capabilities and to pave the way for *heterogeneous* sites. That is, a company may want to run AutoCAD on several different platforms (PCs, Macintosh computers, or workstations) instead of forcing its engineers or designers to leave their machine of choice and use a PC to run AutoCAD.

The Future of Networking

Today, AutoCAD is on the threshold of becoming truly at home on a network. In the years to come, the increasing popularity of networks is bound to shape AutoCAD workgroups and AutoCAD itself even further.

Networking technology has had—and will continue to have—a profound impact on AutoCAD workgroups of all types and sizes. Before long, network connections will be as commonplace as printer connections. When this time arrives, nearly every CAD manager, DP manager, and MIS director will have to be knowledgeable of networks and network applications. The profusion of small local area networks is sure to lead to the growth of metropolitan area networks and wide area networks, which will connect LANs across town, between several states, or even across the oceans (see fig. 3.2). This aspect of technology is covered in depth in later chapters.

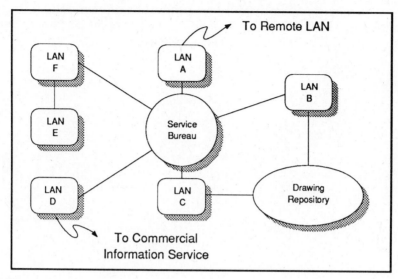

Figure 3.2:
Wide area networks connect local area networks.

Consider the possibility of centralized database facilities in geographical areas with widespread use of LANs. LANs could be connected to a central plan review and repository system for Architecture/Engineering/Construction (A/E/C) users, or to a photoplotting center for electronics firms. These larger networks could serve the general inter-LAN communications needs of subscribers and provide bulletin boards, mail, and message services. WANs would perform similar functions to those that the CompuServe Information Service and others like it now provide on a national scale. Businesses like this are already beginning to appear. Plotting service bureaus are becoming commonplace. Many offer high-speed file transfer and translation services at prices that are quite reasonable, when compared with the cost of purchasing expensive hardware and translation software.

The technological advances being made in networking hardware and software will change networking as it is known today. Hardware is becoming faster and more intelligent. Super-high-speed fiber-optic networking links are becoming popular. Dedicated communications and database servers will likely become superservers with multiple processors. Network software is already headed in directions that will distribute the load of processes across the network and exploit multiprocessor servers. The interface of the network to the user is becoming more transparent while it dovetails with applications programs.

For example, ISICAD, Inc., maker of the CADVANCE 4.0 drafting program, recently demonstrated a hidden-line removal NetWare Loadable Module (NLM) for Novell's NetWare 386. The module enables the file server of a network of CADVANCE 4.0

workstations to participate in hidden-line removal being performed on a workstation. Thus configured, the task is completed in a fraction of the time it would take the workstation alone to finish the job (see fig. 3.3).

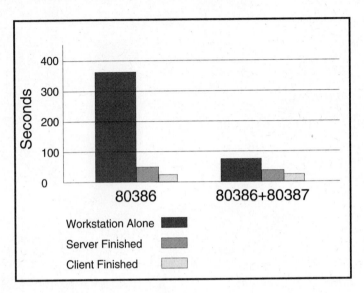

Figure 3.3:
Client/server architecture adds processing power to workstations.

NLM demonstrates the practical application of the *client/server* approach to distributed network processing. This new model for information processing is particularly efficient at providing shared access to a common database. In distributed network computing, application processes can be physically separated. The processes are usually divided between clients (running on workstations) and servers (running on file servers, database servers, and so on.). The client process is frequently referred to as the front end, and the server process as the back end. In a distributed database application, for example, the client sends a request for services to a server. From this, only the results of the request (such as hidden line view and database query) are returned to the client rather than the entire database, which is the case with standard database applications.

The client/server architecture of application development makes even more sense in today's growing use of multivendor and multi-operating-system environments. Centralized database, communications, and other services can allow access by multiple client platforms. Autodesk recently demonstrated its progress in this area by exhibiting an AutoCAD session submitting database queries to, and receiving results from, an ORACLE database server under OS/2.

Summary

The decision to network involves a great deal of planning and preparation. Before installing a network system, particularly for use in an AutoCAD workgroup, users and management must determine whether a network will fit the workgroup's current organization, and whether a network will help the firm achieve its long-term goals. Users also must examine the capabilities of the applications programs to determine whether those packages can function effectively in a network environment. To do so, applications must feature their own file security and management capabilities, or must not interfere with the network's security and management capabilities.

Once the determination is made to network, users and management must prepare for long-term changes in the way they work and think. Commitments must be made to system maintenance and expansion, and decisions must be made regarding the integration of daily routines into the network environment.

The next chapter examines the foundation of AutoCAD performance and functionality: the workstation operating system. If you are not 100 percent committed to your present operating system, or if you are just curious about the alternatives, you should read Chapter 4. Your choice of workstation operating system affects the network operating system you choose. You will learn the pros and cons of the various operating system platforms on which you can run AutoCAD as the first step toward designing a high-performance AutoCAD network from scratch.

Part Two

Planning and Installing an AutoCAD Network

Comparing Operating Systems

Choosing a Network Operating System and Hardware

Designing and Installing the System

Configuring Popular Networks for AutoCAD

Configuring AutoCAD on a Network

4

Comparing
Operating Systems

The first step in implementing an AutoCAD network is selecting the workstation operating system upon which you can build the network. The operating system will greatly affect many of the network design choices you will have to make in the future. If you choose the right operating system for your needs, you can ensure a long and productive life for your network.

A computer's operating system is the most fundamental of all computer programs. By acting as a middleman, the operating system controls all the applications programs you use on the computer and manages all the computer's hardware and software resources. Your operating system's power determines the power of the applications you can run on your computer system. An eight-bit operating system such as DOS, although extremely popular and compatible, limits the capability of applications to take advantage of advanced computer hardware. A 16-bit operating system or environment, such as OS/2 or Windows, improves the outlook, but hardware already has passed on to 32-bit architectures. Forward-thinking CAD managers and businesses should be looking ahead to 32-bit operating systems, such as UNIX and future versions of OS/2. These systems take the best advantage of hardware and yield the highest performance.

Not too many years ago, PC users had no choice at all when they needed an operating system. Mainframe systems had their own proprietary operating systems, and the PC had DOS. DOS has served its purpose, but has lost much of its usefulness relative to the applications it controls. PC-based CAD in general, for example, has exploded into a mainstream application industry, and AutoCAD specifically has outgrown the capabilities of basic DOS in the areas of memory addressing, multitasking, video support, and processor support. To meet the PC user's growing needs, new operating systems have been developed for the PC, and older ones have been adapted to the PC. Autodesk has recognized these new alternatives and has modified many of its products to run under operating systems other than DOS.

This book surveys the major operating system options that AutoCAD runs on: MS-DOS, OS/2, UNIX, and MacOS. Along the way, the advantages and disadvantages of each operating system are explained, and a little background on some related operating system products, such as Windows and DOS extenders, are given. The inherent networking features, or lack of, in each of these options are looked at, as well as some of the market forces that are defining which operating systems ultimately will succeed.

The well-prepared CAD manager must understand not only the operating system(s) he uses, but also should be familiar with the other operating systems currently available. As much as possible, he should understand the ways in which various operating systems can affect AutoCAD system performance and productivity. If you are puzzled by all the claims made about which is the best operating system, this chapter should help you understand the issues more clearly.

New CAD managers should be especially concerned about their choice of an operating system. A new operating system not only offers convenience and power, but also requires a considerable commitment in training and software investment. Armed with this chapter, you should be able to make informed decisions about the operating system features your AutoCAD network or other workgroup needs to grow and prosper.

Graphical User Interfaces: The Prompt Alternative

Each of the operating systems discussed in this chapter supports a *graphical user interface* (GUI, pronounced *gooey*). The concept of a GUI is new to most DOS users. If you have never used a GUI-based operating system, you may be using one soon. All the major operating systems have them now, including—in a limited fashion— the latest versions of DOS. GUIs are rapidly gaining popularity because they are easier to learn and use than the traditional command-line-interface.

AutoCAD provides a semi-graphical interface called the Advanced User Interface (AUI), which is a system of pull-down menus, dialogue boxes, and icon menus. Other common DOS-based GUIs are the Microsoft Windows environment (see fig. 4.1), Digital Research's GEM environment, and many of the popular "paint" programs. Imagine an entire operating system that looks and works this way, and you begin to appreciate the impact that a GUI can have on a user's interaction with the computer.

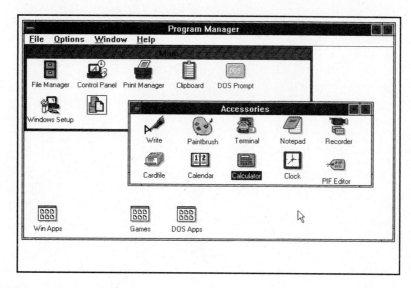

Figure 4.1:
The Microsoft Windows GUI.

Graphical user interfaces resulted from early research done by Xerox Corporation at the Palo Alto Research Center (PARC) in the early 1970s. Computer scientists there researched many aspects of computer technology that are taken for granted today. PARC researchers, for example, studied the enhanced man/machine communication that occurs when a person associates pictures and objects with programs, files, and processes on a computer. Many of the results of this research now are used in the Macintosh interface, which was derived largely from the STAR system developed at PARC. The small on-screen pictures, called *icons*, graphically represent a program's function or a file's contents. An icon for a word processor, for example, might appear as a quill pen. The user relates faster to the pen as a writing instrument than he does to the words *Xywrite* or *Ami*. Similarly, AutoCAD users can more easily recognize hatch patterns by icon menus than by text descriptions.

The mouse also was invented at PARC as an alternative input device to the keyboard. By using a mouse, the user can freely and intuitively move an arrow-shaped cursor across the screen to select windows, icons, and other GUI objects.

Working with GUIs

GUIs do not utilize a command prompt, such as the notorious DOS C:> prompt. Rather, the user controls the GUI system through the use of windows, pull-down menus, and dialogue boxes, which generally are similar to the tools provided by AutoCAD's AUI. The user may "open" several windows, for example, each of which may contain an active but separate program. A windowed interface enables the user to display several programs on-screen at the same time. A GUI's windows can be individually resized, repositioned, and in many operating systems, *iconized*; that is, the user can reduce an active program's window to an icon when the program is not needed or when space is needed for another window. To resize a window, the user can choose a menu command or use the pointer to "grab" the window's border and stretch the border to the desired size. To move a window, the user places the pointer in a special border area, presses a mouse button, and drags the entire window across the screen. Although all windows may be active and processing at the same time, the user can interact with any window simply by moving the pointer into the window and clicking the mouse button.

A GUI enhances file management by representing drives, directories, and files as graphical objects or bits of text. Because the GUI does not display file names as static lists on the screen, the user is not forced to remember and retype drive indicators, directory paths, file names, or extensions when copying or deleting files. As a result, file management and system administration chores become easy and quick. By clicking on a directory icon that looks like a folder, for example, the user can open the directory and display the names of the files contained in that directory. By dragging a file icon from one directory icon to another, the user can move the file to that directory.

Some advanced systems, such as Presentation Manager and the Macintosh, even enable the user to start a program and automatically load a data file simply by clicking on the desired file's icon or name within the GUI. With some GUIs, such as Windows and Presentation Manager, similar programs can be arranged into logical groups for easy access. All GUIs are recognized widely as the easiest way for controlling modern multi-tasking operating systems and sharing data between programs.

Perhaps the greatest advantage to GUIs is the consistent interface they provide, which makes every program easier to learn, use, and remember. Within each system, when the user pulls down a menu (such as File) and selects an option (such as Open), the same familiar dialogue box appears whether the active program is a database, spreadsheet, or graphics package. For AutoCAD and network users, this means that the complexities of AutoCAD and network operating systems are less intimidating when they are hidden behind a familiar and non-threatening interface with which the user is comfortable. AutoCAD has ways to go in completely adopting the same interface as some of the operating systems it runs on, and network operating systems themselves are faced with the same challenge. But seamless integration of all these products seems to be the goal, and progress is being made.

Why DOS is Dying

MS-DOS (and PC DOS for most users of IBM personal computers) is the original operating system for PC users and AutoCAD. AutoCAD began as a product named MicroCAD running on the CP/M operating system. MicroCAD was later named

AutoCAD-80 because it ran on the Z80 and Intel 8080 processors. A parallel version named AutoCAD-86 was developed to run on the IBM PC and Victor DOS-based computers built around the Intel 8086/8088 chips.

You probably are familiar with DOS. More than 90 percent of all AutoCAD packages sold are for DOS systems. DOS comprises the following major features:

- DOS is a single-user operating system.
- DOS is a single-task operating system.
- DOS was written for the 8086/8088 processor.

Figure 4.2 illustrates the basic architecture of how DOS and system hardware and *firmware* interact. Firmware is a hardware component that contains microcode instructions necessary for the computer's basic functions. A figure similar to figure 4.2 is displayed for each of the operating systems and environments discussed in this chapter. These figures are included to help you understand how all the pieces of the system architecture work together and to differentiate between the various systems.

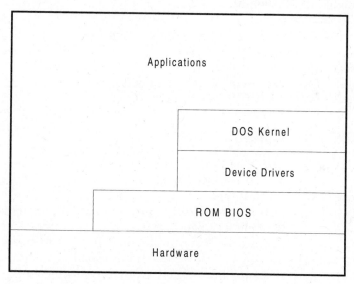

Figure 4.2:
DOS system architecture.

In figure 4.2, you can see that the DOS core program, or *kernel*, communicates with the hardware by device drivers and the ROM BIOS. Application programs, such as AutoCAD, can communicate directly with either DOS, the ROM BIOS, or the hardware directly. What this means is that any application program has several different interfaces with which to perform its duties. The program can have any of the layers with which it communicates perform specific duties for the user. This is advantageous to the application's developer because he can choose how to perform certain tasks. An application, such as AutoCAD, can control video hardware directly and bypass all other layers.

This type of communication has both pros and cons for the user. Application performance may be optimum if the program takes advantage of communications with layers closer to the hardware itself. But it also can make programs less compatible. The hardware in a personal computer was not initially designed to be accessed directly by applications, so few standard procedures are developed for doing so. Some programs leave the hardware in an undesirable condition when they finish using the hardware, leaving an unstable condition for the next program. This is the problem with many terminate and stay resident (TSR) programs. Another disadvantage is that the operating system, which is responsible for controlling the computer, loses control when applications begin to work around it. This prevents the operating system from protecting the computer from incompatible or misbehaved programs, causing more "crashes" and "lock-ups."

Although it falls short of meeting many power users' needs, DOS still remains the dominant personal computer operating system with more than 50 million copies sold. From a networking perspective, DOS' popularity is its only advantage. Any network you choose will have some way of connecting to a DOS workstation and nearly every networking hardware device will support DOS. This makes DOS a "no brainer" if all you need is basic networking capability. DOS' other shortcomings are outlined in the following sections.

Single-User Limitations

Because DOS is a single-user operating system, a DOS-based computer cannot support more than one user at a time. DOS has no concept of differentiating between more than one point of input or output. This limitation prevents you from building a network around DOS alone. You must use, therefore, a network operating system that works with DOS to provide the necessary network functions. Operating systems such as UNIX and XENIX, on the other hand, can support multiple users on the same computer. This multi-user support usually is accomplished by connecting ASCII terminals to the host computer by serial cables. ASCII terminals are simply additional displays and keyboards for input to and output from multiple users. They have no processor of their own. Instead, they rely entirely upon the host computer, hence they are often called "dumb" terminals. Later in this text you will learn about networking programs that work with DOS to provide networking capabilities between personal computers.

Single-Tasking Limitations

DOS can process only one task at a time. Even with TSRs, DOS must stop one program before it can work on another. Many users would like to be able to run a word processor, database, or spreadsheet while they have their AutoCAD drawing loaded. Sometimes a user needs to switch quickly to a text editor from within AutoCAD, without having to go through the DOS shell provided by AutoCAD. Programs such as Quarterdeck Office Systems' DESQview 386 that are installed in an 80386-based computer enable DOS users to perform this type of multitasking, but not without certain drawbacks. DESQview itself, for example, is difficult to configure so that several programs can run concurrently with it. DESQview also is prone to trouble when used with programs that do not comply with its Virtual Control Program Interface (VCPI); AutoCAD, incidentally, does comply with this interface standard. And, although DESQview is capable of character-based windowing, a high-resolution AutoCAD ADI (Autodesk Device Interface) driver cannot be run in a DESQview window. If you are technically inclined and patient, however, DESQview can help you be more efficient.

General Performance and Memory Limitations

DOS was written in eight-bit programming instructions and does not take advantage of 16- and 32-bit instructions now available. This limits performance on 80286-, 80386-, and 80486-based computers so much that AutoCAD Release 10 is the last version that will run on eight-bit computers. Release 11 requires at least an 80286-based (16-bit) PC.

Because it was written for use with the 8086 and 8088 processors, DOS can utilize only 1M of total memory, which is the maximum those chips are capable of handling. Of this memory, the system reserves 384K for its own use, leaving 640K free to store active programs, such as AutoCAD and network drivers. This creates another problem with building a network for workstations based on DOS. When running large, memory-hungry applications such as AutoCAD, DOS seldom has enough memory remaining to load the network drivers needed to create a network. As a result, network developers have had to design ingenious work-arounds to make drivers smaller or use other types of memory. Most of the drives work well, but the added complication is a problem that most network users would rather live without.

AutoCAD is not the only program to outgrow DOS. Many other programs have felt the pinch of the 640K RAM barrier and have searched for memory expansion solutions. One solution was agreed on by Lotus, Intel, and Microsoft as the Expanded Memory Specification (LIM EMS). By taking advantage of a little-used 64K range of RAM addresses (called a page frame) reserved by the system, special bank-switched RAM expansion cards can substitute 16K banks of physical RAM into the addresses dynamically. This solution works most of the time, but it requires that programs be specially modified to take advantage of EMS memory. EMS memory is slower than conventional (up to 640K) memory, and conflicts and crashes are common. AutoCAD can use expanded memory conforming to EMS on any computer and extended memory (explained later) available on 80x86-based computers (80x86 denotes all the five digit Intel CPU chips in that particular family, such as 80286, 80386, and 80486). AutoCAD uses this extended memory as extended I/O page space to hold drawing data.

AutoCAD can use as much as four megabytes of either extended or expanded memory. Figure 4.3 shows a typical memory map of a DOS-based personal computer with expanded memory. The computer's ROM (Read Only Memory) BIOS (Basic Input Output System) and DOS occupy the bottom of the available 640K of RAM. Between 640K and 1024K is the 384K area reserved for uses such as additional ROM BIOS and video buffers. Expanded memory of up to eight megabytes is divided into individual 16K "pages." Four pages at a time can be swapped into the 64K page frame as needed by an EMS driver for use by an EMS-compatible program. When more memory is needed, four more pages can be swapped into the frame. All of this happens quite fast, but slower than a single contiguous block of memory. To help you remember how expanded memory differs from extended memory, you should think of expanded memory as expanding out horizontally from system memory like an accordion.

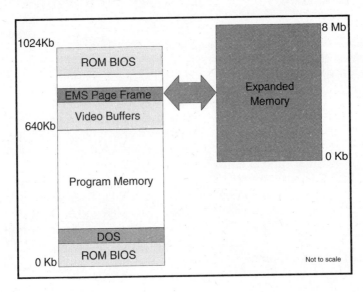

Figure 4.3:
EMS page scheme.

Utilities provided with expanded memory managers are another common solution to memory shortage—or "RAM cram," as it is commonly called. These utilities load mouse, video, network drivers, and other TSR programs into unused areas of high reserved memory, permitting larger programs and more data to reside in lower DOS memory. The best uses for this additional breathing room are for the extended I/O page space addresses required by large amounts of page space, and for larger network drivers that cannot be loaded in high memory areas.

New Releases of DOS

If you are committed to staying with DOS, you might consider using one of the new versions of DOS that are designed to load most of the operating system's resident code (the DOS *kernel*) into extended memory on 80x86 computers. Extended memory is memory that can be accessed only when a program switches an 80x86-based computer into its protected mode. In this mode, the CPU can address up to 16M of memory installed in the computer. (For more information on the various CPUs and modes, see Chapter 14). Figure 4.4 shows how extended memory continues above the 1024K boundary imposed on 8086/8088-based computers. To remember how extended memory differs from expanded memory, you should think of extended memory as extending vertically above the system memory.

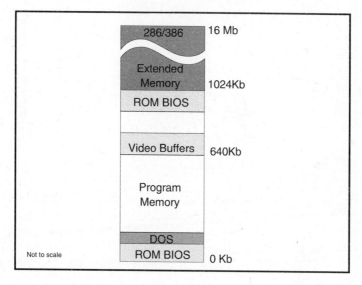

Figure 4.4:
Extended DOS memory map.

The first version of DOS to provide this feature did not come from Microsoft, but from Digital Research. In fact, Novell has recommended Digital Research's DR DOS 5.0 as a solution to memory constraints. Autodesk, however, has received reports from customers of problems running DR DOS 5.0. Microsoft reportedly will follow suit and soon release a version of DOS that also uses extended memory.

These new versions of DOS save users as much as 40K of memory over earlier versions of DOS because they load most of their own program code into extended memory above 1M. This leaves more RAM available for the user's programs and drivers. These new versions also conserve space in the valuable first 640K of RAM by loading device drivers and TSRs into high memory while remaining compatible with Windows 3.0 (Windows is discussed later). As the memory map in figure 4.5 shows, as little as 15K of program code from these new versions of DOS must remain in the 640K RAM pool.

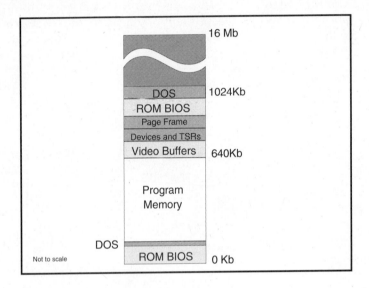

Figure 4.5:
Memory map of DOS versions using extended memory.

In addition to its memory-saving features, the new version of MS DOS is anticipated to give users basic task-switching capabilities once available only from third-party programs. Other welcome enhancements may include a Windows-like shell, file-searching capabilities, undelete and unformat utilities, a user-configurable DIR command, a full-screen text editor, a Quick BASIC compiler, command-line recall and editing, and on-line help.

Using AutoCAD with Extended DOS

As a stop-gap measure to increase the functionality of AutoCAD until other operating systems gain popularity or DOS is improved, Autodesk and other software developers are implementing DOS *extenders*. A DOS extender allows Autodesk to continue to add features and improve AutoCAD without many of the limitations of DOS alone.

A DOS extender is a software product that enables compatible programs to take advantage of the larger memory address spaces of 80286 and 80386 systems. Extended AutoLISP in the 640K version of AutoCAD Release 10 and AutoCAD 286 uses Rational Systems' DOS/16M software to enable users of 80286- and 80386-based PCs to place the AutoLISP interpreter and AutoLISP programs in extended memory. As a result, 128K of the 640K address space remains vacant for drivers and I/O page space. The extender switches the processor into protected mode to access extended memory (to activate the AutoLISP interpreter, for example) and restores the system to real mode for other AutoCAD operations. (The differences between protected and real modes are discussed in Chapter 14.) This switch happens much more slowly on 80286 PCs than 80386s.

The AutoCAD 386 version uses the Phar Lap 386 DOS Extender to eliminate most of AutoCAD's real-mode operation. This technique also is used in Computervision's Personal Designer and VersaCAD/386. In this 80386-only version, AutoCAD has *no* overlays files. Instead, the program is back where it began, as one executable file (only much larger—roughly 1.5M in size). Because this version of AutoCAD is intended for use only with the 80386 processor, Autodesk programmers had to recompile AutoCAD for the 80386 instruction set. This gives AutoCAD a big performance increase, averaging 62 percent better than the regular 286-compatible DOS version.

AutoCAD 386 adheres to the Virtual Control Program Interface (VCPI) developed by Quarterdeck Office Systems and Phar Lap. This interface ensures compatibility between DOS extenders and protected-mode programs. Programs that comply with VCPI, such as Quarterdeck's DESQview 386, can be run with DOS-extender environments. Unfortunately, VCPI provides no security against programs that might crash the computer. On the other hand, Microsoft and several other companies have worked together to develop the DOS Protected Mode Interface (DPMI). DPMI protects the system from failing applications and is supported by Microsoft Windows 3.0. Hence, AutoCAD 386 and other extended DOS applications, such as Paradox 386, cannot be run under Windows without extra protection. If you intend to use an extended DOS environment, such as DESQview 386, IGC's VM/386, or Windows 3.0, make sure that AutoCAD supports its extension interface.

DOS is dying, but it will not be forgotten soon. If you are committed to DOS and have a large investment in DOS applications and training, you should stick with DOS. If you have many 80286 PCs, then AutoCAD 286 is your best bet until you replace them with 80386 PCs. The following are system requirements to run AutoCAD 286 Release 11:

- IBM-compatible 80286 computer
- 80287 math coprocessor
- 640K RAM minimum with 512K of extended memory required to use Extended AutoLISP
- Hard disk

- High-density floppy drive
- DOS 3.3 or later
- Appropriate video, input, and output devices

Autodesk is committed to supporting the 80286-based PC, but AutoCAD 286 is now at the bottom end of the AutoCAD product line.

The 80386-based PC, on the other hand, is fast becoming a corporate standard. AutoCAD users committed to DOS with 80386-based PCs should use AutoCAD's 386 version. If you do not yet have AutoCAD 386, you should consider upgrading to it. The upgrade and installation costs can be quickly offset by AutoCAD 386's fast response and execution times. The following are system requirements to run AutoCAD 386:

- IBM-compatible 80386 or 80486 computer.
- 80287 or 80387 math coprocessor (an 80387 coprocessor is integral to 80486 computers).
- 2M RAM minimum (4M recommended). Memory above 1M must be extended, not expanded, memory.
- 20M hard disk minimum. AutoCAD 386 will occupy 3.3M to 5.3M. The Advanced Modeling Extension (AME) will require an additional 3.4M.
- High-density floppy drive.
- DOS 3.3 or later.
- Appropriate video, input, and output devices.

AutoCAD 386 for DOS is as fast as or faster than any other version of AutoCAD using the same hardware. You should, however, keep your eyes on the alternative operating systems discussed in the following sections. In some situations, they provide a much better platform for AutoCAD than DOS.

Looking Ahead through Microsoft Windows

Microsoft Windows is not a true operating system but has become wildly popular with the release of Windows 3.0. Windows is actually an *operating environment* that sits on top of DOS and acts as a multipurpose DOS extender and GUI. Windows can run on any 80286-, 80386-, or 80486-based PC that has at least 2M of extended RAM.

Windows enables the user to run specially created Windows applications that take advantage of Windows' GUI and other resources. Windows also runs regular DOS programs and enables the user to switch between multiple DOS and Windows programs quickly and easily on a 386 machine. Like other modern operating environments, Windows uses virtual memory technology to help applications break through the 640K barrier and coexist with each other. Windows features a program manager that presents the GUI, and a print manager, which controls printing resources and spools output automatically. Windows also reclaims reserved high memory space addresses for use by applications, in much the same manner as the expanded memory management utilities described earlier. Further, Windows comes with its own disk-caching utility to improve hard disk performance. In short, Windows stuffs all the known DOS performance-enhancing tricks into one bag.

Figure 4.6 shows how DOS is reorganized under Windows so that all communications between layers are restricted to well-defined paths. Contrast figure 4.6 with figure 4.2, which shows DOS running without Windows. At the application level on Windows, several programs can be loaded at the same time and share memory and other Windows resources while presenting the GUI to the user at the uppermost level.

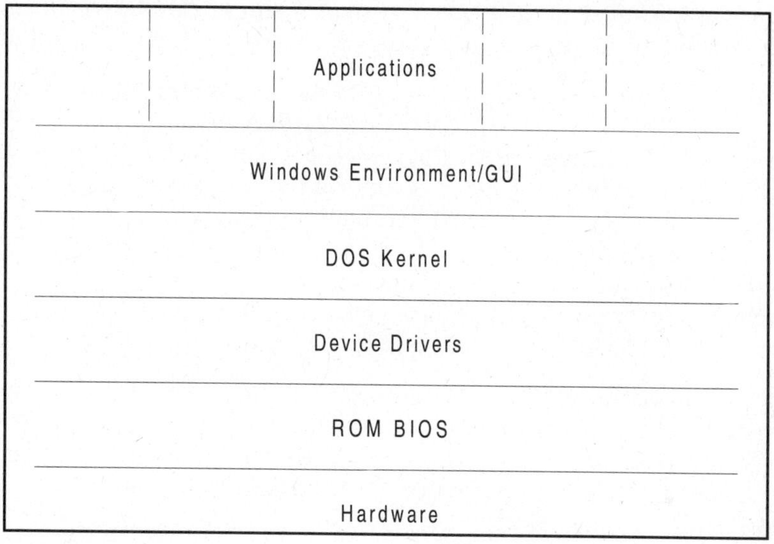

```
┌─────────────────────────────────────────────┐
│   │      │   │ Applications │   │      │    │
│   │      │   │              │   │      │    │
├─────────────────────────────────────────────┤
│         Windows Environment/GUI             │
├─────────────────────────────────────────────┤
│                DOS Kernel                   │
├─────────────────────────────────────────────┤
│              Device Drivers                 │
├─────────────────────────────────────────────┤
│                ROM BIOS                     │
├─────────────────────────────────────────────┤
│                Hardware                     │
└─────────────────────────────────────────────┘
```

Figure 4.6:
Microsoft Windows architecture.

Windows runs in one of three different modes, depending on the computer on which it is installed. On 286-based PCs, Windows runs in either *real mode* or *standard mode*. In either of these modes, the user runs Windows applications in on-screen windows and controls them with a mouse through the GUI. The user also can switch almost instantly to a standard DOS application that runs in full-screen text or graphics modes. The difference between real and standard mode is that real mode uses only 640K (conventional) memory and expanded memory. Standard mode uses the same 640K memory as real mode plus extended memory. However, because of the high overhead required to perform all this trickery, and forcing applications to communicate through all the layers shown in figure 4.6, Windows' performance generally is poor on all but the fastest 286-based PCs.

When installed in an 80386- or 80486-based PC, Windows performs acceptably. When a fast computer is combined with the ease of using Windows applications, a user can be considerably more productive, depending on the work being done. On a 386 machine, Windows can operate in 386 enhanced mode. This mode takes full advantage of the 80386 processor's capability to create "virtual machines." Windows can control multiple applications running at the same time in this mode, and can even allow standard DOS programs to run in windows beside true Windows applications. For more information on the 80386 chip's capabilities, see Chapter 14.

Using AutoCAD under Windows

The Windows package is inexpensive and boasts several built-in accessory programs, including a text editor, a word processor, a simple database, a communications program, a paint program, a file manager, games, and other useful programs.

Unfortunately, Windows is not of much use to the serious AutoCAD user because AutoCAD's performance suffers so much under Windows. AutoCAD is too large a program and relies too heavily upon having access directly to certain DOS layers. Another reason why you might want to stay away from running AutoCAD with Windows is because of the way AutoCAD uses screen space. AutoCAD is a graphics program that makes direct use of video hardware, so it must be run as a full-screen application (that is, not enclosed in a "window"). Also, AutoCAD does not run reliably with many software disk caches and Windows relies heavily on its own disk cache program, SMARTDRV.

In addition, Extended AutoLISP, which otherwise would let AutoCAD run in less memory, also fails under Windows. Windows will refuse to let the Extended AutoLISP DOS extender switch the mode of the CPU. Only the standard DOS versions of AutoCAD (Release 10 for 640K DOS or AutoCAD 286 Release 11) will operate (with limited performance) under Windows.

AutoCAD 386 (either release) is not fully compatible with Windows either, and cannot take advantage of Windows' resources. AutoCAD 386 also needs to have control of the computer's CPU and access to large amounts of memory. Because Windows is loaded before AutoCAD is, Windows takes control. As mentioned earlier, Windows complies with the DPMI interface, whereas AutoCAD complies with the VCPI interface. Because the two are not compatible with each other, AutoCAD is unable to access system resources controlled by Windows.

Some hope does exist for AutoCAD users who want to use Windows, as well. Phar Lap (makers of the AutoCAD 386 DOS extender) recently has added XMS (Extended Memory Specification) support to its DOS Extender. XMS is the same memory specification that Windows uses. Thus, AutoCAD 386 Release 10 and AutoCAD 386 Release 11 programs that have been updated to the new extender, can now run as a full-screen application under Windows in real or standard modes. These configurations, however, still have inherent performance limitations and a computer needs to be equipped with very large amounts of RAM to run AutoCAD 386 and Windows acceptably. Most users who have tried running AutoCAD under Windows have given up running the two together and exit Windows to run AutoCAD, preferring AutoCAD's native performance over Windows' convenience.

To update your copy of AutoCAD 386 with the new extender, you will need to contact your authorized AutoCAD dealer to receive the patch disk named NEWDX, which does not require that you upgrade your copy of AutoCAD. NEWDX also includes several other performance improvements to the DOS extender. Your AutoCAD dealer can perform the fix for you in minutes. NEWDX also is available from the ADESK forum on CompuServe.

In order for AutoCAD to run well under Windows, Autodesk would have to create a version of AutoCAD specifically for Windows. Autodesk, however, has not yet committed to creating such a version, and does not endorse Windows as an operating environment for AutoCAD.

About Windows and Networks

Windows works much better with networks than it does with AutoCAD. Microsoft has big plans for making Windows a part of its overall networking strategy, including client/server computing as was introduced in Chapter 1. Windows 3.0 is the first version of Windows to provide specific support for networks, with more to come in the future.

Windows 3.0 directly recognizes network drives and directories and will let the Windows user attach to those drives while in the Windows' File Manager. Each network drive seen by Windows appears in File Manager with the word NET below it (see fig. 4.7).

Windows 3.0 also recognizes network printers that can be associated with a printer driver and a port on a personal computer. This lets any Windows application print directly to the network printer.

Windows also supports network messages sent and broadcast across the network by users. Windows includes setup features for popular networks, including MS-NET and compatibles, Novell NetWare, and Microsoft LAN Manager, that supply pop-up dialogue boxes for network messages. For more information on Windows and networks, get *Maximizing Windows*, published by New Riders Publishing.

Windows is a good stepping-stone because it has breathed new life into DOS and is paving the way toward advanced operating systems, most notably a future 32-bit version of Windows, Win/32, and OS/2. Windows and OS/2 are almost identical in appearance, and applications developed for one easily can be adapted for the other. In fact, many companies are installing Windows in preparation for an eventual move to OS/2 and a future version of OS/2 should run Windows programs directly, providing an attractive upgrade path. If you want to see into the future of personal computing without much expense and have fun at the same time, start with Windows. Running AutoCAD under Windows is not recommended, but for general computing needs, Windows is an attractive and exciting option.

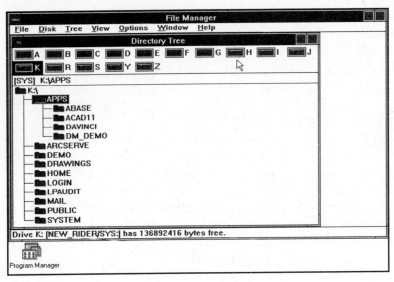

Figure 4.7:
Network drives as seen inside the Windows File Manager.

OS/2: The Future of PCs?

IBM and Microsoft jointly created OS/2 in the hopes that this new operating system would both replace DOS and realize the potential of advanced microprocessors. As was the case with DOS, which was marketed in two nearly identical versions (PC DOS for use with IBM computers and MS-DOS for use with computers made by everybody else), Microsoft licenses OS/2 to IBM and other personal computer manufacturers. These vendors may add their own extensions and enhancements to the operating system to work with their particular hardware and resell it with their computers just like DOS. More than 60 original equipment manufacturers (OEMs) have licensed OS/2 from Microsoft, including the following:

- Apricot Computers
- AT&T Information Systems
- Bull S.A.
- Compaq Computer Corporation
- Dell Corporate Systems
- Everex Systems Inc.
- Fujitsu Ltd.
- IBM Corporation

- NCR Corporation
- NEC Corporation
- Nokia Data systems
- Olivetti SPA
- Peacock GMBH
- Unisys Corporation
- Zenith Data Systems

With all of these vendors selling OS/2, you can be assured that you have a good chance of getting OS/2 with your next computer purchase. Contrary to popular opinion, you do not have to buy from IBM alone to get OS/2.

Understanding the Editions

The OS/2 issue is blurred also because of the different editions of the operating system. In addition to the basic OS/2 operating system named Standard Edition (SE), IBM also offers OS/2 Extended Edition (EE). The Standard Edition includes the main operating system, or kernel, and the Presentation Manager (PM). The Presentation Manager is responsible for the OS/2 graphical user interface in the same way Windows provides the GUI for DOS. IBM's Extended Edition combines OS/2 SE with the following three important programs, which help IBM reach its goal of having similar applications across all its systems:

- *Database Manager* is a nearly functional equivalent of IBM's DB2 mainframe database program, which is built around *structured query language* (SQL).
- *Communications Manager* is a multipurpose asynchronous communications program with emulation support for popular IBM terminals.
- *LAN Requester* provides client support for IBM's connectivity products.

Microsoft does not offer an extended edition of OS/2. Instead, Microsoft allows third-party programs to supply the additional capabilities provided by IBM's OS/2 Extended Edition. IBM also includes hardware support for its own Micro Channel Architecture with its versions of OS/2. Otherwise, Microsoft OS/2 SE and IBM OS/2 SE are exactly the same product; only the names are different. Programs written for one of these operating systems will run identically on the other. DOS programs, however, may not run "directly" on any OS/2 system.

OS/2 is written in 16-bit programming instructions, uses the processors' protected mode, and allows programs to address 16M of memory in 80286, 80386, and 80486 computers. OS/2 programs, including AutoCAD OS/2, are built and operate in much the same way as AutoCAD 386. That is, they are not limited in size to operate in less than 640K, and TSR programs are unnecessary. If you need a second program while one application is active, you simply start the second program in addition to the current one. The new program appears in another window on top of the current application, making both programs available. The OS/2 user interface is described in greater detail later in this chapter.

A 32-bit version of OS/2 should be available soon from IBM (which has taken over most OS/2 development from Microsoft) and should feature a larger segment size, improved mode-switching capabilities, demand paging, and better I/O protection. These features will further optimize OS/2 for 80386 and 80486 computers.

The following hardware is required to run OS/2 on a personal computer:

- 80286-based personal computer (80386 recommended)
- 2M memory (4M or more recommended)
- One high-density floppy disk drive
- 40M (80M or more recommended) fast (under 28 ms recommended) hard disk
- VGA (Super VGA or Extended VGA recommended) graphic display adapter and monitor
- Mouse

OS/2's Advantages over DOS

Microsoft learned its lesson with MS-DOS. Each time Microsoft's programmers added features to MS-DOS, the entire system had to be recompiled and another version released. With OS/2, services are added to the operating system in modules called *dynamic-link libraries* (DLLs). Unlike DOS routines, OS/2 routines are not all compiled into one large file. Instead, OS/2 routines reside in DLL files, which are supplied with OS/2 and can be distributed in modified form as needed, or replaced entire. In order for DOS to support a new display resolution standard, for instance, an entire new version of DOS is needed. With OS/2, only a new DLL file is needed to add the same display support to an existing version of OS/2.

DLLs also let multiple, active programs share operating system code responsible for system services. Presentation Manager is added to OS/2 this way, as is Microsoft LAN Manager support and many other services by applications programs. As figure 4.8 illustrates, several application programs can share a DLL at the same time, instead of having to wait their turn, as in DOS. A single DLL file can be read by each application and, in essence, become a part of each application. Display, mouse, help, and keyboard support are examples of these dynamic link libraries.

OS/2 tackles the inadequacies of DOS by providing many new capabilities, such as multitasking, multiple threads of operation, inter-process communications (IPC), and a virtual memory system. The following sections briefly introduce each of these capabilities.

Multitasking

OS/2 features true *multitasking* capabilities, which means that a user can have several programs running at one time without conflicts. OS/2 uses a multitasking process known as *priority-based preemptive scheduling*. Under this kind of multitasking strategy, OS/2 diverts the CPU's attention from one program to another according to a dynamic, multilevel priority scheme that minimizes system response time. Other multitasking programs and operating systems, such as DESQview and certain versions of UNIX, use *round-robin time slicing*. This method divides the CPU's attention in fixed increments and distributes them to each task in the cycle equally, regardless of importance. Still other multitasking programs rely on a process called *event-dependent scheduling*, which forces certain tasks to wait until others are finished.

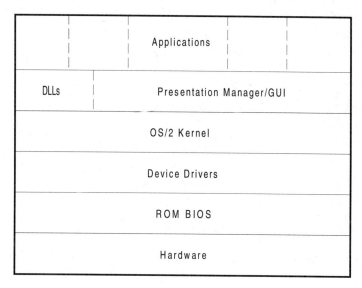

Figure 4.8:
OS/2 system architecture.

Multiple Threads

OS/2 programs also can execute multiple processes—or *threads*—within themselves to increase efficiency. For example, while a program is saving a file to disk (one thread), it also can be accepting input from the user (another thread). Because OS/2 programs use a priority-based scheduling method, the thread that is accepting user input can be assigned a higher priority by the programmer, so that the file-output process does not necessarily slow down the user.

Virtual Memory

If a user attempts to launch a program that requires more free memory than is available, OS/2 can *swap* data, another program's code, or even some of its own program code. The operating system places this information on disk or in another storage area to make room for the new program. Only about half of OS/2 needs to be resident in the system to run, and OS/2 can swap up to a total of 128M of code and data. This swapping capability makes the system appear as though it has much more RAM available than is actually installed. For this reason, OS/2 is referred to as a *virtual memory* operating system.

Inter-Process Communications

In a multitasking environment, multiple programs can execute simultaneously and the user can manipulate the same data in several of those applications. At such times, the opportunity to share that data among programs arises. Through *inter-process communications* in OS/2, programs pass data back and forth in three ways: shared memory, named pipes, and dynamic data exchange.

Shared Memory

The first way programs can share data is by sharing memory. Unlike DOS, which crashes if one program attempts to read the memory used by another program, OS/2 can protect the memory that is used by each program. Programs are free to read the memory occupied by other sessions of the same program. Indeed, if you ran two incidences of AutoCAD under OS/2, when combined they would occupy little more RAM than a single incidence of AutoCAD. Segments of code in memory that are not otherwise busy at work in one session of the program can be used automatically by the other. All the code of both sessions does not need to reside in memory at the same time.

Named Pipes

Two related programs also can communicate through a dedicated high-performance communications channel, called a *named pipe*. Programs use named pipes much the same way as they write to and read from a file. OS/2 programs running on workstations attached to a LAN Manager network, for example, can use named pipes to communicate with each other across the network.

Dynamic Data Exchange

The final option available to programs for communication is called *dynamic data exchange* (DDE). When dynamic data exchange is used, one or more processes act as servers and one or more processes act as clients. Clients issue request messages to servers, and servers answer requests from clients. Basically, DDE processes are parts of a program that not only work for their own program, but can work for other programs as well. DDE is usually used to let programs share the same data. If changes are made to the data in one program, they can be updated automatically in another program by DDE. In order for OS/2 programs to use DDE, however, the programs must be written for the OS/2 Presentation Manager.

AutoCAD OS/2 features dynamic data exchange capabilities and is shipped with sample programs that can communicate with Microsoft's Excel spreadsheet program. Figure 4.9, for example, shows AutoCAD operating as a client issuing requests for data, while Excel acts as a server returning data. Through this particular combination, the user can establish a parametric drafting system. Drawing data can be represented in Excel and AutoCAD can poll Excel for updated information. The process works in reverse as well; if the drawing is changed graphically, Excel updates the associated dimensions.

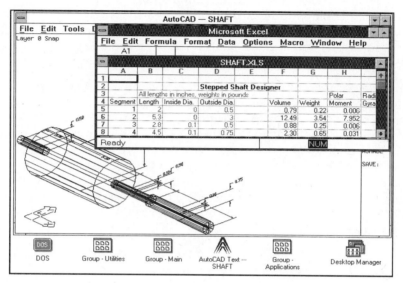

Figure 4.9:
AutoCAD OS/2 communicating with Microsoft Excel through DDE.

> **Note:** Dynamic data exchange in AutoCAD is accomplished and made available to the user through a programming interface introduced by Autodesk in AutoCAD OS/2, known as the AutoCAD Development System (ADS). ADS provides programmers with a set of C language functions. This includes functions present in AutoLISP as well as functions that facilitate DDE and other operations. By programming in C, developers can write larger, faster, and more complex programs than they can by using AutoLISP. These ADS programs are defined as commands in AutoCAD by AutoLISP. The user can then call these programs like an AutoLISP function, or use them as an external process through an AutoLISP function.

OS/2-DOS Compatibility

OS/2 provides backward compatibility with DOS. OS/2 commands are primarily a superset of DOS V3.x commands, with additional commands and utilities for OS/2-specific functions such as managing printer spooling and batch processing. If you know DOS well, you will not have much trouble getting around on an OS/2 system.

The most widely advertised feature in OS/2 of concern to DOS users is the *DOS compatibility box.* When the user double-clicks on the DOS icon, OS/2 switches to real mode and releases approximately 540K (under OS/2 V1.2) of memory for running DOS programs. In contrast, DOS 3.3 provides approximately 576K of free memory for programs, including character-device drivers such as communications and printer drivers. Block-device drivers such as disk and network drivers, however, are not compatible with the OS/2 DOS box. Alternatively, the user can disable DOS compatibility completely, freeing another 500K of extended memory for OS/2 programs. A future version of OS/2 is expected to be capable of executing multiple 640K DOS sessions.

Applications developers can make the switch from DOS to OS/2 fairly easily, by taking advantage of the OS/2 Family Applications Program Interface (FAPI). Programs written to common FAPI specifications run under both OS/2 and DOS. FAPI programs do not take full advantage of the OS/2 Presentation Manager interface, but they can be run in a PM text window. Microsoft Word 5.0 is an example of a FAPI program, in that its executable file is compatible with both operating systems. Most programmers eventually will want to move their products to full PM implementation to take advantage of OS/2's capabilities. FAPI, however, helps developers create functional OS/2 programs more quickly than they would if they had to code OS/2 versions from scratch.

When properly configured, a computer can run both OS/2 and DOS. IBM versions of OS/2 since V1.2, and several OEMs of Microsoft OS/2, have provided *dual boot* utilities that enable the user to choose between the two operating systems. With the help of such a utility, users can migrate to OS/2 slowly, falling back on DOS if necessary for incompatible programs.

Finally, OS/2 also retains the file allocation table (FAT) file system that is used in DOS. The DOS FAT is explained in the following section. The file systems of all other operating systems (XENIX, UNIX, and others) are incompatible with DOS. Only OS/2 permits the user to have a foot in both operating system worlds.

File System Flexibility

The DOS FAT was designed in 1977. The FAT recording method was designed primarily for use with floppy disks and has not kept pace with technology any better than DOS has. For quite some time, users have sought to escape from the restrictive 11-character file name (composed of an 8-character name and a 3-character extension) imposed by the FAT. Ever since the appearance of the first hard disk with more than 32M of storage capacity, users have bemoaned the need for special drivers, controllers, and basic input-output systems (BIOS) to take advantage of larger-capacity drives.

The FAT file system is inadequate in network environments. Novell NetWare, for example, which uses a proprietary file-recording scheme, has 11 file attributes compared with DOS' four file attributes (read only, hidden, system, and archive).

OS/2, since V1.2, has come with an alternative to the DOS FAT system—the High-Performance File System (HPFS). With HPFS, files can have extended file attributes in addition to the attributes used by DOS. This includes the capability to associate up to 64K of binary data, such as icons or other file information, with files. File names also can have up to 256 characters, such as "Widget Corp-flange.heavy duty." HPFS handles spaces, punctuation marks, and case sensitivity.

> **Note:** Extended file attributes are the key to new *object-oriented* environments, such as Hewlett Packard's New Wave operating environment. In an object-oriented environment, the program and the data are "connected" to act as one object, and are synonymous with each other. In a desktop publishing (DTP) scenario under DOS, text is prepared with a word processor, a spreadsheet section can be included, and graphics are done in another program. If any one of the elements needs to be changed, the user must leave the DTP program, make the changes, and import the changed file back into the published document. With object orientation, however, the user simply clicks on the text, spreadsheet, or graphic, and the program that created the file will pop up with the file ready to be edited. Once editing is finished, the program disappears and the change is reflected in all associated files without user intervention. New Wave is available for the Windows environment, but programs must be adapted to work with New Wave.

In contrast to DOS and other operating systems that use a single file system, OS/2 has provisions for installable file systems. OS/2 is unique in that it can use different filing systems for different purposes, whether they are single-user filing systems, network and multiuser systems, or file systems for very large database applications. Users can have the different file systems installed on the same computer in different volumes. Third-party developers can replace the filing system without replacing the entire operating system. HPFS leaves the future open for the inevitable changes that will come. If a higher-technology file system becomes available, it can easily be added to the OS/2 operating system.

Under HPFS, disk-volume capacities increase to seemingly ridiculous limits. HPFS can handle volume sizes up to 2 terabytes (2 million megabytes) and file sizes up to 2 gigabytes (2,000M). Even so, HPFS wastes less storage space on small files than FAT does. With the DOS FAT file system, disk space is allocated in single-sector increments so that an average of 2,048 bytes (one half of a 4,096 byte sector) is wasted per file (the actual size of the file rounded up to the next 4,096 byte boundary). HPFS wastes an average of only 256 bytes (half of a 512 byte sector) per file. This may not seem much, but when multiplied by thousands of files per disk, it can add up to a large amount of expensive disk space going to waste.

HPFS is also faster than FAT in loading files because of its directory-recording scheme. The FAT file system records file names and directory information in a linear fashion in a single space on each disk. HPFS, on the other hand, is more efficient in its handling of file names because the system stores them in an indexed binary tree. When looking for a file, OS/2 goes directly to the directory information.

In addition, HPFS keeps directory and file name information closer to the actual data. Rather than forcing the disk drive's heads to traverse the disk surface back and forth between the FAT table, HPFS maintains the information in directory bands located between 8M data bands (see fig. 4.10). This feature keeps the file and directory information closer to the data itself, minimizing head travel.

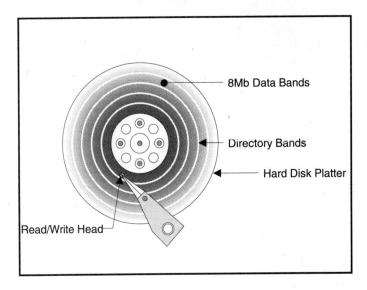

8Mb Data Bands

Directory Bands

Hard Disk Platter

Read/Write Head

Figure 4.10:
HPFS directory and data bands.

HPFS also has the capability to perform "lazy" writes. Lazy writing is a technique whereby the file system writes information destined for disk to a disk buffer in RAM if the drive is presently busy servicing other requests made by another process. When the disk is once again idle, the information in the buffers is written to disk. Altogether, HPFS constitutes a powerful new file system for multitasking and heavy-duty uses.

Even with HPFS installed, OS/2 systems can still read and write FAT files. In fact, users can have both file systems installed on the same computer in different disk volumes. DOS programs running in the compatibility mode can read and write HPFS files (but only if the file name adheres to the old FAT convention). To simplify file transfers, HPFS always formats floppy disks with the FAT file system.

The OS/2 Presentation Manager

OS/2 provides PC users with a new *WYSIWYG* (what-you-see-is-what-you-get) screen display and graphical interface called Presentation Manager (PM). Presentation Manager is included with OS/2 versions 1.1 and later, and is similar in appearance to Microsoft Windows. PM is a hardware-independent, window-based GUI for all programs running under OS/2 that are written for PM. The PM interface enables the user to define multiple display areas (windows) on the screen, with a program running in each window. These windows can be moved, resized, minimized, or maximized. The user can control PM's windows by using a mouse pointer to manipulate on-screen scroll bars, buttons, icons, and borders.

Most programs running under Presentation Manager use drop-down menus exclusively, similar to the drop-down menus in AutoSketch and AutoShade. File operations and user options are controlled by dialogue boxes. Figure 4.11 shows how one of AutoCAD's dialogue boxes looks with the Presentation Manager face-lift.

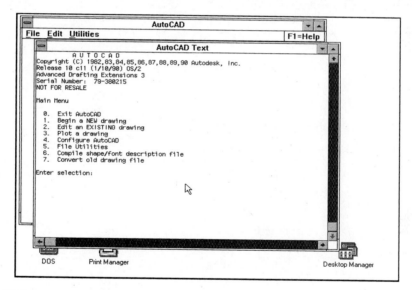

Figure 4.11:
AutoCAD's Presentation Manager interface.

Another benefit to OS/2 users is that all OS/2 PM programs can utilize high-resolution graphics card drivers. OS/2 will work with an EGA adapter, but a VGA, Super VGA, or 8514/A adapter greatly improves not only screen appearance, but productivity as well because more information is visible at higher resolutions. As a result, text does not need to be scrolled as often and windows do not need to be moved as frequently. Because PM specifies a graphics programming interface (GPI), graphics card makers can write drivers for PM at various resolutions and color palettes in much the same way they do for the ADI interface used by AutoCAD for third-party graphics cards. The driver can enhance all screen display with the exception of the OS/2 full-screen text mode. A 1024x768 PM driver, for example, displays AutoCAD OS/2, Microsoft Excel, and WordPerfect for PM all at the same resolution and colors. Several companies, including Renaissance GRX, Compaq, Dell, and Hewlett Packard are preparing TIGA interface PM drivers for their TI 34010 graphics boards. For more information on graphics coprocessor boards and TIGA, see Chapter 14.

OS/2 conforms to IBM's common user access (CUA) specification, which provides a consistent method of displaying options, making menu selections, editing text, and supplying help and other logic in programs on all types of computer platforms, from micros to mainframes. Programs that adhere to CUA are easier to learn, reducing both training and development costs. This type of specification has long been an advantage of the Macintosh interface.

Using AutoCAD with OS/2

AutoCAD and OS/2 are a fine match, especially for people who do more than just draw all day, such as engineers, managers, and AutoCAD programmers. The OS/2 version of AutoCAD is called simply AutoCAD OS/2.

The following are system requirements for AutoCAD OS/2:

- IBM PC/AT, PS/2, or 100% compatible computer
- 4M RAM minimum, 6M recommended
- OS/2 v1.1 or higher with Presentation Manager
- 80287 or 80387 coprocessor
- High density floppy disk drive
- Hard disk
- Presentation Manager-compatible mouse
- Optional digitizer
- Optional Presentation Manager-compatible printer, or plotter

AutoCAD OS/2 provides AutoCAD users with several unique advantages of OS/2. The most apparent is the Presentation Manager (PM) GUI. AutoCAD OS/2 runs within either one or two windows on the PM desktop: one window is for graphics and the other window is for text. The text window is the equivalent of the DOS version's text screen and is either always visible or only visible when needed. Each window can be resized, positioned, maximized to full screen, or minimized to an icon similar to any other OS/2 window.

AutoCAD and Presentation Manager

The most striking feature of the graphics window for DOS users is the absence of the Main menu. AutoCAD users have complained about the Main menu for several years. The graphics window displays immediately when AutoCAD is started, poised to invoke the drawing editor. Here, AutoCAD displays three pull-down menus similar to other OS/2 programs: File, Edit, and Utilities. When in the drawing editor, the File and Edit menus are displayed in addition to the normal pull-down menu selections of the AutoCAD Advanced User Interface (AUI). This new convention may be how future versions of AutoCAD for DOS might look.

File Menu

By pulling down the File menu, a user can begin a new drawing or open an existing drawing file by selecting the file's name from a dialogue box. The dialogue box has drive, directory, and file lists, as well as dialogue box buttons (see fig. 4.12).

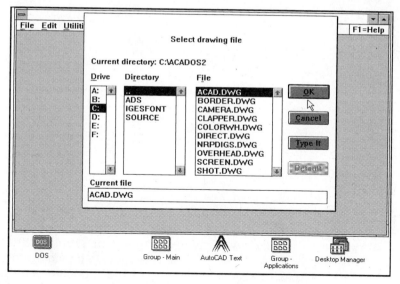

Figure 4.12:
The AutoCAD OS/2 file dialogue box.

The File menu of the graphics window gives easy access to editing, saving, and plotting drawing files, and adjusting the ways AutoCAD uses the PM interface. By selecting Environment from the File menu, users can toggle the AutoCAD screen menu area on or off, toggle the status line of the graphics window on or off, configure the command prompt area with up to three lines (alternatively you can use the AutoCAD text window for command prompt display), save and restore window positions, and toggle the AutoCAD file dialogue box feature on or off. The environment dialogue boxes also let the user select from among any installed OS/2 font for the AutoCAD graphics screen, text screen, and dialogue boxes. Other selections on the File menu let the user set up page sizes and orientations for OS/2 system printers, and to dump a graphics screen (without menus and status line) to the printer—a feature DOS users have longed for (see fig. 4.13).

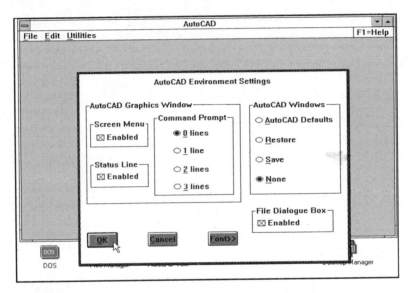

Figure 4.13:
Configuring the AutoCAD OS/2 interface.

Edit Menu

The AutoCAD OS/2 Edit menu controls the Undo and Redo commands, toggles the text window on or off, and controls AutoCAD's use of the OS/2 clipboard. The OS/2 clipboard is a general OS/2 facility for temporarily saving graphics images from Presentation Manager programs. AutoCAD OS/2 includes a clipboard viewer program that gives users access to images contained in the clipboard. The AutoCAD clipboard viewer is started also from the Edit menu. It, too, runs in a window and can be manipulated like the graphics and text windows. From the clipboard viewer, images can be loaded from metafile files and opened or saved from bitmap files. From the Edit menu, users can copy portions of screen images to the clipboard from the AutoCAD graphics window, the text window, or anywhere on the screen for inserting into documents created by other programs. Specific drawing vectors can be copied to the clipboard with AutoCAD's general object selection methods (see fig. 4.14).

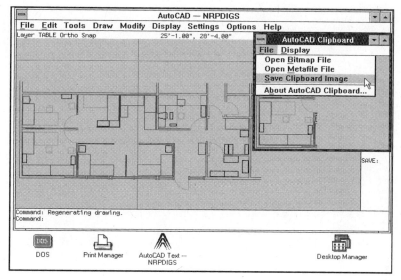

Figure 4.14:
The AutoCAD OS/2 clipboard viewer.

Utilities Menu

Selections for device configuration, file utilities, compiling shape files, and converting old drawings are found on the Utilities menu that is displayed only before entering the drawing editor.

All of the normal selections of the AutoCAD Main menu are still available within the AutoCAD text window. One particularly nice feature of the text window is its ability to buffer up to 1,500 lines of AutoCAD prompts, responses, and messages. By using the PM's slider bars, you can scroll up or down and read messages that would have long since been lost on a DOS system.

How AutoCAD OS/2 Exploits System Resources

With AutoCAD OS/2, a user can use OS/2's multitasking features to do other tasks at the same time as drawing, such as typing a document, editing an AutoLISP program, working in a spreadsheet, or file management. Even multiple sessions of AutoCAD can be run for editing multiple drawings or plotting concurrently. Only the first copy of AutoCAD, however, will have access to the system pointer or digitizer, so only plotting or other "hands-off" tasks, such as running scripts, should be performed in subsequent copies (see fig. 4.15).

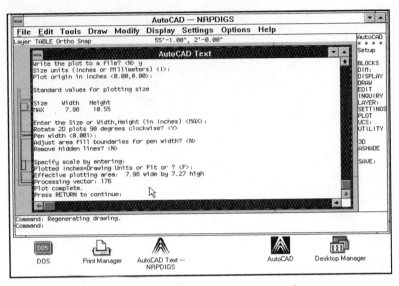

Figure 4.15:

Two copies of AutoCAD OS/2 running simultaneously.

Virtual Memory

Under OS/2, AutoCAD has access to virtual memory for AutoLISP and large drawings. The AutoLISP HEAP or STACK do not need to be configured. The STACK is preset at 20K, large enough for the most robust AutoLISP programs. Autodesk recommends 6M of RAM for AutoCAD OS/2 although it will run with as few as 4M. The 640K DOS version of AutoCAD can run in the DOS compatibility box of OS/2, but not very well; OS/2's DOS session does not provide expanded or extended memory that AutCAD needs to be productive.

AutoCAD OS/2 can make use also of OS/2's dynamic data exchange facility to work cooperatively with other programs and was the first version to include the AutoCAD Development System (ADS) as described earlier.

System Printing

Another OS/2 system resource that AutoCAD OS/2 uses is system printing. AutoCAD users can choose the OS/2 system printer in addition to many standard plotters and printers. When using standard AutoCAD output devices, plotting and printing occurs similar to the DOS version. When configured for the system printer, users can modify page size and orientations settings from within AutoCAD.

When you print to the OS/2 system printer you can take advantage also of the OS/2 Print Manager. The Print Manager acts as an automatic spooler and print job queue for OS/2 programs. Printing happens much faster when processed through the Print Manager because printer data is spooled to a disk file, returning the user to the application much faster. Meanwhile, the Print Manager handles transmission of the print data from the disk file to the attached printer. The user can pause, resume, and delete print jobs with the Print Manager, as shown in figure 4.16.

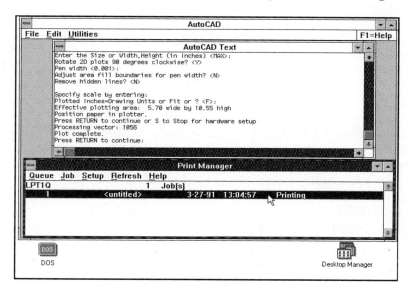

Figure 4.16:
An AutoCAD plot being serviced in the OS/2 Print Manager.

Display Services

All display services for AutoCAD OS/2 are provided by OS/2 itself. AutoCAD OS/2 includes only one display driver: the Autodesk OS/2 PM driver. This single driver interfaces AutoCAD to the display driver used by OS/2 for all displays. No special AutoCAD drivers are needed or upgraded when a new version of AutoCAD comes out. Your video card manufacturer, however, must provide you with a PM driver to take advantage of the card's high resolution modes if you do not want to use it in standard VGA mode. Many video card manufacturers have PM drivers that provide resolution up to 1024x768 in 256 colors. That is the nice aspect of Presentation Manager: instead of having crisp, high resolution display only for AutoCAD, you can have it in all your other PM programs as well.

Multitasking

AutoCAD OS/2 provides complete flexibility for multitasking external programs with the AutoCAD Shell command. Through various options within the ACAD.PGP file, users can have other programs execute in the foreground or background, have AutoCAD wait or not wait until processing is complete before continuing, and have other programs be invisible or visible. With these options users can have almost any program spin off from AutoCAD and perform another task while they continue drafting, or they can turn their attention to the external program.

Input Devices

Normally, a user configures a mouse for use as the OS/2 system pointer. The system mouse can be used with AutoCAD to move the drawing editor crosshairs and to make pull-down menu selection when within the graphics window. Many AutoCAD users, however, need digitizers for use with tablet menus. Digitizer owners can have their digitizer act the same as a DOS AutoCAD digitizer to pick tablet commands and move the crosshairs within the drawing editor. The user, however, also must have a system mouse to access AutoCAD's pull-down menus and for use with other Presentation Manager windows. Autodesk saw this as a handicap and provides a *mole driver* for OS/2 with AutoCAD OS/2. The mole driver lets a digitizer be used for both AutoCAD tablet and screen picks, as well as acts as the OS/2 system pointer. The mole driver can be configured with a dedicated area for digitizer picks, with an area for toggling between digitizer and system pointer modes, or with a digitizer button as a toggle between the two modes.

About OS/2 and Networks

OS/2 was designed with networking independence at its foundation. With DOS (which does not have built-in network support), network drivers must be loaded in the CONFIG.SYS or AUTOEXEC.BAT files. The drivers intercept operating system calls before they get to DOS and act as what is called a *front end*. OS/2, on the other hand, is structured in such a way that front ends are not allowed, meaning all service requests must go through OS/2 first. Software systems such as networks, therefore, must reside on an OS/2 computer as a *back end* and let OS/2 be the front end. A network driver must request that services be redirected to them by OS/2. Thus, network driver programs for OS/2 are known as *requesters*, meaning DOS-based network drivers cannot be used while operating OS/2.

With the proper requester program, an OS/2 workstation can function in a Microsoft LAN Manager, IBM LAN Server, 3Com 3+Open, or Novell NetWare network. Connectivity with LAN Manager, LAN Server, and 3+Open networks is possible through the Microsoft OS/2 Requester. Also, access to NetWare systems is available trough the OS/2 Requester for NetWare from Novell.

The benefits of using OS/2 as the workstation operating system of a network are threefold. The first is freedom from the memory restrictions imposed by networking with which DOS users are familiar. When you network an OS/2 workstation, you will not be left with less usable memory for applications, suc as when you network with DOS.

The next benefit is the capability to run network utilities within a window with your other programs. You do not need to exit an application, for example, to run a utility or command, to change printers, or to send a message. DOS utilities for these kinds of tasks exist as TSRs, but they still use up precious memory and can conflict with other programs. In OS/2, network utilities are just another program and can be run as such, even concurrently.

Finally, OS/2's DDE opens up powerful possibilities for sharing data not only among applications running on the same computer, but also among different computers running on the same network. Several users not only can share the same file on the network, but with DDE, any changes made to that data by one user can update the data of others without reloading the file.

The disadvantages of networking OS/2 workstations are mostly the result of OS/2's current lack of widespread popularity. There are few requestor programs for OS/2, and to make matters more difficult for OS/2 users, not all network interface cards include requester software to work with OS/2. Only the major network interface card vendors are shipping OS/2 drivers so far. Before you commit to OS/2 for your workstations, you should investigate your network hardware and driver options that are presented in the next chapter.

UNIX on the PC

In the late 1960s at AT&T's Bell Laboratories, programmers were working on a new operating system to solve the problems of transferring programs across different computers. Until that time, each computer had a proprietary operating system. The programmers needed an operating system that could be transferred to any hardware architecture, provide the same development tools on any system, and be easy to maintain and extend. To address these needs, the AT&T programmers developed the UNIX operating system.

Distribution of UNIX mainly came through development of the operating system at the University of California at Berkeley. AT&T had licensed UNIX to educational institutions for use in research at little or no cost. With commercial backing by Sun Microsystems and government sponsorship from the Defense Advanced Research Project Agency (DARPA), UNIX soon became the operating system of choice among programmers on mainframes and minicomputers. UNIX became popular because of its power and flexibility, and eventually became the favorite base operating system for engineering workstations.

More recently, before the introduction of OS/2, developers attempted to bring the UNIX operating system down to the PC to drive more powerful applications and take advantage of 80286- and 80386-based computers.

UNIX Features

UNIX is a time-slicing, multitasking, and multiuser operating system. *Time slicing* is a primitive round-robin scheme for scheduling many tasks. In a time-slicing scenario, each active task, in turn, receives an equal amount of the processor's attention. Although it affords equity to all tasks, time slicing gives greater priority to less important processes than the user might like.

UNIX is primarily written in C language with some assembly language routines. Because C language is available on virtually every computing platform, UNIX can be moved to different types of computers without much difficulty. To move UNIX from one platform to another, the developer needs only to recode or substitute assembly language subroutines and compile them with the C source code.

Figure 4.17 illustrates the various UNIX layers. At the bottom layer can be almost any hardware platform, such as a mainframe, a minicomputer, or an 80386-based PC. The second layer comprises the UNIX operating system itself, including, in this case, additional emulation software for running DOS programs directly. The next layer provides distributed network file system and communications support. Additional modules for input and output management come next, such as the X Window System standard for providing windowed access to programs running on remote hosts. Atop it all can rest a UNIX GUI, such as Open Software Foundation's Motif, which is an OS/2 Presentation Manager look-alike. Application programs can have direct access to any layer, similar to the DOS architecture, yet only UNIX has direct control of the system's hardware, providing a stable environment for the application.

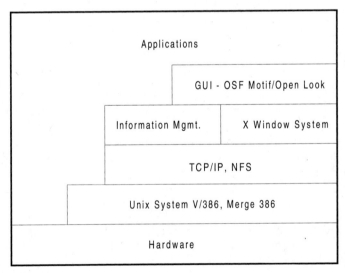

Figure 4.17:
UNIX system architecture.

Like OS/2, UNIX features a virtual memory system that makes free disk space appear as system memory. UNIX also implements a memory-swapping scheme to set aside noncritical memory contents to disk. This swapping makes room for higher-priority programs and data.

Compared with the Macintosh's 32-character and OS/2 High-Performance File System's 256-character file names, the UNIX file system accepts only 14 case-sensitive characters in a file name. UNIX also includes the following features:

- Capacity for files larger than 17 gigabytes
- Built-in accounting of system usage
- A replaceable *shell* (command interpreter)
- A C-language compiler and programming tools
- Built-in communications and networking
- Security features
- Directory structures that can be *mounted* (moved) to any point on the overall directory hierarchy

In Pursuit of a Binary Standard

UNIX has been adapted by many of the major computer manufacturers, such as Apollo, HP, Sun Microsystems, IBM, ITT, and DEC, to fit their business plans and visions. This multi-platform customization, however, has resulted in the lack of binary compatibility among the different vendors and applications (see fig. 4.18). At the height of UNIX customization in 1982, 220 different versions of UNIX existed.

Recently, however, many UNIX vendors have tried to come to an agreement on a standard "shrink-wrapped" version of UNIX. This proposed UNIX would run identically on all processor architectures and reunite the AT&T and Berkeley versions. From this unification movement, however, have arisen two opposing groups: Sun Microsystems and AT&T (alias UNIX International) versus a number of other vendors, including IBM, DEC, Santa Cruz Operation, and HP (known as the Open Software Foundation). Both groups are fighting for the profits from an estimated 65,000 new UNIX installations each month.

A major point of contention between the UNIX groups is the "look and feel" of the new UNIX. Sun and AT&T propose that their *Open Look* GUI developed for the Sun SPARCstation should be accepted as the standard UNIX interface. Open Look will be standard in AT&T's next version of UNIX—System V Release 4.0—which integrates the Sun and Berkeley versions.

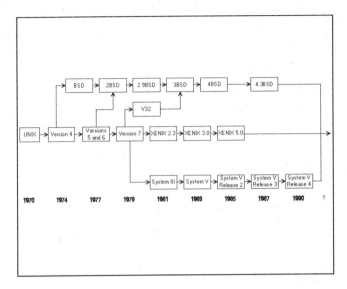

Figure 4.18:
UNIX development history.

The Open Software Foundation, on the other hand, promotes the development of the UNIX operating system on published, nonproprietary standards. OSF proposes a Presentation Manager look-alike GUI named Motif. Motif has a strategic advantage in that it has the blessing of IBM. The OSF version of UNIX, christened *OSF/1*, is built on IBM's UNIX clone, AIX, even though AIX does not use Motif. If Motif wins out, users could see the same easy-to-learn-and-remember interface from Windows on DOS, to PM on OS/2, through Motif on OSF/1. This would make training and retraining much less of a hassle for companies with all of the supported platforms and make developing software for those computers almost universal.

XENIX and Other Flavors of UNIX

Microsoft seized the opportunity to provide UNIX power to scientists and developers who moved to the PC by licensing UNIX from AT&T. Microsoft adapted UNIX to the Intel processor architectures, and in turn, licensed other resellers to sell the PC version of the operating system as XENIX. Because of legal restrictions on the name "UNIX," most versions of UNIX have different names with an X in it, such as AIX, Ultrix, and XENIX. Each version is adapted to run on different computer hardware. AIX, for example, runs on only IBM RISC-based workstations, whereas Ultrix runs on only Digital Equipment Corp. workstations. For IBM-compatible personal computers, Microsoft released XENIX/286 in 1982 and XENIX/386 in 1983. XENIX/286 runs on 80286 and 80386 processors in protected mode, and in the 80386's virtual mode. XENIX/386 also runs on an 80386 in protected mode, and allows a DOS program to run concurrently with XENIX programs.

To give you an idea of XENIX's features, the major reseller of XENIX, the Santa Cruz Operation (SCO), is focused here. All other XENIXs are nearly identical with only a different name on the label.

SCO provides a rich, bundled XENIX environment in its Open Desktop product. Open Desktop includes support for Ethernet networking through NFS, NETBIOS, and LAN Manager interfaces. A SQL database system is built into Open Desktop, as is a convenient feature called *Merge 386*. Merge 386 enables DOS applications to be run unmodified as tasks under XENIX. All this is integrated through the Motif graphical windowing system.

SCO XENIX was the first PC-based UNIX target of AutoCAD *porting* in early 1989. AutoSolid, Autodesk's solid modeling program, was already running on XENIX prior to 1989. Versions of AutoCAD for Apollo, Sun, IBM, and DEC workstations as well were running on their respective versions of UNIX and are supported still today.

Porting refers to the process in which the source code of a program (in this case, AutoCAD, which also is written in the C language) is converted by a *compiler* program running on the target operating system. The program is converted into executable machine language instructions with little or no modification to the source code. With the help of this fairly simple technique and some sophisticated development tools, developers have ported more than 2,500 UNIX and DOS applications to XENIX. Some of the applications include FoxBASE, WordPerfect, and Microsoft Word. Ashton-Tate Corporation and Lotus Development Corporation are currently developing dBASE and 1-2-3 applications for use with XENIX.

Recently, the SCO XENIX and AT&T UNIX versions merged their capabilities. Now the UNIX sold by SCO is named SCO UNIX. This merger happened in between AutoCAD Releases 10 and 11. AutoCAD Release 10 is supported on SCO XENIX and with a patch available from Autodesk can be run on the new SCO UNIX System V Release 3.2. Release 11 of AutoCAD, however, probably will support only the UNIX version.

Using AutoCAD with UNIX

In spite of the divergence of UNIX into many different versions, AutoCAD is available under several of the more popular "flavors" of UNIX. In fact, each new release of AutoCAD is first developed on the UNIX operating system by Autodesk programmers and then converted to DOS and other systems. If left up to Autodesk, UNIX would be the successor to DOS as AutoCAD's primary operating system. This would be a plus to many AutoCAD users because the primary difference between AutoCAD running on UNIX and AutoCAD running on DOS is UNIX's multi-user and multitasking capabilities.

As was explained earlier, UNIX allows multiple users to share the same computer. This can create an economical network of sorts, or a secure way of allowing several people to share one computer, such as for different work shifts. UNIX security also works for the general benefit of a single user in that it can help protect against accidental file erasures and other data accidents.

UNIX's multi-tasking capabilities contribute the most productivity to AutoCAD users. Like OS/2, UNIX can support running multiple programs at the same time. One program can run in the foreground that interacts with the user, and one or more programs can run in the background unattended. The user can switch from one program to another at will.

In the sections that follow, the features and requirements of AutoCAD running on each of the UNIX variants, XENIX, ULTRIX, SunOS, and AEGIS, are described briefly.

AutoCAD and SCO XENIX

AutoCAD Release 10 currently supports SCO XENIX V2.3 or later on the following hardware:

- Compaq DeskPro 80386 or IBM PS/2 model 70 or 80 personal computer
- 80387 math coprocessor
- 4M RAM minimum, 6M minimum recommended
- One high-density floppy disk drive
- Hard disk with 2.5M free to install AutoCAD and swap partition with at least 20M free disk space
- Hercules Graphics Card, EGA, VGA, PS/2 display adapter or ADI-supported display adapter and monitor
- Mouse or digitizer
- Optional plotter or printer

AutoCAD currently does not support the XENIX Motif interface standard described earlier. Instead, AutoCAD runs in full-screen mode in much the same manner that AutoCAD 386 runs under DOS. XENIX creates virtual terminals called *multiscreens* to execute multiple programs. Separate copies of AutoCAD may run on one or more of the multiscreens. XENIX multiscreens are analogous to having several computers that you can control from one keyboard and monitor. To switch between multiscreens, you press the Alt key in combination with a function key associated with a respective multiscreen. Pressing Alt-F1, for example, would switch to the first multiscreen, Alt-F2 would switch to the second screen, and so on. The keyboard, monitor, and system mouse are then active for the current multiscreen.

For output, AutoCAD can use either a plotter configured directly with AutoCAD, or spool plot files in the background. To spool plots, a XENIX command or script file name is set in the AutoCAD environment variable ACADPLCMD or ACADPPCMD. Then, when an AutoCAD plot file is made with the name AUTOSPOOL from within AutoCAD, the file is sent to a spool directory and the real file name is supplied to the XENIX command or script.

AutoCAD and DEC ULTRIX

When used on the DECstation 3100 from Digital Equipment Corporation, AutoCAD runs under a version of UNIX named ULTRIX. ULTRIX uses windowing software called DECwindows that is based on the X Windows System standard. DECwindows is the GUI that is used to display AutoCAD within windows. X Windows is a protocol that lets any computer on a UNIX network control applications running on another computer. That is, AutoCAD may be executed on one computer, for example, yet display and accept input from another.

If you want to run AutoCAD on a DECstation 3100, you will need the following hardware and software:

- DECstation with monochrome or color monitor
- 8M RAM minimum
- ULTRIX operating system V3.1
- DECwindows V2.1
- Local or network access to a TK50 tape drive for installation
- Digitizer optional if AutoCAD is run and displayed on the same computer
- Hard disk with 5M free to install AutoCAD and swap partition with at least 64M free disk space
- Optional printer or plotter

Under ULTRIX, if you want to run AutoCAD on the computer where it is installed, you start AutoCAD normally. If, however, you want to display AutoCAD on the local computer while it runs on a remote computer, you must follow the following steps:

1. Open a window on the local computer.
2. Set an environment variable DISPLAY on the local computer.
3. Establish a network connection with the remote computer.
4. Launch an operating system process on the remote computer.
5. Change to the directory where AutoCAD resides.
6. Set an evironment variable DISPLAY on the remote computer.
7. Start AutoCAD.

AutoCAD then will be using the processing and disk resources of the remote computer, yet will be controlled by the local computer.

Under DECwindows, AutoCAD runs within windows similarly to the way AutoCAD runs under OS/2. That is, when executed, AutoCAD opens two windows—one for graphics and one for text. Each window may be resized and repositioned at any time by using the resize button present with each window. With the shrink-to-icon button, you can choose to close the window to an icon, and the push-to-back button will place the current window behind all other open windows. When iconized, an

AutoCAD window (either text or graphics) will appear as an icon in the DECwindows icon box. These, however, are the only DECwindows controls that can be used on an AutoCAD window. The DECstation version of AutoCAD, however, does use a display list video driver. For more information on display list processing, see Chapter 14.

Changes in locations and sizes of windows are saved between sessions only by going through the AutoCAD Main menu configuration (task 5) process. You can switch between windows simply by moving the system pointer into any window and clicking the mouse button. Text can be pasted into the AutoCAD text window as it can with other programs. For more information on working with GUIs, see the Graphical User Interfaces section earlier in this chapter.

Similar to other UNIX versions, AutoCAD for the DECstation can use either a plotter configured directly with AutoCAD or spool plot files in the background. To spool plots, an ULTRIX command or script file name is set in the AutoCAD environment variable ACADPLCMD or ACADPPCMD. Then, when an AutoCAD plot file is made with the name AUTOSPOOL from within AutoCAD, it is sent to a spool directory and the real file name is supplied to the ULTRIX command or script.

Other than these few differences, AutoCAD looks and behaves under ULTRIX similarly to the way it does under DOS.

AutoCAD and SunOS

Sun Microsystem's version of UNIX, SunOS 3.4 or 4.0, blends UNIX System V with Berkeley Standard UNIX 4.2. AutoCAD runs on top of the Sun Windows or SunView GUIs on the Sun 3, 386i, SPARCstation, and Sun 4 platforms with the following requirements:

- Sun 3, 4, or 386i graphics workstation with monochrome or color monitor and mouse
- 4M RAM minimum, 8M recommended
- Floating point coprocessor (68881 coprocessor for the Sun 3, 80387 for the 386i)
- Hard disk with 2.5M free to install AutoCAD and swap partition with at least 20M free disk space
- Optional digitizer, plotter or printer

By using one of Sun's GUIs, you can run AutoCAD within windows similar to OS/2. That is, when executed, AutoCAD opens two windows—one for graphics and one for text. Each window may be resized and repositioned at any time by using the Frame menu. From the Frame menu, you can choose to close the window to an icon, open a window from an icon, move a window or icon, resize a window, bring a window to the front of all other windows, place it behind all other windows, repaint the window, or quit the program in the window. An AutoCAD window, however, may only be quit from within AutoCAD itself.

Changes in locations and sizes of windows are saved only between sessions by going through the AutoCAD Main menu configuration (task 5) process. The user may switch between windows by moving the system pointer into any window. Text, however, cannot be pasted into the AutoCAD text window as it can with other programs.

AutoCAD for the Sun runs very fast. SunOS is a 32-bit operating system and AutoCAD takes full advantage of that 32-bit power. Multitasking multiple copies of AutoCAD under SunOS is as simple as starting AutoCAD in another window, with the same restriction over digitizers for OS/2. That is, only the first copy has control over the digitizer. Other copies must be used for plotting or other less input-intensive operations.

Another nice feature of SunOS is its capability to associate data files with their applications. On the Sun, double clicking on an AutoCAD drawing file from within SunOS' file and directory manager, Organizer, will automatically begin AutoCAD with the selected file. Also, the Sun platform enjoys popular support from other major DOS application developers. Almost all of your favorite DOS programs have a Sun version and the Sun is the most popular platform for AutoCAD third-party applications.

AutoCAD plots and prints under SunOS similar to the way it does under XENIX. AutoCAD can use either a plotter configured directly with AutoCAD, or spool plot files in the background. To spool plots, a UNIX command or script file name is set in the AutoCAD environment variable ACADPLCMD or ACADPPCMD. Then, when an AutoCAD plot file is made with the name AUTOSPOOL from within AutoCAD, it is sent to a spool directory and the real file name is supplied to the UNIX command or script.

Other than these few differences, AutoCAD looks and behaves under SunOS similar to the way it does under DOS.

AutoCAD and AEGIS

Apollo has two versions of UNIX that AutoCAD runs under: AEGIS and DOMAIN/IX. AEGIS is built on the Display Manager windowing system for the Apollo Domain 3000 and 4000 workstations.

System requirements for AutoCAD on Apollo include the following:

- MC68020- or MC68030-based Apollo Domain workstation with Release 9.7 or later operating system
- 2M RAM minimum, 4M recommended
- Hard disk with 2M free to install AutoCAD
- Optional digitizer, plotter, or printer

AutoCAD for Apollo starts from a single text window that splits into two windows when you enter the drawing editor—one window for graphics and a four line text window. This text window switches to the original text window's size when AutoCAD needs to display a large amount of text or the user presses the Flip Screen key.

AutoCAD's windows can be resized or repositioned with the system mouse and keyboard keys. AutoCAD remembers these new window positions for the current drawing session. With the Domain's programmable keys, a user can switch between any active window.

AutoCAD for Apollo is very fast. AEGIS is another 32-bit UNIX operating system. Multitasking multiple copies of AutoCAD under AEGIS is as simple as starting AutoCAD in another window, with the same restriction over digitizers mentioned for other multitasking operating systems. Only the first copy has control over the digitizer. Other copies must be used for plotting or other less input-intensive operations.

Like the other UNIX versions, AutoCAD can use either a plotter configured directly with AutoCAD or spool plot files in the background. To spool plots, a UNIX command or script file name is set in the AutoCAD environment variable ACADPLCMD or ACADPPCMD. Then, when an AutoCAD plot file is made with the name AUTOSPOOL from within AutoCAD, it is sent to a spool directory and the real file name is supplied to the UNIX command or script.

UNIX Networking

A network built around UNIX can take two different forms. You can network individual UNIX workstations similar to a traditional DOS workstation network. Or, you can have multiple users share a single UNIX-based computer, using UNIX's multi-user capabilities. If you set up a UNIX network like a DOS network, you can use two software systems: the Transmission Control Protocol/Internet Protocol (TCP/IP) standard for communicating between stations and the Network File System (NFS) for creating a shared file and directory structure. Both of these systems are explained in the next chapter. In this section, UNIX's multi-user solution to networking is covered.

For general applications, a fast 80386-based personal computer with 16M of RAM and a 300M hard disk running XENIX or UNIX supports 16 to 24 users with terminals. This adds up to about half the cost of a LAN with PCs on every desk. Many corporate computing plans use this kind of UNIX system for multi-user access to a central shipping-and-receiving, order-entry, and inventory-control database.

A multi-user AutoCAD installation, however, probably will not yield the same results as a non-CAD network. This is because AutoCAD is a computing and input/output intensive program. Most other applications are not nearly as demanding. Although you can design a multi-user AutoCAD installation, you should anticipate hosting only three or four users in order to keep the system performance at acceptable (80286-like) levels.

In addition, inexpensive ASCII terminals cannot be used for a multi-user AutoCAD system. Instead, sophisticated and expensive graphics terminals are used. As a result, many multi-user AutoCAD installations end up costing as much as or more than a regular AutoCAD network with individual workstations, but sometimes perform worse. High-performance graphics display drivers for graphics terminals also are in short supply.

> ***Note:*** One elegant implementation of a XENIX multi-user installation is the SunRiver CADLight terminal, which can be connected to an 80386- or 80486-based host PC running XENIX and AutoCAD. Rather than the normal copper wire serial cable, CADLight terminals use fiber-optic cables capable of transmitting data at a rate of 32M per second, which is three times the theoretical maximum of Ethernet. The host PC is equipped with 12M of RAM (or more), a hard disk large enough for all the connected users, a math coprocessor, and the fiber-optic host adapter. Each CADLight terminal is composed of a desktop module for connection of a monitor, keyboard, one parallel port, two serial ports, and the fiber-optic interface. The display is driven by a display list processor on the host PC. Each terminal can multitask AutoCAD with other XENIX applications, yielding a very flexible and productive system. The Achilles heel of a multi-user UNIX system, however, is that everyone is affected if the CPU goes down. A LAN, on the other hand, keeps running if the applications are installed on the workstations.

Hope for UNIX

Even though UNIX has not been popular among PC users, UNIX may yet become a serious contender as a PC operating system. Two recent developments make this more likely than ever before.

The first development was the 80386 and 80486 processor chips. Before these chips arrived on the market, PCs simply did not have enough horsepower to run UNIX satisfactorily. UNIX was conceived by programmers, for programmers. Programmers require a level of performance that was not available from early PCs. Now, 32-bit personal computers can make UNIX perform well and at much lower cost than traditional UNIX hardware. The availability of this high-performance hardware encourages UNIX developers to write more applications for the PC market, and PC developers to start writing applications in UNIX.

Second, Intel, AT&T, and SCO agreed on a binary standard for UNIX in August, 1990. If UNIX International and Open Software Foundation member companies accept the standard (as is anticipated) and begin adhering to it, most of the barriers to vendor acceptance will fall.

UNIX is a mature, proven operating system and development environment. It has broad appeal and support, and thousands of applications have been written for it.

For businesses with allegiances to major UNIX vendors, such as Sun, DEC, and HP, using UNIX makes good sense. Interconnectivity with other products from the same vendor is a valuable asset and one that should not be taken lightly. If your company has minicomputer or mainframe equipment from those vendors, you should look seriously at their UNIX workstation offerings for your CAD department.

PC users, however, should wait a little longer before jumping to UNIX. Even with the announced binary standard, standardized UNIX applications will take some time to reach critical mass. The necessary UNIX drivers and "accessories" also will take time to arrive. When they do, however, UNIX will stand "toe to toe" with OS/2. OS/2 may have a slight technological advantage, but UNIX will rely upon its proven strengths.

Macintosh

Unlike IBM-compatible users, who can choose from several operating systems, Macintosh users have limited operating system options. The default operating system, appropriately called the Macintosh Operating System (MOS), is included with the purchase of every Macintosh computer. The Mac user also can purchase Apple's version of UNIX, which is named A/UX.

The Macintosh is more an operating *environment* than it is a collection of discrete hardware, operating system software, and applications. Each of these ingredients is tightly interwoven with the others; one cannot operate without the existence of the others. Together, they make a closed system that imposes strict standards for programmers to follow. For a program to run on the Macintosh, for instance, the program must adhere to and use the Mac's graphical user interface supplied by *Finder*, which is included in the Mac package.

Finder is the file and screen manager for the Macintosh. Finder supplies the pull-down menus, windows, and icons for control of multiple programs running in a pseudo-multitasking environment. Users simply double-click on icons to launch programs. Users then double-click on file names and the file tells the operating system what program created it. The program is started automatically and the file is loaded, ready to go. File names on a Macintosh can be up to 32 characters long, store information about the program that created them, and store the file's icon appearance.

What normally is called a TSR program in the DOS world is called a *desk accessory* on the Macintosh. A Mac II user can install as many as 15 utilities without the worries of memory conflicts that DOS users have. An alarm clock, calculator, notepad, scrapbook, and file-finding utility are all included with System. The user can activate these utilities any time by selecting them from the menu bar at the top of the screen.

Using AutoCAD on the Mac

The Macintosh version of AutoCAD is slick and easy to use. While AutoCAD does make some concessions in order to conform to the Macintosh's look and feel, the program still maintains enough of its traditional appearance to distinguish itself as genuine AutoCAD (see fig. 4.19). Most Macintosh enthusiasts criticize AutoCAD, however, for not completely subscribing to the Macintosh look and feel.

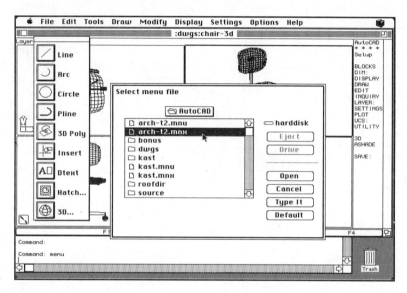

Figure 4.19:
AutoCAD for the Macintosh features the Mac look and feel.

Noticeably lacking in the Mac version of AutoCAD is adequate graphics performance. The Macintosh operating system protects the hardware from direct manipulation by programs similar to OS/2. Consequently, AutoCAD must go through the Mac BIOS and Quickdraw routines to perform graphics display. This rerouting causes AutoCAD to run more slowly on the Macintosh than on equivalent DOS systems. Third-party products are beginning to work around this limitation of the Mac.

The following system components are required to run AutoCAD on the Macintosh:

- Macintosh II, IIx, IIcx, IIci (IIfx recommended) with MOS 6.0 or higher and System 6.0.2 or higher
- Monochrome or color display
- 4M RAM minimum for Finder (6.1 or higher); 8M recommended, especially if Multifinder (6.0.1 or higher) is used
- Hard disk with 4M free disk space for installing AutoCAD
- Mouse
- Optional digitizer, plotter, or printer

AutoCAD is executed on the Macintosh by double-clicking on the AutoCAD icon, a drawing file icon, or an AutoCAD script icon. When you start AutoCAD from its program icon, you are presented with the AutoCAD graphics and text windows that are similar to OS/2. That is, a menu bar displays at the top of the screen with File, Edit, and AutoCAD Utilities menus instead of the AutoCAD Main menu. A text window opens for text display. These windows can be resized independently and positioned on the screen and will remain in position and size when the drawing is opened the next time. The text window will hold the last 65,000 text characters of the current editing session.

At the bottom of the AutoCAD graphics window are four graphic function key buttons corresponding to function keys F1 through F4 of the Macintosh extended keyboard. Each of these buttons can be picked with the mouse or keyboard and can be customized by editing the ***AUX1 section of the ACAD.MNU file.

By double-clicking on a drawing file icon, AutoCAD starts automatically with the selected file. Double-clicking on a script file icon that has its creator set to ACAD also will invoke AutoCAD. By highlighting both a drawing file icon and a script icon and then double-clicking on them, AutoCAD will be started with the selected drawing loaded and the selected script executed.

Figure 4.19 shows that AutoCAD for the Macintosh includes File and Edit menus along with the menu selections of the AUI that are similar to the other operating systems reviewed in this chapter. The Macintosh provides the same functions as the other operating systems, such as Main Menu, Page Setup, Print Screen, Undo and Redo, Show Text, and commands for accessing the Macintosh clipboard. The Mac clipboard also can receive selected drawing vectors for use in other programs.

The similarity between the operating systems ends there, however. On the Macintosh, pull-down menus can display icons only, icons and text, or text only. A different style of display can be set for each menu, if desired. This lets advanced AutoCAD users customize pull-down menus so they take up less screen space. The icons displayed by the pull-down menus also can be customized, and users can add their own icons, Command key equivalents, check marks, and fonts to customized menus.

AutoCAD pull-down menus on the Macintosh also enjoy one other distinction from any other operating system: they may be "torn" off from the menu bar and positioned on the graphics screen for easy picking. The Draw pull-down menu is torn off in figure 4.19. Up to ten pull-down menus can be torn off and visible at the same time, even between drawing sessions. By holding down the Command key and pressing the mouse button, a temporary version of the last used menu will appear for repeating a command. By holding down the Command and Option keys together and pressing the mouse button, the last selected menu will appear torn-off at the pointer location ready for placement.

Altogether, these little user-friendly enhancements make AutoCAD easy to use on the Macintosh. For companies or departments with large Mac investments, the Macintosh version of AutoCAD is the only sensible option.

Macintosh Networking

A tremendous advantage to Mac users is the inclusion of basic networking capabilities within each Macintosh. Every Mac features a serial port for a 230K bytes-per-second daisy-chain connection, and the System software includes Apple's peer-to-peer networking software, called AppleTalk. All that is needed to connect several users is an inexpensive connection module and cables.

AppleTalk does not support large workgroups efficiently, nor does it handle the heavy demands of a centralized CAD network very effectively. AppleTalk does provide the basic file transfer, electronic mail, and printer-sharing services that most small departments and companies need but cannot afford. Additional third-party products are available to boost an AppleTalk network's performance. Alternatively, many DOS networks now also support Macintoshes, including Novell NetWare.

Summary

All the operating systems presented in this chapter offer advantages to certain groups of users and particular business environments. The one you choose for yourself and your workgroup or company depends on your needs, your ability to support a given system, and in some cases, courage.

Even when it is extended, familiar old DOS is still dying. If you are not looking into the alternatives now, you should be. Extended DOS offers the most bang for the buck, but it is living on borrowed time. Few people expect DOS extenders to be around several years from now.

OS/2 is a great environment for people who need to do several things at the same time. It works well for managers, engineers, and developers. OS/2 is not quite fast enough for pure production users, but a faster 32-bit OS/2 is just around the corner.

A binary standard UNIX should perform on a par with future versions of OS/2. UNIX is beneficial to the AutoCAD network for the same reasons OS/2 is, plus UNIX offers the benefit of connectivity to larger systems and is available now.

Do not count the Macintosh out yet, either. Mac followers are loyal, and more powerful engines are sure to come. The Mac also has the advantage that it is the easiest of systems to learn and use.

To help summarize this chapter and put all the important specifications in one place, table 4.3 shows each operating system that has been covered. You can use this table to help you compare hardware requirements and system capabilities.

A CAD manager needs to watch the development of these operating systems and commit to understanding their theory and applications.

Table 4.3
Operating Systems Comparison

	DOS	Ext. DOS	MacOS	OS/2	UNIX
Users Per System	One	One	One	One	Many
Maximum User Memory	640K-8M (Exp.)	640K-16M (Ext.)	32M	16M	3G
Memory Management	Physical Static, Segmented	Physical Static, Segmented	Linear	Virtual, Demand-Segment Swapped	Virtual, Demand Paged
System Security	None	None	None	Protected Mode at OS level	User Passwords, Group-level Permissions
Execution Modes	Real	Real, 16- and 32-Bit Protected, Virtual	16- and 32-Bit Protected	16-Bit Protected	16- and 32-Bit Protected, Virtual
Interprocess Communication	None	None	None	Shared Memory, Message Queues, Semaphores, Pipes	Shared Memory, Message Queues, Semaphores, Pipes
Device I/O	Simple	Simple	Interrupt Driven	Interrupt Driven	Interrupt Driven
Common Network Schemes	MS-Net Novell NetWare, Others	MS-Net, Novell NetWare, Others	AppleTalk, Others	MS LAN Manager, 3Com 3+Open, IBM LAN Server	TCP/IP, NFS, RFS

With a workstation platform and operating system chosen, your next step in building an AutoCAD workgroup is selecting a network operating system and hardware to run it on. Your choices from this chapter will influence your options in the next, so keep them in mind as you continue. If you have decided not to network, you may want to skip the next chapter and proceed directly to Chapter 6, where you will learn how to bring these systems into your business with the least amount of disruption and trepidation.

5

Choosing a Network Operating System and Hardware

No sooner does a CAD system grow beyond its first workstation than the subject of networking comes up. It may not be called by that name, but the problems are the same. Once the system grows into a workgroup of multiple workstations and users, the company must face the logistical problems of peripheral sharing, data and program sharing, and communications.

Workgroup CAD does not necessarily have to lead to an expensive and complicated solution. A basic understanding of networks and their operation, however, can help you implement effective solutions to the problems associated with workgroup computing. In the following pages, you will learn how different networks function and the different technologies that can be combined to build a network to meet any need. You will learn about different network access methods, cabling, and configurations. This chapter gives you the information you need to choose a network operating system that will work with your AutoCAD configuration. You also will learn also how a network can make a difference in the workstation hardware you buy and what to look for in a network file server.

When you interconnect computers, you must delve into a dimension of technology that is largely unfamiliar to most CAD users. If networking issues are unfamiliar to you, you should study this chapter carefully. This chapter explains the various types of networks and describes some of the headaches that managers face when trying to select the right network system. Hopefully, this information will help you make the right choices of network hardware and software that will integrate well into your company. If your network already is running satisfactorily already, you may want to look at Chapter 6, which shows you how to work with dealers. Or, you may want to jump ahead to Chapter 7, which shows you how to configure a network for best AutoCAD performance.

The Lay of the LAN

In its simplest form, a *local area network* (LAN) is a group of personal computers, minicomputers, or mainframes that are connected to each other by a high-speed communications link. The link is considered *local* when the connection is limited to a small geographical area, such as a single office, a building, or a campus. Networks that span larger distances—such as across town (*metropolitan area networks*, or MANs) or across the country (*wide area networks*, or WANs)—require more sophisticated communications technology than LANs do. Most AutoCAD networks are local area networks.

A network enables computers (and their users) to share data, programs, and peripherals, and to communicate with each other. Before the advent of local area networking technology, if you wanted a group of people to share computing resources and communications, you installed a minicomputer or mainframe. That solution still is valid in many circumstances, but LANs take advantage of the popularity of the personal computer in today's business world. Corporate computing has moved from the centralized approach of one computer's holding all the data and power to a distributed approach in which computing power is located at the user's desk. Figure 5.1 illustrates the growth of LAN technology.

In spite of the move to decentralization, some data and resources often should be kept in a central place to facilitate backups, maintenance, and security. Many networks, therefore, employ a *file server*. A file server is typically another personal computer that acts as the heart of a LAN. The file server usually has a large amount of mass storage and provides a single access point for control and security of the network's resources. A file server can be economically beneficial in many circumstances. A file server can house a few large-capacity hard disks, which can be cheaper, more easily accessed, and less prone to failure than dozens of smaller disks in individual PCs spread throughout the network. A file server also can enable several users to share one modem, FAX, and other kinds of peripherals otherwise provided on a one-per-user basis. Modem servers and FAX servers, when included in the network, can support the needs of many users.

A LAN uses special software to transmit files, printer data, and messages over a cable attached to each machine on the network. The machines consists of the file server and individual workstations. The workstations are most often PCs, but may be UNIX-based micros and minis. Each workstation is considered a *node* on the network. The cable usually plugs into a network interface card (NIC), which is installed in each node computer. The network software consists of a portion of the network operating system (NOS), called a *shell*, which resides on each workstation, and a driver that communicates the operating system's needs to the interface card. The network shell intercepts requests for network resources originating from the workstation and directs the requests to the network. The network driver carries out the details of communicating over the network cable through the NIC.

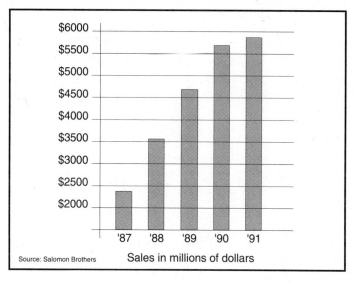

Figure 5.1:
Growth of personal computer local area networks.

How LAN Communication Works

The process of communicating on the network is a complicated symphony of activity. Fortunately, users do not have to contend with network communication details because the details are hidden within the underlying software. The following short section explains a typical communication cycle of a PC acting as a workstation to a LAN file server.

When an application program, such as AutoCAD, requests a service (for example, to read a file on the file server), the workstation software examines the request and determines whether it is for a local service or for a network service. If the request is for a local service (such as video output or floppy disk access), the shell passes the request to the workstation's operating system for processing as though no network software is involved. If the request is for a network service (such as access to a shared disk or printer), the shell redirects the request to the driver for processing. The request does not pass as a constant stream through the cable from the workstation to the file server. The interface card chops the request into *packets* (see fig. 5.2) and transmits them onto the cable with the *source address* and the *destination address*. The source address tells the network which workstation is sending the request. Every networked computer has a unique address. The details of source and destination addresses are handled by the network software. If you think of network addresses like mail addresses, each packet contains the address for delivery along with the sender's address. The destination machine, through the network software, can assemble packets into an ordered collection of data even if the packets are sent out of sequence.

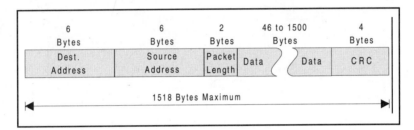

Figure 5.2:
The structure of a network packet.

The file server also contains a network interface card, which communicates by sending and receiving packets. When the file server receives a packet, it sends an acknowledgment back to the shell of the workstation from which the packet originated. The originating machine uses the acknowledgment as an assurance that the receiving machine has the packet. The receiving file server's interface reassembles the packets into the request and passes the request to the main network operating system. The file server's operating system then examines the request. If, for example, the workstation has asked for a copy of a file from a network drive, the network operating system reads the file from disk, breaks the file into packets, and sends the file back to the workstation.

The requesting workstation receives the packets and sends acknowledgments back to the file server, verifying that the packets were received. The workstation interface card and driver software then reconstitute the file and pass it on to the shell. The shell passes the file, at last, to the application and the request is complete. All the while, other computers on the network may be sending and receiving packets of their own.

Protocol Standards

LANs can be constructed in many ways. Each component—the software, the cable, and the interface card—can take on many nonexclusive forms. In fact, thousands of hardware and software products are available to meet almost every networking need.

Of course, when such an array of products exists, standards must be established to ensure that the products can work together without problems. Network technology is addressed by many standards for the *medium* (cable) used, the *topology* (physical arrangement of the cable), and *protocols* (rules the software obeys in communicating on the network).

Because networks can be global as well as local, two standards apply to the connection of dissimilar network systems. These standards allow any node on one network to communicate with any node on another network, regardless of geographic area. Such standards are valuable not only to global network installers and multivendor network installations, but also to many smaller AutoCAD network installations that may need to be connected to a larger system.

The OSI Standard

The International Standards Organization (ISO) has proposed recently the Open Systems Interconnection (OSI) model to define the boundaries of responsibility between individual network protocols. The OSI comprises seven layers that set standards for virtually every level of the network, from network hardware to the user interface. Figure 5.3 describes the OSI model and breaks it down into specific network functions.

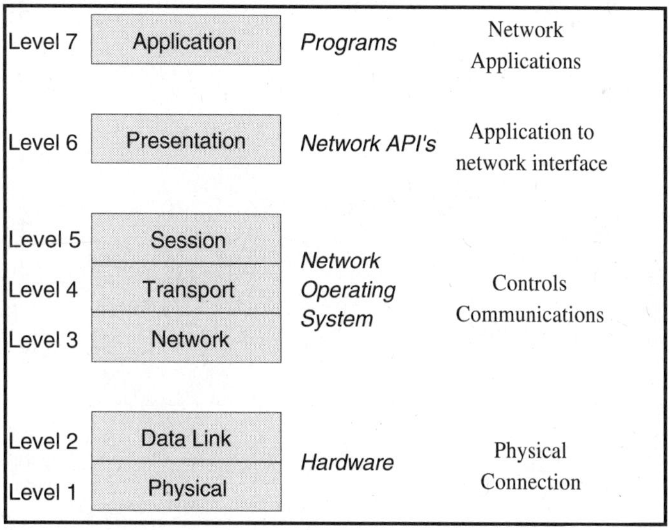

Level 7	Application	*Programs*	Network Applications
Level 6	Presentation	*Network API's*	Application to network interface
Level 5	Session	*Network Operating System*	Controls Communications
Level 4	Transport		
Level 3	Network		
Level 2	Data Link	*Hardware*	Physical Connection
Level 1	Physical		

Figure 5.3:
The ISO/OSI network model.

Not all products conform to the OSI standard yet. OSI compliance, however, has been made a requirement in U.S. government systems and will be required in Europe in 1992. OSI will take time to overcome the more well-established proprietary systems and the TCP/IP standard, which is discussed next.

The TCP/IP Standard

The TCP/IP (Transmission Control Protocol/Internet Protocol) protocol standard has been around for years. TCP/IP was developed in the early 1970s to solve the problems of interconnecting various government, military, contractor, and university computer systems that worked for the Department of Defense. TCP/IP is supported heavily by UNIX computer systems, DEC minicomputers under VAX/VMS, and IBM mainframes. The TCP/IP standard also is popular because it is a requirement of almost every government computer purchase contract.

At one time, TCP/IP support was included with Berkeley UNIX, and this brought the standard into wide acceptance. TCP/IP is the easiest way to network UNIX workstations and add them to other types of networks (see fig. 5.4). TCP/IP is the foundation of the Sun NFS network system used by many AutoCAD networks (Sun NFS is discussed in Chapter 7).

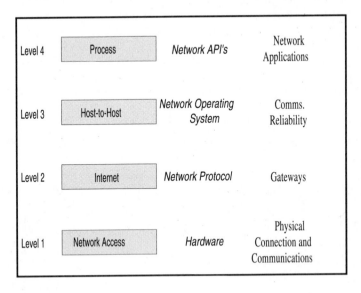

Figure 5.4:
The TCP/IP protocol model.

The other standards, described in the following sections, each make up one or more levels in either the OSI or TCP/IP models.

Access Protocols

If computers are to communicate with each other in an orderly manner, they must follow an established *access protocol*. Access protocols are analogous to the rules of order imposed on people gathered at a meeting, where some of the people may or may not have something to say to the other people.

Two principal network access protocols are used in PC-based LANs today. One is known as *token-passing*; the other is called the *contention-based* access protocol. IBM's Token Ring network uses a token-passing protocol, as does ARCNET, which has been adopted by more than 100 producers of network products. The most popular contention-type protocol is named Carrier Sense Multiple Access/Collision Detection (CSMA/CD). CSMA/CD has been in use since 1975, and is the basis of Ethernet. Ethernet, which was designed in 1980 at the Xerox PARC facility, is accepted universally by the computer industry and is supported by almost every vendor.

Token Ring

To understand a Token Ring network's operation, imagine a group of people holding a meeting around a large table. If someone wants to speak to another person who is sitting across the table, he cannot speak directly to that person. Instead, the speaker must have the people seated between him and the listener relay the message around the table until it reaches the listener. When that message has reached its destination, another person can send a message to someone else, in the same round-robin fashion. Those persons who are not interested in the conversation cannot concentrate on reading a report or some other activity, because they must still relay messages for the person who is speaking. If one person leaves the meeting, the ring is broken and the meeting falls apart.

As the name implies, stations in a Token Ring network communicate by passing a *token*, or special network packet. To send a message on a Token Ring network, a computer must "listen" to the cable until a "free" electrical token is passed to it. The workstation then regenerates the token, attaches a packet containing its request or data with source and destination addresses, and sends the token on to the next computer.

The second computer receives the packet and reads the destination address; if the packet is not addressed to the second computer, it regenerates the token and sends the token and packet down the line. When the destination workstation receives the packet, it reads the packet's data, regenerates and marks the token as received, and sends it out on the cable to the next station.

Once the token comes back to the workstation that originally sent it out, the packet is discarded, and the token is marked as free and sent out again to be used by another workstation. The next station that needs access to the network attaches its message to the free token, and the cycle continues.

Because of a Token Ring's cyclic pattern, the token must be free to circulate in one direction among all workstations. The network, therefore, must form an electrical circle, or ring; this is where Token Ring gets its name. A Token Ring network is connected together through a multistation access unit (MAU) in a star topology. The MAU creates an electrical ring internally and typically has ten ports for workstation connections (see fig. 5.5).

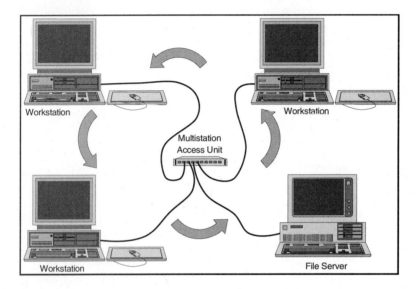

Figure 5.5:
A Token Ring network.

Token Ring originally was rated at a data transfer rate of four megabits per second (Mbit/sec) but a new 16 Mbit/sec version is now available, which greatly increases data throughput. Further, the new Token Ring specification allows for the "early release" of the token, meaning that two packets from different workstations can move around the ring at the same time, increasing throughput even more.

On a Token Ring LAN, every computer gets an equal opportunity to take care of business, just as each person around the table has the chance to speak—in turn, of course. The disadvantage of this protocol is that if one computer has a great deal of data to send or receive and many network nodes are in between the source and destination nodes, the data may take a long time to complete its journey.

Another disadvantage of this network is Token Ring's proprietary heritage and hardware expense. IBM invented the token ring network and is the primary vendor of Token Ring networks, with Proteon, Inc.'s ProNET a distant second. IBM has discouraged other major computer vendors from supporting Token Ring, which means that its equipment and cabling are the most expensive to install.

A Token Ring network does offer advantages, however, including a predictable level of performance. You also can install backup cables that reduce the chance of a network failure should one cable fail. Perhaps Token Ring's biggest asset is that it has the sanction of IBM, which developed the product and supports it as the connection of choice for larger IBM systems.

ARCNET

The Attached Resource Computer Network (ARCNET) is the oldest PC network access protocol and captures an estimated 25 percent of all new LAN systems. ARCNET, developed by Datapoint in the early 1970s, uses a token-passing protocol that is slightly different from the standard Token Ring protocol. ARCNET does not require everyone around the table to relay messages; rather, anyone can elect not to participate in the "ring." Messages bypass nonparticipants and go to the next person. Uninterested persons can leave the meeting without affecting messages or the meeting.

In an ARCNET network, workstations connect by cables to hub devices, which can be either active or passive. An active hub has from two to 64 ports, and distributes and amplifies the signals it receives from the workstations. With ARCNET, the active hub—not each workstation—regenerates the tokens. A passive hub, on the other hand, has only four ports and distributes only signals. Passive hubs are used in networks of four stations or fewer where the signals do not need regeneration. A passive hub also can act as a simple distribution device connected to an active hub. Figure 5.6 illustrates an ARCNET network and shows how each network node maintains the address (ID) of the next active node in the network (NID). The network node sends the packets directly to the node to which the packet is addressed, rather than sending it in a round-robin fashion.

On an ARCNET network, each interface card's address is set by a switch on the card. The card also holds the number of the next address (NID) in a special register. Whenever an ARCNET workstation signs onto the network, it calls the next higher address to see if a workstation exists at that address. If not, or if that workstation has left the network, the first workstation attempts to call the next higher address, and so on, until it receives an acknowledgment from an active workstation. That address is then held in the original workstation's next-address register.

ARCNET is a more reliable scheme than Token Ring because ARCNET permits workstations to join and depart the network. ARCNET eliminates the overhead of repeated retransmissions as the token and packet pass from one address to the next. When a workstation receives a "free" token and needs to send a packet, ARCNET sends the token and packet to the next address. Although ARCNET has a slower 2.5 Mbit/sec rating than both Token Ring and Ethernet (discussed later), an upcoming version will be rated at 20 Mbit/sec.

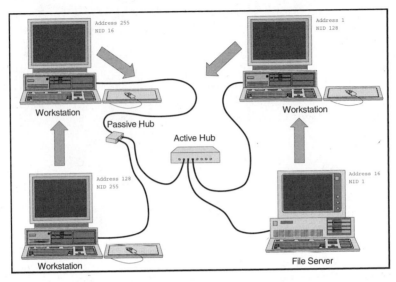

Figure 5.6:
An ARCNET network.

ARCNET offers several advantages. First, it is the least expensive fully functional network to install. Second, it can be run on different types of cable. Finally, ARCNET is easier to troubleshoot than other types of networks, because technicians can use the hubs to isolate faulty components.

On the other hand, ARCNET is currently the slowest of the major networks and is not recommended for applications that demand high performance, such as AutoCAD. In fact, many hardware vendors are concentrating development resources on the newer Token Ring, Ethernet, and other network technologies, which will inhibit the evolution of ARCNET. Further, ARCNET is not supported by 32-bit engineering workstations, such as the Sun and DEC.

Ethernet

The CSMA/CD access protocol (sometimes called a *contention* scheme) is similar to an informal meeting where everyone at the meeting is free to "get a word in edgewise" whenever he can. If person A tries to speak at the same time as person B, person A pauses and listens for an opportunity to try again. In this scenario, a great deal of information can be disseminated quickly—that is, until the meeting gets too big and a conversation cannot be conducted because of interruptions.

All workstations on an Ethernet network "listen" to a shared length of cable called a *bus* (see fig. 5.7). If the workstations do not "hear" any traffic, they go ahead and transmit their packets onto the network cable, in no specific direction, for all other workstations to "hear." When a specific workstation "hears" a packet on the cable with its address, it reads only that packet's data, ignores the other packets, and sends the source node an acknowledgment packet in the same fashion.

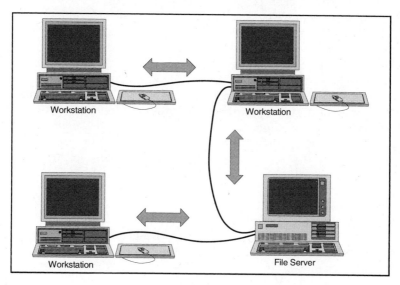

Figure 5.7:
An Ethernet network.

Problems arise, however, when two or more workstations attempt to transmit data simultaneously. When this happens, the packets may collide and become lost. When the packets collide, the voltage on the cable goes up. The interface cards recognize this sign as a collision, stop transmitting, back off for a time, and then begin listening again. If the sending node has not received an acknowledgment packet from the receiving node, it then knows that its last packet was involved in a collision and resends the lost packet. Most well-designed Ethernet networks function efficiently at high loads without reaching chaos (the point at which most packets are colliding and few get through).

Ethernet's advantages include its high speed (at present, a maximum of 10 Mbit/sec) and flexible wiring options (an Ethernet network can run on virtually any medium). It is extensible with bridges and routers, which can break the network into more manageable segments or join it with other network schemes. Ethernet can support multiple protocols for different computers on the same cable, and enjoys the largest direct support of network devices, workstations, and VAX computers. Virtually every network vendor supports Ethernet hardware.

Ethernet does have disadvantages. As an Ethernet network grows, workstations must increasingly contend for on-line time. Ethernet also is more expensive than other schemes, and is more susceptible to wiretapping.

Access Protocol Recommendations

Ethernet is the favorite access protocol among AutoCAD users. Token Ring networks have been too expensive to install, have been too slow, and have only recently begun to gather significant support outside of IBM. Unless you have an existing investment in Token Ring networking hardware, or a need to connect to larger IBM systems, you should consider a different protocol. ARCNET networks also have been too slow, except in large networks, for the big file sizes and rapid system responses AutoCAD users expect. Even though a faster version of it is now gaining interest, ARCNET is not well supported by connectivity products to larger systems. For now, only Ethernet has the performance, economy, flexibility, and acceptance to meet the diverse needs of a powerful AutoCAD network.

Media

Several standards exist for the physical *medium* (cable) that can be used in networks. The Institute of Electrical and Electronic Engineers (IEEE) is the governing group that establishes standards for the different media used by all network vendors. Not all cable types can be used with all access schemes, and some media are more resistant to interference than others. The cable you choose should depend largely on the access scheme and topology you select.

Coaxial Cable

The original medium specified for Ethernet was a 4/10-inch diameter, barely flexible RG-11 coaxial cable, which was affectionately called "frozen yellow garden hose" or "thick Ethernet." The IEEE standard for this cable is named 10BASE-5 because the cable can transmit signals at a rate of 10Mbit/sec, and can stretch a maximum distance of 500 meters between two devices. This cable is the backbone of many large Ethernet networks and is used in industrial environments where large motors and transformers create interference that can corrupt network communications.

Thick Ethernet effectively spans long distances, such as university campuses and office complexes. If the cable must travel more than 500 meters between workstations, a special repeater device must be attached to help signals traverse the greater distance.

A workstation attaches to the cable by a vampire tap on the Ethernet cable and a shielded, four-wire transceiver cable that runs into the computer's interface card. The cable must be terminated on each end of a bus topology with a 50-ohm resistor.

Ethernet also can be used with a flexible 2/10-inch diameter RG-58 coaxial cable, which is similar in construction and appearance to the wire used for cable TV (see fig. 5.8). RG-58 cable consists of a center conductor surrounded by an insulating PVC or Teflon layer. A woven mesh shield covers the two layers and is encased in a tough outer insulation layer. This cable complies with the 10BASE-2 standard that limits its length to 200 meters between devices. Thin Ethernet, as it is called, is the cable most widely used for Ethernet networks today, but a similar RG-62 cable can be used to connect devices in an ARCNET network.

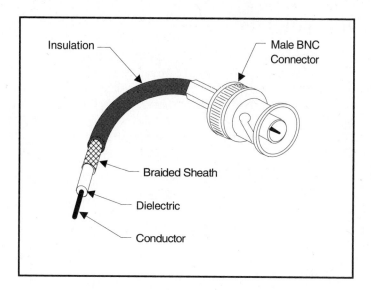

Figure 5.8:
Coaxial cable.

Ethernet workstations are attached directly to the cable with a coaxial connector. The connector attaches directly onto the interface card, which must include its own transceiver (most do). RG-58 cable needs a repeater to span distances greater than 200 meters, and must be terminated in a bus configuration with a resistor. Because it is smaller and cheaper than thick Ethernet, RG-58 cable is often called "cheapernet." Thin Ethernet is much better suited than thick Ethernet to environments where cable must be rerouted.

Ethernet cable provides the highest *bandwidth*, or load capacity, of all the network media options except fiber optic cable (which is discussed later), but is more difficult to install than other choices.

Shielded Twisted Pair

IBM chose a type of *shielded twisted-pair* wiring for its Token Ring networks. The cable is made up of pairs of high-grade multistrand conductors that are twisted around each other to reduce electrical side effects, called *capacitive coupling*. Two pairs are used to connect each workstation to the previous workstation and the next, in keeping with the ring design of the Token Ring network. An extruded aluminum shield surrounds the conductors, protecting them from interference. The whole assembly is heavily insulated and terminates at special connectors. This IBM Type 1 cabling is used only on Token Ring networks, and for good reason—it often costs more than a dollar a foot, which is several times as much as other media.

Unshielded Twisted Pair

The cheapest and easiest medium to install is *unshielded-twisted pair* (UTP) wiring. It is similar to the shielded twisted-pair cable, but is not shielded and has solid 22 or 24 AWG copper conductors. In fact, UTP is the same wire typically used to wire telephone systems. It is widely available and very cheap. It can be connected easily with *punch-down blocks* in a wiring closet (as many telephone system are), and even uses modular RJ-45 connectors, which are similar to phone connectors (see fig. 5.9).

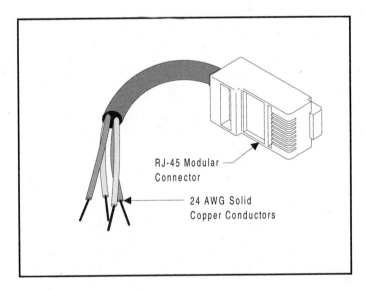

Figure 5.9:
Unshielded twisted pair medium (UTP) wiring.

UTP wiring's similarities to telephone wiring are no coincidence. Many buildings have extra pairs of wires installed when the building is wired for its telephone system. Network hardware vendors have specifically designed the NICs and hubs to take advantage of the extra wiring in existing buildings and to make it easier and cheaper to wire new installations. Ethernet uses two wire pairs: one pair for transmitting and one pair for receiving. A few network vendors, notably AT&T, have been using UTP wiring for years, but only on a proprietary basis. These companies' hubs are not compatible with each other even though they use the same cable.

To ensure compatibility among vendor equipment that utilizes UTP technology, the IEEE recently ratified the new 10BASE-T standard for UTP use in Ethernet networks. The final draft of 10BASE-T was released in September 1990 to manufacturers, so they could ensure that their products would comply with the standard and be compatible with each other. The 10BASE-T specification does not set a limit on the length of cable runs, as the other Ethernet standards do, but establishes a performance level that any segment of cable must meet. Most UTP wiring meets these standards at lengths up to 100 meters, and higher-grade UTP wiring and devices can safely operate at longer lengths—some up to 200 meters. Even so, when shopping for UTP products, beware of products that are compliant only with the 10BASE-T Draft (an earlier version of the standard); there are still a few around. Insist on products whose manufacturers guarantee compatibility with the final standard.

UTP was first certified only on ARCNET networks, but now can be used for Ethernet and Token Ring networks, as well. In spite of its economy, UTP carries with it the lowest immunity to electrical interference of all the media described here. It also is the most susceptible to damage. If necessary, you can run UTP inside conduits to provide extra protection. If great lengths of UTP must be installed in conduit for protection purposes, however, you may find new coaxial cable to be less expensive. Thoroughly test all existing UTP wiring before committing it to network duty.

UTP provides the most aesthetically pleasing installation, because it can hook into standard modular telephone-type wall plates and RJ-45 connectors. For this reason, UTP is a favorite choice in environments where PCs are moved often. You can establish a network connection as easily as you can plug in a telephone. One end plugs into the NIC and the other into a wall jack connected to a hub device (often called a *concentrator*, *media attachment center*, *multiport repeater*, or *wiring center*). UTP's point-to-point connections also simplify network management and troubleshooting, because technicians can isolate workstations and groups without disrupting other users. Network transmission statistics, problem monitoring, and fault isolation are much easier on an Ethernet network using 10BASE-T. Network vendors now have products that support basic network management functions by intelligent concentrators and network management software.

Fiber-Optic Cable

The fastest and most resistant medium available for LANs is *fiber-optic* cable. This medium is similar to the plastic fibers used in monofilament fishing line, but is more closely related to the fiber-optic cable used in high-speed telephone networks. Individual plastic or glass fibers are surrounded by buffer coating and cladding that insulates the fibers, and another tough, protective plastic jacket surrounds the core (see fig. 5.10). Digital light pulses travel through these refractive fibers at very high speeds but with little loss of signal. Fiber-optic cable boasts a high resistance to interference.

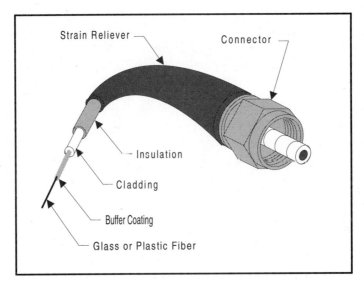

Figure 5.10:
Fiber-optic medium.

Because it is such an expensive medium, fiber-optic cable currently is used only as the backbone medium in large networks, in installations that are at a high risk of interference, and in sensitive data applications. Every termination of a fiber optic cable must be specially prepared, and the ends of the fibers must be polished. For this reason, eavesdroppers have a tough time tapping into a fiber-optic network.

Fiber-optic wiring is gaining popularity in multiuser graphics applications because it can accommodate the high bandwidth needed to transmit high-resolution graphics at acceptable rates. These data transfer rates can be as high as 100 Mbit/sec. Recent developments for a protocol standard in this area have been made under the name Fiber Distributed Data Interface (FDDI). This protocol uses a dual-path, counter-rotating Token Ring topology.

Note: Artist Graphics recently announced its ARTISTAR network system that is based on a UNIX- or XENIX-based 386 or 486 multiuser host system connected to up to four ARTISTAR stations. The user can connect each ARTISTAR station to four extender boxes, which each support high-resolution monitors, keyboards, and pointing devices. These graphics terminals share files, output peripherals attached to the host, and the XENIX version of AutoCAD. Graphics performance at the terminals is extremely fast because of the FDDI data throughput and the popular Artist graphics controllers installed in the ARTISTAR station.

The Thomas-Conrad Corporation, a large networking systems vendor, has introduced FDDI products for traditional distributed processing networks, such as Novell and Banyan, with the name TCNS. Intended for CAD, CAM, digital imaging, electronic publishing, and database server applications, TCNS products let you use standard personal computers instead of terminals.

Media Recommendations

For the typical small AutoCAD network (that is, one with fewer than 12 workstations), thin Ethernet or UTP cable work equally well. Choose UTP if you have good-quality existing pairs of UTP telephone cable already wired into your building. You will need at least two unused cable pairs for each computer, originating near each computer and terminating in a central location suitable for the wiring concentrator. Many installations have only one extra pair, and sometimes the wiring does not meet the specifications to support 10BASE-T. Your network installer can tell you if you can use the building's existing wiring. If you are building a new office, you can safely use 10BASE-T wiring if the wiring is installed by an electrical contractor.

If you do not fit into these situations, and you will be wiring a fairly small area, thin coaxial cable will be easier to connect and cheaper because it does not require a hub device. For long cable runs between floors or across large buildings, use thick coaxial cable. For the ultimate in performance, look into fiber-optic cable if you can afford it.

Topology

Now that you understand the ways in which networks communicate, you can examine the ways in which individual PCs can be connected to permit the protocols to operate. As previously mentioned, you can configure a LAN in many different ways and employ your chosen access protocol over different physical configurations, which are called *topologies*. Most topologies fall into the categories of *bus* topologies and *star* topologies. In special applications, an advanced network design may use a combination of bus and star topologies.

Bus Topologies

The simplest LAN topology is the bus design. Simply defined, a bus topology is a common, shared length of cable. Each workstation attaches at a certain spot along the cable, and each end of the bus terminates at a resistor. If the bus is not terminated, signals can "bounce" back down the cable and disrupt communications.

Ethernet networks typically utilize a bus topology. Ethernet's CSMA/CD protocol requires that all workstations be able to listen continuously for transmissions from the other workstations, and Ethernet's high bandwidth is more easily achieved on coaxial cable. The disadvantage of a bus topology is that should there be a fault in the cable, because it is shared, it will affect the entire network. Bus network installations are typically less aesthetic than other topologies because the bus cable must pass by each workstation.

Star Topologies

In a star (or *cluster*) topology, each workstation has its own cable and a central device provides continuity between the workstations. The central device is most often an active or passive hub in ARCNET networks (see fig. 5.6) or a Multistation Access Unit in Token Ring networks (see fig. 5.5). In 10BASE-T installations, the device is called a hub or concentrator.

In ARCNET and Token Ring configurations, this central device creates the electrical ring required for token passing, and eliminates the need to physically connect workstations into a loop. You can chain together multiple devices to extend the star topology to workstations in other areas to create a hierarchical topology. With Token Ring networks, however, dual cables must run in between the hubs to maintain the electrical ring. A single coaxial cable is sufficient to interconnect hubs in an ARCNET configuration.

In a 10BASE-T network, the concentrator reduces the shared bus length of an Ethernet network to the circuitry within the device (which otherwise would have to extend from one end of the network to the other end) and eliminates the serpentine paths often required by a bus topology. If one of the cables between a hub and a workstation should fail, only that workstation is affected; the remaining stations stay functional.

Topology Recommendations

A star topology can be much more manageable than a bus topology. The star topology enables you to add and move workstations without disrupting the entire network. Star topologies, however, command a higher price than do bus topologies, because the star configuration requires the central piece of hardware. Unless you are planning a medium to large network and you can spread the cost of hubs over many nodes, you should try to stick to a bus. Table 5.1 summarizes your options for combining a protocol and medium with a topology.

Table 5.1
Possible Network Standards Combinations

	Ethernet	ARCNET	Token Ring	FDDI
Thick Coax	Bus			
Thin Coax	Bus	Star/Hier.		
Type 1			Star	
10BASE-T	Star/Hier.	Star/Hier.	Star	
Fiber Optic	Star	Star		Star

Organization of Network Services

A network's purpose is to provide services to the workstations that are connected to it. Networks can be divided into two classes depending on where those services come from; that is, the services come either from dedicated computers or from the workstations themselves.

Centralized Networks

The most powerful networks use one or more dedicated computers to provide network services to the interconnected workstations. These dedicated network "brains" are called *file servers* because their primary task is to provide file services. File servers also provide printing, electronic mail, messaging, and other services. Server-based networks are the easiest to maintain, because network services typically originate from one source. When the source is modified, the services are changed for everyone.

Server-based networks cost more than nonserver-based networks. A network's cost increases substantially when one computer is dedicated strictly to providing networking services. The cost is offset, however, by the server-based network's higher level of performance; when one machine distributes network services, individual workstations do not need to contribute network services.

The file server, however, does not always need to be totally dedicated to providing network services. A nondedicated file server not only provides network services, but also features DOS or another operating systems for conventional application sessions. You can run an application on the nondedicated file server while the machine also acts as file server to the other computers in the network. Both Novell NetWare and Microsoft LAN Manager are available in versions that support nondedicated file servers.

Nondedicated file servers can perform satisfactorily for small workgroups and lightly loaded networks. AutoCAD and other large, power-hungry applications, however, should not be run on a nondedicated server. Such applications simply demand too much power to run well on a nondedicated server, and can degrade system performance.

Peer-to-Peer Networks

In a *peer-to-peer* network, each workstation contributes some of its own resources for use by the other workstations. The responsibility for network services is spread across the entire network. A peer-to-peer network generally is less expensive than a centralized network, because the peer-to-peer arrangement does not require an additional computer to act as a file server. The drawback, however, is that your computer may not always be working for you. At times, your computer may have to do work for someone else, such as printing or reading a file. This overhead generally is undesirable, however, when AutoCAD is in use on the network. Because no dedicated computer holds the network operating system, it must load on each workstation on the network. In DOS-based peer-to-peer networks, the network operating system's own RAM requirements may prevent you from running AutoCAD at all. The following sections help explain why.

Network Memory Requirements at the Workstation

The single biggest complication in designing an AutoCAD network is coordinating the RAM requirements of resident AutoCAD, AutoLISP, ADI drivers, NIC drivers, and the network shell. You must leave enough RAM for I/O page space addressing, or AutoCAD performance will suffer appreciably.

The 640K Pool

As you may remember, the Intel 80x86 processor family (on which the DOS versions of AutoCAD are based) can access only 640K of memory for applications. Applications, such as AutoCAD, must try to occupy that amount of memory, in contention with all the previously mentioned programs and drivers. Various hardware and software work-arounds attempt to salvage unused RAM in the 640K-1024K range for applications to use. Before examining these work-arounds, you should understand how the lower 640K is consumed (see fig. 5.11).

Resident AutoCAD Code

When the DOS AutoCAD program is executed, it loads itself into memory in much the same way other programs do. But because AutoCAD is such a large program, overlay files are needed to store some of its code (this is not the case, however, with AutoCAD 386). Overlay files are the files that end with an .OVL extension and are analogous to the pinbar drafting system and transparent overlays. A draftsman does not keep all the overlays on his board all the time, only the ones he needs to do the work at hand. In the same way, AutoCAD loads only its core functions and then swaps code overlays into memory as needed to perform various drafting functions.

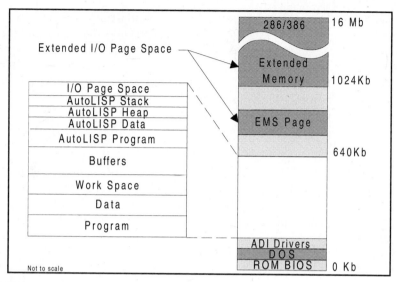

Figure 5.11:

Typical AutoCAD RAM usage.

AutoLISP

Almost every AutoCAD user works with AutoLISP in some capacity, so the AutoLISP interpreter must reside in RAM during most AutoCAD sessions. When stacked on top of AutoCAD, AutoLISP consumes another 76K of RAM, which is not much considering the power that it puts in your hands. Still, RAM is precious. Your settings for the AutoLISP heap and stack affect the overall requirements for AutoLISP. You can reserve a maximum of 45K for your AutoLISP data, but if you can get by with less, the difference can be returned to the pool for better uses. Most users, for example, set the DOS environment variables LISPHEAP and LISPSTACK to reserve the entire 45K for AutoLISP. Typical environment variable settings look like the following:

```
SET LISPSTACK=5000
SET LISPHEAP=40000
```

These settings are placed in the batch file used to execute AutoCAD or in the workstation's AUTOEXEC.BAT file. See the AutoCAD *Installation and Performance Guide* for more information.

By reducing your AutoLISP requirements by a few kilobytes, you may free up the extra RAM you need to squeeze in a network driver. The following settings save another 20K of RAM:

```
SET LISPSTACK=5000
SET LISPHEAP=20000
```

Experiment with the AutoLISP programs you normally use to determine whether you still can run them with less RAM. The AutoLISP VMON (Virtual Memory ON) function may help, or you may have to adjust the LISPHEAP setting up if you receive Insufficient node space error messages. The AutoCAD *Installation and Performance Guide* and *AutoLISP Programmer's Reference* describe these techniques in more detail. If you seldom or never use AutoLISP, you can disable it through AutoCAD's configuration and save the entire 45K.

Extended AutoLISP

Autodesk introduced Extended AutoLISP to solve two problems. The first was to alleviate the constraints on AutoLISP program size and complexity. There is no need to limit AutoLISP heap and stack sizes when using Extended AutoLISP, and programs can be as large as necessary. The LISPHEAP and LISPSTACK environment variables have no effect on Extended AutoLISP. Instead, you can set the LISPXMEM environment variable to limit the amount of extended memory allocated to Extended AutoLISP, so that some of that RAM can be used as Extended I/O page space.

For example, the setting SET LISPXMEM=1024,512K limits Extended AutoLISP to a 512K section of RAM starting at 1024K.

The second problem Extended AutoLISP solved was the lack of memory for memory-resident programs such as network drivers. Extended AutoLISP loads into extended memory and frees memory space in the 640K pool for other programs. You should have at least 512K of extended memory to use Extended AutoLISP, but it can run with less. If you have an 80286-based computer equipped with 1M of RAM and 384K available as extended memory, you probably can run Extended AutoLISP there.

Extended AutoLISP also was a "test bed" for the DOS extender technology that led to the creation of AutoCAD 386. Extended AutoLISP uses the Rational Systems, Inc. DOS extender and AutoCAD 386 uses the Phar Lap DOS extender. AutoCAD 386 leaves plenty of the 640K RAM pool for network drivers. As mentioned in Chapter 4, DOS extender technology is prolonging the life of DOS in the face of UNIX and OS/2.

ADI Drivers

The introduction of the Autodesk Device Interface (ADI) specification in AutoCAD version 2.52 was a mixed blessing. The ADI specification enables hardware vendors to write drivers that take advantage of their own hardware's strengths, and it frees Autodesk of the burden of developing drivers to support hundreds of peripherals and displays. ADI drivers, however, take up more of the RAM pool that is needed for both AutoCAD and other memory-resident programs, such as network drivers and shells. This is one area where the quality of the ADI driver can make a tremendous difference. An efficiently written driver in assembly language can be only one-tenth the size of a sloppy or hastily written driver. The user, however, pays the penalty in wasted RAM. Some of the smallest ADI display drivers are 10K to 20K in size and have all or more of the features of 50K to 100K drivers.

You can work around the ADI driver problem by configuring AutoCAD to use one of its own built-in drivers, but few of them provide the high-resolution displays users have come to love. If you have a mouse, digitizer, or plotter driver loaded in addition to the ADI display driver, you are using up even more RAM.

AutoCAD Data Memory Management

Besides the RAM filled up by AutoCAD and AutoLISP, AutoCAD requires additional RAM to hold drawing files and provide scratch space to perform hiding operations and calculate polylines, curves, and hatches. If you do not have enough memory left after loading network drivers for AutoCAD to manipulate your drawing data, performance will be poor.

AutoCAD uses a *paging* scheme to handle the current drawing file. If you create a 200K drawing file, and AutoCAD has only 35K of RAM left after loading itself and all your drivers, then the drawing file is not going to fit completely into RAM. Paging is a programming trick similar to the overlay scheme AutoCAD uses for its code. Through its paging scheme, AutoCAD loads the drawing file into RAM in *pages* (or portions), depending on the portion of the drawing you are using. The rest of the drawing remains on disk until the program requests another portion.

You can check the amount of available page space by examining the output of the Status command. The number that appears on the line for I/O Page Space is the amount of RAM AutoCAD has left after loading the program, AutoLISP, and drivers into memory, and after allocating memory for other uses. I/O page space is the last block of memory used by AutoCAD, and it shrinks or expands to occupy all the remaining RAM in your computer.

If you have expanded or extended memory installed in your computer, AutoCAD 286 can use up to 4M of it for extended I/O page space. AutoCAD 386 can use much more. AutoCAD's drawing pager uses this page space to place pages in faster RAM, rather than writing them to the slower disk. In order to use all the expanded or extended memory, however, AutoCAD 286 needs to store all the pages' addresses in the 640K pool. Those addresses can eat up a great deal of memory, especially when you have little to spare.

If your system has a large amount of memory, you may unexpectedly receive a warning from AutoCAD 286, stating that the program needs more low memory to make use of the high memory. If you do not have enough low memory to contain all the high-memory addresses, you have two choices. The first choice is to limit AutoCAD's use of your extended memory with the ACADXMEM environment variable, or limit the expanded memory with the ACADLIMEM variable to only as much memory as you have address space for. The AutoCAD *Installation and Performance Guide* shows you how to set these variables. The alternative choice is to maximize low memory to allow for more address space, by using the techniques in the following section, "Relief for RAM Cram."

The ACADFREERAM setting also can affect RAM availability. The DOS environment variable ACADFREERAM notifies AutoCAD of how much memory you want it to reserve for performing polyline curve, hatch, and hidden-line removal calculations. AutoCAD reserves 18K of free RAM by default. If you never use these drafting functions, you can adjust the ACADFREERAM reserve downward to make more room for drivers, page space, and other uses. If you typically work with 3D, hatch patterns, or curves, 18K may not be enough. You can tell AutoCAD to reserve as much as 24K for ACADFREERAM.

Network Drivers

During a typical boot-up, the computer loads the network interface card driver and NOS shell, along with DOS system drivers for hard disks, ANSI.SYS, and others. These drivers and programs limit the space that can be occupied by AutoCAD and its entourage. AutoCAD primarily feels the pinch in the I/O page space, first reducing the number of extended I/O pages that the AutoCAD pager can address, then reducing standard I/O page space. When page space is compromised to the minimum, and additional RAM is needed for AutoCAD to complete initialization, then AutoLISP may be disabled to make room for basic functions.

Just like ADI drivers, NIC drivers come in different sizes and require different amounts of RAM. Different network operating systems also require different amounts of RAM for their shells. Network users find themselves in the same general predicament many AutoCAD users are in; that is, network vendors are continually upgrading their operating systems, which, in turn, expands the size of the shell. If you use AutoCAD on a network, you feel the squeeze from both ends, as both AutoCAD and the network shell get bigger and eat up more RAM. Eventually, something has to give.

Relief for RAM Cram

Autodesk has released two versions of AutoCAD aimed at higher performance, but which make life easier for the networked AutoCAD user. AutoCAD 386 Releases 10 and 11, optimized for use with the 80386 processor, load primarily into the 16M possible in protected mode. Approximately 350K of the 640K memory pool is left for ADI drivers, network drivers, and other resident utilities (see fig. 5.12). By switching to AutoCAD 386, you get not only the advantage of higher performance for AutoCAD, but extra room for network software that could open up more network system choices. AutoCAD 386 requires an 80386SX or 80386DX CPU; if you switch to AutoCAD 386, Autodesk considers the move as a platform change from your current version of AutoCAD. See your AutoCAD dealer for upgrade details and prices.

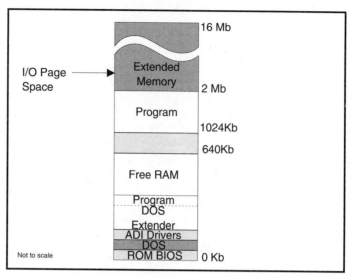

Figure 5.12:

The AutoCAD 386 memory map.

If you cannot move AutoCAD out of the way of network programs, you might be able to move the network shell and other TSRs out of the pool. You may be able to accomplish extra RAM savings by using memory management software. Several *expanded memory manager* (EMM) software packages let you take advantage of any unused addresses in the 640-1024K range. Two capable and popular EMMs are 386^{MAX} by Qualitas Software and QEMM by Quarterdesk Office Systems. These utilities work by assigning RAM to the addresses normally reserved for ROM on the motherboard, hard disk controller, video adapter, and other expansion cards. Once the RAM is assigned, it can be used by utilities provided with the EMM to load pointing device, video, NIC, and other drivers or TSRs into this "high memory."

A few network interface cards rely on hardware enhancements to ease RAM cram. They provide program RAM on the card and special drivers that download to the card before they execute. One example is the Micom-Interlan NP627. These enhanced NICs do not consume as much RAM as standard NICs, but they do cost considerably more.

With your lower DOS memory optimized, you can begin to estimate the maximum network shell size your configuration can tolerate. You can experiment with different sizes by loading unused device drivers or other TSRs and watching their effect on AutoCAD's I/O page space, extended I/O page address space, and AutoLISP. With trial and error deduction, you should arrive at a safe maximum-allowable shell size. You then can narrow your NOS and NIC choices to those shells and drivers that will fit within that space.

Network Security

Many potential network users question whether network security is needed. If they have no need for security now, then they imagine they probably will not need security with the network either. While this is true to an extent, remember that one of the major requirements for network security is not to protect your system from outsiders; it is to protect the network from insiders. You may not think that a network is at much risk from its own users, but most of the security built into network software is designed to protect against accidental damage. This is true even for small networks in which everyone knows everyone else's business.

The type of NOS you buy will impact the security of your network system. Peer-to-peer NOSs that tend to rely heavily on the DOS file system, for example, have no way of preventing users from gaining unauthorized access to files directly from DOS. Further, because the network's files are scattered around the office (decentralized), they are vulnerable to accidental erasure and intentional tampering.

On the other hand, a centralized (server-based) network can justify a different, higher-performance, and possibly proprietary file system. Because shared files do not reside on the workstations, they do not have to comply with the workstations' file system. The server's file system can be proprietary and optimized for networking.

Each network operating system has different security features, but most implement a common set of features that include password protection and privileges to specific network resources such as disk directories or network devices. Chapter 7 describes some of the network security features of several common networks and tells you how those features should be used with AutoCAD.

Network Data Integrity

Although a network gives you the advantage of having to maintain only one set of data, your data is at higher risk of becoming corrupted or lost in a network environment. Different network operating systems take different approaches to the issue of data integrity. Some systems, for example, maintain the DOS File Allocation Table file system. This approach simplifies data maintenance, and lets DOS maintenance techniques be used on the network just as they can be used on a stand-alone workstation. UNIX- and XENIX-based networks also generally adhere to those operating systems' native file systems.

Novell NetWare takes an entirely different approach by implementing a proprietary file system with *fault-tolerant* features much like those found in mainframe systems. Other popular network operating systems, such as LAN Manager, also implement fault-tolerant features. The term "fault tolerance" describes a network's data protection features, including the following:

- Duplication of directory and file allocation tables on the same disk in case one is damaged.

- Read-after-write verification of data with automatic relocation of the data and bad-block marking.

- Disk mirroring that can make two hard disks look identical. If one disk should fail, the other disk is automatically recognized and the system keeps running.

- Disk duplexing, which allows duplication of entire disk drive subsystems. If one subsystem fails, the system falls back to the other. Disk reads also can be performed in parallel, increasing performance.

- Server duplexing, which duplicates entire servers in case any component of one server should fail.

- Transaction tracking, which ensures that an application cannot corrupt files if it fails during a file update.

Although these features are not a substitute for good backup procedures, they greatly reduce the chances that you sometime will have to rely on your backup. Backup strategies are covered in Chapter 11. The more important your AutoCAD data is to your company, the more you need powerful data integrity features in a network operating system—look for them while you are evaluating your choices. Without these protective measures, your data is no safer on a network than it would be on a common workstation, even though networked data is under much greater risk.

Network Output Topologies

The need to share expensive printers and plotters may be one of your major reasons for networking. Networks enable users to share and manage output devices transparently, so that you no longer need to wheel your output devices around the office or to connect them through data switches. Most networks apply the concept of queuing to the management of hard-copy output. Peer-to-peer and server-based networks, however, differ slightly in their approach.

Sharing Peripherals in Server-Based Networks

On a server-based network, each user works in an application and prints data just as if he were working at a stand-alone workstation. The workstation's built-in network shell intercepts the application's output at the printer port and redirects the data to a disk file on the file server. This often happens more quickly than the actual print job takes to complete (the process is similar to AutoCAD's plot-to-file capability), and the user returns to the application and can continue working. A print request is placed in the desired output device's queue. If no other jobs are in progress, the file is spooled to the printer or plotter, which is connected to the file server (see fig. 5.13). If other jobs are waiting to go to the same device, the request is placed at the bottom of the list and must wait its turn on a first come, first served basis. A user can delete a job from the queue or reprioritize it.

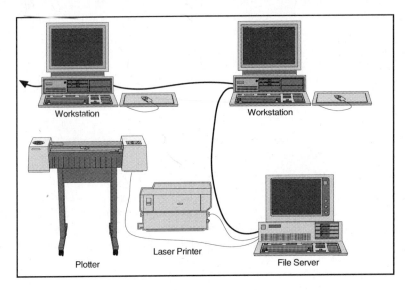

Figure 5.13:
Traditional peripheral location on a server-based network.

If you plan to use a centralized network with a dedicated file server, you probably will attach output devices to the file server. In most cases, the file server resides in a secure area. If you plan to set up a centralized network, you should consider the following points about peripheral sharing:

- Output peripherals can be placed in noise-controlled space so that they do not distract users.
- Printer and plotter supplies can be stored with peripherals for convenience and better waste management.
- Processing overhead for output is carried by the server, not the workstations.
- RAM requirements of the network shell at the workstations are often lower.
- Third-party software is available to allow certain workstations to act as *print servers* and have printers or plotters attached to them, making them

function in much the same fashion as workstations on a peer-to-peer network.

Sharing Peripherals in Peer-to-Peer Networks

Peer-to-peer networks allow you to share peripherals, just as you share programs and data. Most output peripherals attached to a workstation on the network are available to the other users (see fig. 5.14). When a user prints from within an application, the network operating system intercepts the print job. If the destination printer is attached to that workstation, the job is spooled to the workstation's disk file and placed in the printer's queue to await printing. If the destination printer is attached to another workstation across the network, the print job is transmitted to that workstation and written to a file. If the printer is not busy, the job begins to print. Otherwise, the job is placed at the bottom of the queue to await printing.

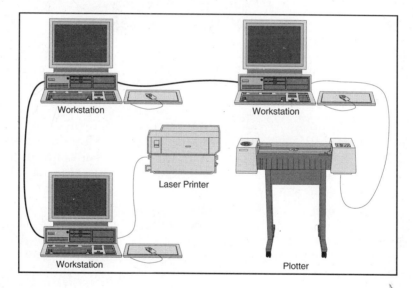

Figure 5.14:
Peripheral location on a peer-to-peer network.

If you plan to set up a peer-to-peer network, you should consider the following points about peripheral sharing:

- If your workgroup is small, you may be able to leave peripherals where they are now and have less disruption.
- You may not want to have plotters or printers attached to workstations. This type of peripheral-sharing setup can create distractions and interruptions when one person attempts to use a peripheral that is connected to another person's workstation.

■ Some network software requires more RAM in workstations with peripherals attached than in other workstations.

■ Background output tasks may reduce the performance of the workstation with a shared peripheral attached.

Conclusions on Peripheral Sharing

In most AutoCAD networks, the centralized, server-based approach works best for the users working on the network, as well as for the performance of AutoCAD. Exceptions include cases in which file servers are too distant from the workstations and access to output devices becomes inconvenient. In this case, output devices located closer to the workstations make more sense. Another exception is with most UNIX-based networks that do not employ a dedicated server.

Network Administration Features

Your network does not have to become large or complicated before you need to find simple but powerful methods of administering the users, directories, security, files, peripherals, and performance. Some operating systems provide better tools for these tasks than others. You should look for the following important administration features in any network operating system:

■ **File management.** Networks can easily grow to include hundreds of megabytes of data and programs in thousands of files. The network should provide utilities that enable the network supervisor to scan files easily and perform maintenance operations across the network.

■ **User management.** User profiles change frequently. People often need temporary or permanent access to new areas of the network directory structure. As a result, users' rights must be changed from time to time. The network should enable the administrator to maintain passwords and track user activity.

■ **Interface maintenance.** Most networks use menus or batch files to make network resources accessible to users. The network should allow the administrator to change these mechanisms easily.

■ **System configuration adaptibility.** Few networks remain static for long. They change as equipment is added and moved around. As the system grows, additional disk storage and RAM are needed to accommodate the increasing demands made on the overall system. Your network should be easy to expand and reconfigure without unnecessarily disrupting ongoing work.

■ **Performance monitoring.** Speed is critical to your network's success. The network should allow the administrator to measure its performance and accurately calculate performance statistics.

■ **Security.** You must be able to identify security breaches. For most users, however, the ability to see the relationships of users rights to the data structure of the network is more important. The network operating system you choose should make it easy for you to see the relationships between users and data security.

Workstation Hardware Considerations

Your network management tasks will be easier if you look closely at your network hardware needs. The benefits of hardware planning are greater for firms that are starting to purchase hardware, but planning also can help those that already have equipment in place. If you carelessly attempt to integrate different combinations of dissimilar equipment, you can create problems and cost your company extra money.

The Merits of a Standard Workstation Configuration

When you are selecting workstation hardware, try to standardize on one configuration for the whole group or company. This means that you should settle on the same type of computer, hard disk, video card, and network card for each user, if possible.

If you purchase only one configuration, you will have to maintain only one configuration for all users, which is easier than trying to maintain a different, and possibly conflicting, configuration at each desk. This makes good sense, particularly when you are selecting a network interface card. Once you find the right software (especially drivers) and the optimum standard workstation configuration, you can easily replicate it on the other workstations and will not need to modify it several times.

CAD manager's workstation, copied to a network drive, and downloaded onto the other workstations. In the case of AutoCAD, all that remains is setting individual workstation parameters. If you have several different ADI drivers to update, for example, you must devote more of your time and energy to system configuration.

A standard workstation configuration provides you with plenty of spares for troubleshooting and replacement. If you keep an extra workstation for training and overflow, you can borrow its expansion cards and other parts to keep "front-line" workstations in operation.

By settling on a proven configuration, you make your relationship with your dealer more trouble-free, too. When the time comes to add a workstation, unless technology has advanced significantly, you can place a typical order. Your users do not suffer from "new computer envy," and you might get a better price from your dealer if he knows he will not have to support some new, unfamiliar product. If you are a frequent customer, your dealer can keep your favorite products in stock.

You should consider two final points about workstation selection. First, when considering a server-based network, managers sometimes assume that network performance is enhanced if more power is placed at the server than at the workstations. In practice, however, this does not work. For example, with a 286-based NOS and all else being equal, a network with 386-based workstations and a 286-based file server will yield higher performance than an identical network with 286-based workstations and a 386-based file server. Just as if the machines were going to stand alone, select them for AutoCAD performance first and leave network performance as a separate issue. The second point concerns workstation hard disk requirements and is covered in the next section.

Workstation Data Storage Requirements

When you are selecting your workstation hardware, be sure to look at your data storage requirements. You will not need as much hard disk space at the workstations in a LAN as you do if your workstations are not networked. Any file that is shared (drawing files, typical details, symbols, and even applications) should be stored on the file server.

If drawings, libraries, and programs are stored on a file server, then less hard disk space is necessary at the workstations. 20M to 40M of hard disk space is sufficient for the temporary files, operating system, and a few personal programs. If you are buying your first computer in hopes of later using it as a file server in a network, however, a larger disk is needed to accommodate many users. In such cases, a 150M to 300M ESDI or SCSI drive is more appropriate.

If you decide to install the AutoCAD program files on each workstation using the strategy outlined in Chapter 8 (which works with any NOS), you will need a hard disk in every workstation.

With, however, a properly sized and configured RAM disk in each workstation and a server-based network, you can even do without hard disks in the workstations. When a RAM disk is utilized, workstations can share AutoCAD program files from the file server and direct temporary files to the local RAM disk. Each workstation can use a bootable floppy disk to store network and video drivers, the network shell program, and batch files.

ADI Compatibility

AutoCAD display drivers for graphics cards use a communications channel called an *interrupt vector* to get services from the CPU. These Autodesk Device Interface (ADI) drivers almost always come preset from the vendor to interrupt 7A, the same interrupt setting that is used by some older versions of Novell NetWare. Autodesk provides these drivers with the capability to use interrupts other than 7A. You must make sure that any display drivers you will be using with NetWare can be reconfigured to an interrupt other than 7A, or either the driver or your network connection may not work.

Network Interface Cards

A good network interface card can save you time and frustration when accessing drawings on a network. NICs also can improve otherwise sluggish system response when performing other routine network tasks. The section that follows describes NIC hardware technology as it applies to AutoCAD performance in either a workstation or a file server.

Several features affect network card performance, including buffer size, driver software, on-board processors or controllers, and I/O scheme. The following sections briefly examine each of these features.

Buffers

An NIC buffer acts like the buffer in a printer. A buffer temporarily holds data as it moves from a fast data channel to a slower one. In the case of a printer, the buffer holds data waiting to be printed, so that the processor can work on other tasks. An NIC buffer holds outbound data destined for the network medium and inbound data destined for the CPU. For AutoCAD users, the rule of thumb for buffer size on a NIC is the same as the one for RAM memory: the more the better. AutoCAD uses larger files than most applications, and a larger buffer will hold more data than a small one. Most major network cards come with 8K to 64K buffers.

Driver Software

NIC driver software is a major influence on overall network performance. The situation is similar to video cards; a high-performance, tightly written driver can make all the difference between otherwise competitive hardware products. This has become especially true in the last year, because most major NIC manufacturers have optimized their hardware designs. In fact, many manufacturers use the same network controller chip. Several NIC vendors have released high-performance drivers that optimally match the data segment of the network packet to the cache buffer size of the network operating system, resulting in more efficient memory use.

On-Board Processors

Before the advent of today's microcomputers, some NIC manufacturers designed NICs with their own processors to offload network overhead from the CPU. These cards were designed primarily to improve network performance in file servers involved in heavy-duty applications, such as AutoCAD. With the introduction of today's hyperkinetic PCs, however, most tests show that these coprocessors do not improve network performance as much as faster CPUs can.

I/O Schemes

The last NIC performance criteria is the I/O scheme employed by the card to transfer network data to the computer's memory, where the CPU can get to it. The most popular schemes used by NICs include I/O port addressing, shared RAM, direct memory access (DMA), and bus-mastered DMA. Every NIC uses one of these methods to transfer data between the NIC's buffers and the host computer's RAM. Some NICs can employ different methods, depending on their configuration.

I/O Addressing

In the I/O port addressing method, data is moved back and forth from the computer's RAM, through the CPU, to the NIC's buffers. This method takes advantage of a designated I/O port, which is similar to a printer port. I/O port addressing is relatively slow (about 1M/sec) compared with other methods.

Shared RAM Addressing

When shared RAM addressing is used, the board is configured so that its buffer area can be addressed within the CPU's reserved high memory area. Network data does not have to go through any of the CPU's I/O circuitry, but is read and written by the CPU like system memory. Shared RAM addressing is much faster than I/O addressing.

Direct Memory Access

Direct memory access allows the NIC to transfer data to and from the host's memory without the aid of the CPU. This memory-addressing scheme enables the CPU to go about its other duties without having to attend to data transfers. In theory, this should result in data-transfer rates higher than either of the two previous methods. In reality, however, DMA transfer rates are controlled by the DMA logic circuitry design of the PC. These rates have not changed appreciably since the original IBM PC. As a result, DMA transfers happen 15 to 20 percent slower than shared RAM access in today's fast machines.

Bus-Mastered DMA

DMA transfer is improved, however, in micro-channel and EISA bus machines that allow the DMA circuitry to be located on the NIC instead of on the motherboard. With these boards, DMA transfers can be accomplished at the maximum rate of the bus (33M/sec for EISA), and with properly designed boards, up to the speed of the system's RAM chips.

Conclusions about Network Interface Cards

From this discussion, you might conclude that a shared-RAM I/O NIC with a large buffer and a top-notch driver is the best choice for an ISA bus computer, such as the typical AutoCAD workstation. If so, you would be right for the most part. An additional complication exists, however. Expanded memory cards, video cards, tape drive controllers, device drivers loaded in high memory, and other expansion cards may use the high-memory addresses also needed by shared-RAM NICs. An unused 32K (or even 8K) range of addresses may not exist under many circumstances, so you may not be able to use a shared RAM NIC. This is why some cards offer shared RAM and DMA I/O schemes on the same card. With such a card, you have the flexibility to use either method, whichever suits the machine better (shared RAM if it has the free address space, DMA if its too crowded). A little performance may have to be compromised by using DMA transfers (so the NIC can coexist with your other devices and drivers), but the alternative is having to remove or disable another card, driver, or utility to make shared RAM addresses available for the NIC—usually an unacceptable solution.

When you are evaluating NICs for AutoCAD workstations, look for an adapter that has the best combination of buffer size, I/O methods, and well-supported driver software. Do your homework ahead of time and find out which high-memory RAM addresses you can use. You will need this information anyway, when you configure the NIC. If you are fortunate enough to be able to afford an EISA or MCA computer, consider a bus-mastered DMA network interface card, especially if the computer will be the file server.

File Server Hardware Considerations

Most AutoCAD networks are built around a computer that acts as a dedicated file server. You probably will have a more difficult time choosing a file server than you would simply finding a cheap PC to store files. If you have to save money, save it on the workstations, not the file server. For the best results, consider several factors. These factors are important in any PC-selection process, but more so when choosing a file server. A file server is not an accessory; it is an integral part of your network system. Extra emphasis must be placed on reliability, performance, and expandability, because they will play important parts in your network's evolution.

Once your network is configured and operating, the file server should not be shut down except for maintenance and repairs. Instead, it should be allowed to run 24 hours a day, every day of the year.

Unlike workstations, which are replaced when performance must be improved, new file servers generally are added to a network to supplement existing file servers rather than to replace them. As a result, your file server probably will be in place for many years to come, which is why you need extra reliability. The first place to look for this reliability is in network hard disk drives. Because the hard disk drives are the weakest part of any PC, look for drives with especially high mean time between failure (MTBF) figures, and which are specially designed for use in file servers.

Maximizing Hard Disk Performance in the File Server

As your network grows and your need for disk capacity and performance increases, you may want to employ special disk configuration techniques within your file server to improve response time. One technique is called *disk duplexing* and the other is *disk mirroring*. The file server you choose, the specific disk subsystem components you select, and your network operating system all determine how easily you can use either or both of these techniques. Major server-based network operating systems, such as Novell NetWare, have built-in disk duplexing and disk mirroring capabilities.

Disk mirroring optimizes data security by repeating every disk write operation on an identical drive connected to the same controller or *channel*. A channel is a discrete data path from one device to another. The drives are mirrored in the sense that they are the identical image of each other. Should one fail, the network operating system automatically recognizes only the intact drive and network operation is not interrupted. With two drives, you only get the actual storage capacity of one drive, but with the security of two. You can think of disk mirroring as an automatic, on-line backup.

Disk duplexing is a method whereby two channels, created by two controllers, are used to connect one or more drives to each controller. When a disk read or write is necessary, the network operating system performs the operation on the drive whose heads are closest to the file's location. If one drive is busy writing when a read is requested, the other drive can read without delay. This lets the network operating system distribute file I/O between the two channels, doubling performance. Your cost per megabyte of data storage is doubled with disk mirroring, but the data transfer rate is doubled with disk duplexing. Figures 5.15 and 5.16 illustrate the physical and logical differences between disk mirroring and disk duplexing.

Using Multiprocessing Power

The more powerful a file server is, the longer it will serve the your workgroup's needs before another file server must be added. Many companies build high-performance PCs that can be used as file servers. At the forefront are new proprietary, *scalable* file servers that can be upgraded to additional processors as network loads increase. Combinations and multiples of 80386 and 80486 processors in these machines can perform *symmetrical* or *asymmetrical multiprocessing* with a network operating system, such as LAN Manager, SCO UNIX, and Banyan VINES. Symmetrical multiprocessing makes several processors in one machine act as one large processor. When another processor is added, the NOS distributes the network load evenly across all the processors.

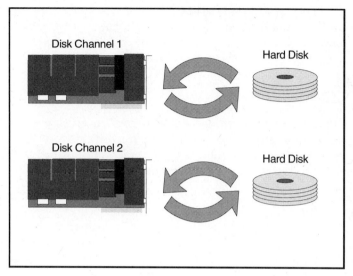

Figure 5.15:
Disk duplexing.

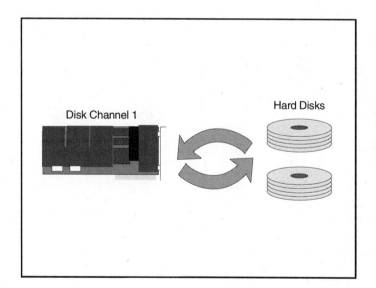

Figure 5.16:
Disk mirroring.

LAN Manager uses an asymmetrical multiprocessing scheme to divide the network load. LAN Manager delegates core functions, such as file and print services, to one processor and assigns server-based applications to the other processor, ensuring the performance and response of each. This idea has been used in the mainframe world for years. Today's multiprocessor PC file server can meet or exceed the performance of a traditional mainframe. Most high-performance file servers feature improved I/O subsystems, bus architectures, and disk subsystems. These features are a necessary part of large client/server networks.

Server Expandability

Networks grow and grow. An expandable file server preserves your investment because it can grow right along with the rest of the network. If you choose your server wisely, you save money down the road because you will not need to buy additional servers or copies of software that is licensed per server.

When shopping for a file server, give consideration to how many total transactions (service requests and replies) the server can provide, not just the amount of data moved by the NIC or disk controller. In addition to expandable processing, discussed earlier, look for plenty of slots. It is not uncommon to have several network interface cards and two disk controllers, in addition to a video card, tape drive controller, one or more I/O port cards, and memory cards installed in a fully exploited file server. Consider an EISA or MCA bus design to take advantage of bus-mastering cards and the additional data bandwidth.

Give preference to tower-type cases with plenty of drive bays with front panel access to mount all your expansion drives.

File Server RAM Requirements

Look for plenty of room for RAM on the file server's motherboard. You should always put as much RAM as possible on the motherboard, instead of on expansion cards. Memory access to expansion cards often is slower than access to RAM on the motherboard. For more information on RAM configurations and memory access, see Chapter 14.

For NetWare networks and systems built on DOS, you probably will want to start with 4M and go up from there, depending on the size of your network. UNIX and LAN Manager networks should start with 8M or more RAM in the file server.

Planning for Plotting Capacity

If you plan to funnel the plots from all your network's users through one or two plotting devices on a network, you should prepare yourself to deal with several installation problems.

When you first plan to purchase a plotter for network duty, try to anticipate the number of plots (per day) that the device will receive from the system's users. Past requirements are usually the best indicator for future use. If your users will need more plots per day than a pen plotter can handle, you should consider buying an electrostatic plotter. Electrostatic plotters handle the high loads produced by many users and do not require as much supervision and maintenance. Both types of plotter technologies are described in Chapter 14.

If you will be setting up AutoCAD on a dedicated file server (running Novell NetWare, for example), you will need an unused I/O port on the file server for the serial or parallel interface required by the plotter. Pen plotters usually need a serial port; most dot-matrix, electrostatic, and laser peripherals need a parallel port.

Most devices other than pen plotters operate on raster data. This introduces an additional, time-consuming step in the plotting process, because AutoCAD produces vector data. The devices typically provide a parallel interface for higher data-transfer rates in an attempt to improve performance. Many also feature a serial interface, but will suffer from performance degradation if the serial port is used. Always use a parallel interface if possible.

If your plotter can not be located near the file server in a dedicated server installation, however, you may have to settle for a serial cable to get from the server to the plotter. Parallel cables can be used only for runs of eight feet or less; dedicated network operating systems, such as NetWare, send output through ports installed only on the file server. The file server and plotter, therefore, must be close to one another. This problem can be overcome with the use of third party *print server* software that can be installed on a workstation located near the desired plotter location. Some network operating systems also come with their own print server software. Print servers enable you to attach plotters (considered as printers) to workstations. Make sure that you know the type of interface you need to use and the data-throughput rates for each interface before you buy print server software.

Some output devices require an ADI software driver or interface adapter in the computer to which they are attached. Remember that TSR drivers can rob memory that is needed for AutoCAD, input device drivers, display drivers, and the network software driver. Additional controller cards that may be required by some output devices not only consume physical slots in the PC, but can take up I/O and RAM addresses needed for network interface cards and bus mice. If the plotter you are considering requires an ADI driver, and if it cannot plot to a file, then it may not work from a file server. Make sure that the file server or workstation that will host the plotter can accommodate all the device's requirements.

Backup Devices

An appropriate backup device and medium can make network backup processes painless and should be a part of every file server purchase. Many people argue that they cannot afford to spend $600 or more on a tape drive for backups that seemingly add nothing to productivity. On the other hand, if you pay a CAD manager or even an entry-level person to oversee the daily backup process and shuffle diskettes, you could pay for a tape drive in just a few months.

The backup density of a tape drive proves that tape is the most economical medium for large-capacity data recording. Even when advanced data-compression techniques are used, high-density diskettes hold only a little over 2M of data each. With several hundred megabytes of shared disk storage in the typical network, a diskette backup scheme would require 150 diskettes or more to complete a full backup.

When you mention a high-capacity tape backup device to many CAD managers, they immediately object to the high price of both tapes and drives. In truth, tape drives are more economical than practically any other medium for backup storage. Considering that high-density diskettes are available for as low as 50 cents apiece, the cost per megabyte of storage media is then about $.42/M. Tape, on the other hand, lowers the cost per megabyte of storage media to $.20/M, less than half the cost of diskettes. DC600XL-type cartridges are available for $30 or less and can store up to 150M. Remember, as your network grows, your backup technician will find it increasingly difficult to handle all those diskettes.

Floppy disks are all right for backing up small hard disks, but tape is a natural for larger hard disks and file server backup storage. Minicomputer and mainframe users have known this for years. A tape drive unit can transfer data to and from the computer at much higher rates than can a diskette drive. Its continuous physical form lends itself to the sequential reading and writing activities typically performed by backup programs. Most tape backup systems use 1/4-inch-tape data cartridges. The typical storage capacities of various tape formats are shown in table 5.2.

Table 5.2
Backup Media Capacities

Medium	Capacity
DC-2000 cartridge	40-160M
Data cassette	60-300M
DC-600 cartridge	60-320M
DAT cartridge	600-1300M
8mm cartridge	2200M

One interesting, high-capacity standard emerging for tape backup is *digital audio tape* (DAT). Using media originally designed to store high-quality audio recordings, this new standard, with high-performance error detection and correction capabilities, helically records digital computer data onto high-quality tape. The helical recording process places tracks of data in diagonal rows across the width of the tape, like the threads on a screw. Large network installations enthusiastically are adopting DAT and 8mm systems for their backup media needs because of their higher speed compared to cassettes and DC-600 cartridges.

Only closed and inactive files, normally, can be backed up. Backup tape drives are installed traditionally on a workstation and are used to back up the file server when all other users are logged off the network. Another traditional configuration is to install the tape device on the file server. The file server, however, must be shut down and rebooted under DOS to execute the backup program. Fortunately, several third-party developers have developed backup programs that can back up data from a file server to an installed drive, even while the network is in use. These programs and others are covered in Chapter 11. It is truly the tape drive software that makes a backup device convenient and powerful. Consider one only in conjunction with the other.

One final caveat about tape drives: make sure that you select a drive that will allow you to restore existing backup data from a new drive if your existing one should fail. Some products are so sensitive about the particular physical alignment of the drives' heads, that even though you replace one with an identical model, it may not be able to restore previously created tapes. This capability to restore previous tapes is crucial if your drive should be stolen or damaged. You will want to be able to replace the hardware, and restore your software and data from your backup tapes. If your drive choice is not compatible among individual units, however, all your backup efforts could be in vain. Ask the vendor for a written guarantee.

Power Protection

With all your valuable data in one central location, it is especially vulnerable to power fluctuations and failures, which could make the data unavailable to the system's users.

Power problems come in a variety of forms. A *spike* is a short yet very-high-voltage condition, as is created when lightning strikes a power line. Most power disturbances are *surges.* A surge occurs when the power level momentarily rises above the 110-volt upper limit of normal power. Surges account for most of the damage to computer hardware and data. A *sag*, or brownout, on the other hand, occurs when the voltage momentarily drops below 80 percent of the normal voltage value. Finally, an *outage* occurs when the power fails completely. Outages may last a few minutes, until the power transmission system compensates for the glitch, or for hours, until repair crews can fix the damage.

Studies performed by IBM and Bell Labs determined that more than half of all power problems last less than six seconds, and occur twice a week on average. To protect your file server equipment and data investment, power protection devices are available to combat power anomalies. Power protection for PCs comes in three basic forms: surge protection, power conditioning, and uninterruptable power supplies (UPSs).

Surge Protectors

Surge protectors are the most popular form of power protection. These devices protect your computer equipment from the voltage spikes that are common to public power sources. They suppress and absorb spikes caused by lightning, switching motors, and other sources, allowing only acceptable maximum voltages to pass through to the computer.

More advanced surge protectors prevent RFI interference from getting to your computer. The surge protector is the minimum acceptable power protection device you should get for all your computer equipment except your file server. Do not operate without one.

Power Conditioners

Power conditioning devices condition the incoming AC sine wave from the power source. They smooth out any ripples, spikes, and dips in the waveform and pass premium-quality power to the PC. Power conditioners are better insurance against power problems than surge protectors, but a power conditioner will not save your data from most power outages.

Uninterruptable Power Supplies

Uninterruptable power supplies provide a finite amount of power reserve to any connected device in case of a power outage or brownout. A UPS should be attached to every network file server. A UPS's basic design uses a battery to store a specific amount of energy in case the AC power source fails. Uninterruptable power sources are broken down into two basic categories: switching-type units and true uninterruptable power supplies.

A switching UPS—or standby power supply (SPS), as it is more appropriately called—permits power to proceed to the computer unaltered under normal operation (except for possible surge protection). But if a power failure should occur, the unit switches the current going to the PC from the wall receptacle to a battery. The switch happens so fast that the computer does not notice that the power was interrupted for a few milliseconds.

SPSs are the least expensive protection type of uninterruptable power supply, and are adequate for many file server installations. They have a small amount of reserve (from five to 15 minutes) to endure most power outages or provide enough time to shut down the file server before their reserve power is exhausted. With many files in use and data held in its disk cache when the power stops, a network operating system has to be shut down ("downed" as network supervisors call it) carefully to avoid interrupting important server processes. Once the power is restored, current is switched back to the receptacle. The battery is recharged while the system is running, and is maintained until it is called upon again.

A true UPS, on the other hand, provides all outgoing power to the PC from a battery. It is kept charged by the UPS's circuitry, and the PC never receives current from the wall receptacle. If normal power fails, the UPS continues to serve power to the PC for as long as the UPS is capable. If you believe that you may be getting poor quality power, you should get a true UPS to isolate at least your file server from your commercial power system.

When shopping for an UPS or SPS for a network file server, first consider output capacity. UPSs are typically rated in volt-amperes (VA) or *watts*. Select a UPS large enough to accommodate all the devices plugged into it: the file server PC, monitor, external drives, printers, and other peripherals needed while the file server is running.

Most devices bear a sticker or other label on the back of the cabinet declaring power consumption in amperes ("amps" for short) or watts. You can calculate the wattage of a device by multiplying the voltage by the amps, times a power (efficiency) factor of 0.6. A printer that draws 110 volts AC at two amps, for instance, consumes approximately 132 watts of power ($110 \times 2 \times 0.6$). Total all values in one system of units (VA or watts) for all devices connected to the UPS. Then select the next larger size UPS for a safety and reserve margin. For a file server with a 200-watt power supply, a 0.4-amp monochrome monitor, and four-amp laser printer, for example, select an 850 or 900 VA UPS:

200w (330 VA)

$110v \times 0.4a$ (44 VA) $\times 0.6 = 27w$

$110v \times 4a$ (440 VA) $\times 0.6 = 264w$

equals 814 VA or 491 watts

Consider the minimum amount of time you (or another authorized person) would need to see that all users log off the network, get to the file server, and bring it down safely. Choose a UPS with a margin for safety above this figure. If it would take you 30 minutes to prepare to down the server, choose a device with at least 40 minutes of reserve power. Most UPS and SPS manufacturers report the amount of hold-up time their units provide in their specifications. During an extended power outage, you will probably not be able to continue business because of the lack of power for lights, copiers, and other office equipment. While 30 minutes is not enough time to get much work done, uninterruptable power protection for your file server will at least let you shut it down in an orderly fashion.

If you decide against a true UPS, compare the switching time or *transfer time* of SPSs. The faster the transfer time, the better; less than ten milliseconds is adequate, under four milliseconds is good.

Look for UPS and SPS models that feature a *UPS monitoring* interface. Popular network operating systems from Novell and 3Com have built-in UPS monitoring supports. A UPS with a monitoring interface provides a jack into which can be plugged a cable. An optional UPS monitoring kit provides an adapter card that installs in the file server and a cable to connect the card to the UPS. Some UPSs connect to the file server with a serial cable to one of the file server's serial ports. If power is interrupted and the UPS begins to discharge (or the SPS switches to its reserve), a signal is transmitted by the cable to the monitoring interface card or serial port. The card then produces a software interrupt that notifies the network operating system that the power has failed. The network operating system then warns all active users by its electronic messaging service to log out as soon as possible. When a user-defined amount of time has passed (corresponding to the amount of reserve power provided by the UPS), the network operating system automatically logs out all remaining users, closes all open files, terminates all pending print jobs, flushes all its cache buffers, and downs itself.

It can do all this, any time of day or night, without human intervention. A UPS with monitoring, by reducing the amount of time needed to prepare the server for downing, can reduce the amount of reserve power you need to buy and provide extra protection against power-related data loss.

Lastly, look for the type of AC wave-form output by UPSs. Some provide square wave power, some pseudo-sine waves. Pseudo-sine wave more closely resembles the ideal AC sine wave that computers expect to receive. And, as always, look for the Underwriters Laboratory safety seal of approval.

A Final Note on Hardware

As a final note on network computer hardware, make sure that the products you are considering are compatible with all the network hardware and software you will be using. Products are becoming more and more compatible with networks, as networks become more common, but problems exist and can be hard to diagnose. Networking involves close and specific ties between all hardware and software at a low level. If you cannot try a network before you buy it, at least get a guarantee that it will work exactly the way you want.

Summary

Choosing a network operating system and hardware is a tough job. Many factors must be taken into account when selecting technology to connect your users. The first step is developing a good understanding of the network's many components. You also should remember one important point: do not underestimate your present and future needs. All too often, network buyers think too small and the network is soon outgrown. If you have to replace an existing network with another system, you must go through the entire process of evaluation, design, procurement, installation, and training all over again. Try to start with a system that can grow with your needs by adding on new features, not replacing old ones.

This chapter has tried to make your network-selection job easier by helping you understand how networks operate and the relationships between network software and hardware. You learned how networks use packets and how networks are made up of layers of protocols. You should now understand the different access protocols of Token Ring, ARCNET, and Ethernet, when to use different types of network cable, and when to consider the different network topologies. You now know the pros and cons of server-based and peer-to-peer networks and how to determine the amount of RAM at your workstations, and how to determine RAM usage. You learned the security, data integrity, output, and administration features to look for in a network operating system. You now should be able to select a capable file server complete with high-capacity disk storage, and expandabilty, a backup device, and power protection.

CAD managers, new or experienced, involved in purchasing and installation decisions, concerned with system performance or troubleshooting, should continue reading in the following chapter. The next chapter shows you how to compile the specifications for hardware and software and looks at the quality and price/performance issues you will face when selecting specific equipment. You will learn how to work smoothly with a computer dealer, create a request for proposal, and schedule, participate in, and test a new installation. You will see how to design an ergonomic CAD work area, and learn about performance benchmarking, as well as systematic troubleshooting.

6

Designing and Installing a System

With your operating system and hardware platform choices made, your next step is to administer the acquisition and installation of your AutoCAD system. Whether you are installing a single workstation or a huge network, the tasks are basically the same.

A system as major as CAD or as complex as a network should be put into use with careful planning, preparation, testing, and a smooth grafting into the infrastructure it supplements. This chapter shows you how to organize your installation with a minimum of risk and disruption to ongoing production.

This chapter is about getting your new system off to a good start. It covers that anxiety-filled period when you are trying to decide which products you need, coping with computer dealers, installing the system without creating chaos, and ensuring that the system works as expected.

This chapter is useful for anyone who is unsure of what to do when faced with the preceding tasks, especially a new or under-experienced CAD manager. This chapter also helps you make educated decisions about buying computer hardware. By assembling the appropriate facts, weighing the evidence, and using good judgment, you can be confident that the equipment you purchase will meet your needs, at a cost you can justify.

Specifying CAD System Hardware

When you set out to select the equipment for your AutoCAD workstations, you face one of the computing world's paradoxes. That is, the choice should be easy because AutoCAD will run on almost any computer you might want to use—IBM machines, PC compatibles, Macintosh computers, and most engineering workstations. Because you have to select from such a vast variety of machines, however, the choice can be difficult.

Some of the CAD manager's toughest decisions deal with hardware selection. This is not because it is difficult to find the best hardware for the job (most of the available products will do well). Instead, it becomes a matter of understanding the different technologies, making cost/performance compromises, and finding the time to research the options. CAD-specific hardware and network equipment change almost daily, and you could easily spend most of your time just trying to keep up with the changes. Further compounding your frustration is the fact that this expensive equipment has a relatively short life expectancy.

If someone else has not already made your hardware decisions, you may know which hardware platform you want to use. If you or your co-workers already have experience with Macintoshes, then you should consider Macintoshes. If you already have Sun or DEC workstations dedicated to design, then those machines would make a good foundation for your AutoCAD network. More than likely, however, you will want to stick with the familiar and cost-effective IBM AT-compatible or 80386-based personal computer.

Market Research

If you want to make sure that you will not invest in soon-to-be-obsolete equipment, then you must research the market. Once you understand the types and variety of options available, you should try to keep your knowledge current. You should find it easier to keep abreast of product developments as they occur than to take periodic "crash courses."

Market research is rightfully the CAD manager's responsibility. Once he understands the hardware options available to his workgroup, the CAD manager can investigate products by talking with hardware manufacturers or software publishers (vendors), by meeting with local user groups, and by reading product literature. This way, the CAD manager can determine whether products actually perform as their manufacturers claim. More important, he can determine whether a specific product can fill his company's needs.

> *Tip:* You can find current information about products, techniques, and trends through professional magazines such as those listed in Appendix D. Nearly all these periodicals carry advertisements for CAD hardware, software, and services. Remember, however, that some products are advertised *before* they are available for purchase, so beware of early marketing hype. Most magazines periodically review products; these reviews can be valuable indicators as to how compatible and effective a product can be.

When you find a product that might fill a particular need, follow up on the ads by requesting product literature from the manufacturer. This literature should contain specifications that can help you determine whether the product will be compatible with other products you are using or considering. If the specifications are not there, request more information from the manufacturer. This step is very important, and should be part of the planning for any computer product purchase.

Whenever possible, try to get the following information from the manufacturer:

- A list of authorized dealers in your area
- Samples of output, if the product is an output device
- A demo disk, if the product is software
- Published reviews and customer references

You always should be wary of new products. Most new products by reputable manufacturers are innovative, higher-performance, better-value alternatives to existing products. New products, however, are prone to bugs and compatibility problems. Even Intel's 80386 processor chip had bugs in its initial version. Infant mortality rates (the rate of failure during initial power-up) are also higher among new products than among tried-and-true existing products. If the manufacturer is a newcomer, the product soon may become an orphan (a product whose manufacturer has gone out of business or no longer supports the product because of limited installed base or resources).

As you may have guessed, then, the key to investing in emerging products is to wait until they have been on the market for some time. Watch for praise and reports of problems from other users. After the product has spread around the computing community a little, any glitches should become public knowledge and a general opinion will have been formed. Watch and listen for it; let someone else be the guinea pig.

Speed and Power

When you are buying AutoCAD workstations, try to remember the following rule of thumb: buy all the speed and power you can afford. The greater the speed at which the system hardware and software can respond to the user's commands, the greater his productivity will be. In the early 1980s, IBM research showed that the average graphics workstation user's productivity could be elevated to that of an expert if system response time was reduced to under four seconds. When response time was reduced to under one second, incredible performance and accuracy gains were achieved (see fig. 6.1).

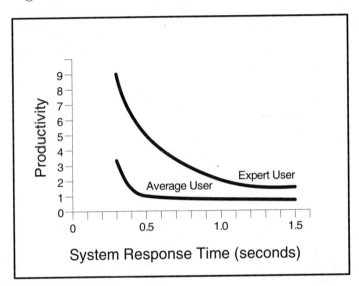

Figure 6.1:
Productivity as a function of system response time.

When searching for AutoCAD hardware, however, you should apply a little common sense to the speed rule. Suppose that you are buying systems for only four users, and you can afford only two state-of-the-art computers, but you could afford four lesser models. The four users with slower equipment will almost certainly out-perform two users with "hot rods."

Price/Performance Analysis

Because cost is always a consideration for any company, the cost of some CAD hardware (and software, especially upgrades) may be hard to justify. CAD hardware, nevertheless, can be proven often to be more than a luxury. Consider, for example, the issue of monitor size and resolution. Monitor sizes typically range from 14" to 20" with resolutions ranging from 640×480 to 1280×1024. Prices for these combinations run from several hundred dollars to several thousand dollars. Although it is less than twice the size of a 14" monitor, a 20" monitor is up to five times more expensive. How, then, can you justify the cost of a 20" monitor?

First, look at the kind of drawings that typically will be produced on the monitor. Will the monitor be used on a workstation that creates only construction details? If so, the monitor usually will not be required to display more than one detail at a time, unless the user needs to see a complete sheet of details for overall composition purposes without having to plot it. A 14" or 16" monitor probably will display one detail at an adequate resolution.

On the other hand, you can more easily justify the expense of larger or higher-end hardware if the user must perform more precise or detailed work, or if greater size is necessary. What if the monitor will be used for facilities management of a university campus, or VLSI circuit design? If these kinds of tasks are involved, you would be crippling the workstation if you purchased a monitor that was less than a 19".

For the sake of argument, assume that the standard 640×480 VGA card and 14" monitor setup costs $750 and a 1024×768 Extended VGA card and 20" monitor setup costs $3000. The difference is about $2250. Management probably will pass on the more expensive monitor unless you can demonstrate the effect of the larger, higher-resolution display (see fig. 6.2).

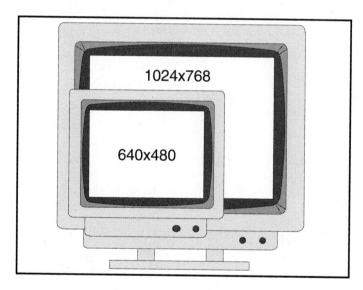

Figure 6.2:
Relative usable screen areas of different resolutions.

Take the facilities management application as an example. On the standard VGA combination, 1/8-inch-high text (on a floor plan with a scale of 1/8"=1'-0") is comfortably readable at a maximum displayable scale width of around 125' worth of the plan on the screen (plus or minus ten percent for individual monitor sharpness and the font used). The Extended VGA combination, however, offers the same degree of readability at a scale width of more than 250'. You can safely say, therefore, that the Extended VGA combination displays twice as much area of a drawing at one time. (The Extended VGA display actually contains more than 2.5 times as many individual picture elements, but in panning to display the floor plan, you could cover the same area in two pans in most cases.) A user working on the lower resolution system, therefore, will have to invoke twice as many display commands to cover the same working area as a user working on the higher-resolution system.

If you assume that the user on the low-resolution system invokes 50 display commands per day (probably a conservative number), and execution of each command consumes 30 seconds (again, this will vary depending on the display hardware and driver used, and assumes a large, complex floor plan as is often the case in facilities management), the handicap would amount to 25 minutes per day spent waiting for the display to redraw. Regenerations, of course, take much longer. Using another conservative estimate of $30 per hour for wages, insurance, other benefits, and floor space, this loss of productive time comes to $12.50 per day wasted, or roughly nine months to achieve payback on the high-resolution system. The following formula can be used to calculate the approximate cost of the lost time. The formula can be applied to any cost justification that can be based upon time saved per AutoCAD command as the result of better hardware or software.

> Time per command execution saved
>> × Commands per day
>> × Total hourly rate of employee
>> × Work days per year
>> = Annual potential savings

Other factors can come into play in this scenario, as well. At 240 days per year, the slower-than-desirable monitor setup costs your company a total of 100 person-hours. Imagine the additonal productivity you could realize if you could reclaim that lost 2 1/2 weeks of work time per year for every AutoCAD user.

This scenario does not consider display-list processing software drivers or graphics-coprocessor-based cards that offer enhanced performance benefits. Nor does it consider the cost to production of a fatigued user frustrated over seemingly continuous display adjustments.

The same principles of cost justification just given can be applied to almost any circumstance. You can use this reasoning to justify digitizers over mice, electro-static over pen plotters, or AutoCAD 386 over AutoCAD 286. The key is to find the point of disparity and follow its effect to the company's bottom line.

If you equate actual cost savings to hardware (and software) features, you should come up with an expected payback period for every purchase decision. Use the payback period, and the ensuing profit period, to justify purchases (or upgrades) to yourself, or to sell ideas to upper management.

Expandability for the Big Picture

Look for products that can be expanded. This is true not only for file servers, but for any computer purchase. Examples are display cards that can accept additional RAM for increased resolution and colors. SCSI interface cards can accept more devices than other types of controllers. Computer chassis with additional drive bays (especially with front panel access) are convenient for adding optional diskette, tape, and optical disk drives. If you specify a half-height hard disk, you can later add another half-height drive with it in one full-height bay. Finally, if you buy a computer system that accepts larger amounts of RAM on the system board, you save the cost of expensive and sometimes slower memory expansion boards. For more information on hardware details, see Chapter 14.

Reliability for the Long Run

Do not underestimate the importance of buying reliable equipment. Look for *mean time between failure* (MTBF) ratings for mechanical devices, such as printers and disk drives. When you consider one product, compare its ratings with those of its more expensive competitors. The extra cost may be worth it and could buy you peace of mind. Much depends on a computer system's reliability; if one machine is down for repairs, it will cost your firm not only in dollars spent for repairs, but in productivity lost as the user waits for the machine to be fixed. Chapter 11 shows you how to calculate the cost of downtime to your company.

AutoCAD always has made great demands on hardware; when pushed hard, the program can tax a computer beyond normal levels. One way this point can manifest itself is compatibility, which is related to reliability. If your hardware cannot be trusted to run with certain software, it is not very reliable. Compatibility is becoming an issue of increasing importance with the growing popularity of alternative operating systems to MS-DOS, such as OS/2, UNIX, and XENIX. Many of the economical clones that attract AutoCAD buyers will not run these operating systems, or the operating system is unavailable in a customized version from the manufacturer. One or more of them probably will be in your future, so carefully check compatibility when you shop.

Armed with your knowledge of operating systems and platforms from Chapter 4 and your plans to network from Chapter 5, you are ready to approach a computer dealer with a set of intelligent specifications for a system that will suit your needs. If your computer dealer is knowledgeable enough, he can help you with all your system needs. If you are skeptical about your dealer's ability, or if you have not yet selected a dealer, read on.

Dealing with Dealers

Your local AutoCAD dealer can be a valuable business partner. Admittedly, some dealers are better than others, and the reasons are simple. CAD is a technical and vertically oriented field; AutoCAD dealers need significant amounts of resources if they are to provide a variety of products and knowledgeable support at competitive prices. Most retail computer dealers cannot justify a strong commitment to such a narrow field. Some that try to make the commitment simply do not carry it far enough.

Your company's best insurance for making the right decisions is to commit to the idea of keeping a competent CAD manager on staff, who can supplement the dealer with internal support and expertise. That is not to say, however, that you should not look for and depend on the help of a qualified dealer. A good dealer can save you many headaches and a great deal of money.

When picking a dealer, look for stability and a history of doing business in your area. Be wary if the dealership frequently changes names or management. Ask for references from businesses like yours, with whom the dealer has worked in the past. Contact them and get their opinion of the dealer's responsiveness and knowledge.

If you were considering buying a car, and if you knew someone who already owned the same model, you would ask that friend for his opinion of the car. Similarly, you should ask professional friends and other business contacts whether they have had any experience with a vendor or dealer. Their first-hand experience can be a valuable resource for you. User groups especially are valuable for this, and members are happy to talk to you about their personal experiences with dealers. In fact, a user group is one of the best places to learn which dealer is offering the best service and prices.

Note: Dealers who are not authorized by the product's manufacturer, yet who will sell you AutoCAD (or other products requiring authorized dealerships) are working in what is called the "gray market." They buy their stock from dishonorable or unwitting authorized dealers at a steep discount, or at overstock sales, close-outs, auctions, or bankruptcy sales. Then they resell the products to the public at discount prices that look good compared to actual authorized dealers' prices. The problems come when you need special support and the gray marketer cannot help you, or when you need to upgrade or take advantage of some other offer that only authorized dealers can provide.

Autodesk works dilligently to reduce the opportunities for gray marketers to get products. If Autodesk catches an authorized dealership selling AutoCAD to another dealer for resale, the authorized dealer may lose his authorization. If you find an unauthorized AutoCAD dealer, or need help in locating an authorized dealer in your area, contact Autodesk at 1-800-445-5415. This phone number is only for dealer assistance, not technical or sales help for Autodesk products. Those questions, of course, can be answered by an authorized AutoCAD dealer. Authorized dealers are the major direct channel of support from Autodesk.

Understanding the Role of Value-Added Resellers

When computer hardware and software become too complex for the end user to support by himself, the need arises for someone who can provide extra expertise. AutoCAD and networking both fit into this scenario. A segment of the computer market has evolved in which the emphasis is placed on specialized hardware and software, training, and support. Companies that specialize in this area are called *value-added resellers* (VARs). They are resellers because they resell products they buy from vendors and distributors. They are called "value-added" because they do not just mark up the price and simply sell products. They add value to what you pay by providing consulting, training, and expertise that many retail stores cannot offer.

VARs often specialize in one or more areas of computing, such as AutoCAD, networking, and accounting. Because they operate in smaller and more specialized markets than the high-volume, commodity dealerships, however, VARs also can pose a risk. A bad VAR—or a bad relationship with a good VAR—can be dangerous and expensive for your company.

You may benefit from working with a VAR if:

- You do not have the time to dedicate to programming, training, market research, and installation.
- Your company does not have the knowledge or expertise to implement all or part of the AutoCAD system.

Most VARs run reputable businesses. They build their reputations on providing complete "turn-key" solutions to automation needs with hardware and software as a "single-point purchase." Cultivating a good VAR relationship begins with finding the right VAR, executing a thorough contract or other agreement, and maintaining clear communications.

If you want to find a good VAR to help you with your AutoCAD network project, you may have several options. Start with a list of the authorized AutoCAD dealers in your area. To be authorized to sell AutoCAD, a VAR must receive special training in the software's capabilities and support.

Contact other people in your trade who have installed the type of system you are considering for references; give preference to VARs recommended by professional associates or local AutoCAD user groups. Vendors of specialized products, such as video cards, sometimes maintain lists of VARs who resell their products and demonstrate the technical expertise necessary to support them. Industry trade shows and magazines are also a good source of potential VARs, and are often the only places VARs have to expose themselves to the market.

For the remainder of this book, any references to a dealer may also mean a VAR.

Choosing the Right Dealer

Once you have found a group of prospective dealers (VARs or otherwise), send an initial inquiry letter to each one, providing and requesting the following information:

- State concisely the products and solutions you are seeking. For example, "My company is evaluating value-added resellers for the purchase, installation, training, and support of four high-speed AutoCAD workstations for the design and documentation of plastic injection molds. The system should provide integrated project tracking, electrostatic plotting, and on-line drawing storage and retrieval by an Ethernet network. Custom menus, AutoLISP programming, and interfacing will be required to control existing numeric-controlled milling equipment."

- Request complete marketing information, including product lines and suppliers.

- Request financial and historical data on the company.

- Request disclosure of the company's payment terms, warranties, support terms, and maintenance policy.

- Notify the candidates that the information they provide will be used in a preliminary review, and request a contact to whom you can forward a request for proposal.

At the end of a reasonable time period, gather the information from all the prospects that respond, and evaluate each. Consider the potential strengths of each dealer, as well as the risks you might incur by hiring that dealer. Each will present a degree of risk in several of the following areas, with more emphasis in some areas than others, as follows:

- **Products and services.** Misrepresentation or misinterpretation of the dealer's ability to provide and support certain products can leave you bearing the full burden of supporting highly specialized technology. Make sure that the dealer is actually authorized to sell and service the brands he is proposing. If you have any doubt, ask to see authorization documents or verify the dealer's authorization with the manufacturer. Some manufacturers will not honor warranties on equipment sold by "gray market" unauthorized dealers.

- **Performance**. After the bulk of the system is in place, you may have problems getting the dealer to see to details, if he is busy seeking other, more lucrative contracts. Carefully check the dealer's references and staff resources.

- **Financial health**. The dealer should provide financial information, which will help you assess the firm's economic standing. If possible, check the firm's payment rating. Dealers are susceptible to cash-flow problems.

■ **Vendor relationship.** Find out which major vendors the dealer represents, and try to get their assurance that they will support their products in case your relationship with the dealer breaks down.

Describing Your Needs with a Request for Proposal

Although most installations go smoothly, even the best plans can be ruined by inadequate communications with dealers and consultants. Your installer is primarily responsible for seeing that your interests are served, but you still should invest a little effort in some insurance. You can make sure that the installer clearly understands your objectives by developing a concise *request for proposal* (RFP). This document does not need to be complicated or legalistic, but should serve only to ensure that all parties understand their roles.

Generally, you should send an RFP to all dealers who respond to your query letter before prices are set or contracts signed. The dealers use the RFP as the basis of their "bids" and respond to the purchaser with proposals (thus the name "request for proposal"). In the proposal, the dealer recommends that the buyer puchase certain products or services at certain prices. The purchaser can then compare all the proposals received from dealers, and select the best deal. The RFP then forms the basis of the contract between the purchaser and the dealer.

Most important, the RFP should be written correctly. A loosely worded RFP can result in quick "canned" responses that do not help you or the installer understand each other. If you make the RFP complex or specific, you may end up requiring products or services that the dealer does not represent, complicating the process. An improperly worded RFP also discourages VARs (or dealers) from responding and, as a result, may limit your final choice of installers.

When you receive the bids from prospective dealers and the incidentals are outlined in the RFP, you will have then a good idea of what the purchase is going to cost. As you determine your needs for every component of the system you are buying, whether it is one AutoCAD workstation or a large network of stations, these needs can be incorporated into the RFP. If you are vague about the equipment or capabilities you need, the dealer may not understand your special requirements until it is too late.

> *Tip:* If you plan to make a very large purchase, you may want to implement it in phases. By phasing in your new system, you reduce the risk of investing too heavily and too suddenly in a project. This approach can be especially comforting if you are not sure about the system's benefits, or when you are working with an unfamiliar vendor or dealer. If the first phase goes well, you can proceed with the rest of the project, or with additional phases, in confidence.

The RFP should clearly state your company's objectives for the desired products and services, but should not necessarily mention products by name; the actual agreement will do that. The RFP also should spell out the terms of the purchase. Prices, payments, delivery and installation schedules, and responsibilities of both parties should all be included with provisions for negotiation at the time the contract is awarded. Be sure to include ownership rights to the source code of any custom software developed for your system. Although the dealer may not agree to give your company absolute ownership of all code (if it uses common "tools"), you should clearly state that your staff wants the right to maintain and customize any software the dealer develops for your company.

Finally, do not forget to include the terms of support calls after the sale. Include the number of calls you want to be able to make during a given period, and what charge you are willing to pay for such calls, if any.

A Sample Request for Proposal

The following is an example of an RFP for a medium-sized manufacturing company:

ACME WIDGETS, INC.
7777 Acme Dr.
Patriotville, MT.

Request for Proposal/Bid

COMPANY PROFILE

ACME Widgets is an aggressive manufacturer of custom-fabricated, exotic alloy parts. The company is three years old and employs 17 people. Annual sales exceed $4 million. ACME Widgets is committed to using personal computers in every aspect of its information processing tasks, especially in CAD/CAM. ACME is soliciting proposals for a local area network to incorporate the company's existing CAD/CAM PCs.

SPECIFICATIONS

The local area network will connect six existing IBM-compatible CAD/CAM personal computers, one pen plotter, and one laser printer, but must be expandable to at least six more PCs.

The file server will have an 80386 or 80486 processor, a minimum of 4M of RAM, at least 300M of disk storage, and a tape backup unit, and will not be of proprietary design.

The network operating system will be a standard, off-the-shelf product intended for PC applications running under DOS, OS/2, or UNIX.

At least 550K of RAM should remain available after loading of the network operating system software on each workstation. Network software may be loadable into high or extended memory, if necessary.

Network resources will include electronic mail, remote log-in, menu interface, and transparent plotter/printer sharing.

The network will be of at least 10Mbit/sec Ethernet or 16Mbit/sec Token Ring design.

The dealer must guarantee the installation for a minimum of 90 days from the date of acceptance by ACME, and provide a separate quotation for a 12-month service contract.

INSTALLATION

The majority of installation must occur during ACME's nonbusiness hours, although approved preparations may be accomplished during regular business hours.

The dealer will supply eight hours of network administration training to one of ACME's employees, two hours of basic network training to six employees, and provide an additional hour of support, if requested.

The dealer will ensure that AutoCAD 386 will run satisfactorily on the workstations once they are connected to the file server and that output will be directed to the network plotter and printer.

The dealer will provide complete documentation of the network installation, including configuration of all hardware and software proposed.

The dealer will install and test all software and utilities provided.

The dealer will create all user accounts and security structures necessary for the six workstation users.

The dealer must complete the installation to the satisfaction of ACME within 30 days of being awarded the purchase agreement.

QUOTATIONS

Bids must be written, with each line item priced individually.

Bids must be received no later than April 5, 1991.

The dealer must submit two references from customers, for whom the dealer has installed solutions. Those solutions must have been operational at least 90 days.

The purchase agreement will be awarded by May 15, 1991.

ACME Widgets, Inc. reserves the right to reject any or all proposals.

Any questions shall be directed to John Doe, CAD Manager, ACME Widgets, Inc.

ACME Widgets, Inc. will pay 50 percent of the winning bid price upon delivery of purchase, and the remaining 50 percent upon acceptance of the solution.

Distribute your RFP only to dealers you believe can provide the products and services you need. Give them adequate time to respond to your request, but note the amount of time each one takes to answer. The response time could be indicative of the service you can expect when you need assistance.

Reviewing Proposals

You can evaluate bids based on the common set of criteria you gave the dealers and their proposed solutions. If you receive more than a few bids that look good, invite sales representatives from the most promising dealers to visit your office and provide more information.

When you review the bids, look not only at the obvious facts, but also for anything that can tell you about the dealer, such as the following:

- Has the dealer performed other installations that are similar to yours? If the proposal refers to such installations, follow up on the information by contacting that installation's owner. There probably is little point, however, in checking into installations that are too new to indicate the dealer's after-sale support.

- Is the bid accurate and complete? Did the dealer address all the items in your RFP per your specifications? If not, does the dealer explain why? Look for miscellaneous items that are not included, such as cables and surge protectors. Call the author of the proposal for clarification if you find details missing. They may have been overlooked, or simply included in the cost but not itemized.

- Does the dealer offer discounts? If so, are they shown by total or by item?

- Do you need further information on some of the items? Write down a list of questions to ask the dealer.

- What pros and cons can you determine for each bid and dealer? Create a weighted score table of all the important factors to help you select a winner (see table 6.1).

Table 6.1
Dealer Scoring Table (10 = Highest; 1 = Lowest)

Category	Dealer A	Dealer B	Dealer C
References			
Accuracy			
Price			
Promptness			
Warranty			
Total			

Taking a Last Look

Before you decide on a dealer, take one last look. Make a visit to the dealer's showroom. Do the surroundings and activities project a competent, professional image? Does the company have a well-stocked and adequately staffed service department? Does the company have its own training facilities? Sit down with your representative and see if he or she really understands AutoCAD and networking issues from *your* perspective. Ask for a demonstration of the dealer's own in-house AutoCAD network, complete with file management and plot spooling. If all goes well up to this stage, you can consider your homework well done; the dealer is probably competent to meet your needs.

Scheduling the Installation

When it comes to installing an AutoCAD system, everyone gets anxious. The designers and drafters who will be using the system get impatient to try out the skills they (hopefully) have been learning and to start automating drawing production. Managers want to get the system running to see if it will do everything they hope (and have been told) it will do, and to start realizing a return on the investment. And of course, your dealer will want to move along smartly so he can get paid.

You will be wise, however, if you move cautiously at first. As soon as you start, you will recognize that organizational procedures need to be in place to keep the whole system manageable. And the most probable time for failure is during the system's infancy.

Try to schedule your installation during a period of reduced activity. Disruption of people and work while in the middle of a "crunch" not only reduces productivity, but might also foster resentment toward the system by those who were affected by the installation. They probably will resent the disruption even worse if they will not be taking advantage of the new system! Of course, the more work you can do during nonbusiness hours, the better. But give yourself plenty of time to complete the full installation, because complications undoubtedly will arise.

Ensuring a Painless Installation

You can make quite a few preparations before the equipment arrives. You can choose workstation locations, for example, and prepare the environment by moving the furniture to maximize space and minimize glare. You also can see that necessary adjustments are made to your power supply system, such as the installation of dedicated circuits and uninterruptable power supplies (UPSs). You can prepare yourself for the installation and configuration process by reading the network operating system manuals ahead of time. Further, if you intend to convert an existing workstation into the file server, it can be prepared now.

The best way to keep onlookers' curiosity satisfied is to report on the installation's progress and to let them know that they can expect a complete demonstration of the system when it is functioning. While you should invite all who are interested to learn about the installation, do not invite everyone who claims to be an experienced user to help with the installation. If you make this mistake, you run the risk of having "too many cooks spoil the broth."

Make regular reports to the steering committee, too. If you keep the decision makers informed of the installation's problems and successes, they will understand the complexity of automation implementation and of your hard work at making it succeed.

Break the project into discrete phases and milestones. If you will be installing a dozen new workstations, start with just one and get it debugged. Tackling the little problems once is much more productive (and cheaper) than trying to replicate the fix a dozen times after everything is installed. Replacements for some items may be required because of unforeseen incompatibilities. By working on one system first, it will be much easier to get your dealer to take a whole group of the same products back.

If you are installing a network, start with the file server (if your plan includes one) and one workstation. When they are functioning, add a few workstations at a time and test each one. By testing a few workstations at a time, you are more likely to find cabling problems, which are one of the most frequent points of failure in a network.

Determining the Dealer's Responsibilities

In most cases, your dealer will perform the majority, if not all, of the hardware and software installation. This is his chance to make good on the claims he made to you before you signed the installation contract. The dealer should provide you with complete records of the system, including configurations of all equipment and software. Issues of compatibility and performance should be settled to your satisfaction before you sign off on the delivery.

Your dealer may provide training before or after the installation. This training should not be considered complete until every user can perform a predetermined list of important tasks on the new system, such as logging into the network (if provided), starting an AutoCAD session, loading a drawing (from the network if provided), plotting or printing a drawing, exiting AutoCAD, logging out of the network (if provided), and performing any other activities the user needs to do his job or that your network provides. The dealer should provide extra training for the CAD manager on network system administration, hardware maintenance, performance tuning, and software configuration.

Participating in the Installation

Even if the dealer handles the entire installation, the CAD manager should oversee the installation process. The CAD manager, after all, must make sure that the system stays in operation after the installer is gone. By participating in the installation, the CAD manager gains insight into the way the system works, learns its possible weaknesses and critical areas, and can avoid trivial service calls.

Few dealers provide the kind of documentation that is necessary to help you manage multiple workstations efficiently. The CAD manager should record the installation and configuration of each component for reference as the dealer installs it. The CAD manager should fill out a form for each workstation. Once the workstation is operational, he should place an electronic copy of this form in the root directory of the machine's hard disk and name it SYSTEM.CFG. Appendix B contains more information on this and other forms included on the *Managing and Networking AutoCAD Disk.* This file is a convenient reference that can be updated easily and will be more difficult to lose than a paper document. Flag the file as read-only to avoid accidental erasure, and keep a hard copy of the document with the other system documentation.

If a network is installed, the CAD manager should prepare a complete diagram of the topology and location of each node, including all peripherals. This diagram will help the system manager identify cable routing for future repair or expansion. If the network uses node addresses, such as ARCNET and AppleTalk, the diagram should clearly indicate each node's network address.

Dealing with Physical Installation Concerns

Years ago, CAD computers had to be installed in special glass rooms with dedicated air conditioning and electrical power, and raised floors. CAD terminals were installed in a nearby room with almost no lighting, and the whole facility had an eerie, mysterious atmosphere.

"Clean rooms" are still used today for mainframe computers, but some people still have the notion that a dedicated, central CAD facility is required, even when PCs are being used. This philosophy easily can lead to a "back room" approach that is not healthy for the company or its people. If you physically isolate your AutoCAD facility, you diminish both its accessibility and effectiveness. Isolation creates an "us versus them" mentality between AutoCAD operators and other staff members, which compromises teamwork and efficiency. This isolation also can lead to the harmful "pigeonholing" of the AutoCAD staff into positions with limited potential and can unnecessarily complicate the company's organizational structure.

Workstation Centralization

Depending on the administrative approach your company takes to its AutoCAD system (whether as a centralized service to others, or as an integrated personal productivity tool), you may not want to install all your AutoCAD workstations in one area.

If your company holds to the centralized view, then a central, dedicated AutoCAD facility makes sense. You can control the environment (lighting, security, interruptions), standardize drawing-exchange techniques, conduct training, and communicate with users more easily than in a noncentralized facility.

If workstations are installed at each user's work area, environmental issues will need more attention. Remember, however, that people often are more productive when they are permitted to remain in their own familiar environment. As a company policy, you should strive to take automation where it is needed, and not to force all employees to adapt to computers. A network works either way; do not let it impose an incompatible structure on your company. If your company is structured into discrete teams by function, and if your AutoCAD operation requires a team of its own, then consider a dedicated server-based network and a small, central computer area. If yours is a small, loosely formed, dynamic workgroup, consider a peer-to-peer or nondedicated system distributed evenly among the users. In short, you should make the solution fit the problem.

Workstation Ergonomics

One of the most overlooked and underestimated factors of AutoCAD installation is the preparation of a work environment to make it conducive to CAD work. The goal of this type of preparation is to optimize workstation *ergonomics*. When companies make the switch from the drawing board to the keyboard, managers often fail to modify the environment adequately. As a result, productivity and user satisfaction are not what they could be.

The manual drafting environment is the opposite of a properly designed AutoCAD studio. Drawing board surfaces are usually higher than the typical CAD worksurface. Manual drafters generally sit on tall drafting stools and lean over their drawings as they work. High levels of direct lighting illuminate the drafters' work area.

The World Health Organization, the National Institute for Occupational Safety and Health, the U.S. House of Representatives Subcommittee on Health and Safety, and the Occupational Safety and Health Administration have studied the effects of the workplace environment on computer operators. These studies concluded that proper installation of furniture, computer equipment, and lighting reduces the risk of a number of health problems, including the following:

- Eyestrain
- Visual discomfort

- Burning eyes
- Neck pain
- Sore shoulders
- Back pain

When you replace a drawing board with an AutoCAD workstation, you should do more than just set the system on a person's desk. The preceding list of health hazards result from poorly fitting the AutoCAD workstation into the existing work space. Glare, viewing distances, contrast levels between display and reference materials, improper seating, and poor posture can all contribute to an environment that robs workers of their ability to concentrate, and robs the company of valuable productivity.

Standards and guidelines exist for the placement of equipment and other environmental factors to reduce or eliminate harmful side effects caused by computer systems. Figure 6.3 shows the recommended specification for an AutoCAD workstation.

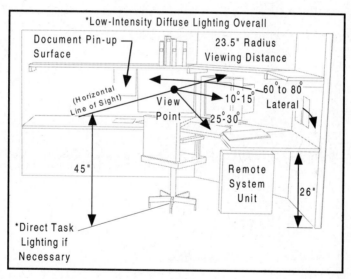

Figure 6.3:
Ergonomic specifications for an AutoCAD workstation.

Testing Your New Installation

After your system has been installed, you and the installer should agree on a reasonable period of time to allow your company to conduct *acceptance testing*. This testing will verify that the goals of the RFP, proposal, and any contract are met. The dealer will want you to accept the installation as soon as possible, because final payment may depend on it. You, on the other hand, will need enough time to ensure that the system operates as desired and without conflicts or discrepancies. The dealer should be helpful in recommending test criteria, but you should set the final test. Any deviation from the specifications should be corrected by the dealer and retested, or the system rejected.

Unless you test your system, you cannot fully ensure that your system has been installed properly and is performing at full potential. Some system conflicts, such as RAM addresses, may show up only under extreme circumstances—the kind you experience when you are putting the finishing touches on the most complicated drawing you ever did, on the night before the drawing is due.

Even though you should give your dealer the benefit of the doubt in his configuration of your system (you did choose him, after all, because of his expertise), you can test each subsystem as it is set up.

Starting with the basic system unit, verify that the I/O ports work correctly by connecting a printer or other device to each port. Then make sure that the device works by sending it some output through a familiar application program.

Math coprocessors often come with diagnostic or demonstration software that can check for proper installation. You also can test their operation with AutoCAD itself. AutoCAD fails to execute if a math coprocessor is absent. If AutoCAD does execute, you can issue commands such as Hatch, Plot, or Hide to exercise the chip and determine whether it is working properly.

Hard disk controller operation is relatively obvious (either it accesses the attached drive or it does not), but the data-transfer rate of the drive subsystem often is not configured for optimum performance, even by dealers who should know better. A diagnostic utility, such as SpinRite by Gibson Research, can determine whether your drive is optimally interleaved. Make note of any RAM addresses your controller may use. Those addresses may conflict with addresses used by some video and EMS adapters. You need this information to determine compatible addresses for any conflicting cards you may be installing, now or in the future.

Video cards sometimes need extra prodding to coexist peacefully with other adapters. Video benchmark tests, such as the one included in the PC Laboratories Benchmark Series, can be helpful when testing the benefit of video shadowing, eight-bit- or 16-bit ROM addressing, and other video adapter options. The PC Laboratories Benchmark suite of tests (distributed by PC Magazine) is available for downloading by modem from the PCMagNet on-line information service. If you are already a subscriber to the CompuServe Information Service, logging onto PCMagNet is as easy as entering **GO PCMAGNET** at any ! prompt. CompuServe then connects you to the PCMagNet system.

Tape backup systems often are the last options to be added to a computer. You may have difficulty configuring the tape backup to one of the few remaining RAM base addresses, interrupt levels (IRQs), and DMA channels. Your best bet is to buy smart and get a tape backup system with a large number of configuration possibilities. Once installed, test it with the manufacturer's software by performing a backup and restore. Verify that the restored data is correct.

The network interface card has to squeeze in there somewhere, too. Some NIC packages include diagnostic utilities that can help you isolate malfunctioning cards. The real test of NIC configuration problems, however, is compatibility of the NIC driver software with your other drivers, such as for video cards and scanners. Load all your software drivers, first individually, then in combinations, and check for proper operation of all their associated peripherals. One final caveat about drivers: you may need to check the amount of available RAM left after all your drivers are loaded. Programs such as MAPMEM.COM by TurboPower Software, Inc. can be invaluable for solving memory usage problems. The following is a sample output from MAPMEM showing memory used by DOS, drivers, and COMMAND.COM:

```
Allocated Memory Map - by TurboPower Software - Version 1.9
PSP     blks    bytes    owner        command line        hooked vectors
-------  ------  -------- ----------   ------------------  ------------------
0008     1       31872    config
11C2     2        3632    command                          22 24 2E FE
12B5     2      578736    free


block    bytes    (Expanded Memory)
-------  --------
    0    589824
    1    262144
 free   2867200
total   3719168
```

MAPMEM.COM is included on the *Managing and Networking AutoCAD Disk* as part of the TSRCOM package of shareware utilities. See Appendix A for more information.

To test your network, begin by making sure that every workstation functions properly with its network interface card and drivers loaded. Then ensure that each workstation can log into the network. Once your system is running with the network, you can use the diagnostic utilities provided with your network operating system (if any) to check for proper communications between workstations, and for transmission errors and throughput over the network.

Soon after installation, you should conduct the acid test for your new system; that is, you should check out all your application programs on the network. Whether you decide to install the programs and data or just data on a file server, or whether you use a peer-to-peer network, exercise all the programs' input and output functions (loading a file, writing a file, and printing or plotting) using network drives. Be sure to change any drive assignments in your applications' configuration that are affected by network drives and modify the paths or drive mappings as directed by your network operating system's documentation.

Benchmarking Performance

Nearly everyone involved in computing is concerned about performance. The marketing campaigns of hardware and software dealers have users forever lusting after faster products. Although you can benefit by staying current with technology, you may not always be able to quantify and justify upgrades for state-of-the-art computers. Benchmark programs give you one means of quantifying computer performance. The justifying is up to you. Remember, however, that benchmark test results are not the final word in performance. The real-world performance you will see may be different. You may, however, want part of your acceptance testing to include benchmark tests.

Empirical testing of computer systems is a mixed blessing. On one hand, testing is sometimes the only way you can quantitatively measure system performance. On the other hand, tests must be interpreted for what they are—a fixed set of instructions (which may not simulate your actual habits) designed to produce measurable results for comparing other systems.

When you use a benchmark test's results to compare systems, remember that any other systems must be configured the same as the tested system, except for the part of the system you are trying to test. Suppose, for example, that you are using a benchmark program to test two computer systems. One has an EGA display and the other has VGA. One runs at 10 MHz and the other runs at 12 MHz. One has a 40 ms hard disk, and the other a 28 ms hard disk. When you run the same benchmark program on both machines, there is virtually no comparison you can make between the two. Each machine's attributes contribute to performance to a greater or lesser extent, depending on what the benchmark is trying to test. If the machines are identical except for the hard disk, for instance, the benchmark would highlight the difference that single factor makes in the performance of the test.

Benchmarks do produce statistics, however, that you can analyze to identify strengths and weaknesses. These statistics can help you make performance decisions. Nevertheless, do not rely solely on such test results when making purchasing decisions, but as one part of your criteria that include vendor reputation, quality, support, and cost-effectiveness. One high-performance graphics adapter, for example, may beat out another in a graphics benchmark by 25 percent. If the winning card is orphaned a year down the road, however, while the benchmark loser still is supported strongly, who really loses? You do if you bought the winning card, because you have to invest in another card in order to get a driver that works with your version of AutoCAD. This points out the need to weigh benchmark results with your other criteria.

Benchmarks almost always simulate a series of non-real-world conditions. Many tests try to get close to working conditions, but ultimately only the end user can determine which devices work best. The bottom line is still this: before signing on the dotted line, if at all possible, try everything out in *your* environment, on *your* work, with *your* people.

Benchmarks can report the performance of your computers and network at various loads and configurations. They can be helpful also in simulating future growth and in testing different hardware settings and software configurations.

Three benchmark utilities are included on the *Managing and Networking AutoCAD Disk*. Perhaps the most useful is the DeLucchi AutoCAD benchmark distributed by the AutoCAD Users Group of San Diego. The DeLucchi benchmark uses a long script to put AutoCAD through a series of operations designed to simulate a user working on a drawing. The benchmark keeps track of the time required to complete certain phases of the drawing and can be useful when trying to optimize AutoCAD configurations between network, local, and RAM drives, regular and Extended AutoLISP, and I/O page space considerations (see fig. 6.4).

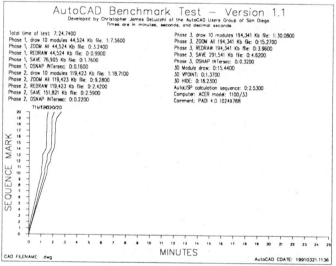

Figure 6.4:
Sample DeLucchi benchmark results.

You can learn more about using the supplied benchmark programs in Appendix A.

Performing System Troubleshooting

If your dealer installs your new workstation(s) and network, everything *should* work correctly. There is still a chance, however, that you may encounter a problem the installer has overlooked. If, on the other hand, you install the system and you do not have much experience with computer system installation, you will almost certainly find something that does not work. How do you find the root of these problems?

A Structured Approach to Troubleshooting

One key to network troubleshooting is to take a structured, system-by-system approach. This method defines a network as an overall system of interrelated subsystems and components (software, hardware, medium, and protocols). This approach isolates the problem by using the process of elimination. That is, you discount operational subsystems and narrow the list of possible problems down to the smallest component. By using diagnostic tools, tests, and replacement parts, you should be able to narrow the search and solve the problem.

If you have added several hardware or software components and something does not work, you probably can isolate the problem by eliminating possible causes one by one until the problem disappears. Once the problem is solved, verify the culprit by reinstalling the last component.

Suppose, for example, that your network printer does not respond to your application. Try the device directly from DOS at the computer where the device is installed. By doing so, you either eliminate or implicate the network. If it still does not work, try the same test with the device connected to another computer. This test enables you to determine whether the original computer was at fault. If the device still does not respond through a different application that is known to work with that device, you probably can be certain that there is a problem with either the device or the cable. Swapping the cable for a new one should illuminate the cause of the problem: either the cable failed or the device failed.

As another example, suppose that a workstation fails to recognize the attached network. If you swap the failed workstation with one known to work on the network and it responds, you can rule out a cable failure. Verify the network board's jumper and switch settings in the failed workstation. If they check out, swap the board for a network interface card that is known to work. If the workstation now does not respond, look at the next lower interface, which is the software. Make sure that the card's driver is correctly configured for that workstation. If the workstation that was swapped into the failed one's place fails, you need to test the cable(s) attached to it. If substituting another cable is impractical, check for a break or short in the cable by testing the cable's resistance with an ohm meter.

By now you should be getting the idea. A few quick steps can isolate the most obscure bug or error. Try to think logically, follow each step of the failed process along its course from beginning to end, and do not be afraid to question everything.

The next best way to troubleshoot networks is to be intimate with your network on a technical level. A network is a creation and nobody knows a creation better than its creator.

Basic Troubleshooting Tips

Although it would take an entire book to cover PC and network troubleshooting in depth, here are some suggestions that might help you with basic problem solving:

- Read all the documentation provided with a product. This probably is the best step you can take to avoid installation problems. Most vendors try to anticipate potential problems and provide adequate installation instructions and manuals. Take time to read them.

- Document each step of the installation. Note the order in which components are installed, any jumper block or DIP switch settings, and every point where a choice must be made. Keep these notes handy when you start troubleshooting, and you may not need to return to manuals or reopen cases to verify settings.

- Use the buddy system if you are not sure about what you are doing. Two heads are better than one. Often, another pair of eyes or a fresh perspective can help you pinpoint a problem.

- Find the products' technical support numbers and keep them handy. Many common problems have solutions or work-arounds that are well known by the vendor's support technicians. Many vendors have toll-free numbers, so advice is free and may save you hours of frustration, delays, and mistakes. But make sure that you have exhausted all the obvious possibilities before you call. The following list contains the 14 most frequent causes of network problems, listed in order, as logged by Novell service representatives:

  1. Unconditioned power (no UPS)
  2. Cabling problems (incorrect cable type, incorrect or loose connectors)
  3. Network shell version conflicts with the workstation operating system version (updated DOS without updated shells)
  4. NetWare coexistence with another network operating system (basic multi-vendor incompatibility)
  5. Unapproved use of the network operating system (trying to make it do something it was not designed for)
  6. Hardware or software configuration conflicts
  7. Disk input/output problems
  8. Expansion cards bad or loose
  9. Hardware speed problems
  10. Remote boot PROM configurations (for diskless workstations)
  11. Environmental (too hot or cold, too much EMI or RFI)

12. Printer protocol problems

13. More than one workstation set to the same network address

14. Network configured for a larger disk drive than the one installed

Summary

Whether you are installing a single new workstation or building a company-wide data communications network, these are the glory days. Everyone is excited about the new equipment, new technologies, and new possibilities.

This chapter has shown you how to make intelligent, prepared buying decisions that will not only pay back the initial investment, but also will provide reliable service for many years to come, even in the face of changing technology. You have learned important factors to consider as you do market research for hardware specifications, and how to prepare an RFP and select the best computer dealer or VAR. This chapter also taught you what to do before and during the installation to make it go smoothly, and how to test and troubleshoot new installations.

In the following chapter you will learn how to configure certain networks in preparation for installing AutoCAD. LAN Manager, Sun NFS, and Artisoft LANtastic are described with a hands-on approach.

7

Configuring Popular Networks for AutoCAD

Once you have decided which components you want to use in your network, such as access protocol, medium, and topology, you can begin to look at the network operating systems that currently are available. The following sections offer overviews of the most popular network operating systems with which AutoCAD is used. These include the following:

- Novell NetWare
- Microsoft LAN Manager or IBM LAN Server, which runs on top of OS/2
- Artisoft LANtastic, which runs on top of DOS
- Sun Microsystems' Network File System, which is an integral part of the Sun operating system, SunOS, for Sun workstations

Use the overviews in this chapter to help narrow down the choices. You will find detailed information on each network's features with tips and techniques on setting each network up to run AutoCAD. Then contact a knowledgeable dealer or the network's vendor for specific information and details about the most recent versions.

Whether you are shopping for a new network, planning to expand an existing network to include your CAD department, or just looking for ways to improve your present network's efficiency, you should find what you need in this chapter. When you are done with this chapter, you will want to study Chapter 8, Configuring AutoCAD on a Network, to find out how you can integrate the network of your choice with AutoCAD.

Taking a Closer Look at Novell NetWare

Most local area networks use the Novell NetWare family of products. Novell currently holds between 50 percent and 70 percent of the LAN market. These systems are built on the concepts of dedicated and nondedicated file servers, a proprietary file system, and sophisticated security and administration features. NetWare products utilize an open architecture that encourages the development of third-party products and supports virtually all network access protocols, media, and topologies.

NetWare is a high-performance product line with minimal RAM requirements. It supports DOS, OS/2, and Macintosh workstations in the same network. NetWare also supports UNIX workstations in its high-end product, NetWare 386 V3.11. Novell's Advanced NetWare product is designed for medium to large businesses and workgroups, and is by far the most popular version of NetWare. This version of NetWare supports up to 100 concurrent users and can utilize 32 drive volumes of up to 256M each, totalling 2G. NetWare also supports up to 12M of RAM in the file server. NetWare requires an IBM Personal Computer AT-compatible or PS/2 computer with at least 2M of RAM and an appropriate network interface card to act as the file server. An optional disk coprocessor board can be used to enhance disk performance. NetWare is designed primarily as a dedicated file server operating system, but a version is available that operates in a nondedicated configuration, so that you can run a DOS program in the foreground on the file server.

All of NetWare's advanced file-serving features are included in Advanced NetWare V2.15, including the following:

- Directory hashing and caching, which maintain the names and locations of disk directories in memory for faster access.
- Disk caching, which keeps frequently read files in memory, and elevator seeking, which performs disk operations according to drive head's position.
- A high-performance, true multitasking, multiuser, multithreaded kernel.
- Read-after-write data verification.
- Directory verification upon power-up.
- Duplicate directory and file-allocation structures that are maintained to ensure data integrity.
- Automatic disk is defect detection and correction capabilities, which can relocate data that is destined for a bad disk block, and then mark the bad block to prevent it from being used again.
- Uninterruptable power supply (UPS) monitoring. In the event of a power failure, NetWare can notify and log out users, close any open files, and shut down the file server.

A powerful on-line help utility incorporates all the user and network supervisor manuals into an indexed text retrieval system. All NetWare commands and utilities can be invoked through an easy-to-use, user-definable menu system and user interface.

Operating System and Hardware Independence

Unlike many other network operating systems, NetWare works independently of the client operating system. That is, NetWare is not a DOS, Macintosh, or OS/2 product, and does not rely on an underlying PC operating system. NetWare is intended to support any workstation operating system the user wants to use. In fact, a NetWare network can incorporate workstations running each of these operating systems (even Windows) and sharing files. NetWare provides transparent access to files and peripherals among all system types within a single network.

NetWare also is media independent. A single NetWare file server can support up to four independent subnetworks that use incompatible protocols and media (such as ARCNET, Ethernet, and Token Ring). NetWare also permits a user on any subnetwork to access any file server on any other connected subnetwork. In addition, NetWare supports a wealth of Novell router, bridge, and other communications products to connect to virtually any other computer, including minicomputers and mainframe systems.

NetWare Security Features

Novell Advanced NetWare has long been recognized as one of the most secure network operating systems available. To protect network resources, you can configure overlapping layers of security at the file, directory, user name, password, and group levels. NetWare uses encrypted passwords, and the CAD manager can require users to change their passwords periodically. You can limit access to the system so that certain users can enter the network only on certain days of the week and times of day. You can even restrict users to specific workstations, files, and network resources, such as disk space. Further, you can enable NetWare features that detect incorrect login attempts and lock the user out after a specified number of incorrect attempts.

> ***Note:*** NetWare is based on the concept of a single network administrator, who is called the *supervisor*. The network supervisor is one of two network users whose security level is automatically created when NetWare is first installed. The other user is an ambiguous user named Guest, which will let any person log onto the network with minimum privileges. The supervisor is the only user who can set up most of NetWare's security measures, and who has unlimited rights on the network. In this discussion, the NetWare supervisor and the CAD manager are the same person. More information on network administration appears in Chapter 9.

Transaction Tracking

System Fault Tolerant (SFT) NetWare and NetWare 386 include a feature called the Transaction Tracking System (TTS), which tracks resource usage by project or department. TTS can assign user-definable charges according to connect time, disk activity, disk space used, and service requests—even according to the time of day and day of the week. TTS can be useful for backcharging certain departments for network usage.

Third-Party Support

Like AutoCAD, Novell NetWare has an open architecture, which enables independent software vendors to develop server-based applications and network utilities that extend NetWare's capabilities. To help third-party software developers get started, NetWare offers the following built-in features:

- A server-based version of the Btrieve database language
- A generic message-handling service, which can be supplemented
- Support for *application program interfaces* (APIs) to NetWare's resource accounting, queue management, network diagnostic, virtual console, and security subsystems
- Support for OS/2 distributed applications, such as SQL servers

Novell offers an SQL database product for SQL developers and NetWare-specific software development tools that can extend the included Btrieve software.

Other Versions of Novell NetWare

As you can see, Advanced NetWare packs a great deal of power. If the package sounds like too much for your needs, Novell also offers an economical, trimmed-down version of NetWare, called ELS NetWare Level II. ("ELS" stands for *entry-level system.*) This smaller version of NetWare supports only eight concurrent users and two internal hard disks in the file server, yet includes all of Advanced NetWare's other features. If your network has no more than four users, you might consider the even trimmer ELS NetWare Level I.

Should you need even more security than Advanced NetWare for extremely sensitive data, you should consider System Fault Tolerant (SFT) NetWare, which adds even more protection against network breakdowns and errors than does Advanced NetWare.

For the ultimate in high performance and expandability, NetWare 386 can support the largest, most complicated networks that are made up of thousands of users and dozens of file servers.

Novell recently announced that it is consolidating its entire 286-based product line (ELS NetWare Level I, ELS NetWare Level II, Advanced NetWare, and SFT NetWare) into a single product, NetWare 2.2. Novell plans to sell NetWare 2.2 in increments of 5, 10, 50, and 100 users at various prices and will incorporate all of the features of SFT NetWare regardless of the number of users supported.

You can upgrade NetWare similarly to the way you upgrade AutoCAD. You can upgrade the lower levels of NetWare to higher levels at any time. Novell only sells NetWare products through trained and authorized resellers who understand their products and can help you take advantage of these features without having to understand the intricate details. This lets you concentrate on AutoCAD.

NetWare Workstation Memory Requirements

Novell's solution to the memory crunch described in Chapter 5 is to provide two network shells that can load most of their code into extended or expanded memory. This gets around the limitation of the 640K of conventional DOS memory used by the standard shell. These shells are available as the NetWare DOS Client Kit V3.01. All three shells use the same NIC driver that must reside completely in conventional memory. Figure 7.1 shows how this flexible shell-loading scheme frees memory space for applications such as AutoCAD and drivers.

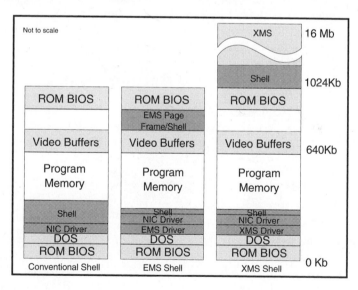

Figure 7.1:
Different NetWare workstation memory requirements.

When it is used, the conventional network shell consumes about 41K of RAM in addition to the 17K used by the NIC driver. This configuration leaves you the least amount of RAM for AutoCAD. For AutoCAD 386 users, however, this will not be a problem. AutoCAD 286 users can have performance problems, though, unless sufficient extended I/O page space is available. The conventional shell is the fastest of the three shell types.

If you have expanded memory installed in your computer, or you use an expanded memory manager, such as Quarterdeck Office Systems' QEMM 386 or Qualitas Systems' 386MAX, to convert extended memory into expanded, you can use the NetWare EMS shell and save about 34K of RAM. The EMS shell loads about 7K of itself in conventional memory and the remainder is loaded into expanded memory. Your expanded memory driver or expanded memory manager will use up some of the conventional memory savings, but the net result will be more memory for AutoCAD. The EMS shell is slightly slower (10-15 percent) than the conventional shell. In most cases, the difference in performance between the conventional shell and either the EMS or XMS shell is not as great as using the conventional shell and restricting memory for use by AutoCAD.

With extended memory, you can use the XMS shell. It also loads a small amount of itself into conventional memory, but only about 6K. The remainder of the XMS shell loads into XMS memory above 1024K that must be under the control of an XMS driver, such as HIMEM.SYS (provided with Windows), or a compatible memory manager, such as QEMM 386. Your XMS driver or memory manager will also consume some of the savings, but you should end up with about as much free memory for AutoCAD as if you used the EMS shell. The XMS shell is slower than the conventional shell, but slightly faster than the EMS shell.

NetWare File Server Memory Requirements

Chapter 5 recommended that you install 4M of RAM in your NetWare file server to begin with, and add more as your network grows. To understand the need for so much RAM in a file server, and to understand better how NetWare works, look at the way Novell NetWare utilizes RAM.

NetWare's memory needs begin with an executable file similar to any other program or operating system. The executable file for NetWare 286, NET$OS.EXE, consumes 450K of memory once it is resident. This is not much, but it is just the start.

NetWare optimizes file performance by implementing a large disk cache in the file server's memory for use by workstations. The cache begins by storing the file allocation table (FAT) of each server hard disk volume in RAM. The FAT basically is an index of the locations of disk blocks on a drive; the larger the disk, the more memory is required for each FAT. NetWare needs 1K of RAM to store the FAT information for every megabyte of disk space. Additionally, NetWare can index the FAT entries for your most important files, especially the large ones (2M or more). Each indexed FAT entry (*turbo FAT*) requires another 1K.

Next, NetWare needs 36 bytes for every directory and file name you expect to create, which can amount to thousands. Do not worry; NetWare assigns all of these parameters for you during installation, and it offers generous default values. You can change many of the sizes later if needed. NetWare occupies 64K of RAM for a dynamic memory pool to manage these buffer areas, print queues, and NIC adapter buffers.

Above all the FAT and dynamic memory information, NetWare places the file cache area, which consumes all left over RAM. This area has no size limitation, and there are no rules of thumb for calculating the proper size. Instead, you must find the optimum size for your particular network; just remember that bigger is not necessarily better. Too much cache adds so much overhead that it can actually be detrimental. Fortunately, NetWare provides statistics on the FCONSOLE utility's summary screen that can help, and more RAM is automatically recognized when you add it. Once your server is up and running, check the value shown with the Disk Requests Serviced From Cache statistic. If it is in the 90 percent range, then your cache is adequately sized. If you have a small network, a small amount of RAM in the file server (2M to 4M), and the requests serviced figure is low, adding more RAM should help improve overall network performance. If you have a larger network with 8M or more of RAM in the file server and the requests serviced statistic is still low, you may need to add another file server to divide the file service load between two disk subsystems.

Any server-based applications loaded on the file server will subtract their memory from the file cache area. So be sure to compensate for large *Value Added Processes* (VAPs) and *NetWare Loadable Modules* (NLMs) with more RAM. Putting additional RAM in one machine and amortizing it over many users is cheap compared to the cost of multiplying productivity lost as a result of being too conservative. To help you calculate server RAM requirements, spreadsheet models on the *Managing and Networking AutoCAD Disk* are provided for you to experiment with. There is one spreadsheet for Microsoft Excel and one for Lotus 1-2-3. For more information on their use, see Appendixes A and B.

Using NetWare's Security with AutoCAD

If AutoCAD Release 11's built-in file-locking capabilities are not used to protect a drawing file that is being edited on the network, then that file's security is the network supervisor's responsibility. Earlier versions of AutoCAD that are run on a network need file protection as well. NetWare alone can supply this file protection. Each of the following sections describes a different level of network security available with NetWare. You can think of these security levels as successively larger layers stacked on top of each other, each layer broadening the security supplied by the layer above it (see fig. 7.2).

Refer to figure 7.2 as you read about each of the following security layers.

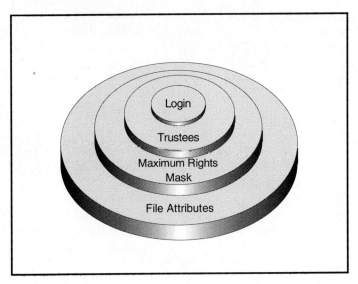

Figure 7.2:
Network security layers.

Password Protection

The file security features that have been described apply at the file and directory levels. To maintain security at the user level, several security features are available.

Network user security starts with user login passwords. NetWare can be configured to require that passwords be a certain length, be changed periodically, and be entered correctly within a certain number of tries before the NOS terminates the login attempt. NetWare can even restrict user access to certain hours of the day and days of the week. You may want to restrict access to your drawings in this way if they contain sensitive or proprietary information.

Trustee Rights

Additionally, each user must be specified as a trustee (or *entrusted*) to work in directories. After logging on, each user can be made to "see" only a certain logical view of the network directory structure. This depends on who logged on to the network, and how the system administrator has configured the system. NetWare can prevent the user from seeing directories that contain sensitive files. The network supervisor may give certain users the right to use specific directories. Such users are trustees of that directory and are entrusted with upholding the "sanctity" of those files by not misusing them.

The supervisor uses SYSCON to assign trustee rights to the user for each directory in which that user will be allowed to work. The user's available directory rights are the same as those used to construct the maximum rights mask at the directory level.

Directory Rights and the Maximum Rights Mask

The network supervisor can use SYSCON to set four specific directory rights to protect entire directories of files with the same security level. These directory rights include the following:

- **Normal.** Most AutoCAD directories can be left safely with the default Normal directory attribute, which permits all file operations to be performed on their contents.

- **Hidden.** The Hidden directory attribute should be used with caution because only a user with supervisor security rights can set the Hidden directory attribute or see a hidden directory's files. No other user can see the directory name or file names when viewing file listings. Only highly sensitive information, therefore, should be maintained in a Hidden directory.

- **System.** NetWare uses the System directory attribute to protect the network operating system files.

- **Private.** The Private directory attribute marks directories as being privately owned and accessible only by their owner. Only the person who created the directory and set the attribute (and the supervisor) will be able to access files in that directory.

To control access to directories even further, the supervisor can use SYSCON to create a maximum rights mask for each directory. This is a type of security template, against which NetWare compares every file operation to determine whether the operation should be permitted. It can be used to globally restrict all users to a maximum level without having to address each user individually. The maximum rights mask may contain any combination of the following rights:

- **R** (Read from files). Required to read an open file.
- **W** (Write to files). The only way a file may be written to a disk (saved).
- **O** (Open existing files). Required to open an existing file for either reading or writing.
- **C** (Create new files). Required if user wants to make new files or subdirectories in the current directory.
- **D** (Delete files). Users other than the supervisor can delete files only if the files reside in a directory with this right.
- **P** (Parental rights). Gives users the right to change the maximum rights mask of the selected directory, to specify trustees (which are explained later in this chapter), and to assign their rights. Prior to NetWare V2.15, parental rights were required to create subdirectories below the selected directory.

- **S** (Search for files). This right enables users to view the names of files in the selected directory. It also will let users view a directory listing of file names in a directory marked as Private if they are the owner.

- **M** (Modify file names/flags). File and directory names, creation dates, last accessed dates, and last modified dates may be changed if this right is granted for a directory.

By default, a directory's maximum rights mask includes all the preceding rights. In most AutoCAD situations, a directory's mask will need at least S, O, R, W, D, and C rights to accommodate AutoCAD's temporary file management and file locking schemes. The remaining rights, P and M, may be omitted if tight security is desired, or controlled with the other security mechanisms such as directory and file rights.

> **Note:** You should not make entire network directories Read-Only by restricting the maximum rights mask to the Search, Read, and Open rights if AutoCAD Release 11 will need to access them. This is referred to as a Read-Only directory in the *AutoCAD Installation and Performance Guide* and in the AutoCAD installation program. This situation should be avoided when using NetWare. AutoCAD will not be capable of creating its own file locks and temporary files in such a case and will not run properly. Instead, you should flag files that have individual file attributes as Read-Only on a file-by-file basis.

File Attributes

In a NetWare network, the supervisor should use the FLAG command to establish individual file rights to certain files on a file-by-file basis. NetWare maintains not only the Read-Only, Hidden, System, and Archive file attributes that DOS does, but several special purpose file attributes. Advanced NetWare file attributes include the following:

- **Read-Only or Read-Write.** Controls the capability of users to write to the file.

- **Hidden.** Hides the file from view of users other than the file owner.

- **System.** Used by NetWare for system files.

- **Shareable or Non-Shareable.** Controls access by multiple users.

- **Modified.** Designates a file as having been changed since it was last backed up.

- **Indexed.** Speeds loading of large files (2M or larger).

- **Execute-Only.** Protects executables from tampering.

- **Transactional.** (SFT NetWare only). Protects files from partial changes because of system failures.

NetWare 386 includes additional file attributes for inhibiting file copying, deleting, and renaming. See your NetWare 386 documentation for more information on these rights.

With the default attribute of Read/Write, any file is vulnerable to accidental over-writing and erasure. Program and library files requiring controlled access should be flagged with the Read-Only attribute, so they cannot be altered or deleted without authorization. This precaution can be extended to menu and AutoLISP files if control over unauthorized editing or documentation is a problem. If a user wants to modify one of these files, he can read the files but must save them under different names in order to edit them. The CAD manager then can check the file for conformance to office standards and documentation before releasing it for general use.

NetWare V2.15 files are individually flagged as Non-Shareable by default, to limit a file's access to only one user at a time. (The Non-Shareable attribute is not available in earlier versions of NetWare.) To allow more than one person to read any file, the file must be flagged as Shareable. All AutoCAD files except user configuration files (described in the next chapter) should be flagged Shareable.

Note: In cases in which a shareable file needs to be edited, such as a menu file or library drawing file, you can protect the file from accidentally being overwritten or from access by other users with the NetWare HOLDON and HOLDOFF commands. Simply execute HOLDON once before you begin editing the shareable file. HOLDON will hold open any files you work on until you issue a HOLDOFF. Other users will not be able to write to the file as long as you are working on it, but they may read from the file for reference.

An Execute-Only file attribute is available for program files in some versions of NetWare. Files flagged as Execute-Only only can be run or deleted but cannot be modified or copied. This security attribute, however, should not be used to protect AutoCAD executable files (*.EXE or *.EXP) because AutoCAD sometimes reads them in pages while executing. When used with other program files, Execute-Only should be used in conjunction with the Read-Only attribute to prevent accidental erasure. More on sharing AutoCAD files is in the next chapter.

Note: All of the rights discussed so far should be set only after AutoCAD installation and configuration. This lets AutoCAD modify several files before being executed.

More on NetWare Security

With all these security layers and combinations possible, a complex, yet flexible security net can be created. Each user's effective rights (the actual rights that he is allowed to exercise on any file on the network) is the intersection of all of the rights levels described earlier. Each level is not mutually exclusive of the others. They overlap each other, and wherever the holes in each line up, the user is granted privileges to a single file (see fig. 7.3).

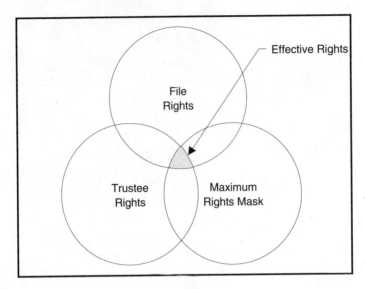

Figure 7.3:
Effective rights is the intersection of security layers.

This multilevel approach to file security may sound like overkill. Remember, however, that a network enables multiple users to gain access to the same files at the same time. When you consider the implications of such a data-sharing arrangement, you begin to appreciate this kind of control over file security.

The effective rights (the combination of all these rights) is the intersection of all applicable security levels: File (attribute), directory (maximum rights mask), and trustee rights. If a user, for example, is named as a trustee with delete rights for a directory, and the directory's maximum rights mask permits the deletion of files within it, yet the file is flagged as Read-Only, it still cannot be erased. For more network security information, refer to your NetWare documentation.

Configuring NetWare for AutoCAD Plotting

You begin configuring NetWare for AutoCAD plotting during NetWare installation by configuring a port (typically a serial port). You will need to tell NetWare all the data communications parameters your plotter needs. These parameters include the number of data, parity, and stop bits, transmission rate in baud, and the type of flow control the plotter uses—whether hard-wired or software. When discussing NetWare printing, you safely can apply the same concepts to plotting—only the actual devices that you use are different.

The 80286-based versions of NetWare can support up to five network printers, two attached to serial ports and three to parallel. NetWare 386 allows printers attached to workstations to be shared on the network as remote printers through a supplied DOS utility. See your NetWare 386 documentation for details.

For each port configured for a printer, NetWare assigns a printer number from 0 to 4. To control printer sharing by multiple users, NetWare creates a corresponding print queue, such as PRINTQ_0 and PRINTQ_1. Each queue serves its respectively numbered printer; for example, PRINTQ_0 serves printer 0 (see fig. 7.4). The queues manage printing requests on a first come, first served basis and provide the means for manipulating print job order and priorities. Print jobs may be moved within the queue or deleted by either the print job's owner or the supervisor.

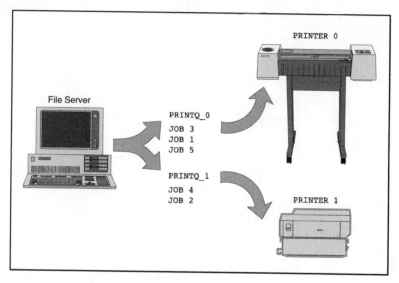

Figure 7.4:
The NetWare printing scheme.

In its default configuration, NetWare spools print jobs destined for printer 0 to PRINTQ_0, printer 1 to PRINTQ_1, and so forth. You can override the default queue mappings by placing special entries in the file server's AUTOEXEC.SYS file:

Printer 0 ADD PRINTQ_0

Printer 1 ADD PRINTQ_1

Printer 2 ADD PRINTQ_2

Spool 0 to Queue PRINTQ_0

Spool 1 to Queue PRINTQ_1

Spool 2 to Queue PRINTQ_2

MONITOR

In the preceding AUTOEXEC.SYS file example, printer 0 is added to PRINTQ_0, printer 1 to PRINTQ_1, and printer 2 to PRINTQ_2. Next, the application output is directed to be spooled to each printer queue by the operating system according to the printer's number. Finally, the file server console MONITOR utility is executed. Each of these steps will be performed each time the file server is booted.

You may cross-assign queues and printers such as sending PRINTQ_1's output to printer 0. This makes it possible for you to have multiple queues serving one printer (PRINTQ_0 and PRINTQ_1 feeding printer 0). In this case, each queue may serve different groups of users and each queue may have a different priority assigned to it. Higher priority print jobs will be printed before print jobs coming from a lower priority queue. Or, multiple printers can accept output from one queue, sometimes called *pooling*. In this case, all print jobs are served by the next available printer or plotter. All devices served by the same queue should be the same type, however, or results could be unpredictable.

Tailoring the NetWare CAPTURE Command

One way to get AutoCAD output into a print queue is to use the NetWare CAPTURE command. CAPTURE redirects parallel output from the workstation to a NetWare print queue.

The CAPTURE command accepts many switches (known in NetWare as *flags*) on the command line that tailor the way it works. These flags are easiest to use in a login script that executes every time a user logs in to the network. With them, you can make CAPTURE do almost anything. CAPTURE's flags include the following:

Flag	Function
/S=*server*	Server name. The default is your default server.
/Q=*queue#*	Printer queue to receive output. Printer queue 0 is the default.
/P=*printer#*	Printer number (0 through 4). The default is printer 0.
/L=*LPT#*	Local printer port from which to redirect output. The default is LPT1.
/C=*copies*	The number of copies to print. The default is one copy.
/J=*job#*	The job definition name. Job definitions are created with PRINTCON.
/F=*form#*	The form number or name. Forms are defined with PRINTDEF.
/CR	Creates a disk file with the specified path and file name. Use the /CR flag if you want to keep the output disk file for later printing without disabling CAPTURE.
/B=*phase*	Banner word or phrase to print on the banner page before your print job.
/NAM=*name*	The user name to appear on the banner page. The default is the user name you logged in under.

Flag	Function
/NB	For no banner to be printed. A banner is printed by default. Because plotters cannot print the unformatted ASCII text of a banner, you should always use the /NB flag in conjunction with print jobs.
/FF	Sends a form feed character to the printer after the job is finished. The /FF flag cannot be used to perform a plotter sheet advance on roll feed plotters.
/NFF	For no form feed character sent. One is sent by default. Although most plotters will ignore the ASCII form feed character sent by the /FF flag, you may want to include the /NFF flag as a reminder that none is performed.
/K	Keep all the data received even if the network connection is lost. By default, NetWare discards partial print jobs. Unless a partial plot is valuable to you, do not use the /K flag.
/A	For Autoendcap (AUTO END CAPture). Automatically closes print jobs when you exit an application and opens a new print job spool file when you enter a new application. The default Autoendcap condition is desirable with AutoCAD.
/NA	NoAutoendcap keeps the spool file open between successive applications. Autoendcap is the default.
/T=spaces	Sets the number of spaces to be produced by a tab. The default is 8 spaces.
/NT	For NoTabs, lets the printer perform its own tab conversion.
/TI=seconds	For TImeout, sets the number of seconds that CAPTURE waits after receiving printer data from an application before it considers a print job ended, and closes the spool file. The default is 0 (disabled). Most networks need a value of five to 30 seconds for AutoCAD and a plotter. On slower computers, vectorizing a plot may cause pauses in plotter data output of many seconds. Setting /TI too low can result in partial plots.
/SH	Shows the current CAPTURE parameters.

Normally, you will want to issue one or more CAPTURE commands in each user's login script to establish network printing for each workstation. Look at the following sample CAPTURE command:

CAPTURE /L=3 /Q=1 /P=2 /J=1 /F=2 /NB /NFF /TI=5

This command captures the output from LPT3 and sends it to PRINTQ_1 for printer 2, using job definition 1 and form 2. The command does not print a banner or issue additional form feeds, and waits five seconds after the application prints before sending the output to the printer as a discrete print job.

To get AutoCAD to send plotter output to the parallel port for CAPTURE to intercept, tell AutoCAD to plot to a file, then specify the parallel port name as the file name (LPT1, LPT2, PRN, and so on). You even can configure a parallel port as the destination of a plot file semi-permanently by configuring the port name as the default plot file name in AutoCAD. Chapter 8 tells you more on how to do this.

Sending AutoCAD Plots Indirectly with NPRINT

You also can get AutoCAD plotter data into a NetWare print queue after a plot file is created on disk by using the NetWare NPRINT command. NPRINT is analogous to the DOS PRINT command, but has many more command flags that give you much better control over your print jobs.

NPRINT uses the same flags as the CAPTURE command, except for the TImeout, Keep, and SHow flags. If your configuration requires any of the flags, such as the Printer flag (/P), to use a logical printer other than 0, add them on the command line or to the batch file you use to process plot files. The default values probably are adequate, although you may want to reset the following flags:

- /J, to specify a particular print job configuration set up with PrintCon
- /F, for specifying a particular medium or pen types that may be assigned to a printer form
- /NB, so that NPRINT does not send banner information that, although it would not plot, adds unnecessary overhead

NPRINT d oes offer one flag that CAPTURE does not: /D (Delete). The /D flag erases the file after it has been sent, and makes file cleanup as automatic as CAPTURE. If you have a reliable plotter, such as an electrostatic, so that you do not need to worry about its pens drying out, you can use the /D flag to keep your plot file directory clean.

Consider the following sample NPRINT command:

NPRINT 9051A112.PLT /P=2 /J=3 /F=1 /NB /D

This command sends an existing plot file, 9051A112.PLT, to printer 2 (a plotter is attached to a file server serial port). A message appears on the file server screen for the plotter operator to load the medium or pens defined for form 1. The file plots using the definition for job 3, no banner information is sent, and the file is deleted when the job is finished.

You can easily place the NPRINT command in a batch file with replaceable parameters and common flags, as follows:

NPRINT %1 /P=2 /J=3 /F=1 /NB /D

In this example, any file name you specify replaces the %1 parameter when the batch file is run. You can create separate batch files for each sheet size that use different form numbers, and give them descriptive names. With the aid of such batch files for common plotting jobs, such as the preceding one, all the user needs to do is pass the batch file the name of the file to plot, as follows:

VELLUM_D H:9051A112.PLT

In the preceding example, VELLUM_D.BAT contains the previous NPRINT command syntax, with replaceable parameter and common flags. You could have a similar batch file with only the form flag changed for a different size media. This batch file would be named VELLUM_E.BAT or MYLAR_D.BAT, if you used a flag that specified that Mylar media and pens be used.

You can run the batch file outside of AutoCAD, from the command prompt or a network menu, from within AutoCAD by the SHELL command, or as an external command defined in ACAD.PGP. An elegant method for this technique with Release 11 is discussed in Chapter 8.

Taking a Closer Look at LAN Manager

Microsoft Corporation's LAN Manager grew from the original MS-Net network operating system, which was based on DOS. MS-Net was modified to work on top of OS/2 as the basic operating system of a file server. LAN Manager has evolved into the network operating system of choice for OS/2 networks that distribute network applications. LAN Manager also works with DOS workstations and is available from Microsoft or from one of several original equipment manufacturers (OEM), including LAN Server from IBM.

Microsoft LAN Manager runs on top of the OS/2 operating system to take advantage of many of the rich features inherent in OS/2. LAN Manager is designed for medium to large LANs and can support up to 254 workstations and concurrent users.

LAN Manager Features

The primary component of a LAN Manager network is the OS/2 operating system. OS/2, with all of its features and powerful capabilities, not only makes a solid platform for a network, it is also a superb choice for a stand-alone operating system. The following are some of the features provided by OS/2 Extended Edition:

- **Presentation Manager**. A graphical user interface (GUI) that displays programs and information in windows.
- **Multitasking operating system**. Lets you work on several tasks simultaneously.
- **Database Manager**. Lets you create and maintain databases.

- **Communications Manager**. Capable of terminal emulation and LAN communications. Also lets you use programs written to the application program interfaces (API's) for communications.
- Printer queues and spooling capabilities.

For more information on the OS/2 operating system, see Chapter 4.

When it is set up on an OS/2 system, LAN Manager provides the network features and OS/2 provides core services, such as the file system, multitasking, and memory protection. On 80386-based servers, LAN Manager installs an optimized network I/O software subsystem and 32-bit HPFS file system. LAN Manager supports multiple processors in the file server, and because it runs in a multitasking environment, the server is nondedicated and can be used as a workstation to run other applications.

LAN Manager is intended as an open network environment so developers can create replacement or supplemental modules for any of LAN Manager's services. LAN Manager excels at connecting to other LAN Manager, Microsoft Network, IBM PC LAN Program, and IBM LAN Server networks with many industry protocols. Some of the different access protocols LAN Manager can use include the following:

- Transport Control Protocol/Internet Protocol (TCP/IP)
- Open Systems Interconnect Transport Class 4 (OSI TP4)
- IBM NetBIOS Extended User Interface (NetBEUI)
- Xerox Network Standards (XNS)

TCP/IP and OSI are discussed in Chapter 5.

For network hardware support, Microsoft and 3Com codeveloped the Network Device Interface Specification (NDIS). NDIS lets any workstation or server under LAN Manager share a common driver. In other networks, workstations and servers usually require separate drivers.

LAN Manager uses a character-based windowing interface to centralize network administration and simplify management. It uses a hierarchical user account system that divides network administration tasks among five different levels of users. The network administrator has full control over printing priorities, scheduling, routing, and security. LAN Manager also provides I/O device sharing for devices such as modems and plotters with printer-like spooling and queuing. The network administrator can manage the network from any OS/2 workstation.

LAN Manager's security features include network administrator workstation protection, password control, centralized log-on for multiple servers, and full account control. A seven-level general security system protects network resources down to the file level. LAN Manager also provides reliability features, including disk mirroring and duplexing, disk defect detection and data redirection, UPS support (discussed in Chapter 5), and file replication.

At the workstation, LAN Manager allows easy operation through a character-based, windowing interface with dialogue boxes. Peer services can be added to OS/2 workstations, giving additional interprocess communications capabilities to host/client server applications. This allows workstations to share peripheral devices with other workstations similarly to a file server. Other features include automated connection and logon management, savable user profiles, and integration with the Windows graphical environment.

Microsoft and IBM are the two main developers of OS/2 LAN Manager products. IBM licenses OS/2 LAN Manager from Microsoft Corp. then modifies it based on IBM OS/2 Extended Edition V1.2 operating system. For the most part, the two LAN Manager products are functionally the same. The information presented in this section is based on the IBM version.

LAN Manager System Requirements

LAN Manager requires that one of the following network adapters be installed in an IBM PC AT compatible or PS/2 computer:

- Token-Ring adapter
- IBM PC network adapter
- IBM ETHERAND baseband adapter
- Any standard Ethernet adapter with an NDIS driver

> **Note:** If connection to an IBM mainframe computer or minicomputer is a consideration, the Token-Ring adapters can take advantage of the 5250 Work Station Feature and 3270 Terminal Emulation communications capabilities that are provided by the OS/2 Extended Edition V1.2 operating system.

A LAN Manager server requires a minimum of 5.7M of RAM and 36.2M of fixed disk storage (3.5M of the RAM and 30M of the fixed disk space are required for the OS/2 V1.2).

Configuring LAN Manager Workstations

Two basic types of workstations can be configured to communicate with a LAN Manager network: *requesters* and *servers*. A requester is a workstation that accesses shared network resources, such as printers, plotters, file storage, and serial devices, that are made available by other workstations running as servers on the network.

The requester can be a workstation that is based on either DOS 3.3 (or higher) or OS/2 Extended Edition V1.2. On systems with OS/2, the requester program is called OS/2 LAN Requester and is included with the Extended Edition of OS/2. The

DOS systems use the DOS LAN Requester program that is included with OS/2 LAN Server V1.2.

An OS/2 requester workstation has the same minimum hardware requirements for the OS/2 operating system as the server (3.5M RAM and 30M fixed disk). A DOS LAN Requester workstation requires 2M available hard disk space and approximately 97K RAM—all but 40K of which can be loaded into either extended or EMS 4.0 (Expanded Memory Specification) memory.

The majority of the DOS LAN Requester program can be loaded into either extended or expanded memory. To load in expanded memory, a 64K page frame must be available. This usually is handled by an expanded memory manager. With QEMM V5.1, all of the DOS LAN Requester can be loaded into higher memory, which leaves more of the 640K base for TSR's and AutoCAD's Shell.

A server is a workstation that shares its network resources with requesters on the network. OS/2 LAN Manager V1.2 requires that at least one workstation on the network have OS/2 Extended Edition V1.2 and OS/2 LAN Server V1.2 installed and be configured as a *domain controller*.

Organizing Domains under LAN Manager

LAN Manager servers and resources are organized into logical groups called *domains*. A domain is a group of one or more servers that share resources with a specific group of users. A network, for example, can have a domain for the group of users in each department, or the group of users on each floor. A network can have more than one domain. Similarly, a domain can have several servers, but must have at least one server. A server, however, cannot belong to more than one domain.

The network supervisor assigns a user ID to each user in the domain. A user ID can be valid on more than one domain in the network, which lets a user log on to any domain (in which he is defined) from any requester in the network. A user, however, may log on to only one domain at a time.

The network supervisor assigns one server within each domain as the *domain controller*. The domain controller is a server that controls communications between the servers and requesters in the domain and must be installed and running so other servers can start. This, in turn, lets users log on to the domain.

For small- to medium-size installations, one domain is sufficient and preferred because it is easy to manage and gives the network supervisor flexibility in distributing resources. In order to use a resource (printer or file set), the user must log in to the domain in which the resource's server is assigned. If a network, for example, has two domains called ADMIN and ENGINEERING, a user named SULLIVAN, who is defined on both domains, can log on to either domain. The user, however, cannot be logged on to both domains at the same time. This would present a problem if the user wanted to plot a drawing located on SRV3 to a plotter located on SRV2. When logged on to ADMIN domain, SULLIVAN has access to the plotter but not the drawing file. When logged on to ENGINEERING domain, on the other hand, SULLIVAN has access to the drawing file but not the printer. Each domain, therefore, should have its own output resources. Otherwise, a plot or print file must be made on the workstation and SULLIVAN must log off of one domain and log onto the domain with the plotter. SULLIVAN then would need to send the file to the plotter.

Using LAN Manager Security with AutoCAD

LAN Manager provides a multi-layered security system that includes access-controlled profiles for resources, automatic logon assignments for users, automatic disconnection from resources when the network is inactive, and mandatory updating of passwords that have reached a specified age.

LAN Manager also provides an optional *replicator* feature that lets a centralized set of files be selectively replicated automatically from a server to one or more servers or requesters. The interval (1-60 minutes) with which the replicated files are checked for changes can be configured by the network supervisor.

The network has two types of users: supervisors that have full access rights and users that have limited access rights. The supervisors can perform administrative tasks from any OS/2 machine on the network using either the User Profile Management full-screen interface, or the command line. Each user is assigned a user ID and optional encrypted password. Users can be organized into groups based on function, department, and resource requirements, such as ACCTG, ADMIN, CADMECH, CADELEC, and CORP MIS. A user's access rights to resources can be defined individually, by group, or by a combination of both. This allows for flexibility in resource assignment.

Each server can keep an audit trail of all attempts to access its resources. The audit trail contains the following information:

- Start and stop status of the server
- Logons with user type indicated
- Logoffs with reasons for disconnection
- Start and stop of resources and reason
- Resource access with resource name and operation
- Access permission violations

Each protected resource is described by an *access control profile* that defines which users and groups have access to a particular resource and their permissions. A network supervisor can create an access control profile using the access control panel on the LAN Manager full-screen interface. The supervisor, for instance, can define the groups and users who have access to a protected resource, and can specify the maximum number of concurrent users for each resource. This lets the supervisor keep the number of users within the requirements of the site license agreements for shared applications, such as AutoCAD.

The access permissions that can be specified in an access control profile are the following:

- **D** (delete). Permits deleting subdirectories and files
- **A** (attributes). Permits changing OS/2 file attributes
- **N** (none). Denies access to the resour
- **X** (execute). Permits only running (not copying) program or command files, such as .EXE or .COM files
- **R** (read). Permits reading, running, and copying files from a directory
- **W** (write). Permits writing to (modifying) files
- **C** (create). Permits creating subdirectories and files
- **P** (permissions). Permits changing access permissions

In order for AutoCAD Release 10 or 11 to function properly as a shared application, users' permissions should include execute, read, write, create, delete, and attributes (XRWCDA). For users who will be creating and modifying drawings from a network drive, read, write, create, delete, and attributes (RWCDA) permissions are needed.

> *Tip:* Accidental erasure of entire drawing sdirectories is possible with delete capabilities. Because both operating systems, OS/2 and DOS, will recognize and enforce a read-only file attribute, you can create an AutoLISP routine that redefines the End and Save commands by doing the following steps:
>
> 1. Strip the read-only attribute from the .BAK file, if it exists.
> 2. Save the drawing file.
> 3. Set the read-only attribute for the newly created .DWG file.
> 4. QUIT the drawing file.

You should name the lisp file ACAD.LSP and configure AutoCAD so it automatically loads in each editing session. This method, however, does not set the read-only attribute of drawing files that are copied to the network drive.

For users who need only to view or plot drawings, only the read (R) permission is needed. The network supervisor can configure the network so file resources for storing blocks, compiling menus and shapes, and using AutoLISP routines have only read permission. The supervisor then can maintain and update the support files by granting himself group permission (RWCDA).

Configuring LAN Manager for AutoCAD Plotting

Printers and plotters must be supported by OS/2 device drivers to take advantage of OS/2 system queues and spoolers. OS/2 contains a variety of drivers and many software products, such as AutoCAD OS/2, LOTUS-123/G, and Microsoft Excel, include additional drivers.

The following are the basic steps you need to configure a plotter or printer for sharing under LAN Manager. They are the same steps as setting up a device under OS/2 itself.

■ Install the OS/2 printer driver through the Presentation Manager (PM) Control Panel.

■ Verify that the correct serial port driver is installed in CONFIG.SYS for your computer.

■ Set the serial port parameters through the PM Control Panel.

■ Add a name for the plotter in Print Manager.

■ Associate the plotter name with the serial port and driver.

■ Add a queue in Print Manager to receive plot jobs.

■ Associate the new queue with the plotter driver and port.

The spooler queue now can be shared within the domain in which it is defined. For more information on these steps, consult your OS/2 and LAN Manager documentation.

If you have a device for which OS/2 does not supply a driver, the device's manufacturer may be able to supply one, or you might locate a suitable driver on a bulletin board. If you cannot locate an OS/2 driver, one more option is available. OS/2 LAN Manager can utilize *external resources* defined on an IBM PC LAN Program V1.32 server (IBM PCLP 1.32). IBM PCLP 1.32 is a DOS-based (V3.3 or higher) network program that can be configured as a server. It lets you configure the device on a DOS server and define the device as an external resource to the LAN Manager domain controller. The device then can be shared within the domain in which it is defined. Because you cannot use OS/2's spooler queues in this situation, you should install a third-party, DOS-based print spooler or plot spooler that is network compatible to run on the IBM PCLP server.

If you are using AutoCAD on an OS/2 workstation, you can start a session of AutoCAD to plot or print a file in the background while you edit a second session of AutoCAD on-screen. The plot data will be spooled automatically to the queue you have selected in Print Manager. Background plots should be started from the Main Menu instead of from the Drawing Editor to ensure that the digitizer is available to the second session.

If you are on a DOS workstation using AutoCAD, you have the following queue options:

- You can configure AutoCAD to plot directly to the device connected to the network, such as LPT2, LPT3, and COM3. The plot data then will go to the spooler associated with that device.
- Or, you can configure AutoCAD to plot to a file, then send the plot file to the appropriate spooler, either using the NET PRINT command, or going through the DOS LAN requester full-screen interface.

The processing time can be reduced by setting the plotter optimization to a lower level when you configure AutoCAD. For more information on these steps, consult your AutoCAD and LAN Manager documentation.

Taking a Closer Look at Sun NFS

Sun Microsystems' Network File System (NFS) is a software standard established for the sharing of resources, such as hard disks, tape drives, and output peripherals (printers and plotters), across a network. While Sun Microsystems pioneered the use of NFS on its UNIX workstations and file servers, NFS has been adopted by most major computer manufacturers and currently is capable of sharing resources across various operating systems and hardware platforms, such as VAX VMS, Ultrix, IBM MVS, and MS-DOS. Generally, the information presented in this section, while written specifically to describe the implementation of NFS on Sun workstations, also is applicable to implementations of NFS on other computers.

NFS creates a peer-to-peer system by letting participating workstations *mount* portions of their own file systems for public access. Any connected workstation, then, has access to the group's collective contributions to the network. A single system administrator mounts or unmounts directories, establishes security for public resources, and manages group security privileges. Individual users maintain security for their private directories.

NFS also allows access to the other workstation computing resources, including processing. A user on the network, for example, can have multiple applications or print jobs running simultaneously on several workstations. Many NFS users take advantage of this capability by using one machine to handle accounting for the entire system.

Because every Sun workstation has an Ethernet port, you can easily install NFS by connecting coaxial cable and setting up user accounts, which are inherent with UNIX. The new peer-to-peer network appears transparent to every Sun user, hence the Sun slogan: "The computer *is* the network."

NFS Features

The following lists the advantages of running AutoCAD on an NFS network:

- **Security**. Access to AutoCAD drawings can be protected by the standard UNIX permission structure. Users and administrators can restrict or control the viewing or modification of their drawings by designating the permission for individuals or groups.

- **File access**. An NFS network lets multiple workstations access any number of common disk resources across the network. For the user on an NFS network, the disk resources, either from an individual workstation or from another system on the network, appear as part of one directory structure or file system. AutoCAD users can have common directories for shared projects and for released and pre-released drawings. These projects and drawings are available for all systems and appear as being part of their local machine.

- **Data integrity**. One of the primary reasons for using AutoCAD on a network is to maintain the integrity of the drawings in an organization. Drawings that are stored in common directories on a network can be managed for access and updating. The inadvertent loss or corruption of drawing data can be avoided by maintaining the drawings in specific directories on the network. A feature of an NFS network is that access to the network is *stateless*. Stateless means that when a drawing is being saved to an unavailable server, the station running AutoCAD will continue to request that the data be written to the server. Once free, the server acknowledges the station and the data is stored.

- **Output resources**. All of the printers and plotters that are connected to the Sun workstations are available to all of the workstations on the network. An AutoCAD user has the capability of using plotters and laser printers anywhere on the network. Plot or print jobs can be spooled automatically to the appropriate workstation. This frees the local workstation to continue productive work and maximizes the usage of expensive printers and plotters.

- **Administration**. The capability to represent common directories on the network as local directories lets a CAD manager establish standards for directory structures among all of the workstations. Also, the CAD manager can establish and maintain access and control over the drawings that are on the network.

NFS Network Topology, Protocol, and Media

The most common Sun workstation network has an Ethernet bus-type network with a TCP/IP transport. A TCP/IP is the low-level protocol that is used to pass messages on Ethernet. NFS uses TCP/IP to transport its messages to other stations on the network. Each workstation requires a transceiver to which the network cable attaches. The cable traditionally has been 50-ohm coaxial cable, known as thick or thin Ethernet cable.

Ethernet over twisted pair wiring, made popular by manufacturers such as Synoptics, uses a star topology rather than a bus topology. Hardware concentrators for this wiring scheme provide the timing and retransmission of packets. The main advantage of the twisted pair star topology is the increased flexibility of physical network reconfiguration; you can move a workstation into a different location on the network without breaking the existing network or affecting other workstations on the network. This cannot be done with coaxial cable.

In a network of Sun workstations, one or more systems can be designated as a workstation/fileserver and common network resources, such as higher capacity disks (1G), tape drives (150M, 2G 8mm), and printers and plotters, reside on the server.

Installing and Configuring NFS

Installation is not necessary for NFS on a Sun workstation because support for NFS is included with the Sun operating system (SunOS). The configuration of the workstations, however, is not pre-configured. A Sun workstation, such as the SPARCstation IPC, comes from the manufacturer with the operating system loaded. When the system is first turned on, the user is prompted with a number of questions, including machine name and network role.

The /etc/exports file, which is an ASCII file, is used to control the local directories that are made available (exported) for access by the other machines on the network. Local directories that are listed in this file can be exported to all or any specific systems on the network. Changes in the exports file are completed by running the exportfs command. The existence of the /etc/exports file also triggers the start of the nfs *daemons* (nfsd) and the mount *daemon* (rpc.mountd) at boot time. These daemons are programs that run in the background and that process the NFS requests for *mounting* and accessing the local resources. Mounting is the process by which other systems request and get access to remote directories. For the AutoCAD user, the export file should include directories on the local hard disk that contain or will contain information that is needed by other users and systems on the network.

Once the systems have been configured for the network, the CAD manager must decide on the directory structure of the data across the network. Will one central machine be on the network that has all of the disk resources? Or, will the disk resources be spread out across a number of systems?

When you configure the network to have a central system that acts as the fileserver for the network, you simplify the administration of the drawing data by keeping the drawing data on one machine. Only one machine's disk with drawing data needs to be backed up, and all of the directory structure resides on that one machine. All drawings that are accessed and modified, however, will be served by that one system, and performance of the network will depend on the speed and throughput of its disk and controller. In addition, the file server and its disk are a single point of failure that could render the entire network unusable if they go down.

Alternatively, by distributing network disk resources over a number of machines, you avoid the problems associated with having the network depend on a single critical component. A number of workstations can have disks available to provide network disk space for projects and drawings. The failure of any one system would restrict access only to the directories on that one system and the network would continue to function.

The administration of a distributed network where critical data is found on a number of systems, however, is more difficult and calls for a higher degree of organization and planning. Programs and utilities that let a CAD manager monitor parameters, such as disk usage, become more crucial and network-wide backup and restore capability becomes a necessity.

Using NFS' Security with AutoCAD

File security for AutoCAD running on Sun workstations is governed by the ownership and permission structures found in the UNIX operating system. By using these elementary controls on drawing security, the network administrator can develop a simple but effective plan for managing the Sun AutoCAD network.

User Accounts

The first level of security in a Sun AutoCAD network is user accounts and passwords. All users of the network must have a user account that identifies them to the network, provides them with a home directory on the network, and gives them file access and privileges based on the characteristics set for that user. The CAD manager typically is in charge of setting up and maintaining the user account information, either through an automatic script such as is available under SunOS 4.1.1, or manually, as outlined in the following list:

- Add an entry for the user in /etc/passwd on the system that is the Network Information Services (NIS, formerly YP, or yellow pages) server. NIS is a network database of resource information, such as user accounts and passwords, for each machine that makes network administration easy.

- Add the user to specific defined groups in /etc/group, as covered in the next section.

- Transfer the information to the rest of the network's NIS clients and slave servers using the ypmake(8) procedure. ypmake(8) passes the NIS database information to the other NIS clients on the network.

- Create the user's home directory.
- Copy your organization's default files, including .login, .cshrc, .mailrc, and shell scripts for starting AutoCAD, into the user's home directory. The default files control the user environment, such as CONFIG.SYS and AUTOEXEC.BAT files do for DOS users.
- Change ownership, group designation, and permissions for the user's home directory, as well as the files contained therein.
- Establish an initial user password for the account by running the command yppasswd username, which is a command line entry.

Passwords

Once a user's account has been established, security is maintained by the user's password at login. The primary means for controlling access to the network is through passwords. No one can log into the network as a user without a user account and password. If someone is not authorized to use the network based on user accounts and passwords, no access at any level is possible. The CAD manager can ensure the security of the network by establishing accounts only for those individuals who need access to the network, by making sure that every user has and maintains a password that changes periodically, and by not having "house" accounts, which give no indication of who is using the network.

The second step in maintaining system security is to design a file access structure that lets selected users access and control drawing files. This structure should take into account your company's organizational structure, flexibility, degree of control desired, and need for document control.

File Access

The next level of security, once the user's access has been validated, is file permissions. The UNIX operating system allows read (r), write (w), and execute (x) permission for each file or directory on the network. These permissions can be set for three categories of users:

1. The owner of the file or directory
2. The group of users associated with the file or directory
3. All others not in the first two categories

Through these permissions, the CAD manager can control access to the files and drawings that are produced with AutoCAD.

Configuring NFS for AutoCAD Plotting

An essential feature of using AutoCAD on a Sun NFS network is the capability to use network plotters and printers. Because AutoCAD on a Sun workstation runs on the

UNIX operating system, multitasking is available to the user. The user can run two or three sessions of AutoCAD simultaneously under the SunView window environment. This capability enables the user to edit multiple drawings at the same time, or plot one drawing while working on a second. With the multitask Sun environment, the user gains time that is lost by regens, hidden line removal, plotting, and dxf file generation, and increases AutoCAD productivity.

A DOS environment, on the other hand, does not provide multitasking capabilities. When AutoCAD plots a drawing, for example, the system is dedicated to the plotting task and is unavailable for other work. Large plot buffers, background spoolers, and stand-alone plot servers make DOS work similar to a multitasking environment, but at added expense, decreased flexibility, and added load to the operating system. Under a Sun NFS network, however, not only can the plot be sent out in the background because of the UNIX multitasking capabilities, the plotter can be installed on a separate machine to be accessible by all systems on the network. Performance on the local workstation is optimized by off-loading the burden of spooling to the networked system.

To take advantage of the network transparent plotting capabilities, AutoCAD's default plot name must be set to AUTOSPOOL and an environment variable, ACADPLCMD, must be set. The following is an example of setting the ACADPLCMD variable:

demo% setenv ACADPLCMD lpr -Php -r -s %s

In the preceding syntax, the lpr command is the standard UNIX printing program. The -Php option tells lpr to use the printer named hp, whereas the -r option tells lpr to remove the spooled file after it has been plotted. The -s option tells lpr to create, if possible, a symbolic link to the spool file rather than copying it to the spool directory. The %s variable is used by AutoCAD to substitute its own spool file name.

When this environment variable is set, you can plot as normal in AutoCAD, but the output is spooled automatically to the plotter. The spool file directory is set by the AutoCAD configuration item, Default Spool Directory, and is called var/spool/acad.

NFS RAM Considerations for AutoCAD

Autodesk recommends that the workstation have three times the drawing size in free memory (RAM) available so the entire drawing and temporary files can be loaded into RAM. This configuration yields the highest system performance because writes to the disk and network will be minimized. The free memory is exclusive of the RAM allocated to UNIX (up to 2M), the window environment (300K for Sunview, 1M for OpenWindows), and AutoCAD (1.7M). Sunview is the original Sun window environment in which AutoCAD was designed to run. OpenWindows, on the other hand, is the newest Sun window environment and uses the Open Look GUI. Although AutoCAD Release 10 will run in OpenWindows, Release 11 is the first AutoCAD program that conforms to the Open Look GUI. A SPARC IPC with 8M RAM running

OpenWindows and AutoCAD, for example, uses between 4-5M of RAM, which lets AutoCAD operate on a 1M drawing completely in RAM. For each additional copy of AutoCAD, the system needs to have 1.7M plus three times the drawing size available in RAM. Two sessions of AutoCAD running on this system would have 7M allocated, leaving 1M available for the two sets of drawings and temporary files.

Running Additional Sessions of AutoCAD

Additional sessions of AutoCAD can be started by executing ACAD from the command line or through a shell script. Because AutoCAD accesses the digitizer through direct interaction with the serial port, only one session of AutoCAD can use the digitizer. Additional sessions of AutoCAD configured to use the mouse, however, can be operated concurrently. The following are some reasons to have multiple sessions of AutoCAD:

- During long regens, the user can work on another drawing.
- The user has multiple reference drawings.
- The user can work on multiple drawings interchangeably.
- Drawings can plot in the background.

UNIX Script Files for AutoCAD

C-shell script files, similar to batch files in DOS, simplify and standardize the way users start up AutoCAD on a Sun system. The following is a sample script file, acadmouse, that starts AutoCAD Release 10:

```
#!/bin/csh
#acadmouse
#Script file to start up AutoCAD on a Sun workstation
#
setenv ACADCFG /home/acad/mousecfg
setenv ACAD /home/acad/acad/
setenv ACADBGCOLOR black
setenv ACADPLCMD lpr -Php -r %s
setenv ACADFASTDRAW yes
/home/acad/acad/acad
```

In the preceding script file, the AutoCAD files have been installed in the /home/acad directory. The ACADCFG variable is set to the directory that contains the configuration file for AutoCAD, acad.cfg_hostname. Hostname is the name of the machine on which AutoCAD is authorized to run. The ACAD directory is set to the directory that contains the support files, such as acad.pgp. The AutoCAD background color command, ACADBGCOLOR, which has values of black, white, and gray, is set to black. Next, the ACADPLCMD plotter command is set to use the UNIX lpr command with options that output be directed to printer hp and that the spool file be removed at the completion of the plot. Then, the ACADFASTDRAW flag is set to yes. This enables the built-in display list processor, which allows for a greater degree of zooming before regeneration is necessary. Last, the AutoCAD executable program /home/acad/ acad/acad is called up.

Use of shell scripts to start AutoCAD gives the user and CAD manager flexibility in running AutoCAD in standard configurations. The preceding script, for example, can be copied to acadtablet by only changing the ACADCFG environment variable to /home/acad/tabletcfg. In this manner, the user, without reconfiguring AutoCAD each time, immediately can start a mouse or tablet-configured version of AutoCAD. Similar scripts can be written to account for different plotters, printers, and background colors.

Taking a Closer Look at Sun's PC-NFS

Sun Microsystems' PC-NFS lets MS-DOS based personal computers share the same network resources that are available to Sun workstations. Through PC-NFS, PCs can access network directories as if they were local hard disks and can access network plotters and printers as if they were local DOS printers. In addition, PC-NFS includes utilities systems that support TCP/IP utilities, such as *telnet, rcp,* and *rsh.* Telnet lets a DOS user log on to the Sun system and emulate a VT100 program. The RCP utility lets a DOS user copy a file between a remote machine and the PC, while the RSH utility lets the DOS user execute remotely a UNIX command on the Sun. These utilities, however, are base utilities and generally are not used because PC-NFS provides more functions.

AutoCAD running on a PC-NFS network is streamlined by common directories for drawings, projects, and peripheral sharing. AutoCAD drawings that are created on a PC can be modified by someone using AutoCAD on a Sun without any file translation or modification. A mixed AutoCAD network of PCs and Suns running PC-NFS/ NFS lets you preserve existing MS-DOS hardware and equipment, while taking advantage of the file security, drawing data integrity, and resource sharing of workstation NFS.

PC-NFS Features

The advantages of running AutoCAD on a PC-NFS network are the following:

- **Security**. Access to AutoCAD drawings can be protected by the standard UNIX permission structure. Users and administrators can restrict or control the viewing or modification of their drawings by designating the permission for individuals or groups.

- **File access**. A PC on a PC-NFS network has similar access as Sun workstations to common disk resources across the network. The user of PC-NFS sees disk resources from NFS servers, such as Sun workstations, as logical DOS disks. AutoCAD users can have common directories for shared projects, or for released and pre-released drawings available for all systems. These drawings appear as being part of their local machine.

- **Data integrity**. Drawings that are stored in common directories on a network can then be managed for access and updated. Loss or corruption of drawing data because of multiple copies of drawings on multiple computers can be avoided by maintaining the drawings in specific directories on the network.

- **Output resources**. All of the printers and plotters that are connected to the Sun workstations are available to all of the PCs on the network. An AutoCAD user can use plotters and laser printers anywhere on the network that appear as local printers LPT1:, LPT2:, and LPT3:. Plot or print jobs can be spooled automatically to the appropriate Sun workstation. This frees the local workstation to continue productive work to maximize the usage of expensive printers and plotters.

- **Administration**. PC-NFS uses a windowed configuration program, NFSCONF, to manage the choices for logical drive assignment, printer redirection, and system identification. Some administration tasks must be run or installed by the CAD manager on the Sun workstation.

PC-NFS Topology, Protocol, and Media

PC-NFS is a software product that requires the use of an Ethernet adapter card that resides on the AT bus. Some widely available cards from manufacturers such as 3COM and Western Digital are supported directly by PC-NFS. Cards from other manufacturers such as Everex come with their own PC-NFS drivers supported by the card manufacturer. Both 8- and 16-bit cards are supported, but the capability to load drivers into the adapter's RAM generally is not supported. The same network topologies, protocols, and medias are supported in PC-NFS as in Sun's NFS. Chapter 5 describes loading drivers into NIC RAM in more detail.

Sun PC-NFS 3.01 requires DOS V3.1 or higher. AutoCAD generally is run on AT-class or better machines with hard disks, although XT-class machines and floppy-only disks are supported. PC-NFS uses about 70K of conventional memory for its device drivers; high-memory products, such as Quarterdeck's QEMM or RYBS' HI386, can be used to load some or all of the drivers into high memory. See the section entitled, "Relief for Ram Cram," in Chapter 5 for a more detailed discussion on RAM considerations.

Using PC-NFS Security with AutoCAD

File security for AutoCAD running on a PC-NFS network is governed by the same ownership and permission structure found in the UNIX operating system on Sun workstations.

PC AutoCAD users must have user accounts and passwords on the Sun workstation for file security to be in effect. The accounts and passwords can be established as outlined in the Sun NFS section. Access to and modification of users' files are protected through the UNIX permissions so the user can store individually controlled drawings, and view, but not modify, released drawings.

Configuring PC-NFS for AutoCAD Plotting

Network resources, such as printers and plotters, can be used by DOS AutoCAD users in a similar fashion to those on the Sun workstation. Up to three printers or plotters can be assigned to DOS designators LPT1:, LPT2:, or LPT3:. The print devices can be configured to spool the job by a hot-key combination after a pre-set time, or after exiting the application program. You also can choose the type and degree of print job filtering for the specific printer or plotter.

Miscellaneous PC-NFS Features

One of the most common Sun PC-NFS network configurations is a Sun workstation running AutoCAD that acts also as an NFS file server. The Sun provides a fast, multitasking machine for AutoCAD, as well as providing the network capabilities, such as file and peripheral sharing, for the PCs. In contrast to the traditional PC network that centers on a dedicated PC server, the multi-purpose Sun server provides the traditional server functions as well as adding an AutoCAD station. This allows you to have two choices when the needs of your organization grow: you can add PCs running AutoCAD that are low in price, but also are low in performance and have only single-task capabilities, or you can add Sun workstations that can be high in price, but have multitask capabilities that lead to higher productivity.

Taking a Closer Look at Artisoft LANtastic

Artisoft Inc.'s LANtastic has moved from being a relative unknown to being one of the most recognized names in networking. This success has been built on the premise of minimalistic networking. LANtastic is a peer-to-peer, DOS-based (DOS 3.1 or higher) network designed for small- to medium-size businesses and workgroups and can support up to 300 nodes, of which any can be servers.

The LANtastic Network Operating System (NOS) is designed to work with Artisoft's 2 ms and Ethernet cards. LANtastic also is available in an adapter independent version that will work with any network adapter that has a NetBIOS (Network Basic Input/Output System) interface, including many EtherNet, Arcnet, and Token-Ring adapters. Artisoft sells its own NetBIOS software for Western Digital and Novell Ethernet adapters, as well as marketing its own NetBIOS for parallel and serial ports, called LANtastic-z, which is sold with a two-user version of its NOS.

Because of its peer-to-peer orientation, LANtastic makes server requirements trivial. Any PC can be a server, although best results are obtained with faster 286- or 386- based machines. LANtastic's low RAM requirement is one of its strongest selling points and is a major reason why it is popular with AutoCAD users. A workstation node requires less than 14K of RAM and a server requires a minimum of 40K. If a server is not intended to run AutoCAD (or other demanding programs), LANtastic can be told to use the total amount of RAM in the system.

Although LANtastic is an inexpensive LAN with minimal RAM requirements, it does include some exotic features, such as electronic mail, optional network voice mail, shared CD-ROMS and WORM drives, disk caching, and an optional remote-control capability that is useful for plotting. These capabilities put LANtastic in the same league as bigger network players, such as Novell.

LANtastic, of course, does lack in some areas. Because it is DOS based, LANtastic cannot work easily with Macintosh, OS/2, or UNIX workstations. LANtastic also lacks explicit hooks for wide area networking (WAN), but soon repeaters and bridges will be available that work with LANtastic.

Storage limitations on LANtastic are limited only by the version of DOS that is on the system. These limitations include hard disk partition size and memory size. File and record locking are provided by the DOS Share command. If no file or record locking is on a network, more than one user can modify a file at the same time. Share prevents this and lets only one user modify a file at one time.

LANtastic has no special provision for data integrity and relies on the mechanisms of each server to assure data integrity. For critical applications, however, commercial mirroring disk controllers are available that provide data redundancy. On a simpler level, setting Verify On in DOS provides an additional level of security, but at the cost of disk speed.

LANtastic Features

One of the most important capabilities in a low-cost network is shared printing and plotting. LANtastic fulfills this requirement admirably by providing multiple print queues and by letting any parallel or serial port on any server be shared. Queues can be manipulated from any workstation provided that the user has that privilege assigned to his account.

Any significant weaknesses in LANtastic generally are a result of its peer-to-peer nature, rather than any flaws in its design. If you have every workstation on a network be a server, you cannot maintain any form of central administration without difficulty. LANtastic can maintain records of who logs in and logs out, but these records are held on each server. Distinct passwords and accounts must be established for each server and data must be backed up from each server. Because each user has control over their own machine, they sometimes do careless things, such as turning off the computer while someone else is accessing it, which hangs up the person who is accessing the server.

LANtastic's problems, however, are not detrimental to a small workgroup network. With only a few computers running on it, LANtastic provides an attractive and inexpensive alternative to a sneaker-net network. In smaller LANtastic installations, each computer typically is run as a stand-alone system with its own copy of AutoCAD and local drawing storage. The network is used mainly to transfer files and gain access to a common plotter or printer. Because each system has a local hard disk, network traffic is low and performance is good.

In workgroups of more than three or four computers, however, the administration troubles of many separate servers outweigh LANtastic's advantages. In fact, the first major LANtastic pitfall is having too many servers and too little administrative control. The other problem with larger peer-to-peer networks is the tendency to use production AutoCAD workstations for network plotting, printing, and data file storage. Although no hard and fast rule exists against doing this, using an AutoCAD workstation for anything but the lightest server duties will hurt both its performance and the network's. The ideal arrangement for medium-size or larger networks is to assign one or more systems as dedicated servers to handle data files, programs, and plotting. By allocating all of a server's RAM to network tasks and caching, AutoCAD performance can be increased to nearly the same level as dedicated network operating systems.

The performance of LANtastic, similar to any other network, is limited more by the network configuration and hardware than by software. With thought and care, you can have a large, yet fast LANtastic network. On the other hand, through carelessness, you can have a smaller network that does not perform very well. AutoCAD, because it is a processor-intensive program, requires large amounts of the computer's time for good performance. If LANtastic spends too much time performing network server tasks instead of AutoCAD tasks, AutoCAD performance will decrease.

LANtastic probably should be used in smaller groups even though it is capable of competing against Novell in large networks. In smaller networks with as few as two computers, LANtastic often is used when the cost and complexity of a Novell system is prohibitive. For AutoCAD users, LANtastic is valuable when older equipment must be used. LANtastic networks with up to ten AutoCAD stations using a PC AT computer for a file server and a PC XT computer for plot servers is not uncommon.

LANtastic Configuration Options

AutoCAD can be configured a number of ways on a LANtastic network, but only two methods usually are used. One is to essentially ignore the network and use it only for file transfers. The other is to use the network with dedicated servers as a centralized storage, plotting, and management system.

Configuring LANtastic as a Peer-to-Peer Network

In existing AutoCAD installations where only a few computers are set up, a peer-to-peer LANtastic configuration is easiest and least expensive to use. If you plan to use LANtastic in its simplest form, you will find that it intrudes little on the operation of AutoCAD. AutoCAD 386, in particular, because it has modest base RAM requirements, will get along fine with LANtastic even when configured as a server. The only real conflict between AutoCAD 386 and LANtastic is in the area of shell space. The Shell command in AutoCAD 386 provides a limited amount of working memory that is reduced by the presence of LANtastic. You can do several workarounds for this problem. Older versions of AutoCAD 386 can be updated to gain a larger shell space with a program, NEWDX, available from AutoCAD dealers. The Shroom command, shipped with AutoCAD 386 Release 11 and available from CompuServe, swaps out the AutoCAD executable from base RAM, giving a larger shell space. The only penalty with Shroom is the time required for disk access.

In its non-386 specific versions, however, AutoCAD presents more of a problem. For best operation, AutoCAD needs as much free RAM as possible; 640K is ideal, but probably unattainable. The LANtastic NET_MGR program includes an option to establish server parameters. All the parameters should be set for minimum values if AutoCAD is to be run on the server. If you have a 386 computer, use a program such as Qualitas 386-to-the-MAX or Quarterdeck QEMM to load the LanBIOS and redirector in high memory. This will preserve base RAM for AutoCAD's use. To avoid RAM problems all together, do not configure an AutoCAD system as a LANtastic server.

The LANtastic server program does not affect a computer's performance to any great degree by its presence alone. But, when used heavily in conjunction with AutoCAD, LANtastic will slow down the computer. Because of this, you should think carefully when configuring your network. If possible, avoid using one AutoCAD system's disk as a storage depot for other systems' blocks and drawings. With a peer-to-peer configuration, this means either duplicating drawing libraries on each computer, or storing them on a computer that is not used for AutoCAD. Duplicating the library may take more storage space and management, but will be faster.

When using a LANtastic print queue for background plotting or printing on an AutoCAD system, you should recognize that the queue will not send data as fast as AutoCAD does alone. The best results are obtained by using a station that is dedicated to plotting and printing. Even an old PC XT computer is adequate for this.

Configuring LANtastic as a Server-Based Network

As with Novell, LANtastic offers the option of putting everything or just drawings on the server. The only practical difference between AutoCAD configured on a Novell server and on a LANtastic server is the minor detail of drive mapping. The following, for example, are two equivalent statements, one for Novell and one for LANtastic, that assign the local J: drive to the ACAD directory on the server SYS:

Novell: MAP J:=**SYS:ACAD**

LANtastic: NET USE J: **\\SYS\ACAD**

In Novell, the drive mapping can be changed by changing directories. That is, if you execute the preceding Novell command and change to the J: drive, you will find yourself in the J:\ACAD directory. From there you can change directories, even moving to the root directory (in which you would likely have no privileges). In LANtastic, however, the drive mapping is more strict. If you execute the preceding LANtastic command and change to the J: drive, you will find yourself in the J:\ directory, which corresponds to the ACAD directory on the server. You will not be able to change to the server's root directory because your computer will believe it is in the root directory of the J: drive. You will be able to change to subdirectories under the server's ACAD directory.

Using LANtastic Security with AutoCAD

Security in LANtastic is managed by a program called NET_MGR. By using NET_MGR, the network supervisor sets up user accounts and passwords on each server. NET_MGR also creates links allowing network access to the server's individual directories. Each of these links includes an access control list (ACL) that provides security to allow or prevent access on an individual or group basis. LANtastic's access control can be limited to read, write, create, delete, or execute files.

In NET_MGR, each network directory can be assigned the following access control list flags on a user-by-user basis:

R   Read access

W   Write access

C   Create file

M   Create directory

L   Allow file look-ups (DIR's)

D   Delete files

K   Delete directories

N   Rename files

E   Allow program execution

A   Allow file attributes to be changed

I   Directory supports indirect files

P   Allow physical access to devices

The I and P flags only are of interest in special situations. For more detail on these flags, you should refer to the LANtastic users manual.

When wildcards (*) are used to specify user names, groups of users can be created. All the AutoCAD users on a server, for example, might have their name prefixed by the word ACAD_. The entire group then would be referred to as ACAD_* (see fig. 7.5).

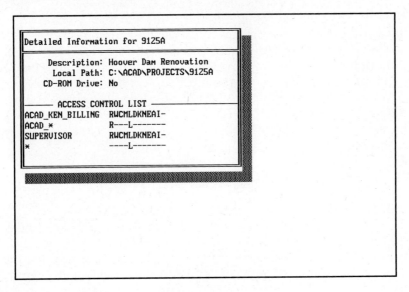

```
Detailed Information for 9125A

    Description: Hoover Dam Renovation
    Local Path: C:\ACAD\PROJECTS\9125A
    CD-ROM Drive: No

        ACCESS CONTROL LIST
ACAD_KEN_BILLING   RWCMLDKNEAI-
ACAD_*             R---L-------
SUPERVISOR         RWCMLDKNEAI-
*                  ----L-------
```

Figure 7.5:
A sample of the ACL flags assigned to a project directory.

In figure 7.5, both the supervisor and Ken Billing have full access to the directory. Members of the ACAD group have the capability to read files, whereas everyone else (*) has the capability only to list a directory of the files. The following table lists the recommended ACL settings that an AutoCAD user would need in each AutoCAD-related network directory:

AutoCAD directory:	R—L—E—
Configuration directory:	RWC-LD-NEA—
Project directory:	RWCMLDKNEA—
Library directory:	R—L———

For best security, you should remember that LANtastic automatically confers *parental* rights. That is, if a right is assigned in one directory, that right applies in all its subdirectories.

Configuring LANtastic for AutoCAD Plotting

Similar to other network operating systems, LANtastic does not understand the difference between a plotter and a printer. This is no real problem, of course, so long as *you* understand the difference. A plotter queue is defined in the NET_MGR program similarly to a network directory. The difference is that the name is proceeded by an @ (see fig. 7.6).

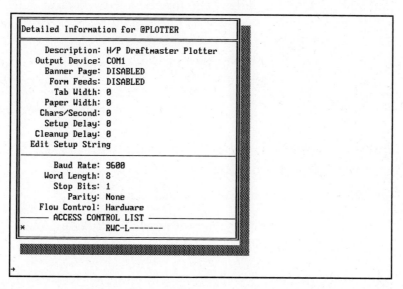

```
Detailed Information for @PLOTTER

        Description: H/P Draftmaster Plotter
      Output Device: COM1
        Banner Page: DISABLED
         Form Feeds: DISABLED
          Tab Width: 0
        Paper Width: 0
       Chars/Second: 0
        Setup Delay: 0
      Cleanup Delay: 0
      Edit Setup String

          Baud Rate: 9600
        Word Length: 8
          Stop Bits: 1
             Parity: None
       Flow Control: Hardware
      ———— ACCESS CONTROL LIST ————
 *                    RWC-L--------
```

Figure 7.6:
Detailed information on a typical plotter setup.

> **Tip:** You should not send banners or form feeds to plotters because they only will confuse the plotter and possibly ruin your plot job.

Under the Edit Setup String option, you can define an initialization string to be sent to the plotter before each job. A different initialization string can be made for each queue, and more than one queue can be made for each plotter or printer. An initialization string can be used to send a form advance command for roll feed plotters. Alternatively, under the same option LANtastic can be instructed to send the contents of a file at the beginning or end of each print job. These files, called setup and cleanup files, can contain either ASCII or binary information.

On some plotters—those that can plot twice on the same paper without reloading—the cleanup file can be used to plot a title block. This is done by plotting a title block to file and telling LANtastic to use it as a cleanup file.

The setup and cleanup files can be used with printers to change their operating mode. Some printers, for example, support HP-GL/2 plotting language. When you use the setup file, the printer can be initialized in the HP-GL/2 mode for plotting. The cleanup file can be used to change the printer back to normal mode. Another significant use of the cleanup file is for sending an *off-line* command to the plotter. On cut-sheet units, an off-line command will let you reload media before the next plot. Another method for pausing between plots is to use the printer control option in the NET program to stop the queue. Then use the one-job command to send one plot at a time. The disadvantage of this is that it is not automatic and requires the NET program to be run.

The plotter, similar to a network directory, has ACLs. The P (physical connect) access code can be used to bypass the print queue, but it can cause problems. If two users, for example, try to plot at the same time, one of the computers can hang up. To redirect output to a plotter, you should use either of the following two NET commands:

NET USE LPT1 \\SYS\@PLOTTER

NET USE COM1 \\SYS\@PLOTTER

When you redirect COM ports, AutoCAD often will carry on a two-way conversation with plotters unless you are plotting to file. With HP plotters, for example, AutoCAD will query the plotter for the hard-clip limits. You should configure AutoCAD to plot to file and then substitute the DOS device name (such as LPT1, LPT2, LPT3, COM1, or COM2) as the file name.

Because AutoCAD sometimes fails to send an end-of-file character at the end of a plot, LANtastic must be instructed on how long to wait for the plot to end, such as the following:

NET LPT TIMEOUT 30

This statement instructs LANtastic to wait for 30 seconds of inactivity before the output queue is closed. Optionally, when you press Control+Alt+PrintScrn at the same time, you will close the queue manually. To send information to the queue from the DOS prompt, you should use the NET command instead of the DOS Print command:

NET PRINT{/BINARY}{/VERBOSE} filename device {comment {copies}}

In the preceding syntax, the /BINARY command directs the device to print the file in binary mode. The /VERBOSE command displays the file names as they are queued. Then, the filename variable gives the pathname of the file to print. You can use wildcards to name the pathname. The device name, such as LPT1, is given by the device variable. The comment variable lists any text that is associated with the print job. If the comment variable is omitted, the filename is listed. The number of copies to print is defined by copies variable.

In the detailed plotter information in NET_MGR, the characters-per-second rate can be set. When set to zero, for example, LANtastic tries to find the optimum rate. The rate can be set manually up to 32,767 characters-per-second. For serial ports, for example, 9600 baud translates to 960 characters per second so you should leave the rate set to zero. For plotters with parallel interfaces or printer-plotters, you may have to experiment to find a rate that is fast enough, yet does not degrade the server's performance on other tasks.

For the fastest plotting with the least network degradation, you should set up a separate plot server. The plot server can be as simple as an XT computer with a couple of ports, to as sophisticated as a 386 with a 387 math coprocessor. With an XT computer, the server captures plot data generated from CAD stations and spools it out to the appropriate printers and plotters. If you use a 386-based computer, on the other hand, you can run AutoCAD and plot jobs when you need them.

Note: You do not need to purchase a license of AutoCAD for your plot station so long as you plot from the Main Menu and not the Drawing Editor. In the Release 11 network version, plotting from the Main Menu does not use any of the floating AutoCAD licenses for the network.

Artisoft sells a program called Network Eye that lets you control other computers over the network from any workstation. This program is suited ideally for controlling a plot server. Network Eye, however, does not work in graphics mode, so you cannot run a Drawing Editor session remotely. In a practical sense, Network Eye lets you run a plot server from your seat, rather than having to walk down the hall.

Miscellaneous LANtastic Features

LANtastic, because it is DOS- and NetBIOS-based, can use a wide variety of third-party hardware and software. Cyco AutoBase, ACS Telecom AutoEDMS, and CAD Systems Unlimited Slick! are NetBIOS-based and provide significant drawing management capabilities for LANtastic users.

If you need to manage large numbers of drawings, LANtastic supports CD-ROM, WORM, and re-writable optical disk drives. LANtastic generally supports most brands and models of optical drives, but check with Artisoft's up-to-date compatibility list before you purchase one.

Summary

In this chapter, you have taken a tour through the favorite networks of AutoCAD users. Each has features that make it attractive for certain reasons. Microsoft LAN Manager and Sun NFS give you a protected option for running AutoCAD on a file server with a high performance, multitasking operating system—an ideal worksta-tion for the busy CAD manager. Sun's PC-NFS, Artisoft LANtastic, and the peer services of LAN Manager all give you workstation-to-workstation features that let you distribute your network resources to your needs. Also, NetWare, LANtastic, PC-NFS, and LAN Manager let you keep comfortable old MS-DOS, as well as your investment in DOS software, intact.

Novell NetWare is the most popular network operating system, as well as the best performer. Artisoft LANtastic, however, wins the hands down vote for the budget-conscious or small group network shopper. LANtastic does not sacrifice much in power compared to the larger networks and has attractive RAM requirements.

The next chapter is the heart of this book. Chapter 8 describes how to configure AutoCAD for any network. First, you will learn the advantages and disadvantages of installing AutoCAD on a file server as opposed to on each workstation. Next, con-figuration options that are common to all versions of AutoCAD are presented with particular emphasis on network plotting and optimizing AutoCAD performance on a network. The chapter also shows you how to use AutoCAD Release 11's network-specific features, especially file locking and external plotting command links.

8

Configuring AutoCAD
for a Network

Once your network is up and running well, your next step in building an AutoCAD network is to install AutoCAD and configure it properly. To get AutoCAD to perform at its best on a network, you must exploit almost all of AutoCAD's configurable options. In the past, you probably skipped over these options when you configured AutoCAD on a stand-alone computer.

In this chapter, you will learn how to integrate AutoCAD almost seamlessly into a network environment. The following sections discuss AutoCAD installation options and performance issues, and explain general plotting procedures that can be used on any network. This chapter first examines the issue of whether AutoCAD should be installed on the file server or on each workstation, and then looks at AutoCAD installation concepts that are common to any version of AutoCAD. The chapter concludes with a discussion of AutoCAD Release 11's specific network features.

You should use this chapter as a guide to implementing AutoCAD on your own network. Although this chapter describes techniques that work with any network, they may not be ideal for your circumstances or the way you work. Wherever possible, the text covers most of the reasonable alternatives. If you already have an AutoCAD network, you should study this chapter for ideas that can help you further streamline your installation.

For the purposes of illustrating these configuration concepts, the DOS versions of AutoCAD are used in the examples in this chapter. The other versions of AutoCAD work similarly, with slight variations in the way environment variables and network drives are specified. See the AutoCAD *Installation and Performance Guide* for details on configuring AutoCAD to your specific platform.

Weighing Your Installation Options

You can choose from two basic methods of configuring AutoCAD and manipulating drawing files on a network. The method you choose depends on the type of network you have. On a network with a dedicated file server (such as Novell NetWare) you can run AutoCAD in either a *server-based* or *workstation-based* configuration. The method you choose determines where you install the AutoCAD program—on the file server itself, or on each individual workstation.

If you have a peer-to-peer network such as Sun NFS or Artisoft LANtastic, you probably would find it impractical in most cases to install AutoCAD in only one central location. In these cases, you should install AutoCAD on each workstation.

Your choice of configuration also depends on two management factors: your tolerance for risk, and the convenience with which the configuration can be managed. The following sections discuss server-based and workstation-based AutoCAD configurations, as well as the advantages and disadvantages of each.

Server-Based Configurations

In a server-based configuration, AutoCAD is installed only on the file server. That is, you specify a logical drive and directory on the file server when prompted during the AutoCAD installation program. You do not install the program at each workstation, as you would when the workstations stand alone, but you will use the same AutoCAD INSTALL program. The file server serves the program, drawings, symbols, menus, and other files to the workstations. The operating system, network shell files, device drivers, and configuration files are the only permanent files that need to reside in the workstations. The configuration files include ACAD.CFG for all platforms, plus the files ACADDS.OVL, ACADDG.OVL, ACADPP.OVL, and ACADPL.OVL for AutoCAD 286.

In a server-based configuration, the system must contend with many temporary files. After you learn how to create multiple configurations on a network, this chapter will show you how to create custom configurations that control temporary file placement for best performance. Figure 8.1 shows the network traffic between an AutoCAD workstation and a file server in a server-based configuration. The following sections show you how to control each of the configurable files.

The Advantages of a Server-Based Configuration

The server-based configuration offers several advantages. With only one copy of the program on the network, program files are more manageable. You can flag most program files as read-only to protect them from accidental erasure or other damage.

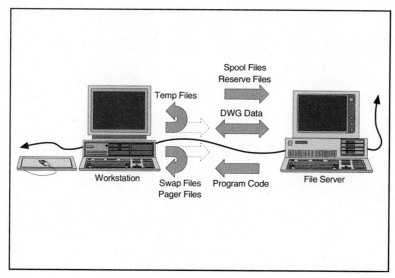

Figure 8.1:
Network traffic reduced by custom configuration.

A server-based configuration also simplifies software upgrades for your entire organization. When it is time to upgrade an application in a workstation-based configuration, you must move from one machine to the next, installing, configuring, and testing each one (which can take many hours, or even days in a large company). In a server-based configuration, however, you can install and test the new version in parallel (in a different subdirectory at the same directory and security level). When the configuration is complete, you can redirect users' menus and batch files to the new version of the program and then remove the old version from the system with minimal disruption.

Normally, to satisfy software licensing requirements, one copy of AutoCAD must be purchased for each workstation that will be using the software. In a server-based configuration, however, you must install only one copy. AutoCAD Release 11 is an exception and has a "floating" license requirement, which can actually save you from buying AutoCAD licenses. Complete details are explained later.

Configuring AutoCAD for Multiple Workstations

Normally, when AutoCAD is installed for a single user, you configure the program just once unless you make additional configurations for different hardware combinations. To configure one copy of AutoCAD for many workstations, you must create one set of configuration files (ACAD.CFG and possibly ACADDS.OVL, ACADDG.OVL, ACADPP.OVL, and ACADPL.OVL) for each user on your network. You still can have multiple configurations for any one user with different hardware combinations. In fact, you can have any number of configurations so long as only the maximum number of licensed users are active at one time.

To make each of these configurations with a single copy of AutoCAD, set the ACADCFG environment variable to the destination for each workstation's configuration files before you configure AutoCAD. This is done most easily in a batch file (such as ACADNET.BAT) that is used to launch AutoCAD on the network. This batch file can reside on the workstation's hard disk or in each users private directory on the network. A line pointing ACADCFG to a network directory might look like the following:

    SET ACADCFG=I:

In this example, drive I is a network drive letter corresponding to the user's home directory on the file server. When AutoCAD executes the batch file, the file server places the configuration file(s) for that workstation in the specified directory.

Instead of setting ACADCFG to a network drive, you also can set it to a directory on a hard disk on the workstation, such as ACADCFG:

    SET ACADCFG=C:\ACADCFG

Set ACADCFG from each remaining workstation to its own local drive and directory or network home directory and configure AutoCAD for that workstation. Each workstation also should have a batch file ACADNET.BAT that sets all necessary environment variables, loads any ADI drivers before executing AutoCAD, and unloads drivers after exiting from AutoCAD, according to that workstation's individual requirements.

For each configuration, however, the environment variable ACAD should remain set to the network drive where the AutoCAD program is located:

    SET ACAD=J:

In this example, J is a network drive letter corresponding to the directory on the file server where AutoCAD is installed. The variable ACAD helps AutoCAD find its support files on the network instead of the workstation's hard disk. See the AutoCAD *Installation and Performance Guide* for more on maintaining multiple configurations.

You will encounter several more DOS environment variables to set for AutoCAD as you continue in this chapter. At the end of this chapter, you will find a sample ACADNET.BAT that uses each of the variables presented in this chapter. You also will find tips on writing and running an ACADNET.BAT file of your own.

Managing AutoCAD 386 Swap Files on a Network

The Phar Lap DOS Extender for AutoCAD 386 can add another twist to the server-based configuration scheme. The DOS Extender uses the root directory of the drive containing ACAD.EXE as the destination for its *swap files* by default. A swap file is a type of temporary file that the DOS Extender makes to hold program code that it does not need at the moment, in order to make more RAM available. The DOS Extender makes two types of temporary files. The larger of the two is the swap file itself (400K by default), which holds pages of program code. This file is named according to the time AutoCAD is executed and therefore has a name made up of eight hexadecimal digits, such as 0B152638. The swap file has no extension. The DOS Extender also creates a swap reserve file (100K by default), which reserves disk space ahead of the actual swap file, to ensure that AutoCAD does not run out of swap space. The swap reserve file has the same file name as the swap file, but with the extension SWR.

Because only one copy of the ACAD.EXE program exists for all the users on a network, and because the program is installed on a network drive, the DOS Extender will try by default to create all users' swap files in the root directory of the file server volume. This is undesirable, however, for two reasons. First, the root directory of a server volume is generally off-limits to user files; users usually do not have the right (and, as a result, AutoCAD does not have the right) to create files in the file server's root directory. Second, because AutoCAD is executing in each workstation's RAM, swap files' traveling to the network drive unnecessarily add to network traffic.

The AutoCAD 386 package includes the program CFIG386.EXE. You can use this utility to modify the DOS Extender portion of the AutoCAD executable file for different memory and swap-file settings. Individual settings for these parameters are not saved in the ACAD.CFG configuration file, which holds the other hardware parameters. You can use CFIG386 in two ways to configure AutoCAD to send both swap files to the same directory on the workstation's local hard disk for better performance.

Configuring Swap-File Directories with CFIG386

First, you can create a directory on each workstation's hard disk to hold the swap files. In this example, that directory is called TEMP on drive C. Once that directory is created on every workstation, use the SWAPDIR switch to make each workstation send its swap files to its own TEMP directory. Using supervisor's rights, change to the network drive containing ACAD.EXE and invoke the utility, as follows:

```
I:\> CFIG386 ACAD.EXE -SWAPDIR C:\TEMP
```

Of course, you do not have to name the directory TEMP. If you use this redirection method, simply substitute the desired directory's name in the preceding syntax line.

This directory must exist on each workstation on the network before you execute AutoCAD, and the disk must have plenty of free space. The swap files' default sizes are only the minimums. Thus, each swap file and its swap reserve file will consume 500K (400K + 100K) when AutoCAD begins. As you edit more and larger drawings in a single session, the swap file will continue to grow as needed and may expand to many megabytes.

Second, each workstation can store its swap files in a different directory. You can set up this swap file scenario by taking advantage of the DOS Extender's "runtime" environment variable. By using an environment variable, you can, in effect, tell the DOS Extender to check with the DOS environment for the location of the swap file directory every time AutoCAD is executed.

To do this, you must first configure the DOS Extender in ACAD.EXE to use a variable like ACADSWAP, as follows:

I:\> **CFIG386 ACAD.EXE %ACADSWAP**

Next, use the ACADSWAP environment variable in ACADNET.BAT to specify the SWAPDIR switch string when AutoCAD is run. In ACADNET.BAT add a line:

SET ACADSWAP=**-SWAPDIR** *d:swapdirectory*

In this generic syntax, *d:swapdirectory* is the drive and directory where you want the swap files directed on the workstation. When the batch file executes, the SWAPDIR switch and swap directory are recognized by the DOS Extender *for that instance of the executable only* because it is executing in *that workstation's* DOS environment. Each workstation must have its own ACADNET.BAT with corresponding ACADSWAP settings. Optionally, you can use a shared ACADNET.BAT and specify the locations of individual swap directories by establishing another environment variable in each user's login script if your network uses them (provided that each user works at only one workstation).

Controlling AutoCAD 386 Code Paging with CFIG386

You can configure one other DOS Extender switch to improve AutoCAD's network performance. The NOPGEXP switch prevents AutoCAD from reading code pages over the network. Even though AutoCAD 386 is a single executable file and does not use overlays (as do the 640K DOS versions), it still reads its program code in pieces (pages) from the disk-based executable file as needed (often repeatedly). This technique frees RAM for drawing data, which in turn reduces the need to read paged drawing data from the disk. Performance is enhanced when most of the drawing data can be stored in RAM rather than paged from the disk, because byte for byte, AutoCAD usually can swap program code more efficiently than it can page drawing data.

On networks where AutoCAD is installed on a shared drive, however, this periodic reading of one executable file by many users results in frequent disk accesses and network traffic that should be avoided. You can redirect this traffic to the local hard disks so that it does not effect others on the network. You do this by configuring the DOS Extender to read the entire executable into the workstations' RAM and to swap code pages to the local drives along with the data pages it is already sending to the local drives. This option uses the NOPGEXP switch, as follows:

I:\> **CFIG386 ACAD.EXE -NOPGEXP**

The NOPGEXP switch cannot be set with a DOS environment variable, so you will have to use CFIG386 to modify ACAD.EXE if you want to disable code paging across the network.

Controlling CFIG386 with CFIGPHAR

In each of the preceding cases, CFIG386 modifies AutoCAD's executable file to use the parameters you specify at the DOS prompt. If you want, you can clear the changes you have made and restore the executable file's default settings by using the CLEAR switch and re-entering default values, as follows:

I:\> **CFIG386 ACAD -CLEAR**

I:\> **CFIG386 ACAD -MINSWFSIZE 400000 -SWAPDEFDISK -SWAPCHK OFF -INTMAP 8 -VSCAN 20000**

As you can see, however, this is quite a bit of typing to do on the DOS command line. If you misspell anything, an error will result.

You also can view the current switch settings for SWAPDIR and the other configuration switches by executing CFIG386 without any switches, as follows:

I:\> **CFIG386**

AutoCAD displays the settings as follows (your settings may vary):

```
Configured switch values:
     -minswfsize 400000
     -swapdefdisk
     -swapchk off
     -intmap 8
     -vscan 20000
```

But this, too, can be inconvenient. Alternatively, you can run the menu-based configuration utility CFIGPHAR.EXE, which presents you with the current settings and eliminates long command-line entries. CFIGPHAR is a *preprocessor* for CFIG386, which presents defaults and options in a menu-driven interface. When you have made all your selections for CFIG386's switches, the utility creates a batch file called CONF386.BAT, which you must run to execute CFIG386 and make the actual modifications (see fig. 8.2).

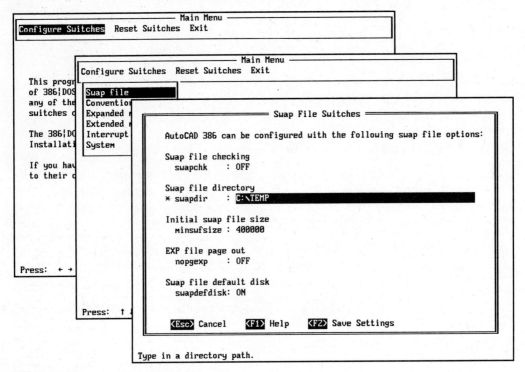

Figure 8.2:
The CFIGPHAR configuration utility.

See the AutoCAD *Installation and Performance Guide* for more information on running CFIGPHAR.

Managing AutoCAD 286 Overlay Files on a Network

In many situations, users start AutoCAD once a day and move from drawing to drawing. This means the AutoCAD executable file ACAD.EXE is loaded across the network rather than being loaded from a local hard disk. In most cases, the executable file does not take longer to load from the file server than from the local drive because network file access speed can exceed local file access speed.

This loading can be faster for two reasons. In the first case, most file server hard disks are faster than hard disks installed in workstations. Most networks can easily handle the output from these fast disks, so the network usually does not slow down the file between the file server's hard disk and the workstation's RAM. Also, remember that most server-based networks implement a large disk cache in the file server. Once ACAD.EXE is read into this cache by the first workstation, subsequent requests from workstations for ACAD.EXE will be read from the file server's cache, not from the hard disk. After the first transfer, therefore, the program basically is read from the file server's RAM to the workstation's RAM. Even if neither of these cases occurs, because ACAD.EXE is loaded infrequently, any traffic caused by loading ACAD.EXE is a small price to pay for increased network manageability and control.

The situation changes a little, however, if you use the 640K DOS version of AutoCAD, because this version of the program relies heavily on the use of overlay files. This version of AutoCAD loads a smaller ACAD.EXE into RAM, to preserve memory. When a nonresident portion of the program is needed, it is read from an overlay file on the disk. These overlay files should not be left in a shared AutoCAD directory and read repeatedly across the network as needed by different AutoCAD commands on multiple workstations. This arrangement can bog down even a high-performance network.

To hold down network traffic and maintain the server-based configuration, you can employ the same technique used by many stand-alone DOS users. At the start of a daily editing session, the user can download the overlays from a directory on the file server to a virtual disk at the workstation. The workstation can access overlay files more quickly from a virtual disk than from its own hard disk. Additional downloading time is required for these files only after power has been interrupted at the workstation. If you leave your workstations running continuously to minimize hard disk wear, then this is hardly a compromise. The only prerequisite is that each workstation must have enough RAM to fit all the overlays in a virtual disk (about 806K for Release 10, 945K for Release 11) in addition to memory needed to edit large drawings.

To accomplish this, create a subdirectory on the file server below your normal AutoCAD program directory. Give the new subdirectory a name such as \OVL and copy the following AutoCAD program overlay files to it:

    ACAD.OVL
    ACAD0.OVL
    ACAD2.OVL
    ACAD3.OVL

When the files have been copied into the new directory, delete them from the AutoCAD directory. Otherwise, AutoCAD will find the overlays there and will not search for them on the workstations' virtual disks.

Configure each workstation for a virtual disk of at least the combined sizes of the overlay files. If you have enough spare RAM, move ACADL.OVL and ACADVS.OVL to the OVL directory and increase the virtual disks to accommodate them, as well. These are the overlays for the AutoLISP interpreter and AutoCAD's message overlay file. Do not move ACADL.OVL if you use Extended AutoLISP. In any case, do not move the Extended AutoLISP gateway overlay ACADLX.OVL or the AutoCAD machine type overlay ACADM.OVL.

Next, if you are running AutoCAD Release 10 or an earlier version, place the new virtual drive letter (in this case, D) in the DOS path of each workstation that will use virtual disk overlays. This is the only way to get AutoCAD to look at the virtual disk because the environment variables point elsewhere: ACAD points to the shared AutoCAD network drive for menus, fonts, linetypes, and other files; ACADCFG points to the local directory that contains the AutoCAD configuration file(s), temporary and pager files (discussed later), and swap files. With Release 11, you can add the virtual disk to the ACAD environment variable "path" because Release 11 accepts multiple directories:

    SET ACAD=**J:;D:**

In this sample syntax, J is the network drive corresponding to the AutoCAD directory on the file server, and D is the virtual disk at the workstation.

Finally, go to the batch file that you use to launch AutoCAD, and add lines that test for the existence of the overlay files on the virtual disks. If the files are not found in the virtual disk, the batch file will copy them from the \OVL subdirectory to the virtual disk. The lines should look like this:

    IF NOT EXIST D:*.OVL ECHO Downloading AutoCAD overlays, please wait…
    IF NOT EXIST D:*.OVL COPY J:\OVL*.OVL D:

When configured this way, ACAD.EXE loads into local RAM from the network drive and begins to execute. AutoCAD first looks for its overlays in the current directory (preferably a drawing directory), then in the drawing directory if it is not also the current directory. AutoCAD then looks for its overlays in the directory(s) specified by the ACAD environment variable, where Release 11 finds its overlays. Release 10 then searches along the DOS path until it found its overlays. Any other file searches finally looks in the location of ACAD.EXE.

Coordinating Protected-Mode ADI Drivers

Real-mode ADI drivers are no problem in a network configuration. Simply load them as you normally would with ACADNET.BAT or AUTOEXEC.BAT. Protected-mode ADI drivers, however, require a trick.

A protected-mode ADI driver is a device driver that is designed to work in the processor's protected mode along with AutoCAD 386, which runs only in protected mode. A normal ADI driver, however, works only in real mode. When a real-mode ADI driver is used with AutoCAD 386. the processor must switch to real mode to service the ADI driver, and then back to protected mode for AutoCAD. A protected-mode driver allows the processor to remain in protected mode, resulting in better performance and, because there are no memory size constraints with protected mode, more features.

Unlike a real-mode driver, which is an executable EXE or COM file, the protected-mode driver (EXP) is loaded by AutoCAD when the program loads. The protected-mode driver is unloaded when AutoCAD terminates, releasing any memory it occupied. Normally, you place the EXP file in the same directory as AutoCAD, to help AutoCAD find the file. In a network configuration, however, you should not place the EXP driver file in the file server's AutoCAD directory unless several work-stations will share the driver file. If you install many assorted drivers in the AutoCAD directory, you may become confused when trying to determine which driver is used with which computer. Also, some drivers assume that you will have only one pro-tected-mode driver and they use the magic driver names that help AutoCAD find the drivers automatically. AutoCAD can use only one driver with each magic name, so you cannot install multiple drivers with magic names. See the AutoCAD *Installation and Performance Guide* and your driver's documentation for more on magic driver names.

Each workstation's drivers (for the mouse, video, virtual disk, and other compo-nents) should be installed on the workstation's local hard disk. This keeps the drivers from becoming mixed up with other drivers and also makes troubleshooting easier. When you load the drivers on the workstation rather than on the file server, however, you must let AutoCAD 386 know where to look for the drivers. To inform AutoCAD of a driver's location, use the following DOS environment variables in the ACADNET.BAT file for each workstation using a protected-mode ADI driver:

SET DSPADI=*d:\path\DisplayDriverFilename*

SET DGPADI=*d:\path\DigitizerDriverFilename*

SET PLPADI=*d:\path\PlotterDriverFilename*

d:\path\DeviceDriverFilename is the drive, path, and file name of the protected-mode ADI driver to load for the desired device.

Conclusions on Server-Based Configurations

Although you may need to spend some time configuring AutoCAD on a file server, your time will not be wasted. Most of the file redirection happens automatically once AutoCAD is configured. Other file activity is automated by the ACADNET.BAT batch file. In every case, you only have to set up the program once; it should work from then on. The alternative is to configure AutoCAD on a workstation-based network, which could cost you more in network manageability and control, as well as addi-tional AutoCAD licenses. This is covered in a moment.

Opponents of the server-based scheme argue that your installation is significantly more vulnerable to downtime because the whole workgroup must depend on one machine to keep working. If AutoCAD is installed only on the file server and the server goes down, no one can access the program. Further analysis, however, shows that the server-based configuration is no more vulnerable than the workstation-based scheme, for the following reasons:

- The file server *should* be the most reliable computer in your company. It should have the best hardware and the best power protection. Combined with the benefit of fault tolerance built into most network operating systems, your risk of downtime due to a file server failure is much less than that of a workstation failure.

- If the file server does go down, chances are that your drawings and libraries are on it anyway, so continuing stand-alone will not be of much use. This situation also is true, however, for workstation-based networks. To eliminate reliance on the network for drawing storage, you would need to eliminate the network entirely, along with its benefits.

- Most network plotters are connected to the file server. If the server goes down, no hard copies will be possible until it is restored. This situation is also true for most workstation-based schemes. Yet, as in a workstation-based network, a plotter still can be connected directly in a server-based network.

You must know your own needs, and weigh the pros and cons of application serving, if you want to determine whether the server-based configuration will work for you. If you have a small workgroup, a reliable file server, and enough extended memory to create a virtual disk (if applicable), and if AutoCAD is not a mission-critical application (requiring guaranteed 24-hour uptime) for your company, then you will find the server-based approach manageable and convenient. If you are ready to start setting up your server-based configuration, continue reading with the section titled "Common Configuration and Operation Techniques for All Versions of AutoCAD." Chapter 9 also offers practical information on server-based installations.

Workstation-Based Configurations

As the alternative to the server-based configuration, you can install AutoCAD on every workstation as if it were not networked, and use the file server only to store drawings, symbol libraries, menus, and AutoLISP files, and to share output devices. In a workstation-based configuration, your network-related configuration choices are fewer than they are if you use a server-based configuration. These choices will be limited to configuring a shared prototype drawing, a default plot file name, a spooler directory, network node names, or external plotting command links. No other special steps are needed. Each of these topics are discussed in the following section.

These configuration options are common to both the server-based and workstation-based schemes. Follow the directions according to the version of AutoCAD you are using. Server-based users should follow them, as well.

A workstation-based network offers the following advantages:

- Workstations are not dependent on the file server for AutoCAD, but only for data and output.
- The system is easier to maintain for CAD managers who are not comfortable with DOS and knowledgeable of AutoCAD's file-accessing habits.
- A workstation-based network may be easier to configure and maintain in large workgroups that use diverse hardware and operating systems.

As mentioned earlier, the workstation-based network's primary disadvantage is that every workstation must be treated individually, requiring considerably more time and energy than the server-based network.

Common Configuration and Operation Techniques for All Versions of AutoCAD

Until the appearance of Release 11, AutoCAD was merely "networkable." The program had several configuration options to help make it more cooperative in network environments, but Autodesk did not officially support the program's use with networks. Before version 2.6, which was introduced in 1984 (when local area networking became popular for PCs), AutoCAD had no network features at all.

Each of the network configuration features of AutoCAD version 2.6, Release 9, and Release 10 are explained in the following sections.

Whether your system is server-based or workstation-based, you should handle several procedures the same way for any configuration. The following sections describe steps you should take in configuring and operating AutoCAD regardless of the scheme you choose or version of AutoCAD you use. These steps include recovering from an AutoCAD 386 crash, configuring a shared prototype drawing file, making network plotting easy, configuring a default plot file name and plot spooler directory for automatic network plotting, and assigning network node names.

> **Note:** Beginning with Release 9, all AutoCAD binary files (DWG, HDX, MNX, SHX, SLD) and ASCII files (HLP, LIN, LSP, MNU, PAT, SCR, SHP) are compatible across all supported platforms without requiring any special configuration. This means that you can have a network with PCs running the 640K DOS version, AutoCAD 386, AutoCAD Xenix, Sun workstations, DEC workstations, and even Macintoshes, and they can share files.

AutoCAD drawing files are upwardly compatible, but they are not downwardly compatible. That is, a Release 11 user can edit drawing files that were created with Release 10, but once it has been edited by Release 11, the drawing no longer can be edited with Release 10. You can use a utility program to translate drawing or DXF files between versions. You will need to implement a translation procedure on your network if users will work with different versions of AutoCAD sharing files. See your authorized AutoCAD dealer for information on these translation utilities.

Recovering AutoCAD 386 Swap Files

When AutoCAD 386 (Release 10 or 11) crashes, it leaves the swap file and the swap reserve file (SWR) behind. Together, these "orphaned" files take up at least 500K of disk space; this abandoned space remains unusable until the files are deleted. If a drawing is being edited at the time of the failure, the drawing file also remains locked. Fortunately, these conditions are easily repaired.

If any swap files are orphaned because the workstation locks up or another type of sudden termination prevents AutoCAD from automatically erasing the files, then the files will exist only on the workstation's disk and will not dirty up the file server. When a crash occurs, however, AutoCAD does not reclaim the workstation disk space used by those files the next time you execute the program. Everyone who uses AutoCAD 386 on the network should understand that, if the program crashes, they should either delete the swap files from their hard disk or ask the network administrator to clean up the orphaned files.

Cleaning Up with CHKDSK

AutoCAD 386 also may leave unallocated disk clusters if AutoCAD crashes. These disk clusters were allocated to the swap file, but were not yet written to when the crash occurred. The only way you can tell is by using the CHKDSK command after a crash.

To reclaim the disk space occupied by a crashed swap file, run the DOS CHKDSK utility with the *fix* option, as follows:

    C:\TEMP> **CHKDSK /F**

Note that, in this example, the swap files have been redirected to a directory named TEMP, on the workstation's hard disk. After you issue the CHKDSK command, DOS displays a report and prompt similar to the following if any disk clusters were left by AutoCAD when it crashed:

    437 lost clusters found in 13 chains.

    Do you wish to convert the chains into files (Y/N)?

Your numbers will vary. If you respond **Y** at this prompt, DOS allocates the clusters to a file that can be deleted. Because the file is of no use, however, you can safely answer **N**; DOS frees the clusters for use by another file.

Caution: You should check with your CAD manager or system administrator before attempting to run CHKDSK on a network drive. Some networks cannot use CHKDSK.

Erasing Orphaned Swap Files

After you get rid of any unallocated disk clusters. You should eliminate any spurious swap and swap reserve files. At the crashed workstation's DOS prompt, delete any swap files from the swap file directory. To do this, you first will need to find the swap file's name. Use the DOS DIR command to view a listing of all files with no extension (remember that the primary swap file has only a hexadecimal file name with no extension), as follows:

C:\TEMP> **DIR *.**

The "star-dot" (*.) wild-card combination will display all file names in the current directory with no extension. This list should contain any orphaned swap files. It also will contain the names of any subdirectories of the current directory:

```
Volume in drive C has no label
Directory of C:\TEMP
ACAD11      <DIR>       2-28-91   9:21a
07351D05        397312   3-13-91   7:54a
        2 File(s)  23486464 bytes free
```

If AutoCAD had not started to swap data into the swap file when the crash occurred, the swap file will contain zero bytes but still use up space in the DOS file allocation table. You can refer to the files' dates and times to safely erase any swap files that you are certain are no longer in use. If you check for swap files on a workstation and AutoCAD is not running, then any swap files listed at this point are not being used and can be deleted. If you check for orphan swap files on a network drive, be certain that the swap file does not belong to an active user or that no one else is running AutoCAD, or you may delete their active swap files.

Similarly, you can use a wild card to view a list of orphaned swap reserve files, as follows:

C:\TEMP> **DIR *.SWR**

```
Volume in drive C has no label
Directory of C:\TEMP
```

```
07351D05 SWR   100000   3-13-91   7:53a
     1 File(s) 23486464 bytes free
```

You can safely delete swap reserver files the same way you delete swap files.

Unlocking a Crashed Drawing

As soon as possible after any AutoCAD crash, you should unlock the crashed drawing so that others can use it. You should be able to unlock the drawing from any workstation. Select Option 6, Unlock file, from the File Utility menu, and then enter the locked drawing file's drive, path, name, and extension (DWG). The original file name must be entered, not the lock file name. AutoCAD displays the login name of the user who was working on the file when the crash occurred, displays the time and date when the drawing was locked, and prompts you to answer whether you want to unlock the drawing file:

```
          AUTOCAD (R)
Copyright (c) 1982-90 Autodesk, Inc.  All Rights Reserved.
Release 11 (10/17/90) 386 DOS Extender
Serial Number: 117-10004482
EVALUATION VERSION — NOT FOR RESALE
Licensed to:   Ken Billing, New Riders Publishing
Obtained from: Autodesk, Inc. - None

File Utility Menu

  0.  Exit File Utility Menu
  1.  List Drawing files
  2.  List user specified files
  3.  Delete files
  4.  Rename files
  5.  Copy file
  6.  Unlock file

Enter selection (0 to 6) <0>: 6

Enter locked file(s) specification: GADGET.DWG

The file: GADGET.DWG was locked by Ken at 9:16 on 11/5/1990.

Do you still wish to unlock it? <N>
```

If you respond **Y** to the prompt, AutoCAD releases the drawing. You can use wild cards to unlock groups of files in a single operation. If the drawing file no longer exists for some reason, the lock file is essentially orphaned. You will, however, still be given the opportunity to proceed with unlocking the file, which will remove the lock file.

Sharing a Prototype Drawing and Menu

You may want to configure a prototype drawing if you elect to use a server-based or workstation-based installation. If you use a custom prototype drawing or menu, you will need to configure AutoCAD to use it for all workstations. This is true whether you have one copy of AutoCAD installed on the file server, or a copy installed on each workstation. Even if you do not change any of the settings in the prototype drawing, you will need to load any customized menu you may have into the prototype drawing so it will be the default menu for all your network users.

Start by creating a copy of the ACAD.DWG file and giving the copy another name. You should use a copy of ACAD.DWG in case you permanently want to revert to AutoCAD's default settings as your prototype drawing. Use a name for your copy of ACAD.DWG that will be easy to recognize as your prototype drawing. A form of your company name is a good candidate because the file will be recognized as a company-wide drawing.

You can use AutoCAD's defaults for any new drawing (while a different prototype is configured) by using the equal sign when specifying a new drawing name. To start a new drawing GADGET, for example, with AutoCAD's default settings, enter **GAD-GET=** as the new file's name. AutoCAD will recognize the equal sign and use its own defaults, which are stored internally.

If you have installed AutoCAD in a server-based network, leave the copy in the network directory containing AutoCAD. If, on the other hand, you have installed AutoCAD in a workstation-based network, move the copy to a network directory for shared AutoCAD files and make sure that all users have security rights to use the file.

Start AutoCAD from any workstation, using the ACADNET.BAT batch file you have made with the network-specific AutoCAD environment variables explained earlier. Edit renamed the copy of ACAD.DWG you made, setting any new defaults you want in effect for all new drawings, and use the Menu command to load the menu that you want every AutoCAD user to use. End the drawing so your changes are saved.

Then, from each AutoCAD workstation, start AutoCAD with ACADNET.BAT and select Main menu option 5, Configure AutoCAD. Choose option 8, Configure operating parameters, then option 2, Initial drawing setup. Enter the full drive, path, and file name of your renamed and edited copy of ACAD.DWG when the following prompt appears:

```
Enter name of default prototype file for new drawings
  or . for none <acad>:
```

Exit from the configuration menus, saving your configuration changes when prompted. The next time that workstation (and all others that you configure this way) executes AutoCAD, it should load the new prototype drawing and menu. You can make changes to your new prototype drawing (when it is not locked by another user) and they will be reflected every time a new drawing is begun with a network configuration.

Network Output Made Easy

Part of the awkwardness of using a general-purpose network operating system (such as the ones presented in this book) to support AutoCAD stems from the networks' lack of direct plotter support. They each have powerful printer-control facilities, including spooling and queuing, but they are designed for printing to printers, not plotters.

If you want to use these network printing features for plotting, you must use a little imagination and think of your plotter as a printer (at least as far as the network is concerned). These networks do not know the difference between a printer or plotter. They assume that every networked output device has basic printing capabilities. Generally speaking, these printer facilities do work well for controlling plotters. By taking advantage of some DOS and AutoCAD capabilities, you can make them perform like a dedicated AutoCAD network operating system.

> **Note:** This section uses the terms "print" and "printer" to remain consistent with network printing terminology. You may assume that they refer to plotting.

Normally, when you are logged into a network and print from within a network-aware application program, the output is directed to a temporary disk file (called a *spool file*) on the file server. This file is then assigned automatically to a printer *queue*. A queue is a list of spool files waiting to be printed. Each queue entry is spooled (transmitted), in turn, to the printer to which it is mapped (associated). The network operating system automatically erases the spool file when the print job is complete.

Redirecting AutoCAD Plotter Output

With single-user programs that do not recognize networked printers, a network command or utility usually is used to redirect output from the workstation's parallel printer port to a spool file and printer queue on the file server. This is the fundamental means by which you can adapt a network's printing facilities for use with plotters. A network output utility usually can intercept AutoCAD plotter output and redirect it to a network print queue.

> **Note:** Plotter drivers that perform hardware handshaking will not work with the technique described here because the driver does not directly communicate with the plotter. See the other plotting techniques described later, or try to configure your plotter without hardware handshaking.

These network output utilities unfortunately cannot redirect the serial port output that is used by most plotters. Parallel plotters, of course, are no problem. As a result, most networks offer no direct way to spool AutoCAD serial plotters.

You can circumvent these limitations by using the DOS file names for parallel ports—LPT1, LPT2, and PRN. DOS treats devices as though they are files. Because AutoCAD can plot to a file, you can substitute parallel device names for disk file names. Thus, you can simply tell AutoCAD to plot to a file, and then select the other plot parameters as you would if the plotter were connected locally. When prompted for the file name, enter **LPT1** or **PRN** if you have your network configured to intercept output there, or **LPT2** if you have a local printer connected to LPT1 and are redirecting printer output from LPT2. Do not enter a trailing colon (as in LPT1:) or the plot will abort. The network redirection utility or command should grab the plotter commands at the parallel port and redirect them to the same type of spool file on the file server that it creates with parallel printer output. It gives each file a unique name, protects it while it is being printed, and then deletes it when finished. In these respects, network printing is similar to the popular DOS plot spoolers used in non-networked installations.

To connect your serial plotter to the file server, just set it up as a serial printer according to your network's documentation; your network operating system will not know the difference. Configure the printer queue that is to receive your plotter spool files to send its output to the file server's serial port.

Sending Plot Files Manually

You also can perform network plotting by using AutoCAD's capability to plot to a file and then invoking your network's native print command. Most network operating systems have a command for printing from files instead of applications. This technique is similar to the use of DOS parallel port file names, except that you give the plot file an actual disk file name. The file should be sent to a directory set up on the file server specifically for plot files, such as \ACAD\SPOOL. This technique does not apply, of course, if you have a networked plotter connected to your local workstation.

After AutoCAD has plotted a drawing to a file, you must issue your network's print command from the command line. You can use the AutoCAD Shell command, or more conveniently, define a command in the ACAD.PGP file, such as the following:

NETPLOT,*command,memory,prompt,***0**

NETPLOT is the command you execute at the AutoCAD command prompt, *command* is your network's print command, and *memory* is the amount of RAM you need AutoCAD to set aside to run the network print command. If you want AutoCAD to prompt you for a file name to print, enter the prompt in place of *prompt*.

When you use this method, however, remember that the network does not automatically delete the plot file. You must delete the file yourself after it is plotted. Using your network's print command is approximately the same as assigning a spool file to a printer queue. This technique is handy if you want to keep the plot file until it can be plotted later; perhaps at night in a batch of files to a roll-feed plotter, or at some other designated plotting time.

You can plot a drawing to a file either on a network drive, or on a local hard disk. Preferably, however, you should maintain a directory on the file server dedicated to storing plot files, for two reasons. First, all plot files created by users should be directed to a network drive for easier management and monitoring. Second, program-to-device communications between your network print command and the plotter will then have to traverse only the serial channel between the network hard disk and the plotter. This is better than the same communications over the network cable, adding to overall network traffic, which would be the case if the plot file resided at the workstation. While the plot file has to be transmitted from the workstation to the file server in either case, it is usually faster to plot to the network drive because the plot data will go directly into the file server's disk cache first, which is faster than a local hard disk.

You may better understand how this works if you consider that the entire plot file transmission will take place in two phases no matter where the plot file is first created. The first phase occurs when AutoCAD writes the file to disk (either a network drive or a local drive). The second phase occurs when the network print command transmits the file to the plotter. By plotting to a file (the first phase), you save time because it is much faster than transmitting a plot file to a plotter (the second phase). This is why plot spoolers are so popular; they take care of the slower plot file transmission phase for you so you can go back to work. By sending the file slowly from the local hard disk to the network plotter (which will usually create an additional spool file anyway), you degrade network performance for the other users for a longer period of time.

Using Plot Spoolers on a Network

Plot spoolers work just as well for managing network plotting as they do for individual workstation plotting. The plotter, however, must be attached to a workstation or other computer (called a *plot server*) that can run the plot spooler program. A dedicated file server cannot run a DOS program, so a plot server must be set up. The plot server can be an AutoCAD workstation or an obsolete computer dedicated to transmitting plots and managing a plot file directory.

A plot spooler program handles the communication of the plot file to the plotter (this communication is handled by the network print command in the technique described in the preceding section). The only difference is that the plot spooler program works more automatically and gives you better control over your plots. Plot spooler programs are usually TSR programs that can send the plot file in the background while another program runs in the foreground. Most spoolers now recognize high drive letters, so they work well with networks. Some spoolers can even "watch" a directory for the appearance of plot files and automatically send them to the plotter. A plotter operator can load and maintain the plotter and manage the plotting sequence with the plot spooler.

If you already have printer server or queue management software that you use to supplement your network's printing facilities or setup printer servers for local printers, then you probably can use them to send plot files to local or network plotters. Think of a plot file as being any other printer file, and a plotter as being the same as a printer.

Automating Plotting with a Default Plot File Name

If you use a plot spooler or intend to use the plot file redirection technique described earlier, you can standardize your plot file names, make them identifiable, and make the process more transparent to the user by using AutoCAD's default plot file name feature.

AutoCAD normally offers the default drawing name as the default plot file name when plotting or printing to a file. This lets you accept the default, either from the keyboard or in a script, and each drawing will have a corresponding plot file. Instead of having the extension DWG, as the drawing file has, each plot file has the extension PLT. A print file receives the extension LST.

When you standardize file names for every plot file, you work at an advantage because certain plot spoolers can recognize certain file names. You can configure a plot spooler to monitor a spool file directory for plot files. The plot spooler directory should exist on the file server for the reasons described in the section on sending plot files manually.

AutoCAD recognizes the special default plot file name AUTOSPOOL (notice the nine characters, as opposed to DOS' eight-character limit) as its signal to assign standard plot file names and to use the plot spooler directory when it creates plot files. You also can enter **AUTOSPOOL** as the plot file name from the keyboard at plot time. The plot file names it assigns are based on the following three factors:

■ The output type. AutoCAD begins the file name with *V* (for vector) for files created for plotters, or *R* (for raster) for files created for printers. Your plot spooler should use the V and R to distinguish between files destined for a plotter or printer, respectively.

- The exact time the file was created. AutoCAD uses the current time to complete the file name. The remaining seven characters used to express the current time are in hexadecimal format, as used by AutoCAD 386 swap files.

- The workstation creating the file, established by AutoCAD's Network node name option, which is described later. AutoCAD uses the three-character node name to form the plot file's extension.

Thus, a plot file's name might be V3146940.WS1. If the same drawing were made for a printer, created at the same time and on the same workstation, it would appear as R3146940.WS1. The CAD manager can check the spool file directory periodically to see if any spool files are waiting to be plotted, and if so, when they originated. By using the file's date and time, you can determine when the files originated to aid in troubleshooting or resource management. Any file names that begin with a $, yet look like spool file names otherwise, are plot files that have not been completed because AutoCAD still is adding plotter commands to them. AutoCAD changes the $ to either V or R when the plot or printer plot is finished. Your plot spooler should ignore these files.

Note: As a general rule, AutoCAD uses the dollar sign in the file name or extension of all of its temporary files. Avoid deleting any of these files while AutoCAD is running.

When you use the plot file redirection technique, you can assign the DOS file name for a device as your default plot file name. Substitute the name, such as LPT1, for AUTOSPOOL at the Default plot file name configuration prompt. After you save your configuration changes, the DOS device file name will be the default for all subsequent plots made to files. Your network operating system will have to redirect the plotter output from the DOS device to its own printer spool file or AutoCAD will hang up when it does not find a real device at the port. You will, however, want to use this technique only when you desire to plot right away. No plot file will be available to send later or to transmit with a third-party plot spooler.

Assigning the Plot Spooler Directory

Used in conjunction with the plot file name AUTOSPOOL, the plot spooler directory lets you integrate AutoCAD with your own plot spooler program or network print command. You can save the name of this directory with the other configuration information.

AutoCAD offers a default directory name of \SPFILES for DOS systems and /usr/spool/acad for UNIX systems. You can give the directory any name, but a suggested file server directory name is one parallel to your AutoCAD working drawing directories, such as \ACAD\SPOOL. All AutoCAD users should be trustees of this directory with security rights necessary to create and write to files. The user managing the plot spooler will need security rights to search, open, read, and delete files as well.

The directory must exist before it is used, and it is a good idea to keep it cleared of other files and not to use a directory that is used for other files. If a file beginning with a V or R gets placed inadvertently in the directory, your plot spooler may try to send the file to your plotter or printer with undesirable results.

Placing Temporary Files for Best Performance

To enable you to edit drawings of unlimited size, AutoCAD must have a mechanism to deal with limited amounts of RAM. AutoCAD handles RAM limitations by temporarily placing unneeded data on disk to make room in RAM for frequently used information. AutoCAD uses some of these temporary files to store temporary data, but not in RAM. The other type of file, called a *pager file*, is for temporarily setting aside unused drawing data. Select option 5, Placement of temporary files, from the Operating parameters menu, to specify where AutoCAD will place both types of these temporary files. This can be advantageous to non-network users as well as those who are connected to a network. If you can direct these temporary files to the fastest possible disk medium, performance increases when AutoCAD has to transfer data to and from disk.

AutoCAD, by default, stores all temporary files in the same directory as the drawing. This is not desirable for networks where drawings reside on the file server because of the increased network traffic and resulting lower performance. Consequently, the network user should use this option to direct temporary files to a local drive with plenty of free space—at least twice the space required by the drawing being edited. You can use AutoCAD's Status command to check the amount of free space remaining on a temporary file disk. When configured to a directory other than the drawing directory, AutoCAD's Status command displays the free disk space in each directory.

If you can direct the temporary files to a virtual disk, AutoCAD's performance will be almost the same as if all the data were stored in RAM. If you can use a virtual disk, make it large enough to hold more than twice the expected size of the finished drawing. If you also want to place the drawing itself on the virtual disk, the disk should be at least three times the size of the drawing file to accommodate all the temporary files.

Even when you configure your system so that temporary files are directed to the local hard disk, some unconfigurable temporary files will continue to be written across the network. For AutoCAD 386, these will be pager files with names like AC$PG1.$AC. The file name is made up of the network node name (described in the next section) AC$ (by default), the letters PG (short for page file), a number indicating the order of the page file (1 in this case for the first page file), and the file extension $AC.

For AutoCAD 286, these unconfigurable files will be similar to AutoCAD 386's pager file and others used for different purposes. Their extension is always $A (note that this extension has two characters, rather than the three used by AutoCAD 386). The AutoCAD 286 temporary file, for example, that holds the current editing session's changes and will become the new DWG file is named AC$EF.$A. The file name is made up of the network node name AC$ (by default), the letters EF (short for entity file), and the extension $A.

Alternatively, if you have AutoCAD 386, you can use the AutoCAD 386 environment variable ACADPAGEDIR to tell AutoCAD 386 where to place its drawing page files. Add a line to ACADNET.BAT setting ACADPAGEDIR to the directory on your local hard disk, such as the following:

        SET ACADPAGEDIR=**C:\TEMP**

The directory \TEMP can be created on every workstation, or ACADPAGEDIR can be set in individual ACADNET.BAT files for each workstation to a different directory for more flexibility. Note that ACADPAGEDIR will override any setting made by configuring the Placement of temporary files option, so you can temporarily override the configuration if you need to.

Because they must be capable of ensuring that you can update the current drawing file, these pager and temporary files cannot be redirected. Also, never erase a pager or any other temporary file while you are working in AutoCAD or the program will crash. If you use high-quality network interface cards and disk subsystems, temporary file transfer should not pose a problem until a large number of AutoCAD workstations are active at the same time. Even then, temporary file traffic is no greater than the traffic created when many users access any large database. AutoCAD's own files are the only ones that should create traffic because of their size. Even these, however, can be fine-tuned.

Assigning Network Node Names

If several users attempt to edit different drawings in the same directory, the unconfigurable pager and temporary files from the concurrent AutoCAD sessions will have identical file names by default. Unless you assign unique names to each workstation, the multiple temporary files, although different for each user, will overwrite each other because they will have identical names. A *network node name* is a name used to identify each configuration of AutoCAD on the network. AutoCAD lets you give each configuration a unique name to use for the temporary files created by that configuration. If you install AutoCAD once on the network file server, you can set a network node name in the configuration file that resides on each workstation. If you install AutoCAD on every workstation, those configuration files should have a network node name assigned as well.

AutoCAD accepts a three-character string to use when creating file names for all the temporary files. If the workstation's network node name is set to WS1 (for workstation 1), AutoCAD 286 names its temporary entity file WS1EF.$A. AutoCAD 386, on the other hand, names its first pager file WS1PG1.$AC. The next workstation could be WS2, and so on, so that every workstation creates unique temporary files.

The network node name also becomes the extension for spool files if the AUTOSPOOL name is used. A plot file, therefore, created by this workstation with the AUTOSPOOL feature appears similar to V3146940.WS1. With this feature, you can tell not only the device type for which the file is destined, but when it was created and where.

Tip: To make file ownership easier to determine, you can set the workstation's node name to match the user's initials.

Release 11 Network Features

AutoCAD Release 11 includes the same network features of version 2.6 (Release 8), and Releases 9 and 10, plus many new features that address the network application prerequisites listed in Chapter 3. Autodesk now supports AutoCAD for networks, and this position has been awaited eagerly by those who have struggled with networking until now. The following sections discuss Release 11's network features and their suggested uses.

Server Authorization

When you purchase AutoCAD Release 11, you have the option of licensing it for one or more users. If you license your package for only one user, you may install the program on one computer for use by one person at a time. In a network environment, however, Release 11 can be installed on a file server and authorized for the maximum number of *concurrent* users, which may be less than the total number of networked computers. You will be charged the full price of a copy of AutoCAD for each user for which you request authorization.

If, for example, you have six AutoCAD workstations on your network, but only four of them use AutoCAD at the same time, you can license AutoCAD for four users in any combination at $14,000 (4 × $3,500 suggested retail price), and install it on the file server. Otherwise, you would need to purchase six copies of AutoCAD at $21,000 (6 × $3,500) and install them on all six workstations in order to give any four out users immediate access to AutoCAD at any given time. Optionally, you could have two users work at one of the four licensed workstations when the workstations are not being used by their primary owners.

By centralizing AutoCAD, as in the first scenario, you save the price of two copies of AutoCAD. In your situation, however, you may have to purchase an authorization for every workstation. Many AutoCAD dealers extend discounts for additional authorizations beyond the first seat even though Autodesk has no official tiered-site licensing policy. You also can extend your authorization at any time without performing an additional installation. If you need to authorize additional users, you must have supervisor-equivalent network security access to AutoCAD's program files.

If you install AutoCAD for more than one user, such as for the server-based configuration, you will be asked for a server authorization code at the end of the first configuration after installing AutoCAD. This code is an eight-digit hexadecimal number that identifies your AutoCAD package as having been licensed for a particular number of users. You also will need an Advanced Modeling Extension authorization code for the number of concurrent AME users. AutoCAD does not request the AME authorization code until you load AME the first time.

The first time you run AutoCAD after installing it, you are escorted through the usual initial configuration process for specifying the devices that AutoCAD will use. After you select a display device, pointing device, and plotter or printer, AutoCAD prompts for the first login name:

    Login name:
    Enter default login name or . for none <>:

This is the login name of the person who will be using the current configuration of AutoCAD (controlled by the ACADNET.BAT batch file, which was executed to begin AutoCAD). If you executed the ACADNET.BAT on your own workstation and configured AutoCAD to use the devices installed in your workstation, enter a login name as you wish to use it for starting AutoCAD. It does not need to be the password you use to log into the network. Login names are explained in more detail in the next section.

AutoCAD then presents a prompt requesting the maximum number of concurrent users for your AutoCAD package:

    Server Authorization
    AutoCAD's serial number is 117-10004482
    Enter the maximum number of users for this package <1>:

Your serial number will be different. Enter the number of users you wish to authorize, up to the maximum number for which you are authorized. The next prompt asks for the authorization code you received with your AutoCAD package:

    Enter server authorization code for this package <O>:

Answer with your eight-digit hexadecimal number. Configuration continues with a prompt about running AutoCAD from a read-only directory:

    Do you wish to run the executable from a read-only directory? <N>

Unless you have a 3Com network or another network that requires directories containing executable files be read-only, answer **N**. As the final step in server authorization, AutoCAD prompts for a password:

```
Enter a password to restrict unauthorized changes
to the server authorization or . for none <>:
```

If you are a CAD manager or other authority in your company, you may want to enter a password at this prompt. AutoCAD asks for this password any time an attempt is made to change the server authorization to add or subtract authorized users. AutoCAD cannot be re-authorized without the password. If you assign a password, make sure that the right people in your organization know where it can be found in your absence, or AutoCAD will have to be reinstalled. If you enter a period, no password will be required from any person who attempts to change your AutoCAD authorization. The number of authorized users is directly associated with the authorization code, so no one can add users without a new code from Autodesk.

All your server authorization information is then encrypted and saved in the login file ACAD.PWD. You should make a backup copy of ACAD.PWD before anyone logs into AutoCAD in case the original becomes corrupted or erased. You then can restore ACAD.PWD without having to go through the entire configuration and authorization process again.

Note: Do not make ACAD.PWD read-only. The file is updated with user login names as users execute AutoCAD. If you are running AutoCAD from a read-only directory, ACAD.PWD must reside in a read-write directory.

Changing the Server Authorization

In the future you may want to add users to your AutoCAD license. You will not need to buy additional software and reinstall AutoCAD, but you will have to pay for the additional users to receive a new authorization code for your existing installation and receive additional manuals for the new users.

You can enter your new authorization code by selecting option 11, Server authorization and file locking, from the Operating parameter menu. Change your server authorization number only when no other users are executing AutoCAD. AutoCAD responds by displaying your current server authorization information:

```
Server authorization:

Your current server authorization is 9DEB49E5

The maximum number of users for this package is 3

The AutoCAD executable resides in a read/write directory.
```

WARNING: This information should only be changed while no other users are currently executing the program.

Do you wish to change it? <N>

Your numbers will vary. Enter **Y** to update your authorization. AutoCAD repeats the authorization steps you originally went through and gives you an opportunity to change the server authorization password if you want to.

AutoCAD Login Names

AutoCAD now requires the user to enter a login name before accessing the Drawing Editor, whether the workstation is networked or not. Logging in to AutoCAD does not log the user in to a file server; rather, AutoCAD uses the login only to track the number of active users against the authorized number, for associating lock files with a particular user, and for creating unique temporary file names in shared directories. A default login name is first set during the personalization process of initial installation and is entered as the license holder, which is probably your company's name.

You can change the default login name to a user name by selecting option 10, Login name, from the Operating parameters menu. If more than one person will use a single workstation, a single period (.) should be entered that will cause AutoCAD to prompt for a login name each time the program is invoked at that workstation.

If no default login name is set during the configuration, the user, when entering the Drawing Editor, is greeted with a dialogue box that contains the default login name, and which accepts a new login name of up to 30 characters. A check box is provided to save the login name as the default in ACAD.CFG, so that the dialogue box need not be completed each time the same user enters the Drawing Editor. The normal text editing functions are available for editing the string before clicking on the OK button (see fig. 8.3).

If fewer than the maximum number of licensed users are logged in, the login will be successful. If the maximum number of users are already logged in, AutoCAD tells the user that he is not allowed to proceed:

Login Failed: The maximum number of users has been reached.

Try again later.

Press RETURN to continue:

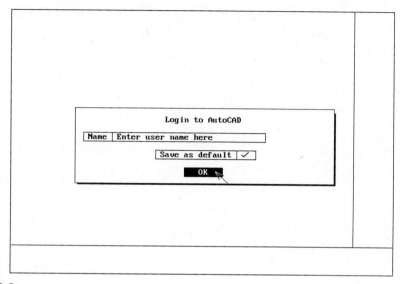

Figure 8.3:
AutoCAD's login dialogue box.

Note: If AutoCAD terminates abnormally (whether it is installed at the workstation or not), the number of active users (known by AutoCAD) is not decreased. This can result in an apparent shortage of user authorizations depending on how many people were logged into AutoCAD when the termination occurred. If the maximum number of authorized users were active when the termination occurred, then the next attempt by a user to log into AutoCAD (other than the one who was using AutoCAD when it crashed) will be denied access.

If you log back into AutoCAD under the same login name, you will cause AutoCAD to recover the user authorization. The user may then continue the session or make the authorization available to someone else by exiting AutoCAD. If recovering the authorization is not possible (because the user is not present, or the password is not known), the ACAD.PWD file may be deleted and restored from your backup copy (while no one is logged into AutoCAD) to release all authorizations.

File Locking

AutoCAD now provides built-in file-locking capabilities, to prevent users from over-writing files that are already in use. If AutoCAD is authorized for only one user, you can toggle file locking on and off by selecting option 11, File locking, from the Operating parameters menu. If you have installed AutoCAD as a server, this option is called Server authorization and file locking. File locking is on by default. You cannot disable file locking when AutoCAD is configured as a server.

To perform the locking, AutoCAD creates a 128-byte lock file for each lockable file opened during a session. Before opening any file, AutoCAD determines whether a lock file exists for that file. The lock file identifies the login name that was used when the file was locked, and records the time when the file was locked. The lock file's name is made up of the original file name, but the file-name extension's last character is changed to *K*. Most files are locked only while the file is being read or written, but drawing and temporary files are locked for the entire drawing session. Table 8.1 lists the files AutoCAD locks by extension, the associated lock file extension, and the conditions during which it will be locked.

Table 8.1
AutoCAD Release 11 File Locking

File Type	Lock File Type	Conditions
ADT	ADK	When creating an audit report file
BAK	BKK	When creating a backup file as a result of the End or Save command
CFG	CFK	Configuring AutoCAD
DWG	DWK	While in the Drawing Editor with a new or existing drawing
DXB	DBK	Reading a DXB file with the Dxbin command
DXF	DFK	Reading a DXF file with the Dxfin command
DXX	DXK	Writing a DXF file with the Attext command's DXF option
FLM	FLK	Writing a filmroll file with the Filmroll command
IGS	IGK	Reading an IGES file with the Igesin command
LIN	LIK	Reading or writing a linetype file with the Ltype command's Define option
LST	LTK	Writing a printer plot file with the Prplot command or from Main Menu option 4, Printer Plot a drawing
MNX	MXK	Reading or writing a compiled menu file with the Menu command or when entering the Drawing Editor
OLD	OLK	Renaming a drawing file during conversion from an older version with Main Menu option 8, Convert old drawing file

Table 8.1—continued

File Type	Lock File Type	Conditions
PLT	PLK	Writing a plot file with the Plot command or from Main Menu option 3, Plot a drawing
PRP	PRK	Writing an ADI printer plot file with the Prplot command or from Main Menu option 4, Printer Plot a drawing
PWD	PWK	Updating the login file
SHX	SXK	Writing a compiled shape or font file with Main Menu option 7, Compile shape/font description file
SLD	SDK	Displaying a slide file with the Vslide command
TXT	TXK	Reading an attribute extraction template file
XLG	XLK	During Xref Attach, Detach, and Reload
$AC	$AK	While in the Drawing Editor with a new or existing drawing

Table 8.2 lists files that are not locked when accessed.

Table 8.2
Files Not Locked

File	Description
BK*n*	Emergency backup file
HLP	Help file
HDX	Help index file
LSP	AutoLISP program file
MAT	Materials file
MSG	Message file
PAT	Hatch pattern file
PGP	Program parameters file
SCR	Command script file
SHP	Shape and font definition source file
SLB	Slide library file
UNT	Units file

Each lock file is created in the same directory as the file that is locked. This may result in many lock files being sent over the network, but at 128 bytes each, the overhead should not be noticeable. Also, each user will need appropriate privileges for every directory that may receive a lock file even though the user may never actually change any files.

Note: If you have several copies of AutoCAD sharing files on the same network, you should configure all copies of the program alike, so that file locking is either on or off.

Nonlocking copies recognize locked files opened by locking copies. Locking copies, however, still can open and save to unlocked files opened by nonlocking copies. Locking copies also lock out nonlocking copies besides overwriting any changes.

You should not run earlier versions of AutoCAD on the same network with Release 11. Any drawing files created by earlier versions that are then edited by Release 11 will become incompatible with the earlier version. You then will need to perform some translation in order to use an earlier version of AutoCAD with that drawing again.

Rather than using the more secure method of file locks at the operating system level, Autodesk implemented these file locks in AutoCAD Release 11 to maintain compatibility in mixed network environments. All platforms of AutoCAD recognize the same file locks. Unfortunately, AutoCAD's lock files are *not* foolproof. Files manipulated by ADS or AutoLISP, for instance, are not locked.

Tip: Autodesk recommends that you provide each user on your network with their own copies of any AutoCAD menu files (MNX) that you use. Users can place these files in their own network directory or on their own hard disk. Menu files are locked only while AutoCAD reads the menu at the beginning of a session, after creating a plot or printer plot, or when you explicitly load it with the Menu command. A single menu file may be shared, however, provided that the menu source file is not compiled while the menu is in use. File contention caused by simultaneous attempts to load the same menu files may become a nuisance on larger networks. This contention may happen when many users are trying to load the menu at the same time, such as first thing in the morning or right after lunch. You may want to provide individual compiled menus if contention causes problems.

In order for files to be completely safe, file security must be handled by the operating system, which itself allows or denies access to files. Instead, AutoCAD's file locks are recognized only by AutoCAD. Files locked by AutoCAD still are vulnerable to intentional or accidental operations performed through DOS or any other DOS file utility.

You should use a network drawing manager to help protect your drawings, use AutoCAD's File Utilities or Files command for copying, renaming and erasing files, disable DOS shells wherever appropriate, and make maximum use of your network's file security.

Note: If you use your network's file attributes to make any drawing files read-only, such as shared symbols, details, or prototype drawings (including ACAD.DWG), AutoCAD will alert you with a message when the drawing is opened for reference or plotting:

WARNING: That file couldn't be opened for writing due
to "Access denied error".

The warning means that AutoCAD cannot open the file with write privileges or make the old drawing into a backup file. You still can bring the drawing into the Drawing Editor for reference or plotting, but you will not be able to save any changes you make. If you attempt to do so, AutoCAD displays the following message:

Drawing file is write protected.

To make changes to a read-only drawing, you must remove the read-only restriction or make a copy of the drawing with another name and make the copy read-write. Avoid making files read-only on a by-user basis. Users with read-write privileges can overwrite drawings opened by read-only users.

Working with AutoCAD File Locks

If a user attempts to access a file that is locked by another user, AutoCAD suspends the current operation with a message such as the following:

Waiting for file: J:GADGET.dwg.

Locked by Ken at 3:26 pm on 03/12/91.

Press Ctrl-C to cancel.

If the user does not want to wait for the file to become available, and needs to perform some other operations, he can press Ctrl-C and return to the Main Menu or the command prompt, depending on where the file request was made. If the user wants to wait for the file, as would be the case with a menu file (MNX) that is accessed momentarily, AutoCAD repeats the message 12 times before denying access, and the user is returned to the point of file request:

Access denied: J:GADGET.dwg is in use.

Press RETURN to continue:

A user should not wait for a long time or repeatedly attempt to access a drawing file that already is in use. A file-sharing violation error, reported by DOS, can result if the file's current owner attempts to save the file while another user has a request pending for that file:

    Share violation error reading drive A directory information
    Retry, Fail ?

The designation of drive A occurs because DOS does not recognize network drive letters. Answering **R** causes DOS to retry saving the file until the requesting user stops trying to access the file. Answering **F** causes AutoCAD to save the file with the extension SV$. Any changes can be misplaced easily because the file will need to be renamed to be used:

    File could not be renamed J:GADGET.dwg.
    It is saved under the name J:GADGET.sv$.

If the file becomes available before the access attempt is denied, the operation will resume. Lock files are deleted automatically whenever a file is released. See the section titled "Unlocking a Crashed Drawing" for more information.

External Reference Files

Although *reference files* are not specifically a network feature, they have more potential on a network than on stand-alone workstations. An external reference file is a drawing file that you can make appear within another drawing strictly for reference purposes (see fig. 8.4). Reference files are used in much the same way as normal AutoCAD blocks, but a reference file's actual drawing data remains in its original file and is not imported into the referencing drawing. You can snap to the reference file's geometry, and control the file's visibility by layer, but you cannot edit the reference file itself from within the referencing file.

A civil engineer's drawing of a building site, for example, can reference the actual building plan, which is maintained by the architect. If the architect changes the size or shape of the building, the changes will appear automatically in the civil engineer's drawing the next time the engineer loads the reference file. The architect's changes, however, are not highlighted, and the engineer has no other indication that any changes have been made. Both drawings can exist on a file server (in a server-based or workstation-based network) or on another workstation (in a peer-to-peer network).

Reference files enable several people to work on a complicated drawing, each of them contributing different parts that can be combined to create the final drawing. If any part needs to be changed, only the individual part drawing needs to be updated, and every other drawing that references that part will be updated the next time it is loaded. Reference drawings themselves may contain other reference drawings, or be "nested" at several levels.

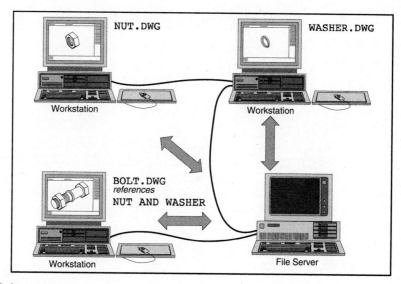

Figure 8.4:

An example of AutoCAD external reference files.

If a reference file is moved or erased inadvertently, AutoCAD displays the following message when it tries to load the reference file into the current drawing:

    **Error resolving Xref filename

If the file is not found and reattached, only a notation of the file's name appears in the drawing, and the reference file's data will be unavailable to the drawing that referenced it.

External Reference File Locking

AutoCAD external reference files are drawing files that are the same as any ordinary drawing, and are subject to AutoCAD's file locking when they reside on a network. AutoCAD, however, opens reference files only long enough to read them into the current drawing, in much the same way as it treats blocks. The AutoCAD file lock also exists only for this period of time. A fundamental difference, therefore, between active AutoCAD drawings can be summed up in two rules:

- You may edit or reference a drawing that someone else is referencing.
- You may not edit or reference a drawing that someone else is editing.

If you edit a drawing that someone else is referencing, you may save your changes. Other users, however, cannot update their references until you exit from the drawing because the reference drawing will be locked (by you). They then can see the changes by invoking the Xref command's Reload option.

Linking AutoCAD to External Plotting Commands

AutoCAD Release 11 DOS versions now have a way to combine the default plot file name and an ACAD.PGP command with two new environment variables to make network plotting transparent and automatic without extra software. These features have been in Release 10 versions on other platforms, but have only now made it to the DOS platforms. This facility works well especially with the DOS PRINT or COPY commands, or NetWare's NPRINT command within a batch file. The environment variables are ACADPLCMD and ACADPPCMD. They use a special replaceable parameter (%%S) to represent the current spool file name and "hook" into the operating system to permit background plot transmission. You can use ACADPLCMD for plots created with the Plot command or Main Menu option 3, Plot a drawing, and ACADPPCMD for plots made by Prplot or Main Menu option 4, Printer Plot a drawing.

With AutoCAD configured for a default plot directory and the plot file name set to AUTOSPOOL (as described earlier in this chapter), you need to add the appropriate environment variable settings for ACADPLCMD or ACADPPCMD in ACADNET.BAT similar to the following:

SET ACADPLCMD=VELLUM_D %%S

In this example, ACADPLCMD passes the name of the last spool file created through %%S to a batch file named VELLUM_D. The batch file would receive the plot file name and pass it on to NPRINT through the DOS %1 replaceable parameter:

NPRINT %1 /P=2 /J=3 /F=1 /NB /D

This batch file executes a network print command, such as NPRINT for NetWare, with the necessary switches to plot the spool file only with a print job definition used for vellum media and D-size extents. See Chapter 7 for more information on setting up NetWare print jobs.

Next, open the ACAD.PGP file and create an entry for each external plotting link. The following sample releases 24K of memory and executes the batch file VELLUM_D without prompting for a file name:

VELLUM_D,VELLUM_D,24000,,0

Now, any time the AUTOSPOOL plot file name is used, AutoCAD vectorizes the drawing into plotter commands and sends them to the plot file directory with a unique name, according to the parameters explained earlier in this chapter. When the plot file is complete, the external command specified by the environment variable ACADPLCMD or ACADPPCMD (and enabled by ACAD.PGP) is executed and passed the plot file name through %%S. AutoCAD lets the command (in our example a batch file containing a network print command with other parameters) execute (possibly in the background), and program control returns to the user. All this happens without requiring input from the user, and AutoCAD calmly responds:

    J:\SPOOL\filename.ext is currently being printed

> **Note:** This technique does not work with real-mode ADI plotter or printer drivers, and may not work with earlier protected-mode ADI plotter or printer drivers. If it does not work with your protected-mode driver, contact your plotter vendor for an update.

The Complete ACADNET.BAT

Many of the configuration choices in this chapter were implemented by setting AutoCAD environment variables to tell AutoCAD how to work when it is run. To pull all these variables together for you, an example of a complete ACADNET.BAT file follows. You can use it as a checklist for your own ACADNET.BAT, modify it, or place the commands at the end of your AUTOEXEC.BAT. Whatever method you use, be sure not to add any trailing spaces at the end of each line or you may have problems. Always end each line immediately after the last character by pressing Enter.

You may need to expand your DOS environment size for a batch file with this many variables. If you receive the error message: Out of environment space when you execute ACADNET.BAT, you will need to include a line in your CONFIG.SYS file to enlarge the default DOS environment from 160 bytes:

SHELL=C:\COMMAND.COM /E:256 /P

This example expands the DOS environment space to 256 bytes. If you continue to get DOS error messages, increase this amount until they subside. If you keep COMMAND.COM in a different directory, substitute it in the example above. See Appendix A for information on the ENVLIST utility included on the *Managing and Networking AutoCAD Disk* that can help you fine-tune your DOS environment space. See your DOS reference manual for more information on the SHELL command.

A Sample ACADNET.BAT

```
rem Create a logical drive mapping to your network's
rem AutoCAD directory first, or place it here.

rem Use this section only if your network has no way
rem of appending network drives to the DOS path.
set OLDPATH=%PATH%
path=J:;%PATH%
```

```
rem Saves the current DOS path while you run AutoCAD
rem Substitute your network AutoCAD drive for J:

set ACADCFG=C:\TEMP
rem Substitute your configuration file directory for C:\TEMP

set ACADSWAP=-SWAPDIR C:\TEMP
rem Only needed for AutoCAD 386
rem Substitute your swap directory for C:\TEMP
rem You must configure ACAD.EXE for ACADSWAP with CFIG386 first.

set ACAD=J:;J:SUPPORT;J:AUTOLISP
rem Substitute your network AutoCAD drive for J:
rem Use additional directories for supporting files such as
rem symbol libraries, external reference files, and AutoLISP.

set DSPADI=C:\SYS\ADIDISP.EXP
rem Only needed for AutoCAD 386 protected mode ADI drivers
rem Substitute your driver directory for C:\SYS
rem Substitute your driver name for ADIDISP.EXP if needed
rem Repeat as necessary for DGPADI or PLDADI

set ACADPAGEDIR=C:\TEMP
rem Only needed for AutoCAD 386
rem Substitute your pager directory for C:\TEMP

set ACADPLCMD=C:\SYS\SPOOL %%S
rem Substitute your external plotter utility directory for C:\SYS
rem Substitute your external plotter utility name for SPOOL
rem Repeat if necessary for ACADPPCMD

set ACADALTMENU=J:\3RDPARTY\AWESOME.MNU
rem Only needed for swapping tablet menus with pick X25
rem See the AutoCAD Installation and Performance Guide and
rem the AutoCAD Reference Manual for more information
rem Substitute your alternate menu for J:\3RDPARTY\AWESOME.MNU

acad %1 %2
rem Start AutoCAD, passing any command line arguments for a
rem drawing name and script name as replaceable parameters

path=%OLDPATH%
rem Restore the DOS path if you saved it above
```

```
set OLDPATH=
set ACADCFG=
set ACADSWAP=
set ACAD=
set DSPADI=
set ACADPAGEDIR=
set ACADPLCMD=
set ACADALTMENU=
rem Clean up the environment for other programs when done
```

If any of these variables' meanings are unclear to you, review the appropriate sections earlier in this chapter.

Summary

The process of configuring AutoCAD for a network can be a complex task. The trouble will be worth it, however, when you begin to see how easy it makes your other workgroup management tasks.

In this chapter you have learned the fundamental differences between configuring AutoCAD on a server and using the file server only to share files. You learned how to configure one copy of AutoCAD to serve many users without their individual files' getting in the way of each other. You also learned how to make a prototype drawing and menu file shareable by many users who are running AutoCAD on their individual workstations. The configuration options that are common to all AutoCAD versions were shown in this chapter, as well as Release 11's new network features.

In the next chapter, you will find out how to build on the last two chapters to make your AutoCAD network even more manageable. You will learn how to manage Sneaker nets (in case you do not have a network yet), how to put the centralization of a server-based network to best use, how to make network security organization easier, and how to make your network easier for your users to work with by installing a network drawing management program.

Part Three

Managing the AutoCAD Office

Network Management Techniques

AutoCAD Management Methods and Economics

System Maintenance and Development

Managing AutoCAD Users

9

Network Management Techniques

The term "network management" is hard to define. Basically, it is the job of keeping the conglomeration of network hardware, software, and cable working efficiently. Some days, the job's biggest challenge can be as simple as plugging in a loose cable. At other times, however, network management can involve days of complicated troubleshooting. The process can include daily disk maintenance, security maintenance, or complete network reconfiguration. The network manager's job description can include an almost endless list of duties that collectively equal doing whatever it takes to keep the network running with minimal or no downtime.

This chapter looks at some of the concepts you can apply to help make management of your CAD resources easier and eliminate the network as an excuse for unsatisfactory production.

Managing AutoCAD without a Network

Even if you decide not to connect your AutoCAD workstations with a physical network, you are in fact operating a network of sorts. That is, your users are organized together for similar, if not identical, purposes and they share common goals. They should be communicating and sharing information and resources in much the same ways as physical networks do. Network management in workgroups without physical interconnection, however, requires more discipline than does a formal network. The formal network facilitates much of the control itself through built-in security and other structures.

261

Without an electronic connection between computers and peripherals, users are forced to deliver files and messages to one another personally, usually on floppy disks. Because its users must run back and forth from one station to another, this old-fashioned system often is called a *sneaker-net*. AutoCAD workgroups have used this type of system for years, and it is the reason for many of their problems.

Peripheral Sharing without a Network

When properly managed, a sneaker-net can effectively serve the needs of several users, even in an AutoCAD workgroup. But when the group grows to more than four users, the need arises for a faster, safer way to share files and peripherals. Indeed, the need to share peripherals (plotters, in the case of AutoCAD) is often the primary reason that managers investigate the possibility of creating a network. Unless management is willing to invest in a plotting station or peripheral-sharing cabling scheme, users may find it impossible to share a pen or electrostatic plotter if they are separated by an appreciable distance. With a little more investment, peripheral sharing (enhanced with automatic spooling, high-speed transmission, and queue management), file sharing, security, and communications capabilities also can be gained. But not every company has the capital or the justification for a network. For them, and many other unique business scenarios, a sneaker-net must suffice.

Without a real network, peripheral sharing must be accommodated in one of three ways:

- By installing a cabling system with manual or automatic data switches to connect each computer alternately to a printer or plotter

- By installing a dedicated or nondedicated computer or other device as a plotting station to send hand-delivered plot files to a connected plotter

- By physically moving and directly connecting the plotter from computer to computer as needed

None of these solutions calls for an inordinate amount of management, only the right hardware and some common sense.

Managing Personal Communications without a Network

A sneaker-net requires that interpersonal communications be conducted through old-fashioned but time-honored means—notes, memos, intercom system, water cooler, and personal interruptions. You can do little (and should not have to do much) to manage these types of communication. In a non-networked environment, however, the concern is that not enough of the right kind of information sharing, coordination, and updating is happening the way it should. A network can make possible (and even enforce) adequate communications and messaging that makes use of your users' time and efforts more efficiently.

File Sharing without a Network

File sharing in a sneaker-net environment can be a nightmare if not effectively managed. If only one or two people are working on a project, they can easily swap files with little confusion. The scenario changes, however, when multiple users are working on several projects, especially if the workers operate at different levels or in different shifts. The confusion over responsibility for files can result in multiple and often disparate copies of files, incomplete backups, lost revisions, or even lost files.

Typically, these failures occur like this: a file begins life on one workstation, either by creation or exchange from another department or company. Inevitably, someone else needs to change the file, so it is copied onto that user's workstation, and he edits the drawing. Meantime, changes can still be made to the original as it resides on the first workstation. If either file is copied to the other workstation without having its name changed, someone's work will be overwritten. Who is responsible for seeing that the files are backed up? If the wrong copy is backed up and later restored to another workstation, the problem has spread. If you consider the number of users and files on the system at any given time, you can understand why file sharing can be a problematic process.

Some sneaker-net users manage the sharing of files by relying on the *Golden Disk* or *Master Disk* strategy. This system permits only one authorized copy of every file. The copy may reside on the hard disk of a designated workstation operated by the project leader or CAD manager, or on a secure diskette, possibly with one diskette for every file. Admittedly, this is not a very cost-effective use of diskette storage space, but considering the low cost of diskettes and the alternative of mismanagement, the advantages may justify the cost. If the file is located on a hard disk, it will be easier to back up along with other files. Backing up dozens of individual diskettes is an inconvenient chore and off-site backups are not likely to be maintained.

The diskette system works best for library files, such as standard details. Because these files seldom change, they are easy to maintain on floppy disks. Standard details also can be inserted into a drawing from a floppy disk more easily than symbols, which are needed more frequently. Further, detail drawings (which may be used only once per project) are not good candidates for permanent storage on a hard disk because they require so much disk space. Symbol libraries, on the other hand, because of frequent access and menu programming, do not lend themselves well to the Golden Disk system from a practical standpoint. These files need to be maintained across all workstations, but one authorized master copy still should be the goal, with immediate updating of workstation files should any changes be made to the master copy.

Working copies of drawing files may be made only from the Golden Disk. If the Golden Disk is a diskette, the user must "take possession" of the diskette as long as changes are being made to the file. When he is finished with the file, the user copies the file back to the diskette and stores it in an approved location. From this location, the Golden Disk may then be "checked out" by someone else. Appropriate measures should be taken to ensure that the original file cannot be changed until it is overwritten by the updated copy from the user who checked it out. Another way to protect the copy is to set the file's attributes as read-only or hidden after copying, and restore them when the authorized copy is returned.

In any case, a Golden Disk system requires strict compliance in order to succeed. If an unauthorized copy of the file is used to make hard copies for checking or approval, or is transferred to the Golden Disk, the system fails. Although file dates and times can help in tracking the most recent version of the file, they cannot be of help when more than one copy of the file has been changed. File sizes are not an accurate indicator either, because a changed file can be either larger or smaller than the original file.

Regardless of the system of file sharing you use for your sneaker-net, it requires close observation, management, and the full cooperation of everyone involved if it is to be successful.

Monitoring Network Performance

With an electronic network, you must carefully monitor network performance to ensure a high level of system responsiveness. As the load placed on the network grows, system response may slow slightly. System load can increase as existing users gain more comfort and expertise with the network and make more demands on it, and again as new users are added to the system.

Many new network managers fail to monitor network performance and become discouraged when network performance begins to decline. They become frustrated because, as the network grows, users begin to complain about how slow the network has become.

> ***Note:*** Because networks come in many different varieties, it is almost impossible for this book to tell you how to monitor your own specific (and, in many ways, unique) network. And because every network is different in the way it is used, the habits of its users, their expectations, the company's budget, and the company's needs, it is equally difficult for one book to tell you how to upgrade your network's performance when the time comes. Suffice it to say that you need to monitor your network's performance the best you can, however that may be. This book only can provide you with some basic suggestions.

Benchmark test results and network usage statistics provided by the network operating system or third-party management utilities can aid the CAD manager in forecasting network degradation. With this information, management can formulate an upgrade or configuration strategy ahead of time to ensure that system response keeps up with the demands of the users. Check with your network dealer or user group to see how other network managers monitor their networks and the means they use to judge their system's performance. Many of the network-related periodicals listed in Appendix D contain regular columns and feature articles on network performance.

When time comes to upgrade, it may consist of purchasing duplexed hard disks, faster drives or network cards, a better or additional file server, or an upgrade for the network operating system. The solution to your network performance problems depends on where your network bottleneck is. Your network dealer should be able to help you identify the network bottleneck and suggest remedies.

A common example of one way to improve performance on the typical Ethernet network is by splitting one network into two smaller network segments. Ethernet networks usually start out small and grow into one large network. This causes performance to decrease as the network grows. You can split the network by installing two network cards in the file server, creating two network segments where only one existed before (see fig. 9.1). You then can reconfigure the network operating system to recognize the new segment. The new card may be a different type than the first, letting one server support two different network segments. Your single file server, for example, can support both a Token Ring segment and an Ethernet segment. You can set up each segment to meet different needs within your company; the Ethernet segment may serve your CAD department, for example, while the Token Ring segment serves the company's administrative office.

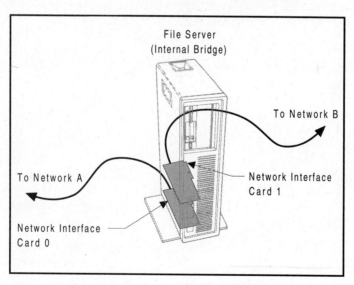

Figure 9.1:
Dividing a network to improve performance.

You can divide any type of network into smaller subnetworks to bring network performance back to the level it was when the network was small. The key to managing your network's growth and performance, however, is consistent monitoring.

To help you create a history of network performance, a performance benchmark utility is provided on the *Managing and Networking AutoCAD Disk*. This utility is the Novell PERFORM3 program designed and used by Novell to test the *throughput* rate of Novell networks. Throughput is a measurement of the volume of data transferred over time from one or more network nodes to the server in the writing and reading of files. For more information on PERFORM3, refer to Appendix A.

Organizing Network Security

Network security procedures, along with network configuration, help you control and manage your network. Without adequate network security, your network not only becomes vulnerable to intrusions, but also can become unwieldy. The CAD manager or network supervisor should be responsible for network security. Even if you are not directly responsible for the network, you still should understand network security because it may effect the way you configure and operate AutoCAD.

Each network operating system implements network security in its own way. Further, your networking needs determine the manner in which you handle network security. Still, to manage network security successfully, you must administer protection at each of the following three levels:

- Physical security
- User identification
- File access

The following sections briefly examine these aspects of network security.

Physical Security

You achieve physical security in basically the same manner for both formal networks and non-networked systems ("sneaker nets"). By limiting personnel access, maintaining secure diskette storage strategies, and using the key lock provided on most systems, the CAD manager can eliminate most criminal activity or mischief on the network.

Your company already may enforce restrictions on personnel access. These restrictions may determine who has keys to the office, the days and hours people may get into the office, and sometimes even security personnel. If your company used supplemental security for its paper drawings before CAD, you should consider extra security for your AutoCAD system. Lock away diskettes, tapes, and other media.

You can secure workstations with the key lock if your machines have them. Some companies use security devices that prevent theft of the entire computer.

These methods are all right against criminal acts, but by taking advantage of network technology, the CAD manager can further limit the casual mischief and accidental security breaches that interfere with or even cripple the system's operation.

User Identification

Password security is your second line of defense; every network has some form of password-protection scheme. Every user should be assigned a unique password, and should have to use the password to gain access to the system. If you allow the users to select, maintain, and protect their own passwords, however, passwords may be misused or neglected. Unless the CAD manager takes a systematic approach to establishing and maintaining password protection, unauthorized access to the network cannot be prevented. Your network operating system may have password-maintenance features that can force each user to have a password, force passwords to be changed regularly, establish minimum password lengths, limit login attempts, and lock out user accounts after too many invalid access attempts. Check your network's documentation for your network's password features and enable those features that seem appropriate for the amount of user identification your workgroup needs.

By assigning a unique network password to each user, the CAD manager can make sure that passwords do not consist of users' names, nicknames, or names of relatives. Although users can easily remember such "personalized" passwords, unauthorized entrants to the network can easily guess them. You should assign passwords that are not easily associated with their assigned users, and that will be difficult for an unauthorized user to guess. Again, check your network documentation for any restrictions it places on passwords for total length and allowable characters.

A good way to create difficult passwords is to form them from multiple, random words, such as the system used by the CompuServe Information Service. Initial CompuServe passwords combine two random words that are joined by a random punctuation character, such as SANCTION&CHEESE or PARANOIA^MANNER. You can easily create such passwords by opening a dictionary, closing your eyes, and pointing at the page. The word under your finger becomes part of a password.

> **Tip:** Assign new passwords every month, and make sure that all users understand that network security is for their own good. Your system's users must understand that they should not divulge their passwords to other users. If users want to access other users' computers or files, they should use their own passwords or discuss the matter with the CAD manager, rather than exchanging passwords.

File Access

In a workgroup environment, files seem to propagate almost endlessly. Security at the file-access level, however, is probably the most difficult to maintain of all the network security levels. Nevertheless, the CAD manager must assign network file and directory rights to limit users' access to certain types of files and directories. This task is much easier if the manager maintains well-organized groups of users with equivalent rights, and designs the file server's directory structures to make files as self-protecting as possible.

Controlling File Access by User Groups

Many popular networks let you manage users by grouping them according to their file-access needs. Even if your network does not provide for user groups itself, you can use groups of user names on your own to help you organize the security features the network does have.

As you set out to establish user groups within your organization, examine the needs of each user who will need access to the server's files. Then categorize the users according to security requirements. Only one or two people, for example, need unlimited access to files, those being the CAD manager and the network supervisor (if the CAD manager is not also the network supervisor) or a trustworthy alternative CAD manager. These two people constitute the group of users at the supervisor security level.

Your company's AutoCAD users usually need equivalent access, including the following:

- READ and WRITE access to project drawings
- READ access to details, symbols, menus, and AutoLISP functions
- EXECUTE access to applications
- READ and WRITE access to application temporary and configuration files
- No access to system files

Everyone else, such as clerical personnel and users-in-training, may need only a subset of the AutoCAD users' rights.

By establishing a security template for each level of network user, the CAD manager can quickly and consistently apply security to users at different levels as needed. A security template is a list of network user groups, the users in each group, and the rights they are granted at each security level. The security levels may be at the directory level or the file level, or both. The template may be only on paper as a record of your file security plan, or implemented in software through your network's security features. If a security change needs to be made, it needs to be made only to one section of the template, and the effects will apply to all users who have equivalent rights. A simple security template might resemble table 9.1.

**Table 9.1
A Sample Security Template**

Directory Group	Supervisory Users	AutoCAD Others	All
APPS\ACAD11	Unrestricted	Execute	None
PROJECT*	Unrestricted	Read-Write	None
APPS\LIB*	Unrestricted	Read-Only	None
APPS\LSP	Unrestricted	Read-Only	None
APPS\SPOOL	Unrestricted	Read-Write	None

Your directory and security structure may look different. To add security protection to a new directory, you can set security restrictions for the group of AutoCAD users for that directory and it will be effective for all its members.

Controlling Network Security by Directory Levels

You can further simplify network security management by structuring the file server's directories so that they control file access. In table 9.1, notice how user security is consistent at the third and fourth directory level. If you organize network security by directory level and plan network directories with security in mind, you and your users can keep track of current network security without much hassle.

You should place system files only in the root directory and in first-level directories. The designated network supervisor and CAD manager have unlimited access to this level. AutoCAD users need only enough access to facilitate normal network operation.

Second- and third-level directories are available to AutoCAD users only on a "need-to-know" basis. Applications programs should reside at this level, along with protected files for symbols, menus, details, prototypes, and AutoLISP libraries.

Fourth-level directories should be provided for work-in-progress and personal files. Typically, every user needs more relaxed access to directories at this level. You probably should not bother to nest directories beyond five levels; this is usually unnecessary and difficult to maintain. By allowing users to have write and create rights at the third and fourth level only, you isolate the areas to which they can cause either intentional or unintentional damage (see fig. 9.2).

The CAD manager's power to control user access is a serious responsibility and should not be abused. The CAD manager may be tempted to make the network overly secure, thereby making it difficult for the users to gain authorized access to the files they need.

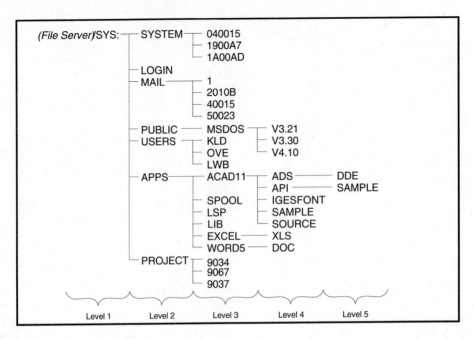

Figure 9.2:

Security layers can correspond to directory levels.

The User's View

Another important goal of effective network management is not to intimidate or bury the AutoCAD user with complex management and security procedures. If the user views the network as being overly complicated and frustrating to use, he will resist the CAD manager's efforts to promote the network and will need more hand-holding and support.

To avoid this type of user reaction, the manager should try to make the network as transparent to the user as possible, with the goal of not requiring the user to know anything about the network itself. For example, you can create batch and script files to automate repetitive and complex logins, path mappings, directory switching, program execution, and egress.

Automating Session Setup with Login Scripts

Network login scripts give you one way to exercise control transparently, logically, and with little effort. Only a few lines of commands are needed to make intelligent decisions that affect every user. Consider, for example, the following portion of a

NetWare login script. This single script establishes network drive mappings for all three of the user groups listed in table 9.1:

```
REM Greet the user by name
WRITE "Good %GREETING_TIME, %LOGIN_NAME."
REM Conceal drive mappings from displaying
MAP DISPLAY OFF
REM But show any errors
MAP ERRORS ON
REM Set up drives to system directories for all users
MAP INSERT S1:=SYS:PUBLIC
REM Test for user SUPERVISOR
IF LOGIN_NAME = "SUPERVISOR" THEN MAP *1:=SYS:SYSTEM
REM Test for AutoCAD users and set them up with personal
REM directories, network AutoCAD directory in their path, shared
REM support directories, and shared drawing directories
IF MEMBER OF "CAD" THEN BEGIN
MAP *1:=SYS:USERS\%LOGIN_NAME
MAP INSERT S2:=SYS:APPS\ACAD11
MAP *2:=SYS:APPS\SPOOL
MAP *3:=SYS:APPS\LSP
MAP *4:=SYS:APPS\LIB
MAP *5:=SYS:PROJECT
REM All others can have further statements beginning here,
REM and they will not have access to AutoCAD
```

By using a login script such as this one, you can make individual user login scripts shorter or even unnecessary. Look for similar ways to automate user network logins in your network software.

Using Batch Files To Control User Movement

Network management can tax your comprehension of batch file and operating system usage. Time spent on perfecting this automation logic will pay off in a more reliable and more fully automated system. By using batch files, you can put little-used capabilities to good use for network control. In the initial network design phase, for example, the CAD manager should determine whether to make attachment to the network a requirement or an option for each workstation. If the network is considered an integral part of the workstation, then the network connection and login sequence should be placed within each computer's AUTOEXEC.BAT file. The following batch file lines prevent the user from cancelling a batch file during boot up, and automatically log the user into a NetWare network. You could place these or similar lines in your own AUTOEXEC.BAT or other network login batch files:

```
REM Turn off command echoing
@ECHO OFF
REM Redirect standard input from the keyboard to the nul device (none)
CTTY NUL
REM Load the NIC interrupt driver
IPX
REM Load the network shell program and attaches to the network
NET3
REM Switch to the first network drive (your network drive letter may vary)
F:
REM Restore input to the keyboard so the user can log in
CTTY CON
REM Execute the LOGIN utility
LOGIN
```

In this example, the user, while logging in to the network, cannot drop to DOS and circumvent the network management efforts controlled through menus or other means. This technique makes good use of DOS' capability to redirect standard input and output. Thus, the Ctrl-C or Ctrl-Break combinations are useless to stop the process. A batch file can be used any time to enforce network security or management. You can use the same technique in any batch file to make sure that users follow assigned procedures.

Tip: Use a good menu system to conceal your batch processes from the user. Most network operating systems include a good menu interface for the selection of programs and tailoring of the network session. Third-party developers produce excellent menus that go beyond those provided with the operating system and add features that are unavailable from the network vendor. Some third-party menu systems, for instance, enable the system supervisor to disable menu exiting, which further enhances security.

Making Network Output Easier

The CAD manager should not underestimate the convenience of automating the output process with the techniques described in Chapter 8. Users notice everything management does to streamline peripheral selection. Your users probably are accustomed to having direct access to output peripherals. Contention over output, especially in an AutoCAD environment, can be extremely frustrating. If the output bottleneck was bad before you set up the network, do not substitute it for anxiety over peripheral setup procedures; automate them wherever possible with batch files and other techniques. Integrate output parameters in your batch files and add menu system submenus if necessary to make peripheral management easier.

Taking a Look at Network Drawing Management Programs

The remainder of this chapter examines two network drawing management programs: AutoBASE by Cyco International and Drawing Manager by Nehalem Bay Software, Inc. Such programs can help you manage your AutoCAD drawings on shared network drives. You install one of these programs on your file server, and all users access the drawing management program before invoking AutoCAD from within the management program.

Each network drawing management program maintains its own database of drawing information, independent of AutoCAD. The program places a layer of security between the user and AutoCAD, filtering user requests for drawings through its own database and security facilities. All network AutoCAD users must use the drawing management program, however, for the program's security features to be effective. Users who do not run the program can easily get around the security schemes and cause file-sharing problems.

The programs described here are only two representative examples of network drawing management programs. This information is presented only to show you what a drawing management program can do for you, and to explain some of the features you should look for. Many other such programs exist—each with its own personality and features. The key to selecting a drawing management program is to find one that works as you do. The more intuitive the program's operation is, the easier it will be for your people to use it and to take advantage of its features.

AutoBASE

AutoBASE is perhaps the most ambitious product to come from registered Autodesk developer and network integrator Cyco International. AutoBASE is basically the bigger brother to Cyco's already-popular AutoManager program. AutoManager was one of the first AutoCAD drawing-viewing programs on the market. AutoBASE provides AutoManager-like facilities to network users.

AutoBASE creates a database of information about your network drawings and enables you to access the database through a paradigm that works in much the same manner as a Rolodex. That is, each drawing on your network has an index card. The card can contain all sorts of information about that drawing, including the drafter's name, the project's name, discipline, revision number, and so on. AutoBASE can keep track of the dates an AutoCAD drawing was created, last changed, and the elapsed time spent in the Drawing Editor. AutoBASE also maintains network information, such as the availability of the current drawing, the name of the user who is currently working on a file, and amount of time a user has had a drawing checked out.

To access an AutoCAD drawing, the AutoBASE user selects the card for the desired drawing. AutoBASE displays textual information for that card on-screen, and provides a fast graphical display of the drawing file (see fig. 9.3). From within AutoBASE, the user can launch AutoCAD and go directly into the selected file. AutoBASE locks the drawing card while the drawing is in use, preventing other users from working on the same drawing while the first user has it open.

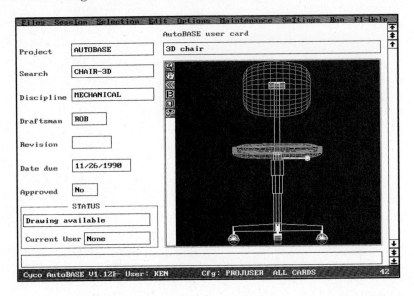

Figure 9.3:
AutoBASE displays drawing files tracked within its database.

To create a new AutoCAD drawing, the user first gives AutoBASE required information about the new drawing. AutoBASE then starts AutoCAD with the name entered in the AutoBASE card. AutoBASE cards easily can be added, edited, and deleted at will.

The AutoBASE Field-Path Relation

AutoBASE maintains relationships between data stored in a drawing card and the location of the drawing on the network. Relationships are set between drawing card data items called *fields* and portions of the drawing's path. In AutoBASE, this is called a *field-path relation*. Through AutoBASE, you can change either one and AutoBASE will reconcile the other so that they still relate.

Suppose, for example, that you create a network directory structure with a directory named PROJECT as the parent of many other directories. These subdirectories are named with project numbers and contain drawings for individual projects, such as 9034, 9035, and so on. AutoBASE can create a field-path relation between the project numbers in a drawing path (such as \PROJECT\9034\9034A201.DWG) and a data field for the project number on the drawing's card (PROJECT # = 9034). If a user begins a new drawing for that project and specifies the project number on the drawing's card, then AutoBASE stores the drawing in the appropriate directory automatically without further user intervention. Similarly, you can import existing drawings into AutoBASE and have AutoBASE draw information from the files' locations to fill in fields on the drawings' new database cards (see fig. 9.4).

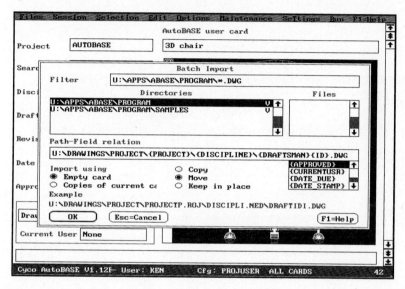

Figure 9.4:
Importing drawings according to a field-path relation.

Alternatively, you can export one or more AutoBASE drawings for use elsewhere, or for archiving. AutoBASE makes the drawings unavailable to other users. The actual drawing files can be copied, moved, or left in place.

Searching an AutoBASE Database

Because your database of network drawings easily can grow to thousands of individual files, AutoBASE enables you to find drawings in several ways.

Browsing with the Viewer

The easiest way to find a drawing is to use the AutoBASE graphic display to browse through drawings until you find the drawing you are looking for. This method is especially useful if you do not know the name or data field information of the drawing you need. You can quickly step through AutoCAD drawings and AutoBASE displays each one in a graphics window. As soon as you determine that you do not need the current drawing, you can step to the next drawing, quickly scanning many drawings in seconds. The AutoBASE viewer has viewer commands for zooming and panning, and viewing named views saved within AutoCAD. You also can control AutoCAD block and layer visibility within the viewer.

Viewing the Database as a List

If you know what information is contained in a drawing, you can browse through the entire AutoBASE database. This method is faster than viewing individual drawings, but does not enable you to view the drawings themselves. Rather, you view the entire AutoBASE database as a list (see fig. 9.5).

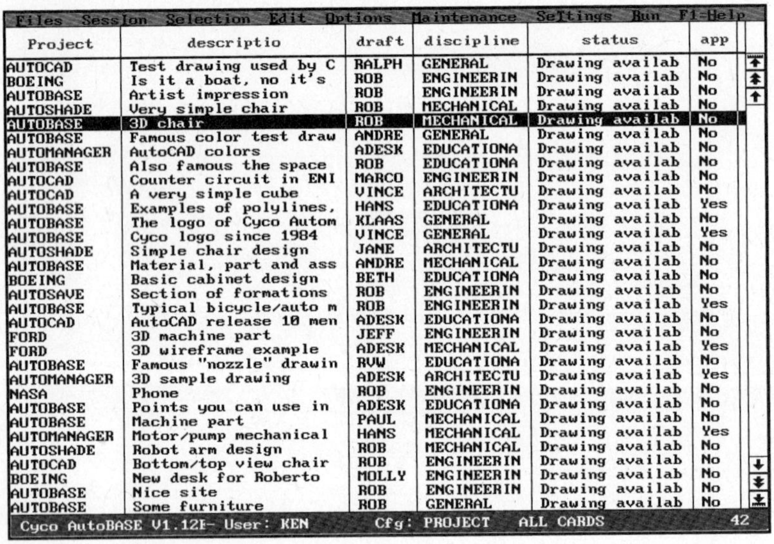

Files Session Selection Edit Options Maintenance Settings Run F1=Help

Project	descriptio	draft	discipline	status	app
AUTOCAD	Test drawing used by C	RALPH	GENERAL	Drawing availab	No
BOEING	Is it a boat, no it's	ROB	ENGINEERIN	Drawing availab	No
AUTOBASE	Artist impression	ROB	ENGINEERIN	Drawing availab	No
AUTOSHADE	Very simple chair	ROB	MECHANICAL	Drawing availab	No
AUTOBASE	3D chair	ROB	MECHANICAL	Drawing availab	No
AUTOBASE	Famous color test draw	ANDRE	GENERAL	Drawing availab	No
AUTOMANAGER	AutoCAD colors	ADESK	EDUCATIONA	Drawing availab	No
AUTOBASE	Also famous the space	ROB	EDUCATIONA	Drawing availab	No
AUTOCAD	Counter circuit in ENI	MARCO	ENGINEERIN	Drawing availab	No
AUTOCAD	A very simple cube	VINCE	ARCHITECTU	Drawing availab	No
AUTOBASE	Examples of polylines,	HANS	EDUCATIONA	Drawing availab	Yes
AUTOBASE	The logo of Cyco Autom	KLAAS	GENERAL	Drawing availab	No
AUTOBASE	Cyco logo since 1984	VINCE	GENERAL	Drawing availab	Yes
AUTOSHADE	Simple chair design	JANE	ARCHITECTU	Drawing availab	No
AUTOBASE	Material, part and ass	ANDRE	MECHANICAL	Drawing availab	No
BOEING	Basic cabinet design	BETH	EDUCATIONA	Drawing availab	No
AUTOSAVE	Section of formations	ROB	ENGINEERIN	Drawing availab	No
AUTOBASE	Typical bicycle/auto m	ROB	ENGINEERIN	Drawing availab	Yes
AUTOCAD	AutoCAD release 10 men	ADESK	EDUCATIONA	Drawing availab	No
FORD	3D machine part	JEFF	ENGINEERIN	Drawing availab	No
FORD	3D wireframe example	ADESK	MECHANICAL	Drawing availab	Yes
AUTOBASE	Famous "nozzle" drawin	RVW	EDUCATIONA	Drawing availab	No
AUTOMANAGER	3D sample drawing	ADESK	ARCHITECTU	Drawing availab	Yes
NASA	Phone	ROB	ENGINEERIN	Drawing availab	No
AUTOBASE	Points you can use in	ADESK	EDUCATIONA	Drawing availab	No
AUTOBASE	Machine part	PAUL	MECHANICAL	Drawing availab	No
AUTOMANAGER	Motor/pump mechanical	HANS	MECHANICAL	Drawing availab	Yes
AUTOSHADE	Robot arm design	ROB	MECHANICAL	Drawing availab	No
AUTOCAD	Bottom/top view chair	ROB	ENGINEERIN	Drawing availab	No
BOEING	New desk for Roberto	MOLLY	ENGINEERIN	Drawing availab	No
AUTOBASE	Nice site	ROB	ENGINEERIN	Drawing availab	No
AUTOBASE	Some furniture	ROB	GENERAL	Drawing availab	No

Cyco AutoBASE V1.12E- User: KEN Cfg: PROJECT ALL CARDS 42

Figure 9.5:
Viewing the AutoBASE database as a list.

From the list, you can get a broad overview of the database and pick out candidate drawings for viewing. You can adjust the list so that it shows data from any of the fields that AutoBASE tracks. You also can adjust the width of the database's columns. Still, this method may be inconvenient if you know specific information from any of the AutoBASE fields.

Keyboard Index Searches

Each database can contain several different indexes, which sort drawing cards according to one or more database fields. For example, you can have an index for projects, discipline, or an arbitrary search field that you design within a card configuration. One index is active at all times. You can search through the active database index simply by typing the known field entry. AutoBASE matches the characters you type with the current index's entries. This method lets you browse through drawing files with the same index entries or quickly home in on a particular drawing that has a unique index entry (see fig. 9.6).

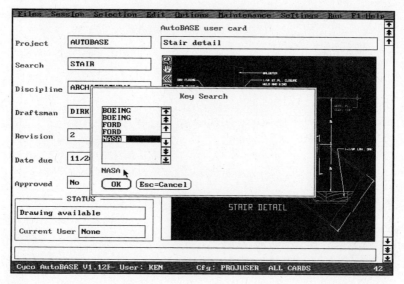

Figure 9.6:
Searching the project index by keying in field entries.

AutoBASE Selection Sets

AutoBASE lets you build selection sets of drawing cards in much the same way AutoCAD lets you build selection sets of drawing entities. You can compile an AutoBASE selection set in four ways.

The first and easiest method is just like picking single entities for an AutoCAD selection set. You can add individual drawing cards to a selection set as you browse through the database while using any of AutoBASE's search methods. When you are finished selecting cards, you can have AutoBASE make your set of drawing cards the current selection set for further review.

The second method utilizes simple text searches for a character string within any of AutoBASE's fields. The string can be part of a word, an entire word, or multiple words that occur in any visible field (see fig. 9.7).

When AutoBASE concludes its search, the number of active drawing cards is reduced to only those that satisfy your text search. You then can browse through the drawings visually, use a different search method, or refine your search.

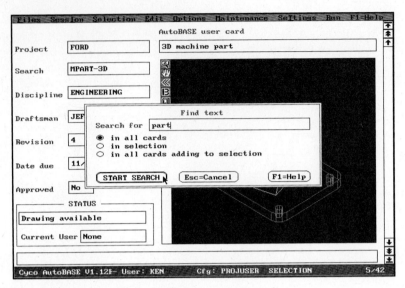

Figure 9.7:
Performing a simple text search on all cards.

The third search method involves specifying a search string within one or more particular drawing card fields. This method lets you be less generous with the number of cards you are willing to accept (see fig. 9.8).

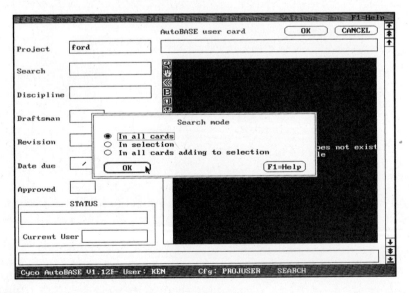

Figure 9.8:
Performing a text search confined to a specific field.

The resulting drawing cards will contain fields that match your selected search strings.

The fourth search method enables you to be very logical and precise in the way you match search values. For any visible field, you can search according to various predefined criteria. Figure 9.9 shows the different criteria built into AutoBASE for this type of search.

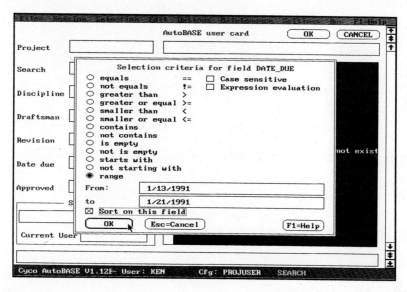

Figure 9.9:

Searching a field according to logical criteria.

This method is especially helpful when you must conduct a search based on variable data, such as dates and ranges.

AutoBASE Configuration Files

AutoBASE enables you to create different configurations of AutoBASE data within a drawing card for different classes of AutoBASE users or different purposes. In this sense, an AutoBASE configuration is not a configuration of hardware devices, but a configuration of information that is presented to the user—the card's layout, if you will. The figures so far in this section show a typical user card configuration. You also can have a supervisor's card configuration to display more information about drawing files and AutoBASE users (see fig. 9.10).

AutoBASE also accepts other card configurations for other uses. You can load any configuration at any time, and the AutoBASE screen updates to reflect the changed layout. You will learn how to create AutoBASE configuration files a little later.

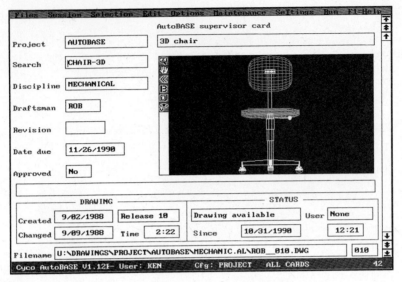

Figure 9.10:
A supervisor configuration for an AutoBASE card.

AutoBASE Extras

AutoBASE has several features that go beyond mere drawing selection and tracking. Most of these functions make AutoBASE easier to use, and enable the CAD manager to manage drawings more easily.

Printing Reports

You may, at times, want to keep a hard copy of your database information about drawings. AutoBASE lets you print configurable reports from database field data to a local printer, network printer, or a print file. A report can contain information for a single card, a selection set of cards, or the entire database. Report layouts are created by a designated AutoBASE supervisor.

Controlling Users

AutoBASE requires that you set up user accounts for all persons who use AutoBASE. You can manage login names, assign passwords for security, establish network or local drive paths for temporary files, and view a user's login status (see fig. 9.11). If a user has crashed while in AutoBASE, you can log him out again.

For additional security, you can limit access to any AutoBASE function to users, the supervisor, or both (see fig. 9.12).

If a user is not permitted access to a certain function, that function is grayed-out on the user's menu and cannot be activated.

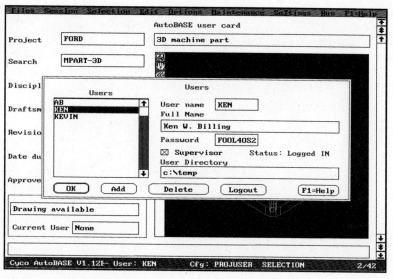

Figure 9.11:
Controlling AutoBASE user accounts.

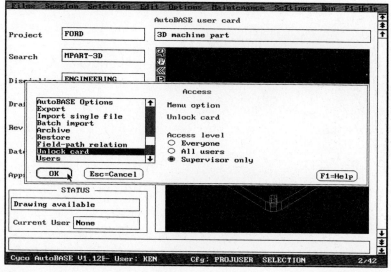

Figure 9.12:
Limiting AutoBASE option access.

Managing Databases

AutoBASE gives the CAD manager, or whoever is designated as the AutoBASE supervisor, complete flexibility in designing and managing AutoBASE databases.

The AutoBASE package includes the AutoBASE Database Editor program (ABD Editor), which can be run from within AutoBASE itself (see fig 9.13).

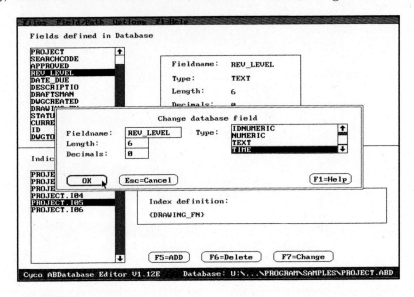

Figure 9.13:
The AutoBASE Database Editor program.

The ABD Editor enables you to do the following tasks in AutoBASE:

- Create new databases
- Control fields that are defined within existing databases
- Control the indexes defined within existing databases for searching
- Pack databases
- Rebuild indexes
- Change drawing file locations according to the field-path relation

Through ABD Editor, you can easily build a database to suit your every need.

Customizing AutoBASE

AutoBASE affords you many customization options. AutoBASE not only allows you to create your own database formats, as explained above, but it also allows you to change the program's appearance (with the exception of the pull-down menu bar and the status line). The AutoBASE package includes another program, the AutoBASE ScreenPainter. The AutoBASE ScreenPainter gives you user interface design capabilities formerly reserved for software engineers. The program is an interactive screen designer that can manipulate AutoBASE field names, value boxes, borders, drawing windows, buttons, drawing lists, and reports (see fig 9.14).

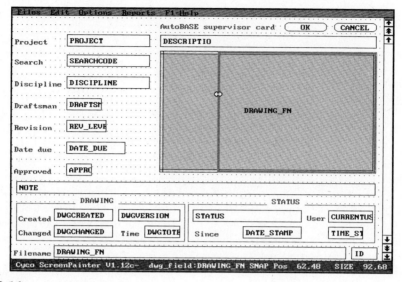

Figure 9.14:
The AutoBASE ScreenPainter.

Using a mouse, you can insert, position, and resize any element of the AutoBASE screen by simply dragging it across the screen. ScreenPainter features snap and grid facilities to ensure accurate screen layouts. Once you have designed a new screen layout, ScreenPainter saves it as a configuration, ready for selection by AutoBASE users when they work in the AutoBASE database.

Conclusions about AutoBASE

AutoBASE is a very flexible network drawing management package that is designed to work with most DOS-based networks. AutoBASE's strongest feature is its capability to tie its database together with automatic file management. With AutoBASE, your directory structure automatically conforms to your database structure, and vice versa. AutoBASE also is the most customizable network drawing management package currently available. You do not have to conform to the program's view of how a network database should look. Rather, Cyco gives you tools to create your very own drawing databases and user interfaces. If you enjoy customizing AutoCAD, you will love customizing AutoBASE. Finally, if you already use AutoManager, AutoBASE will make you feel right at home. The same graphical user interface that controls AutoManager is reproduced in AutoBASE.

AutoBASE's drawbacks are a result of its strengths. Because directory structure creation is so automatic, the directories that AutoBASE makes may be more difficult to work than you would like. This will depend on the way you establish the field-path relation in AutoBASE. Fortunately, the program lets you decide how you want the relation to work. AutoBASE also takes no particular advantage of network operating system security or printing facilities. You are on your own in managing those aspects of your AutoCAD network.

For more information about AutoBASE contact:

Cyco International
1908 Cliff Valley Way
Suite 2000
Atlanta, GA 30329
(404) 634-3302

Drawing Manager

Drawing Manager, by Nehalem Bay Software Incorporated, is another database-type product for network drawing management. Drawing Manager is different from AutoBASE in several fundamental ways. First, Drawing Manager is not limited to AutoCAD users; it also supports Intergraph Microstation users and files. Second, Drawing Manager is designed to integrate specifically with Novell NetWare and uses the same menu-style interface as NetWare (see fig. 9.15). Drawing Manager cannot run on other networks.

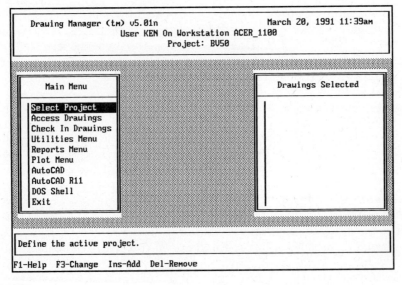

Figure 9.15:
The Drawing Manager menu-driven interface.

Third, Drawing Manager must copy drawing files to the workstation. If your network uses diskless workstations, you must take extra steps to enable Drawing Manager to function.

The Drawing Manager Library Paradigm

Drawing Manager uses a public library as its model for managing AutoCAD drawings. If you want to edit a drawing, you must first "check it out." While you are
editing that drawing, no other Drawing Manager users may check it out. When you
are finished editing a drawing, you check it back in to Drawing Manager for use by
others.

To make new drawings available to Drawing Manager users and to have them managed by Drawing Manager, you can import new drawings residing on the network or
check in new drawings residing on workstations.

Using Drawing Redundancy

To ensure that your drawings are safe from breakdowns, Drawing Manager always
maintains two copies of the file—one on the network file server hard disk, and one
on the hard disk of the workstation that last edited the drawing. Drawing Manager
keeps the two copies straight with records in its database and by using two different
directories on the workstation.

When you check a drawing out from Drawing Manager, the program not only makes
a notation of the drawing's status, but also copies the drawing to the workstation for
editing. Drawings destined for editing go to a working directory (named WORK) on
the workstation's hard disk. You can control the location of this directory on each
workstation by setting a DOS environment variable for each workstation. This is
where you load the drawing into AutoCAD (see fig. 9.16).

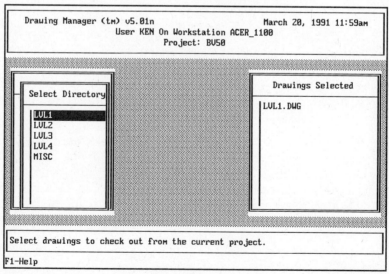

Figure 9.16:
Checking a drawing out of Drawing Manager.

After you have finished editing a drawing, you are returned to Drawing Manager, where you can check in drawings you have edited, update the file server copy for safe keeping, or relinquish the drawing if you do not want your changes to be saved to the network (see fig. 9.17).

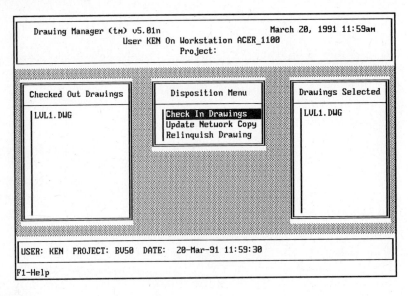

Figure 9.17:
Checking a drawing back into Drawing Manager.

If you check your drawing in, Drawing Manager updates the network copy of the drawing and moves the workstation copy to a directory named RESOLVE on the workstation. The copy residing in RESOLVE maintains redundancy with the network copy in case of a file server failure. You cannot edit the RESOLVE copy through Drawing Manager. If you need to edit the same drawing again, you must check it out once more; Drawing Manager then makes another copy of the network drawing in the WORK directory.

If your file server fails, you can rebuild the file server back up to the point of the failure by using the RESOLVE directories on the workstations. Drawing Manager features a recovery option that can perform the updating automatically. After you have performed a compete backup of the file server, you can clean out local workstations' RESOLVE directories by using Drawing Manager's DM_BAK program. DM_BAK flags all the files in RESOLVE as erasable and Drawing Manager itself removes the redundant copies along with its own time and lock files.

Working with Drawing Manager Projects

Drawing Manager stores drawings on the file server in separate directories—called *projects*—according to job groups. These projects make it easy to organize drawings consistent with your office projects. This system also allows your file server's directory structure to parallel office project names without making the user navigate through directory trees. The user needs only to select a project to work on; Drawing Manager displays the appropriate directory's contents for drawing selection. The contents may be project drawings, or further directory divisions, each containing its own drawing files (see fig. 9.18).

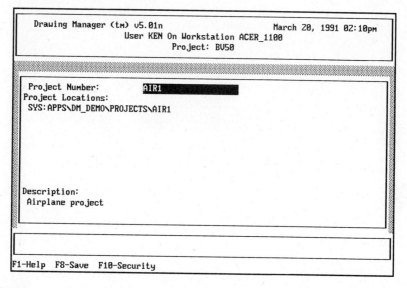

```
Drawing Manager (tm) v5.01n                    March 20, 1991 02:10pm
              User KEN On Workstation ACER_1100
                        Project: BV50


    Project Number:        AIR1
    Project Locations:
    SYS:APPS\DM_DEMO\PROJECTS\AIR1






    Description:
    Airplane project



F1-Help  F8-Save  F10-Security
```

Figure 9.18:
Project directories named according to project names.

You can lock entire projects so that works-in-progress cannot be modified. You also can assign specific trustees to a project and give them specific NetWare file rights so that only authorized persons can access project drawings (see fig. 9.19).

Drawing Manager supervisors can archive or unarchive entire projects. In the archiving process, Drawing Manager copies all a project's drawings to another destination and flags the drawings' records in the Drawing Manager database as archived. Unarchiving reverses the flagging process and makes the drawings available once again.

Searching for Drawings

Drawing Manager helps you find drawing files by allowing searches of its database. The program displays a form, into which you can fill in known information about the drawing you need. You can fill in any number of fields, and DOS-like wild cards are allowed (see fig. 9.20).

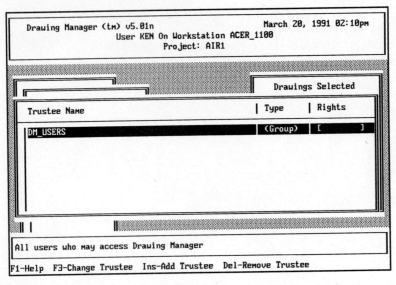

Figure 9.19:

Adding a trustee to a project named AIR1.

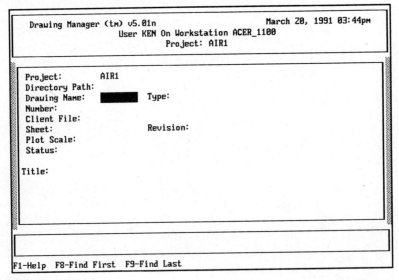

Figure 9.20:

Searching for a drawing in Drawing Manager.

Once your search is completed, you can browse through the drawing records that match your search criteria, view drawings, select drawings for checking out, or delete database records.

Working with Drawings in Drawing Manager

Once you have selected a project from Drawing Manager, the program displays a list of the drawings that Drawing Manager is tracking in its database. From this list, you can select one of a variety of operations to perform on a drawing (see fig. 9.21).

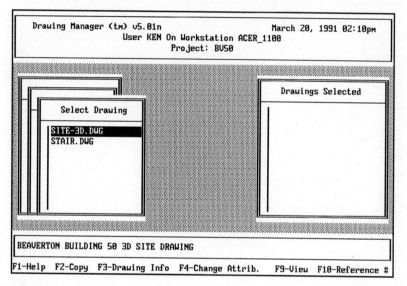

Figure 9.21:

Selecting a drawing from Drawing Manager.

You can build a selection set of drawings to check out as a group so that you do not have to return to Drawing Manager to check out another drawing. Or, you can have Drawing Manager copy a drawing to your workstation WORK directory, so that you can use it as a template for a new drawing or to extract blocks from. You also can view a drawing's database information; that is, the information that was entered when the drawing was imported into Drawing Manager (see fig. 9.22).

While the drawing information is displayed, you can add a memo to the database for others to read when they access the drawing (see fig. 9.23).

You can make individual files within a project read-only to secure them from editing, or you can view a drawing without checking it out by way of a bundled copy of Drawing Librarian by SoftSource (see fig. 9.24).

Aside from its basic drawing viewing capabilities, Drawing Manager can launch AutoCAD automatically and offers many other useful features:

- View up to 25 different drawings at once in multiple viewports
- Create slide, HP-GL, and various DXF files

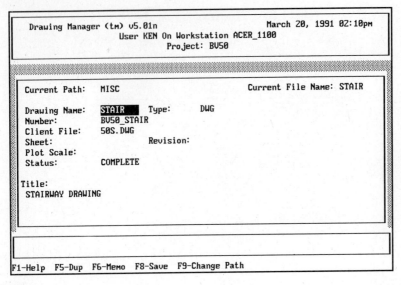

Figure 9.22:

Viewing database information for a drawing.

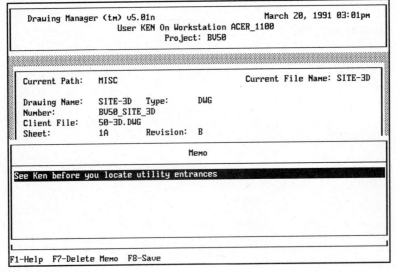

Figure 9.23:

Adding a memo to a drawing record.

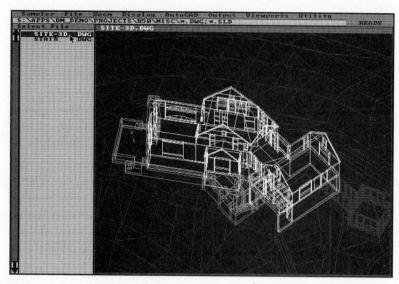

Figure 9.24:

Viewing a drawing from within Drawing Manager.

- Print the currently displayed drawings with file names
- Print individual drawings, slides, or DXF files
- Rename, copy or erase individual files, copy or erase groups of files
- Red-line drawings
- Link external notes to drawings
- Group multiple drawings into projects similar to Drawing Manager for recall
- Execute Drawing Librarian scripts
- Execute an external text editor

Any time that a drawing file name is visible within a Drawing Manager menu, you can have an optional 20-character reference number displayed instead (see fig. 9.25).

The reference-numbering feature is handy if your organization uses part numbers or drawing numbers that do not work well as file names. You can toggle between the file name and reference number as needed.

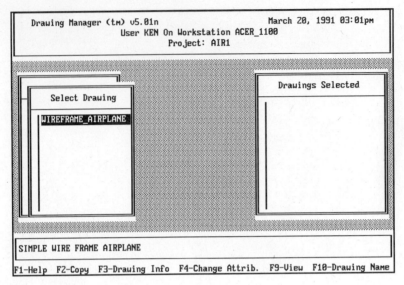

Figure 9.25:
Optional reference number displayed instead of file name.

Drawing Manager Reports

Producing reports from Drawing Manager is easy and thorough. Drawing Manager allows you to produce reports on database information held for either the current project or all projects. Different report formats are available for all drawing details, checked out drawings, or only project drawings. You can create reports of Drawing Manager user accounts and track time usage just as easily. For a complete report of all drawing activity on a monthly basis, Drawing Manager can print an audit trail of all transactions made through the database according to various criteria (see fig. 9.26).

Any report can be printed to the screen, a printer, or to a file for future reference. Drawing Manager produces a complete audit trail file for each month, so you can go back and refer to any month's activity.

Plotting through Drawing Manager

Because Drawing Manager is designed specifically for NetWare, it gives you direct access to NetWare printer queues for network plotting. Drawing Manager allows you to select existing NetWare print queues to associate with network plotters (see fig. 9.27).

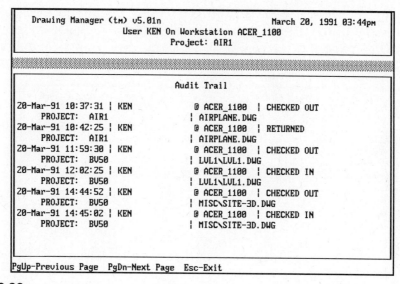

Figure 9.26:

A Drawing Manager audit trail.

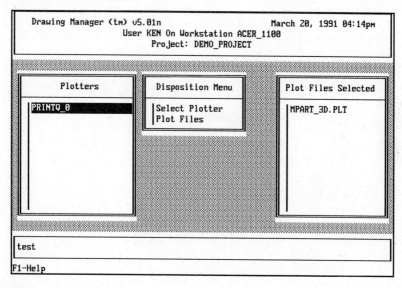

Figure 9.27:

Selecting a network queue for a plot file.

Whenever you return to Drawing Manager from AutoCAD after creating plot files, it gives you a chance to plot those files through a network queue. You can queue plot files (which are automatically listed) that you have created in your WORK directory.

After you submit the plot files for plotting, Drawing Manager displays a screen similar to the NetWare PCONSOLE utility, which shows your plot's sequence in the network queue (see fig. 9.28). When the plot is completed, Drawing Manager moves your plot files to the RESOLVE directory for replotting, redundancy, or cleanup.

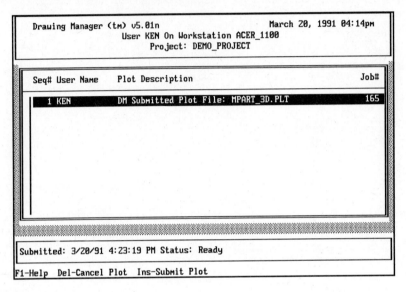

Figure 9.28:
Plotting a file through Drawing Manager.

Conclusions about Drawing Manager

Drawing Manager is a capable network drawing management solution for Novell NetWare users who desire maximum security for their files. With Drawing Manager's redundant file scheme, you can always be sure that you can keep working after a breakdown. Drawing Manager integrates seamlessly with the NetWare security structure and print queues, eliminating the need to do extra setup for plotting or security administration. The NetWare-like menu interface has a zero-length learning curve for users who already are accustomed to NetWare.

Drawing Manager's biggest disadvantage is that, in large networks or with large drawings, it creates a great deal of network traffic while copying drawing files between the file server and workstations. Further, Drawing Manager is not very customizable. The user is limited to report formats that are built into Drawing Manager, and the user may not customize the database format to suit specific needs.

For more information on Drawing Manager, contact:

Nehalem Bay Software Incorporated
5331 SW Macadam
Suite 243
Portland, OR 97201
(503) 228-8680
(800) 525-9974

Summary

Network management can be summed up as the act of maintaining the glue that holds together all the dissimilar and disjointed aspects of network computing, making it look and perform as though it were originally designed that way. This chapter has examined several ways of maintaining that glue, including sneaker-net management techniques, performance monitoring, security organization, and techniques that can help you make the network more transparent to its users. These all contribute to a more streamlined and efficient workgroup system.

The CAD manager must make a conscientious effort to manage the network well while not creating any more work than is necessary for the system's users. Although much of network management boils down to experience, the suggestions in this chapter and throughout this book will give a new CAD manager a jump on the experience curve.

The next chapter looks at some of the more conceptual ways CAD management can be improved through resource management, project management, system documentation, CAD layer standardization, and financial practices.

10

AutoCAD Management Methods and Economics

In business, daily operation is where the rubber meets the road, the payback is reached, and concepts become reality. Here is where CAD managers spend most of their time and energy keeping the total system—equipment, software, users, and processes—healthy and integrated.

This chapter explores some of the techniques the CAD manager can use in facing his day-to-day responsibilities. You will read about some common pitfalls and their solutions. You will be introduced to project management software and learn how the software uses classic project management methods to describe projects, the kinds of graphic documents these programs produce, and how they can help you schedule and track CAD resources.

This chapter also describes documentation conventions and offers suggestions for file naming and documenting projects, drawings, libraries, and procedures. Two A/E/C layering guidelines are discussed so that you decide which may be better for your company. The chapter's final sections discuss some of the dynamics of basic CAD business economics, and show you how to determine whether you AutoCAD system has paid for itself and whether to charge your customers for it.

Management Responsibilities versus Production Duties

In most AutoCAD workgroups, especially small ones, the CAD manager is responsible for overseeing the AutoCAD operation in addition to other duties as an engineer, designer, or draftsman. This is logical because the network should not require full-time attention. Unfortunately, however, conflicts can arise between the CAD manager's dual functions.

The CAD manager's superiors need to understand that the overall CAD system and the network are not "maintenance-free" appliances. These systems require a certain amount of fine-tuning, adjustment, and preventative maintenance each day. What is more, the network's users need ongoing tutoring and support. Otherwise, the network will suffer and may eventually fail.

Similarly, CAD managers need to keep their own mission firmly in mind. A CAD manager can become quite provincial about a CAD department and a network. Upper managers have certain expectations about what the CAD department is going to do for the company, the amount of commitment they are willing to justify, and the CAD manager's role in the overall picture. These expectations must be met, just as system duties must be performed. This often requires setting some difficult priorities, delegating responsibilities to others, and compromising at times.

System users need to balance their desire for maximum support on the one hand and what may seem like arbitrary or indifferent treatment by management on the other hand. This balance can be attained through cooperation and better understanding of each person's jobs and responsibilities. Prioritization of job tasks and compromise can become important to the user. The user, for example, may notice minimal benefits when he takes the time to fill out log forms to document and track CAD projects. On the other hand, the CAD manager can benefit greatly from properly documented paperwork because it makes system management easier. Log forms are discussed later in this chapter.

One way to keep the system healthy is to schedule a period of time each day for maintenance, such as batch file adjustments, backups, file and directory maintenance, and other nonemergency activities. This daily routine can last from a half hour a day on up, depending on the network's size. Larger networks demand more time in proportion to the number of users supported. Of course, you must devote more time to routine maintenance on some days than others. Tell all your coworkers that you will be doing system maintenance chores at the same time every day. Of course, minor "fires" break out frequently in any company, and you must put them out as quickly as possible. Everyone in the organization should know that you are available to handle these instances, but unless it has a direct impact on productivity and cannot wait until the next scheduled maintenance period, it should wait.

The CAD manager needs to exercise good judgment and prioritize tasks when both network support and production demands increase. Neglecting either one can be dangerous. During "crunch" periods, some CAD managers perform their routine network maintenance chores during the lunch hour, so that work on the network is performed while everyone else is on break. You may not be able to schedule the network maintenance period before or after business hours without putting in a great deal of overtime, but when the pressures of production are on, this type of schedule might be what is needed to see that the network stays fit.

Managing Your CAD Resources

If you are responsible for establishing other AutoCAD users' schedules and production activities, then you face additional management headaches. You must balance your department's resources against the amount of time that is available to meet the company's production requirements.

Of all the resources you have on hand, the equipment is the easiest to manage. Equipment can run 24 hours a day without tiring, its skill level is constant, and it never complains. Next to the skill of the people who run the equipment, however, CAD production is most dependent on the performance of hardware. System response time and Price/Performance Analysis was covered in Chapter 5. For more information on specific hardware issues, see Chapter 14, CAD Workstation Hardware.

Once you have your hardware in place, you are dealing with a relatively fixed performance level. Beyond that level, you must make more efficient use of the hardware to improve productivity, especially plotting.

Managing Plotting

One of the first things people notice about any CAD system is that they have far fewer up-to-the-minute "hard copies," or paper drawings, to look at. Some hard copies, in the form of plots, may be laying around the office. These hard copies, however, almost always are dated because of the ongoing work on the drawing. In a CAD office, the original drawings are not laying around for easy inspection; they are stored invisibly on a disk. In the traditional drafting office, viewing a drawing is as simple as looking over someone's shoulder. If you look over a CAD drafter's shoulder, however, you may find that he is zoomed into a tiny part of a very large drawing. If his screen is displaying a view of an entire drawing, you probably will not be able to see the details very clearly.

Using Viewing Software for Drawing Review

This reduction of drawing "originals" can be inconvenient and can make drawing review and mark-up a problem in high-production AutoCAD offices. Operators do not always have enough time to run complete sets of plots for marking up because plotting ties up computers too long.

One answer is to use drawing viewing software. A handful of AutoCAD utilities enable you to view AutoCAD drawings without using AutoCAD itself. The utilities are typically used to help manage drawing files. Because they do not have to maintain the drawing's database, the utilities can display files much more quickly than AutoCAD can. These programs are ideal for displaying files when you need to locate a particular drawing, or when you can get by with just viewing drawings instead of plotting them.

Most of these utilities can be run on a basic workstation without a math coprocessor or a high-resolution video monitor. These utilities often have their own display commands for zooming and panning around a drawing for closer inspection. If you connect a viewing-only workstation to the network, users do not need to exchange drawing files from an AutoCAD workstation; the files can be viewed from the network.

Viewing workstations have other benefits, too. They can help convert conservative individuals to electronic drafting by letting them experience the power of the computer in a cheap and safe way. These users need only the viewing software, access to the drawing files, and perhaps a mouse.

A few viewing utilities even feature rudimentary mark-up capabilities. They confine the viewer to drawing basic lines and text, which the utility stores on a reserved layer in the drawing file. A CAD specialist can load the "marked-up" drawing file and respond to the marks with the full power of AutoCAD. Figure 10.1 shows a sample AutoCAD drawing with markings, viewed with the CADVIEW II utility by Control Systems, Inc.

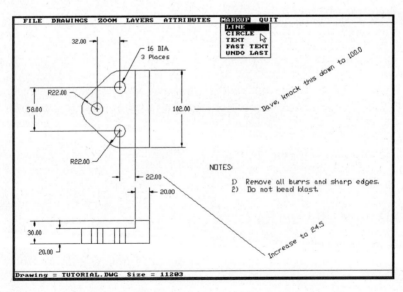

Figure 10.1:
An AutoCAD drawing, electronically marked with CADVIEW II.

Some other popular drawing viewing programs include Cyco International's AutoManager, Slick! by CADsystems Unlimited, Inc., Drawing Librarian Professional from SoftSource, AutoVue from Cimmetry Systems Unlimited, and AutoView from Premier Design Systems.

Breaking the Plotting Bottleneck

When your department is caught in a plotting crunch, you must make compromises or allowances to achieve a certain amount of output (in the form of finished drawings) in an allotted period of time. In other words, if your plotter needs 16 hours to complete a project's plots, you must begin plotting no later than two days before the deadline. Ideally, plotting should begin even earlier to leave a margin for error and to allow for a final check of the drawings.

How often have you worked on a project when at least one minor change *was not* made during the last two days before your deadline? In the "good old days" of manual drafting, changes were no big deal. You simply pulled the drawing and made the change. With a CAD system, however, the entire drawing may need to be replotted.

Some companies have turned to pencil plotters, so that they can more easily make changes to final plots. The affected area can be erased and corrected manually, as is done in traditional drafting. Companies that are contractually required to submit ink plots, however, have perfected the technique of erasing the error with a solvent-impregnated eraser and then replotting only the layers or windows that contain the changes.

One way to minimize replotting and to ease the deadline plotting crunch is to plot noncritical and static drawings ahead of time, leaving more time to concentrate on more dynamic drawings. Typical detail, schedule, and legend sheets are good candidates for early plotting. Try to plot finished sheets as soon as possible after they are completed, not when they are due.

Using the Demonstration Version of AutoCAD for Plotting

You also can use one other little-known strategy for eliminating plot processing time at AutoCAD workstations. It involves using the demonstration version of AutoCAD. The demonstration version of AutoCAD is exactly the same as the retail version, except that the file output commands, such as Save and End, are disabled. Yet, the demo version can view, edit, and plot drawings normally, and only costs about $100.

You can install the demonstration version of AutoCAD on a plot server PC that is connected to your plotter, and plot batches of drawings by scripts or with the help of a human operator. Because all the plot vector processing is performed at the plot server, your AutoCAD workstations do not need to plot the drawing information to a PLT file. They need only to set up the drawings' plotting views and scales per your standards, and the plot server can handle the rest.

To run the demo version of AutoCAD, the computer must meet the same minimum hardware requirements needed to run the production version of the program. You can even connect two or more plotters to the plot server by additional serial or parallel ports, and control all your plotters from one point. If you have a network and connect the plot server to it, drawing loading becomes almost effortless from shared directories instead of from diskettes.

Your AutoCAD dealer probably uses the demonstration version of AutoCAD; see if he can get you a copy to increase your plotting production.

Using Plot-File Server Devices

Another alternative is to use stand-alone plot-file server devices. These devices are most appropriate for sneaker-net plotter sharing. The device consists of a small cabinet with a floppy diskette drive that reads a plot file from the diskette and transmits it to an attached plotter. AutoCAD users need only to plot their drawings to files at their workstation, copy the plot file to diskette, and insert it into the plot server. The disadvantage of such devices, however, is that they are limited in plot file capacity to the floppy diskette capacity. This is not a problem for most drawings, but complex plot files with a large amount of text and hatches may be too large for even a high-density floppy diskette. In these cases, the plotter must be connected directly to the workstation.

Using Outside Plotting Services

One final option is to look for a competent service bureau in your area. Often, such a service can help you through a plotting crunch if it has its own plotter. Many service bureaus can accept plot files in a number of common formats, including AutoCAD drawing files. These services usually can pick up your plot files and deliver the plotted hard copies back to you. If you make reprographic copies of your finished plots anyway, you may save money and time by having the service bureau perform both processes. Be sure, however, to investigate the service bureau's capabilities. Run some test plots by the bureau to make sure that its staff completely understands your plotting requirements.

Assigning Workstations

Another equipment management issue is the pairing of workstations with users. If all your workstations are identical, then this is not a problem. But most companies have computers of varying sophistication, such as 386s, fast ATs, slower ATs, and maybe even XTs. The question of who gets to use which machine is often determined according to seniority. Veteran or senior employees get the fastest, best equipment, with lower-performance computers going to users with less authority and responsibility, on down to the new guy who has to use the least capable machine in the office. To some degree, this arrangement is as it should be. Seniority should be respected and rewarded, as long as it does not interfere with productivity.

If you assign a high-speed, high-resolution, 386-based computer to an engineer who spends an hour a day using AutoCAD, and give an XT with an EGA monitor to a full-time drafter, then you probably are not deploying your resources as efficiently as you should. Each workstation should be placed where it will do the most good, result in the highest overall productivity, and produce the best return on equipment investment. Investment recovery is covered later.

One of the best uses for older, less productive equipment is for AutoCAD training. You can set up an obsolete workstation for manual drafters who are waiting for a workstation of their own, or for managers to use in exploring AutoCAD for themselves. A training station goes a long way toward getting your staff and managers to accept CAD, and sends the message that AutoCAD is accessible to everyone. Team spirit and cooperation are encouraged, and understanding of the system and its capabilities is spread.

A more equitable solution with the equipment and users in the previous example might be to apportion equipment with more emphasis on function rather than seniority alone. Engineers involved part-time in CAD and drawing viewing could receive entry-level 80386 or 80386-SX workstations; full-time production drafters could receive high-powered 386s; designers doing modeling, presentation graphics, and other computer-intensive tasks could get 80486s; and 80286s or XTs could be used as training machines and plotter servers.

Scheduling Workloads: Some Valuable Tips

Any resource can be defined as a source of ability to accomplish a task. Always remember that your total CAD resources are only part hardware—the human component is there, as well. When you manage human resources, you should rely on different strategies than the ones you use when managing equipment. Human resources have to be handled in an impersonal way as well as in a personal way. The personal side of human resource management takes into account each individual's ambitions, talents, and weaknesses. This side of management is covered in Chapter 12. The impersonal aspect of human resource management, on the other hand, regards human resources in the same manner as time, financial, or other resources. This part of human resource management is explored here.

Here are some tips on scheduling human resources:

■ Work with the managers in your company to develop a clear set of priorities for the completion of projects. Determine in advance the lengths to which people will be expected to go in order to meet deadlines, and then identify the circumstances that could force your staff members to go to those lengths. Communicate these expectations to all workers and try to adhere to them. Changes in policy are easier to understand and not seen as arbitrary judgments if they are in light of business priorities rather than made in the heat of a deadline.

■ Strive to put some cushion in schedules for overruns, errors, and unforeseen circumstances. If every project is placed back-to-back and one deadline slips, all the others will be affected. With so much depending on hardware, simply authorizing overtime may not be enough to get the whole schedule back on track. Remember that if you do not back yourself into a corner, you will not have to fight your way out.

■ Monitor all incoming work carefully. The CAD department often inherits "little" jobs because the CAD staff can get them done so easily and quickly. But these little jobs can become leaches on your productivity and jeopardize higher-priority work. Set up a system that allows for all work to be authorized.

■ Encourage open communications so that everyone working on the same project is made aware of any changes. By its nature, CAD work is more isolating than manual drafting. Compensate for isolation by holding regular project meetings.

■ When you estimate the amount of time that will be required for certain projects, try to classify drawings into types that you can deal with more easily. A/E/C firms, for example, classify drawings into different types such as floor plans, sections, elevations, details, and riser diagrams. Calculate the average amount of time required to complete a typical drawing in each class. Then, based on your averages, assign a flexible time limit on new drawing tasks. Keep a record for each drawing class to help refine the averages. This will make your planning efforts more accurate.

■ Look for reusable data and geometry that can be built early and referenced or reused by others. Remember: draw it once, copy it forever.

■ Assign related drawings, if possible, to teams that work well together, or to the same person. Maximize the talents at your disposal and take advantage of them. Also, take advantage of the individual talents and aptitudes for certain drawing classes when assigning tasks.

Using Project Management Software

The CAD manager must keep track of resources, time, costs, tasks and deadlines, and all this can be an arduous challenge when confronted with multiple projects. The job grows larger when there are more people to manage, because less time is available to keep everything straight. Project management is a science that attempts to bring order and logic to the meeting of a challenge. Several good PC software programs are available to assist in project management. The figures for the example in this section were made with Timeline by Symantec Corp. Other good project management programs include Microsoft Project by Microsoft Corp., SuperProject Expert by Computer Associates, and Primavera Project Planner by Primavera Systems, Inc.

In the science of project management, a project is any activity or group of activities that has an objective, has a beginning and an end, takes place over time, uses human or material resources, and involves fixed or variable costs. Traditional project management methods force you to look at the overall picture of each project, break it down into definable tasks and events, decide which resources will be applied to those tasks and when, and organize the project before it starts. The methods do not make decisions for you, but they can help you organize the tasks so that you can make better decisions.

Outlining a Project

The first step in project management involves *outlining* the project, or defining the project in terms of steps or phases. Each task and event gets listed in order of occurrence, leading ultimately to the project's objective. You can begin by breaking the project into large phases and adding detail as the lesser steps are identified. Then you can use any of four common methods for organizing, planning, and controlling the project. These four methods are the Gannt chart, the PERT chart, the CPM diagram, and the WBS flowchart. The PC enables you to use any of the methods easily, and lets you switch between them when one may give a better perspective on some aspect of the project than another.

To understand these four methods of project management, consider the following example of a project to design a satellite reception station. Figure 10.2 shows the project as an outline within a project management program. You can see how individual project tasks and phases are indented to show the project's overall hierarchy. Short notes help provide description or task goals. Plus signs at the beginning of task names indicate where some tasks have subordinate tasks that are not visible. Those tasks have been collapsed within the outline.

```
                                          Press [/] for Main Menu
Mechanical Housing              Resource:
SUMMARY, 10 months,  2-May-88 thru 17-Mar-89.   Future.

Task Name                          Notes
   Outdoor Electronic Unit
      Low Noise Amplifier          Identify vendors for joint effort (early i
         Prelim Design             Sketchy, just enough for RFP from vendors
         Identify Vendor           Concentrate on Taiwan & Japan
         1st Article from Vendor   Kicks off spec negotiations
         Testing                   1 or 2 technicians for testing
         Negotiate Specification   Give on heat/cold req, stand on pricing
         Vendor Rework             Reiterative testing
      Microwave Down Converter     Integrated in same housing as LNA
      IF Down Converter            Can be done in-house
      Mechanical Housing
         Prelim Design             Enough for size of vendor's drop-in
         Detailed Design           Manufacturing spec
         Vendor Manufacturing
         Integrate Down Converters (microwave & IF)
   Indoor Electronic Unit          Compare stndaln & PC-based costs/benefits
    + PC-based Option              Flexibility, expandability, std repl parts
    + Standalone Option            Low profile, cheaper in quan over 300/mo
 + Antenna System
             SATELITE End: 28-Nov-89
```

Figure 10.2:
The sample satellite project in outline form.

Under the outdoor electronic unit phase, component assemblies are listed, such as the low noise amplifier, microwave down converter, IF down converter, and mechanical housing. The second phase includes designing the indoor electronic unit and consists of two optional paths of design: a PC-based option and a stand-alone option, each with its own tasks collapsed. The third phase finishes the job with the antenna system design.

While it includes all the steps for completion of a project, the outline does not accurately indicate the flow of the project. Some of the steps can be performed out of order or concurrently. Such is the case in the real world with large design and drafting projects. Some tasks have to be completed before others can begin, some tasks do not matter, and others may be spread out over time. Further, a project outline does not take into account the interdependence of tasks.

CPM Diagrams and Dependencies

You can graphically depict the interdependence of tasks through a *critical path method* (CPM) diagram, or *network* diagram. CPM does not have anything to do with *computer* networking. The critical path method was developed to help manage the U.S. Navy Polaris submarine project in the 1950s. A CPM depicts each task as a box and connects tasks that are dependent on each other with lines that direct the flow of the project (see fig. 10.3).

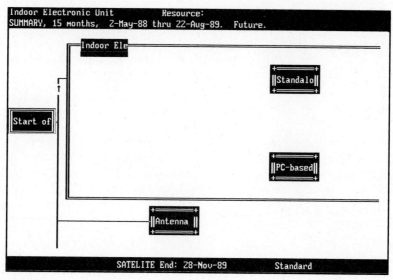

Figure 10.3:
A CPM diagram of the satellite project.

Relationships between tasks and events are known as *dependencies* in project management terms. The task that must be completed first is called the *predecessor*; the task that follows is the *successor*. Tasks can have complete or partial dependencies, and may be interdependent in various ways. If a successor task is completely dependent on a predecessor task, the successor cannot begin until the predecessor has finished. This type of dependency is known as a *finish-to-start* dependency. In the satellite station example in figure 10.3, the antenna system phase can be performed in parallel with the indoor electronic unit, which contains both the PC-based and stand-alone options.

A *partial* dependency describes the relationship that exists when one task can begin only after another has started. Work on the IF down converter, for example, can begin only after the microwave down converter has begun. The second task, however, does not have to wait until the first task is complete. This is a *start-to-start* dependency. There are *start-to-finish* and *finish-to-finish* dependency types, too, and any one task can have multiple dependencies. The major benefit of the CPM diagram is that it enables you to identify tasks that can be performed in parallel, if no dependencies prevent them. From this, you can begin to see how the computer can help keep track of all a project's tasks.

CPM diagrams also are valuable in determining the critical course of events that must proceed consecutively and on schedule in order for the entire project to be completed on time. This course of limiting events is known as the *critical path*. Other tasks may have spare time before or after them, which is known as *slack*. Most project management programs display the critical path of a project differently than the other tasks. Recognition of critical events helps a manager focus extra attention on them to ensure that they proceed smoothly. A project management program that is capable of working in CPM format can keep track of all of a project's dependencies for you. All you have to do is decide the individual relationships. A network diagram shows these relationships in graphical form.

Gantt Charts

One of the main reasons for formal project management is to reconcile the project with the time available. A network diagram does not accurately depict the dimension of time. Professional project managers typically use a *Gantt chart* to depict the effect of time on tasks and events. A Gantt chart shows tasks as horizontal bars across a time scale. Tasks are listed in outline order on the left side of the chart and the length of their horizontal bars represents the duration of each task (see fig. 10.4).

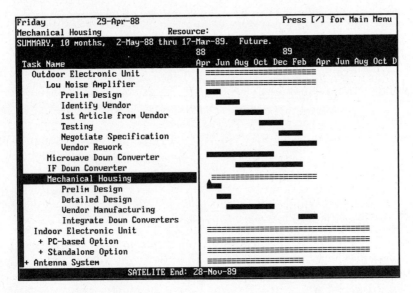

Figure 10.4:

A Gantt chart of the satellite project.

The Gantt chart is one of the most useful tools of project management. With one glance at a Gantt chart, you can see the duration of tasks, the flow of the project from start to finish, and critical dates that are known as *milestones*. Some project management programs also let you see in Gantt form which tasks or events are the limiting factors of the project's completion, or its critical path.

PERT Charts

You also can visualize a project with the help of a *program evaluation and review technique* (PERT) chart. This type of chart is a variation of the CPM chart. A PERT chart looks like a CPM chart but attaches a best, worst, and most probable completion time to each task. Armed with this information, the CAD manager can quickly evaluate different scenarios and identify weak areas in the plan.

Other Resource Management Tools

If a task is to be completed, you must assign a resource to that task. Resources are usually the *real* limiting factor in completing a project on time. Almost any job can be done on schedule if you can assign many resources to it. A resource can be an individual, a group of people, or one or more machines. Project management programs keep track of the resources you assign to tasks in a project, and most let you assign anticipated and actual costs to track expenses for the project. By tracking actual costs against planned costs, you can hone your estimating skills and create more accurate budgets.

A good project management program keeps track of the amount of time for which resources are committed to tasks. The program should be capable of generating a *resource histogram*, which should enable you to see if you have enough people assigned to a project (or more important, not enough), whether overtime will be necessary, or when a deadline is unreasonable. A resource histogram is a vertical bar chart of resource allocation (see fig. 10.5). With it, you can see immediately if you have overloaded someone, or if someone can handle some more work. Careful examination of the histogram helps forecast slow periods or the need to add more staff to lighten the load on others. Figure 10.5 shows that the IF engineering group is scheduled at maximum usage from July through January working on the IF down converter.

With all the potential sources of conflict—task dependencies, deadlines, time, and resources—problems are bound to arise. Otherwise you would not need to use project management strategies. The project management program is to project management what a spreadsheet is to accounting: it enables you to perform quick "what if" analyses of problems so that you can make better decisions more quickly.

Project management programs can help you by an approach known as *automatic resource leveling*. When it recognizes a conflict between resources and the schedule, the program automatically can optimize schedule dates to take into account any slack periods. Or, the program may delay critical dates (and the project as a whole) to accommodate the amount of resources you have assigned. In many cases, however, you must manually reorganize or reschedule the project to make everything possible and reasonable.

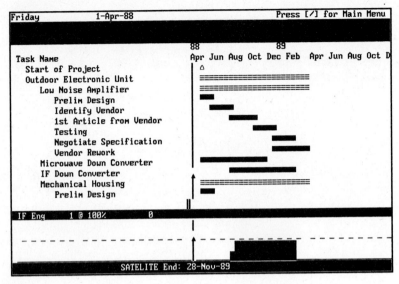

Figure 10.5:
A resource histogram of the satellite project.

Once you have reconciled the schedule and resolved all the conflicts, you can use your project outline as a model for the project. By entering actual amounts for time and resources expended on tasks, and actual completion dates, you can compare your estimates to the actual dates and expenditures. This can be an invaluable tool for honing your estimating skills on future projects. Reports produced by a project management program can be valuable for summarizing progress to upper management, posting work assignments for staff, coordinating with other groups, and justifying costs for additional equipment, software upgrades, and personnel.

Establishing a Drawing File-Naming Convention

By using project management techniques to organize projects and their subordinate tasks, you can get a clearer picture of your department's projects and more efficiently juggle deadlines and resources. Still, you must organize many details that otherwise would interfere with your CAD system's smooth operation. One such detail is file naming. Some operating systems, such as the ones discussed in Chapter 4, will let you be descriptive with your file names. Yet, in cases where users must exchange drawing files, long and descriptive file names may not be practical. For the purpose of illustrating how these forms can be used, look at an example of a simple file-naming convention. While operating within the constraints of the lowest common file-name format (DOS), a file-naming convention should accomplish the following basic functions:

- Make file identification easy
- Group like drawings into logical sets
- Uniquely identify each drawing with minimal likelihood of repetition

The following file-naming system uniquely identifies files in ways familiar to A/E/C professionals. If you work in a non-A/E/C trade, you may be able to adapt the system to the special needs of your profession. The file-naming system is based on the DOS "8.3" file naming limitation; that is, the system uses the DOS file-name convention, which allows for an eight-character root name and a three-character extension. UNIX, Macintosh, and OS/2 HPFS users can adapt this file-naming system to those file systems, or use it as-is for file exchange with DOS systems.

By incorporating your existing standard for drawing numbering into a file-naming convention, you can easily correlate the drawing files with finished plots. This file-naming system will make your files easily recognizable by anyone who is familiar with your drawing-numbering system. The similarity between the systems helps to integrate manual practices with CAD procedures.

Identifying Individual Projects

Most A/E/C firms assign each construction project a four-character project number or code. This code then can be used to refer to that project in correspondence, documents, accounting, and other project management activities. The four characters include the last two numbers of the year in which the project was awarded to the firm, and a sequential number for the project within that year. A project number of 9024, for example, would represent the 24th project the firm had acquired during the year 1990. Under this system, the numbers 9024 become the first four characters for the name of any drawing file that is associated with that project.

Identifying Classifications of Work

In many large A/E/C projects, drawings are exchanged between architectural firms, engineering consultants, and other contractors. The lead architectural firm usually archives all the drawings produced for the project, copies of which often are passed on to a facilities management firm and the building's owner. In order to separate and identify drawings produced by different disciplines, a unique fifth character is used in drawing file names. In the A/E/C trades, the following codes may be used to classify the various disciplines involved in the project:

- *A* = Architectural
- *S* = Structural
- *H* = HVAC

- *P* = Plumbing
- *E* = Electrical
- *C* = Civil
- *L* = Landscape
- *I* = Interior Design

Identifying Drawing Sheets

The majority of AutoCAD users in the A/E/C industries use a system for numbering each drawing sheet. This system is built on a discipline classification system like the one just shown. To approximate this system in the drawing file name, the discipline character (A, S, or I, for example), is followed by a code number that represents the drawing type within the discipline class. The sample file-naming convention uses the following drawing-type codes:

- 1 = Floor plans
- 2 = Sections
- 3 = Elevations
- 4 = Details
- 5 = Schedules

On the actual drawing sheets, the initial drawing-type number is followed by a sheet number, which increments with each new drawing in the class. On the page, the drawing-type number and the sheet number often are separated by a decimal point. Therefore, drawing sheet A2.1 represents the first section drawing in the architect's drawing set. If this sheet is a part of project number 9024, the AutoCAD file for this drawing would then be 9024A201.DWG (see fig. 10.6).

> **Tip:** Larger firms may easily exceed 100 projects per year. For these occasions, the two-digit year pair can be reduced to a single digit, to make room for three project numbers in the file name. If the sample file name was for the 134th project of 1990, 9024A201.DWG would become 0134A201.DWG.

Using Different Extensions to Identify and Protect Drawing Files

One of the primary limitations of any file-naming system used with AutoCAD is the fact that all AutoCAD drawing files must use the DWG extension. After drawings have been released, however, you can use different extensions to further distinguish different kinds of drawings. If a drawing has gone through one revision, for example, you can give it an RV1 extension. You can use different extensions to distinguish project phases (PH2), departments (MFG), or disciplines (CVL).

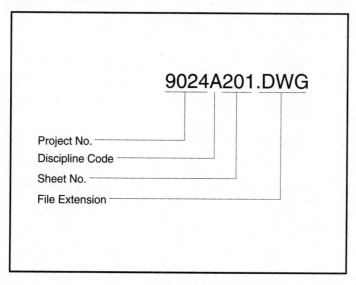

Figure 10.6:

A file name constructed using the sample file-naming convention.

You and your fellow workers should heed one important caveat when changing extensions in AutoCAD files. That is, the assumption must be made and understood that the files require renaming before they can be used. But that is the beauty of it. Completed, checked, authorized, and released drawings cannot be mistaken easily for working copies and therefore cannot be modified easily. When you require users to rename files, you reinforce the use of any approved procedures you may have for making edits to classified drawings.

The following batch file, ACADEXT.BAT, is an example of how you can automate file naming to make it easy and safe for the user. The batch file uses replaceable parameters for a drawing name, an existing extension, and a new extension to maintain backups and to keep file names straight for the user:

```
@echo off
rem * * * * * * * * * * * * * * * * * * * * * * * * * * * * * * * * * * * * * * * * * * *
rem * ACADEXT.BAT file from the book Managing and Networking AutoCAD   *
rem *          (c) 1990 by New Riders Publishing                        *
rem * This batch file accepts three parameters [dwg-name], [current-ext], *
rem * and [new-ext]. It is used for maintaining different versions of the *
rem * same drawing, but with different extensions, changing them as needed to *
rem * allow AutoCAD to edit them.                                       *
rem * This batch file only works with PC-DOS or MS-DOS versions 3.0 or later *
rem * It also only works for one file at a time. You must exit AutoCAD after *
```

```
rem * making changes to each drawing file passed to ACADEXT or only the first*
rem * file will be named properly.                                            *
rem * Provided as-is for educational purposes.                                *
rem * * * * * * * * * * * * * * * * * * * * * * * * * * * * * * * * * * * * * * *
rem Help the lost
if %1 == ? goto help
if %1 == help goto help
:chkdwg
rem Don't proceed if a .DWG file already exists
if not exist %1.dwg goto chkold
echo
echo Drawing file %1.DWG already exists.
echo ACADEXT cannot continue.
echo Correct the situation and try again.
goto end
:chkold
rem Check for the file name and extension given for editing
if exist %1.%2 goto chknew
echo
echo Drawing file %1.%2 not found. Check the parameters given.
goto help
:chknew
rem Don't proceed if a file with the [new-ext] given already exists
if not exist %1.%3 goto docopy
echo
echo Drawing file %1.%3 already exists.
echo Continuing would overwrite %1.%3.
echo Correct the situation or choose a different [new-ext] and try again.
goto end
:docopy
rem Files are okay, but check one last time with the user
echo
echo ACADEXT is about to attempt drawing file renaming.
echo If a %1.BAK file exists, it will be copied to %1.OLD.
echo Do you wish to continue? Press Ctrl-C now to abort.
pause
rem Get rid of any existing .OLD files
if exist %1.OLD echo Removing previous %1.OLD...
if exist %1.OLD del %1.OLD
rem Save any existing .BAK files just in case
if exist %1.BAK echo Copying %1.BAK to %1.OLD...
if exist %1.BAK copy %1.BAK %1.OLD
if exist %1.BAK del %1.BAK
```

```
echo
rem Make .DWG file for AutoCAD
echo Copying %1.%2 to %1.DWG for AutoCAD...
copy %1.%2 %1.dwg
rem Call ACADNET.BAT and pass the drawing name
rem Place your startup script name after %1 if you want
echo Launching ACADNET.BAT...
call acadnet %1
rem If no changes were made, leave the drawing name as it was
if exist %1.BAK goto finish
echo No changes were made to %1.DWG.
echo Resetting %1.DWG to %1.%2...
del %1.DWG
goto end
:finish
echo
rem If the drawing was changed, give it the [new-ext] extension
echo Renaming %1.DWG with new extension to %1.%3...
rename %1.DWG %1.%3
rem Let the user know what he got
echo The latest version of %1 is now %1.%3.
echo Backup file %1.BAK is for %1.%3.
echo File %1.%2 remains intact.
goto end
:help
echo
echo Parameters are [dwg-name] [current-ext] [new-ext]. Use no periods.
:end
```

You can use ACADEXT.BAT as shown or as a model for your own drawing file management batch files.

Identifying Special Directories

You also can apply this file-naming convention to your directory names. When the project number is used for all or part of a directory name, the label is easily recognized and entered. Directories might be named 9024, 9034, 9035, and so on. Do not forget that with DOS a directory also can have an extension, such as 9024.PH2 for phase two, 9024.AD1 for addendum one, and 9024.STR for structural drawings. These extensions may be confusing to recognize or type. But if the directory names are integrated properly with menus, batch files, or drawing management systems to automate directory selection, most users will not have to work with them directly, giving you good drawing organization.

Documenting Your CAD Department

By using project management techniques to organize projects and their subordinate tasks, you can get a clearer picture of your department's projects and more efficiently juggle deadlines and resources. Still, you must organize many details that otherwise would interfere with your CAD system's smooth operation. By documenting these details, such as file and directory names, you can more accurately keep track of them and administer the system more easily. You also should collect information about drawings, symbol and detail libraries, standards, equipment, and procedures into a form that is easily updated and readily accessible. This type of documentation encourages compliance, acceptance, and understanding by the entire CAD staff.

The following sections describe some of the forms you can use in documenting your CAD department's operations. You can use these forms just as they are presented here, if they meet your needs, or you can modify them to suit your work. Each form is included in electronic form on the *Managing and Networking AutoCAD Disk* to save you designing and typing time. For more information on the electronic files, see Appendix B.

Project Logs

Most projects contain many drawings, each of which needs a unique file name. Loading drawings into AutoCAD just to find out what they contain is time consuming and counter-productive. A project log form can help you easily identify all the drawings related to one project. This form also makes selection of new drawing names easier by eliminating the need to search for the last drawing name used by a file-naming convention. The form lists project numbers assigned for each project, the drawing title, and the sheet number. You can give a copy of the project log to other firms that may be working on the same project and need to know your drawing names and titling information. Project log forms should be kept in a three-ring binder with drawing log forms, which are discussed in the following section. See Appendix B for an example of a project log form.

Drawing Logs

Whether or not a drawing contains attribute information, much nongraphical data gets saved in drawing files. Even with drawing standards and prototypes, some of this information may need to be recorded for other purposes, adding another dimension to drawing documentation. Drawing information, such as who started the drawing, when it was started, the drawing's scale, layers used, revision history, release dates, authorization, checker, and location, is important to efficient and complete administration. If users have blank drawing log forms, they can jot down drawing information when they begin or edit a drawing. When a user is done with a drawing, the form goes into a drawing log binder along with the project log forms. All the information anyone might need about a drawing is in a centralized location. See Appendix B for an example of a drawing log form.

Catalogs

Your completed project and drawing logs become catalogs of your AutoCAD work. You probably will have other files that could use cataloging, too. Specifically, AutoCAD blocks and AutoLISP files should be cataloged for easy reference. Once cataloged, you should find that your symbol libraries and AutoLISP functions get used more often. This improves productivity while reducing or eliminating duplication of existing work.

Creating a Block Library Catalog

Every AutoCAD installation accumulates a multitude of symbols, typical details, and other blocks. Blocks, while being the functional equivalent of drawings, do not need to be tracked in the same fashion as finished drawings, but they do represent one of the most under-organized resources in most AutoCAD installations.

Symbol and detail catalogs can help you organize blocks into logical groups, so that users can easily find the right symbol or detail. If users can find the right block for a particular purpose, then they are more likely to use approved standards and not waste time creating replicas. When a new block must be created, it can be cataloged with a plot that shows its appearance, scale, insertion point, and file name. You can organize the catalog into general drafting symbols, and list blocks according to their discipline, function, or other use.

You can reproduce the symbol and detail catalogs to make sure that all users have access to a copy. Such resources encourage a modular approach to drafting and boost productivity. See Appendix B for an example of a block library catalog page.

Creating an AutoLISP Library Catalog

How many times have you encountered a problem, and you knew you had an AutoLISP program to solve the problem, but you could not remember the program's name? You probably could have worked around the problem by the time you found the file and identified it. If your organization uses AutoLISP extensively, you should create a catalog of AutoLISP functions. Its pages should contain functions grouped by operation for easy location. For example, you might organize the catalog according to the following divisions:

- Text functions
- Dimensioning functions
- Graphics editing functions

- User support functions
- Entity handling functions
- File management functions

Each function should have a short entry that shows the function's file name, its purpose, arguments, global variables, explanation of prompts, and location. See Appendix B for an example of an AutoLISP function catalog page.

Standard Procedures Documents

When you establish standard drawing procedures in your CAD department, you promote consistent and uniform drawings, which makes them look neater and more organized for your clients. When your CAD specialists all understand and follow the same standardized procedures, you can more easily switch drafters in the middle of a drawing, if necessary, without affecting drawing quality or appearance.

Once you have worked on your AutoCAD system for a while, you will discover standard procedures that should be followed for the creation, filing, backup, plotting, and management of drawings. Standard procedures help eliminate confusion over these activities and stimulate productivity by getting everyone to follow tried-and-true procedures that are the fastest and most reliable.

A standard procedures document can be included with the block and AutoLISP catalogs in a comprehensive CAD manual containing all the CAD documentation you want to distribute to AutoCAD users. In it you might include your file- and sheet-naming conventions, directory organization of the workstations and file server, start-up and shut-down sequences, plotting procedures, revision guidelines, and any other repetitive procedure that require explanation and compliance.

The standard procedures document should be compiled by the CAD manager in a tutorial style that is easy to understand. A CAD manual of this kind can save you days in training new users. You should insist that all the system's users comply with the outlined procedures, but you also should encourage users to suggest alternative procedures and methods. Make sure that you keep all copies of the CAD manual and its forms up to date. Few things discourage compliance more than obsolescence. Give a copy or two to other key managers and principals, so that they can see that your job is more than just riding herd over a bunch of PCs and that you really do manage the system. This will go a long way to helping others understand your job's value to the company.

Choosing an A/E/C Layer Guideline

One particularly frustrating aspect of AutoCAD management, especially for A/E/C managers, is adopting a consistent and practical method for the naming of AutoCAD drawing layers. Layer-standard selection is a troublesome task for A/E/C firms because of the frequent exchange of their drawings and reuse by other companies. Companies in the machine, electronics, and other design disciplines typically prepare drawings only for their own internal use and, therefore, can use whatever layer-naming scheme works best for them. Also, few other disciplines have the potential to require as large and varied a layer-naming structure as the A/E/C trades require. If you are not an A/E/C professional, you can skip down to the section on CAD economics.

For the A/E/C trades, a layer-naming system must meet many requirements. The layer system should be able to describe different classifications of building materials, such as concrete, metals, and wood. It needs to be flexible enough to accommodate different phases of work, such as existing, remodeling, and future construction. It must make provision for each of the different trades, including architectural, structural, mechanical, plumbing, fire protection, electrical, landscape, and civil, as well any other specialty consultants, such as medical, security, and chemical. Technically speaking, a layer system should be adaptable to any CAD system. Also, the system should be easy to enter by way of wildcards and logical divisions, so the user can manipulate classes of entities by common attributes.

Until just a few years ago, little work had been done to define layering guidelines. Users defined their own layer names unless they were compelled to use the layers already defined in a third-party program that they used. Third-party vendors made no attempts to reach a consensus on layer names, and professional organizations left the problem in the hands of the users and vendors. Recently, however, layer guidelines have progressed and have finally forced the industry into examining its layering needs. As yet, no definite layering standard has emerged that meets the needs or expectations of every kind of CAD user. Several groups, however, have proposed solutions to the layer management issue.

The 16-Division CAD Layering Protocols

One solution to the problem of layer guidelines is a system based on the Construction Specifications Institute (CSI) 16-division format. The 16-Division CAD Layering Protocols were developed by Hawaii architect Robert Hartman in 1986. The system was adopted by the Hawaii Society, American Institute of Architects (AIA) in 1987.

CSI is a national organization of A/E/C professionals representing the construction design and manufacturing trades. Long before CAD layering became an issue, CSI organized the 16-division format as a means of standardizing construction specifications. The 16-division format has been adopted as the basis for the indexing of building materials in the popular Sweet's catalogs and is used as the chapter headings for *Architecture Graphics Standards*, which is the bible of architectural drafting. The CSI format is well-known throughout the A/E/C industry and is almost universally accepted. As a result, the CSI format requires minimal adaptation on the part of users, and is easily mastered.

The CSI as an organization, however, does not officially endorse the 16-Division CAD Layering Protocols. It has formed a drawings subcommittee to develop standards for drawing sizes and organization, a CAD layering standard, and a drafting symbol standard.

Understanding the Layer Names

The 16-Division CAD Layering Protocols are reproduced in Appendix C. You can refer to it as the layer names are described. The 16-division format for CAD layer names is a system of five-digit numerical names. The first two digits specify the major division of work, using the same numbers used in the CSI 16-division format. Therefore, if the layer name begins with the numbers "02," then the layer relates to civil engineering or landscape work. Layer names beginning with "09" and "16" relate to interior finish work and electrical work, respectively.

The name's next two digits denote a specific category of work within the major division. If a layer name's first four numbers are "0340," for example, then the layer is part of the concrete division (denoted by the 03), and deals specifically with precast concrete (denoted by the 40).

The layer name's fifth digit is a modifier that further describes the layer, as shown in the following list:

- 00001   Existing to remain
- 00002   Existing to be removed
- 00003   New
- 00004   Text
- 00005   Dimensions
- 00006   Hatch patterns
- 00007   User defined
- 00008   User defined
- 00009   User defined

The layer number 08520, for example, is suggested for aluminum windows. Division 08 covers doors and windows, and 52 is the category for aluminum windows. The final number could create up to nine separate layers for the display of various attributes of the window.

Pros and Cons of the 16-Division CAD Layering Protocols

Aside from the fact that the layer names are recognized easily by construction professionals, the 16-Division CAD Layering Protocols offer other advantages. Primarily, the system's layer names can easily be integrated into specification documents. By extracting layer names from drawings, specification writers can create a checklist of specification sections to prepare. Sophisticated CAD systems can even extract this material directly from the drawing database to form the foundation of project specifications.

Another advantage of a 16-division scheme is the ease with which you can manipulate layer names with wild-card characters. You can use the layer specification **16***, for example, to manipulate all the electrical layers at one time. Similarly, the specification ***5** operates on all dimension layers simultaneously.

Further, because a 16-division scheme uses numerals rather than words or letters to classify layers, the system eliminates language barriers. A knowledgeable designer or drafter can use the 16-Division CAD Layering Protocols whether he speaks English or not.

The disadvantages of the 16-Division CAD Layering Protocols are few, but worthy of consideration. Some building components appear to belong in multiple layers. A stone floor, for example, could just as easily be drawn on layer 09600 (stone/masonry flooring) as it could on layer 04400 (stone masonry). Interpretation and judgment leave some room for inconsistency. Opponents also argue that a 16-division scheme requires too many layers. Proponents, on the other hand, reply that only those layers that are used need to be present.

A 16-division scheme, further, does not inherently support multifloor projects. While few users combine all the floors of multiple-floor projects in the same drawing file because of performance reasons, some do on small projects. In such cases, a user-definable digit or some other variation of the standard must be used. Again, the fifth digit modifier of the 16-Division CAD Layering Protocols allows for several user-definable layers in each minor classification.

In order to use the 16-Division CAD Layering Protocols, users must be familiar with the CSI 16-division format and its numbering system. The layer name A-WALL , for example, is easier to recognize as containing walls than is the layer name 06100. Perhaps the most common objection to a CSI-based system is that it forces the user to select building materials too early in the project, or perform time-consuming layer reassignments later. Often, when a building design is beginning, the designer is more concerned with the placement and spatial relationships of building assemblies, not their composition.

So far, the 16-Division CAD Layering Protocols have been adopted by many major industry groups, including the U.S. Air Force and Shell Oil of Canada. Version 3.0 of the complete 16-Division CAD Layering Protocols is reproduced in Appendix C. For current information on the state of the protocols, contact:

Bob Hartman
Facilities Data Management
P.O. Box 675

Gig Harbor, WA 98335
(206) 857-2185
(206) 857-2186 (FAX)

Mr. Hartman also publishes a quarterly newsletter named *CAD+Healthcare Facilities*, which chronicles the acceptance of the 16-Division CAD Layering Protocols, news on their evolution, views on their usage, and contains information on using AutoCAD to design health care facilities.

AIA CAD Layer Guidelines

In 1988, a CAD layering task force was established by the national AIA to study the CAD layering problem and to develop guidelines to help CAD users overcome the problem. The committee includes the following groups and industries:

- American Institute of Architects (AIA)
- American Consulting Engineers Council
- International Facility Management Association
- U.S. Army Corps of Engineers
- U.S. Naval Facility Command (NAVFAC)
- National Bureau of Standards

This committee set out to formulate hierarchical layer guidelines to emphasize drawing types and building assemblies without as much attention to detail as is paid by the CSI-based standards. A draft of the task force's guidelines on CAD layering was presented at the A/E/C Systems '89 show in Anaheim, CA for comment by the construction industry. The formal results were presented at the following year's show in Atlanta, GA in the form of another CAD layering standard. The complete AIA CAD Layer Guidelines are reproduced in Appendix C. You can refer to it as the layer names are described.

Understanding the Layer Names

The AIA layer system conforms to an alphanumeric *1-4-4-modifier* format. The first character describes the construction category represented by the layer, such as *A* for architectural work, *E* for electrical work, and *M* for mechanical work. The first four-character field denotes major drawing groups, such as elevations, details, and sections. The second four-character field subdivides the major groups into minor groups, such as symbols, dimensions, and notes. A user-definable, variable-length modifier can be added to the layer name for further subdivision or description.

To accommodate remodeling, multifloor projects, and 3D drafting, the first hyphen in the format can be substituted by a character to identify those situations. Further, each category is divided into one group of layers for scaled information and another for symbology and annotations. S-PLFL, for example, is the layer for drawing structural foundation plans, and A-FLOR-IDEN is reserved for architectural floor plan room numbers and names.

Pros and Cons of the AIA CAD Layer Guidelines

One advantage of the AIA layer system is that users can easily identify layers by their names. The four-character mnemonics give the reader a hint as to the objects that reside on each layer. Another advantage is the convenience of using logically named layers. For example, you design building walls on a layer named A-WALL. Because of its hierarchical nature and the use of standard mnemonics, wild cards work equally well for this layer system. A specification of **S*** manipulates all structural layers at once, ***SECT*** sorts out only the layers in each major group associated with building sections, and ***NOTE** lists all layers with notes and call-outs.

Even though it is supported by so many powerful industry organizations, the AIA system has its disadvantages. It provides easily recognizable divisions, but it forces the user to learn another classification system and translate it to the CSI format if working with construction specifications. Further, the scheme's 11- to 16-character layer names require extra keystroking, especially if you want to use a separate layer for annotations for each graphic element. Some CAD programs cannot handle the longer names, and programs that use number-based layers must cross reference the names to a numeric equivalent.

Another disadvantage is that unusual drawing types, such as remodeling and 3D designs, are not addressed adequately and integrated into the name. These situations leave open the possibility that the use of a modifier in the space occupied by a hyphen can be mistaken easily. Finally, the AIA guidelines provide no information about the materials used in a building; in some cases, this type of information is an obvious advantage to the user. Whereas the 16-Division CAD Layering Protocols, for example, enable you to extract layer names to create a materials checklist for a building, the AIA CAD Layer Guidelines require you to place material information within nongraphic attributes, requiring an additional layer of complication.

The Need for Vendor Leadership

Unfortunately, no concensus on layer standards yet exists among major A/E/C third-party vendors, and each addresses layer-naming in a different way. In the third-party vendor community, however, several major applications provide either rigid systems or flexible guidelines and translation features. One major developer, LANDCADD Inc., makers of a highly successful landscaping and site-planning package, has adopted the 16-Division CAD Layering Protocols for use in its software.

The popular AEC Architectural and AEC Mechanical tablet menus by Autodesk and Archsoft, Inc. force the user into a fixed, predefined set of layers. These layers are required for operation of their encrypted AutoLISP functions, and all layers must be present whether they are used or not. This approach to layering has been widely criticized for its inflexibility. But because it is the system promoted by Autodesk, it is accepted by many companies.

Archsoft, Inc. recently joined with Chase Systems, Inc., makers of productive and sophisticated piping and HVAC menu systems, to form ASG (Archsoft Group). The company now markets flexible menu systems for all A/E/C trades that incorporate customized layer systems. ASG's Layer Master program can translate layer names in one or more drawings to other systems by using template and cross-reference files. Indeed, a practical and easy-to-use menuing system supported by AutoLISP routines can make any layering standard nearly transparent to the user. Neither the advantages or the disadvantages should be apparent.

The solution to the layer-naming issue seems to rest with the user. None of the systems produced so far seems to satisfy everyone and every circumstance. The "best" system, perhaps, is one that lets the user work in his favorite standard and then translate it to one or more other systems. The Layer Master system may be the closest attempt yet.

Deciding which system is best is a subjective process, but one that you should stick with once you have made the choice. By maintaining consistent layer names across projects and over time, you make your drawings more organized and more easily maintained. If you are in an architectural firm, you should consider all the choices and the requirements of your consultants before choosing a layering standard. Temper that information with your designers' preferences.

If you work for a consulting engineering firm, you may prefer the 16-division layering system because you probably will know what materials you will specify for each job. By translating the layer names through an AutoLISP program, you can accommodate your clients who use other systems.

On the other hand, if your company does not fit into any of the preceding scenarios, you can breathe a sigh of relief that you do not have to join the layer debate. By all means, though, develop a logical set of standard layer names that is flexible to allow for unforeseen circumstances. Your layer-naming scheme should be easy to use, have classification information that is based on industry standards, create easily recognizable names, and be intelligent enough to store drawing layer data in the names.

CAD Economics

A CAD department and its parent company are in a vital state of mutual dependency. The CAD department cannot function without the parent company's commitment of resources and faith in the department's ability to produce. Likewise, the company cannot profitably deliver its product unless its CAD department can complete accurate documents in a timely manner. This interdependency depends on effective communications and unselfish cooperation. The next section discusses some of the dynamics of this relationship, including the ways in which each partner can benefit from and contribute to the relationship, and the part a CAD manager plays in overall company management.

Profitability and Return on Investment

At times (especially for those enamored with technology), maintaining the proper perspective on a CAD department and its mission is difficult. That mission should be to leverage AutoCAD and other computer technologies for the purpose of improving the company's position in its marketplace and increasing the bottom line. The company's executives, however, can more easily maintain their perspective on the CAD system's role. They often have not been as smitten with the power of computers as AutoCAD users have (although executives may be smitten with other forms of power) and executives are naturally more objective about CAD's impact on the company. By educating upper managers about the role of CAD, as described in Chapter 12, you can make them more sympathetic to the challenges of CAD implementation. But overall, if managers are supplying strong leadership, upper management's objectivity is not a bad thing.

Instead of struggling against executive objectivity, use it to your advantage. You should not, for example, complain about the need for hardware upgrades in an unwarranted manner or if you are not prepared to defend your point of view. If you are sure your case is valid, however, present it in economic terms, and be sure to point out the profit period.

From the moment your AutoCAD system is installed, you need to find ways to measure the system's profitability. Although an AutoCAD system is valuable in many ways (it acts as a valuable database, for example, helps increase drawing quality and accuracy, and produces other revenues through additional services), the CAD system's most important benefit is the savings it creates in production overhead. These savings equate to profit for the company. Managers have difficulty expressing these savings, however, in terms of a universal formula for every circumstance. But at the least, the formula should include the one factor that executives can appreciate most: savings in labor over manual methods.

If you can quantify the savings created by the CAD system, you can use the results when:

- Measuring return on investment (ROI)
- Identifying the most productive applications for AutoCAD
- Scheduling, estimating, and bidding on future projects
- Justifying the AutoCAD system's growth and development
- Providing feedback on performance

Calculating the return on investment can be difficult, or even impossible, because exact costs in some areas may be hard to total. You can obtain a reasonable approximation, however, that can serve as a benchmark as time with the system increases. Here is one formula for calculating return on investment (ROI):

$$\text{ROI} = \frac{((CP\text{-}CN)xC\text{-}O)\text{-}((MP\text{-}MN)xCxM\text{-}O)}{I}$$

In this formula, *CP* represents the total annual available CAD production hours. *CN* represents the system's nonproductive hours. *C* is the total compensation and benefits package. *O* equals associated operating costs for CAD or manual drafting. *M* is a productivity multiplier, which is equal to the total annual available manual production hours. *MP* equals productive manual drafting hours, *MN* equals nonproductive manual drafting hours. *I* is your net investment in the AutoCAD system.

The ROI formula calculates the gross savings of CAD as the difference in total labor costs of CAD compared with manual drafting costs. Labor costs include the total available production hours less the actual or estimated nonproductive hours spent in meetings, telephone calls, research, and so on. Multiply the net hours of each drafting method by the CAD specialists' and manual drafters' hourly compensation and benefits rates, respectively. This results in the cost of labor per person. Apply a productivity multiplier determined by actual comparison of test drawings completed both by manual means and with AutoCAD (or other documentation) to the CAD labor costs. If by historical evidence or testing, for example, you determine that a particular drawing type (or the average of all types) yields a 2:1 productivity factor for CAD, then the multiplier applied to *manual* labor costs would be 2. The result should be total labor cost figures for both manual and CAD methods; the difference between these two figures should be your company's gross savings.

Subtract from each side the associated operating costs. These include lease or rent payments for equipment, maintenance, initial loss of production (compared to manual methods), facility preparation (if applicable), floor space costs, training, consulting fees (if any), and supplies. The difference between the two sides now equals the basic comparative costs and savings. Do not be surprised if more than 50 percent of your direct costs for CAD is from support-related items and services. Capital investments in hardware and software typically only comprise 30 percent of the total investment. Today, typical total costs for an AutoCAD workstation run about $25,000 for three years. This includes a three-year lease cycle, shipping, installation, insurance, the cost of leasing, maintenance, initial and follow-up training, and customizing.

Your total savings should take into account any additional and indirect savings or benefits, such as manufacturing savings as a result of more efficient processes (including automated CNC program generation, and reduced prototyping and reworking), reduced overtime expenses, elimination of subcontracts, and tax savings. If CAD places your company in a position of providing new services or entering new markets, such as facilities management, these additional revenues should be credited to the CAD column. The difference between CAD and manual drafting at this point will be total CAD savings.

Finally, divide this difference by your net capital investment in hardware and software, after any tax breaks, including depreciation. The end result equals your approximate annual return on investment.

Three major variables can affect ROI, either in dollars or the amount of time spent until a break-even point is reached:

- **Time.** As a long-term investment, CAD generates proven returns if managed properly. Over-sensitivity toward short-term returns, however, may jeopardize long-term benefits. For example, reluctance to invest in adequate training in the near term pushes higher productivity ratios further over the time horizon.

- **Hard CAD costs.** The price of CAD hardware is falling steadily, reducing the incremental investment required to add more workstations. More sophisticated software enables greater productivity.

- **Labor costs.** These costs must be examined in light of each company's industry and production cycle. Although CAD is most profitable when implemented at the design level, designers demand higher salaries than do production people. Designers, moreover, are involved in more nonproduction hours (as far as CAD ROI is concerned), resulting in greater system slack time.

You must analyze (possibly on a per-designer basis) whether fewer hours with AutoCAD by a designer are more productive than a full-time dedicated CAD specialist. Although it is not recommended solely on the basis of accelerating ROI, multiple shifts or similar tactics that improve the utilization rate of the equipment will improve ROI. Table 10.1 illustrates the average portion of a day spent by different personnel in performing various duties.

In the *Other* category in table 10.1, work may include any *productive* activity that does not require direct interaction with the CAD system. You should perform time studies of your own personnel and use the results to determine how utilization affects productivity and costs.

Table 10.1
Average Personnel Utilization Rates

	Drafting %	Other %	Nonproductive %
Drafters	80	5	15
Checkers	30	55	15
Designers	60	25	15
Engineers	25	60	15

A key point to remember when calculating ROI is not to expect it all to come back immediately. Implementing AutoCAD is analogous to planting a crop in a field. There is a time for planning, investing, cultivating, and harvesting. Return on investment will be low during the cultivation period when you are involved heavily in training and system development. The harvest does not begin until the entire system—hardware, software, human resources, and management—has matured. You must be realistic about how soon you expect your investment to ripen.

Charging Back versus Overhead

Once CAD costs are quantified, companies want to know how to allocate them. The method used for allocating CAD costs depends largely on the type of business in which the company is involved. Many organizations have a single product or focus, such as a public utility company. For them, charging CAD costs back to a single project does not make sense. Instead, most assume that CAD costs are part of the total overhead, or perhaps will be allocated to the entire engineering department.

For other organizations, such as architectural or engineering firms (especially ones that may not use CAD resources on some projects), loading some of the burden for CAD support on a non-CAD project will adversely influence the project's bottom line. If you account for CAD time (and therefore costs) on a project-by-project basis, you highlight CAD's effectiveness in those projects. Using the figures obtained from the ROI formula, an hourly rate can be charged to CAD projects for each hour of CAD use. Even if the figures are used only for estimating, they help measure how well CAD was managed and implemented in that case.

In the past, CAD time was sometimes billed separately to clients and customers. This billing procedure, however, is seldom done today except in special cases. Most design clients today assume that CAD will be used on their project, so they do not expect to pay extra for CAD time.

One benefit of allocating CAD as overhead is absorbing research and development costs. Because these activities tend to benefit all projects either directly or indirectly, the costs also should be shared. Another benefit is that if CAD is made a part of your company's business plan and is understood to be just another way of doing business, then it really is just overhead. CAD is easier to account for, especially if you use CAD data for other uses, as explained in Chapter 11. If you, for instance, use presentation images produced for one project to help you land another project, should you attribute the costs of producing the images to the original project, or should you absorb them in the new project? If you consider CAD as an overhead expense, you should not care where the costs go.

When you examine the positive and negative financial impacts that CAD has on your company, you can be in a much better position to plan for future growth and development. If financial analysis shows that CAD has a positive impact, then you have grounds to ask for a portion of that profit for improving the weak areas in your system, or for research and development. If you are struggling financially with CAD, then even more emphasis should be placed on proper training and other implementation factors.

You are the CAD department's representative as a business partner with the entire company. If your company is committed to CAD, then you and the company need each other. You need company leadership and support if you want to increase your productivity ratio into the highest ROI ranges.

Your CAD department, on the other hand, is needed by your company to improve its position as a technological power, to improve its productivity, and position it for the future. This only will happen as senior management views CAD as a business tool instead of a technology toy. Management at large is beginning to develop this enlightened point of view, as major technological investments have become ingrained in the companies' products.

As a business partner, you have certain responsibilities beyond the day-to-day management of the CAD system and its users. You must magnify the strengths that make your company uniquely competitive. With so much riding on CAD, however, one of your priorities must be to ensure that the CAD system stays reliable and its fault tolerance is high, as is discussed in Chapter 5 and Chapter 11.

The relationship between the CAD manager and upper management must be one in which each is committed to look after the best interests of the other and be dedicated to the other's long-term success. Without it, neither one will be satisfied. If the CAD department is not supplementing the company's goals, the company will not support CAD. If the CAD department is not supported from the top, it will not have the resources to provide the productivity returns or other benefits that management wants or needs.

As in any relationship, the CAD manager and the upper management have to be patient and understanding with one other. When finances for CAD expansion or upgrades are elusive, trying harder to make profits on every project through better management of CAD resources is needed. Hopefully, your effort through the rough times will be remembered when the harvest comes in.

Remember that people are afraid of change, especially in the way they work. They need time to adapt to the changes and to build trust in the system. They also need to trust you, because you are the one in charge of the system and have more power over it than they do. People will even resist change when they know it is in their best interest, so your job becomes more difficult to persuade them to sacrifice short-term comfort for long-term benefits.

These changes will affect the entire company. To minimize the detrimental affects, involve the other departments in your organization to promote communication and enthusiasm for the CAD system. Everyone from the user and management level to the finance and accounting level should feel a sense of ownership in the system. People will support you if they feel that they have something to contribute to the system and something to gain from it.

Summary

The CAD manager faces many challenges in his daily routine, such as effective resource management, scheduling problems, and system documentation. This chapter has explored these problems, as well as some popular layering guidelines and the basic economics of CAD-system implementation.

Chapter 11 describes comprehensive maintenance procedures for expensive CAD equipment, and shows you how to make these maintenance strategies work for you. You also will look into the issue of data backup and discover several practical scheduling strategies. Chapter 11 concludes by examining some of the ways for importing and exporting AutoCAD data, and explains why you may want to master several drawing-translation techniques.

System Maintenance
and Development

Experienced computer users often say, "It's not a matter of *whether* you will lose data, but *when.*" This caveat illustrates the critical need to be prepared at all times in case a system's data becomes lost or corrupted. Data loss can happen in many ways, including natural disaster, user error, software glitches, or hardware malfunction. Because the danger of data loss is always present, system maintenance is one of the CAD manager's most important functions.

Proper maintenance not only protects you from *permanently* losing your data, but it also helps keep your expensive hardware operating at peak performance and accuracy. A neglected hard disk, for example, can slow down system response time, thereby costing additional man-hours, and neglected output devices can damage hard copy quality.

This chapter discusses simple measures you can take to prevent or solve these and other simple problems. The following sections show you how to calculate the cost of system downtime, how to perform basic maintenance on critical pieces of hardware, how to develop a backup strategy, and how to archive your drawing data once a project is complete.

This chapter also looks more closely at using your AutoCAD database as a central information resource for many of the business activities your staff may be performing manually. Later sections show you how AutoCAD can share drawing data with other programs, and describe each of the data formats AutoCAD can produce. You also will learn ways to use these formats for nondrawing purposes, including creating bills of materials, marketing, and others.

All CAD managers should read at least the first half of this chapter, which deals with system maintenance. You may find some ideas there that you had not considered in your own system maintenance plan. If you are not interested in expanding your AutoCAD system, you can skip the second half of the chapter, which shows you several techniques for developing your system for use in nondrawing tasks.

Downtime Economics

Whether it affects one workstation or an entire network, downtime costs your company money—lots of money. The cost is greater, of course, in the case of a network than in the case of a stand-alone workstation. Many business managers, however, see computer downtime as only a nuisance. A breakdown robs them of time and capital required to replace failed hardware, but they do not realize the greater cost in terms of lost productivity, lost momentum, and lost business. These are the same managers who balk at the cost of higher-quality hardware, despite its better *mean time between failures* (MTBF) ratings, more adequate power protection, and other fault-tolerant system features.

A recent study of 100 MIS and network managers of Fortune 1000 companies revealed some startling statistics:

- On average, a network becomes disabled 23.6 times per year.
- The average system breakdown lasts 4.9 hours.
- On average, $606,000 in revenue is lost each year because of system failures.

While the median values of the frequency distribution curves associated with these findings were substantially lower, they underline just how real the economic threat of downtime actually is. You may not work for a Fortune 1000 company, but downtime is expensive. Another study shows that most companies experiencing a data disaster lasting ten days or more are either bought up by another company or declare bankruptcy within a year. How is that for expensive!

Understanding the Effects of Downtime

A loss of data on your network file server (or any PC, for that matter) can happen as a result of various events. The most common cause is the user, who inadvertently erases a file before realizing that he needs to keep it. An error caused by a program also can corrupt data or otherwise render it unusable. The best-known cause of this is a software virus. A LAN is an extremely fertile place for viruses to proliferate. There even have been cases recently of network-specific viruses designed to bring down certain PC LAN installations. Of course, data loss can occur at any time because of a power failure. Faithfully backing up your data is your *only* course of recovery from these disasters.

Consider for a moment all that is involved when a breakdown occurs. First, hardware may need to be replaced. Someone (usually the CAD manager) must take time to discover the problem and identify the failed component(s), and then find and procure a replacement component, which must be installed and tested. Lost data may need to be restored, and the incident documented (as it always should be).

All the while, the failed equipment's users are less productive. If they cannot work manually, then they may not be productive at all. The company loses the total of their salaries and wages as well as the product of their labors—revenue the data was expected to generate.

Further, companies that suffer such hardware breakdowns run the risk of losing additional business over the long term. Using the average statistics given earlier, the average networked company stands to lose the equivalent of more than two weeks' time due to combined network disabilities each year (23.6 breakdowns × 4.9 hours = 14.45 work days) unless above-average precautions are taken. How much more business do you think your company could do with two *more* weeks in every year? Surely enough to pay for the additional support it takes to minimize or eliminate your downtime in the first place.

Calculating the Cost

An actual cost can be attached to network downtime. First, divide the gross income produced by your company by the number of employees. This calculates the amount of revenue each employee is expected to produce annually. Next, divide this figure by the 2000 working hours in one year, and you arrive at the hourly revenue value of each employee. Finally, you can calculate lost revenue by multiplying this value by the product of the number of users affected and the downtime's duration, as follows:

$$\frac{\dfrac{Gross}{Employees}}{Annual\ Hours} \times Users \times Duration$$

Suppose, for example, that the following figures apply to your company. The preceding formula would work out this way:

$4 million annual gross income / 24 employees = $166,666

$166,666 / 2000 hours = $83.33/hr.

$83.33/hr × 12 users = $1000/hr. cost of downtime

This scenario assumes that no critical data is lost, or that lost data (data changed since the last backup) is restored right up to the time of failure. It does not account for data that must be rebuilt, which *adds* to the cost of downtime. You double your costs when you must rebuild data, because you pay for it not only the first time it is created, but also when it must be recreated. Not every breakdown causes a loss of data, but if your file server's hard disk fails any time after a backup, some data will be lost. Backups are your *only* safeguard, and yet an estimated 70 percent of all network users have no backup plan at all. Backup strategies are discussed a little later in the chapter.

You can use even more sophisticated methods for quantifying downtime economics and analyzing the risks associated with networked systems—methods that can predict with reasonable accuracy when your network will fail. But they are very complicated and do not apply well to the typical small network. The important point is that both the CAD manager and upper management must understand that along with increased automation and integration come increased and expensive risks that should not be taken lightly. You can begin by keeping your equipment running in top shape.

Periodic Maintenance

Regular maintenance of your equipment is a proven technique for minimizing expensive downtime. You do it for your automobile. Why not do it for your much more sensitive computer systems? Which one do you rely on more for your livelihood?

While computers (fortunately) do not fall out of tune or suffer from fouled spark plugs, some components still fail from mechanical wear, heat fatigue, and user neglect. Periodic maintenance can be as simple as scheduling an hour or so a week or month for each computer, on a rotating basis, for preventative maintenance.

Maintaining Hard Disk Drives

You should begin your disk maintenance routine by erasing files that are no longer needed. Unused or forgotten files consume expensive disk space and may even prompt you to expand your hard disk capacity unnecessarily. By keeping your hard disks "lean and mean," you can postpone costly hard disk upgrades and avoid messy Disk full errors. Eliminate unauthorized and unneeded copies of drawings, symbols, and other files. Use your choice of a disk management program, such as XtreeNet from Xtree Company, Norton Utilities from Symantec, or PC Tools Deluxe from Central Point Software, Inc. These programs allow you to see an overview of your network directories and work with files easier.

Defragmenting Files

Another hard disk clean-up technique is *defragmentation*. Almost all files are saved in more than one 512-byte block. When the disk has plenty of free space, files tend to get recorded in contiguous blocks, one after another. Through constantly repeated file changings, recordings, and erasings on a hard disk's surface, the logical grouping of blocks in proximity to each other becomes disrupted. Fragments of files become scattered around the disk, in the computer's attempt always to make use of *any* available space.

Disk performance begins to suffer as the drive reads and writes portions of each file to various physical locations on the hard disk that are distant from each other instead of adjacent. Several utility programs are available that can reorganize these fragments back into consecutive (and sometimes fewer) storage units, restoring the performance that a hard disk was designed to deliver. Examples of these kind of programs are Disk Optimizer by Softlogic Solutions, Inc., and PC Tools Deluxe by Central Point Software, Inc. In simple terms, these programs work by sorting a disk's file allocation table so that each file is written into consecutive blocks wherever possible. Then they read each file into RAM and rewrite it to the new locations on your disk. Figure 11.1 shows the difference that defragmentation makes on a file.

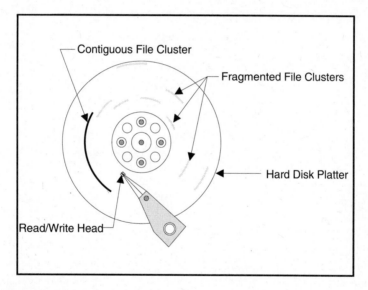

Figure 11.1:
File blocks before and after optimizing.

Note: File fragmentation is generally a bigger problem in workstation hard drives than in file servers. Most network operating systems that use dedicated file servers implement a huge disk cache in the file server that minimizes file accesses from the disk. Hard disk reorganization utilities typically do not work with these operating systems. Usually, the only way to reorganize the file structure of a file server disk is to perform a total file-by-file (not image) backup of the disk, reformat the disk, and restore the entire disk's contents. An image backup will simply restore the disk to its previous fragmented state.

Improving Disk Interleave

Some hard disk utilities can verify that your hard disk and controller are configured to the correct *sector interleave* value. Diskettes and hard disks are divided radially into many sectors. Sector interleave is the order in which a hard disk reads these sectors as the drive's head passes over the disk surface while the disk is spinning. Many drives do not efficiently read sectors in sequence, but skip one or more sectors depending on the data throughput rate of the drive, controller, and the computer's bus.

Only one optimal interleave setting exists for each combination of these three hardware components. If the interleave is too high, the computer must wait for the disk to rotate until the correct block comes under the drive head. If the interleave is too low, the block passes under the drive head too soon, and another revolution must occur before the block is "in sync" with the drive head. The illustration in figure 11.2 shows the effect of different interleave settings on the same drive.

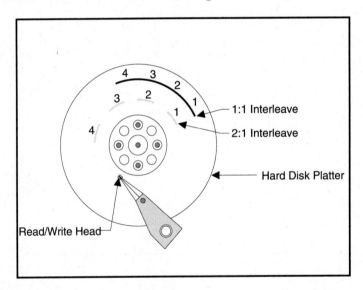

Figure 11.2:
Optimum interleave improves disk performance.

Examples of programs that can optimize disk interleave are Gibson Research's SpinRite, and Disk Technician Gold by Prime Solutions, Inc. These types of programs analyze your disk's interleave to determine an optimum value for your configuration. Then they perform a nondestructive format of your hard disk and place the existing data into the correct sectors. Some programs can also diagnose some early signs of hard disk wear, such as format integrity, bad block marking, and actual mechanical wear.

Cleaning Floppy Disk Drives

Do not forget about floppy disk drives when you perform periodic maintenance. A quick cleaning with an inexpensive head-cleaning diskette can remove the debris that can collect on the head and cause data errors. Neglected, dirty diskettes and airborne dust can accumulate inside floppy drives. With the drive's cover off, use a compressed air canister to blow out the dust before using the head-cleaning kit.

Output Device Maintenance

Networked printers and plotters see extra heavy duty. Networked users can easily send a print or plot job to the network and forget about it; before they had the network, they might not have bothered to go over all the hurdles required to print or plot a file. When networked, output devices receive much greater utilization than when they are dedicated only to a single user.

Because of this greater use and dependency, networked output devices deserve more preventative attention than non-networked devices. Your entire workgroup depends on their smooth operation, and your company is dependent on their reliability and accuracy. You should include them in your overall preventative maintenance plan.

Most printers' and plotters' user manuals include instructions for minor maintenance. Be sure that you observe at least the minimum recommended maintenance intervals for these devices. Networked output devices, however, should be serviced *twice* as often as non-networked output devices.

Dot-Matrix Printers

When servicing a dot-matrix printer, remove any tractor feed mechanisms, sheet feeders, and covers after disconnecting the printer's power cord. Check for any integrated circuit chips that may be loose in their sockets or circuit boards that may need to be reseated. Clean out any paper debris and dust. Check all moving parts for smooth operation, then clean and lubricate the drive gears and the print head's guides. Check the printer's gears for excessive backlash, which can cause poor character alignment. Adjust or replace the gears, if necessary.

Use platen cleaner to clean ink off the platen to prevent drying and cracking. The print head itself should be cleaned of built-up ink, which is the major cause of print-head failure. Many mail-order computer suppliers carry printer-cleaning kits that contain cleaners and lubricants that are specially formulated for use in computer printers.

Laser Printers

When servicing a laser printer, you typically should remove excess toner, clean the corona wire, and clean the fuse bar assembly. Some printers include most of these parts in a cartridge that is replaced whenever you replace the toner cartridge. Check your user manual to verify the maintenance procedures for your particular model. Newer Hewlett-Packard laser printers include a special cleaning sheet that cleans the entire paper path when fed through the printer.

As a normal product of the printing process, laser printers produce harmful ozone gas, which is absorbed by a filter. The odor given off by an old electric drill when its armature and brushes are worn, for example, is caused by ozone. (Electric current passes over the excessive clearance caused by wear, producing the ozone gas.) If your laser printer has seen very much use, you should replace the filter if you notice the distinctive odor of ozone near the printer when it is in operation.

Pen Plotters

While internal maintenance of your pen plotter should be left to qualified service personnel, you can take preventative measures to keep your plotter working properly.

Wipe down all external surfaces with a 50-50 mixture of isopropyl alcohol and water in a soft cloth or sponge to remove ink spills and other residue. Do not use abrasive cleansers, detergents, or solvents. Rinse with a clean cloth and water. Dry with a soft lint-free cloth.

You can use a damp cotton swab to clean around paper edge sensors and pen holders to remove dust, lint, and ink. Clean pen carousels with cotton swabs moistened with pen-cleaning fluid or alcohol. Allow these parts to dry thoroughly before you use the plotter again. Replace any worn or damaged carousel seals.

To help ensure the plotter's continued accuracy, clean the paper pinch wheels and grit wheel surfaces. Using the brush supplied with your plotter, or a stiff toothbrush, remove debris from these parts as you manually rotate them. Maintain your plotter pens according to the manufacturer's recommendations. If you suspect that your plotter's accuracy has diminished, seek a qualified technician who can accurately test and calibrate the plotter.

Electrostatic Plotters

Because they incorporate advanced technology, electrostatic plotters require more attention than most other peripherals. Following the directions outlined in your plotter's manual, open the plotter to expose the writing assembly. Remove the unused media and clean the media compartment of paper debris and dust.

Next, check the writing head for stains or corrosion. Using the cleaning supplies and procedures recommended by your plotter manufacturer, clean and polish the writing head and developer. Replace worn or corroded writing head assemblies. Clean the pinch rollers or other media transport mechanisms, reload the media, and reassemble the plotter.

Wipe down all external surfaces with a 50-50 mixture of isopropyl alcohol and water in a soft cloth or sponge to remove toner spills and other residue. Do not use abrasive cleansers, detergents, or solvents. Rinse with a clean cloth and water. Dry with a soft lint-free cloth.

The extended maintenance requirements for your plotter may require flushing the toner delivery system with dispersing fluid. Do this according to the manufacturer's recommendations.

Finally, generate several test plots to make sure that you reassembled the plotter correctly and that it is performing satisfactorily.

Miscellaneous Checks

The periodic checkup is a good time to look for strained cables that could lead to a failure. Give computers, monitors, and keyboards a good external cleaning and get around to those pesky little adjustments and bugs that you can never seem to make time for. Do not forget to log all work in a system log book. It will provide a clear record of performance on the machine's part and yours.

Service and Maintenance Contracts

An extended warranty or service contract makes a lot of sense, especially for plotters. Your system's success depends on equipment's being on-line 100 percent of the time.

Plotter service contracts are usually quite reasonable, considering the extent of coverage these agreements offer. A single billable service call for the most trivial problem, such as plugging the plotter into a power receptacle, can easily cost more than several years' worth of service contract charges. Some service contracts even include provisions for scheduled preventative maintenance visits to keep your plotter healthy.

Plotter service technicians usually charge well over $100 per hour, and usually charge a one- or two-hour minimum fee for service calls lasting less than an hour. Plotter parts also are extremely expensive. A service contract could well be your only hedge against very untimely and expensive repairs.

If you do not feel comfortable maintaining or servicing your equipment yourself, or if you simply do not have the time, you should consider contracting a maintenance company to do the work for you. Off-site maintenance services exist in most major cities. They can schedule periodic maintenance visits to perform all the diagnostic and cleaning chores discussed here and more for a nominal fee. Just make sure that the maintenance company knows exactly what services to perform, and understands the extent of its liability.

The Science of Backups

Your data may well be worth more to your company than all its computer equipment combined. Yet, surveys reveal that 35 percent of all respondents *never* back up their data! Backups are the cornerstone of the CAD manager's job and traditionally at the top of his job description. You have already read *why* you need to do backups, now you will learn *how* to do them more efficiently and easily.

Backups should be the CAD manager's most painless task. If backing up your workstation or server disks is a hassle, you will be less prone to do it. Backing up should take a minimum amount of your time. Ideally, all that should be required is to insert a new tape into the drive each day. Your network system should be designed and installed so that working data is centrally located and backups are performed unattended. Also, the integrity of the backup process should be verifiable. You should regularly test your backup system's ability to restore files accurately.

Scheduling Backups

Most companies that do backups keep only one spare set of data in case of an emergency. They use the last set of backup media to do the next backup. In non-networked sites, many users simply pull out a box of diskettes on Friday and use a third-party backup program. The user sits and watches the file names go by as he dutifully feeds his diskettes into the machine. It is a boring job that takes precious time. If his company is lucky, he *may* feel like doing it again next Friday.

With a well-designed backup scheme and the right equipment, your backups should take only a moment each day—and it should happen every day. You should not, however, simply recycle the same backup medium every day.

What if you found out that you had been working with the wrong version of a base drawing all week? With only a daily backup record, the previous week's work would be lost or ruined. Or, what if you found out (too late) that your backup scheme was missing a whole subdirectory that had been created three weeks ago?

There are several ways to schedule backups, again, according to the amount of work you do. But all backups should be kept according to some sort of generational scheme. These schemes are sometimes known as the *grandfather/father/son* system. That is, at least three generations of data are kept current at all times. The frequency of the generations should vary with the amount of revision that occurs in your use of CAD and the amount of work you do.

The Volume/Calendar Backup Strategy

One of the easiest ways to schedule backups is on a volume/calendar basis (see fig. 11.3). If you can fit your entire file system onto one tape, for instance, then it does not hurt to do a *full system backup* every night. But if you have hundreds of megabytes of on-line data and programs, and much of it is static, then you could do a full system backup once a month, a *partial backup* of all dynamic files once a week, and an *incremental backup* of only the files that change daily. In a five-workday scenario, this would take seven sets of media.

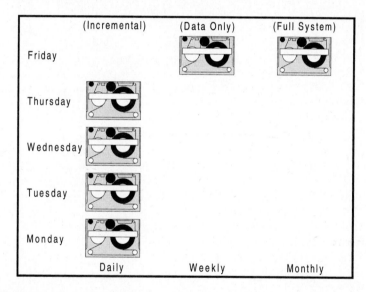

Figure 11.3:
A volume/calendar backup schedule.

The Grandfather/Father/Son Backup Strategy

Another backup system keeps backups according to the same schedule, except that the content of the backups is more generational and the backups rotate according to age (see fig. 11.4). This system requires at least nine sets of media. You perform daily backups as usual, using a new set of media for each backup session. Thus, a backup history is saved for each day of the work week. After one week has passed, on Friday for example, instead of overwriting last Friday's data, that backup is placed on a weekly cycle. After the second week passes, another weekly backup is set aside, and once again on the third and fourth week. At the end of the fifth week, a monthly tape is set aside and the previous monthly tape is then returned to the weekly cycle for use during the current week.

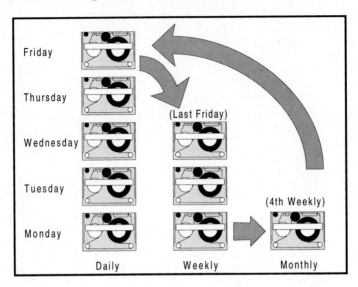

Figure 11.4:
A grandfather/father/son backup schedule.

In this way, one backup set contains data from a month ago, one set is saved for each week until the current week, and there is a set containing data from each day of the current week. With this system, you are assured of having several different time periods from which you can restore your data. By adding 10 more tapes to the schedule, you can extend the backup history a full year by maintaining a tape for each month.

The monthly and weekly sets (at least) should be kept off-site where they will not be susceptible to the same catastrophes as your equipment on-site. Keep a copy of the backup software used to create the backups with the media sets, too. If a new system must be configured in order to restore them, and the backup software was lost in the catastrophe, the correct backup software version could mean the difference between a successful restoration and unusable data. Also, all backups in this type of system should be (at minimum) partial backups of all data, configuration, and security files. You need not bother to do daily backups of application programs and unmodified system files that can be reinstalled from distribution diskettes. An occasional full backup of the full file structure any time it is modified should be sufficient.

Other Backup Strategies

The last backup strategy (see fig. 11.5) is for those who really want to get organized, and whose data is especially sensitive to timeliness. This system is based on a mathematical formula that increases the number of backup sets in proportion to time, with the most frequent number of backups made most recently.

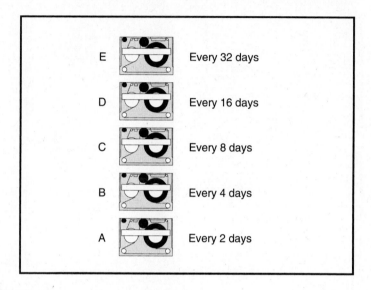

E   Every 32 days

D   Every 16 days

C   Every 8 days

B   Every 4 days

A   Every 2 days

Figure 11.5:
An exponential backup frequency strategy.

A similar application of this algorithm is the Tower of Hanoi game, which consists of three pegs on a board and five progressively larger rings placed on one of the end pegs. The goal of the game is to move all the rings to the peg on the other end of the board by moving them one at a time to either of the other pegs. The trick is to never place a large ring on top of a smaller ring.

You can implement the Tower of Hanoi backup method with as many tapes as you wish, with each tape representing a backup frequency of a power of two. For example, with five backup tapes, one tape is used every other day, one tape every four days, one every eight backups, one is no more than sixteen days old, and one is used only after 32 days. Adding a sixth tape to the system would give you a backup history extending back 64 days (see fig. 11.6). If you used five tapes, which were labeled A through E, the basic pattern would look like this:

ABAC ABAD ABAC ABAE

Applied to a five-workday schedule, and by repeating the pattern, the schedule would look like this:

ABACA BADAB ACABA EABAC ABADA BACAB AEABA CABAD ABACA
BAEAB ACABA DABAC ABAEA BACAB ADABA CABAE...

			1 A	2 B	3 A	4
5	6 C	7 A	8 B	9 A	10 D	11
12	13 A	14 B	15 A	16 C	17 A	18
19	20 B	21 A	22 E	23 A	24 B	25
26	27 A	28 C	29 A	30 B		

Figure 11.6:
The Tower of Hanoi backup schedule.

Backup Program Requirements

You can select from a wide variety of backup software to facilitate your backup tasks. All programs can do the basic job of copying your disk's contents. But a few special features help the best of these programs make your backups easier.

In general, the software should be easy to use. Although a program may be totally capable of doing anything you want it to, if the process is overly complicated or awkward, the program's power may remain hidden and the program may go unused. Look for a program with a well-designed, logical, and descriptive menu interface. The menu interface should help you learn to use the program and all its options. A macro facility can also be very helpful in recording frequently used sequences of keystrokes. If a program does have a macro capability, make sure that you can edit the macros, either within the program itself or by using a standard text editor. Then you can make changes to macros in the file instead of having to repeat the sequence.

The backup program should support command-line execution, so that it can be invoked by a batch file or log-in script. All the pertinent menu options should have command-line counterparts. Options and commands should be easy to apply for file selection by inclusion or exclusion of wild cards, dates, extensions, types, or file structures.

Security-File Backup

For use on a Novell network, the backup program should have some provision for backing up and restoring the server's security and system files. These files are hidden from the average DOS program, and contain all file ownership, group membership, user trustee rights, user IDs, and passwords. Without these files, you would not be able to reconstruct the network back to its status just prior to time of failure. Restore these files before restoring any data that may belong only to one user, because ownership of files cannot be transferred from one user to another during the restoration process. In the case where the entire file server disk structure must be restored, if the user does not yet exist on the system at the time the attempt is made to restore the data, it will be lost if that person does not also happen to be the user performing the restoration.

Unattended Backups

The backup program should provide some sort of timing function so that you can schedule the backup to occur unattended while nobody is working on the network and all files are closed. Sometimes this capability is provided as a separate program. It may be a TSR that enables the computer to be used normally until the appointed backup time, or it may be an executable that prevents use of the computer until after the backup. Unattended backup is advantageous not only for strategic reasons, but also for security.

If you do not want to need to be present when initiating the backup, and the software cannot be automated to perform it according to a schedule, then you must give someone else security clearance equal to yourself to perform the backup for you. Supervisory security clearance should be extended only for more important reasons than mere convenience. While the security of your scheduled process for an unattended backup must still be equal to the network supervisor's, it is far better for the backup to happen sometime in the middle of the night, and for a predictable duration, than if it happens at the hands of an unpredictable human operator.

Types of Backups

The program should allow for both *file-by-file* and *image* backups. A file-by-file backup stores files as discrete entities, just as your hard disk does. From this type of backup, you can restore any one file independently of the rest of the backed-up data. This is the type of recovery you will use the most to restore one or more files that get corrupted or accidentally erased. The backup software creates an index of all the directories and files to be backed up on the tape, just like a FAT. When a file must be restored, the software can scan this index for the correct file, advance to it, read the file, and write it to the disk. The disadvantage of file-by-file backup is that the disk must have a working operating system installed before a restoration can be made. Hence, in the case of a complete disk failure, a file-by-file backup will not be useful for restoring the network operating system and boot files.

An image backup essentially takes a binary snapshot of the entire disk at the time that the backup is made. The software bypasses the file server's operating system and reads the disk directly, beginning at the first track and sector and progressing to the last, ignoring the directory structure. Every fragment of a file is faithfully reproduced on the tape. This "brute force" method is much faster than file-by-file backup. Because you do not need the services of a working network operating system to restore an image backup, it is the best way to backup up the NOS along with all its security information. You should perform an image backup of the drive containing your network operating system, both after you install the software and every time you upgrade or change its configuration. Otherwise you will need to completely reinstall and reconfigure the software in the case of a failure of that drive.

Unfortunately, image backup has its disadvantages, too. With most backup programs, the only way to restore an image backup is to restore the entire data set, overwriting the entire disk's contents in the process. Some programs have the ability to read the disk's FAT and assemble the file's pieces off the tape before writing them to disk. All this thrashing makes individual file restoration from an image backup slower than the file-by-file method. Further, not all backup programs are able to recognize bad blocks on the target disk during a restoration. Because the program bypasses the operating system (which knows where the bad blocks are) it may try to write data to the bad blocks, which almost every disk has. Finally, because an image backup is a faithful reproduction of the disk from which it was made, it can be restored only to a disk of the same type. This prevents you from upgrading to a larger disk in the case of a failure, or transferring files to a another system with a larger or smaller drive.

Miscellaneous Requirements

An intelligent backup program either waits for opened files to close, or catalogs them for backup after the other files on the disk are backed up. Poor backup software may lock up or abort if it encounters an open file. And no matter what the reason, the backup program should have some way of telling you which files it could not back up so that you can take care of them. If you have a large network, make sure the program you are considering will handle your largest (multimegabyte) files and directory structures.

You also should test any application programs with the backup program you choose for incompatibility during backup. If you purchase a program that can back up the network while it is in use, make sure that as the backup program passes over any open files it does not cause errors in the programs that opened them. Organize your programs and data on separate drives or volumes. Then you can easily backup all files of either type without specifying individual directories.

Some backup programs also employ data compression and/or error detection and correction algorithms to compress disk data onto the backup media, thereby requiring less media space (up to a 2:1 ratio). These schemes require more time to complete, of course. Error correction should be automatic and ensure data integrity to and from the backup or compression process. Vendors often call this correction process "write verification."

Also look for a program that will allow *tape spanning*. Normally, you will want to buy a tape drive with at least enough capacity to back up your file server's largest volume. Try to buy a device that is large enough to accommodate all your anticipated future growth. But inevitably, your network will grow beyond it. If your backup software allows tape spanning, it will prompt you to insert another tape when the first one fills up. This tape swapping may make it hard to perform a complete backup unattended, but at least you do not need to buy another tape drive.

Traditionally, tape backup of network file servers has been performed from a workstation. The network operating system itself was the only program allowed to run on the file server, and there was no provision to launch utility programs. However, some newer backup programs enable you to install the backup device inside the file server and act as an extension of the operating system. These are installed as a Value-Added Process (VAP) or NetWare Loadable Module (NLM) with NetWare. The backup is initiated from a workstation by loading the user interface.

With the backup in a more protected physical location with the file server, data security is enhanced and complex workstation configurations are not further complicated. Also, the file server's processing resources can be put to use while the network is up and running, so that backups can be loosely monitored by the CAD manager without constant supervision.

Other useful features are available in some network backup programs. Some programs can back up workstation hard disks as well as the file server's hard disk. These programs ensure that everything on the network is secured, regardless of user negligence. Some have built-in backup scheduling and tape management features. Still other programs perform continuous backups as data is modified, thus leaving nothing to chance.

Whatever system you use, be sure to hold your own "fire drills" periodically and test your backups to be sure they are working properly. Restore a directory or two to a test area and see if the files are accurate. Test a restoration of your security data, as well. Do not forget to test again if you make any changes that could affect the backup system—upgrading DOS, your network operating system, and backup software or hardware.

Archiving Your Work

Another axiom of computer technology is that no matter how big a hard disk is, the data stored on it will increase to fill all the available space. Sooner or later, something must go in order to make room for more timely data. You cannot expect to continue adding disk space in order to keep all your department's data on-line all the time—especially when much of the data is seldom, if ever, used.

Archiving is the process of storing completed projects on disks or tapes in much the same way as you store backups, only in a more specific form. Rather than backing everything up onto one media set, archiving is the process of removing individual project data from a current storage device to a long-term storage medium when the project is complete. By removing infrequently used or unused data from the file server's disk(s), you reduce the hard disk space you need to buy and make more efficient use of the space you have. Archiving also protects inactive files from most of the hazards associated with on-line data. You can create and maintain a "library" of past project data, just as you do with paper or film drawings.

By using your tape drive as an archiving device, you further justify its cost for backups. Simply make two archive tapes of each project, one for on-site and one for off-site storage. Large architectural or engineering projects can easily total dozens of megabytes of data contained in many drawings. Storing them all in one discrete cartridge encourages and promotes organized maintenance. A catalog of archived drawings and a notation on the individual file's drawing log help you locate archived drawings easily.

You can even purchase archive programs that can monitor your entire disk system and dynamically archive any type of file. The system supervisor can specify how long any file should be allowed to go unaccessed. The program maintains an index of all the files on the hard disk, and if one has not been used by the end of the prescribed period, it is automatically archived to the backup device. Some files, such as operating system files, can be excluded from the archiving process. Some systems also allow automatic restoration of files should one be requested. Access times can be very slow because the file must be found on the tape and restored to the disk, but an archiving capability can really help in space-sensitive situations. Such systems are known as *archive servers* and can also double as the backup system.

A cheap but effective method of creating archives is to use a *file compression* program such as PKZip or LHArc. These programs are capable of quickly compressing files down to a fraction of their original size for storage, exchange, or transmission by modem. When the file needs to be opened, a complimentary decompression program expands the file back to its former state in seconds. Compression programs can squeeze AutoCAD drawings by as much as 90 percent or more, with about 75 percent being average. Their application as archiving programs is enhanced by the fact that they can combine many source files into one compressed file. All the drawings for a particular project or job can be included in one file often small enough to fit on a floppy disk. These programs also can perform error-checking during decompression to ensure that the file that comes out of the archive is the same as the one that went in.

Building on the Initial Investment

Once a system is in place and the human and electronic components are performing as planned and production is acceptable, the tendency is to settle in and watch as technology goes on by. So long as AutoCAD is doing what it is supposed to do—produce drawings—what more should you ask? This is not to say that users should be slaves to technological advancement and blindly adopt every newer, bigger, and faster development. But there are times when upgrading makes sound business sense and provides intellectual gratification. System upgrade is just one part of system development. Progressive system development also means looking for what *could* be, exploiting your system's full potential of your hardware, software, personnel, data, and being alert for what you *are not* getting.

The following sections discuss computer hardware and software upgrading and replacement, and examine general system development strategies for your entire automation system and the role it plays in your business. By continually customizing, refining, and perfecting, you can extract maximum productivity from your system while holding the line on upgrade costs.

When To Consider Software Upgrades

Hardware upgrades usually are equated with speed enhancement, but software upgrades usually are another story. Remember, hardware *runs* software. Faster hardware enables you to do the same job in less time. Software upgrade decisions should be based upon the idea of doing the same job *better*. Software upgrades, for the most part, mean investing in additional features. Features sometimes even come at the expense of some performance—witness AutoCAD Release 9. While it added significant and exciting new features, it was slightly slower than AutoCAD version 2.6.

Your decisions about upgrading software should be based on a demonstrated need for the new features that a new version of software has to offer. What if your company needs AutoCAD to do something it does not yet do? If a new release of the program included this desired feature, and if the feature would enable your company to do a better job for its clients, then you probably should upgrade to the new release.

On the other hand, many companies upgrade their software (and not just AutoCAD) for the wrong reasons. All too often, the only business impact this has is the wasted expense of installation, troubleshooting, debugging, conversion, and training. A poor decision may be made on the basis of an eager salesman's pitch, an overly ambitious user, or ignorance.

Many users, however, are forced to upgrade for business reasons unrelated to software features. Many companies that must exchange drawing files with other companies, for example, find that they have to upgrade simply to overcome the "upward-compatible only" nature of AutoCAD. If a major client or business ally upgrades, a company also may have to upgrade to remain compatible. This condition is prevalent in the A/E/C industry where drawing exchange has become a way of life. The condition is aggravated when a company has no use for the newer program's additional features. AutoCAD's 3D capabilities are a good example. While few would argue that 3D features are a valuable aspect of the program (in fact, AutoCAD would be considered incomplete without them), many companies are frustrated when they must pay for upgrades that include such features, when they never even work with 3D models.

To keep installation costs down when you do need to perform a software upgrade, you can use a specific technique to ensure that it is done smoothly and without incident (see fig. 11.7). By installing the new software in parallel to the old, you can properly debug the installation and configuration without needing to rush, and without causing downtime for your users. You can run test data through the new program and check for normal output and performance before you need to use it in actual production. Install the software in a directory structure identical to the one used for your existing software—only along side of it and with a slightly different top directory name—instead of on top of the old software.

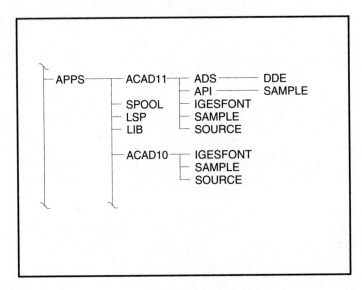

Figure 11.7:
A sample parallel directory structure for software upgrades.

Once you are sure that the new program operates as expected, you can easily adjust the batch files or menus your users invoke to start the new program. Then the old software can be deleted from the system. If your workstations are not networked, the principle is nearly the same. You can install the new software on your system and thoroughly test it. When you are satisfied that it will pass muster with all your other configurations, you can back up your copy of the new program and restore it over the old software on other machines.

Using AutoCAD all around the Office

A considerable amount of work goes into an AutoCAD drawing; once the hard copy is produced, you may be inclined to believe that the electronic drawing is almost disposable. But if you develop your AutoCAD system to its full potential, you will find that the drawing data can be put to other valuable uses throughout your company. Your AutoCAD database contains a wealth of information that can help you with your other information needs.

The remainder of this chapter deals with system development. While maintenance is crucial to your system's success, it is still only part of a larger picture. You also must find ways to develop your AutoCAD system to bring it to its full potential and maximize your company's return on its CAD investment. Here, "system development" means the integration of your AutoCAD system into business areas beyond just drafting. One of the most fundamental ways to develop your system is by linking AutoCAD data to other programs you may or may not already have. Some programs can link to AutoCAD almost invisibly; others require the use of intermediate files, such as DXF, IGES, DXB, HP-GL, and EPS (see fig 11.8).

The following sections show you, in general terms, how you can develop your system , and introduce several interesting uses for your AutoCAD database.

Dynamic Data Exchange

By far, the easiest and most direct way to exchange data between AutoCAD and another program is through *dynamic data exchange* (DDE). This capability is currently available to AutoCAD only in the OS/2 environment. The advantages of OS/2 are discussed in Chapter 4. Under OS/2, AutoCAD communicates with other programs through a special DDE program written with ADS and provided with AutoCAD OS/2. Dynamic data exchange provides a "hot link" between programs, so that they can share data in real-time without messy intermediate files. DDE enables two programs—such as AutoCAD and a spreadsheet program—to act as one program.

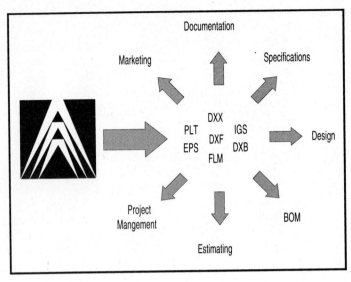

Figure 11.8:
Reusing the AutoCAD database.

Chapter 4 describes one example of DDE in action, in which AutoCAD communicates with Microsoft Excel to exchange dimensional data about a stepped shaft. If the shaft is modified in AutoCAD, the dimensions stored within Excel are updated automatically. Likewise, if a dimension is changed within Excel, the AutoCAD drawing is updated. The ADS application provides the "doorway" between AutoCAD and DDE. DDE, on the other hand, is the "hallway" between AutoCAD and Excel.

As another example of DDE, consider the use of AutoCAD with the ORACLE database server by Oracle Corp. AutoCAD can submit SQL database queries to and receive results from ORACLE through DDE. This adaptation of DDE capabilities gives the user another way to graphically view and change data. By selecting a graphic entity and executing commands, the user can query a large, nongraphical database for information related to the entity. When you select an AutoCAD block of an airplane sitting on a runway, for instance, you are provided data on flight schedules, passenger lists, terminal numbers, and so on. The link works in reverse as well. If you query the ORACLE database for all planes departing within the hour, the AutoCAD blocks are highlighted for easy location. The data-exchange possibilities are almost endless.

When ADS becomes available for other platforms than OS/2, users will at least be able to perform dynamic data exchange in other operating environments. But they must be environments that provide interprocess communications capabilities themselves. AutoCAD and ADS cannot do it alone. The most likely candidates to take advantage of this capability would be Windows, the Macintosh under System 7.0, the UNIX, and possibly the DESQview environment. So far, these environments do not have sufficient interprocess communications capabilities to communicate with ADS, or ADS is not yet available in those environments. The alternative is to use intermediate files.

Reviewing Import/Export Formats

If your chosen platform does not support DDE, you will need to use intermediate files to exchange data with other programs. You can extract drawing information by using simple AutoCAD commands to create intermediate files for in-house use or exchange with other CAD programs. These files are called *intermediate files* because they are neither the origin of the data, nor the final form, but simply are used as a vehicle to transfer data from the former to the latter.

Because users often need to exchange AutoCAD data with other CAD programs and extract drawing information, AutoCAD can produce several intermediate file formats. Each file format has advantages for certain purposes. These formats cannot only be read into different CAD programs, but also can be utilized by traditional database, spreadsheet, word processing, and graphics programs. By understanding these formats, you can put them to use in developing your system to reuse some or all of your AutoCAD drawing data for other purposes.

Some third-party applications can even produce their own intermediate files. For example, design programs can perform analyses that can produce input files for AutoCAD in an intermediate file format. Some of these design programs can create virtually completed drawings.

You must carefully manage these data exchange processes between programs to ensure integrity and accuracy, but you should find that the extra work is worth the results. By making your AutoCAD database do more work for you, your company benefits more from its investment in CAD technology and AutoCAD becomes a more integral part of your company. This can, in turn, prove beneficial to you when you need support and commitment from upper management. The following sections explore several import/export processes as well as the management pitfalls associated with maintaining and exploiting a multiple-application database.

In order to use AutoCAD drawing data with other programs or create data for use by AutoCAD, your program must be able to use one of AutoCAD's exchange file formats. The AutoCAD drawing file format itself (DWG) has never been made available to developers of other programs, and is not likely to be made public knowledge. The DWG format changes with nearly every new release of AutoCAD. If third-party developers were able to use the DWG format, they would be constantly redesigning their products to keep up with Autodesk's changes to the format, and customers would not be able to wait.

Some third-party developers have reverse-engineered the binary drawing file format and discovered its hidden structures, but for most uses this process is unnecessary and very problematic. As an alternative, Autodesk provides several ways for AutoCAD to read and write files for use by other programs. Each format has its strengths for certain purposes. The DWG format is subject to change at any time, whereas exchange formats are documented and guaranteed to remain upwardly compatible with future releases.

DXF: The Universal Format

The *drawing interchange format* (DXF) is AutoCAD's primary file format for use by other programs. An AutoCAD DXF file completely describes the entire drawing right down to block tables, attributes, linetypes, and layer names. Everything that exists in the DWG file is reproduced in a DXF file.

A DXF file is an ASCII text file that is easily read and manipulated. The DXF format has become a de facto standard format for file exchange between CAD programs and is supported almost exclusively by non-CAD programs that use AutoCAD drawings or create complex graphic data for use in AutoCAD. Further, you can edit a DXF file to make it downwardly compatible with earlier versions of AutoCAD. This type of editing is much more difficult to perform on a DWG file.

Examine the following partial listing; it is taken from a DXF file made from the NOZZLE sample drawing that accompanies the AutoCAD program. The partial listing shows the drawing file's data in DXF format:

```
   0
SECTION
   2
HEADER
   9
$ACADVER
   1
AC1009
   9
$INSBASE
  10
0.0
  20
0.0
  30
0.0
   9
```

This data is easy to read, compared to a DWG file. In DXF format, the drawing data is divided into sections containing numeric values that describe the geometry in the drawing and the AutoCAD environment.

AutoCAD creates DXF files by using the Dxfout command to export either full drawings or only selected entities. The Dxfin command can read a DXF file into a new or existing drawing. To create a new drawing with a DXF file, start a new drawing with AutoCAD's default drawing parameters (`NEWDWG=`). When you import DXF data into an existing drawing, you bring in only the entities section of the DXF file. The block definitions and layer names are not imported. Rather, they are overridden by the current drawing's data. Using the Dxfout and Dxfin commands, you can effectively transfer all your drawing data to another program and back again with changes. Further, you can use the Attext command's DXF option to create DXF files that contain only attribute data. These files have the extension DXX to distinguish them from other DXF files.

For example, you can use AutoCAD's "little brother," AutoSketch, to begin drawings for embellishment in AutoCAD later. AutoSketch is a great program for getting people to start using CAD without intimidating them with the complete AutoCAD package. Like its "big brother," AutoSketch can create and read DXF files, so you can exchange drawing files between the two programs.

The Dxfout command also allows for the creation of binary DXF files. A binary version of a DXF file is smaller than an ASCII version, and can be processed several times faster. For very large or complex drawings, look for binary DXF capability in third-party programs.

DXF files are a convenient and accurate way to share data with other graphical and nongraphical programs. For more information on how you can make your own programs that use DXF files, see *Customizing AutoCAD* or *Maximizing AutoCAD Vol.I: Customizing AutoCAD with Macros & Menus*, and *Inside AutoLISP* or *Maximizing AutoCAD Vol.II: Inside AutoLISP*, also by New Riders Publishing.

IGES Data

The *initial graphics exchange standard* (IGES) is the second-most popular exchange format. The IGES format, however, is more commonly used to transfer data between PC CAD programs and minicomputer or mainframe CAD programs. IGES is an internationally used exchange format that is not specific to any one CAD program.

IGES is primarily dedicated to the description of standard product data and graphics. Because IGES is a public-domain format that is universally applicable to any CAD system, however, it does not accurately translate the proprietary data structures of some CAD programs, including AutoCAD.

IGES translations to and from AutoCAD traditionally have met with limited success. Attributes, associative dimensions, wide polylines and solids, 3D entities, text, and other entities usually translate poorly if at all. But, if you absolutely have to exchange data with another CAD system and IGES is the only solution short of the more expensive alternatives (such as a direct translator, scanning, or redrawing) then IGES is better than nothing at all.

Always carefully check translated drawings (whether in IGES or DXF format) for accuracy. You may have to do some clean-up, or your client might not get everything he bargained for. A separate document included with AutoCAD, *IGES Interface Specifications*, documents the correlation between AutoCAD entities and their IGES representations.

Now look at a portion of an IGES file that was produced from the NOZZLE drawing. Like its DXF counterpart, this file is an ASCII text file, but the resemblance ends there. See if you can decipher some of the information contained in the file's header:

```
IGES file generated from an AutoCAD drawing by the IGES                    S0000001
translator from Autodesk, Inc., translator version IGESOUT-3.04.S0000002
,,23HC:\ACAD11\SAMPLE\NOZZLE,10HNOZZLE.IGS,14HAutoCAD-Z.0.9A,12HIGESOUT-G0000001
3.04,32,38,6,99,15,23HC:\ACAD11\SAMPLE\NOZZLE,1.0,1,4HINCH,32767,      G0000002
3.2767D1,13H901116.091320,1.3446413D-8,1.3446413D1,11HKen Billing,22H Ne  G0000003
w Riders Publishing,6,0;                                                  G0000004
     124        1        1                            00000000D0000001
     124                          2        0                   D0000002
     108        3        1                            00010000D0000003
     108                 1                                     D0000004
     108        4        1                            00010000D0000005
     108                 1                                     D0000006
     108        5        1                            00010000D0000007
     108                 1                                     D0000008
     108        6        1                            00010000D0000009
     108                 1                                     D0000010
     410        7        1        1        2        1 00000101D0000011
     410                 1                            PROFILE  D0000012
```

DXB: The Forgotten Format

AutoCAD can import and export drawing data in another binary format, called the *drawing interchange binary* (DXB) format. DXB files do not contain as much data as DXF files do, but they can be valuable when only graphical data is needed without blocks, attributes, or other complex data. The only problem with the DXB format is that, even though it is documented in the *AutoCAD Reference Manual*, it is not used very often. The DXF and IGES formats meet practically every need.

You can use AutoCAD's Dxbin command to import DXB files. By configuring AutoCAD for an ADI plotter driver and selecting the DXB file output option, you can output a DXB file from AutoCAD.

To date, the best use for DXB files has been within AutoCAD itself. A DXB file is essentially a plot file that describes the view of the drawing that was current when the file was made. You can use a DXB file to create new 2D drawings from 3D drawings such as 3D floor plans. Often, several 3D edges will align over one another. Before Release 11, with its duplicate vector elimination feature, this caused time-consuming multiple pen strokes when the drawing was plotted. With the help of a DXB file, a 2D version of a view (such as an elevation or plan) can be made quickly and edited to remove the extra vectors. Release 11 paper space now enables you to create multiple views of the same 3D model, however, so this editing technique will likely die out.

Also, before Release 10's Dview command with its own perspective projection and clipping, you could get the same perspective effects and depth clipping by using AutoShade. You simply made a filmroll file of the 3D model, imported it into AutoShade, applied the desired perspective and clipping, and output a DXB file with AutoShade's Make DXB option. Then you read it back into AutoCAD to create a line drawing.

Perhaps these work-arounds will give you some ideas of how you can put DXB files to use on your needs. In fact, several of the isometric illustrations appearing in this book were produced by DXB plotting views of 3D models, importing the DXB files into new drawings, exporting the resulting 2D drawings to DXF files, importing them into a graphics illustration program for embellishment, then converting them to Encapsulated PostScript format and importing them into a desktop publishing program. This may seem like a long process, but the process exemplifies the beauty of both AutoCAD and intermediate files. AutoCAD is the most powerful tool for 3D modeling; the graphics illustration program is more powerful for publishing-type graphics. The combined time of modeling and conversions was much less than trying to make one tool do something it could not, and the intermediate files create the bridge between the two.

You can think of DXB files as plot files that you can import back into AutoCAD. But be aware that DXB output of a drawing has the same effect on drawing entities as plotting—text characters, arcs, curved polylines, and circles become tiny vectors and the converted drawing will not contain any block or attribute definitions.

HP-GL Files

You also can use plot files to exchange AutoCAD graphics by creating *Hewlett-Packard Graphics Language* (HP-GL) files. AutoCAD creates an HP-GL file when you configure any HP plotter to plot to a file (PLT). Like the DXB file, an HP-GL file describes only the graphics in the area that was plotted, and with short line segments rather than graphic primitives such as curves and circles. These line segments are expressed as a series of plotter control commands that tell the plotter how to plot the drawing.

The HP-GL file fragment that follows shows you the pen movement commands (PU, PD, PA, etc.) that move the pens from coordinate to coordinate across a sheet. Other programs can use these commands to reproduce a drawing faithfully. Again, this listing was taken from AutoCAD's sample NOZZLE drawing file:

```
.(;.I81;;17:.N;19:IN;SC;PU;PU;SP1;LT;VS36;PA-1278,-1365;PD;PA-1268,
-1373;PA-1255,-1378;PA-1243,-1380;PA-1230,-1378;PA-1218,-1373;PA-1207,
-1365;PU;PA-1200,-1393;PD;PA-1126,-1320;PU;PA-1180,-1409;PD;PA-1018,
-1246;PU;PA-1180,-1409;PD;PA-1195,-1420;PA-1211,-1428;PA-1230,-1433;
PA-1248,-1433;PA-1266,-1428;PA-1283,-1420;PA-1298,-1409;PA-1876,-831;
PA-1887,-816;PA-1895,-799;PA-1900,-781;PA-1900,-763;PA-1895,-744;PA-1887,
-728;PA-1876,-713;PA-180,982;PU;PA-131,996;PD;PA-1842,-715;PA-1854,-730;
PA-1862,-747;PA-1866,-765;PA-1866,-783;PA-1862,-802;PA-1854,-818;PA-1842,
-833;PA-1282,-1393;PA-1270,-1402;PA-1256,-1408;PA-1241,-1410;PA-1226,-1408;
PA-1212,-1402;PA-1200,-1393;PU;PA-1278,-1365;PD;PA-1809,-835;PA-1820,-820;
PA-1828,-803;PA-1832,-785;PA-1832,-767;
```

HP-GL is the most widely used and accepted plotter language today, so it is also offered as an import format in several popular graphics and desktop publishing programs for importing graphics.

EPS Files

Another plot file option available to you is the Encapsulated PostScript (EPS) file. PostScript is the industry-standard page description language by Adobe Systems. This language is designed for desktop publishing to describe both typeset text and graphics. The PostScript language is used by many popular laser printers, such as the Apple LaserWriter, and by professional typesetters, such as the Linotronic.

Many graphics and desktop publishing programs use Encapsulated PostScript as a universal intermediate file format for graphics exchange. EPS files contain basically the same data that the program sends to a PostScript printer, but a few of the statements are arranged differently so that applications can use the data.

AutoCAD automatically creates EPS files whenever you configure a PostScript device as the plotter and plot to file. So, just like DXB and HP-GL plot files, you do not even have to own the configured device to take advantage of the data formats.

EPS files, however, usually do not display in an application once they are imported. If you try to view an EPS file on-screen, you probably will see only a box surrounding the image's outline and two diagonal lines intersecting at the image's center. Some other applications, however, can produce EPS files with a *tagged image file format* (TIFF) preview section. TIFF files (TIF) are bit-mapped graphics images that simulate gray-scale shading. By using an EPS file with a TIFF preview section, you can see an on-screen representation of the EPS file's printed output. Regrettably, AutoCAD does not include TIFF previews when it produces EPS files.

The following example is a portion of the EPS file for the NOZZLE drawing:

```
%!PS-Adobe-2.0 EPSF-1.2
%%BoundingBox: 21 78 584 461
%%Title: From AutoCAD Drawing "NOZZLE"
%%Creator: AutoCAD
%%CreationDate: 11/29/1990 8:23:4
%%EndComments
/m /moveto load def
/l /lineto load def
/s /stroke load def
/n /newpath load def
1 setlinejoin
1 setlinecap
20 20 translate
0.240000 0.240000 scale
3.000000 setlinewidth
n
%Pen 1
1472 982 m
1478 978 l
1485 977 l
1492 978 l
1498 982 l
1478 967 m
1471 972 l
```

SLD Files

The simplest exchange format to use for AutoCAD graphics is the slide (SLD) file. A slide file contains a binary, resolution-dependent vector list for recreating the view that appeared on the AutoCAD screen when the slide was created. Slides are a "quick-and-dirty" method of capturing the current display for later reference, usually while another drawing is loaded. You also can use slide files for putting on "slide show" presentations of AutoCAD drawings. You can easily set up a slide show by writing a script to display precreated slides. Many AutoCAD users rely on AutoCAD's on-screen slide shows to make presentations to clients instead of fumbling at the computer manually. Slide shows give you impressive results without much work.

You can easily create slide files within AutoCAD by using the Mslide command. Simply compose a view of your drawing the way you want it, and execute Mslide. To view slide files, execute the Vslide command. Vslide merely repaints your display with the vector list from file. To return to your current drawing, issue the Redraw command.

An AutoCAD script can display many slide images by repeatedly issuing the Vslide command. You can tell Vslide to preload slides (which may take a few seconds) by placing an asterisk before the slide name in the script file. To pause a slide for viewing, you use the Delay script command with the number of milliseconds (1 second equals 1000 milliseconds) to pause. The entire script automatically repeats if you include the Rscript command. To play a slide show script, simply issue the Script command and provide the name of your ASCII script file. You can stop a script by pressing Backspace or Ctrl-C.

You can create a script file with any text editor or word processor that creates ASCII text files. Just place each command on a separate line in the order you want them to execute. Here is an example of a script file that runs a slide show:

```
VSLIDE SLIDE1
VSLIDE *SLIDE2
DELAY 2000
VSLIDE
VSLIDE *SLIDE3
DELAY 2000
VSLIDE
VSLIDE *SLIDE4
DELAY 2000
RSCRIPT
```

For more information on the slide file format, consult the *AutoCAD Reference Guide*. To learn how to create slides or libraries of slide files, see *Inside AutoCAD* or the *AutoCAD Reference Guide*, by New Riders Publishing.

FLM Files

The final output file format that AutoCAD creates for exporting drawing data is the filmroll file (FLM). A filmroll file is the means by which AutoCAD exchanges 3D drawing and scene data with the AutoShade rendering program. You use the Filmroll command to create filmroll files within AutoCAD.

A filmroll file contains descriptions of all surfaces in the current drawing, independent of 3D view or viewports. Information about the last view used in the drawing, including any perspective information, also is saved. The file also contains any AutoShade-specific information you may have added by AutoShade blocks inserted into the drawing with the AutoShade commands provided by ASHADE.LSP. These blocks include attributes for light locations and types, camera locations and targets, scene definitions (which are combinations of different cameras and lights), and surface finishes. If you have Autodesk RenderMan, you also can insert RenderMan setup blocks and surface property blocks that transfer information to the FLM file.

Filmroll files are not in ASCII format and are not published by Autodesk. Presently, AutoShade is the only program that can use FLM files. Later in this chapter you will get an idea of the things you can do with AutoShade and Autodesk RenderMan. Upcoming sections also suggest ways you can integrate these products into your AutoCAD information system.

Using AutoCAD with Design Programs

One of the first places you can use AutoCAD drawings and exchange formats is within your own engineering department. Aside from exchange between CAD programs, DXF files are used most often by engineering analysis and design assistance programs. You can develop procedures in your system that enable users to export AutoCAD drawings by DXF files for either engineering design analysis or design assistance.

In the case of analysis, a complete drawing can be extracted via DXF and analyzed externally. The analysis program may report or display design conflicts using criteria or methods that are too difficult to implement in AutoCAD alone. No matter how large or small they are, discrepancies must be corrected within AutoCAD.

Design assistance programs use DXF files to help in the design process (see fig. 11.9). Initial single-line diagrams and sketches showing basic routing or structure are output and read into a design program. Within the external program, specific design criteria can be met according to nongraphical data and placement specified. Very often, this is done using a spreadsheet-like interface in which the user deals primarily with numbers. The external program then creates a new DXF file containing detailed graphical data, which can be imported into a new AutoCAD drawing file to become the design document.

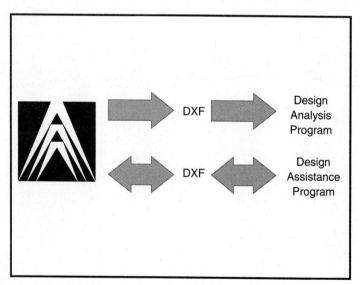

Figure 11.9:
Design analysis versus design assistance by DXF files.

The main difference between these two techniques is that the design analysis process is only one-way. Depending on your needs, this may be sufficient, but it can be limiting. A much more interactive approach is provided by the design assistance program, where conflicts can be dealt with immediately and the results displayed, even if not graphically.

Bill of Materials Programs

One of the first uses of AutoCAD drawing data with external programs was for the creation of bills of materials. In fact, simple source code for BILLMAT.BAS was included with several early versions of AutoCAD.

BILLMAT is an example of a simple BASIC language program that processes DXF data created by the Attext command. BILLMAT uses material information stored in attribute definitions within blocks in a drawing. BILLMAT can accumulate totals of identical entries from the extracted data file. With these totals, you can maintain parts inventories, estimate production costs, or perform any other purpose where drawings represent quantities of materials. The following bill of materials report is an example of data extracted from an AutoCAD drawing of an electronic schematic diagram and processed with BILLMAT.BAS:

```
Enter extract file name: counter

Scan extract file for field names - complete.
Read attributes from extract file - complete.
Assign costs to items - complete.
Sort attributes to report order - complete.
Suppress duplicate items - complete.
```

PNAME	PVALUE	PSPEC1	PSPEC2	COST
C01	2.5uF	150V	10%	1.23
C02	2.5uF	150V	10%	1.23
C03	50pF	150V	10%	0.35
C101	.01uF	150V	10%	0.79
C102	.01uF	150V	10%	0.79
C11	2.5uF	150V	10%	1.23
C12	2.5uF	150V	10%	1.23
C13	50pF	150V	10%	0.35
C91	2.5uF	150V	10%	1.23
C92	2.5uF	150V	10%	1.23
C93	50pF	150V	10%	0.35

```
Subtotal: 11 items, cost:  10.01
```

N01	NE2	0.65		
N11	NE2	0.65		
N91	NE2	0.65		

```
Subtotal:  3 items, cost:  1.95
```

PNAME	PVALUE	PSPEC1	PSPEC2	COST
R01	47K	.5W	10%	0.08
R02	47K	.5W	10%	0.08
R03	470K	.5W	10%	0.08
R04	47K	.5W	10%	0.08
R05	47K	.5W	10%	0.08
R06	47K	.5W	10%	0.08
R07	47K	.5W	10%	0.08
R08	100K	.5W	10%	0.08
R101	1.2K	.5W	10%	0.08
R102	100K	.5W	10%	0.08
R103	47K	.5W	10%	0.08
R104	15K	.5W	10%	0.08
R105	4.7K	.5W	10%	0.08
R106	1640	.5W	5%	0.08
R107	4.7K	.5W	10%	0.08
R11	47K	.5W	10%	0.08
R12	47K	.5W	10%	0.08
R13	470K	.5W	10%	0.08
R14	47K	.5W	10%	0.08
R15	47K	.5W	10%	0.08
R16	47K	.5W	10%	0.08
R17	47K	.5W	10%	0.08
R18	100K	.5W	10%	0.08
R91	47K	.5W	10%	0.08
R92	47K	.5W	10%	0.08
R93	470K	.5W	10%	0.08
R94	47K	.5W	10%	0.08
R95	47K	.5W	10%	0.08
R96	47K	.5W	10%	0.08
R97	47K	.5W	10%	0.08
R98	100K	.5W	10%	0.08

Subtotal: 31 items, cost: 2.48

PNAME	PVALUE	PSPEC1	PSPEC2	COST
V01	6SN7			7.55
V101	6Y6			8.50
V102	6L6			12.95
V11	6SN7			7.55
V91	6SN7			7.55

Subtotal: 5 items, cost: 44.10

Total items: 50   Total cost: 58.54

The first column lists electronic parts used in the drawing. The other columns track various data assigned to each part as attributes within the drawing. BILLMAT totals quantities of parts for each section of like parts and their associated costs. At the bottom of the report, BILLMAT presents a total item count and price.

If you still have one of the earlier versions of AutoCAD, you may have the BILLMAT.BAS file. You can use it as-is or modify it for the kind of work you do. Other, more sophisticated programs are now available to fill nearly every BOM need. By using such programs, you can easily extract instance information from AutoCAD drawings.

Estimating from AutoCAD Drawings

Architects and engineers have long dreamed of being able to create job cost estimates based on the information in CAD drawings. Cost estimating is a time-consuming yet vital activity of almost every A/E/C firm. Accurate estimates ensure that project bids will create a reasonable profit and help establish reasonable budgets, while enabling the bidder to remain competitive with other bidders.

Without the computer, cost estimating is a tedious skill requiring intimate knowledge of construction techniques, flawless math skills, unquestionable accuracy, and a modest amount of good judgment. Many construction professionals question why, since CAD drawings contain all the information they need (with great accuracy), there are not programs that will use the drawing database to produce costing information.

The problems with automated estimating technology have been that a manual estimator has to make hundreds of assumptions and decisions during the process of estimating the materials used in a project. Further, he must reference hundreds of prices for those materials as well as labor and installation rates for various areas of the country. Also, the majority of CAD drafting traditionally has been done in 2D, which does not provide information about the third dimension of buildings. The estimator had to compensate manually. These problems are further complicated by the difficulty of refining the estimating program logic to recognize and correctly handle 3D drawings.

But with the growth of 3D drafting and more powerful computers has come progress in computerized estimating. Several estimating programs are now available that interface to AutoCAD through one of the intermediate file formats discussed earlier. One example, Precision CAD Importer by Timberline Software Corp., allows the exchange of estimating data between AutoCAD and Timberline's Precision Estimating Plus software through another third-party template. Precision CAD Importer takes a file generated by the template (created according to Timberline specifications) and brings it into Precision Estimating Plus to create an estimate. Precision CAD Importer also updates the estimate any time the drawing changes.

Any third-party developer can create a template for creating files compatible with Precision CAD Importer by receiving a tool kit from Timberline. The kit is a series of programming routines, examples, and documentation for designing a template file. Several major AutoCAD third-party developers have plans for incorporating Precision CAD Importer templates into their products, including ASG-Archsoft Group and DCA Engineering Inc. If you are a serious AutoCAD customizer, you can create your own custom templates with the Timberline kit and integrate them as part of your overall system development plan.

Other estimating programs for AutoCAD include EZ-Estimate Plus from LANDCADD, Inc. and SELLECT Estimating Interface by SELLECT Designs, Inc. Others are listed in the *AutoCAD Sourcebook*.

Using Renderings and Animation To Sell Your Products

By taking advantage of AutoCAD's exchange files, you can make valuable contributions to your company's marketing and presentation efforts. At the very least, you can use AutoCAD slides and a simple script to show examples of your work in a fresh and interesting way. You learned how to make a slide script earlier in this chapter. You can create impressive visual aids with 3D slides and plots whose hidden lines have been removed. Shaded renderings of your AutoCAD drawings produced with AutoShade and filmroll files are even more realistic. Going a step further, you can use Autodesk RenderMan to make lifelike images of your products or services. By adding motion to your drawing geometry, you can create your own desktop animations with Autodesk Animator and your AutoCAD slide files and AutoShade rendering files.

AutoCAD gives you a number of ways to make better presentations of your designs. All you have to do is incorporate one of the following programs into your marketing, presentation, or documentation plans. Be sure to use the proper version of the AutoCAD drawing that is the source of your intermediate file. If your designs change often, you will want to set up your own procedures for making sure that designs and presentations are coordinated.

AutoShade Renderings

AutoShade (a separate program from AutoCAD) uses the filmroll files discussed earlier. Once the file is read into AutoShade, the program can display richly colored renderings of any surfaces in your 3D models using simulated lighting and camera-like perspective projection (see fig. 11.10). Your 3D drawings begin to look solid when you treat them with AutoShade.

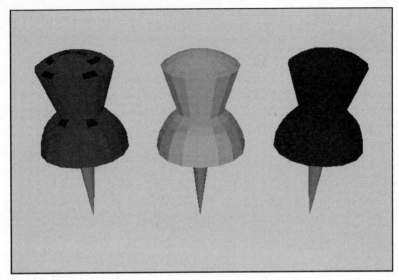

Figure 11.10:
A faceted AutoShade rendering from an AutoCAD drawing.

Shaded renderings enable you to visualize how your completed product will look after it is machined, cast, molded, or otherwise built. AutoShade can help you see the surfaces of your drawing in ways that AutoCAD cannot. You can use these shaded images for design verification or for product presentations without the labor and expense of making a physical prototype or waiting to reconcile design problems in the field.

AutoShade 2.0 adds exciting new possibilities for *photo-realistic rendering* (the creation of images that rival photographs in clarity). In addition to the basic surface-shading capability illustrated in figure 11.10, AutoShade can produce smooth-shaded images by utilizing the Gauraud shading algorithm to smooth the edges between the adjacent surfaces depicted in the filmroll file (see fig. 11.11).

AutoShade 2.0 also includes an interface to produce RenderMan Interface Bytestream (RIB) files. These RIB files can then be rendered with Autodesk RenderMan or any other compatible renderer. RenderMan is a description language similar to PostScript; RenderMan, however, describes entire scenes complete with the appearance of textures, materials, transparency, and shadows (see fig. 11.12).

The greatest difficulty in working with rendering programs (and animation, which is discussed later) is the time involved. Most of these processes can take many hours to perform—even on the fastest computers—when complex 3D models are used. Your challenge is to coordinate the time these processes need with drawing production and design modifications. Often, you can have these programs do most of their work at night. You can begin a rendering or animation compilation before you leave the office in the evening and have it finished and waiting for you in the morning.

Whenever this is not possible, or when design modifications force you to repeat the process, you must use your best project management skills to avoid timing conflicts. For these cases, use the project management tips presented in Chapter 10.

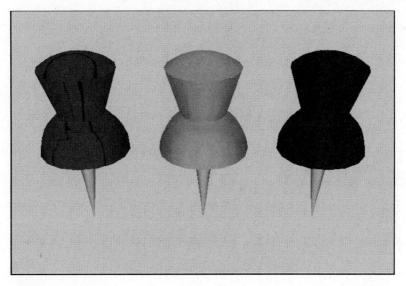

Figure 11.11:
Smooth shaded rendering made with AutoShade 2.0.

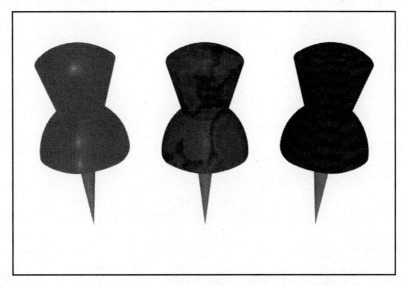

Figure 11.12:
An AutoCAD drawing, rendered with surface shaders in Autodesk RenderMan.

AutoCAD in Motion

You can produce basic animations of walk-throughs or part movements with Autodesk Animator to add real impact to your presentations. Animator can use your AutoCAD slides and AutoShade renderings as frames for your own short "movies." Your movies can let the viewer fly around or through a skyscraper or a microchip. You can simulate mechanical linkages, gears, anatomical movement, or virtually any motion.

Animator lets you combine your renderings with sophisticated yet easy-to-use 2D optical effects, titling, color editing, traditional cel animation, and much more. You can use the Animation Tool Kit (available from Autodesk) to automate the creation of AutoShade filmroll files for smooth camera motion or even kinetic (animated) drawing parts.

The complexity of your animation dictates how involved you are in managing the project. A single animation, for instance, may require hundreds of files and many megabytes of data, requiring plenty of disk space and a fast machine on which to do your animations.

By using Autodesk Animator, your company will be portrayed as having really harnessed the power of CAD and its technology. For more on the possibilities of using animation with AutoCAD and organizing an animation project, see *Inside Autodesk Animator*, also from New Riders Publishing.

Importing AutoCAD Drawings into Text Documents

By importing CAD graphics into your brochures, specifications, advertising, product literature, manuals, and other documents, you can make them more accurate and concise. Several of AutoCAD's exchange and output file formats let you import AutoCAD drawing data into your own documents for publishing.

Most major desktop publishing programs for PCs have provisions for importing AutoCAD slides, plot files, or DXF files. Ventura Publisher can import AutoCAD slides, EPS files, or HP-GL plot files with good results (see fig. 11.13). Aldus Pagemaker can use only AutoCAD EPS plot files.

Even though slide files are easier to create in AutoCAD (and smaller), the results are not as good as HP-GL files. For best results, plot your drawings to files using twice the size you intend for the final graphic. The improved resolution you get by reducing it will look much better. Also, be sure not to specify pen widths that are too large or too small. Widths that scale down to below one printer pixel width will not print at all. Experiment with your printer to see which pen widths look best.

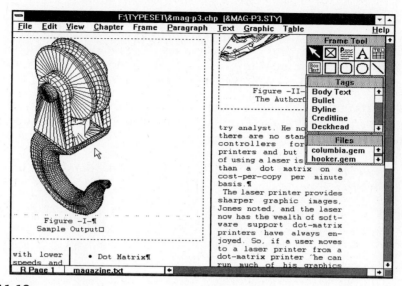

Figure 11.13:
An AutoCAD drawing imported into Ventura Publisher.

Even the major word processors can import AutoCAD graphics easily. Microsoft Word owners can import HP-GL or EPS files directly into Word documents. WordPerfect owners can import the same formats plus DXF files, but must first convert them to WordPerfect's own WPG format by using the GRAPHCNV program supplied with WordPerfect.

The way you manage the publishing of your AutoCAD drawings is perhaps the least labor-intensive activity presented in this section. Only one output file needs to be created for each drawing imported into a document. You just need to be sure it is from the latest version of the drawing.

Only through trial and error, however, can you get the best printed results. You may have to experiment with your program, AutoCAD's different output files, and your particular drawings to find the best combination.

The strategic placement of a diagram or illustration could save you a lot of extra narrative text that might confuse the reader. Just think of what this book would be like without any pictures and you begin to get the idea. Yet every picture in it was created and placed entirely electronically.

Using Drawing Data To Manage Projects

You may want to integrate project management methods into your system development plans. Chapter 10 introduced project management programs that can help you manage project resources and schedules. AutoCAD Release 10, however, added several system variables that can help in tracking the actual time your operators take to complete drawings. The system variables store time information within the drawing file itself for use by the Time command. This information can help you track drawing time whether you use a project management program or not.

The TDINDWG system variable, in particular, contains the amount of time that the current drawing has spent in the AutoCAD Drawing Editor. AutoCAD updates this value with each editing session, so that the current value contains the accumulated total amount of time spent on the drawing. You can extract this value from your drawings for use in time billing, project estimating, scheduling, and many other uses.

The following AutoLISP program, LOGHRS.LSP, creates a small text file containing the number of decimal hours spent in the current drawing. It undefines the AutoCAD End and Save commands when it loads and redefines them with AutoLISP replacements.

You can create the program yourself by typing the following listing into your text editor or word processor and saving the program as an ASCII text file named LOGHRS.LSP. LOGHRS.LSP also is included on the *Managing and Networking AutoCAD Disk* (MN Disk). See Appendix A for information on installing LOGHRS.LSP from the MN Disk.

```
;*
;*    AutoLISP File for Managing and Networking AutoCAD MN DISK - (c) 1991
;* New Riders Publishing. All Rights Reserved. Version 11.00 for PC-DOS/MS-DOS
;*               Developed by Kenneth W. Billing
;*
;
;When file loads, save CMDECHO status, suppress it, then undefine END and SAVE
(setq cmdeko (getvar "CMDECHO"))
(setvar "CMDECHO" 0)
(command "UNDEFINE" "END")
(command "UNDEFINE" "SAVE")
;Define a new END command that gets the current hours spent in drawing
;then calls the file logging function, passes it the hours, does a real END
(defun C:END (/ hrs)
  (setq hrs (rtos (* (getvar "TDINDWG") 24)))
  (loghrs hrs)
  (command ".END")
  (princ)
)
;Define a new SAVE command that gets the current hours spent in drawing
;then calls the file logging function, passes it the hours, does a real SAVE
(defun C:SAVE (/ hrs)
```

```
(setq hrs (rtos (* (getvar "TDINDWG") 24)))
(loghrs hrs)
(command ".SAVE")
(princ)
)
;Generic file logging function used by both END and SAVE
(defun loghrs (hrs / tfile)
  (setq tfile (open (strcat (getvar "DWGNAME") ".TIM") "w"))
  (write-line hrs tfile)
  (close tfile)
  (princ)
)
;Restore CMDECHO after the file loads, kill its variable, notify user
(setvar "CMDECHO" cmdeko)
(setq cmdeko nil)
(prompt "\nLOGHRS.LSP loaded...")
(prompt "\nAutoCAD END and SAVE commands redefined.")
(princ)
```

LOGHRS.LSP works by extracting the Julian day value held in TDINDWG and converting it into decimal hours. LOGHRS.LSP writes this time to a small file in the current directory with a name composed of the current drawing name and the extension TIM (for "time"). Once LOGHRS.LSP is loaded at the beginning of an editing session, every time the AutoCAD End or Save commands are used, a new time file is written. The Quit command, however, is unaffected because TDINDWG ignores time spent in sessions that are quit without saving.

You should load LOGHRS.LSP into AutoCAD at the beginning of any editing session for which you want to track time. One way to load LOGHRS is to use the AutoLISP Load function at the AutoCAD command line:

(Load "LOGHRS")

LOGHRS.LSP must exist somewhere in the AutoCAD search path for AutoCAD to find it. You also can load the program by adding a line to your AutoCAD menu that creates a macro similar to the following:

[LOG HRS]^C^C^C(if (not loghrs) (load "LOGHRS") nil)

AutoCAD loads the file when you pick LOG HRS.

Tip: The easiest way to ensure that LOGHRS gets loaded is to add it to your ACAD.LSP file. This will automatically load LOGHRS any time you start AutoCAD. If you do not have an ACAD.LSP file, simply rename LOGHRS.LSP to ACAD.LSP.

You can look at time files with a text editor or word processor to see how long a drawing has been in the AutoCAD Drawing Editor. You also can view a TIM file's contents by using the DOS TYPE command. The files are not locked while AutoCAD is active on a network, so you can view the files while a drawing still is being edited. In this case, however, the time will be accurate only to the last time the drawing was saved.

You can create a basic project management system by reading all these files for a single project into a database program or other program of your own making. Because times are logged in decimal hours, they can be added or subtracted without formatting values in and out of combinations of hours and minutes.

> **Note:** Be aware that when you block out an entire drawing (as many people do to purge the file of unused symbols), you reset the TDINDWG variable to 0. Plotting and printing time is not added to the total time. If an operator quits a drawing, TDINDWG loses all the time spent in the drawing since the last Save or End command was issued for the file.

You can modify LOGHRS.LSP to include data from the following system variables:

- TDCREATE, which stores the Julian date on which the current drawing was created
- TDUPDATE, which stores the Julian date on which the current drawing was last updated with an End or Save command
- TDUSRTIMER, which stores the amount of time elapsed in the AutoCAD User timer

TDUSRTIMER values are stored in the same format as TDINDWG. TDCREATE and TDUPDATE, however, use the Julian date system that is more difficult to work with. For more information on the AutoCAD Time command system variables see the *AutoCAD Reference Manual*.

Other Tips for Managing System Development

When you use AutoCAD for activities beyond just drafting, you take on additional management responsibilities. For starters, you must make sure that everyone involved plainly understands who is responsible for the conversion, importing, and updating of the additional files created during these nondrawing processes.

You also must answer the following questions:

- Will exporting and conversion of data be the CAD department's responsibility, or the responsibility of those people who will receive the files?

- Where are intermediate files (slide, DXF, plot, and others) to be stored? On the network or on local hard disks?
- Who is responsible for updating and backing up these files?

Including an illustration of a preliminary design in a final document could be disastrous, as could using the wrong estimating data. Again, plan the organization and all the systematic steps before you actually implement any new process. You will be glad you did.

Committing to Research

Recognizing areas in which you can use AutoCAD to improve your company's efficiency, image, and bottom line is easier than actually making it happen. Developing custom applications and integrating third-party applications into your method of operations does not happen by itself. The CAD manager must have the permission and resources to explore these opportunities. The CAD department is one area in every company that should have a research and development plan and budget, whether the company as a whole is involved in R&D or not. Even the best CAD manager can do only as much as he is authorized.

It may take a lot of internal "selling" on your part to convince management that R&D is valuable. To help sell R&D, use one data-sharing technique as a pilot project. Gather evidence that shows that the technique can be profitable to your company if implemented. Perhaps you can test the technique on a small but real project. Make examples of other companies that have implemented similar techniques. Calculate the savings or other benefits and produce the best report and presentation you can. Then present your ideas to management on a level that they can best appreciate. Perform a demonstration if possible. Few business leaders, when approached in this way, with adequate evidence, will decline to approve implementation. If your pilot is successful, then approach management about committing to authorized, ongoing research and development of new ideas and methods.

Research and development is vital to the growth of your CAD department and of your company. Business, people, and profits stagnate unless companies commit to adequate research and development of new processes. Research and development require special support on the part of management and extra effort on behalf of the CAD manager. A clear commitment must be made by both to see that every opportunity possible for advanced application of technology is evaluated for cost-effectiveness and productivity potential.

What is good for the CAD manager, to a lesser degree, is good for other users, too. Allowance should be made for others to explore seldom-used program features and to experiment with new methods for common operations or problems. When properly applied, this time will pay for itself in happier users and in higher productivity as they apply the new techniques they have learned. They will enjoy their job more if they find they can be trusted to make the best use of their time and that they are being encouraged to try new ideas and look for improvements. Everyone likes to feel that his input is important.

Summary

A great deal of time and effort go into the design and installation of any CAD system. As this chapter has shown you, however, the work doesn't stop once the system is in place. The CAD manager must be committed to performing routine, timely system maintenance if the system is to continue running. He also must be committed to system development, if the system is to grow and if the company is to maximize the return on its CAD investment.

This chapter has offered you many tips to use in these two important areas. You learned how to calculate the cost of downtime, how to maintain disk drives and output devices, how to schedule backups and choose a backup program, and how to archive your finished work.

This chapter also discussed the value of system development through upgrading software safely and using AutoCAD data with other programs. You learned about the various data formats that AutoCAD can use to communicate with other programs, so that you can get more mileage out of your AutoCAD data.

By keeping your hardware and software maintained, you can keep two out of the three ingredients for high-production CAD running smoothly. When you involve users in R&D, you are bordering on user management. The next chapter covers the delicate job of fine-tuning the most important component of the CAD productivity scenario: the user.

Chapter 12 looks at the four biggest areas of user management a CAD manager must deal with: selecting CAD specialists, training AutoCAD users, motivating employees, and evaluating performance fairly.

12

Managing AutoCAD Users

The CAD manager's least computer-related responsibility is the management of his system's users. Yet no other resource has a greater impact on a company's productivity. A CAD system encompasses not only computer hardware and software, but also the people who use those technologies, and the procedures and methods that tie them all together. Many CAD managers do not see the management of AutoCAD users as a factor or a priority in the overall success of their AutoCAD operation. This attitude, however, only hampers their quest to reach their automation goals.

People come in all different types, as you know, and they create management problems very different from those caused by hardware and software. This chapter examines each phase of managing a CAD specialist. It shows you how to choose the best CAD people to begin with—whether from within or without—what traits to look for, and how you can test for AutoCAD knowledge. Next, you will learn about the different types of training available for AutoCAD users and upper management, and which methods may work best for your company.

This chapter also examines basic issues of personnel development and workgroup motivation, which are two factors that can keep your people performing at their best. Finally, you will learn methods for evaluating user performance constructively, so as to identify areas in which your staff needs additional development.

A large company may have its own personnel department for finding prospective employees and a dedicated department for training. You may have an immediate supervisor whose job is to perform personnel motivation, provide leadership, and conduct personnel evaluations. In such a case, your role in the CAD department may be limited to technology management and minimal personnel involvement. If your interests lie more with technologies, you may want to skip ahead to Chapter 13.

If you work for a smaller company that has no dedicated personnel and training departments, however, and if you are directly responsible for daily user management, then this chapter is for you.

Selecting CAD Specialists

The best way to end up with talented, team-oriented people, of course, is to begin by hiring the right people. If you are inexperienced in interviewing and hiring personnel, the following sections provide basic, time-proven tips used by experienced managers and businesses.

Even before you select a dealer to install your new system, and well before the system is even designed, you should choose and begin to train the people who will be using the new system. They, and others in your company, will need time and information in order to adjust to the ways in which AutoCAD is going to affect the way they work and feel about their jobs.

Whenever management brings up the idea of installing a CAD system, many drafters and designers naturally ask, "Does this mean that my job will be eliminated?" Fears about being replaced by computers are a holdover from the early days of office automation, when clerical personnel *were* replaced by machines. The fact is, however, that most CAD systems do not replace any existing jobs, although they might defer the need to hire new employees. In reality, a company with a well-managed CAD system can simply do more and better work with the people it has, rather than doing the same amount of work with fewer people. CAD buys the designer the time he needs to perform more design analyses and perhaps to create more information and documentation than before. AutoCAD-trained employees are not at risk of losing their jobs. On the contrary, their additional training and skills make them an even greater asset to the company.

Promoting from Within

You might already have hired the right person for that new job, so whenever possible, promote from within. Most companies have learned the benefit of this practice. It places the cost of replacement at lower levels of responsibility, training, production, and compensation. Generally, you can find and hire an entry-level person much more easily than you can acquire an engineer with AutoCAD experience or a talented CAD designer. Further, within the CAD department, you can more easily train and manage a person you already know and have worked with. But more important, internal promotion builds on your company's strongest resource: the people in whom it has already invested time, energy, and resources. A policy of internal promotion sends a message to everyone in the company that they are valued for their skills and knowledge.

Older individuals seem to be especially susceptible to fears about their roles with the advent of CAD. After having spent many years perfecting their skills and building seniority, they fear that CAD will erase their advantages over younger, less experienced peers. Anxieties over the threat of suddenly being less skilled than a more computer-literate peer can inhibit their acceptance and willingness to embrace the new system. Changes in office systems and procedures threaten to disrupt the accepted and familiar ways of the past.

While it may be difficult to "teach an old dog new tricks," it is still certainly possible, and drafting veterans can bring a lot of practical job experience to bear on AutoCAD drafting problems. They already know the best ways to accomplish nearly any drawing task, and they require less supervision. If they also have the gift of being able to apply those methods with AutoCAD, you can hardly go wrong.

Younger transferees from the manual drafting department to the CAD department should be approached with more emphasis on laying down the fundamentals and procedures of electronic drafting, than on the transitional approach used with senior converts. In these cases, build on any existing CAD education or training. Use your own experience for real-world applications of what they may already know. In this way you will get more cooperation from them, than you would if you challenge or dispute their knowledge.

Recruiting for Keeps

If you must look outside the company for new employees, for whatever reason, you might get lucky and find an applicant who has all the right attributes already. More often, though, you need to look for applicants who have the potential to be developed into the type of person you want.

Successful recruiting depends on knowing specifically what you are looking for before you interview—that certain combination of education, experience, skills, personality, and attitude that will make a valuable addition to your team. Once you know what you are looking for, stick to it. Do not give in to scheduling pressures or get discouraged and hire less than what you need. Wait if you must.

One key mistake made by many employers is eliminating the cause of vacancies created by employees leaving. Unless you objectively track and examine the reasons for job turnover, you may end up losing new hires, as well. If there is a consistent problem with the position, you could lose still more people—even your most trusted and valued employees. Studies show that it costs an average of $6,000 cash and 22 man-hours to hire a CAD technician. You can ill afford to go through the hiring process very often.

Starting with Education

You can reduce recruiting costs by participating in cooperative education or employment programs. In a co-op program, you agree to hire a student while he is still in school, and he earns academic credits for the work he does for you. Your company gets the benefits of the latest in technical education, while you help train a young professional who, if he stays, will tend to remain much longer than a different recruit.

AutoCAD-specific training has become considerably easier to find in recent years. High schools are teaching AutoCAD as part of drafting and design curriculums. Many community and junior colleges use AutoCAD in their engineering, technical, and architectural programs. Private technical institutions provide excellent AutoCAD training. AutoCAD is also part of practically all university-level architectural and engineering programs.

As a result of this emphasis on CAD training, however, many schools are falling behind in training of drafting fundamentals, including geometric construction, drawing composition, tolerancing and dimensioning, and isometric and perspective projection theory. Today's CAD systems have become so automated and easy to use that many of these functions can be performed without a solid understanding of what they actually mean. Consider only applicants who have demonstrated a thorough comprehension of these areas.

Building with Experience

Experience can, of course, make up for a multitude of shortcomings in other areas. Someone who is accustomed to doing the kinds of drawings your company needs may be preferable to candidates with other qualifications. Throughout this book, the emphasis has been on supplementing a solid understanding of business and practice with technology—understanding that comes best from experience.

Applicants for AutoCAD positions should possess as many of the following traits as possible:

- Professional attitude and abilities
- 3D visualization skills
- Verbal and written communication skills
- Ability to think linearly as well as abstractly
- Ability to interpret and follow detailed instructions
- Problem-solving skills
- Organized, self-disciplined, self-motivated
- Interest in and enthusiasm for CAD
- Ability to apply CAD theory and knowledge to practical use

- Creativity and original thinking
- Intelligence to handle complex technology
- Curiosity and the desire to learn
- Perseverance and patience
- Oriented toward detail and accuracy

Looking for Certified Operators

Some experienced employee candidates may come to your interview with credentials from a CAD operator certification program. There is growing interest and support among AutoCAD users, employers, and educators for professional certification programs for CAD operators, which establish levels of competency in AutoCAD knowledge and application. Two such programs have begun on a national scale. You also may want to support your employees so they can obtain certification through one of these programs as part of their overall development.

The AutoCAD Operator Certification Examination

One program began under the auspices of the *Authorized AutoCAD Training Centers* (ATCs), and a two-part qualifications test also has been developed. Designated as the *AutoCAD Operator Certification Examination* (AOCE), this test is intended to measure an examinee's knowledge and application of AutoCAD capabilities. Upon remitting a $95 testing fee, the examinee may take the one-hour, 150-item multiple choice test and the two-hour practical examination. The entire test is given quarterly at the 152 ATC locations throughout the U.S. and Canada. A certified score is given to each examinee, and those achieving qualifying scores also receive a certificate. An examinee may have his scores sent to potential employers, as well. Two additional levels of certification may be added if the AOCE is accepted by the CAD industry at large. For more information on the AOCE exam, contact your local ATC or the SPOCAD Center of Gonzaga University at (509) 484-6808.

NACO Certification

The *National Association of CAD/CAM Operators* (NACO) certification program is even more ambitious. NACO is a nonprofit professional organization founded solely for the recognition, advancement, and promotion of CAD operators. Certification through NACO is possible at one of seven different levels. The testing is neither software- nor hardware-specific at the lower levels, but discipline and software specialization are required at the higher levels. Certification is awarded, as follows, for required combinations of training, experience, and testing:

- **Level 1**. Verified resume, NACO membership, CAD industry involvement, expressed intention to advance to higher levels

- **Level 2**. Level-1 certification plus six months of full-time CAD employment
- **Level 3**. Level-2 certification plus participation in an approved formal training class
- **Level 4**. Level-3 certification plus one year of full-time CAD employment and passage of the Level-4 NACO examination or approved equivalent experience
- **Level 5**. Level-4 certification plus passage of the Level-5 NACO examination and accomplishment in a recognized discipline
- **Level 6**. Level-5 certification plus passage of the Level-6 NACO examination in animation and modeling, architecture, civil, electrical, mechanical or structural engineering, fire protection, piping, or PCB layout; two years of full-time CAD employment; one year of supervisory experience
- **Level 7**. Level-6 certification plus CAD program customization and computer knowledge sufficient to pass the Level-7 NACO examination

NACO membership dues are $50 and testing fees are $45, $55, or $145, depending on the level of the test taken. For more information on the NACO certification program, contact:

NACO
10801 Hammerly
Suite 220
Houston, TX 77043
(713) 932-8473
(713) 932-6352 (FAX)

Testing Job Applicants

Employers also can quantify applicant qualifications by administering an in-house examination during the interview process. Some companies use their own examination, but commercial automated testing software also is available. One such program is *AutoCAD Evaluator* by CAD Studio, Inc., which tests for AutoCAD knowledge through an interactive, automated examination. Figure 12.1 depicts a typical sample question.

The program stores the applicant's test results and basic information in a database that documents the testing process, as shown in figure 12.2.

You can use the AutoCAD Evaluator to compare two applicants according to test categories (see fig. 12.3).

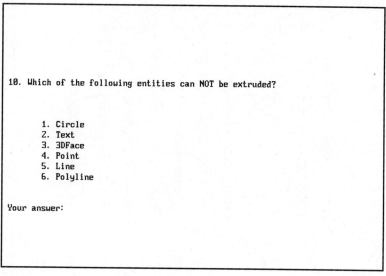

```
10. Which of the following entities can NOT be extruded?


            1. Circle
            2. Text
            3. 3DFace
            4. Point
            5. Line
            6. Polyline


Your answer:
```

Figure 12.1:

An AutoCAD Evaluator test question.

```
      Name:  Veteran P.E., John, Q.
   Address:  7 Sirene Circle
             Yourtown, ST 00000              Individual Information


 Home phone:                       Test date: 11/15/90
 Other phone:                      Years of experience: 6
 Soc. Sec. #: 3                    Latest version used: 11

      Category                     Percent Correct
   Getting Started and Utility Commands        100%
   Edit and Inquiry Commands                   100%
   Entity Draw Commands and Hatching           100%
   Display Controls and Plotting               100%
   Entity Properties and Drawing Aids          100%
   Blocks and Attributes                       100%
   Dimensioning                                100%
   Special Features and Drawing Interchange    100%
   Customizing and System Libraries            100%
   Working in 3D                               100%

 Time Taken: 1.62 minutes       Aggregate Score:     100%

        Work history                    Print    ESC-Prev Menu
```

Figure 12.2:

An AutoCAD Evaluator test score report.

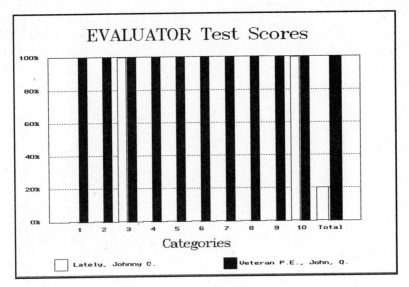

Figure 12.3:
An AutoCAD Evaluator comparison of test scores.

While such tests can give you a general view of an applicant's AutoCAD knowledge, they should be recognized for what they are—tests taken by people who may be anxious about being tested. No test can take into account the emotional effects of the testing process. Use test results only as one part of the hiring process, along with the other qualities previously described.

Structuring the CAD Department

If yours is a large company employing many CAD users, you may find that some structure is necessary to delineate levels of responsibility and aptitude within your CAD department, and to provide hierarchical opportunities for placement and advancement. Barge, Waggoner, Sumner & Cannon, a Nashville-based design firm, uses the following five-level structure for describing various CAD positions. You might consider this example for your company as shown, or adapt it as you wish to your own organizational needs and size. Large companies also may find this type of organization valuable when a single CAD manager cannot handle all of the various responsibilities offered in Chapter 2. This structure delineates skill, training, and responsibility levels for delegating some of the CAD manager's duties to other staff.

1. **CAD Trainee.** This is an entry-level position. The trainee is assigned to learn basic CAD skills and techniques. The trainee typically is a high school graduate with one year of drafting experience. Entry-level trainees generally require close supervision.

2. **CAD Operator.** Under general supervision, the CAD operator produces routine CAD-generated drawings from sketches and notes that have been screened for unusual or difficult problems that may require closer supervision. The CAD operator usually is a high school graduate who has one or two years of CAD experience or a technical associate's degree, including course work in CAD and one year of drafting experience.

3. **Senior CAD Operator.** This operator produces CAD-generated drawings, working directly with other designers and Engineers/Architects/Professionals (E/A/Ps). The senior CAD operator is responsible for developing standard methods of CAD production and should be able to work independently with occasional advice from the CAD supervisor to support the design E/A/P with preliminary and final designs. This operator also may be responsible for the training of new operators. The senior CAD operator should have a high school diploma, two or three years of CAD experience, and at least five years of design and drafting experience or applicable technical education.

4. **CAD Supervisor.** This operator supervises and coordinates the work of a group of CAD operators. The CAD supervisor may assist the design E/A/P with the production of CAD-generated designs. The supervisor also may function as shift supervisor and oversee tape backups and file recovery, troubleshooting, developing user commands, and the automation of the firm's CAD effort. The CAD supervisor should have a high school diploma, three to five years of CAD experience, and at least five years of design and drafting experience and applicable experience or course work in computer science or programming. The CAD supervisor receives supervision and guidance on overall objectives, critical issues, new concepts, policy matters, unusual problems, and developments from his supervisor. In turn, the CAD supervisor supervises and coordinates the work of a group of CAD operators.

5. **CAD Applications Analyst.** This position combines the role of the CAD system manager and applications programmers. The CAD system manager is responsible for general supervision of the CAD department and oversees the day-to-day operation of the computer hardware and software, troubleshoots problems, and analyzes hardware and software requirements for new applications. Applications programmers are responsible for design, development, and modification of computer programs and may occasionally coordinate the efforts of a small group of technicians. In some cases, the CAD system manager and CAD supervisor can function as the same person. A CAD applications analyst should have four years of CAD experience and an associate's technical degree with work in computer science or equivalent experience. Supervision is essentially administrative with assignments given in terms of broad general objectives and limits.

Committing to Training

In CAD firms, many upper-level managers operate under the misconception that once the hardware, software, and people are in place, there is no need for further training. Compounding this problem is the inability of most CAD managers to develop and manage effective training programs. Without the right initial or ongoing training, productivity is sacrificed, potential is lost, and human resources stagnate. Every major corporation has learned that training is a key to growth, productivity, and the effective use of technology.

User proficiency is directly related to the quality and quantity of training each user receives. More proficient users need less hand-holding by the CAD manager. This is especially true in networked installations, where the network adds another layer of complexity to the user's daily routine.

Training should be specifically tailored to each person's existing knowledge level and position. Consider the following types of training programs:

- Basic microcomputer operation for support staff, pre-trainees and management (if necessary)
- Basic AutoCAD operation and fundamentals for CAD trainees, management, and closely related support staff
- Advanced AutoCAD for accomplished and promising users
- AutoLISP programming for the CAD manager-in-training, CAD programmer trainees, and key advanced users
- Vertical application training, when applicable to business needs, where available, and for third-party applications
- Network supervisor training for the CAD manager of networked installations
- Personnel management for the CAD manager or other lead individuals
- Software upgrade training for the CAD manager to pass down to others

Training can be accomplished in a variety of ways, ranging from formal classroom training for key users to the simple encouragement and guidance from an experienced peer.

Management Training

For any training program to be successful, it must have the commitment of management. Training should be instituted early and equally for every person whose work relates directly or indirectly to the CAD department. That includes not only CAD users, but management personnel and support staff, as well. Table 12.1 shows the results of a recent survey of information systems (I/S) executives about the most important issues they believe they face in the 1990s. "Information systems" is a term used loosely to describe computer-based information systems as a whole; CAD is just one type of information system. Notice in the table that educating senior management on information systems ranked second. Educating middle management ranked twelfth. Most of the issues listed apply to the CAD manager's job in one way or another.

Table 12.1
Top 20 Issues for U.S. Information Systems Executives in the 1990s

1. Reshaping business processes through I/S
2. Educating senior management on I/S
3. Instituting cross-functional information systems
4. Aligning I/S and corporate goals
5. I/S strategic planning
6. Boosting software development productivity
7. Utilizing data
8. Using I/S for competitive breakthroughs
9. Developing an information architecture
10. Cutting I/S costs
11. Improving the I/S human resource
12. Educating middle management on I/S
13. Updating obsolete information systems
14. Improving software development quality
15. Promoting the I/S function
16. Integrating information systems
17. Managing changes caused by I/S
18. Instituting executive support systems
19. Connecting to customers or suppliers
20. Selecting and integrating packaged software

Training upper-level managers in basic AutoCAD concepts and operation gives them a better understanding of their system's capabilities, strengths, and shortcomings. Through training, managers gain an appreciation for the skills of the system's users and become better equipped to direct the company's AutoCAD applications. They also begin to recognize the value of the CAD manager's position. If you offer basic AutoCAD training to support staff and related departments, you make these people better able to support the CAD department and coordinate their activities with it.

AutoCAD-specific *training* for management might end there, but general CAD *education* does not need to stop. Many valuable tutorials and seminars in upper-level

CAD management and CAD's business implications are conducted each year at conferences such as those offered by A/E/C Systems, AutoFact, and NCGA. These sessions are chaired by recognized experts and leaders in the industry who have learned the secrets of successful CAD implementation. Encourage your managers to attend. A list of popular CAD-related conferences and seminars is included in Appendix D.

Many different ways of facilitating user training are available, with advantages and drawbacks to each. Some of the more common ones are described on the following pages.

Outside Training

Off-site training usually involves sending someone to a class offered by the vendor or dealer as part of the system purchase, or to a third party, a technical school, or a community college. Such courses can be very productive in the presentation of theory and general practice. Their refined curricula are designed to stress understanding of the software's use. They are usually short-term and condensed in nature, and the user advances rapidly along the learning curve. Outside of the pressures and distractions of the office, the student is free to concentrate on the material. There may be a high number of instructors per student, which results in more personal attention, and there are usually a variety of classes offered at different skill levels. Classes are often scheduled in the evenings and on weekends to coordinate with student work schedules.

To set up a training agreement with your dealer or some other training center, first determine what your training needs are according to the preceding list and which groups of students you want to train with help from an outside party. Then find out what types of training the center is qualified to perform. If the training center cannot train your people in the areas that you need, you may have to look elsewhere. If you have chosen a training center, you need only match its schedule with your students' schedule. Your dealer, however, may be able to do the training on a much more flexible basis, either during work hours or after work. If customized training is in order, be sure that both you and the dealer or consultant agree to specific terms of course content, duration, cost, scheduling, and results—all of which may vary widely.

For Autodesk software, the nationwide system of Authorized AutoCAD Training Centers offers consistently high-quality certified instruction. Look for one near you, or contact your dealer for more information.

The major disadvantage of off-site instruction is the lack of application to specific trades. Such courses must be general in nature to meet the broad range of students' needs. If yours is not a mainstream application of AutoCAD, you may find off-site training less than adequate to fully prepare students for your needs.

In-House Training

Conducting training courses on-site is a formidable task, but potentially very rewarding and effective. The workplace becomes the classroom because that is where the equipment is located.

Management's commitment to training is tested when time is scheduled to draw employees away from projects for training. Some managers are tempted to interrupt training for a "quick little job" or "emergency," or to postpone training when deadlines are imminent.

Class organization and preparation can require too much time if the CAD manager himself is to teach the class. The CAD manager must also have sufficient expertise and teaching skills in the first place. Class procedure can incorporate study by the employee on his own time, classroom lecture and discussion, interactive exercises, and practical application to project drawings.

The advantages, though, are many. Trade-specific training teaches the student not only the basics, but can also include company policies, procedures, and standards. The class is made up entirely of employees who will be working together, so interaction and team spirit are high. Students can work on their own familiar workstations with known performance capabilities and configuration. Progress can be supervised more closely and reviewed more often. Course emphasis can be more easily altered to meet the level of progress, and students are more likely to get the individual attention they need. Total training costs are lower without the addition of travel, lodging, and meals to the basic tuition. Further, assignments can be based on productive work, lowering costs even more. By being involved in the education of each employee, the CAD manager gains valuable understanding about individual strengths and weaknesses that can be utilized in his project assignments and scheduling.

To set up your in-house training program, first determine who will do the teaching. If no one within your company is knowledgeable enough to conduct the classes, your dealer may be able to provide the instruction. Outside consultants often specialize in AutoCAD training at client's sites and in specific trades. If you select an outside company to do the training, that consultant should have his own curriculum built already, or be able to structure a custom training program to fit your company goals. As with outside training, be sure that both you and the dealer or consultant agree to specific terms of course content, duration, cost, scheduling, and results.

If you want to conduct the training yourself, you need to develop your own course outline. You may want to use an existing textbook or tutorial for part or all of your course. Begin by defining in specific terms the goals you intend to achieve, such as teaching the students how to draw and dimension a three-view drawing according to your company's standards, or how to prepare a basic floor plan drawing to scale. Then break the task down into manageable segments so that you can test user progress. Examine the end result you wish to achieve and determine whether any concepts need to be introduced and conditioned early, such as 3D visualization or scale relationships. This allows you to develop individual lessons that build the student's knowledge and skills in easily attainable and measurable steps. Provide enough theory lecture so that all students understand the concepts, but base skill development on practical exercises that demonstrate the concepts in real-world terms, such as your own projects. Use each successive lesson to build on the preceding one and pace the class so that you are progressing neither too quickly nor too slowly for your students. Schedule the classes so that time is available to apply what they have learned to work projects, yet not so far apart that the class seems unending. Provide for a rewarding conclusion to the class with a meaningful milestone so that the students go away from the class wanting more.

Independent Study

When only one or two potential students exist, off-site training is too expensive or impractical, or management support for formal training is low, individuals may need to take their training needs into their own hands. Management can support these self-starters by allowing them to use company equipment during off hours. For these individuals, a little encouragement, supervision, and opportunity provided by the CAD manager may be all they need to gain skills and improve proficiency. They can proceed at their own pace without interrupting production, and difficult topics can be repeated as often as necessary.

Many of New Riders Publishing's other titles for AutoCAD are intended to teach various aspects of AutoCAD operation and application. Audio, video, and interactive *computer-aided instruction* (CAI) formats are available for some topics.

Audio tapes are intended for the student to hear while sitting at his workstation, following the instructions and performing exercises. The tape can be paused while the student performs lengthy operations. Although audio tapes have become less popular with the proliferation of videotape players, they can be useful in circumstances in which specific instruction is needed and either the student or instructor is unavailable for meeting. A workbook often supplements the audio tutorial and adds testing and other information.

Training videos are becoming extremely popular, especially with third-party software vendors, as a means of demonstrating and training the use of their software. Often, much more complex concepts and demonstrations can be taught through this medium than through any other. These videos provide visual confirmation that the student has achieved the proper results, and the hands-on experience serves to boost confidence and improve retention of the subject matter. A printed manual is sometimes included. Both audio and video courses can be produced easily in-house. Video teaching aids can be very helpful in group instruction.

Computer-aided instruction programs are especially effective for helping "computerphobic" students overcome their fear of doing something wrong or "breaking" the computer. CAI programs can allow branching in the instruction, depending on the student's progress or interests, and can automate testing and feedback. Companies with development expertise can create their own CAI courses as an easy way to instruct users in operations, standards, and procedures.

Many of these media, books, tapes, videos, and CAI programs are frequently advertised in leading CAD magazines. For a listing of CAD-related periodicals and other publications, see Appendix D.

Training Costs

AutoCAD training is expensive, but it is the best investment you can make to ensure the success of your CAD operation.

Companies can spend twice the value of the hardware and software to train and support each PC user. This illustrates the commitment that these companies are placing on long-term training.

Expenses for training include not only tuition and textual, audio, video, or CAI materials, but also wages and salaries for students and instructors, costs of travel, lodging, and meals. Further, you must allow for lost production time during training for existing users and low production time for new users. Management and other departments must be made aware of the impact that training and initially low production will have *before* training starts. Production schedules and deadlines may be affected, especially if key people are involved in the training. The extent to which management is truly committed to training and the long-term success of AutoCAD will be reflected in how graciously this training is planned and accepted when it begins.

Conducting Productive Personnel Evaluations

Regular, constructive evaluations are another important part of a person's professional development. You do not need to offer a compensation adjustment with every evaluation, but small, frequent bumps in salary tend to be more effective in sustaining morale than annual reviews. Try to give performance reviews at least every six months, every three months during the early years. A lot can happen in six months, even as quickly as time seems to fly.

Everyone likes to know where he stands. People also like to know whether management is satisfied with their performance. Studies have shown that people actually want to succeed, and if given the proper environment and sufficient opportunity, they want to do well. A proper environment includes positive feedback. If you neglect to keep your team members informed of management's perception of their performance, you stall their personal development. Employees also become anxious if they are denied feedback from management. Schedule one meeting a year with each employee, away from the job, over a meal or in some other informal atmosphere, where the entire focus is on his career development. Learn each employee's goals, obstacles, gripes, and what he enjoys about his job.

Try to keep an "open door" policy—not one that means, if your employee does not like how things are, *"There's the door!"*—but one that means your door is always open for people to come in and informally (without fear of retribution) discuss their ideas and concerns with you. Organize your management structure as flat as possible so that higher levels of authority are as accessible as they can be. When approached with complaints, listen twice as much as you talk. This is especially important in environments where CAD users are more isolated, and have less contact with others.

In some organizations, other managers and executives above the CAD manager may have very little knowledge of what a CAD drafter's job entails. If you work in such a company, it may be up to you to prepare objective evaluations of your team members. An evaluation should be a positive and constructive experience that builds the foundation for higher levels of professional growth in the employee. It is a good time to administer positive feedback along with constructive criticism. Try to review the time period since the last review of that employee and determine areas where he made significant contributions to the company's goals and demonstrated excellence. Criticism should be limited to examining specific breakdowns in performance in the light of their causes and how the employee can work to improve in those areas. Carefully examine past accomplishments as an indicator of future performance; mediocre progress is not likely to improve without inspiration. Make it clear how improvement meets the company's business objectives, and how it will enhance advancement potential. Criticism should never take on personal connotations. It should be made clear that, as much as it applies to the job, personalities and social behavior are kept separate from job performance. The evaluation should reflect this. No matter how much you like a person socially, you must be objective about his performance for the good of the company.

An evaluation should review each distinct aspect of a person's job performance. An example of an evaluation form is provided in Appendix B and on the *Managing and Networking AutoCAD Disk*. You can use it as-is, modify it to suit your company and your job descriptions, or use it to supplement your company's own form. See Appendix B for more information.

If some areas are hard to quantify, try contrasting each person against your best performers. You should not, however, discuss comparisons with the reviewee. Identify areas that need development, then provide opportunities for the reviewee to improve in those areas.

You also need to be prepared to handle the eventuality that some employee's performance will not be as good as expected, and may be unsatisfactory. This is when being a responsible CAD manager can be tough. Do not wait until evaluation time to deal with problems of any kind, especially performance. When you begin to see that an employee is not producing the way you expect for someone of his training, experience, and responsibility, you need to determine the cause of the problem. Is it because the person lacks training? Confidence? Willingness? Try to put yourself in the other person's shoes to understand the problem, then try to alleviate it.

Everyone has slumps now and then, but do not tolerate poor performance for long periods. CAD is too critical to your company's mission and too expensive to allow poor performance. Not everyone will make it to super-user status. Some will achieve only satisfactory competence. And some will not work out at all. Be prepared to deal with the latter. Usually, approaching the person openly and honestly works best. If it is clear that someone cannot meet the requirements necessary for the CAD team, maybe another position would suit him better. If not, termination may be your only alternative.

Motivating the CAD Workgroup

Perhaps the most difficult aspect of CAD management to master, yet the one with the most profound effect on productivity, is the management and motivation of people after hiring and training. Hardware and software contribute to productivity and make it possible, but without the involvement and cooperation of people, the best CAD system imaginable is useless.

All else being equal, leadership is a tough enough issue to tackle. But quite often the CAD manager finds himself in a new position of authority over his former peers. This situation can be good if the peers respect the CAD manager's knowledge and experience, and feel part of the same team. But it can be difficult when that authority must be exercised to its fullest in order to enforce compliance with established procedures. The key is good leadership.

As was mentioned at the beginning of this chapter, CAD managers of large companies may not be involved in this area of user management. Also, as was shown in the first chapters of this book, CAD managers tend to come from a technical background, not a managerial one. But for the CAD manager of the smaller firm or others where he needs to provide CAD workgroup motivation, this area may be a special challenge to overall CAD system development.

Personnel management is a broad and varied topic with its own world of resources, methods, philosophies, and trends. The following pages offer just one example of a basic, easy-to-use approach to leadership and user motivation that you can use in your daily relationships with users. You may want to do additional research in this area for your own development if you find it interesting and useful.

Leadership Styles

In his book *The Situational Leader* (Warner Books, 1984), Dr. Paul Hersey proposes three skills as essential to both success and effectiveness in leadership. He defines leadership success as the ability to get the job done as planned, and effectiveness as the ability to build ongoing cooperation. There is a big difference between the two when applied to management.

Many managers are successful in getting others to meet project demands through intimidation and manipulation, but the attitude that remains with the subordinate is not one that will make the next job any easier. In fact, that person's future with the company is probably limited. Due to resentment, he is not likely to progress, even if he wanted to. He will also be tempted to accept the first reasonable offer to go to work for someone else.

Effective leadership not only gets the job done, but the leader obtains the cooperation of others by using the following three skills:

- Understanding past behavior, and recognizing the motivation behind the behavior that either contributed to, or hindered, the achievement of goals

- Predicting future behavior on the basis of past behavior, and projecting how a person will behave in similar or dissimilar circumstances the next time he is called on

- Directing, changing, and controlling behavior, and having the responsibility for—and the ability to influence—the behavior of others through positive reinforcement

Instead of relying on one management style to meet the needs of every person or circumstance, a CAD manager (or any leader, for that matter), must be flexible enough and equipped to handle each situation with the right style for the job. Leadership style is the pattern of behavior (words and actions) in the leader as perceived by others that affects their behavior. Management theorists classify management behaviors as being either *task behavior* or *relationship behavior*.

Task behavior is the extent to which a leader communicates the who, what, where, when, why, and how of job duties to an individual or group. Task behavior is the kind of one-way, directive instruction issued by a driving examiner. The examiner is not interested in building a relationship with you, but only in seeing how well you can perform the dictated maneuvers.

Relationship behavior is a different matter. It comprises the actions of supporting, encouraging, listening, teaching, and other two-way or multi-way communications. Parents, for example, should strive to practice high levels of relationship behavior with their children. These same practices concerning actions and attitudes—within reason, of course—can be beneficial in the workplace, as well.

Because successful managers exhibit different combinations of both types of behavior, a model capable of describing differing amounts of each type is necessary. Figure 12.4 illustrates the four possible combinations of these behaviors.

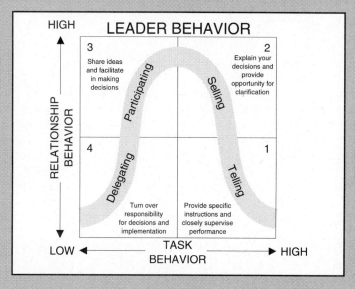

Figure 12.4:

A leadership behavior model. (Copyrighted material from Leadership Studies, Inc. Used by permission. All rights reserved.)

Each combination results in a different leadership style that can be applied in different situations. Each style is described in the following short sections.

Style 1

Style 1 leadership is characterized by high amounts of task behavior and low relationship behavior. This style is most effective when used in situations where clarification and discussion are unnecessary. A quarterback calling plays in the huddle is an example of this type of leadership. The tasks are understood by the other players, who simply need to know what to perform and when. A CAD manager might use this style when reassigning users because of a shift in project priorities (for example, "Dave, you help Scott finish the detail drawings, and Mary, see if you can give George a hand with the assembly diagrams").

This style is dominated by directing others. If a question arises, it should of course be handled, but if someone does not understand what he should be doing, he should be addressed afterwards individually by using a different style.

Style 2

Leadership Style 2 combines a high level of task behavior and a high level of relationship behavior. Instructions are still given as to the tasks and goals, but equal emphasis is placed on understanding them, and in building cooperation and rapport. This style is particularly appropriate when initiating a new employee, who needs to know the facts about his job, but also needs to be encouraged, welcomed, and put at ease so that he can relax and perform well.

Style 3

Relationship behavior dominates over task behavior in Style 3. The emphasis is on promoting discussion, contribution, and candor. The "how-to" is usually understood and secondary. Style 3 would be appropriate when a CAD user has accepted an unusually difficult task, such as one with an abnormally short schedule. Or, another example might be a difficult task in which the user lacks confidence, but he may be familiar with the techniques necessary to complete it. In this case, the CAD manager should provide the support and encouragement that user needs in order to stretch his abilities and build confidence. The manager should also be available and approachable if the user encounters any difficulties, and be ready to help him through them.

Style 4

This style contains low amounts of both task and relationship behavior, and is the ideal condition. When users are entirely capable of any task they might be asked to perform, are well informed as to when and how it should be completed, and are confident and self-motivated, they require little or no direction and only minimal encouragement. Other than supplying reinforcement by recognition of jobs well done, the manager can leave the users to do their jobs with little direction or input.

Readiness Levels

Recognizing when to apply each of the four leadership styles requires that you be able to assess where the follower is. If the leader is doing his job right, and other factors such as the temperament of other associates, the personality of the organization, the demands of the job, and the time constraints are reasonable, then the remaining factor leading to success is readiness.

In this sense, readiness is the ability and willingness of a person to accomplish the task. Each person has a different readiness level to perform a task. Some people's readiness is higher, some lower. Readiness levels may also be different for different portions of a task. For example, a person's readiness to complete a building section drawing may be average overall. He may be an excellent drafter, able accurately and quickly to construct the building's shell geometry. His readiness for this part is high. However, he may not be able to conceptualize well three-dimensionally. If he has difficulty imagining the relationships of the trusses, ceiling, walls, and floor, his readiness for this part is low. In this case, his readiness for the job should be examined in separate parts.

Readiness is the combination of a person's ability (knowledge, experience, and skills) and his willingness (confidence, commitment, and motivation) to do a certain job. Ability and willingness are dependent on each other, too. If a person has plenty of ability, he will generally be willing to do the job. If not, he needs motivation. If he has plenty of confidence that he can do a job even though he may not have the experience or skills, he will often succeed anyway, and gain knowledge and skills in the process. The difference in both cases is motivation—supplied by good leadership.

Figure 12.5 illustrates the degree of follower readiness as a relationship of ability and willingness.

HIGH	MODERATE		LOW
R 4	R 3	R 2	R 1
Able & willing or motivated	Able but unwilling or insecure	Unable but willing or motivated	Unable & unwilling or insecure

FOLLOWER READINESS

Figure 12.5:
Relationship of follower readiness to ability and willingness. (Copyrighted material from Leadership Studies, Inc. Used by permission. All rights reserved.)

This model of the readiness factor is helpful in identifying the one readiness level out of four that each person brings to a project. Each readiness level is described as follows, as each might exist in one person in different stages.

Readiness Level 1

The follower lacks the necessary abilities to perform the task and has neither the confidence, commitment, nor motivation to do so. This might be the case with some older drafters' reluctance to learn about computers and AutoCAD.

Readiness Level 2

The follower lacks ability, but is confident or motivated enough to try. Once the older drafter sees that he cannot "break" the computer and learns how accurate and powerful it is, he begins to be motivated to learn more with the help of others.

Readiness Level 3

The follower is able, but is unwilling or lacks confidence. The drafter has learned all the skills he needs, but is apprehensive when given his first project to complete on his own.

Readiness Level 4

The follower is able, willing, and confident. After a time, the drafter is now competent and enjoys using AutoCAD to make himself more productive. He enjoys learning about AutoCAD, which has sparked new interest in his vocation. Combined with his experience on the drafting board, he is now a top employee.

The practical application of these principles relies on being able to match a leadership style to each of the four readiness levels, and modifying the follower's behavior appropriately. Each person within the CAD workgroup and each task that needs to be done, may require a completely different style and approach. Additionally, a person may require different leadership during the process of one task. Your success in leading others will rely on your ability to diagnose each situation and act accordingly.

To help diagnose the readiness level and select the leadership style with the highest probability of effectiveness, find the readiness level in the model shown in figure 12.6. By constructing a vertical line from that point up to where it intersects the leadership model curve above, the correct leadership style is identified. A single-word description of each style appears on the curve. Style 1 is characterized by "Telling" others what, where, when, and how things need to be done. "Selling" exemplifies Style 2, because the leader is involved in two-way explanation and justification as well as providing direction. Style 3 is described as "Participating," because the leader and follower both participate in decisions and ideas. "Delegating" characterizes Style 4, where much of the responsibilities for meeting goals is turned over to the follower.

In the example shown in figure 12.6, you would use the Style-3 approach with a Level-3 follower. Because the person is able, yet unwilling or unsure, you should share ideas with the person and help him make decisions to get through the task at hand.

Depending on the circumstances, other words might better describe the leadership activity. Alternatives are given as follows:

Style 1	Style 2	Style 3	Style 4
Telling	Selling	Participating	Delegating
Guiding	Explaining	Encouraging	Observing
Directing	Clarifying	Collaborating	Monitoring
Establishing	Persuading	Committing	Fulfilling

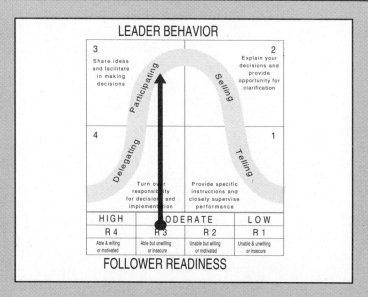

Figure 12.6:
Example of matching leadership style to follower readiness. (Copyrighted material from Leadership Studies, Inc. Used by permission. All rights reserved.)

In R1, for example, conditions in which the followers have very low readiness levels, you should provide all the direction, instruction, support, and encouragement you can (Style 1). R4 situations, in which the followers are both able and willing, should be dealt with using Style 4. Once you point them in the right direction, give them plenty of slack and just ask for progress reports.

Most situations, though, will fall in between these two extremes. Unable but willing followers (R2) need a Style 2 leader, providing direction and instruction, and commending accomplishment and growth. R3 situations, in which the follower knows what needs to be done and how to do it, call for Style 3 (emphasis on relationship behavior over task behavior). The job of cultivating confidence in these followers is perhaps the toughest leadership challenge of all.

Promoting versus Pigeonholing

Instead of hiring for a generic position, take the time to define the available job positions in your company and identify their potential career paths. Some common CAD job descriptions are proposed at the beginning of this chapter. Make sure that everyone understands his job description, its duties, and its potential. When hiring a new employee, tell him about others in your organization who have filled that position on their way to higher ones. Emphasize the potential for advancement, and be prepared to move people up when they demonstrate the ability to fulfill the demands of higher positions.

The temptation exists, once a person becomes profitable and productive in one capacity, to try to keep him there. This is a very short-sighted strategy. Despite the productivity, that person may become bored with his job if it lacks challenge and advancement. Instead, he should be encouraged to specialize in an area that interests him. By allowing every person the opportunity to fulfill his professional potential, the company will realize even greater productivity and growth.

Many companies become reliant on one or more individual experts. On the expert's side, this may seem like job security, but it can easily lead to burnout. On the company side, it can be risky depending on the expert abilities of a few among many. Experts should be encouraged and supported in sharing their knowledge with others. This relates to the need to commit to training. Use your in-house experts as instructors and spread the knowledge around.

Using Other Positive Motivators

In many recent employee satisfaction surveys, the single biggest factor in job satisfaction is the feeling of appreciation for work done well. Positive reinforcement has long been recognized as a positive motivator. Just as a mouse can be taught specific behaviors with rewards, so too people will remember to do those things that bring rewards, whether tangible or not. Providing compensation commensurate with performance is a critical step in rewarding the efforts of others. As much as you can, make it possible for top performers to earn significantly more than equivalent positions in other firms in your area. Also, try to reward CAD-skilled people beyond their non-CAD equivalents. It takes extra dedication and aptitude to excel at AutoCAD. Demonstrate your company's commitment to the success of CAD by rewarding those who most help it succeed. Do not use salary surveys to make policy.

While most CAD managers do not have control over the pay of others, you should exert your influence on upper management to provide pay incentives for exemplary performance. Keep in mind, though, that pay is only one of many motivators. Do not concentrate on pay at the expense of other methods. As pointed out in the surveys mentioned earlier in this chapter, compensation is usually not a high priority when people leave a company. Usually, if people perceive that they are valuable, appreciated, informed, and feel like they have control over their careers, they will stay in a position that may pay less than they are due. Possibly your own experiences can attest to this. Would you rather be paid well for a job you hated, or could you get by with less in a position you enjoyed. Improving the environment and opportunities available to people is nearly free compared with trying to pay them enough to stay. Paying them more may motivate them slightly, but only for a short while, and it will not actually motivate them to do great things, give 110 percent, or excel. It is the intangible things that motivate people.

Compensation, a nice office, and a generous benefits package are merely examples of what is called hygienic factors. They raise the level that people are willing to tolerate when other conditions are undesirable. If things get very tough otherwise, or very often, hygienic factors can prolong their tolerance. Without them, the employee may very likely go elsewhere. Try to eliminate demotivators wherever possible, especially double standards for management and staff. This type of thing only leads to stratification and resentment.

The second highest response in surveys is often "feeling important and involved." When people feel like they are integral to the success of the company's goals and that they are involved in decision-making processes, morale is improved and they work better. You can improve moral in users by soliciting their input on decisions that affect them and by keeping them informed about what is going on around them, how jobs are progressing, how the company is doing, and future plans. Because of the nature of CAD, users can easily become isolated. You can supply the social interaction needed to provide a balance with that isolation by communicating in these ways.

When you do not control pay, you must do whatever you can to provide positive reinforcement. One way is to use praise. While this may seem trite, in practice it can be an effective motivational tool. Here are some tips on administering praise:

- Recognize steady performance, not just extraordinary achievement.
- Recognize good performance even when goals or schedules are not met.
- Use written praise when appropriate. Copies forwarded to superiors or placed in the employee's file can help get that employee recognized during salary reviews and ensure that performance is not forgotten.
- Praising employees in the presence of their peers can motivate others, as well.
- Try to be as specific as possible about what the employee did that is praiseworthy.
- Do not wait too long to give praise. It loses impact with time.
- Be sincere. Token or constant praise is ineffective.
- Be unpredictable in delivering praise. If it is only administered on the morning after a deadline is met, and in private within your office, people will come to anticipate it.

Summary

User management is the most difficult task a CAD manager will face. It separates true managers from mere system administrators, who have little or no interaction with users or impact on their productivity. Finding that diamond of a candidate (sometimes in the rough), and polishing him into a power user through effective training and leadership can be a very rewarding process. It also will pay dividends in your own fulfillment.

In this chapter, you have learned ways to find better people through solid recruiting practices, and learned the qualities that make a good AutoCAD specialist. You learned the importance of training and how to implement different training programs in-house, through a training center, or through independent study. Finally, you learned how to perform evaluations of your people.

Chapter 13 looks at custom AutoCAD applications that can be used with AutoCAD directly or through the exchange files discussed in the last chapter. Chapter 13 also discusses the management aspects of developing your own AutoCAD applications or other software development projects.

Part Four

Expanding and Upgrading Your AutoCAD System

Custom AutoCAD Software

Understanding AutoCAD Workstation Equipment

Illustration courtsey of Autodesk, Inc. Sausalito, California

13

Custom AutoCAD Software

AutoCAD was designed to provide an alternative to manual methods of graphical communication. As such, it was designed to serve thousands of purposes equally well, but as a result, it serves only a few purposes especially well. If your AutoCAD system is to fulfill its real potential, you must customize it to fit your particular purpose. Just as each drafting and design studio has its own particular resources (custom templates, references, expertise) that make it special, a well-equipped AutoCAD system should have special tools of its own.

So, how do you get from a shiny new workstation and shrink-wrapped AutoCAD package to a customized, optimized, integrated system that lets you work as productively as possible? Should you customize the system yourself, in-house? Should you buy special-purpose third-party programs off the shelf? Or, should you hire a consultant to tailor a solution to fit your needs?

In this chapter you learn the ins and outs of all three choices, so that you can confidently chart the best course for your department or company. The chapter begins by helping you shop for an existing third-party application. You will apply many of the same basic principles introduced in Chapter 6, such as evaluating both products and vendors, to the third-party software market. You then will learn about some Autodesk tools that can help you create your own customized application in-house. Finally, this chapter examines some reasons why you might want to enlist the help of a consultant, and tells you what you might expect from one.

If you are serious about AutoCAD productivity, then you should study this chapter closely and start planning your own custom AutoCAD application. If you already have one or more custom AutoCAD applications that work well for you, you may want to move on to Chapter 14 and learn more about CAD workstation hardware and upgrades.

Taking Advantage of the AutoCAD Engine

Many integrated and vertical-market applications, especially databases, function on the principle of a general database *engine* hidden behind a business-specific *front end*. The engine performs the raw data manipulation, organization, and storage functions, while the front end does the data-formatting, display, and output chores. The front end is customized to fit the business problem at hand, but the engine can work with any properly designed front end.

In the case of custom AutoCAD applications, AutoCAD is the engine. Most AutoCAD applications are front ends composed of one or more of the following elements:

- Custom menus with special-purpose macros
- AutoLISP programs
- Block libraries
- Shape files
- Hatch patterns
- Custom linetypes
- External executable programs

For a quick example of AutoCAD customization, look at the AutoShade interface that is packaged with the AutoCAD program. When you select ASHADE from the AutoCAD screen menu, AutoCAD displays options that let you produce a filmroll file that can be used by AutoShade. AutoCAD also loads a special ASHADE.LSP file, which contains scene composition and manipulation commands. When you select a menu macro, the program inserts special blocks into the drawing to hold data that describe the locations and types of lights and cameras. You can make a filmroll file that combines multiple lighting and camera possibilities into your various "scenes." The custom ASHADE components become the front end, with which you interface to get the AutoCAD engine to produce the filmroll file. Each ASHADE component is customized to adapt a particular AutoCAD feature to the specialized needs of AutoShade. Each of these AutoCAD customization techniques is fairly well known, but a new realm of customization is beginning to take shape.

With the help of the AutoCAD Development System (ADS), programmers can write larger and faster programs and subroutines than they can create by using AutoLISP. ADS applications can be written in high-level languages, such as C, and eliminate the need for executable programs to be external to AutoCAD because they run within AutoCAD. ADS applications make more sophisticated front ends possible or even give the AutoCAD engine a new "cylinder" or two by supplying basic functions that AutoCAD does not have. These programs are fast because they can be compiled into directly executable files, which do not need the slower interpretation required by AutoLISP programs. ADS programs, like AutoLISP programs, are loaded into memory, and the programmer can *call* them just as he can call AutoLISP programs. The capability to run ADS programs is currently only available in AutoCAD OS/2 Release 10 and AutoCAD 386 Release 11, but it soon will be available on all other platforms except possibly the Macintosh and DEC VAX versions. Although not many ADS programs are available yet from third-party developers, ADS makes the possibilities for AutoCAD applications almost limitless. Look for ADS capabilities when you consider custom AutoCAD applications.

The Third Party is Bigger than the First

To meet the needs of vertical applications (specialized fields needing specialized tools), an entire software industry has developed. This industry is both separate from and dependent on Autodesk. This vertical software industry is separate in that the companies involved are not part of Autodesk, but they are dependent in that they all rely on Autodesk to provide software tools, documentation, and support so that they can develop AutoCAD "add-on" products.

AutoCAD was created as a general-purpose drafting program that could be customized easily by others, and Autodesk intends to keep it that way. AutoCAD has a long-standing reputation as the most customized of all PC-based CAD programs, with more than 800 aftermarket applications (at last reckoning) amounting to a $2.5 billion industry. If all the developers of these and other unadvertised applications were counted, they would probably outnumber Autodesk employees three-to-one.

Autodesk has several ways of supporting third-party developers with information, documentation, software development tools, and recognition. One of those ways is through a generous Registered Developer program, which encourages customization and extension of AutoCAD's menus, macros, and commands. Companies in this group produce software that customizes or augments AutoCAD to fulfill many different special design and drafting needs, for architecture, engineering, facilities management, manufacturing, and almost every other field with a substantial AutoCAD user base. A well-designed and supported third-party application can save your company thousands of dollars in production costs and training by providing powerful tools that simplify many AutoCAD tasks.

Autodesk's registered developers are informed about Autodesk's technical and business directions. These developers receive marketing, sales and development resources from Autodesk, and share common client and dealer resources. In return, a potential developer must produce evidence of acceptable levels of product marketability, technical competence, and satisfied clients.

Autodesk recently implemented a Strategic Developer program above the Registered Developer program to recognize exceptional developers and their products, and to provide higher levels of cooperation. Look for either developer status in any third-party products you consider. They represent stable and competent companies.

Because these specialized fields can be narrow, however, there is sometimes not enough competition to force developers to provide the best products. And, as you may already know, no two approaches to a problem are quite alike. Your particular needs may not be properly met by just any third-party program in your given field. Carefully scrutinize products and developers to be sure that any third-party program will meet your current needs, and that it also will be expandable, customizable, and well-supported enough to meet your future needs.

Finding the Right Application

To determine how to best exploit AutoCAD's potential, start by assessing your needs. Exactly what do you want to do with AutoCAD? Begin by identifying your drafting discipline, whether it is public utilities engineering, circuit design, or any other field. Third-party applications for AutoCAD exist for the following tasks, and many others:

- Architectural design and drafting
- Facilities planning and management
- Landscape design
- Project management and scheduling
- Site planning and civil engineering
- Structural engineering
- Mechanical engineering analysis
- Mechanical engineering design, drafting, and documentation
- Machine tooling and NC part programming
- Manufacturing production and process planning
- Desktop publishing and presentation graphics
- Electrical design and engineering
- Electronic design and engineering
- GIS and mapping
- Process industry design
- Autodesk product customization tools
- Database management
- General design and drafting utilities
- Graphics translators
- Input and output options

- Systems management
- User interface enhancements

Once you have identified your drafting discipline, you need to narrow it down. Do you want to do on-line design through the application, as well? How does your company work now? Do engineers sketch out designs and pass them on to drafters for documentation? Is there a clear and wide division between the two efforts? Or is it a gray area where engineers and designers draft their own designs as they go? Will they continue to design on paper after the automation of drafting? If you can answer such questions, you can more easily decide on the kind of product you need.

Most AutoCAD third-party applications lean toward drafting automation, not design automation, and many good programs are available. If you want to automate both design and drafting, you might consider starting out slowly and trying a drafting automation package first. Some applications take a modular approach that enables you to add modules as your automation plans grow.

Or, you might want to bite the bullet and bring in a full-blown design automation program at the start, even during your initial AutoCAD system design phase (covered in earlier chapters), and work people into it as production demands allow. Studies have conclusively shown that the greatest productivity gains and return on investment come when design is accomplished on the system. Look hard at the people who will be using this system. Are they capable and motivated enough to change their ways? Maybe the change to CAD alone is all they can swallow at first. Once you have a good idea what you are looking for, you can begin shopping.

Taking Another Look at Market Research

Does this sound familiar? Market research for AutoCAD hardware and networks is covered in Chapter 6, and many of the same concepts apply when you are purchasing third-party software packages to enhance your AutoCAD system. Certainly, you should screen ads and specifications for information on programs, but the best proof of performance is found when the product is put to use. You can base your hardware judgments on easily definable, measurable performance. In general, however, software has very few standards and specifications to govern performance and suitability for a given task.

The best of the vertical-market applications manufacturers advertise both in publications devoted to their field and in AutoCAD-related magazines. You will find many of these publications listed in Appendix D.

Your local AutoCAD user group is the best place to learn of other companies' experiences with third-party packages. Look closely at products developed by companies that are in the same business as your company. Often, companies whose main line of work is engineering or manufacturing cannot find an application that meets their own criteria closely enough, so they produce their own. If the program works especially well, they distribute it commercially. These products tend to work better than those developed by companies that employ more programmers than engineers.

Another great source of information is the ADESK forum on the electronic information service CompuServe. Many experienced AutoCAD users and dealers actively discuss AutoCAD-related issues in the forum, and can give you the benefit of their experience and knowledge.

Evaluating Products

By their nature, most AutoCAD add-ons do not lend themselves to a working demo disk. The open architecture that makes AutoCAD so customizable also leaves third-party products vulnerable to copying and other types of license infringement. To create a working demo disk, the developer may need to include so much of the actual program that users would have little incentive to buy the real thing; they could just use the demo disk.

Some developers, however, have little trouble making a self-running demo. You may be familiar with these already, as most companies choose to make this kind. You cannot do any actual work with these demo disks, but you can sit through a slide show of screen images while you press the space bar or some other key to go to the next page. Text explains the program's features, and, in most cases, you can see the graphic output of the program on the screen as it actually would appear.

Self-running demos can give you a good idea of a program's procedures and flow, which can be important. If the program performs a task in the same manner as you would, your learning experience will be easier and more comfortable. If the program takes detours to which you are not accustomed, however, you may require an entirely different approach to solving the problems, or you may need training to use the program.

If you or someone on your staff is an experienced AutoLISP programmer and can get a look at the actual program, tear it apart. A careful examination of the code should reveal whether the programmers who created it knew what they were doing.

Check the update record of any program you consider purchasing. Users become frustrated when a new release of AutoCAD comes out with a powerful new feature, but an important add-on program does not appear on the market for another year. Consider the popular AEC Architectural and Mechanical packages, which were originally developed for use with AutoCAD around Release 2.5. These add-on programs were capable and fairly powerful, if not elegant. When AutoCAD Release 9 appeared with its increased 3D capabilities, however, many AEC Architectural owners had to wait almost until Release 10 came out before the add-on was updated. AEC Mechanical was never updated.

As you examine a front-end program, pay attention to the interfaces it exploits. AutoCAD supplies many ways to produce and edit a drawing database. Some ways work better for some purposes than others. For example, suppose that you are evaluating an application that automates process piping design. It might provide an external (to AutoCAD) executable program for entering design parameters, and then create an input file from which AutoCAD can draw the resulting layout. The developer may write a script file of every command necessary to draw the layout with AutoCAD's own editing commands and supply coordinates that the commands expect. Or, the program may produce a DXF, DXB, or IGES file of the actual drawing, which would only need to be imported into AutoCAD. A very sophisticated developer could even cause the program to output a finished AutoCAD drawing file.

Depending on the size and complexity of the layout, a script file would be the slowest and most awkward approach to a drafting problem. A DXF file would be much faster and more reliable, while a binary DXF or DXB file would be smaller and marginally faster. A more interactive approach would be to implement a parametric design interface within AutoCAD, which would enable the designer to create and alter the design, and see the effects of his decisions graphically. The external approach previously described would require importing the input file into AutoCAD, verifying it, and, if modification were necessary, abandoning the drawing, exiting AutoCAD, and starting all over again.

And in all cases of implementing a major piece of software, do not underestimate the amount of training necessary to bring everyone up to speed with it. A new system will surely affect production schedules, and so other departments up and down the line need to be made aware of the upcoming slowdown. Plan ahead before you try to integrate a third-party program into your system.

Evaluating Developers

Do not just check out the program itself; check out the developer as well. The best program in the world is not going to do you good for long if the developer goes out of business or discontinues support for the program shortly after you buy it. Ask not only how long the company has been developing AutoCAD applications, but also how long it has been working on the program in which you are interested. If the program is "fresh out of the oven," it may contain undiscovered bugs. Unless you are willing to take risks to test new software, keep your options open.

Try to get references from the developer. Talk to other firms that use the program, if possible, and find out if the software met their expectations. Be sure to ask about the program's learning curve, the developer's level of support for the program, and the developer's user support record. Remember, if you buy the program, you may need to make a major investment in training and support, so do your homework.

Try to find out how many people the developer has committed to supporting the application. If the product's technical support staff is very small, you may lose support when you need it most.

Find out if the company is a registered developer with Autodesk. If so, then it receives valuable technical support and product information directly from Autodesk, which helps the developer build better products more quickly. Such a company also will have met minimum customer and dealer requirements for acceptance by Autodesk.

Finally, on the odd chance that your authorized AutoCAD dealer is familiar with the product, get his recommendations. Perhaps he has sold and installed the program before, and may have experience with the developer. If not, perhaps he can contact the developer for you.

The Hazards of Customizing Third-Party Programs

As specialized as third-party add-on packages can be, none is likely to exactly match the way your company does things. The program's symbols, annotations, and dimensions might be different from your company's standards. You will want to be able to correct these discrepancies, and possibly even to supplement the package yourself.

Some developers, however, take a closed approach when it comes to making their AutoLISP, shape, and menu source code available for customization by end users. All software developers are sensitive about the fruits of their labor being copied, in whole or in part, for unlawful purposes. To keep people from stealing portions of their AutoLISP programs, some programmers use encrypting utilities to scramble AutoLISP code into nearly indistinguishable gibberish. Developers can protect their programs' menus by supplying only the compiled MNX file instead of the MNU source file. Shapes can be handled the same way.

Your company, for instance, may have an unusual standard size or format for dimension text. Yet, your third-party application may control dimension appearance with values built into encrypted AutoLISP routines. If you use the application's dimension routines with your own standards on the same drawing, the two dimension types will make your drawing look inconsistent and sloppy. If the application uses nonencrypted AutoLISP code, however, you could make the dimensioning adjustment relatively easily.

No one can make changes to the package you buy if the source code is not included, so insist on receiving source code and assurances that you can augment the package if you need to. If the package does not offer this, you should look elsewhere for a more open product.

Creating Your Own Applications

Sometimes the only way to get the application you need is to create the application in-house. If your company has been using AutoCAD for years, you may already have the people who can put together a good add-on package. If you are just getting into AutoCAD, however, your users probably will not be ready to take on a task like this for quite some time. Your users should have a good understanding of each area of AutoCAD customization to complete a major AutoCAD application, especially knowledge of menu macros and AutoLISP.

While it is not within the scope of this book to teach you specific customization techniques, the following pages will highlight some of the tools available from Autodesk to help make the process smoother and more predictable. For in-depth coverage of AutoCAD customization, see *Customizing AutoCAD* or *Maximizing AutoCAD Vol. I: Menus and Macros* and *Inside AutoLISP* or *Maximizing AutoCAD Vol. II: Inside AutoLISP*, by New Riders Publishing.

An in-house software-development project should be as carefully managed as any other costly undertaking. You can keep costs down and get positive results by borrowing a few tips from traditional electronic data processing management. Software development is one of the most labor-intensive activities an organization can undertake, in relation to returns. It will take much longer to pay back the investment of an in-house software project than to buy a new product in finished form. Further, software development can sap the productivity of some of your most highly talented and highly paid personnel, and their performance (whether good or bad) on the project will have far-reaching effects on your CAD endeavor's profitability.

Finally, as you look at the cost of a software-development project, do not forget that more than just a raw programming effort is required. You should break the project into the following phases, and consider how each phase fits into the big picture:

- Analysis
- Design
- Programming
- Documentation
- Training
- Maintenance

Each phase brings a perspective to the project that can help the project succeed in the long run. Analysis and design supply the planning perspective, programming and documentation are the products of planning, and training and maintenance ensure that the product is understood and remains useful. The pages that follow provide you with some practical tips for these phases.

The Autodesk Software Development Kit

Autodesk provides a group of software tools to aid in the actual development of AutoCAD applications. These tools collectively are referred to as the Autodesk Software Development Kit (SDK). The SDK supplies individual tools in three different areas depending on the area of AutoCAD customization you are working in: ADS programs, AutoLISP programs, and general-purpose tools for common areas in either environment.

The AutoLISP development tools in the SDK include the AutoLISP Pretty Printer, AutoLISP Beautifier, AutoLISP Prototyping Environment, the Kelvinator, and Protect. The SDK includes the Function Call Tracer tool for ADS application developers. General-purpose SDK tools include the DOS Memory Mapper, Menu File Editor, and Linked List Library.

Each development tool is described briefly in the following sections. Your authorized AutoCAD dealer can help you get a copy of the AutoCAD Software Developer's Kit from Autodesk. Or, if you like, you can download any one of the SDK's tools, or the entire SDK, from ADESK forum on CompuServe.

AutoLISP Pretty Printer

The AutoLISP Pretty Printer function is an AutoLISP file named PPRINT.LSP. PPRINT is a function used with AutoCAD that accepts AutoLISP symbolic expressions and reformats them with proper indention for easier reading and documentation. PPRINT normally sends its formatted output to the screen, but it also can be made to send its output to a file that can be edited. PPRINT is useful for formatting and saving expressions entered within the AutoCAD Drawing Editor, for isolating and formatting unformatted subroutines as stand-alone functions, and for reformatting functions that have been "stripped" of white space.

AutoLISP Beautifier

The AutoLISP Beautifier, LB.EXE, is a stand-alone program that performs much the same function as PPRINT.LSP, only outside of AutoCAD. LB accepts an input file that contains the AutoLISP code to be formatted, and can accept an output file name for the finished product. Additionally, LB will accept arguments that make the output file either all upper- or lowercase, customize the width of output lines, customize the spacing intervals for nested code and for piping standard input. LB is much faster than PPRINT and is more appropriate when working with large programs.

AutoLISP Prototyping Environment

The AutoLISP Prototyping Environment (APE) consists of several AutoLISP programs that aid in the development of AutoLISP code by making the AutoLISP interpreter more interactive. Once loaded in AutoCAD, the APE provides two basic functions: an AutoLISP command line editor named ERL, and an AutoLISP command line processor (CLP) that takes over the AutoCAD command line processor.

ERL lets you enter a line of AutoLISP code and move about through the characters. ERL also lets you edit the code with EMACS standard key sequences. EMACS is a text editor based on editable macros. ERL lets you perform functions such as jumping backward one word by using the key combination Alt-B. If you prefer another combination, however, ERL contains functions that will let you redefine the key combinations associated with the function.

The CLP program runs AutoCAD specifically to develop and test AutoLISP code. Once invoked, CLP remembers some of the AutoLISP lines you have entered and their results, lets you use ERL on any lines at the current CLP prompt, monitors parentheses matching, and provides two symbols for macro-like shorthand. CLP also lets you enter, execute, and edit AutoLISP code unlike the standard AutoLISP interpreter environment. CLP has useful history and redo functions that let you recall an earlier line of code for editing or execution, and includes provisions for adding your own watchdog processes, called *daemons*. Daemons monitor input and perform a prescribed action when certain input appears.

Kelvinator

The Kelvinator, KELV.EXE, is a stand-alone program that translates one or more related AutoLISP files into encrypted gibberish. KELV takes a commented, formatted, and indented AutoLISP file and deletes the comments, translates all variable names into random, yet rule-based aliases, and removes line breaks and indention. KELV has facilities for multiple file handling so that separate AutoLISP files that reference variables and functions within each other remain operable. These facilities also let the user define certain parameters of KELV's operation. Kelvinated AutoLISP files protect the developer from casual code theft and reverse engineering. If you receive Kelvinated or encrypted AutoLISP code, be sure the developer has provided means by which you can customize the program with user-definable variables, functions, or blocks.

Protect

PROTECT.EXE is a stand-alone program provided by Autodesk for developers with especially sensitive security needs. PROTECT encrypts an AutoLISP file according to a user-supplied key character. The resulting encrypted file nearly is impossible to decipher. Whereas a Kelvinated AutoLISP file is readable yet nearly meaningless, an encrypted AutoLISP file displays the message AutoCAD PROTECTED LISP file when someone attempts to read it. A Kelvinated AutoLISP file even may be encrypted with PROTECT for maximum security. If you receive encrypted AutoLISP files from a developer, you should observe the same preceding precautions for Kelvinated files.

For your own in-house development, you may decide to use either or both methods to discourage users from tampering with your company's development efforts and to prevent accidental or intentional migration of programs to competitors.

Function Call Tracer

The ADS Function Call Tracer (FCT) comprises programming-language-specific files that can be incorporated into a developer's ADS application. The FCT functions intercept calls to the ADS library and create a file that tracks the activity of the ADS functions. The file tells you which functions were called and when, and what data was passed between them and the developer's functions. This information can be valuable in debugging an ADS application developed for the AutoCAD environment.

DOS Memory Mapper

The DOS Memory Mapper, DOSMAP.EXE, can be a useful tool for troubleshooting AutoCAD software and hardware configuration, as well as an aid in software development. DOSMAP is a stand-alone utility that displays technical information about the configuration of 80286- and 80386-based personal computers running DOS versions 3.0 and 4.0. DOSMAP creates a text file that contains the following series of dumps of the DOS environment:

- Equipment configuration dump
- Memory table dump
- Memory control block chain dump
- Driver table dump
- Device control block dump
- File control block dump
- Buffer control block dump
- Logical disk table dump
- Program table dump
- Interrupt table dump

With the help of these dumps, you can determine how memory and other hardware are being used by various programs such as TSRs and device drivers, and how much free memory remains and its location.

Menu File Editor

The Menu File Editor (MFE) is a series of C-language functions that a developer can include in his ADS application to build custom AutoCAD menus on the fly. These MFE functions can be invoked as a result of conditions observed by daemons, described earlier. MFE makes it possible to create custom menus without requiring close attention to menu file syntax, and in a more natural, higher-level context. MFE uses a master input file in menu format and creates custom AutoCAD menu output files that can be compiled and loaded by AutoCAD. MFE eliminates the need to design AutoCAD menus that encompass every possible combination of diverse menu needs in complex AutoCAD applications.

Linked List Library

The Linked List Library is a series of C-language functions that enable a developer to implement abstract data structures called *linked lists*. Linked lists are especially useful in developing programs for multiple platforms and in increasing the modularity of programs.

Autodesk has committed to updating and expanding the SDK with even more and better tools as the technology becomes feasible. If you are interested in customizing AutoCAD, you should watch for developments in this area.

Using a Consultant To Create Custom Applications

If your staff is not comfortable with the idea of creating customized applications in-house, you might want to consider hiring a consultant to help you devise custom solutions.

You should consider hiring a consultant if any of the following conditions apply to your organization:

- Production schedules do not give the CAD manager enough time to organize a software project.
- The CAD manager does not have the ability to define the problem and develop solutions.
- The CAD manager does not have the authority or responsibility to carry out the project.
- The business climate does not leave any room for waste in development or training time.
- You need the consultant's specialized knowledge, training, or techniques.
- You need an objective outside viewpoint, possibly because of conflicts or communication problems within the company.
- You have small, specialized projects that must be completed quickly, on an as-needed basis.
- You need to supplement in-house expertise.

Choosing a Consultant

A good CAD/CAM consultant should be able to identify your specific performance problems and recommend solutions in the areas of software, hardware, personnel, management, and organization. Before contacting a consultant, you should first verify the need for outside help, and then clear up any reservations that anyone in your organization might have about bringing in an "outsider." The complete cooperation of everyone affected is necessary for any project to succeed. Call one or more meetings in order to exhaust all other alternatives and discuss any problems.

The first meeting with a consultant should be a two-way interview in which the consultant outlines his experience and capabilities, and you describe the objectives that you hope to achieve with his help. You should interview as many potential consultants as you need to find the most qualified one.

While you are interviewing consultants, ask for references of previous (yet recent) clients, and follow up with them. You also may want to ask the consultant about any professional affiliations he may have, such as the *Independent Computer Consultants Association* or others that demonstrate credibility and accountability.

Ask the consultant to provide you with a proposal for actions to be taken with a tentative time-line and schedule of fees for the engagement. If you decide to hire the consultant, set up a formal schedule and agree to the following points with the consultant:

- The terms of the agreement, whether verbal or written, including conditions of extension and termination
- Exact services to be rendered
- Requirements of the client (your company)
- The staff member to act as your company's contact person for the consultant
- Compensation, either as an hourly rate, an agreed limit not to be exceeded, or a flat rate, possibly including reimbursable expenses
- Description, licensing, and rights of any software developed
- Indemnity and insurance
- Confidentiality
- Warranty
- Payment terms
- Successor and assigns
- Extent of the contract

Once work has begun, you should talk with the consultant regularly, with progress reports and intermediate reviews. He should provide your staff with training on using the new system, including maintenance instructions to the CAD manager, and he should make periodic follow-up visits to ensure acceptance and satisfaction. If these points are applicable to your project and desirable, you may want to include them in the written agreement. Usually, however, only very large development projects with long schedules require written contracts and most consultants avoid the hassle and expense of contract preparations. Nevertheless, you should involve your company's legal department if you decide on a written contract.

Working with a Consultant

To understand how your firm might develop a relationship with a consultant, consider the following example.

The ACME Industrial Screen Door Company has just installed a new AutoCAD system to help in the design and drafting of its patented screen doors. The system is up and working fine, but ACME's CAD manager, Ted, is busy adjusting to his new duties and does not know much about AutoLISP.

ACME's screen doors are made of thin sheets of stainless steel, perforated with holes spaced at different intervals, and of different diameters, depending on the amount of wind shear expected at the client's site. ACME's engineers calculate the wind force and design a custom hole pattern for each of ACME's screen door models, then have ACME's drafters make drawings for the shop floor where the doors are made.

ACME executives are pleased with their new AutoCAD system because it makes such nice-looking drawings. The executives, however, are perplexed as to why they do not seem to be getting the kinds of productivity improvements their dealer told them to expect. The executives continually question Ted as to why the CAD system is not performing up to their expectations, and charge him with finding a solution to the mediocre productivity levels. Ted tries everything he can think of to speed up the computers, fine-tune their configurations, and optimize his network, but the improvements do not make the noticeable difference his superiors are looking for.

Then Ted has a revelation: what if the computers could calculate the optimum hole spacing and sizes automatically from a set of parameters entered by the engineer? The engineers would only have to know dimensions for the screen doors and enter field data about wind conditions. Once the doors were drawn parametrically, the engineers could verify the designs and pass the drawings on to the draftsmen over the network for finishing touches or embellishment. By using such a program, ACME could produce more custom designs per engineer-hour, drawing accuracy would improve, and drafters would not get sick of using the Array command. As mentioned earlier, however, Ted does not know enough about AutoLISP to customize his system to perform these tasks. He decides, therefore, to find a consultant.

Ted sets up a meeting with a CAD consultant who specializes in AutoLISP. They agree on terms that would have the consultant create a custom AutoLISP application for ACME that will do everything Ted envisioned.

Ted agrees to provide all the data the consultant needs to design the AutoLISP program to ACME's door specifications. Ted also agrees to work with the consultant as a liaison between the consultant and ACME, and the consultant agrees to make regular progress reports to Ted. Ted and the consultant sign a short written contract that includes the following stipulations:

- Licensing rights for ACME to use the application and modify it in the future
- Indemnity for the consultant should any ACME screen door designed with the program fail or cause an accident
- Confidentiality to ensure that the consultant does not tell ACME's competitors about the company's patented door designs
- A warranty stating that the consultant must fix any bugs found in the program, that cause deviations from ACME's specifications

Summary

AutoCAD is a powerful engine, but you must customize it with a good front-end if the system is to perform to its potential. You can do this by buying a ready-made application, if you shop carefully and wisely, or you can make your own.

In this chapter, you learned about the AutoCAD add-on product industry and what to look for in a specialized product. This chapter showed you some customization tools that you can get from Autodesk (just as Registered Developers do) to make the job easier. Finally, you learned how to go about finding and engaging a CAD consultant.

Chapter 14 offers a detailed look at CAD hardware you should consider for upgrades or for parts of a new workstation. The chapter is a complete survey of an entire personal computer system configured with all types of peripheral devices. The chapter explains basic operation of each component, as well as the advanced features that many components provide for the best AutoCAD performance.

14

Understanding AutoCAD Workstation Equipment

How did you decide on the last automobile you bought? Can you still stand behind that decision today? If you answer yes to the latter question, then you made a well-educated decision, or you are still enamored of the car that first captivated you. If you answer no, then you may have been swayed by the allure of the car's beauty or performance without regard for its reliability or economy.

It may not be fair to compare the claims of enhanced productivity through techno-logical innovation to the fascination of automobiles. Still, a computer buyer can be sold on a lemon of a hard disk just as easily as a car buyer can be won over by a poorly designed turbocharger. Because all CAD managers are faced with the prob-lem of keeping up with technology, this chapter's goal is to explain technological advances and help you make informed buying decisions.

This chapter is intended not only for CAD managers, but for anyone interested in getting the most for the money when shopping for new PC hardware. Whether you are planning an entire new department or a single dedicated AutoCAD workstation, looking to upgrade components in an existing machine, or just "window shopping," this chapter will help you understand the technology and its application to AutoCAD. The following PC hardware components are looked at in this chapter:

- Central processors
- Math coprocessors
- PC bus designs
- RAM
- Quality details

■ Hard disks
■ Auxiliary storage
■ Video graphics
■ Monitors
■ Input devices
■ Output devices

Some hardware features are critical if an AutoCAD workstation is to perform optimally. This chapter describes each component of a personal graphics workstation
and explains how that component can increase performance and reliability in an
AutoCAD environment. Armed with this information, you can confidently decide
what hardware features are worthy of your consideration, and which ones to leave
for the impulse buyer.

When To Consider Hardware Upgrades

Face it, the state of the art in computers is a fast-moving target. Most computer
users are bewildered by the pace of technology development. You research the
products, compare values, specify components, and no sooner do you place your
order than something better is announced or the price drops. It is perhaps similar to
finally talking yourself through the "sticker shock" of buying a new car, and then
finding out the second you drive off the lot that it depreciates a thousand dollars.

At any one time, thousands of computer buyers are waiting for the right time to
make a computer purchase—waiting for the next CPU to come out, waiting for the
price of RAM to come down, or waiting for some other feature to appear or improve.
Often, as in the case of simply waiting for the price to fall, the money saved in the
eventual purchase is spent in the meantime on lower productivity, which could have
benefited from meeting your need for a productivity solution the first time the product was available. Many experts agree that you are far better off just making the
most informed purchase decision you can in any particular technology/value "window," and then putting it to work immediately toward your return on investment.

From a practical standpoint, it is hard to go wrong in postponing hardware upgrades as long as possible. As long as your essential equipment is still running
reliably, you are just dollars ahead. From a business standpoint, however, how
much is the performance differential costing you between, say, a new display list
processing video card and your old standard EGA card? If the new card saves the
user just one hour a day, it will probably pay for itself in a month. This ties together
with the effect of system response discussed in Chapter 6.

CAD Equipment: Past and Present

CAD hardware technology has undergone changes as rapidly as microcomputer technology. Vacuum tubes and toggle switches have been replaced with silicon chips and scanners.

To illustrate the rate at which technology has advanced, consider the TX-2 computer that Ivan Sutherland used to develop his Sketchpad program. The TX-2 was created in 1956, and included the following features:

- 64K of 6 ms vacuum-tube memory
- 4K of 4.4 ms transistor memory
- A 36-bit processor
- The equivalent of two 9M tape drives for storage
- 592 toggle switches
- 37 push buttons in addition to the keyboard.
- A 7"x7", 1024x1024 resolution monochrome display.

The TX-2 was one of only a few systems like it in the world. By comparison, today you can buy a 32-bit personal computer with 100 times the memory, ten times the storage, and four times the display for the cost of a used car in nearly any city in the country. You can only imagine what Sketchpad could have been if Sutherland had today's technology.

Today's CAD operator has many options from which to choose when setting up a workstation. You can invest in state-of-the-art CAD equipment without having to spend unheard-of amounts of money. You can keep down your costs by purchasing a reliable PC, but still have the option of upgrading to a higher system as your needs change.

Today, a typical CAD workstation might have the following features:

- 80386-based PC
- Math coprocessor
- 4M-8M RAM
- VGA monitor
- Mouse or digitizer tablet
- Pen plotter

From this workstation, you can upgrade to an 80486 CPU, increase your RAM, install graphics cards or add an additional monitor, or add a scanner to increase input options. This system also can be included in a network, if that is the route that you need to take.

The following sections discuss each component of a CAD workstation, and provide recommendations on many types of CAD hardware components.

Central Processors

The *central processing unit* (CPU) chip is the computer system's "brain." The CPU controls the computer circuits' function according to a set of instructions contained in the ROM BIOS or basic input/output system chip. The features of BIOS chips are covered later.

Some debate surrounds the superiority of various CPU chips in computers. For the majority of AutoCAD users today, this debate is taking place in the IBM-compatible world, which is dominated by chips produced by Intel Corporation. Millions of computers are now based on Intel processors with the designations of 8086, 8088, 80286, 80386-SX, 80386, and 80486, with rumors of the 80586 chip coming. The Macintosh II computers feature the Motorola 68020 and 68030 processors with a 68040 on the way. News of the revolutionary *reduced instruction set computer* (RISC) chips, which are different from the Motorola and Intel chips, is causing excitement in the industry.

The following sections examine each of these processors and explain their meaning to AutoCAD users.

The Intel Family

Today the name Intel is synonymous with personal computers, but it has not always been so. Back when the IBM PC still was on the drawing board, Intel was just another chip maker in a crowd of solid state device manufacturers. Then, when IBM selected the 8088 as the CPU for the PC, Intel's future was changed forever. Intel has been the single source of CPUs for all of IBM's personal computers since then. Intel also has picked up the business for nearly all IBM compatible computers built. Only in the last several years have companies such as Advanced Micro Devices and Harris been able to supply special high speed or low power copies of Intel chips to computer manufacturers.

Intel has produced what could be called a family of microprocessors. All of these chips have a name beginning with the number 80 and all except the 8088 end with the number 86. A single digit in between the two numbers identifies another chip in the series, such as 80286, 80386, and 80486. Hence, they are termed collectively the 80x86 family. Each successive chip design is a little bigger, a little faster, and a little more complex than the previous generation chip design (see fig. 14.1).

Each of the following sections describes one of the members of the Intel family, the computer it appeared in, and how it relates to AutoCAD.

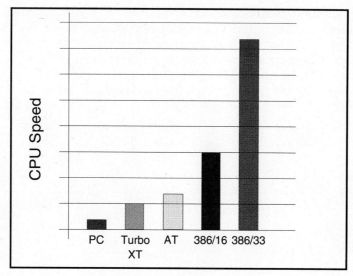

Figure 14.1:
Relative speed comparison of common Intel processors.

The Intel 8086

The 8086 processor was the first CPU chip Intel produced in the 80x86 family of microprocessors. Introduced in 1978, the 8086 processor was designed to move and manipulate program code and data in a 16-bit-wide path both *inside* and *outside* the chip. Paths outside the processor lead to memory chips, control circuits, and expansion cards installed in the computer. Paths inside the chip lead to the processor's individual data manipulation areas. The 8086's main problem was that it was not as much of a commercial success as the Intel 8088 was. The 8086 recently has made a slight comeback, however, after being chosen for the IBM PS/2 models 25 and 30.

The Intel 8088

In 1981, IBM built its first PC using the 8088 processor. The 8088 moves 16 bits of data at a time inside the chip, but only eight bits at a time outside the chip (hence the different name). Computers equipped with the 8086 processor actually outperform computers using the 8088 processor when operated at the same frequency. The 8088 processor, nevertheless, still is being used by millions of IBM PC and compatible owners.

The Intel 8088 processor (and a computer built around it) runs at a maximum speed of 10 MHz (megahertz), more than twice the speed of the original IBM PC, which ran at 4.77 MHz. The 8088, however, does not provide acceptable performance for most professional AutoCAD applications, and soon will no longer be supported by

AutoCAD. In order to accommodate the older, slower 8088, AutoCAD must wait at points in the program for timing-dependent operations. These wait instructions take up a modest amount of memory. Because most AutoCAD customers are moving on to more powerful processors for their workstations, Autodesk can strip out the wait instructions from AutoCAD, add more features, and speed up the program. Autodesk has done this in the AutoCAD 386 version, and soon will follow suit in other versions as well.

> **Tip:** If you still use IBM XT-class computers, now is the time to upgrade to a newer, faster processor. If you are on a tight budget, you may be able to improve your system's performance simply by adding a processor upgrade card. The Intel Inboard 386 PC, for instance, replaces your 8088 processor with a 16 MHz 80386 processor that provides additional memory. The performance will not be as good as a PC that is built specifically for an 80386 processor, so if you can afford to, replace the entire computer.

The Intel 80286

The first *power user's* chip, the 80286, was introduced in 1984 in IBM's AT-model computer. Originally, the 80286 processor ran at speeds of 6 or 8 MHz, and compatibles have since soared to 20 MHz. IBM's PS/2 models 50, 50Z, and 60 all use the 80286 processor. Its architecture includes 16-bit data paths internally and externally, and a new mode of operation called *protected mode*. Earlier processors operated in *real mode*. Real mode enables the processor to *address* (recognize) a total of 1M of memory. This was an enormous amount of memory considering that early PCs featured only 64K of memory.

The 80286 processor remains compatible with the earlier standard of real mode, but also can switch into protected mode, which enables the chip to address 16M of memory and support memory management and multitasking. In protected mode, applications can run at one of four privilege levels, which keep system functions from interfering with each other. These privilege levels often are compared to a set of four concentric rings. The operating system is generally trusted with running at ring zero, where it is protected from applications that are running at ring three.

The 80286 processor's extra memory and other features gave software developers the opportunity to create more powerful programs and manipulate more data. The 80286's biggest drawback, however, is that it must be reset to switch from real to protected mode. This requirement makes the 80286 impractical for many uses. Further, the processor is unable to take advantage of many of the more powerful applications and operating systems now available. Even so, the 80286 has been commercially successful, and offers adequate performance for many AutoCAD applications.

> **Tip:** For 80286 owners who need more power, the Intel Inboard 386 AT adapter card, or an equivalent card, replaces the 80286 processor with a faster 80386 one. Many AT-type computers also can accept the new 80386-SX replacement modules that plug into the 80286 chip's socket.

The Intel 80386

The Intel 80386 processor has become the standard for high-performance computing. First used in the Compaq Deskpro 386 in 1986, and since used in the IBM PS/2 model 80, the 80386 processor was the first processor to use 32-bit data paths and operate at a clock speed of 16 MHz. Currently topping out at 33 MHz, the 80386 is acceptable for all but the most demanding applications.

By adding *virtual memory* capabilities to the 80386 processor, Intel expanded the 80386's memory-addressing capability to 4 gigabytes (4000 megabytes) directly and to 64 terabytes (64,000,000 megabytes!) using virtual memory. A computer with virtual memory capabilities can put contents of memory aside on a disk or other medium, and load up to 4 gigabytes of new data into memory.

> **Note:** Benchmark programs report the number of millions of instructions per second (MIPS) that a computer is capable of completing. MIPS are a measure of the computer's net throughput—independent of processor type, speed, and other factors—and can be thought of as the computer's "horsepower" rating. While AT-compatible computers can reach a performance level of only 2 to 3 MIPS, 80386-based computers generally perform at a rate of 5 to 6 MIPS.

The 80386 processor can operate in *virtual 86* mode as well as real and protected modes. Virtual 86 mode is similar to virtual memory and virtual disks, and uses software to disguise a hardware device or medium so it appears as another device or medium. This new mode enables the processor to divide its attention into multiple real-mode images of 8086 processors. This means the 80386 can behave as though it were really more than one computer, and can run multiple programs simultaneously.

Unlike the 80286 processor, the 80386 does not require resetting when switching between real and protected modes. Setting a bit through software allows the 80386 to flip back and forth between modes almost effortlessly. Programmers now can write software that takes advantage of the 80386's mode-switching power. These 80386 programs perform functions many times faster than the same program in nonoptimized form. AutoCAD's Extended DOS and Xenix versions are optimized for the 80386 processor. AutoShade 386, AutoSolid, and 3D Studio also are 32-bit software products.

The Intel 80386-SX

The 80386-SX processor basically is a scaled-down 80386, in much the same way as the 8088 is a scaled-down 8086. The 80386-SX processes instructions internally in 32-bit portions, but externally it performs like the 16-bit 80286 processor. In 1988, computer manufacturers began to build systems around the 80386-SX. These new systems offered the economy of the 80286 and the power of the 80386.

The 80386-SX can run 32-bit software, but is not as fast as the full 80386 because of the narrower external data path. The primary purpose of the 80386-SX processor was to ease the user's transition between the 16- and 32-bit worlds, and to compete with other chip manufacturers who had begun to clone the 80286. As a result, however, the SX probably will fade away over time. AutoCAD users should be aware that much of AutoCAD processing is external to the CPU in the form of disk access, video, memory, and input devices. For very little extra money, you can get an 80386 and avoid wasting money on transitional products. The extra performance justifies the extra cost of investing in a full 80386-based computer.

The Intel 80486

The present generation of processors is the 80486, introduced in 1989. The 80486 is the most powerful PC processor currently available, and can operate at speeds of 25 MHz to 33 MHz. Future versions of the 80486 are expected to top out at speeds of 50 MHz. The 80486 is a marvel of modern electronics, packing 1,180,235 transistors into a piece of silicon that takes up less than one square inch of space. The 80486 combines an enhanced 80386 chip with some of its typical support chips, including an 80387 math coprocessor (which is covered later in this chapter), a memory cache controller that enables the fast processor to use slower RAM, and 8K of high-speed cache RAM to act as a buffer between the processor and slower main memory.

Every processor uses a timing clock within itself to synchronize all of its processes. This clock acts as the processor's "heart" and each tick is a heartbeat. Combining all of these support chip functions on one piece of silicon lets the 80486 processor do its job with fewer ticks of its internal clock; the 80486 is not just a compact 80386. Table 14.1 compares the 80386 and 80486 chips' capability to execute typical programming instructions. By performing the same task in less heartbeats, an 80486 can get more work done than an 80386 can in the same amount of time. Computers built around the 80486 handle even the most arduous tasks with ease by placing minicomputer power on the desktop.

Table 14.1
Intel 32-bit Processor Execution: A Comparison

Instruction	80386	80486
Load	4	1
Store	2	1
Reg/Reg	2	2
Jump (taken)	9	3
Jump (not taken)	3	1
Call	9	3

The Motorola Family

Motorola is best known for its contribution to radio and television technology, but the company also has developed a reputation as a manufacturer of fine CPU chips. Motorola's chips never have been used in a DOS machine, but rather have found homes in Macintosh computers and a few UNIX computers, such as the Sun 3 workstations. Motorola, like Intel, has created an entire family of microprocessors that are based on the same basic design. Unlike Intel, which has increased both of the bus widths of its processors incrementally, Motorola's 68000-series processors all have 32-bit internal data buses. Motorola's external data buses began at 16 bits, but have since increased to 32 bits.

The Motorola 68000 processor's personal-computing debut was as the basis for the original Apple Macintosh. The Macintosh II incorporated a 16 MHz 68020 processor that is roughly equivalent in performance to an 8 MHz AT. The Mac IIx, IIcx, IIsi, and IIci computers use 68030 processors that have different speeds, similar to an Intel 80386 processor. Apple's recently announced Macintosh IIfx, equipped with a 40 MHz 68030 processor is reported to be equivalent to Intel's 80486. The Motorola 68040 also includes a floating-point coprocessor and the equivalent of 1.2 million transistors.

Table 14.2 compares the Intel and Motorola processors.

Other than the growth of the data bus, the capability to use virtual memory, and the faster exectution speeds, no significant differences among the early Motorola 68000 chips and the later chips exist. Motorola has no added modes of operation like the Intel family, but has been more *evolutionary* than *revolutionary*. This lets software for the original Macintosh run equally well on the latest Mac II, unlike Intel 80386-specific software that cannot run on an 8088.

Table 14.2
Intel and Motorola Processor Comparison

Model	Introduced	Data Bus	Internal Bus	RAM Capacity	Virtual Memory
Intel 8086	1979	16	16	1M	No
Intel 8088	1981	16	8	1M	No
Intel 80286	1984	16	16	16M	Yes
Intel 80386	1986	32	32	4G	Yes
Intel 80486	1989	32	32	64T	Yes
Motorola 68000	1980	16	32	16M	No
Motorola 68020	1986	32	32	4G	Yes
Motorola 68030	1987	32	32	4G	Yes
Motorola 68040	1990	32	32	4G	Yes

For Macintosh AutoCAD users, the same principle applies to processor selection that PC AutoCAD users abide by: "Buy the most power you can afford." Minimum requirements and recommendations for running AutoCAD on the Macintosh are listed in Chapter 4.

Aside from the architectural differences between the two processor families, there are fundamental differences in the way Motorola and Intel chips are programmed. Programmers generally prefer the Motorola over the Intel, but both chips can accomplish the same tasks.

RISC Processors

A reduced instruction set computer (RISC) processor may be in your future. As microprocessors have evolved and gotten faster, their instruction sets have expanded to include more commands and options. As a result, the time required to execute an instruction (*E-time*) has decreased because of the processors' faster speeds, but the time required to interpret more incoming instructions and their options (*I-time*) hinders processor performance. RISC processors are designed to reduce the number of options for instructions whose E-time is the most critical. Processors, for instance, often perform 20 percent of their total number of instructions 80 percent of the time. This is similar to an AutoCAD user who repeats many commands more often than other commands—a few instructions are used the most. RISC chips are built so that these often-used instructions are interpreted faster and frequently used combinations of instructions are combined into one instruction.

The end result is RISC processors are capable of much higher performance than traditional CISC (complex instruction set computer) designs, such as the Intel family. RISC processors are gaining widespread attention in the CAD and scientific worlds. RISC processors can be manufactured around the same basic system as other processors, but offer lower cost-to-performance ratios.

One example of a RISC-based computer is the DEC 3100, a 14-MIPS UNIX-based workstation built around a MIPS Computer Systems, Inc. R2000 processor. The DEC 3100 delivers roughly 2 1/2 times the power of the best 80386 computer. Another RISC computer is the Sun Microsystems SPARCstation 1, which is less powerful but more economical than the DEC 3100, and which is becoming popular with software developers and AutoCAD users.

Intel Corporation also is capitalizing on RISC technology with its 64-bit, 27-MIPS i860 RISC processor. Capable of operating as a CPU or a graphics coprocessor, the i860 will be valuable to AutoCAD users when graphics cards emerge that can use the i860 to perform complex 3D construction and shading calculations. Computer makers Olivetti and Stratus have announced commitments to use the new i860 chip. The i860 is seeing first duty as a CPU in IBM's new Wizard board that installs in a PS/2 Model 80 computer. The Wizard board is reported to outperform other RISC processors by orders of magnitude that are equal to one-half the power of a Cray 1 mainframe computer. Microsoft also is rumored to be developing the structures to port OS/2 to the i860—a move that is sure to give both the chip and OS/2 more appeal.

If you are shopping for a new AutoCAD workstation, you have more choices now than ever before. Plenty of power is available in each processor type mentioned here. Each has a "best fit" in any particular AutoCAD workgroup. Macintosh fans should consider the hot new Mac IIfx or a IIcx with display-list accelerator. If you are a diehard DOS user, you should consider only 80386- or 80486-based PCs, because they are the only DOS-based machines that have enough muscle to carry you into the future. For the all-out power user not afraid to dig into UNIX, the RISC-based SPARCstation is a sure bet.

Math Coprocessors

In order to operate more efficiently in scientific and technical applications, nearly every IBM-compatible computer supports installation of a *math coprocessor*. These special chips are designed for one purpose; that is, they perform mathematical operations that otherwise would have to be handled by the central processing unit.

Many scientific and graphics applications—including AutoCAD—require that mathematical calculations constantly be made. Math coprocessors perform these calculations with exacting precision, and generally can do the work in as little as one-tenth the amount of time required by the CPU. If the coprocessor is to accomplish these tasks, however, the application must contain instructions for the coprocessor. When the CPU encounters these special instructions, the CPU simply passes them to the math coprocessor. The CPU then skips ahead to the end of the coprocessor instructions, and either waits to receive the answer from the coprocessor or performs other tasks.

Your system must have a math coprocessor if you want to run AutoCAD. Early versions of AutoCAD performed double-floating-point-precision mathematics by extensive instructions written within the program. Once the math coprocessor became standard equipment on AutoCAD workstations, Autodesk replaced the program's built-in math routines with simple coprocessor instructions. This change created more space for new AutoCAD features.

> **Note:** If a math coprocessor is to operate efficiently with a CPU, the two chips must operate at the same speed. If the CPU runs at 33 MHz, for example, then the math coprocessor must also run at that rate. The math chip, however, can be rated higher than the CPU and still work. You can, for example, match a 33 MHz math coprocessor with a 25 MHz CPU, but not the reverse. If you install a faster coprocessor than the CPU, you cannot make any program run any faster than if the two chips had the same speed rating.

Intel

The Intel 80x86 processor family can perform mathematics functions on integers only, and must rely on software to manipulate more complex numbers used by programs such as AutoCAD. To give the central processor more power, Intel designed a *floating-point coprocessor* (FPU) to complement each CPU. A floating-point coprocessor is a processor chip that is capable of working with much greater numbers, both in total numbers of digits and in decimal fraction precision, than a general-purpose processor. The 8086 and 8088 processors use the 8087 math coprocessor; the 80286 uses the 80287; and the 80386 uses the 80387. The 80486, as mentioned before, has an 80387 equivalent built in.

Motorola

Motorola offers math coprocessors for use in Macintosh computers. The 68020 central processing unit, for example, is complemented by the 68881 chip. The Motorola 68030 CPU can operate with the 68882 math coprocessor. The 68040, described earlier, includes its own floating-point arithmetic unit.

Other Math Coprocessors

Intel is not alone in the math coprocessor market. Among other companies, Integrated Information Technologies, Inc. (IIT) and Cyrix Corp. have successfully cloned Intel's math chip designs. Cyrix, in particular, claims that its FasMath chip design is faster than Intel chips.

Two other math coprocessor chips are the Weitek (pronounced *way-tek*) 3167 and 4167 Abacus chips. A Weitek 3167 can be used in an 80386-based computer and a 4167 in an 80486-based computer. Both Weitek chips often are used in RISC-based engineering workstations. Weitek's math chips utilize a different design than Intel's. Unlike the Cyrix and IIT chips, Weitek chips cannot interpret Intel coprocessor instructions. Even though the Weitek chips have proven to perform several times faster than Intel math coprocessors, the Weiteks are incompatible with programs written for an Intel chip. Further, the Weitek chips also are much more expensive than their Intel equivalents.

Because AutoCAD is written to take advantage of Intel math chips, Weitek coprocessors cannot yet be used with AutoCAD. New products from Autodesk, including 3D Studio and Autodesk RenderMan, can recognize and take advantage of an Abacus chip. Because of the enormous amount of math required to perform realistic shaded rendering, 3D Studio and RenderMan run much faster with an Abacus chip installed. If you are going to use either of these products extensively, an Abacus would be a wise investment.

You may run into problems if you need to use both an Intel and a Weitek coprocessor—the former for AutoCAD and the latter for rendering and animation. A few computer manufacturers have anticipated such a dilemma and provide support for both chips in their machines. Either coprocessor is selected as needed depending on the software being run. The majority of PC makers support only one or the other chip. You must decide which program you want the better performance for. Just remember, however, that AutoCAD must have an Intel coprocessor, whereas your other programs may use either chip. If you need all the power an Abacus chip can give you, you will need to find a computer that will accept both chips, or own two computers—one with each chip.

Conclusions

Regardless of its brand, a math coprocessor accounts for only about 15 percent of AutoCAD's performance. The rest of the program's performance is divided between video, disk, and other input/output functions. Even if another math coprocessor chip operated twice as quickly as an Intel chip, AutoCAD's performance enhancement would still be 15 percent at most. These chips often are more expensive than Intel chips and are not authorized by Autodesk, so the CAD manager only should consider purchasing one as a first purchase, and not as a replacement for an existing coprocessor.

Expansion Buses

A computer's *expansion bus* is the path between the CPU and the expansion cards that are installed in the computer to provide additional memory, graphics or network support, disk control, and other services. The expansion bus is an integral part of the computer's main circuit board and is not removable. Many PC manufac-turers are now divided over the type of engineering that goes into this important data path. Only the Macintosh hardware developers seem to be immune to the controversy; all Macintosh II models have the same expansion bus called NuBus. The lack of a unified design standard, such as the standard that once existed for PC- and AT-class computers, may influence your future computer-buying decisions.

IBM published the expansion bus design used in the IBM PC, and forged the stan-dard for other expansion buses. Other manufacturers designed adapters to work with the IBM bus, and ultimately copied it in their own computers to compete with IBM.

The PC expansion bus initially was an eight-bit bus that ran at eight MHz and was adapted to the externally eight-bit 8088 CPU. Later, the AT came with a 16-bit bus that had been physically widened to adapt to the 16-bit 80286. The 16-bit bus remains identical to the eight-bit bus in most other respects, and was later termed the Industry Standard Architecture (ISA) bus when a 32-bit, compatible design was invented (discussed later).

Operating at a data transfer rate of 16M per second, this 16-bit bus is fast enough for the highest-performance peripherals and adapters when used in a single-user computer. Adapter cards designed for the eight-bit PC still work with the 16-bit bus and provide upward compatibility. This bus still is being designed into most 80386- based, 80386-SX, and 80486-based computers being sold today.

The IBM Micro Channel Architecture Bus

IBM once led the world in compatible personal computer design. With its PS/2 family of personal computers, however, IBM introduced a new bus design called Micro Channel Architecture (MCA), which is not compatible with earlier designs. If other PC manufacturers want to duplicate MCA in their new machines, they must license the design from IBM. IBM intentionally set the licensing fees for the new bus so high as to prevent other manufacturers from profitably building competitive computers based on the MCA bus standard. IBM's licensing stance regarding MCA runs counter to the original concept of PC design, which left the door open for other manufacturers to create both complementary and competing hardware.

Still, this new bus design has brought the microcomputer another step closer to minicomputer and mainframe technology. MCA is designed for newer, more power-ful processors and multitasking operating systems that can be accommodated by earlier bus designs. The expansion bus in most MCA computers runs at 10 or 14.3 MHz with a data transfer rate of 20M/sec up to a maximum of 160M/sec. MCA separates the CPU and the expansion bus into two subsystems, enabling the bus to be controlled by *bus masters*. Bus masters are devices such as disk controllers and network interface cards that move data across the bus without the help (and over-head) of the CPU. The MCA bus can support up to 15 bus masters, including the CPU.

All bus masters in an MCA computer are coordinated by *central arbitration point* circuitry. This circuitry resolves any conflicts between bus masters according to a built-in or programmed priority. Bus masters can send data across the bus to any other card (bus master or not) acting as a *bus slave*. A bus slave simply receives data sent to it but cannot initiate a data transfer itself as a bus master can.

The EISA Bus

In response to MCA and IBM's licensing policy, several manufacturers of PC-compatible computers banded together to design their own expansion bus. The resulting bus design is called Extended Industry Standard Architecture (EISA), and is compatible with the earlier ISA bus. The EISA bus follows the evolution from the 8-bit to 16-bit bus by widening it to 32 bits. EISA also adds powerful enhancements that are similar to those used in IBM's new bus design, including direct memory access (DMA), support for multiple processors, and a 33M bit/sec data-transfer rate to keep pace with more powerful processors and bus masters.

Conclusions

Before you buy into any expansion bus standard, you need to be aware of the differences, advantages, and disadvantages of each design. Because costly adapters can be used with only one type of bus or the other, buying both types leads to redundancy and incompatibility. Recent studies have concluded that for typical single-user computers, neither the MCA nor the EISA bus and its expensive adapter cards are much of an advantage over high-performance ISA components. In multiuser and file-server machines, however, the newer buses can accommodate the higher loads that the ISA bus cannot.

Your bus purchasing decision will be guided also by the type of computer you intend to buy. No 80286-based EISA machines are available, while few EISA machines with 80386 CPUs are on the market. The EISA bus is most prevalent among 80486 computers. Yet, all types work equally well together if networked and they rarely have any compatibility issues.

Until one expansion bus design emerges as the new standard, companies with allegiance to IBM probably should buy into IBM's MCA plan to protect their investment and preserve their service contracts. Companies not partial to IBM equipment and those opposed to proprietary designs should support the new EISA standard.

ROM BIOS Features

A computer's *read-only memory* (ROM) works in much the same fashion as a write-protected disk; that is, the computer can read information from ROM but cannot write information into ROM. A computer's *random-access memory* (RAM, discussed later in this chapter), on the other hand, can be read by the operating system and its contents changed by the user or application program. ROM and RAM also differ in that ROM chips are physically larger than equivalent RAM chips, but ROM chips hold less memory and operate at slower speeds.

ROM circuitry is used to contain a computer's *basic input/output system* (BIOS). A computer's ROM BIOS contains instructions that perform the following functions:

- Power-on self testing of circuits and devices
- Bootstrap loaders for the operating system
- Keyboard support
- Display support
- Serial port support
- Parallel port support
- Real-time clock support
- Print screen control
- Hard disk support
- Floppy disk support
- Other support as defined by the manufacturer

The ROM BIOS essentially behaves as the middle-man between the operating system and the computer's hardware.

Most modern ROM BIOSs provide support for the majority of popular devices used in an AutoCAD workstation, such as the following:

- Up to four serial ports for the addition of mice, digitizers, scanners, and plotters.
- Up to three parallel ports for printers and parallel plotters.
- High-density 5 1/4-inch and 3 1/2-inch floppy disk drives.
- A wide range of hard disk drive types.

Note: The ROM BIOS must contain the specifications of any hard disk it is to support in order for the computer to communicate with the drive. This usually includes parameters for the number of recording heads, sectors, tracks, and other information. Newer AT-compatible and 80386-based computers normally have 47 or more drives specified in their ROM BIOS. This feature is especially important to AutoCAD users. Because AutoCAD workstations often have very large hard disks (100M to 300M), a ROM BIOS compatible with your disk size should be installed or you may need a special disk driver. You also should have ROM BIOS support for larger hard disks used in network servers if you plan to relegate the workstation to server duty. Some ROM BIOSs come with empty drive types that allow the owner to customize a drive number to fit any unsupported drive types.

AutoCAD users also can benefit from additional ROM BIOS features, such as ROM shadowing and video BIOS shadowing.

ROM Shadowing and Video BIOS Shadowing

ROM shadowing is a feature that enables the BIOS to load a copy of itself into faster RAM and redirect the operating system to look for BIOS instructions there. ROM chips typically operate at 200 nanoseconds or more, while RAM chips usually run at 80 to 100 nanoseconds.

> **Note:** A nanosecond is a unit of time (one billionth of a second) used to measure the fastest rate at which a memory chip can operate. With ROM chips, a nanosecond is the amount of time the chip takes to read the data held in memory. With RAM chips, a nanosecond is used also to measure the length of time between successive refresh cycles needed by the chip to maintain stored data.

When a program requests access to the display, keyboard, drives, or ports, the request is usually made through the ROM BIOS. If the instructions for these devices are held in the same memory as the program, the program does not have to slow down for those operations as it would if the ROM were not shadowed.

When *video BIOS shadowing* is used, the system takes video BIOS instructions that are held in ROM chips on the graphics adapter itself, and copies those instructions into faster RAM. CGA color and monochrome BIOS instructions are included in the main ROM BIOS. BIOS instructions for EGA, VGA, and other standards, however, are stored in ROM chips built onto graphics adapters. Some video cards include software that will perform the video BIOS shadowing if the system ROM BIOS does not.

The system generally performs shadowing by using a portion of RAM between the 640K available to DOS and the 1M limit of the 80x86 processor. Unfortunately, this is the space also used by the hard disk controller, network adapters, expanded memory page frames, and other adapters, and software utilities, such as Quarterdeck Software's LOADHI.COM and Microsoft Windows' HIMEM.SYS. Your system's configuration determines which types of shadowing you can use. If you choose a system that can utilize ROM BIOS shadowing and video BIOS shadowing, your system's device accesses and video performance will increase considerably.

BIOS and Operating System Compatibility

Because it is the middle man between your hardware and the operating system, the ROM BIOS must be compatible with the operating system. Popular operating systems such as DOS, UNIX, XENIX, and OS/2 are usually supported by the BIOSs of major manufacturers. OS/2, however, requires a much closer tie to hardware than other operating systems, especially when used with network operating systems.

Most of the major vendors of IBM-compatible systems use BIOS chips supplied by a few quality vendors. American Megatrends, Inc. (AMI), Award Software, and Phoenix are all reliable brands. Some features may be found on one computer, yet not on another computer with the same brand of BIOS. Always check for the features you need and get written guarantees of compatibility. You should never *assume* your system has compatibility with any particular operating system.

RAM

Many people say, "You can never be too thin or too rich." Computer users, however, say, "You can never be too thin or too rich, or have too much RAM." Random Access Memory (RAM) determines a computer's capacity to work with programs and data; you generally can put to good use any amount of RAM you may have installed in a personal computer. The memory is termed *random access* because any memory location in a RAM chip may be accessed at random, as opposed to in sequence.

RAM Chip Design

RAM chips come in a variety of sizes, styles, and types. The first PCs used 36 *dual inline package* (DIP) 64K RAM chips arranged in four banks of nine chips for a total installed memory of 256K. Nine individual chips are required for each 64K of contiguous memory: one chip for each bit in a byte, and one chip for a parity bit that ensures data integrity. The DIP design features two rows of eight pins on each side of a chip. A variation of the traditional DIP design places the chip on its edge. Both rows of pins exit the DIP chip from one side rather than two. The result is a chip that takes up less horizontal space than other DIP chips, a constant concern of computer manufacturers. This edge-wise DIP design is most often used in special video RAM chips that usually need to occupy even smaller areas than conventional memory. DIP chips currently come in 64K, 256K, and 1M capacities.

Other chip designs have followed the original DIP, such as SIMM and SIP. After years of arranging nine chips in a row for PCs, manufacturers began producing a small circuit card that contains nine individual chips, hence the name Single Inline Memory Module, or SIMM. Single Inline Package (SIP) is a variation of the SIMM module that uses short pins for each connector contact (see fig. 14.2).

SIMM memory is typically cheaper than equivalent amounts of DIP memory because of the reduction in overall packaging and connector costs. SIP memory is less popular and slightly more expensive than DIP memory. SIMM chips also are easier to install and remove than are either SIP modules or DIP chips. SIMM modules are available in 256K, 1M, 2M, and 4M capacities.

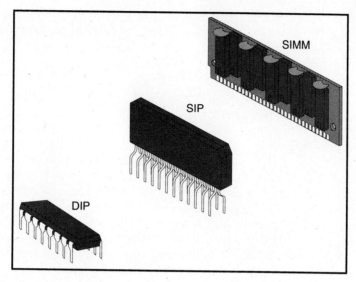

Figure 14.2:
Standard memory chip package designs.

An IBM-compatible computer's main circuit board (often called the *motherboard* or the *planar board*) often is designed to accept only one type of memory package, and usually in only one capacity. Hence, a particular computer only may accept SIMM memory packages in 256K or 1M capacities. If the motherboard has eight connectors for SIMM modules, then the computer probably can hold 1M (4 × 256K), 2M (8 × 256K), 4M (4 × 1M), or 8M (8 × 1M) of memory. If you want to install additional memory in an eight-connector motherboard, you must install a memory expansion card to hold additional modules.

Static RAM versus Dynamic RAM

Memory designs often vary from one manufacturer to another. In current 80386-based computers, some manufacturers install 60- or 80-nanosecond chips that are able to keep pace with the CPU at slower speeds, such as 16MHz. When designing their computers for faster CPU speeds, manufacturers have had to resort to using *static* RAM.

Static RAM is different from the *dynamic* RAM usually used for computer memory. Dynamic RAM chips must be refreshed at frequent intervals (equal to their speed rating) or they lose their data. Most dynamic RAM chips are unable to operate with today's fastest computers without slowing down the processor. Static RAM chips, on the other hand, are designed without the need to be refreshed periodically so they can operate in faster computers. They will, however, still lose their data when power is removed. At first look, you might think that it is more logical to use static RAM rather than dynamic RAM. Static RAM, however, is more expensive than dynamic RAM; computers built entirely with static RAM would be very costly.

Memory Caching

Many computers now are built with small amounts of static RAM (32K to 256K), which acts as a buffer between the CPU and main RAM. This buffer is called a *cache*. By adding a static RAM cache to the computer, the manufacturer can use slower, cheaper 100-nanosecond dynamic RAM chips as the system's main memory. The system passes data in small chunks to the *cache*, using a technique that stores the most recently used data in the cache in case it is needed again. When the CPU finds the needed data in the cache, the successful search is called a *hit*. If the CPU must read information into the cache from slow memory because the information needed was not in the cache, the unsuccessful search is called a *miss*. Some cache schemes load additional information ahead of the request, trying to anticipate what the computer will need next. A caching scheme can help the manufacturer match slow RAM to a fast processor; most designs yield hit rates of 90 percent or more.

If a system has a fast CPU and slow RAM, but does not implement a caching scheme, then the CPU must pause while RAM responds to data requests. These pauses are called *wait states*. During a wait state, the CPU pauses for one or two ticks of its internal timer, enabling the slower system RAM to catch up with the CPU and fill requests for data. Wait states result in modest performance penalties.

Conclusions

When you first purchase a computer for AutoCAD use, you should check the RAM requirements and recommendations for the version of AutoCAD you will be using. Chapter 4 lists RAM amounts for most platforms. Then you should get as much RAM as you can afford in the largest-capacity modules or chips possible. The types of drawings you work with also will determine the optimum RAM configuration for your needs. A network will have a negligible effect on your total RAM needs, but will be a factor on DOS machines, as is described in Chapter 5.

If, for example, you can afford 4M of memory and you have connectors for eight modules, the computer's motherboard should have four 1M RAM modules. You later can add four more modules to boost your RAM capacity to 8M.

Suppose, however, that you decide to purchase the same system with only 2M of RAM, which is installed in 256K modules. If you later discover that you need more memory, you must either purchase a memory expansion card and additional chips, or replace the original 256K modules with 1M modules. (Most motherboards cannot accept both 256K and 1M modules.) If you add the expansion card, you pay not only for the card itself, but you may sacrifice performance because the CPU will be forced to communicate with RAM through the expansion bus at a slower speed and possibly via a narrower data path. If you swap the smaller modules for larger ones, you end up with four 256K modules that you can no longer use in your machine. You would pay for the first 2M twice: once for the original modules and again for the replacement 1M modules.

When shopping for an IBM-compatible computer, look for a system that utilizes a RAM cache. The larger the cache, the better the performance. A large cache is more likely to contain the data your program needs and will run a little faster than an equivalent computer with a smaller cache and much faster than one with no cache at all.

Quality Details

The CPU, math coprocessor, expansion bus, BIOS, and RAM components are basic parts of a computer. The basic computer generally comes as a single package in a single cabinet from one manufacturer. Before you go on to examine some of the expansion cards that also may occupy the cabinet (but which may be made by other manufacturers), you need to understand a few other details that determine the basic unit's overall quality.

FCC Certification

The first quality indicator to look for in a computer is on the outside of the computer case. Look on the back of the computer for its Federal Communications Commission (FCC) rating. Every computer sold in the United States must bear an FCC sticker with an ID number and rating. The ID number identifies the manufacturer who applied for the rating, and the rating is a measure of the amount of EMI (electromagnetic interference) and RFI (radio frequency interference) the device emits.

EMI is interference generated by motors and other devices that produce magnetic fields. This type of interference can cause problems for appliances that rely on magnetic waves, such as television picture tubes. The disk drives and fan are the only parts of a personal computer that produce EMI, and then in only small amounts.

RFI is another story. RFI is caused by electronic circuits and devices that produce radio waves at frequencies high enough to interfere with radio, television, and other equipment that send or receive radio waves. High-resolution graphics adapters in particular, and high-speed computers in general, produce significant amounts of RFI.

You can "hear" RFI if you have a portable radio. Tune the radio to a static-free station and adjust the volume to a comfortable level as though you were going to listen to it. Starting several feet away from a running computer, slowly move the radio toward the computer and listen for the telltale sounds of RFI; it sounds like very fast Morse code. Listen to the radio when your computer performs different operations, and see if you can distinguish between video output, disk input or output, and CPU number crunching. RFI also can be seen on the screen of a television that is near a running computer.

An FCC rating of *A* generally means that the equipment is designed to provide enough protection for an industrial-type environment, in which sensitive television and radio equipment generally is not used. A Class A rating is the lowest acceptable rating a computer can receive, and it does not flatter the manufacturer. An FCC rating of *B* requires that the computer be sufficiently protected against emissions for installation in a home environment, and means that the manufacturer did his homework right. Only a Class B computer can be advertised, sold, or leased for use in a home. This is the class to look for when shopping for a computer for your office. Avoid Class A computers that can be sold only into commercial or industrial locations.

Most computer manufacturers design *shielding* into a computer chassis to help contain EMI and RFI inside the computer. Shielding includes metal panels behind the sculpted plastic panels common with many computers. Manufacturers also can reduce RFI through costly engineering of electronic circuits. Some choose to save the money on this type of engineering so they can deliver their computers at a lower price than their competitors, and many receive a lower FCC rating as a result.

Still, some computers are sold every day that have earned an FCC class B rating, but which are junk in other respects. So do not rely strictly on FCC ratings when making your purchasing decisions.

Motherboard Construction

Look for quality construction in the motherboard. You do not have to be an electrical engineer to recognize a few characteristics of quality. A keen eye and a little common sense will suffice.

The first criteria is the number of layers that make up the motherboard. Modern printed circuits usually are made of multiple layers of etched circuits, sandwiched together to form one thick board. Most of today's computers use four- or six-layer motherboards, but some still try to get away with only two layers. This type of motherboard is much cheaper to build and sell, but can cause reliability problems, especially if combined with shoddy circuit design. Problems may not surface until months later or when you start installing expansion cards in certain slots of the computer.

Simply by looking with the naked eye, you may not be able to tell how many layers a motherboard has. If you are looking at a non-mainstream PC, you should ask the vendor how many layers are on the motherboard. Four-layer boards are common. If the computer has a six-layer board, the manufacturer probably went to great lengths to create a high-quality board in a small amount of desk space, or attempted to minimize RFI and other undesirable side effects of high-performance design.

Another tip-off to quality motherboard construction is the presence of hand-wired jumpers or components on the top or bottom side of the board. Sometimes last-minute design changes must be made or errors are found that require wires or electronic components to be fastened by hand. If you spot even one or two wires, or more than one resistor clinging to a board, you should start asking questions.

Other Details

Look for plenty of steel in a computer chassis, not only for shielding, but for strength. If a computer chassis is made of thin, flexible steel, the motherboard and expansion cards can become loose, twisted, or warped when the computer is moved. This may cause component connections to strain or chips to loosen, resulting in sporadic failures. At the very least, a strong chassis provides a consistently tight-fitting case.

When looking at the case, notice how many options it allows you for installing disk drives. Some cases provide only two half-height drive openings in the front of the case, while others have as many as five or more. Installation options allow you to install additional diskette drives, removable hard disks, tape drives, and optical disk drives. If you even need to load the machine fully, drive access will be important.

Find out if the drive bays can accept half-height drives, full height, or 3 1/2-inch form factor, and in what combinations. Almost all drives, except for extra-high-capacity hard disks, are now half-height units, and 3 1/2-inch drives are becoming popular. Look for flexibility in options, as well as additional 3 1/2-inch bays.

Full-size desktop and tower-style computer cases provide the most options, while small-footprint and mini-tower cases conserve desk space at the price of expansion slots and drive bays. Know whether you can afford to give up options in the future before you buy back some of your desktop today.

Hard Disks

A good hard disk is a necessity for best AutoCAD performance. Hard disks were invented in the early 1970s by IBM for their larger systems and were first called Winchester disks. Each hard disk drive contains many magnetic disks called *platters*. Each platter is a precisely machined metal disk coated with an ultra-thin magnetic film. Small read/write heads float over each disk surface on a microscopically thin cushion of air as the disks spin at a high speed (3600 RPM). The heads are positioned over magnetic rings on the disks, called *cylinders*, by arms that connect the heads to a small motor for moving the heads back and forth to different cylinders. All these mechanical parts are housed in a hermetically sealed container to keep out dust and debris that could damage the drive. Sophisticated electronics decode the magnetic patterns on the disks into streams of data that are transmitted to a controller board for translation into information the computer can use.

The hard disk options available today incorporate various capacities, speeds, interfaces, and other factors.

Disk Size

Size is probably the most frustrating limitation of a hard disk. In the best of all worlds, your computer's hard disk always would be large enough to hold all your programs and data. In the real world of computing, however, a new saying has gained popularity: "The number of files on a hard disk will expand to fill the available space." In practice, you may find it difficult to keep noncritical programs and old data from filling up expensive hard disk space.

The capacity of a hard disk is measured in megabytes. The number of megabytes a drive can hold depends on the number of platters it contains, the number of platter surfaces used for data (up to two per platter, one on each side), the number of cylinders it is able to divide each platter into, and the number of sectors it divides each cylinder into. In addition, some hard disks use varying schemes for recording data onto each cylinder that can affect drive capacity. Hard disk drives have been manufactured with storage capacity ranging from 5 and 10 megabytes in the first PCs to new drives for file servers that have 1.2 gigabytes of space.

Ideally, an AutoCAD workstation's hard disk should be big enough to hold all the programs that the user needs, including AutoCAD and other necessary AutoCAD programs, third-party enhancement packages, word processors and text editors, spreadsheet and database programs, and utilities. The hard drive also must accommodate the maximum amount of data that must remain on-line at any one time, including all current drawing files, block libraries, and drawing-exchange files (such as DXF or IGES files).

If you add in working space for backup and temporary files created by programs, printer and plotter spooling files, operating systems, and a margin for error and growth, you probably should get at least a 40M disk for each machine. Count on buying at least a 60M to 80M disk for machines that utilize larger operating systems, such as OS/2, UNIX, and XENIX, or more heavy-duty programs, such as desktop publishing, finite-element analysis, or graphics programs. Just remember, no matter how much you buy, someday it will not be enough.

Disk Speed

You cannot buy too much disk speed either. An 80386 PC can accept data from the disk just as rapidly as the disk can dish it out. When you work with very large (1M or more) drawing files, a fast hard disk will pay for itself in increased productivity.

Hard disk drives are rated according to the speed with which they can access data recorded on the disk. This access speed is measured in milliseconds (1/1000ths of a second), and normally represents the average time required for the drive to reposition its read/write heads over random data locations on the hard disk's platters. The first PC hard disks had access speeds of 80 ms to 100 ms, which is very slow by today's standards. Most XT-type drives now are rated at around 65 ms. Early ATs featured hard drives that operated at about 40 ms, and later models had drives with speeds of 25 ms to 30 ms. Today, a fast drive operates at about 15 ms to 18 ms, but tomorrow's drives undoubtedly will be faster.

Drive Interface Standards

Drives that operate at speeds faster than 25 ms typically require an improved interface (that is, the method by which data is transferred from the drive to the expansion bus) to take advantage of those speeds. The original ST506/412 interface was used in the IBM PC, XT, and AT computers. The XT could not accept data as quickly as the interface could transfer, but the AT handled the ST506/412 interface well. For today's drives, however, the ST506/412's maximum throughput rate of 5 million bits per second is too slow.

The SCSI Interface

With the advent of computers that were faster than the AT, manufacturers had to develop new interfaces that matched the disk to the potential of the processor. The Small Computer System Interface (SCSI, pronounced "scuzzy") is a method that creates an expansion bus of its own that allows up to eight SCSI devices of any type to be attached. SCSI was adopted by Apple for the Macintosh family of computers and only recently has received support from IBM. SCSI controllers and drives are often used in network file servers and high-powered workstations. SCSI enables hard disks, tape drives, optical disks, and other devices to share one controller with higher data transfer rates than the ST506/412 interface.

Theoretically, several different SCSI devices (such as hard disk drives, optical disk drives, and tape drives) can be added to a single SCSI controller. They are connected in a daisy chain with a single cable leading to and from each drive and terminated on one end at the controller. This sharing of a single controller makes expansion cheaper than using other equivalent options. Some SCSI devices and controllers, however, are not compatible with each other, and timing problems can arise when using drives that are slow to power up with faster starting drives.

The ESDI Interface

Another high-performance hard disk interface is the Enhanced Small Device Interface (ESDI). This interface specifies a data transfer rate of 10 million to 20 million bits per second, more than double the ST506/412 rate. An ESDI controller and drive install and connect in much the same fashion as a ST506/412, yet cost a little more. Aside from its improved performance, the ESDI is hard to tell apart from a ST506/412 by sight.

The IDE Interface

A popular new drive interface pioneered by Compaq Computer Corp is the Integrated Drive Electronics (IDE) interface. Rather than mounting control circuitry on a card installed in the expansion bus, IDE drives carry their controllers on the drive. A simple electronic connection card in an expansion slot or dedicated drive interface plug on the motherboard is used to connect the drive to the computer. IDE drives are attractive to small footprint computer manufacturers because an expansion slot can be pared (in addition to slots saved by other integration methods) without sacrificing expandability.

Recording Methods

You also can improve hard disk performance by altering the pattern that is used to record data onto the magnetic media. One such method is Run Length Limited (RLL). The standard encoding scheme is called MFM (Modified Frequency Modulation). MFM is the most common format for personal computer hard disks. RLL is a convention that records data into a more compressed format on the disk, transferring about 50 percent more data per disk. By placing more data into the same amount of space, an RLL drive can output more data per revolution than a ST506/412, MFM drive. RLL technology, however, is not compatible with ESDI or SCSI interfaces. RLL is not as fast as either of those newer methods, and is only found on smaller capacity (30-80M) drives. RLL controllers must be matched to RLL-certified drives in order to work reliably.

Disk Caching

For several years, computer users have relied on software that improves hard disk performance through a technique called *disk caching*. Now users can purchase hardware products that perform disk caching. A disk cache works in much the same manner as a memory cache, which was described earlier. While a memory cache buffers information between the CPU and RAM, a disk cache buffers data between the CPU and the hard disk.

When a software disk cache loads, it sets aside a small amount of RAM to intercept data that is being transferred between the hard disk and the CPU (see fig. 14.3). When the CPU requests information from the hard disk, the disk controller writes into RAM not only the requested information, but additional data from nearby sectors. The additional information is read into RAM under the assumption that the CPU may need the additional data soon. If the CPU requests the anticipated data, the data is already in RAM and ready for use. The CPU can read data from RAM much more rapidly (.3 ms to .5 ms) than from the drive (15 ms or longer). Software disk caches, however, consume precious system RAM, and may interfere with other programs. AutoCAD, for example, has problems with many software disk caches.

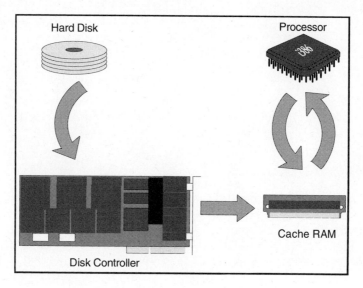

Figure 14.3:
Caching hard disk controller.

Disk caching is now possible in hardware. The RAM for the cache and the software instructions is all contained on the disk controller. If the disk controller contains all the required cache RAM, the cache does not require any system RAM. Further, because hardware circuits and microcoded instructions affect only the controller itself, compatibility with programs is increased. Many of these new caching controllers enable the user to expand the cache RAM, and accept different interface modules to accommodate different drive types and requirements. Caching disk controllers, however, cost considerably more than noncaching controllers.

Conclusions

If you are serious about AutoCAD productivity, or will be working on very large drawings, you probably should not blindly accept the first disk drive a computer dealer recommends. Take a good look at your short-term and long-term needs, and consider which drive size and interface (such as ESDI or SCSI) will best meet those needs. Buy the fastest drive you can afford for any size and interface.

If you do not foresee networking the computer, you should buy a fairly large and fast drive according to the preceding recommendations. ESDI and SCSI interfaces are standard with large (100M or larger) drives, as are access times in the 15 ms to 20 ms range. For a file server drive, follow the guidelines in Chapter 5. If the drive will be part of a computer that is networked to a central file server, you can economize by selecting a smaller drive. See Chapter 5 also for network node considerations. Remember, each type of interface must be matched with a specific type of drive. For the ultimate in disk performance, you should consider hardware caching.

Auxiliary Storage

You probably do not need to keep all your programs and data on a hard disk within a 15 ms reach. Other types of storage devices work well for seldom-used programs, backups, archives, and reference data.

Removable Hard Disks

Hard disks usually are permanently installed in a computer, but not always. A *removable hard disk* works like a permanently installed disk drive, but is portable. You can easily remove the mechanical portion of the drive from the computer chassis, leaving the electronic interface behind. The drive then can be taken to another location, slid into another computer chassis that has an identical interface, and used on that computer.

Removable hard drives are handy for securing highly sensitive data, sharing data, and for persons who want to take their work home without transferring files to floppy disks.

Removable hard disks, however, usually are much more expensive than their permanent counterparts, and are not interchangeable among manufacturers.

Bernoulli Drives

A close cousin to the removable hard disk is the *Bernoulli drive*. A Bernoulli drive is permanently installed, but uses removable media. Bernoulli cartridges look like 3 1/2-inch floppy disks with metal shutters and rigid plastic cases, but are 5 1/2 inches square. This type of drive boasts access speeds comparableo AT hard disks (22 ms to 40 ms) and comes in 10M, 20M, and 44M capacities. Bernoulli drives require their own controller and are twice as expensive as the same size hard disk, but they are convenient for maintaining backups, keeping large programs and libraries off-line yet easily accessible, sharing data, and keeping large archives.

Tape Drives

The *tape drive* is still the most popular backup device. Tape drives provide high data transfer rates, enormous capacity, and economical media. If you use a tape drive, you can back up hundreds of megabytes of data without changing tape cartridges.

Cartridges are available in capacities ranging from 40M to 2.8G. You also can program the drive to execute a backup in the middle of the night while nobody is working. Large tape cartridges make random file access impractical, however, so tape drives generally are reserved for use in backing up and restoring data.

A tape backup unit usually is standard equipment for a network, whether installed in a file server or a workstation. Tape drives for network backup are covered later in this chapter.

CD-ROM Drives

Shortly after the introduction of digital audio compact disks, computer hardware manufacturers began working on ways to adapt the basic technology to the storage of computer data. A *compact disk* (popularly known as a CD) is an aluminum alloy disc encased in clear plastic. The disk's surface is covered with millions of microscopic pits, which are burned into tightly packed tracks. As the disk is spun, a laser beam is focused on a track. When the beam strikes an area between two pits, the beam reflects back to a receiver; when the beam encounters a pit, the light is deflected. The receiver circuitry interprets these laser beam pulses as digital information. Audio CDs store the digital translation of musical sound.

A *CD-ROM* (which stands for Compact Disk—Read-Only Memory) is a compact disk that can be read but not written to. A computer CD-ROM drive features the same basic mechanism that is used in audio CD playback equipment. Rather than using converters that translate the digital information into analog sound signals, a CD-ROM drive uses a digital computer interface, which enables the computer to accept the CD's signals as data. Some new CD-ROM drives also include digital-to-analog circuitry, which enables them to play audio CDs as well as computer disks. You should never attempt to play a computer CD on an audio CD unit; you probably would not hear anything worth listening to, and you might even damage your amplifier or speakers.

CD-ROM's best application is the publication of very large (550M or larger) information databases, programmer's libraries, statistics, dictionaries, thesauruses, encyclopedias, and other reference works. Of interest to AutoCAD users, building materials manufacturers and suppliers are now beginning to put their products' specifications, details, and catalog data on CD-ROMs. The most notable of these is the popular Sweet's catalog. Autodesk has begun to use CD-ROM as a medium to distribute drawing archives to dealers for product demonstrations.

In the years since its inception, CD-ROM has not become as popular as experts predicted. This is due to several factors, including the following:

- CD-ROM drives for computers are expensive, costing more than $500, compared to less than $200 for audio units.
- CD-ROM titles are expensive, typically costing more than $100 each.

- Data-retrieval software is slow.
- Access times for CD-ROM drives are slower than other media.

WORM Drives

Take basic CD-ROM technology, add the ability to write to the disk in the drive, and you get a *WORM* (Write Once Read Many) drive. This type of drive enables you to create computer CDs that contain *your* data, rather than someone else's data. WORM drives work by using a special disk material that allows the drive's laser to burn pits into the disk, creating a finished disk in the same manner a compact disk factory does. Once written, however, the data cannot be erased. But with a capacity of 200M to 1000M (depending on the manufacturer) and costing less than $100, a WORM disk is an affordable way to save large amounts of data. Be prepared, however, to spend some money on the initial cost of the WORM drive. Drives start at around $2500.

WORM drives work well for archival storage of large amounts of data. The drive also gives you fairly quick access to large numbers of archived files. But WORM drives quickly are losing their appeal to the rewritable optical drive.

Rewritable Optical Drives

Erasable optical drives take laser disk technology one step further. Unlike compact disk drives, which use laser optics to burn pits into the disk, rewritable optical drives use laser optics to heat the surface of a special optical disk. Once the disk is heated, a magnetic read/write head reverses the magnetic polarity of particles in the medium, creating digital information. Rewritable optical drives read, write, and erase data just like conventional magnetic recording devices can, but the optical devices offer the storage capacity of CDs.

Rewritable optical drives seem to be catching on, as witnessed by the NeXT, DEC, and HP computers, which feature rewritable optical drives as standard equipment. The drives are expensive ($4000), as are WORM drives, and cartridges cost around $250 each, but if you want the ultimate in mass storage capability and speedy retrieval, you will find no better solution.

Conclusions

Most auxiliary storage devices are a luxury. You often can get by without them unless you have a particular need for one, such as a CD-ROM for databases or a rewritable optical drive for very long-term and mass archival. Without a tape drive, however, backing up a large hard disk is time consuming, monotonous, and tedious. You should expect to buy a tape drive, either one for each computer, or a portable one that can be shared by several workstations. You also should invest in a large-capacity tape drive for your network. See Chapter 5 for information on network backup devices.

Video Graphics

Color graphics cards and monitors come in a variety of standards and capabilities, and are one of the most rapidly changing areas of personal computer technology. Fortunately, all that change is to the benefit of AutoCAD users. Few other components can make the AutoCAD workstation more comfortable and interesting to use than a high-resolution color graphics adapter.

Graphics adapters once were categorized in terms of the number of colors they could display, and the resolution (fineness) of their image. Now, you can categorize a graphics adapter by several additional criteria:

- Graphics coprocessor or frame buffer
- Type of RAM used
- Bus width
- For AutoCAD graphics, display list processing support

Video Resolution Standards

The resolution of a graphics display is determined by the number of individual picture elements (*pixels*) that the graphics card can display on the monitor. Generally, the more pixels, the better the resolution. The more pixels the system supports, however, the more image data the system must manipulate, slowing down the display process.

MDA and CGA

In the beginning, the IBM Monochrome Display Adapter (MDA) and the Color Graphics Adapter (CGA) were the only adapters on the market. The choice was simple: if you wanted to work with graphics programs, you got the CGA; if you worked only with text, then the MDA was better.

An MDA card is limited in that it only can display text on a monochrome (single-color) monitor, but its resolution is not bad at 720×348 pixels. The famous Hercules graphics card enables a monochrome monitor to display graphics. Monochrome monitors, however, are not well-suited to AutoCAD graphics, because these monitors cannot display colors that help the user discern layers and segregate information.

The CGA standard supports a maximum resolution of 640 pixels in the horizontal axis, and 200 pixels in the vertical axis. The resolution can be displayed in two unexciting colors: black and white. The CGA can display four colors at 320×200 pixels, but the resolution is so low that the image appears jagged.

EGA

The Enhanced Graphics Adapter (EGA) is the most popular display standard to date. With a resolution of 640×350 pixels in 16 colors (which can be selected from a 64-color palette), EGA gives applications a sharper, more colorful appearance. The additional colors made available by EGA sparked a revolution in the mid-1980s as computer owners flocked to buy the new adapter.

The forgotten standard was the Professional Graphics Controller (PGC) that was introduced at the same time as the EGA. With a resolution of 640×480 and 256 colors (from a palette of 4,096 colors), PGC was meant for serious graphics users. But when the EGA increased in popularity and buyers saw IBM's $4300 price for the PGC adapter and monitor, PGC slowly faded away. The EGA standard became so popular that vendors started building boards that pushed the resolution of the EGA beyond 640×350. EGA then could take advantage of the capabilities of an exciting new product: the NEC Multisync monitor.

The Multisync monitor was the first monitor capable of displaying multiple video standards. The board makers initially inched up to 640×480 resolution, equaling that of the PGC. They next ventured to 752×510, and finally all the way to the Multisync's maximum of 800×600 pixels, or *SuperEGA*. With the proper software driver and a Multisync monitor, SuperEGA owners can have high resolution graphics for AutoCAD at a reasonable cost. The explosion of graphics card vendors developing high-resolution EGA cards was responsible, in part, for the advent of the Autodesk Device Interface (ADI). ADI allows vendors to be independent of strict display specifications.

VGA

The current display standard is the Video Graphics Array (VGA). This new plateau was introduced by IBM with its PS/2 family of microcomputers. Its models 50, 60, 70, and 80 all come with VGA integrated into the system board. The VGA standard displays at 640×480 resolution, but with 16 colors out of a possible 256. The VGA also can display the Multi Color Graphics Array (MCGA) standard of 320×200 pixels in 256 colors out of a possible 262,144. MCGA video is standard on IBM models 25 and 30. Autodesk Animator uses MCGA mode to create fascinating animated presentations.

IBM designed the VGA display system to implement *analog* output. Earlier display systems used only TTL (digital) output. In a digital video system, each of the three signals—red, green, and blue (the three primary colors that combine to make every other color)—from the display board are on in one of two intensities or off. In an analog system, the three color signals are on in 64 different levels of intensity, or off, creating 262,144 possible colors. Whether a display board can produce all possible colors simultaneously at a given resolution depends on the amount of video memory installed on the board and the software's capability to use them.

As with the EGA card, third-party video card makers grabbed the VGA standard and ran with it to distinguish their products from the original. As a result, SuperVGA adapters are now available that display the 320×200 and 640×480 modes of plain VGA, as well as the 800×600 mode made popular by SuperEGA cards. The 1024×768 16 color mode, once dominated by very expensive, high-end display boards, also became a choice for the PC user. This mode is included in several cards, called Extended VGA, which can display 256 colors at each mode up to 800×600. These cards are economical choices for users who need to create an occasional shaded rendering or digitized broadcast-type video.

At the announcement of their VGA display standard, IBM also announced a high-resolution *8514/A* standard. 8514/A stands for IBM's 8514 Color Display monitor that is required for 1024×768 resolution, and analog signals (/A).

Designed for more demanding applications than VGA, the 8514/A adapter produces 256 simultaneous colors when IBM's Memory Expansion Kit is installed; the adaptor displays 16 colors without the kit. The 8514/A is the second of IBM's display adapters to use a graphics coprocessor. The other adapter was the PGC, discussed earlier. While the PGC was built around improved 3D vector drawing, the 8514/A's processor is intended to improve 2D graphics performance required by Windows and OS/2 Presentation Manager environments. The 8514/A is having moderate success as a standard because of IBM's many loyal customers.

The 8514/A has been widely criticized, however, for its *interlaced* display format. In normal operation, an image is drawn on the monitor in one pass (*noninterlaced*). Interlacing, on the other hand, is a process whereby the display adapter creates an image by drawing every other scan line on the monitor, and then beginning over and drawing in the skipped scan lines. If a monitor with *long persistence* phosphors is connected, or if the graphics adapter operates at a high enough refresh rate, then interlacing appears identical to noninterlaced displays at the same resolution.

Phosphorus dots (*phosphors*) on the inside of a monitor screen glow when struck by electrons controlled by the graphics card. The term "long-persistence" means that the chemical particles continue to glow for a short period after the electrons have stopped striking them. In a long-persistence monitor, therefore, the phosphors do not fade out as quickly as in shorter-persistence monitors. If a short- or medium-persistence phosphor monitor (as most are) is attached, or if the adapter's refresh rate is slow enough, then interlacing will produce an annoying flicker of the image. The drawback to long persistence is that if the image is moved on-screen, the phosphors fade slowly and cause *ghosting* or streaking. In an interlaced display system, the adapter and monitor must be correctly matched to minimize ghosting and flicker.

XGA

IBM recently announced another video standard, the Extended Graphics Adapter (XGA). IBM designed this standard to accommodate the high number of colors needed for the multimedia applications yet to come. Multimedia applications will likely incorporate digitized images from broadcast-type video sources. The XGA standard specifies a noninterlaced display with at least 1024×768 resolution and a 70 Hz refresh (vertical sync) rate. The XGA is designed to accept additional memory, which can increase the available resolution to 1280×1024. The number of colors also is adjustable from 4 bits per pixel (16 colors) up to 24 bits per pixel (16.7 million colors).

VESA

In the rush to take advantage of the 800×600 resolution capabilities of the NEC Multisync monitor, graphics board makers designed their own specifications for producing an 800×600-pixel image. For the end user, this meant that many products were incompatible in the 800×600 mode. Each of the other video standards—CGA, EGA, VGA, and 8514/A—were established by industry-leading IBM.

By implementing differing scan frequencies, video mode numbers, and programming methods, each vendor was, in effect, redesigning the wheel. In an effort to encourage a standard set of specifications for the SuperEGA and SuperVGA display (many VGA cards can display 800×600), NEC founded the Video Electronics Standards Association (VESA). NEC has been joined by most of the leading computer graphics products manufacturers, including the following:

ATI Technologies, Inc.	Maxon Systems, Inc.
Autodesk, Inc.	Metheus Corp.
Binar Graphics	Mitsubishi Electronics America
Capetronics USA (HK), Inc.	Nanao USA Corp.
Chips and Technologies, Inc.	Nokia Data
Cirrus Logic, Inc.	Oak Technology
Compaq Computer Corp.	Orchid Technology
Datamedia Corp.	Panacea, Inc.
Edsun Laboratories, Inc.	Philips Consumer Electronics
Eizo Corp.	RasterOps
Everex Systems, Inc.	Relisys
Genoa Systems Corp.	S3, Inc.
Goldstar Technology, Inc.	Seiko Instruments USA
Headland Technology, Inc.	SGS Thomson, INMOS Division
Hewlett-Packard Co.	Sigma Designs
Hitachi, Ltd.	S-MOS Systems
Intel Corp.	Sota Technologies
Integrated Information Technology	STB Systems, Inc.
JVC Information Products of America	Tandy Electronics, R&D

Tatung Company of America, Inc.	Tseng Laboratories, Inc.
Taxan Corp.	Western Digital Imaging
Tecmar, Inc.	Willow Peripherals
Texas Instruments	Yamaha Systems Technology
Trident Microsystems, Inc.	ZyMOS Corp.

By the fall of 1989, VESA had accomplished its goal of producing a specification for the electrical circuitry, timing, and programming of 800×600 displays. This standard is now supported by nearly every VGA and monitor manufacturer. VESA's recent efforts have been in the Super VGA, 8514/A clone, monitor-timing, and multimedia arenas. VESA's Super VGA committee has proposed BIOS extension standards for accessing the Extended VGA modes for 1024×768-resolution, 256-color, and 132-column displays.

VESA also has focused efforts on the 8514/A video standard, to persuade IBM to distribute unpublished information on the programming details of the 8514/A adapter. Without specifications and guidelines from IBM, which considers the specifications proprietary, support for the 8514/A has been slow in coming. VESA's monitor-timing committee passed a monitor refresh rate specification of 72 Hz, which enables a monitor to support both 800×600 and 1024×768 noninterlaced resolution. The new specification also conforms to European standards, in preparation of new marketing opportunities for manufacturers when the European Economic Community opens its doors to foreign commerce in 1992. Altogether, VESA's efforts should result in more compatible and less expensive products.

When evaluating VGA boards and graphics software, look for compliance with the VESA standard, to ensure compatibility with other VESA products.

Graphics Coprocessors

As display resolutions have improved and color palettes broadened, graphics card manufacturers have recognized the need to improve graphics performance through the use of *graphics coprocessors*. Graphics programs take as much time to address one pixel at 320×200 as they do at 1024×768. All things being equal, it takes several times longer to create a high-resolution screen than it does a lower-resolution screen. Additional colors require even more processing overhead and increased memory.

Additional processors located on the graphics card increase graphics drawing functions speed, in much the same way that math coprocessors accelerate arithmetic functions. That is, the program sends graphics operations to the graphics coprocessor, freeing the CPU to perform other tasks. Popular graphics cards with coprocessors include products from Matrox, Control Systems, Nth Engine, and Renaissance GRX. Coprocessor-laden boards cost more than processor-less boards, and often display only at one resolution, making them either useless or overkill for common business programs. But for dedicated AutoCAD and engineering workstations, graphics coprocessors provide the best graphics performance.

The rise in popularity of graphics coprocessor boards increases the necessity for graphics interface standards. Presently, a few standards exist that the AutoCAD shopper should watch.

Graphics Interface Standards

Each of the following graphics interface standards represents a solution to interfacing applications programs to a graphics coprocessor chip. Graphics functions for boards without coprocessors are handled by the computer's CPU. With a graphics coprocessor board, however, the board uses a driver program to intercept the graphics instructions, translate them into commands that the coprocessor can understand, and transmit them to the graphics board, bypassing the CPU.

The 8514/A Interface

The 8514/A Adapter Interface specification provides a common way for applications to use the 8514/A. Programmers can take advantage of the coprocessor's power without knowing the graphics-board intimately. Further, IBM can modify the board to add enhancements, and as long as the board stays compatible with the Adapter Interface, existing applications will remain compatible.

The DGIS Interface

The Direct Graphics Interface Standard (DGIS) is a wide-reaching specification for graphics coprocessor chips, including Intel's 82786, Texas Instruments' 34010, and Hitachi's ACRTC. DGIS provides a common interface to all three chips for applications programmers, as well as easy access to many applications for adapter manufacturers. In theory, everyone wins with DGIS, including the software vendor, the graphics card makers, and the user. In practice, however, few boards have begun to support DGIS, partly because of the popularity of Texas Instruments' graphics chips and interface standard.

The TIGA Interface

The programming standard for TI's 34010 and 34020 graphics chips is the Texas Instruments Graphics Architecture (TIGA) specification. These chips are being used by more and more graphics card manufacturers every year, and many graphics programs are beginning to provide configuration for this interface.

If you are looking for a high-performance graphics accelerator, look for compatibility in your graphics programs with one of these graphics interface standards to protect your investment in these exotic products.

Display List Processing

Another way graphics performance can be improved is through a technique known as *display list processing*. Display list processing maintains a list of the individual display components (vectors) of a graphics image in a separate memory area. By manipulating this list while edits are being performed (instead of regenerating the display after the edits are done), the graphics adaptor avoids a lot of processing overhead and disk activity. This technology was first pioneered by the high-end graphics card vendors, but recently was brought to Super and Extended VGA cards by driver software specialists (see fig. 14.4).

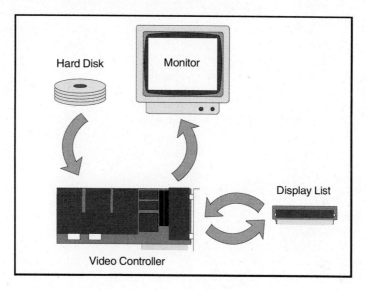

Figure 14.4:
Display list processing technology.

Conclusions

Today's low-priced, high-performance 16-bit Extended VGA cards with display list processing drivers are too good to pass up. High-end, expensive dedicated display cards often are no faster than Extended VGA cards. Look for proven designs from a reliable manufacturer with demonstrated support for AutoCAD driver upgrades.

Monitors

Monitors come in many sizes and resolutions. To work properly with any given display adapter, a monitor must be able to synchronize itself to two different frequency signals produced by the graphics card. The first, the horizontal sync signal, controls the rate at which one full line is drawn across the width of a screen. The other, the vertical sync signal, controls the rate at which one full screen is produced.

To produce displays at different resolutions with clarity, each resolution standard requires these signals be driven at different frequencies. Most resolutions display at a vertical scan frequency of 60 KHz, or 60 screens per second, to make the display appear continuous. Horizontal scanning frequency specifications for the most common resolutions are listed in table 14.3:

Table 14.3
Signal Frequencies of Common Video Standards

Standard	Resolution	Hor. Freq.	Ver. Freq.
CGA	320×200	15.575 KHz	60 Hz
NTSC (TV)	525×262	15.735 KHz	60 Hz
EGA	640×350	22.1 KHz	60 Hz
VGA	640×480	31.47 KHz	70 Hz
SuperEGA	800×600	35 KHz	60 Hz
8514/A	1024×768	35.52 KHz	43.5 Hz
Extended VGA	1024×768	48.5 KHz	60 Hz

Monitors create characters and graphics by a matrix of dots. Each dot on a monitor screen can display any color that the monitor is designed to produce. Monochrome monitors produce only one color: white, amber, or green. TTL monitors, typically used by EGA display systems, can produce 16 distinct colors. Analog monitors attached to VGA and other video controllers capable of producing hundreds of colors, can display any color.

In color monitors, each dot (pixel) is made up of three smaller, closely spaced dots—one from each of the primary colors (red, blue, and green) arranged in a triad, or triangular pattern. All other colors are created by varying the intensity of these three colors. The individual color dots are so small and closely spaced that the human eye cannot discern the difference between them, only the resulting color produced by them.

Each color dot is excited by an electron beam produced by a color gun located in the back of the tube that is aimed at the dot by electromagnetic fields produced in the tube's neck. Circuitry in the monitor produces the scanning pattern that moves the beam horizontally across a thin perforated metal screen, or *shadow mask*, which is placed behind the phosphor-coated display screen. The shadow mask casts a shadow onto the display screen, only permitting a carefully designed pattern of beams to pass through. The three color guns are mounted in the tube so that their electron beams converge as they pass through the holes in the shadow mask. The beams separate as they diverge on the front side of the mask to ensure that each beam hits its intended phosphor dot. The shadow mask also controls the diameter of the beam that strikes the phosphor dot. Only 1/4 to 1/3 of the beam is allowed to reach the screen; the rest is blocked out.

In some monitors, either by design or as a result of manufacturing processes and imperfections, the beams in a monitor tube may not meet precisely at the shadow mask. This is known as *misconvergence*. Misconvergence results when the individual color dots are incorrectly spaced. This poor spacing produces pixels that are not uniform in shape or size and which produce poor color quality. Perhaps the most common evidence of misconvergence in monitors is characters that appear fuzzy around the edges of the display, yet sharp in the middle. This is a result of poor engineering and cannot be adjusted with the monitor's controls. Figure 14.5 shows a cut-away of a typical color monitor with the area around one pixel enlarged to show how the three beams diverge from the shadow mask to illuminate their corresponding color dots and create one pixel.

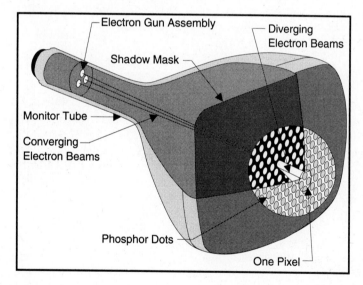

Figure 14.5:
Typical color monitor design.

The matrix of pixels in every monitor is measured in resolution, as described earlier. *Dot pitch* is a measurement of the spacing between the dots that make up a matrix. Dot pitch, for instance, can be thought of in the same way as the dots per inch (DPI) rating of a printer. With monitors, pitch is the distance between consecutive dots. In general, the smaller the dot pitch, the finer the matrix and the sharper the picture. Most monitors have dot pitches between .26mm and .33mm.

Other monitor specifications contribute to overall display quality and effectiveness of the dot pitch. These specifications include convergence error (the less the better), multisyncing capability (the capability to display many resolutions, the more the better), number and accessibility of controls, use of glare-reducing screen coatings, multiple types of input connectors, autosizing circuitry (adjusts display size for different resolutions), and correct color production.

Conclusions

In a professional AutoCAD workstation, the display system is no place to cut corners. The graphics display is the fundamental interface between the user and the system. The better the communication between the two, the more productive they will be. When looking for a computer monitor, make certain that the monitor will operate safely at all the sync frequencies you intend to use. Avoid interlaced resolutions. Few systems can produce flicker-free displays in interlaced modes. As refresh rates (horizontal sync frequencies) climb, acceptable interlaced performance may come. Monitor display quality is a subjective topic even though it can be measured scientifically. Refer to reviews in reputable computer magazines, and plan to spend time in front of a monitor before you buy it.

Auxiliary Input Devices

Auxiliary input devices provide an additional physical link between a user and the AutoCAD system besides the keyboard. Many different types of input devices are available, including mice, trackballs, digitizers, voice input, and scanners. Some other effective input devices such as light pens, dial sets, joysticks, and touch screens are available, but are not of interest to most AutoCAD users because they generally are not accurate or practical enough. If someone in your office must work with a disability, however, you should investigate as many alternative input devices as possible. Light pens, touch screens, and voice input devices may be very helpful for persons who have difficulty manipulating a keyboard, digitizer, or other hand-held devices.

Mice

Mice are small, inexpensive input devices that have become popular since the introduction of the Macintosh computer. Mice have proven their usefulness in desktop publishing and CAD, and are becoming more popular with computer users for use with other programs and graphical user interfaces (GUIs), such as OS/2 PM and Windows. You cannot use a mouse to input geometry from existing drawings, but many AutoCAD users find the mouse to be a sufficient input device.

A mouse operates by decoding light or magnetic impulses, which are produced when the mouse is moved across a desktop or pad. The mouse's software translates this motion into a form recognized by the host computer. When the mouse is moved, the user sees a cursor or pointer move across the screen.

Most mice feature one or more buttons, which enable the user to select commands from menus and pick points on-screen, and are best suited for programs that require those types of input.

Resolution

Mouse resolution is the number of discrete points reported by the mouse for a given distance when moved across a surface. A low-resolution mouse must be moved farther than a high-resolution mouse to achieve the same amount of on-screen cursor movement. The higher a mouse's resolution, therefore, the better the mouse. Currently, mice come in resolutions of 200 to 1000 dots per inch (dpi).

Motion-Sensing Technology

Mice work upon two underlying technologies—mechanical and optical. Mechanical mice use encoders that translate movements of the ball inside a mouse into digital signals by transferring the movements with wheels and shafts. Optical mice use a light-emitting diode (LED) to produce a light beam that is reflected off of a special pad under the mouse. A grid printed on the pad interrupts the light beam at intervals as the mouse is moved over the pad. As the beam returns to the mouse, the beam is received by an encoder device that transforms the light pulses into a digital signal.

Opti-mechanical mice use a combination of the two technologies—mechanical wheels that rotate perforated disks that lie between the LED and encoder (see fig. 14.6).

Mechanical mice have a slight advantage in that they do not require a specific pad. They may be rolled across any surface. Optical mice are not prone to the build-up of dust and other debris on mechanical wheels. Opti-mechanical mice are a compromise.

Buttons

Most mice feature one, two, or three buttons. Some types of mice have more buttons, but the usefulness of the extra buttons depends on the program in use. AutoCAD can take advantage of up to 16 buttons. Most other programs only accommodate the two-button standard set by the Microsoft mouse.

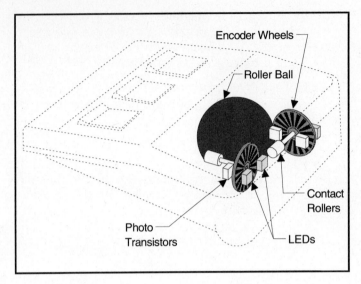

Figure 14.6:
An opti-mechanical mouse.

Mouse Software

When comparing mice, you also should consider the type of driver software that is provided with each mouse. Generally, the mouse must communicate with the application program through a driver that translates the mouse's digital signals into the equivalent cursor movements expected by the program.

Scaling is a useful function of the mouse driver for AutoCAD. To understand how scaling works, try to imagine the mouse as having a two-speed transmission. When the mouse is moved slowly, the driver is in low gear and moves the cursor on-screen slowly; when the mouse is moved rapidly, the driver shifts into second gear and the mouse movements are multiplied by a scale factor to speed up the cursor movements. Scaling enables the user to move the cursor precisely for accurate point placement and to cross the screen for picking commands from a menu, in the least amount of desk space possible and with the least effort.

Finally, driver compatibility is a concern. Drivers that are compatible with the standard set by the Microsoft mouse are more likely to be supported by programs than mice that use their own format.

Trackballs

A *trackball* is a variation of the mouse concept; that is, a trackball is essentially a mouse turned upside-down. Trackballs are the same device made popular by video arcade games, and use the same technology as a mouse to translate physical movement into cursor movement. Instead of moving the mouse across a hard surface, however, the user uses his fingers to roll a protruding ball while the device remains stationary.

The trackball's big advantage is that it requires less deskspace than a mouse does. On the other hand, the motions required to move the cursor on-screen are less natural than those necessary to use a mouse. Some users find it difficult to move the cursor with a button depressed, and have problems accurately placing objects with a trackball. With diligence, however, a user can become as proficient with a trackball as with a mouse.

Digitizers

The *digitizer* is the hands-down favorite input device of AutoCAD users. Digitizers control cursor movement and point selection in much the same manner as mice do, but digitizers are more accurate than mice, and provide other useful features.

A digitizer works by sensing a tiny magnetic field produced by the *puck* (the portion of a digitizer that resembles a mouse) when it is moved over an electronic grid inside the digitizer's *tablet*. This location method allows the computer to know *absolutely* where the puck is in relation to the tablet. With mice, the computer only knows where the mouse is *relative* to its last reported position. Hence, if a mouse user reaches the edge of his desk before the cursor reaches the edge of his display, he must pick the mouse up, reposition it away from the desk edge, and continue to roll it across the desk in the same direction in order to complete the operation.

A digitizer user, on the other hand, configures an area on the tablet surface to correspond to his screen area, and when the puck is moved to the edge of the tablet area, the cursor will be at the edge of the screen. This ability also allows the digitizer to be configured with *hot-spots*. A hot-spot is an area on the tablet that corresponds to certain program commands when a puck button is pressed while the puck is positioned within the prescribed area.

The digitizer reports absolute coordinates to input existing drawings. By aligning the puck's crosshairs with points on a paper drawing taped to the tablet surface, for example, the user can create an electronic copy of the paper drawing.

Digitizers normally come with resolutions over 1000 dpi, and digitizer pucks normally have four buttons. Many provide optional pucks with eight, 12, or 16 buttons, and an optional stylus. The stylus is a more natural device for some users in that it closely resembles a pencil. Many digitizers can be made to emulate mice through special drivers, and can be used with other graphics or business programs.

Scanners

Another input device for the digitizing of existing drawings is the *scanner*. Using much the same technology as a facsimile machine, these devices can "read" a drawing, converting its geometry and text into a *raster* image. CAD programs such as AutoCAD store drawing geometry in the form of *vectors* that describe the endpoints and directions of lines, arcs, circles, and polylines. A raster image is a representation of geometric objects as they conform to a matrix of points.

Some scanners come with software that can analyze the raster image, and attempt to recognize the geometric entities that the image originally contained. The software then converts the dots back into line segments in a process known as raster-to-vector conversion.

The current problem with raster-to-vector conversion software is that most of it is not intelligent enough to distinguish text, line widths, hatches, and fills for what they are, but converts them all into short line segments. The software also cannot make intelligent decisions about line endpoints when it encounters an intersection. This results in large drawing files in relation to the same drawing stored in AutoCAD format. Scanned files, nevertheless, can be useful as templates, over which a more accurate drawing can be traced.

Progress is being made at making scanner software more aware of text fonts, line widths, and repetitive patterns. Scanners are becoming an attractive solution to the problem of entering existing paper drawings.

Voice Recognition

The only command input more intuitive than voice recognition is telekinesis. Great strides have been made in voice recognition technology in the last several years. As a result, advanced telecommunications technologies are becoming more practical for AutoCAD and fairly economical.

Voice recognition input systems respond to spoken words and phrases and convert them into commands and macros. The user wears a microphone, similar to those worn by telephone operators, which is connected to an interface card installed in the host computer. The interface card uses complex algorithms and instructions to associate commands and macros with sound patterns received by the microphone. The user *trains* the system to recognize his voice, and when he speaks certain phrases while using AutoCAD, the appropriate commands are executed. A pointing device, such as a mouse or digitizer, still is necessary to supply cursor movement, but command entry can be very rapid when voice recognition technology is used.

One might think that voice recognition would be the ultimate input device for word processors, but such is not the case. Voice recognition requires large amounts of RAM to hold the dictionary necessary to recognize continuous speech, as well as large amounts of processing power to be able to recognize and differentiate many words. Current voice recognition technology allows for about 200 words or phrases to be learned. With its own on-board processors, the system can recognize these phrases and enter the corresponding macro almost instantaneously—fast enough to provide the user with an uninhibiting interface to AutoCAD's commands.

Conclusions

The AutoCAD input devices you choose depend on your own preferences. Some people do not like mice, while others like to keep their eyes on the screen instead of moving back and forth from a digitizer tablet. Mice have the advantage of low cost (under $100), good accuracy, and wide support by most programs. Digitizers are more expensive ($350 and up), but they are more accurate and almost as versatile as mice. Digitizers also allow one-pick command and macro entry, and allow digitizing of paper drawings. Some people use both mice and digitizers.

Voice recognition is more expensive ($1000), yet fast, and best suited to continuous AutoCAD use in an undisturbed environment. You will need either a mouse or digitizer to go with a voice recognition system. If you frequently have many paper drawings to convert, you should invest in a scanner to top out your workstation.

Output Devices

Once an AutoCAD drawing is completed, a hard-copy representation usually is necessary. This physical evidence of the electronic object can take many forms and can be produced by many different types of devices. These peripherals each use different technology to produce a tangible design. They include pen and electrostatic plotters, dot matrix and laser printers, and a few special-purpose devices.

The hard-copy output of an electronic drawing is the most important result of the entire AutoCAD process. The hard copy is the ultimate reason for the existence of all the other equipment that makes up an AutoCAD workstation. As when selecting a high-quality monitor, you should not cut corners when you choose your system's output device. Your company will depend on the output device for reliable operation and trust in its accuracy. Look for accuracy, reliability, and speed—in that order— when you evaluate output devices.

Pen Plotters

Pen plotters are the oldest and best-known CAD output peripherals, and probably have seen the least amount of change over the years. Although pen plotters have generally become faster, smaller, "smarter," and less expensive, they still represent mature technology. Most of the changes in plotter technology have taken place in the areas of pen design and motor technology.

Plotter Motor Technology

Pen plotters use one of two different methods to move the pen and/or the paper as they plot. Some plotters use primitive *stepper* motors. Stepper motors operate as the name suggests: the motor shaft *steps*, or turns in very small increments, as electricity is supplied. Plotters based on stepper motors typically create lower-quality output than plotters built with *servo* drives, because stepper motors can move only in fixed increments, limiting resolution.

Plotters based on servo drives, however, produce smoother movements than stepper motors. A servo-driven plotter is controlled by optical encoders, which give it better control over pen motion, higher speeds and resolution.

Paper Size

Plotters are classified according to the maximum paper size they can accept. Common sizes are A, B, C, D, and E. If you are certain that you will never need to produce E-size plots, then you probably should not invest in an E-size plotter. Remember, too, that larger plotters generally perform no better than smaller plotters, and you may pay significant premiums for the extra paper width.

Pen Types and Speed

The plotter pen is the weakest link in the pen plotter performance chain. Of all the parts in a pen plotter, the pen is the most likely to fail, yet is the single greatest contributor to plot quality. Recent improvements in pen technology have resulted in pens that transport ink to the plotting media more quickly, inks that flow more rapidly while retaining their ability to block light during the reproduction process, and longer-lasting pen tips that use more durable materials.

In high-production environments, the plotter can become a productivity bottleneck. This is why a plotter's pen speed is so important. Pen speed is usually expressed in centimeters per second (cm/sec) or inches per second (in/sec). The practical limit of most liquid ink pens (used for final plots) is 24 to 30 in/sec. Although a slower plotter can save money, a high-speed plotter may pay for itself many times over in time savings alone. Loaded with roller-ball pens or pressurized ink cartridges, a high-speed plotter can produce check plots quickly and economically.

Plotter specifications often mention acceleration, which is the measurement of the ability of a plotter to get the pen up to full speed. Acceleration is measured in Gs, or multiples of the force of gravity. Generally, the higher the G rating, the better the plotter.

Miscellaneous Plotter Features

Other specifications to look for in a plotter include the following: resolution or step size (the smallest unit of distance the plotter can move), and repeatability or accuracy (the plotter's capability to accurately repeat geometry). Both of these factors largely determine how well a plotter can produce accurate and detailed plots.

Plotter options to look for include the following: internal buffers that can hold plotting instructions from the host computer and allow it to return to work faster (the larger the buffer the better); roll-feed options that allow a plotter to load fresh media and produce multiple plots unattended; built-in plot optimization (the capability to sort pen movements for the greatest economy of movement); and compatibility with popular programming interfaces, such as HP-GL, which are supported by many programs.

Although plot optimization can decrease overall plot times, AutoCAD can perform several levels of optimization itself. Hardware optimization, therefore, is not particularly useful unless you are going to use the plotter with other programs that do not perform plot optimization.

You might be tempted to save money by buying a single-pen plotter. These plotters, however, require an operator to change pens when different widths or colors are required. Many companies have purchased single-pen plotters and regretted the inconvenience and interruption that these devices can cause.

Electrostatic Plotters

For heavy production environments, an *electrostatic plotter* is recommended. Current models can complete a full E-size plot in 1/4 the time required by a pen plotter. Once the plot is *rasterized* by the plotter (converted from pen-movement instructions to a dot image), actual plotting can take only 30 seconds for an E-size sheet. Plotting time is constant for a given sheet size, usually expressed in inches of paper per second (IPS). Compare that to pen plot times that vary widely, with 20 minutes being average for a moderately dense drawing.

An electrostatic plotter does its magic by passing specially treated paper or film in close proximity to thousands of *styli* that are spaced at 200 to 406 per inch. The styli emit 600-volt electrostatic charges in tiny (.0025") dot patterns that represent the vector information received from the host. As the media is passed over a wide trough of liquid toner vapor, the toner adheres to the charged dots and quickly dries. By performing multiple passes with different toners, multiple color plots are possible (see fig. 14.7).

Because of the need to convert vector information into raster format, electrostatic plotters often contain their own hard disks, as well as microprocessors, to perform and store the calculations necessary. This additional hardware contributes to their higher cost over pen plotters.

Dot-Matrix Printers

Impact-printing technology that was once relegated to text output has become viable for graphics hard copy, thanks to products such as the Da Vinci Graphics and JDL 24-pin color printers. These printers can create color plots up to D-size that rival the quality of pen plotters. Standard narrow and wide carriage 24-pin printers are popular for quick check plots and are well supported by AutoCAD drivers. Not all dot-matrix printers require the pen and media maintenance that plotters do, so they can be convenient for offices that do many smaller format outputs.

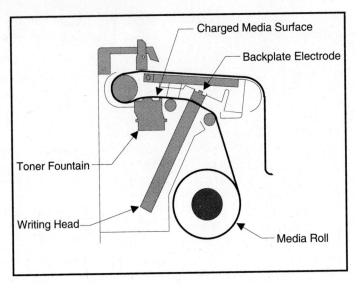

Figure 14.7:
The electrostatic printing process.

Laser Printers

The same laser technology that works so well for word processing and desktop publishing is making its way to AutoCAD users. A laser printer creates rows of charged dots on the paper by reflecting a laser beam off a spinning multi-sided mirror. The laser turns on in small bursts to energize individual dots. The spinning mirror moves the intermittent beam across the sheet horizontally. When the beam reaches the edge of the paper, another mirror face is exposed to the beam and realigns the beam with the opposite edge. Successive rows of dots are formed by minute vertical movements of the paper on rollers. Resolution can be varied through the laser control and paper-movement circuitry.

Laser printers are similar to electrostatic plotters in speed and quality. The potential for higher-resolution laser plotting exists, because the machines' dot density is not restricted to the physical density of styli, as in electrostatic plotters.

Other Devices

Several other output technologies are available for special purposes and media. These include thermal wax color printers for rendering, 3D plotters for modeling, film recorders for slide production, and NTSC boards for screen capture to video tape.

Conclusions

If you need to create production drawings in low volume, or if you need presentation-quality output, select a high-quality pen plotter from a reliable manufacturer. The plotter should be as large a format as your largest anticipated drawings. For medium-volume environments, such as small to medium-sized networks, add a roll-feed option so the plotter can run unattended. In high-volume environments, such as larger networks, you should consider only an electrostatic or laser plotter. In any installation, dot matrix and laser printers can provide quick, small and medium format drafts.

Hardware Equipment Recommendations

If you need to replace a computer or purchase a multiple-computer system from scratch, you may want to model your new system after the following standard configurations for complete systems. These configurations should give you a feel for the preferred combinations of the preceding components, when used to run AutoCAD in a professional setting. Costs have been considered in these standard configurations, and have been kept at a reasonable level, so these systems may not be necessarily the ultimate "dream" machine for your company. Further, remember that these recommendations may be obsolete by the time you read this. Prices are falling in every category of computer hardware and what may have been cost-prohibitive when this book was written could be a good value today or in the future.

Recommendations for DOS and OS/2

If you plan to run DOS or OS/2 on a stand-alone workstation, but not on a network, your best value is an IBM-compatible 80386-based computer running at 33 MHz with an ISA bus and static RAM cache. You should equip it with an 80387-33 Intel math coprocessor. If you also plan to use Autodesk RenderMan or 3D Studio often, try to buy a PC to which you can add the Weitek 3167 chip. Make sure that the PC has a popular ROM BIOS that supports ROM and video BIOS shadowing. Start with 4M RAM for a DOS system, and 8M if you plan to use OS/2, and try to get a machine that will let you add more RAM without buying an expansion card. Be certain that the motherboard is made by a major manufacturer and is free from major reworkings. You should opt for a full-size or tower case; stay away from FCC class A computers.

Most computers in this class come preconfigured with an 80-150M ESDI or IDE hard disk. You may think this is more space than you will need, but the difference between the bundled price and one with a smaller hard disk usually is insignificant. You also will not regret the extra space.

Ask the dealer about your drive controller options. While a caching controller will cost you hundreds of dollars more, some standard controllers have extra large (up to 32K) data buffers that can help. If the drive is slower than 23 ms, ask for a faster model. Although the PC may come with disk caching software, you should avoid using it with AutoCAD unless you are brave and know what you are doing with it.

Be sure to get a video card that is supported by AutoCAD drivers (and PM drivers for OS/2) regardless of the display standard or resolution. Insist on cards that have drivers for the current release of AutoCAD. You also need to find out how you can get updates for the card, and if you will need to go through your dealer or the vendor's BBS. Finally, ask your dealer about display list drivers. Several top SuperVGA and Extended VGA cards work very well and often come bundled with better computer systems.

When purchasing a monitor, you should choose a 16" multiscanning-type monitor. This type of monitor is larger than the normal PC monitor, yet is still affordable and has a fine dot pitch (under .30mm). Be sure to try out the monitor before you buy it to make sure that it has consistently sharp and true-color images. The monitor should be free from flickering and you should be able to fine-tune the picture brightness and contrast.

If you have room in your budget, buy an 11"-x-11" digitizer and tablet menu with a multi-button puck so that you can digitize paper drawings. Also, you should buy an easy-to-use tape drive so that you have no excuse for not backing up your files.

This system will cost you around $5000, depending on the components you select, where you buy them, and how the reseller prices the package. But the system is a solid combination that should pay you back soon and serve you well for years.

If you plan to add this computer to a network, you can choose a computer with a compact *footprint* (but with no fewer expansion slots than would be available in a full-size cabinet) and with less disk storage capacity. A footprint is the desk space that a computer case takes up. You will need one more slot than normal for a network card, but you will be able to share disk space with other users.

Recommendations for Macintosh

Macintosh users have an easier time shopping for a system than PC users, but also have fewer choices of components. For professional AutoCAD use, you should get a Macintosh IIci with 8M RAM and a 68882 math coprocessor. With this, add the 80M 20 ms SCSI hard disk and optional 40M tape backup unit. Choose a supported digitizer if you use third-party programs with tablet menus and replace the Mac's standard video and monitor with high-resolution units from companies, such as RasterOps, CalComp, SuperMac, and Radius. Your total cost should be somewhere around $15,000, which is quite a bit more than an equivalent DOS workstation, but you will have a powerful and versatile workstation suitable not only for AutoCAD, but for multimedia as well.

Recommendations for UNIX

For UNIX lovers and discontented DOS power users, the Sun SPARCstation IPC is attractive particularly for AutoCAD because of Sun's unique value and performance. The SPARCstation IPC comes standard with a 15.8 MIPS SPARC chip with integrated floating-point logic, 8M of RAM, and a 16" 1152×900 resolution color display. The SPARCstation also comes with a 207M hard disk, a high-density 3 1/2-inch floppy drive that works with both UNIX and DOS diskettes, a built-in Ethernet connection if you decide to network, a SCSI expansion port for additional disk and tape drives, and a mouse. Each SPARCstation comes with both the Berkeley and AT&T versions of UNIX installed, along with TCP/IP and NFS networking support, the OPEN LOOK GUI, and useful utilities.

The SPARCstation is packaged (except the monitor and mouse) in an attractive small-footprint cabinet and costs around $10,000. When you add the optional 150M tape drive for approximately $1600, your hunger for power should be satisfied.

Summary

This chapter has examined hardware issues for the AutoCAD workstation and on the "PC side" of the network. Hopefully, the discussion has made you more aware of AutoCAD workstation hardware technology, and put you in a better position to know what you need and how to support it.

If you need to upgrade any of your equipment, use this chapter as a guide as you do your product research. If you need to replace equipment or start up a workstation, look at the recommendations and conclusions that are given with each component listed. The final decision on any hardware purchase, however, rests with you and your company. Not all the components listed in this chapter are needed for every company. Some, in fact, may sit on your desk or in the corner collecting dust because they were purchased without much forethought. Others, still, may be expensive and require some getting used to initially, but will pay for themselves many times over in performance enhancement and project quality.

The MN
Disk Software

The *Managing and Networking AutoCAD Disk* (MN Disk) contains shareware and freeware utilities collected from a variety of sources. These programs can help you manage your AutoCAD system more effectively, whether your workstations are stand-alone or networked. You do not need to have any of the utilities in hand while you are reading *Managing and Networking AutoCAD*. You can use the utilities independently of each other.

> ***Note:*** The MN Disk is not included with your purchase of *Managing and Networking AutoCAD*. The disk is an optional product that must be purchased separately. If, after reading this appendix, you want the MN Disk, first check with the bookstore where you purchased *Managing and Networking AutoCAD*. Many computer bookstores that stock New Riders books also carry the optional disks. If your bookstore does not carry the MN Disk, you can order the MN Disk directly from New Riders Publishing by calling the toll-free order hotline at (800) 541-6789. Be sure to specify either 5 1/4-inch or 3 1/2-inch high-density format.

The MN Disk contains two types of programs: AutoCAD utilities and network utilities. The following sections provide a short description of each utility to help you decide whether it will be useful to you. While most of the network utilities are specific to Novell NetWare networks, some of them can be used on any type of network. When a utility is NetWare-specific, its description says so. Each description also contains either a figure showing the program's full screen interface (if it has one) or a short example of the text that is displayed when the program is executed from the DOS command line. These examples should help you to evaluate whether a given program will be useful to you and what to expect from it.

471

Almost every program on the MN Disk includes its own documentation, which tells you how to install and use the program. Be sure to read all the included documentation before you use any of the programs. If you have a problem with one, you should contact the program's author directly for assistance. Most of the programs' documentation tells you how to contact the developer in their documentation. Many of the programs are supported by the authors in various forums on the CompuServe electronic information service. New Riders Publishing cannot provide technical support for software created by other developers, but will help you if you have any problems installing the MN Disk itself.

Understanding Shareware, Freeware, and Public-Domain Software

The MN Disk contains three types of programs: shareware, freeware, and public-domain software. These terms do not describe the programs themselves, but describe the method by which the programs are distributed to users. *Freeware* programs are distributed by their author for the free use of anyone who wants them. The MN Disk's freeware utilities have been posted on electronic bulletin boards, such as CompuServe, or distributed through other means so that users can try them at no cost. You are not expected to pay for these programs; their creators distribute them for the advancement of computing and the satisfaction of helping others. They are, however, copyrighted by their authors and may not be modified in any way or distributed in any other form than the form in which you received them.

Public domain programs are similar in that they are distributed for the free use of everyone. Their authors, however, have released all their rights to the program into the public domain. This means that the author does not intend to support the program and it has become public property. As such, these programs may be modified to perform a different function or improved and then re-released into the public domain for others to use or modify.

Shareware programs also are distributed by their makers to electronic bulletin boards, user groups, and other organizations. Shareware is a concept of software distribution that allows programmers and developers to distribute their wares for profit without the expense and complexity of traditional publishing, such as duplication, manufacturing, marketing, sales, and distribution. Shareware makes software affordable by cutting out the middle men, and shareware programs are easy to find and evaluate. The shareware system also makes software easier to update and sometimes easier to support.

Unlike freeware or public domain software, however, shareware programs are not free. When you receive a copy of a shareware program, you are granted a limited time period to evaluate the software. If, after that period has expired, you decide that you want to use the software, you are obligated to register it with the author or company. Otherwise, you should discontinue its use.

> **Note:** Please register any MN Disk shareware programs that you decide to use beyond the trial period. The on-disk documentation tells you how and where to register the shareware programs. By registering your shareware programs, you encourage talented and progressive programmers to continue distributing their efforts in this way. Many shareware programs are better than their commercial equivalent, yet much cheaper.

Installing the MN Disk Utilities

Each of the MN Disk's utility programs have been compressed into an individual file. This technique conserves disk space so that the MN Disk can hold more programs. Each utility is actually made up of several files—usually an executable (EXE or COM) file, its documentation (a DOC file, a READ.ME file, or something similar), and any supporting files the program needs in order to run. If, after reading the descriptions, you want to try a program, take the following steps to copy the program onto your hard disk.

First, use the DOS DISKCOPY command to make a backup copy of the MN Disk, then store the original disk in a safe place. If you have only one floppy disk drive (presumably named drive A), place the MN Disk in drive A and enter the following command:

    C:\> **DISKCOPY A: A:**

The operating system may prompt you to swap disks until the copy is complete. Notice that the MN Disk is a high-density diskette, meaning that you cannot copy it in a low-density (360K) drive.

Next, read or print the disk's READ.ME (or similar) file to find any last-minute changes or instructions. Any instructions appearing in READ.ME take precedence over the instructions in this appendix. The READ.ME file is ASCII text that you can read with any word processor, text editor, or by issuing the DOS TYPE command. To read the file from DOS, use the MORE filter as follows:

    C:\> **MORE< A:READ.ME**

The file will display in pages, pausing at the end of each page. You can press any key to view the next page.

Next, change your current directory to the destination where you want the utility to be installed. Some of the AutoCAD utilities require that certain files be installed in your AutoCAD directory (usually named \ACAD) or placed in a directory on your AutoCAD search path. Install the AutoCAD utilities temporarily in a directory on your hard disk, and then read their documentation; carefully follow the utilities' instructions even if they differ from the instructions presented here.

You may want to create one directory for all of the MN Disk utilities you want to try. For example, you might create a directory named **MN-DISK** directly off the root directory, then make it the current directory, as follows:

    C:\> **CD**
    C:\> **MD\MN-DISK**
    C:\> **CD\MN-DISK**
    C:\MN-DISK>

Then make the drive containing the MN disk current. For each utility you want to install, use the installation batch file INSTALL.BAT on the MN Disk with the compressed file name given in the program's description and the drive letter of the destination disk. To install the program BENCHM, for example, enter the following command:

    A:\> **INSTALL BENCHM C:**

The batch file decompresses the utility you specify into the current directory of the hard disk you specify. Once the decompression is complete, look for the documentation file for that utility and read it for more details on any further installation requirements.

If you encounter problems while decompressing a utility on the MN Disk, make sure that you are executing the installation batch file from your floppy disk, not from the hard disk. Also make sure that you have plenty of disk space available on the destination drive; the files on the MN Disk typically decompress to more than twice their size. If you are still having problems, you can call the New Riders Publishing Technical Support Hotline at (503) 661-5745 and a technician will assist you.

AutoCAD Utilities

The MN Disk includes two AutoCAD benchmark programs, as well as a shell program that makes AutoCAD easier to start. The programs should work with any version of AutoCAD and do not require a network. See each program's documentation for individual requirements.

The Delucchi AutoCAD Benchmark

Christopher Delucchi (pronounced "de-luke-ee"), founder and chairperson of the San Diego AutoCAD Users Group, created this AutoCAD benchmark to quantify AutoCAD performance on various workstation configurations. The AutoCAD benchmark has been distributed as freeware on many bulletin boards and has become a popular standard for testing relative performance of AutoCAD hardware and configurations.

You can use the Delucchi AutoCAD benchmark to compare different configurations of a version of AutoCAD. The program enables you to test AutoCAD's performance when different settings are used in CONFIG.SYS, when different amounts of extended or expanded memory are allocated as extended I/O page space, or when AutoCAD overlays or other files are placed in a RAM disk. The benchmark can test different versions of AutoCAD on workstations to help you (not conclusively) make upgrade decisions. You also can use the benchmark to discover the effects of different hardware configurations on AutoCAD performance. The test should even highlight any variances in performance caused by updates in video card drivers, and can show you the performance differences between standard video drivers and drivers that support display list processing.

The test issues a combination of AutoCAD commands in much the same way as an actual user would. The test uses a large script to pump the commands into AutoCAD. The test exercises a variety of AutoCAD commands so that each of AutoCAD's overlays are used when the test is run with the 640K DOS version. This allows the results to be compared against other platforms, especially ones that do not use overlays, such as UNIX. The commands create a single drawing module that is drawn and moved into a row of 10 modules. After a row is completed, it is copied and moved until the drawing consists of an array of 80 completed modules. This part of the test examines the effects of growing file size on system response. At strategic points during the test, Redraw, Zoom, and Regen commands are executed to test video performance. To test floating-point coprocessor performance, a complex mathematical equation is solved 500 times. Finally, the test orders AutoCAD to draw a module in 3D, select a new viewpoint, and a perform a Hide operation (see fig. A.1).

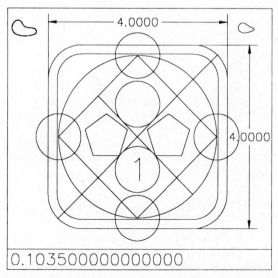

Figure A.1:
A typical drawing module from the Delucchi AutoCAD Benchmark.

While the test puts AutoCAD through its paces, an AutoLISP routine keeps track of the elapsed times for each section of the test. When the test is finished, a report file is written to the disk in comma-delimited format (CDF). You can import this file into many spreadsheet and database programs for further analysis. The test also uses AutoCAD to create a graph of the results that can be plotted or printed (see fig. A.2). The results list individual times for each section of the test for detailed comparison.

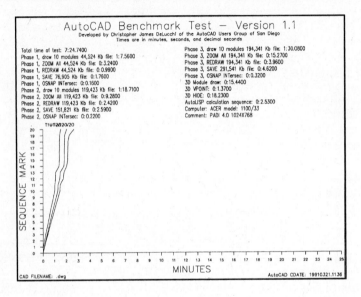

Figure A.2:
A Delucchi benchmark results graph.

When interpreting the results of the benchmark, the user needs to remember that this (or any) benchmark is not the last word in performance. Every part of the system influences the results. Video hardware and software, the amount of memory, the hard disk, and even the configuration of AutoCAD can sway the results. If one part of the system is upgraded, the test's outcome can be affected in unpredictable ways.

Watch your favorite AutoCAD BBS for the upcoming version of the AutoCAD Benchmark. It should test the 3D drafting features of the newer versions of AutoCAD much better than the current benchmark can.

The Delucchi AutoCAD Benchmark is freeware from Chris Delucchi. To decompress it, type **INSTALL BENCHM** *d:* at the DOS prompt.

GRPERF

GRPERF is a performance benchmark that tests different graphics adapter hardware and drivers with AutoCAD Releases 10 and 11. The test records the time required to perform five redraws of one or more test images at nine magnifications, each one twice as large as the last. The times for each magnification are averaged after the program discards the fastest and slowest times, and then averaged for all magnifications of a single test image. The resulting scores are then reported in tabular or bar graph form as an index relative to a standard 25MHz 386 PC with 640×480 VGA and the standard AutoCAD driver (see fig. A.3).

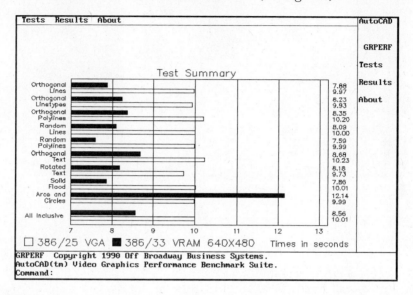

Figure A.3:
The results of a sample GRPERF test.

GRPERF is freeware from Off Broadway Systems. To decompress it, type **INSTALL GRPERF** *d:* at the DOS prompt.

LAUNCHCAD

LAUNCHCAD is an improved Main Menu interface for AutoCAD. If you use LAUNCHCAD, you do not need to remember exact file names and syntax when selecting Main Menu options. LAUNCHCAD displays directory lists and lets you set up Main Menu parameters, including plotting and AutoCAD configurations, from a pull-down menu interface. LAUNCHCAD creates and executes a unique script file that will start AutoCAD from any location on the hard disk using parameters you specify, including a working directory, prototype drawing, and starting command (see fig. A.4).

LAUNCHCAD can be executed in a loop, so you always return to LAUNCHCAD. You also can execute LAUNCHCAD from within the AutoCAD Drawing Editor.

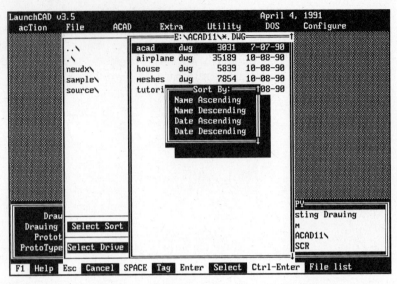

Figure A.4:
The LAUNCHCAD menu interface.

LAUNCHCAD contains file maintenance features that let you copy, erase, rename, and execute files. LAUNCHCAD also can delete all BAK files from a directory. The program's menu offers selections for a text editor, a drawing viewer, a file lister, and other third-party external utilities of your choice. These utilities, however, are not included with LAUNCHCAD. Hypertext help also is included.

LAUNCHCAD is shareware from Mountain Software. To decompress it, type **INSTALL LC351** *d:* at the DOS prompt.

TSRPLOT

TSRPLOT is a shareware plot spooler that is similar to many commercially available plot spoolers. TSRPLOT loads as a 67K terminate-and-stay-resident (TSR) program and performs foreground or background plot spooling to a Hewlett-Packard plotter. TSRPLOT spools HPGL plot files residing either on the workstation or on a network drive. The program's execution priority is user-configurable. TSRPLOT can use either COM1 or COM2 serial ports and can be removed from memory (see fig. A.5).

TSRPLOT has two valuable automated features typically found on commercial spoolers: Auto Plot and Auto Feed. Auto Plot enables TSRPLOT to continuously monitor a local or network drive for the existence of plot files conforming to a user-definable mask (for instance, *.PLT) and automatically spool the files once they are created by AutoCAD. TSRPLOT also can automatically delete plotted files. The Auto Feed feature can be configured to feed a new sheet on roll-fed or sheet-fed plotters.

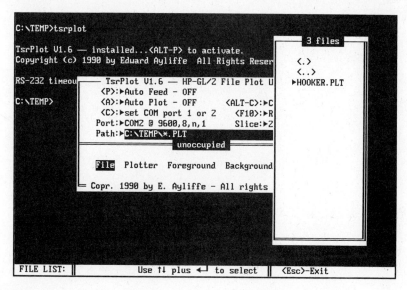

Figure A.5:
The TSRPLOT menu.

TSRPLOT is shareware from J. Edward Ayliffe. To decompress it, type **INSTALL TSRPLT** *d:* at the DOS prompt.

Network Utilities

The following utilities are designed for use on an existing network. Some of the utilities are useful for integrating AutoCAD with a network, while others simplify general network management. Several of these programs can be used only with Novell NetWare. For specific versions and other requirements, see the program's documentation.

AT.COM

AT is a handy little (2448 bytes) TSR that executes a batch file or other program at a specified time on a workstation. You can set up the program to execute multiple events at different dates and times, or relative to the time AT was invoked. AT is convenient for scheduling backup procedures or batch plotting for late at night or on weekends. The following example executes a hypothetical batch file that logs a user into the network and performs unattended backups. In the first line, the backup event is scheduled with AT.COM. In the second line, the event is verified by requesting a list of events held by AT.COM:

```
C:\> AT 6:00PM DOBACKUP
C:\> AT ?
#  TIME  DATE  EVENT
01 18:00 01/09 DOBACKUP
C:\>
```

Even if you are not on a network, you can use AT to do all sorts of routine maintenance chores.

AT is freeware from Bill Frolik. To decompress it, type **INSTALL AT** *d:* at the DOS prompt.

BINDARC

BINDARC is a command-line utility that archives the NetWare bindery files that contain NetWare user, group, and security information into files suitable for backing up. Normally, the bindery is inaccessible to backup programs. With BINDARC, you can make sure that this information is backed up with your data in case of an emergency. Otherwise, the users, groups, and security structures must be recreated from scratch. BINDARC creates files that are compatible with the BINDREST utility, which is included with NetWare. BINDREST can restore the files created by BINDARC.

The following example shows BINDARC creating a BINDREST-compatible archive file for the New Riders file server:

```
J:\SYSTEM> BINDARC
BINDARC v1.0 - Bindery archive utility for NetWare v2.1x and v3.x
Copyright (c) 1989 by Jeff Chumbley
Backing up NetWare v2.15 bindery for server NEW_RIDER.
Beginning backup of bindery . . .
Backup of bindery complete!
J:\SYSTEM>
```

BINDARC is public-domain software from Jeff Chumbley. To decompress it, type **INSTALL BINDARC** *d:* at the DOS prompt.

ENVLIST

ENVLIST makes the DOS environment space easier to manage. The program reports the amount of space used by lines in AUTOEXEC.BAT or other batch files. If you invoke ENVLIST from the DOS command prompt, the program displays the amount of space used by each statement, as well as the total environment space used. The following example shows the ENVLIST utility at work. The numbers at left report the number of bytes allocated for each statement ENVLIST finds in the DOS environment list to the right:

```
C:\> ENVLIST
(22)        COMSPEC=C:\COMMAND.COM
(11)        PROMPT=$P$G
(23)        PATH=C:\;C:\DOS;C:\UTIL
(14)        LISPHEAP=35000
(15)        LISPSTACK=10000
(20)        ACADCFG=\acad11
(12)        ACAD=\acad11
Total bytes used:  117
```

ENVLIST saves time in counting SET statement characters to fine-tune memory usage. Each character in a SET, PROMPT, and COMSPEC statement decreases your available DOS enviroment space by one byte. If you later execute another batch file that sets additional variables, you could exceed the default 160-byte limit. This will result in DOS displaying an "Out of environment space" message. ENVLIST can show you when you need to expand the DOS environment space, and by how much.

ENVLIST is freeware from an unknown source. To decompress it, type **INSTALL ENVLIST** *d:* at the DOS prompt.

FILESCAN

Even when you use AutoCAD Release 11's file-locking feature, your system's users can have problems when they try to share files on a network. AutoCAD Release 11 tells you only when a drawing file was locked (if you are denied access) and by whom. It does not tell you if the file is still open unnecessarily. If that person's workstation has crashed, the drawing file is still locked, but not still held open by AutoCAD running on their workstation because that session of AutoCAD is not still running. The drawing will need to be reopened by the same user, or else the file lock must be deleted.

FILESCAN displays a list of the files on a NetWare network that are held open by NetWare for one or all connected workstations. With the results, you can tell if it is safe to unlock an inactive (yet locked) drawing. You also can use FILESCAN to check file usage before you execute AutoCAD, to determine whether the file you want to use is busy. This capability also is valuable to Release 10 users who want to protect files from being edited simultaneously.

The following example output shows various drawing files held open by different users and the users' connection numbers:

C:\> **FILESCAN**

Con	User	Files
1	Supervisor	
2	Ken	vol1:project\9034\9034a202.dwg
3	Chris	vol1:project\9067\9067i309.dwg
4	Kevin	vol1:project\9037\9037c103.dwg
5	Sstuple	vol1:project\9034\9034a201.dwg

5 Connections, 4 Files

C:\>

FILESCAN is freeware from Manth-Brownell, Inc. To decompress it, type **INSTALL FSCAN** *d:* at the DOS prompt.

LOGOFF

LOGOFF is a replacement for NetWare's LOGOUT command-line utility. Normally, when you are logged into a network, NetWare appends any mapped drives to your DOS path. Depending on your network's configuration, a login script may change your COMSPEC variable to point to a copy of COMMAND.COM on a network drive. Once you log out, however, your path may retain the mapped drives assigned by NetWare. This uses up DOS environment space and slows down directory searches on your local disks. It also can result in Invalid drive in search path error messages. Unless you reset COMSPEC to a local drive when you log out, you can receive Invalid COMMAND.COM...System halted messages, and your computer will lock up. LOGOFF can help in both cases. The following example shows the local DOS path restored by LOGOFF at the end of a network session:

G:\> **LOGOFF**

Computer Tyme LogOff * Version 1.1 * Release Date: 09-17-90

Copyright 1990 by Marc Perkel * All Rights Reserved

KEN logged out from server NEW_RIDER connection 2.

PATH=c:\;c:\dos;c:\dos\bat;c:\dos\util;c:\acad11;

G:\>

LOGOFF searches your DOS path and removes network drive and directory paths that you can no longer access. The program also searches local drives for COMMAND.COM to re-establish COMSPEC, if necessary. As a result, LOGOFF slims down the DOS path and reduces the DOS environment space usage while you are not working on the network.

LOGOFF is freeware from Computer Tyme. To decompress it, type **INSTALL LOGOFF** *d:* at the DOS prompt.

MOVE

The MOVE command-line utility is handy for safely moving files from one directory to another. This utility frees you from first copying files to a new directory and then deleting the files from the original directory. MOVE supports options for quiet mode, overwriting, file attributes, strictly copying or deleting, and supports pipes and redirection. In the following example, MOVE is moving the file TEST.FIL from the root directory of drive C to the directory \TEMP in one step instead of the usual two:

```
C:\> MOVE TEST.FIL \TEMP
Moving C:\TEST.FIL ———>> C:\TEMP\TEST.FIL
C:\>
```

MOVE is freeware from Computer Tyme. To decompress it, type **INSTALL MOVE** *d:* at the DOS prompt.

NETUTIL1

NETUTIL1 is a collection of 17 small command-line utilities for NetWare networks. Because of their fairly technical nature, the programs in this collection are valuable to the budding NetWare guru. Most of the programs can redirect their output to a file or printer for future reference. Others return DOS ERRORLEVEL codes that are useful for constructing intelligent batch files. The programs can be helpful in system troubleshooting, and are generally faster and more convenient than the Novell-supplied utilities.

Program	Description
ACCESS	Returns the calling station's bindery access level
ADDRESS	Returns the calling station's physical card address
DRIVES	Shows drive information for all 26 letters, A through Z
LOGINS	Lists all users created on the network and the last time they logged in
NCSTATS	Displays technical information about the network disk cache
NETDRVS	Displays information about the physical drives installed in the file server
NETMISC	Displays miscellaneous information about the file server and its configuration
NETOBJS	Lists all bindery objects, their type, and privileges

Program	Description
NFSTATS	Displays technical information about the network file system
NIOSTATS	Displays technical information about the network's packet I/O system
NMSTATS	Displays information about the network drive table
NTSTATS	Displays information about the network transaction tracking system
SERVINFO	Displays information about the current server and connections
STIME	Synchronizes the file server time to that of your workstation
TESTIPX	Verifies that IPX has been loaded
TSTNBIOS	Verifies that NETBIOS has been loaded
TSTSHELL	Verifies that a network shell (such as NET3) has been loaded

NETUTIL1 is freeware from David Hendrickson. If you like NETUTIL1, look for NETUTIL2, the second in the series, on a local bulletin board. To decompress NETUTIL1, type **INSTALL NETUTIL1** *d:* at the DOS prompt.

PERFORM3

PERFORM3 is a network throughput benchmark utility created by Novell for NetWare networks. PERFORM3 measures the number of kilobytes per second of data sent from any number of workstations concurrently through a file server to its disk. PERFORM3 sends test files of various lengths from 1 byte to 64K in variable increments, and each test can run for a user-specified number of seconds. The results are written to a text file for future reference and to an output file suitable for use with PLOTOUT, a graphing program that is included with PERFORM3. PLOTOUT displays the results of a PERFORM3 test as a colorful bar graph for easier interpretation (see fig. A.6).

You can use PERFORM3 to measure throughput for a single workstation, or you can run the program on an entire network to simulate an immense load. The results are useful for monitoring network degradation as your network grows, for determining the optimum packet length for systems with configurable packet size, for measuring possible improvement after a network operating system or hardware upgrade, or for comparing your network with others that are similar.

PERFORM3 is freeware from Novell, Inc. To decompress it, type **INSTALL PER-FORM3** *d:* at the DOS prompt.

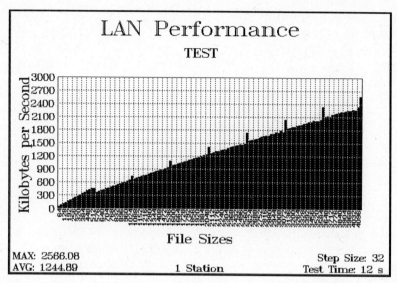

Figure A.6:
A sample PLOTOUT graph of PERFORM3 results.

QLIST

QLIST is a simple command-line utility that lists the print jobs in NetWare print queues. QLIST is faster than the Print Queue Information screens of NetWare's PCONSOLE. When executed at the DOS command prompt, QLIST displays the on-line status of the first two printers, and statistics for the queue name you specify on the command line. If there are no jobs in the queue, QLIST says so.

QLIST shows all the print jobs pending for the queue with their priority number, application and file name (if possible), banner name, spool file size, the name of the user who submitted the job, the date and time the user sent it, and the job's current status. The following example shows printers 0 and 1 on-line and running, and a print job 719,633 bytes long submitted by user KEN currently being printed from print queue PRINTQ_3:

C:\> **QLIST PRINTQ_3**

Printer 0 is on-line and running. Printer 1 is on-line and running.

Print Queue: printq_3

Priority	File Name	Banner Name	Size	User	Queued	Status
1 Ventura -	mnlappa.chp	LST:	719633	KEN	1/30 16:48	Active

QLIST is public-domain software from Bill Wildner and includes C language source code. To decompress it, type **INSTALL QLIST** *d:* at the DOS prompt.

SERVERAM

The spreadsheet file SERVERAM.WK1 is a Lotus 1-2-3 spreadsheet that calculates the approximate amount of RAM required in a NetWare file server for any given configuration. A Microsoft Excel spreadsheet SERVERAM.XLS is included for Excel users. SERVERAM accounts for all the configurable RAM amounts for a NetWare file server, including the number of users, hard disk size, VAPs and NLMs, number of network adapters, and print queues.

Use SERVERAM to determine the amount of RAM you need in order to install NetWare for the first time on a file server. Round up the answer to the nearest megabyte or other physical RAM boundary imposed by your hardware, install that much, and then watch the network statistics as described in Chapter 5. Add more RAM as needed to bring the number of File Requests Serviced from Cache up to 90 percent or more (see fig. A.7).

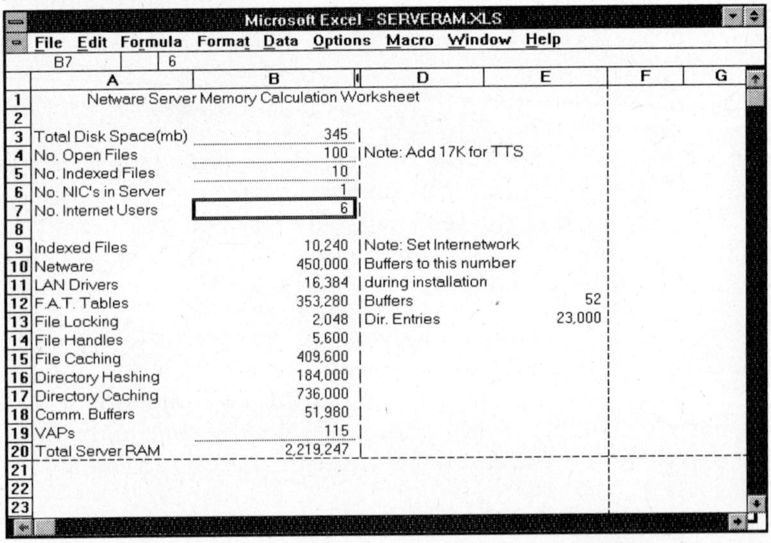

Figure A.7:
SERVERAM calculates the file server's RAM requirements.

You also can use SERVERAM to estimate the amount of extra RAM needed for a file server reconfiguration with larger hard disks, more users, or other parameters.

SERVERAM is public domain. The original Lotus file is from an unknown source. The Excel file was translated by the author. To decompress it, type **INSTALL SERVERAM** *d:* at the DOS prompt.

SHNET

SHNET is a tiny TSR program that works around the problems that cause older versions of AutoCAD to display the Error swapping to disk error message when used on a Novell network. If you do not have AutoCAD configured to redirect pager files to a local drive, and if you receive this error message when executing the Shell or Sh command, you should try SHNET. The following example shows SHNET loading into memory where it does its job without further display:

G:\> **SHNET**

(c) '88 Cyco automation, the Netherlands

(SHNET) Acad shell command works with Novell networks now.

G:\>

SHNET is freeware from Cyco International. To decompress it, type **INSTALL SHNET** *d:* at the DOS prompt.

TSR Utilities

The TurboPower Software TSR Utilities are an indispensable collection of command-line utilities for controlling TSR programs and managing DOS memory. You can use these utilities to view memory usage by TSRs and drivers, check available free memory, remove TSRs from memory without rebooting the PC, disable individual TSRs without removing them, and block out portions of memory for testing TSRs with application configurations, such as AutoCAD. Two utilities, MARKNET and RELNET, can unload the NetWare shell without rebooting to make more RAM available for other purposes.

The following example shows MARKNET first loading into memory and writing the machine's memory and register status to the file **C:\MARKNET.MRK**. Next, the NetWare IPX protocol stack and DOS shell are loaded as usual. You then can proceed with a network session until you needed the extra memory occupied by IPX and NET3. Last, RELNET is used to remove IPX and NET3 from memory back to the point MARKNET was loaded. It then restores the computer's memory and registers from the C:\MARKNET.MRK file:

C:\> **MARKNET C:\MARKNET.MRK**

MARKNET 2.9, by TurboPower Software

Stored mark information in C:\> MARKNET.MRK

C:\> **IPX**

Novell IPX/SPX v3.01 Rev. A (900507)

(C) Copyright 1985, 1990 Novell Inc. All Rights Reserved.

LAN Option: G/Ethernet AT by Gateway Communications, Inc., V2.B1

Hardware Configuration: IRQ = 12, I/O Base = 2C0h, no DMA or ROM

C:\> **NET3**

NetWare V3.01 rev. A Workstation Shell for PC DOS V3.x

(C) Copyright 1983, 1988 Novell Inc. All Rights Reserved.

Attached to server NEW_RIDER

Monday, February 4, 1991 12:18:34 pm

C:\> **RELNET C:\MARKNET.MRK**

RELNET 2.9, by TurboPower Software

Memory release above C:\MARKNET.MRK

C:\>

The TSR Utilities are freeware from TurboPower Software. To decompress them, type **INSTALL TSRCOM** *d:* at the DOS prompt.

UGRAPH

UGRAPH can help you quickly and graphically track server usage (see fig. A.8). UGRAPH displays a NetWare file server's current utilization statistics. Primarily, UGRAPH displays the current server utilization rate for the past 30 seconds as a bar graph that scrolls horizontally across the graph window. The program also shows current connection and dynamic memory group statistics normally found on NetWare FCONSOLE utility screens. The display can be updated at user-definable intervals, with the default being once every second.

UGRAPH is freeware from DBNet Software Solutions. To decompress the program, type **INSTALL UGRAPH** *d:*.

XMETER

XMETER is a software-metering program for use on Novell NetWare networks. With XMETER, you can control the number of users working with AutoCAD (or any other executable program) to match the number of software licenses you have. This is valuable when AutoCAD is installed on more workstations than you have licenses for, or when running older versions of AutoCAD installed on the file server.

XMETER uses NetWare *semaphores* to keep track of the number of programs that are active at one time. A semaphore is simply a flag that XMETER creates in the global NetWare environment with a name you specify. The semaphore then can be assigned a number each time XMETER is run before executing another program. With XMETER in a shared batch file used to invoke AutoCAD, you can specify the number of users you will allow, and can optionally log program usage to a file for reference. XMETER returns DOS ERRORLEVEL codes to allow conditional branching within your batch file to handle exclusions however you decide. You usually should display a message to the user to the effect that they must wait to execute AutoCAD until later when another AutoCAD session is terminated.

XMETER is shareware from Computer Tyme. To decompress it, type **INSTALL XMETER** *d:* at the DOS prompt.

ZERO7A

ZERO7A is a utility to free interrupt 7A on older (v2.0a and SFT v2.1) NetWare networks when you must use an AutoCAD ADI driver that cannot be configured to use a different interrupt. Execute ZERO7A after loading the network shell and before loading the ADI driver.

ZERO7A is freeware from an unknown source. To decompress it, type **INSTALL ZERO7A** *d:* at the DOS prompt.

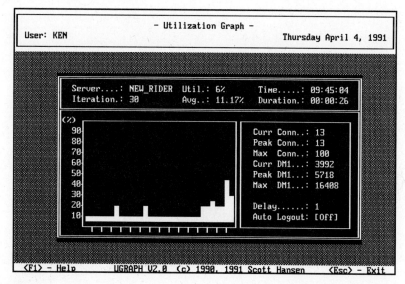

Figure A.8:
Example of the UGRAPH display.

The MN DISK
Sample Forms

This appendix contains several sample documentation forms that are designed to help you with the administrative duties of managing your CAD department. You can use these forms just as they appear here, or you can edit them to suit your needs. All the forms are included in ASCII format on the *Managing and Networking AutoCAD Disk*, so that you can easily import them into any word processor or text editor. The disk and this appendix include the following forms:

- System configuration log form
- Breakdown log form
- AutoLISP library catalog form
- AutoLISP function header
- Project log form
- Drawing log form
- Block library catalog form
- CAD specialist evaluation form

Each form is reproduced in this appendix, along with suggestions that should help you use the forms. For more information on documentation, see Chapter 10.

System Configuration Log

If you are responsible for the performance and maintenance of more than two personal computers, you may have trouble remembering all the hardware expansion cards, software drivers, and configuration parameters used in each machine. If you maintain a simple electronic file in the root directory of each machine, however, you can "check under the hood" of each computer as easily as you can pop up an ASCII text file.

This section describes a simple text file you can place in the root directory of each personal computer in your department (or the whole company). The file is named SYSTEM.CFG. Because this file's name is similar to the machine's CONFIG.SYS file, users can easily recognize SYSTEM.CFG as a configuration file and protect it as they would protect any other file that is relevant to the computer's performance.

You can use the DOS read-only file attribute to protect the file from accidental erasure. To mark the file as read-only, enter the following command at the DOS prompt:

C:\> **ATTRIB +R SYSTEM.CFG**

When any part of the computer's configuration changes, you can reverse the read-only attribute by issuing the following command:

C:\> **ATTRIB -R SYSTEM.CFG**

You now can edit the file to reflect any changes that have been made to the computer's configuration, and then reset the read-only attribute when you are done.

Your SYSTEM.CFG file should resemble figure B.1.

You probably will find it helpful to keep a folder or three-ring binder of printouts of each computer's SYSTEM.CFG file, as well as other information about your computer system. Such printouts also are helpful for substitute CAD managers, service personnel, and consultants.

The folder or binder should contain the following information, along with the SYSTEM.CFG printouts:

- The quantity and location of all computers.
- The network software configuration. For NetWare, include the choices used in the generation of the operating system, such as the file server network card driver, network address, node-addressing method, interrupt level, I/O base address, RAM buffer address and range, DMA channel, and communications buffers. If you have a different network, include the information used and selections made to configure them.
- Network operating system installation options. For NetWare, include the partition sizes, cache buffer size, number of open files, directory hashing, directory caching, and file server names. If you have a different network, include the information used and selections made to install them.
- Network printers and plotters, including their numbers or names, queue names, and any defined forms and print jobs.

System Configuration

| PC# | Make: | | Model: | | Serial#: |

Motherboard

| CPU: | | MHz | FPU: | | MHz | BIOS: | | Bus | MHz |

| RAM: | MB | Style: | | Ns | | KB Cache | ☐ System ROM Shadow | ☐ Video ROM Shadow |

| Convent. Memory: | KB | Expansion Memory: | KB | ☐ EMS | ☐ XMS | ☐ COM1 | ☐ COM2 | ☐ LPT1 |

Device Drivers

#1:		#4:
#2:		#5:
#3:		#6:

Drives

Hard Disk Controller:	☐ MFM ☐ RLL ☐ IDE ☐ ESDI ☐ SCSI ☐ Integral
Floppy Drive #1 Make:	Model:	☐ 1.44MB ☐ 1.2MB ☐ 720KB ☐ 360KB
Floppy Drive #2 Make:	Model:	☐ 1.44MB ☐ 1.2MB ☐ 720KB ☐ 360KB
Hard Drive #1 Make:	Model:	MB	Cyl.	Hd.	Sectors
Hard Drive #2 Make:	Model:	MB	Cyl.	Hd.	Sectors

Expansion Cards

Video Adapter:		Res.:	Colors
I/O Adapter:	☐ COM1 ☐ COM2 ☐ COM3 ☐ LPT1 ☐ LPT2
Network Adapter:	IRQ:	DMA:	I/O Addr.:	Mem. Addr.:
Other:

Peripherals

Monitor Make:	Model:	Inches Diagonal
Pointing Device Make:	Model:	Interface:
Printer Make:	Model:	Interface:
Plotter Make:	Model:	Interface:

Misc:

Figure B.1:
The system configuration log.

- Software serial numbers, technical support, and customer service phone numbers.
- System and group login scripts or other network user profiles. Include user login scripts if there are not too many.
- An explanation of user rights assignments on your network.
- An explanation of your backup procedures.
- Printing and plotting procedures.
- Copies of maintenance agreements.
- Breakdown logs (these are covered in the next section).

Breakdown Log

Nobody likes breakdowns, but they do happen. If you want to get your system going after a breakdown, you must methodically examine the symptoms until you find the cause. A breakdown log can help you identify patterns of behavior common to certain types of breakdowns in your system, and also can help you remember how similar problems have been resolved in the past. If the same problem occurs on another machine, you may be able to find the solution by looking in the breakdown log.

You should fill out a breakdown log immediately after you recover from a breakdown; you may not remember all the details days or months later. Keep all breakdown logs, printer dumps, and error messages together in your folder with the system configuration logs.

The breakdown log should resemble figure B.2.

AutoLISP Library

If you maintain a well-documented AutoLISP library, you encourage your staff to use and maintain the programs. AutoLISP programs easily start "collecting dust" or become lost soon after they are acquired. If their function is understood and they are accessible, however, the programs will be used and the users will not have to waste time looking for them.

One way to encourage their use is by making an AutoLISP catalog available to users, either as part of their own CAD manual or as a master catalog. The catalog should include a page for each AutoLISP program. Individual pages make it easier to update and add programs as they become available. Each page should list everything a user needs to know about how to use the program. To make programs easier to find, categorize them according to type, such as Text Manipulation, Editing Routines, and Database. If you are really sophisticated, you can even index the catalog.

Your AutoLISP catalog entries should resemble figure B.3.

Breakdown Log			
PC#	Date:	Time:	User:

App(s)
Active:

TSR(s)
Active: □ Network
                                                              Connected

Device Drivers
Active:

Description:

Probable
Cause:

Action
Taken:

Comments:

Completed by:

Figure B.2:
The breakdown log.

AutoLISP Function		
File Name:	Location:	Programmer:
Other Functions Required:		
Argument names and purposes:		
Global variable names and purposes:		
Purpose:		
Instructions:		

Figure B.3:

A sample AutoLISP catalog form.

AutoLISP File Header

Good programming techniques also help you get the most from your AutoLISP programs. Chapter 13 offers suggestions on managing software development. One good programming technique is putting documentation in the code itself. By placing basic information about the program at the head of the file, you make the original programmer's intentions clear for the user. If the user must try to decipher someone else's program without documentation, he can waste many valuable hours.

If file-loading speed is an issue, you might try using a public domain "stripper" program. The stripper program creates an *object* file from a fully commented *source* file; the object file is free of comments and *white space* (formatting). The source code files could have the extension LSC (LISP Source Code) and be kept in a secure directory, which is available only to authorized programmers. The stripped object files (LSP) can be made public. Because the stripped, or otherwise optimized, versions are very difficult to alter, users should be discouraged from tampering with them.

Following is a suggested standard header for AutoLISP source code files. This type of header is used and promoted by Autodesk, Inc. and expert programmers. One AutoLISP program, HED.LSP, automatically produces a similar header in existing, non-documented programs.

```
;  ********************************************************************************
;
;  DRAWMAN.LSP     (c) 1987 Autodesk, Inc.
;
;  Author: Kelvin R. Throop
;
;  Drawing revision control - A programming example using entity handles.
;
;  This program implements a crude revision control system for drawings. It
;  is supplied purely as an illustration of what can be done using handles and
;  a very small amount of AutoLISP. It does not purport to be either a full-
;  function drawing manager or the basis for implementing one.
;
;  The program requires the file REVINFO.DWG, which it inserts as a block
;  with invisible attributes when the user logs out. All blocks are inserted on
;  layer $REV and become the reference for RLIST, FINGER, SELUSER, and
;  SELECO. The revision information can then be referenced when you log
;  back on (i.e. LOGON).
;
;  Function          Description
;  --------------    ------------------
;  C:LOGON           Log onto drawing management system
;  C:LOGOUT          Add revision block at end of drawing session
;  C:END             Automatically log out user at end of session
```

```
;   C:RLIST          List revision information
;   C:FINGER         Identify who changed an entity
;   INCHAND          Increment handle
;   C:SELUSER        Select entities added by user
;   C:SELECO         Select entities by engineering change order
;
;   Global Variables  Description
;   -----------------------  -----------------
;   Files Created     Description
;   ------------------   -----------------
;   Algorithm
;   -----------------
;
;   ***************************************************************************
;
```

Project Log

Once a project's drawings are in AutoCAD form, and all the evidence of the job is on a hard disk, you may have trouble seeing the bigger picture of the job, such as how many total drawings are in the job, their exact titles, numbers, and revision and release dates. Check sets of hard copies help, but usually do not have all the information that is needed to track the drawings over the entire life of the project. Hard copies also are inconvenient when you need only a small detail about a drawing.

By keeping a project log for every job, you make coordination and information management easier. With an up-to-date collection of information about the drawings in a project, drafters and designers can easily locate drawings and track the job's progress. When the project log is properly maintained, the project manager does not have to round up all the information in person. Keep the project log in a three-ring binder followed by a drawing log form (discussed later in this appendix) for each drawing in the set.

Your project log should resemble figure B.4.

Drawing Log

Without drawing management software (and even with it, in some cases), managing many drawings among many users is a hassle. By completing and updating a drawing log for each drawing as it progresses, you place drawing facts in one place. Users can rely on the logs for information about drawings, and do not need to load drawings to verify details and revisions. Have your CAD users keep the log handy and add drawing information while they work on a drawing.

Your drawing log should resemble figure B.5.

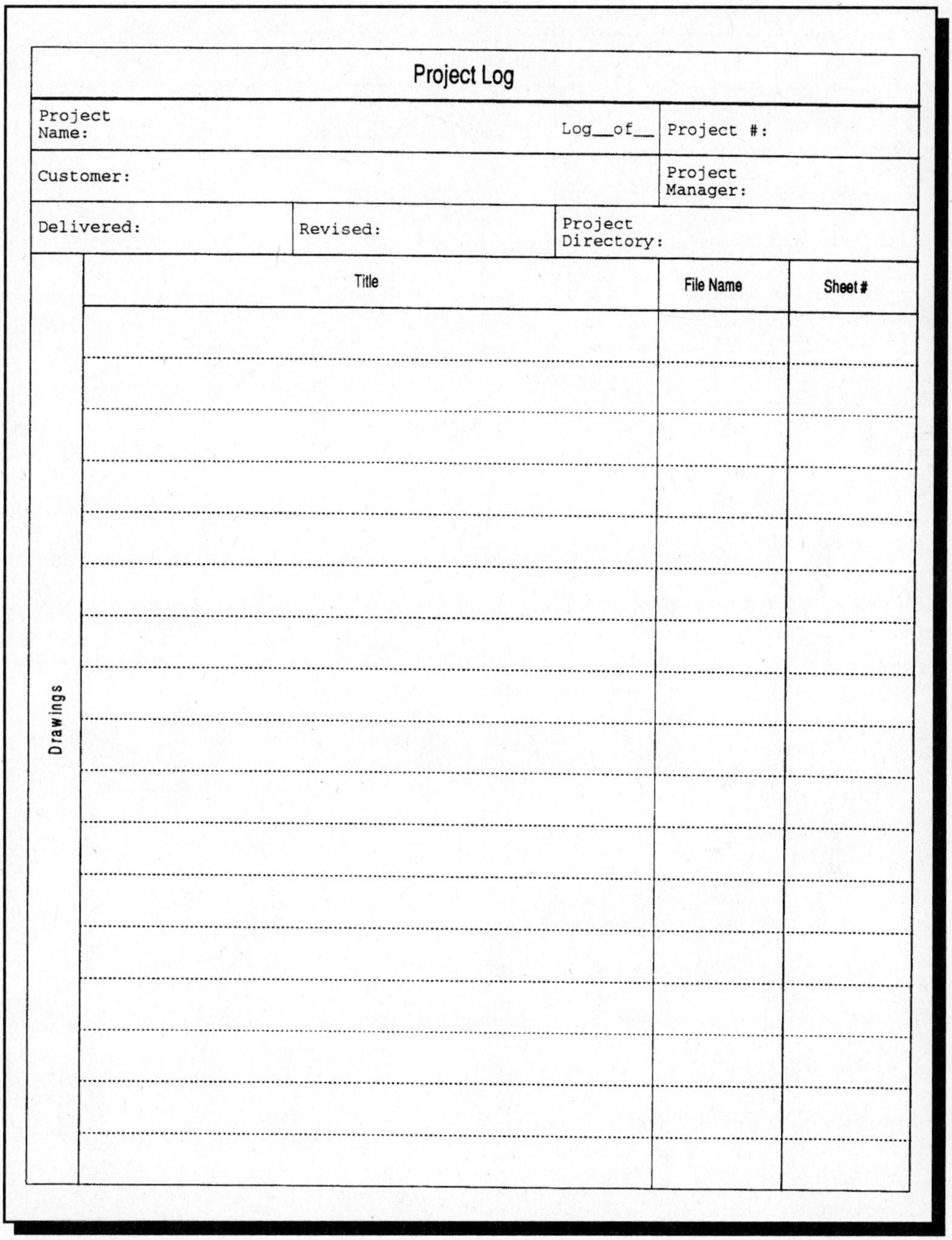

Project Log				
Project Name:		Log__of__	Project #:	
Customer:			Project Manager:	
Delivered:	Revised:		Project Directory:	

	Title		File Name	Sheet #
Drawings				

Figure B.4:
The project log.

Drawing Log		
Title:		File Name:
Scale:	Plot Size:	Project #:
Drawn By:	Checked By:	
Date Began:	Released:	
External File References:		

Revisions

Date Revised	Description

Non-Standard Blocks, Styles, Layers, Linetypes

Name	Description

Figure B.5:
The drawing log.

Block Libraries

Even if all your working drawings are organized and documented, other drawings in your office, such as symbols and typical details, still need to be managed. If you truly believe the cornerstone of CAD is "draw it once, use it forever," then you need to keep track of your drawing "building blocks." Ideally, most of your symbols and typical details either are referenced by menu macros or parametrically drawn on the fly. They should be kept in specific shared directories on a network, in standard directories on each workstation's hard disk, or even organized into separate floppy disks. If they are organized this way, your blocks should be used correctly and consistently. If they are not organized in a similar fashion, drawing consistency and quality may suffer because users will not be able to find and use approved, predrawn symbols and typical details.

Symbols and typical details should be organized and documented in the user's CAD manual. Information about often-used symbols should be included in a block library catalog. A typical block library catalog contains plots of symbols at scale, insertion points and insertion layers, proper pen weights, and associated AutoLISP routines (see fig. B.6). Commonly used details should be documented in the same way symbols are. The locations of each library should be noted for easy retrieval.

AutoCAD Specialist Evaluation Form

If your company does not have an evaluation form for documenting employee reviews, you might want to consider a form similar to the one that follows. Even if your company does use an evaluation form, it may not be specifically targeted at AutoCAD users and their jobs.

The following form uses a cumulative point system to award an overall score. Points are awarded on a scale of one to ten in the areas of general performance and technical performance. The form also is applicable if you still have some manual drafters. You can use one form to review both methods.

Give the employee one copy of the completed form during the review session, and keep one copy on file for reference. This gives the employee a tangible record of his performance review from the previous period. At the next review, you and the employee can use the previous form to compare past performance with current performance.

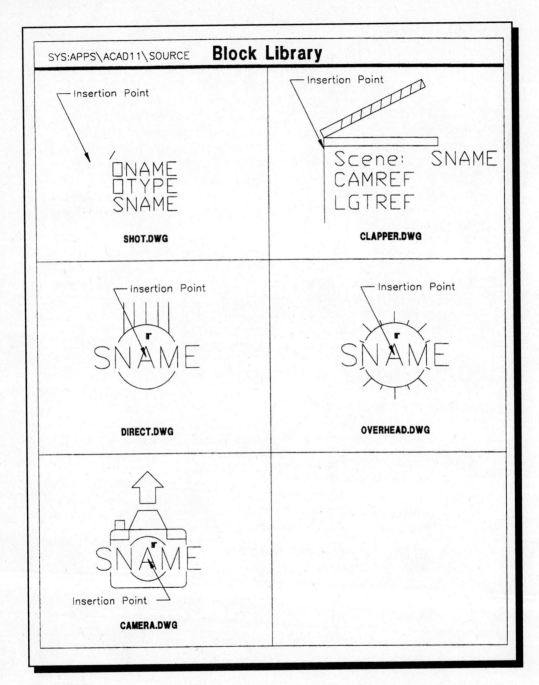

Figure B.6:
Example of a block library catalog page.

DRAFTSPERSON EVALUATION FORM

for _____

date _____

Each of the following items is scored on the basis of 0 to 10 with 10 representing a "perfect" rating.

The Overall Evaluation score is determined by adding the individual scores together. An Overall Evaluation score of 190 represents the "perfect" employee.

Overall Evaluation Score: _____

A. GENERAL PERFORMANCE

1. Pride in the finished product

   Does the employee display a desire for the finished product to appear neat, well organized and easy to read, as well as providing all the information required by the user of the product?

   Score _____

2. Motivation

   Is the employee eager to learn and to complete each assignment efficiently and to the best of his ability?

   Score _____

3. Creativity

   Does the employee offer ideas for new solutions to problems, and connect previously used solutions to new problems?

   Score _____

4. Initiative

   Does the employee carry through assignments from start to finish, within the limits of his ability, without close supervision?

   Score _____

5. Attitude

   Does the employee approach assignments with a positive frame of mind?

   Score _____

6. Attention to detail

   Is the employee's work complete, including clarification of points or ideas not obvious to the user?

   Score _____

7. Work to capacity

   Does the employee work to full capacity during heavy load periods, and use slack time for self-improvement of relevant skills?

   Score _____

8. Work with other employees

Does the employee strive to maintain a cooperative and harmonious atmosphere with other employees in the work environment?

Score _____

9. Punctuality

Does the employee consistently arrive for work on time, and make efficient use of time during company hours?

Score _____

B. TECHNICAL PERFORMANCE

1. Ability

Is the employee's technical ability commensurate with the responsibilities given? Does the employee display confidence in his ability and produce competent and professional work?

Score _____

2. Errors

Does the employee make more than the expected number of errors in his work? Does the employee accept identification of errors in a professional and constructive context?

Score _____

3. Cleanliness

Does the employee produce clean drawings free from smudges, excessive lead dust, and extraneous marks?

Score _____

4. Spatial Composition

Does the employee produce well organized drawings that are easily read and with consistent margins?

Score _____

5. Coordination

   Does the employee adequately coordinate drawing progress with the design staff to ensure timely completion and aesthetic appeal of the drawing?

   Score _____

6. Linework

   Does the employee consistently produce good quality linework of appropriate weights and types, and with complete intersections?

   Score _____

7. Lettering

   Does the employee produce readable and quality lettering? Does the employee often misspell words?

   Score _____

8. Symbols

   Does the employee consistently produced dark symbols of standard shape and size?

   Score _____

9. Detail

   Does the employee strive to render sufficient detail in appropriate drawings that lend a sense of realism to the project?

   Score _____

10. Subject Knowledge

    Is the employee eager to learn more concerning the design of the systems he drafts, and to apply that knowledge toward more accurate and complete drawings?

    Score _____

C. OVERALL EVALUATION COMMENTS

_____

_____

_____

A/E/C Layer
Guidelines

Both the AIA Task Force's CAD Layer Guidelines and the 16-Division CAD Layering Protocols are reproduced in this appendix in the forms that were current when this book was published. The 16-Division CAD Layering Protocols also are included on the *Managing and Networking AutoCAD Disk* in ASCII format, in a file named 16LAYER.TXT. For recommended usage and other information on both sets of guidelines, see Chapter 10.

AIA CAD Layer Guidelines

The AIA CAD Layer Guidelines use a hierarchial naming scheme that is based on abbreviations for data classes rather than numbers. Included is a long format that is more readable, and a short format that is easier to type. The format you use depends on the complexity of your drawings and the way you use menus and macros to assign layers. Both formats are shown in the listing that follows. The guidelines are divided into major groups by a discipline letter in the following manner:

Letter	Designates
A	Architecture, interiors, and facilities management
S	Structural
M	Mechanical

Letter	Designates
P	Plumbing
F	Fire protection
E	Electrical
C	Civil engineering and site work
L	Landscape architecture

Drawing information is divided into minor groups according to building assemblies or construction systems. Each minor group is described with a four-character abbreviation, such as WALL, DOOR, or GLAZ.

Within each minor group, layers are subdivided with a four-character modifier. The modifier is used for building-specific or drawing-specific information concerning elevations, sections, details, 3D models, or user-definable information. The following tables offer some modifiers for building and drawing information:

Building Information

Long Format	Short Format	Layer Description
*-****-IDEN	***ID	Identification tag
*-****-PATT	***PA	Cross-hatching and poche
*-****-ELEV	***EL	Vertical surfaces (3D drawings)
*-****-EXST	***EX	Existing to remain
*-****-DEMO	***DE	Existing to be demolished or removed
*-****-NEWW	***NW	New or proposed work (remodeling projects)

Drawing Information

Long Format	Short Format	Layer Description
*-****-NOTE	***NO	Notes, callouts, and key notes
*-****-TEXT	***TE	General notes and specifications
*-****-SYMB	***SY	Symbols, bubbles, and targets
*-****-DIMS	***DI	Dimensions
*-****-PATT	***PA	Cross-hatching and poche
*-****-TTLB	***TT	Title block, sheet name, and number
*-****-NPLT	***NP	Nonplot information, and construction lines
*-****-PLOT	***PL	Plotting targets and windows

The following layer is common to all major groups:

x-RDME *x*RD   Read-me layer, not to be plotted, information on file organization

In the long format, each group is separated by a hyphen to improve readability. In the short format, the discipline letter is combined with the first two letters of the minor group abbreviation and the first two letters of the modifier abbreviation.

AIA CAD Layer Guidelines

Architecture, Interiors, Facilities
Building Information Layers

Long Format	Short Format	Layer Description
A-WALL	**AWA**	**Walls**
A-WALL-FULL	AWAFU	Full-height walls, stair and shaft walls, and walls to structure
A-WALL-PRHT	AWAPR	Partial-height walls (not on reflected ceiling plans)
A-WALL-MOVE	AWAMO	Movable partitions
A-WALL-HEAD	AWAHE	Door and window headers (shown on reflected ceiling plans)
A-WALL-JAMB	AWAJA	Door and window jambs (not on reflected ceiling plans)
A-WALL-PATT	AWAPA	Wall insulation, hatching and fill
A-WALL-ELEV	AWAEL	Wall surfaces (3D views)
A-DOOR	**ADO**	**Doors**
A-DOOR-FULL	ADOFU	Full-height (to ceiling) door: swing and leaf
A-DOOR-PRHT	ADOPR	Partial-height door: swing and leaf
A-DOOR-IDEN	ADOID	Door number, hardware group, etc.
A-DOOR-ELEV	ADOEL	Doors (3D views)

Architecture, Interiors, Facilities
Building Information Layers

Long Format	Short Format	Layer Description
A-GLAZ	AGL	Windows, window walls, curtain walls, glazed partions
A-GLAZ-FULL	AGLFU	Full-height glazed walls and partitions
A-GLAX-PRHT	AGLPR	Windows and partial-height glazed partitions
A-GLAX-SILL	AGLSI	Window sills
A-GLAX-IDEN	AGLID	Window number
A-GLAX-ELEV	AGLEL	Glazing and mullions (elevation views)
A-FLOR	**AFL**	**Floor information**
A-FLOR-OTLN	AFLOT	Floor or building outline
A-FLOR-LEVL	AFLLE	Level changes, ramps, pits, and depressions
A-FLOR-STRS	AFLST	Stair treads, Escalators, and ladders
A-FLOR-RISR	AFLRI	Stair risers
A-FLOR-HRAL	AFLHR	Stair and balcony handrails and guard rails
A-FLOR-EVTR	AFLEV	Elevator cars and equipment
A-FLOR-TPTN	AFLRP	Toilet partitions
A-FLOR-SPCL	AFLSP	Architectural specialties (toilet room accessories, display cases)
A-FLOR-WDWK	AFLWD	Architectural woodwork (field-built cabinets and counters)
A-FLOR-CASE	AFLCA	Casework (manufactured cabinets)
A-FLOR-APPL	AFLAP	Appliances
A-FLOR-OVHD	AFLOV	Overhead skylights and overhangs (usually dashed lines)
A-FLOR-RAIS	AFLRA	Raised floors
A-FLOR-IDEN	AFLID	Room numbers, names, targets, etc.
A-FLOR-PATT	AFLPA	Paving, tile, and carpet patterns
A-EQPM	**AEQ**	**Equipment**
A-EQPM-FIXD	AEQFI	Fixed equipment

Architecture, Interiors, Facilities
Building Information Layers

Long Format	Short Format	Layer Description
A-EQPM-MOVE	AEQMO	Moved equipment
A-EQPM-NICN	AEQNI	Equipment not in contract
A-EQPM-ACCS	AEQAC	Equipment access
A-EQPM-IDEN	AEQID	Equipment identification numbers
A-EQPM-ELEV	AEQEL	Equipment surfaces (3D views)
A-FURN	**AFU**	**Furniture**
A-FURN-FREE	AFUFR	Free-standing furniture (desks, credenzas, etc.)
A-FURN-CHAR	AFUCH	Chairs and other seating
A-FURN-FILE	AFUFI	File cabinets
A-FURN-PNLS	AFUPN	Furniture system panels
A-FURN-WKSF	AFUWK	Furniture system work surface components
A-FURN-STOR	AFUST	Furniture system storage components
A-FURN-POWR	AFUPO	Furniture system power designations
A-FURN-IDEN	AFUID	Furniture numbers
A-FURN-PLNT	AFUPL	Plants
A-FURN-PATT	AFUPA	Finish patterns
A-FURN-ELEV	AFUEL	Furniture (3D views)
A-CLNG	**ACL**	**Ceiling information**
A-CLNG-GRID	ACLGR	Ceiling grid
A-CLNG-OPEN	ACLOP	Ceiling and roof penetrations
A-CLNG-TEES	ACLTE	Main tees
A-CLNG-SUSP	ACLSU	Suspended elements
A-CLNG-PATT	ACLPA	Ceiling pattern
A-ROOF	**ARO**	**Roof**
A-ROOF-OTLN	AROOT	Roof outline
A-ROOF-LEVL	AROLE	Level changes
A-ROOF-STRS	AROST	Stair-treads and ladders

Architecture, Interiors, Facilities
Building Information Layers

Long Format	Short Format	Layer Description
A-ROOF-RISR	ARORI	Stair-risers
A-ROOF-HRAL	AROHR	Stair handrails, nosings, and guardrails
A-ROOF-PATT	AROPA	Roof-surface patterns (hatching)
A-ROOF-ELEV	AROEL	Roof surfaces (3D views)
A-AREA	**AAR**	**Area calculations**
A-AREA-PATT	AARPA	Area cross-hatching
A-AREA-IDEN	AARID	Room numbers, tenant identifications, and area calculations
A-AREA-OCCP	AAROC	Occupant or employee names
A-ELEV	**AEL**	**Interior and exterior elevations**
A-ELEV-OTLN	AELOT	Building outlines
A-ELEV-FNSH	AELFN	Finishes, woodwork, and trim
A-ELEV-CASE	AELCA	Wall-mounted casework
A-ELEV-FIXT	AELFI	Miscellaneous fixtures
A-EELV-SIGN	AELSI	Signage
A-ELEV-PATT	AELPA	Textures and hatch-patterns
A-ELEV-IDEN	AELID	Component identification numbers
A-SECT	**ASE**	**Sections**
A-SECT-MCUT	ASEMC	Material cut by section
A-SECT-MBND	ASEMB	Material beyond section
A-SECT-PATT	ASEPA	Textures and hatch-patterns
A-SECT-IDEN	ASEID	Component identification numbers
A-DETL	**ADE**	**Details**
A-DETL-MCUT	ADEMC	Material cut by section
A-DETL-BND	ADEMB	Material beyond section-cut
A-DETL-PATT	ADEPA	Textures and hatch-patterns
A-DETL-IDEN	ADEID	Component identification numbers

Architecture, Interiors, Facilities
Drawing Information Layers

Long Format	Short Format	Layer Description
A-SHBD	ASH	Sheet border and title block line work
A-SHBD-TTLB	ASHTT	Project title block
A-SHBD-LOGO	ASHLO	Office or project logo
A-PFLR	APF	Floor plan
A-PLGS	APL	Large-scale floor plan
A-PCLG	APC	Reflected ceiling plan
A-PROF	APR	Roof plan
A-PXFU	APX	Fixtures and furniture plan
A-PEQM	APE	Equipment plan
A-PMFN	APM	Materials and finishes plan
A-PDEM	APD	Demolition plan
A-PARE	APA	Area calculations
A-POCC	APO	Occupancy plan
A-P***	AP*	Other plan drawings
A-ELEV	AEL	Interior and exterior elevations
A-SECT	ASE	Building and wall sections
A-DETL	ADE	Details
A-SCHD	ASC	Schedules and title block sheets
A-****-NOTE	A**NO	Notes, callouts, and key notes
A-****-SYMB	A**SY	Symbols, bubbles, and targets
A-****-DIMS	A**DI	Dimensions
A-****-PATT	A**PA	Cross-hatching and poche
A-****-TTLB	A**TT	Title block sheet name and number
A-****-NPLT	A***NP	Nonplot information and construction lines
A-****-PLOT	A**PL	Plotting targets and windows

Structural
Building Information Layers

Long Format	Short Format	Layer Description
S-GRID	SGR	Column grid
S-GRID-EXTR	SGREX	Column grid outside building
S-GRID-INTER	SBRIN	Column grid inside building
S-GRID-DIMS	SBRDI	Column grid dimensions
S-GRID-IDEN	SGRID	Column grid tags
S-FNDN	**SFN**	**Foundation**
S-FNDN-PILE	SFNPI	Piles and drilled piers
S-FNDN-RBAR	SFNRB	Foundation reinforcing
S-SLAB	**SSL**	**Slab**
S-SLAB-EDGE	SSLED	Edge of slab
S-SLAB-RBAR	SSLRB	Slab reinforcing
S-SLAB-JOIN	SSLJO	Slab control joints
S-ABLT	**SAB**	**Anchor bolts**
S-COLS	**SCO**	**Columns**
S-WALL	**SWA**	**Structural bearing or shear walls**
S-METL	**SME**	**Miscellaneous metal**
S-FRAM	**SFR**	**Framing plan (beams, joists)**
S-FRAM-BEAM	**SFRBE**	**Beams**
S-FRAM-JOIS	SFRJO	Joists
S-FRAM-DECK	SFRDE	Structural floor deck
S-ELEV	**SEL**	**Elevations**
S-ELEV-OTLN	SELOT	Building outlines
S-ELEV-PATT	SELPA	Textures and hatch-patterns
S-ELEV-IDEN	SELID	Identification numbers

Structural
Building Information Layers

Long Format	Short Format	Layer Description
S-SECT	**SSE**	**Sections**
S-SECT-MCUT	SSEMC	Material cut by section
S-SECT-BND	SSEMB	Material beyond section-cut
S-SECT-PATT	SSEPA	Textures and hatch-patterns
S-SECT-IDEN	SSEID	Identification numbers
S-DETL	**SDE**	**Details**
S-DETL-MCUT	SDEMC	Material cut by section
S-DETL-BND	SDEMB	Material beyond section-cut
S-DETL-PATT	SDEPA	Textures and hatch-patterns
S-DETL-IDEN	SDEID	Identification numbers

Structural
Drawing Information Layers

Long Format	Short Format	Layer Description
S-SHBD	SSH	Sheet border and title block line work
S-SHBD-TTLB	SSHTT	Project title block
S-SHBD-LOGO	SSHLO	Office or project logo
S-PFND	SPF	Foundation plan
S-PFSR	SPS	Structural framing plan
S-PCOL	SPO	Column plan
S-P***	SP*	Other structural plans
S-ELEV	SEL	Elevations
S-SECT	SSE	Sections
S-DETL	SDE	Details
S-SCHD	SSC	Schedules and title block sheets
S-****-NOTE	S**NO	Notes, callouts, and key notes
S-****-TEXT	S**TE	General notes and specifications
S-****-SYMB	S**SY	Symbols, bubbles, and targets
S-****-DIMS	S**DI	Dimensions

Structural
Drawing Information Layers

Long Format	Short Format	Layer Description
S-****-PATT	S**PA	Cross-hatching and poche
S-****-TTLB	S**TT	Sheet name and number
S-****-NPLT	S***NP	Nonplot information and construction lines
S-****-PLOT	S**PL	Plotting targets and windows

Mechanical
Building Information Layers

Long Format	Short Format	Layer Description
M-BRIN	**MBR**	**Brine systems**
M-BRIN-EQPM	MBREQ	Brine system equipment
M-BRIN-PIPE	MBRPI	Brine system piping
M-CHIM	**MCH**	**Prefabricated chimneys**
M-CMPA	MCM	Compressed air systems
M-CMPA-CEQP	MCMCE	Compressed air equipment
M-CMPA-CPIP	MCMCP	Compressed air piping
M-CMPA-PEQP	MCMPE	Process air equipment
M-CMPA-PPIP	MCMPP	Process air piping
M-CONT	**MCO**	**Controls and instrumentation**
M-CONT-THER	MCOTH	Thermostats
M-CONT-WIRE	MCOWI	Low voltage wiring
M-DUST	**MDU**	**Dust and fume collection system**
M-DUST-EQPM	MDUEQ	Dust and fume collection equipment
M-DUST-DUCT	MDUDU	Dust and fume ductwork
M-ELHT-EQPM	**MELEQ**	**Electric heat equipment**
M-ENER	**MEN**	**Energy management system**
M-ENER-EQPM	MENEQ	Energy management equipment
M-ENER-WIRE	MENWI	Energy management wiring

Mechanical
Building Information Layers

Long Format	Short Format	Layer Description
M-EXHS	**MEX**	**Exhaust system**
M-EXHS-EQPM	MEXEQ	Exhaust system equipment
M-EXHS-DUST	MEXDU	Exhaust system ductwork
M-EXHS-RFEQ	MEXRF	Rooftop exhaust equipment
M-FUEL	**MFU**	**Fuel system piping**
M-FUEL-GPRP	MFUGP	Fuel gas process piping
M-FUEL-GGEP	MFUGG	Fuel gas general piping
M-FUEL-OPRP	MFUOP	Fuel oil process piping
M-FUEL-OGEP	MFUOG	Fuel oil general piping
M-HVAC	**MHV**	**Hvac system**
M-HVAC-CDFF	MHVCD	Hvac ceiling diffusers
M-HVAC-ODFF	MHVOD	Hvac other diffusers
M-HVAC-DUCT	MHVDU	Hvac ductwork
M-HVAC-EQPM	MHVEQ	Hvac equipment
M-HOTW	**MHO**	**Hot water heating system**
M-HOTW-EQPM	MHOEQ	Hot water equipment
M-HOTW-PIPE	MHOPI	Hot water piping
M-CWTR	**MCW**	**Chilled water systems**
M-CWTR-PIPE	MCWPI	Chilled water piping
M-CWTR-EQPM	MCWEQ	Chilled water equipment
M-MACH	**MMA**	**Machine shop equipment**
M-MDGS	**MMD**	**Medical gas systems**
M-MDGS-EQPM	MMDEQ	Medical gas equipment
M-MDGS-PIPE	MMDPI	Medical gas piping
M-PROC	**MPR**	**Process systems**
M-PROC-EQPM	MPREQ	Chilled equipment
M-PROC-PIPE	MPRPI	Process piping

Mechanical
Building Information Layers

Long Format	Short Format	Layer Description
M-REFG	**MRE**	**Refrigeration systems**
M-REFG-EQPM	MREEQ	Refrigeration equipment
M-REFG-PIPE	MREPI	Refrigeration piping
M-SPCL	**MSP**	**Special systems**
M-REFG-EQPM	MSPEQ	Special systems equipment
M-REFG-PIPE	MSSPI	Special systems piping
M-STEM	**MST**	**Steam systems**
M-STEM-CONP	MSTCO	Steam systems condensate piping
M-STEM-EQPM	MSTEQ	Steam systems equipment
M-STEM-LPIP	MSTLP	Low pressure steam piping
M-STEM-HPIP	MSTHP	High pressure steam piping
M-TEST	**MTE**	**Test equipment**
M-ELEV	**MEL**	**Elevations**
M-ELEV-OTLN	MELOT	Building outlines
M-ELEV-PATT	MELPA	Textures and hatch patterns
M-ELEV-IDEN	MELID	Identification numbers
M-SECT	**MSE**	**Sections**
M-SECT-MCUT	MSEMC	Material cut by section
M-SECT-MBND	MSEMB	Material beyond section
M-SECT-PATT	MSEPA	Textures and hatch patterns
M-SECT-IDEN	MSEID	Identification numbers
M-DETL	**MDE**	**Details**
M-DETL-MCUT	MDEMC	Material cut by section
M-DETL-MBND	MDEMB	Material beyond section
M-DETL-PATT	MDEPA	Textures and hatch patterns
M-DETL-IDEN	MDEID	Identification numbers

Mechanical
Drawing Information Layers

Long Format	Short Format	Layer Description
M-SHBD	MSH	Sheet border and title block line work
M-SHBD-TTLB	MSHTT	Project title block
MSHBD-LOGO	MSHLO	Office or project logo
M-PPIP	MPP	Piping plan
M-PDUC	MPD	Duct plan
M-PEXD	MPE	Exhaust duct plan
M-PHVA	MPH	Hvac plan
M-PSTM	MPS	Steam piping plan
M-PWCH	MPW	Chilled water piping plan
M-PMED	MPM	Special medical
M-PCON	MPC	Controls plan
M-P***	MP*	Other mechanical plans
M-ELEV	MEL	Elevations
M-SECT	MSE	Sections
M-DETL	MDE	Details
M-SCHD	MSC	Schedules and title block sheets
M-****-NOTE	M**NO	Notes, callouts, and key notes
M-****-SYMB	M**SY	Symbols, bubbles, and targets
M-****-DIMS	M**DI	Dimensions
M-****-PATT	M**PA	Cross-hatching and poche
M-****-TTLB	M**TT	Sheet name and number
M-****-NPLT	M***NP	Nonplot information and construction lines
M-****-PLOT	M**PL	Plotting targets and windows

Plumbing
Building Information Layers

Long Format	Short Format	Layer Description
P-ACID	**PAC**	**Acid, alkaline, and oil waste systems**
P-ACID-PIPE	PACPI	Acid, alkaline, and oil waste piping
P-DOMQ	**PDO**	**Domestic hot and cold water systems**
P-DOMW-EQPM	PDOEQ	Domestic hot and cold water equipment
P-DOMW-PIPE	PDOPI	Domestic hot and cold water piping
P-DOMW-RISR	PDORI	Domestic hot and cold water risers
P-SANR	**PSA**	**Sanitary drainage**
P-SANR-PIPE	PSAPI	Sanitary piping
P-SANR-FIXT	PSAFI	Plumbing fixtures
P-SANR-FLDR	PSAFL	Floor drains
P-SANR-RISR	PSARI	Sanitary risers
P-STRM	**PST**	**Storm drainage systems**
P-STRM-PIPE	PSTPI	Storm drain piping
P-STRM-RISR	PSTRI	Storm drain risers
P-STRM-RFDR	PSTRF	Roof drains
P-EQPM	**PEQ**	**Plumbing miscellaneous equipment**
P-FIXT	**PFI**	**Plumbing fixtures**
P-ELEV	**PEL**	**Elevations**
P-ELEV-OTLN	PELOT	Building outlines
P-ELEV-PATT	PELPA	Textures and hatch patterns
P-ELEV-IDEN	PELID	Identification numbers

Plumbing
Building Information Layers

Long Format	Short Format	Layer Description
P-SECT	**PSE**	**Sections**
P-SECT-MCUT	PSEMC	Material cut by section
P-SECT-MBND	PSEMB	Material beyond section
P-SECT-PATT	PSEPA	Textures and hatch patterns
P-SECT-IDEN	PSEID	Identification numbers
P-DETL	**PDE**	**Details**
P-DETL-MCUT	PDEMC	Material cut by section
P-DETL-MBND	PDEMB	Material beyond section
P-DETL-PATT	PDEPA	Textures and hatch patterns
P-DETL-IDEN	PDEID	Identification numbers

Plumbing
Drawing Information Layers

Long Format	Short Format	Layer Description
P-SHBD	PSH	Sheet border and title block line work
P-SHBD-TTLB	PSHTT	Project title block and project name
P-SHBD-LOGO	PSHLO	Project or office logo
P-PPLM	PPP	Plumbing plan
P-PDRA	PPD	Storm drainage
P-PSAN	PSA	Sanitary drainage plan
P-P***	PP*	Other plumbing plans
P-RISR	PRI	Plumbing riser diagrams
P-ELEV	PEL	Elevations
P-SECT	PSE	Sections
P-DETL	PDE	Details
P-SCHD	PSC	Schedules and title block sheets
P-****-NOTE	P**NO	Notes, callouts, and key notes
P-****-TEXT	P**TE	General notes and specifications
P-****-SYMB	P**SY	Symbols, bubbles, and targets

Plumbing
Drawing Information Layers

Long Format	Short Format	Layer Description
P-****-DIMS	P**DI	Dimensions
P-****-PATT	P**PA	Cross-hatching and poche
P-****-TTLB	P**TT	Sheet name and number
P-****-NPLT	P***NP	Nonplot information and construction lines
P-****-PLOT	P**PL	Plotting targets and windows

Fire Protection
Building Information Layers

Long Format	Short Format	Layer Description
F-CO2S	**FCO**	**CO_2 system**
F-CO2S-PIPE	FCOPI	CO_2 sprinkler piping
F-CO2S-EQPM	PCOEQ	CO_2 equipment
F-HALN	**FHA**	**Halon**
F-HALN-EQPM	FHAEQ	Halon equipment
F-HALN-PIPE	FHAPI	Halon piping
F-SPRN	**FSP**	**Fire protection sprinkler system**
F-SPRN-CLHD	FSPCL	Sprinkler head (ceiling)
F-SPRN-OTHD	FSPOT	Sprinkler head (other)
F-SPRN-PIPE	FSPPI	Sprinkler piping
F-STAN	**FST**	**Fire protection standpipe system**
F-PROT	**FPR**	**Fire protection systems**
F-PROT-EQPM	FPREQ	Fire system equipment (fire hose cabinet extinguishers)
F-PROT-ALRM	FPRAL	Fire alarm
F-PROT-SMOK	FPRSM	Smoke detectors or heat sensors

Fire Protection
Building Information Layers

Long Format	Short Format	Layer Description
F-ELEV	**FEL**	**Elevations**
F-ELEV-OTLN	FELOT	Building outlines
F-ELEV-PATT	FELPA	Textures and hatch patterns
F-ELEV-IDEN	FELID	Identification numbers
F-SECT	**FSE**	**Sections**
F-SECT-MCUT	FSEMC	Material cut by section
F-SECT-MBND	FSEMB	Material beyond section
F-SECT-PATT	FSEPA	Textures and hatch patterns
F-SECT-IDEN	FSEID	Identification numbers
F-DETL	**FDE**	**Details**
F-DETL-MCUT	FDEMC	Material cut by section
F-DETL-MBND	FDEMB	Material beyond section
F-DETL-PATT	FDEPA	Textures and hatch patterns
F-DETL-IDEN	FDEID	Identification numbers

Fire Protection
Drawing Information Layers

Long Format	Short Format	Layer Description
F-SHBD	FSH	Sheet border and title block line work
F-SHBD-TTLB	FSHTT	Project title block and project name
F-SHBD-LOGO	FSHLO	Project or office logo
F-PSPR	FPS	Sprinkler plan
F-RISR	FRI	Sprinkler riser diagrams
F-PFPE	FPF	Fire protection equipment plan
F-P***	FP*	Other fire protection system plans
F-ELEV	FEL	Elevations
F-SECT	FSE	Sections
F-DETL	FDE	Details

Fire Protection
Drawing Information Layers

Long Format	Short Format	Layer Description
F-SCHD	FSC	Schedules and title block sheets
F-****-NOTE	F**NO	Notes, callouts, and key notes
F-****-TEXT	F**TE	General notes and specifications
F-****-SYMB	F**SY	Symbols, bubbles, and targets
F-****-DIMS	F**DI	Dimensions
F-****-PATT	F**PA	Cross-hatching and poche
F-****-TTLB	F**TT	Sheet name and number
F-****-NPLT	F***NP	Nonplot information and construction lines
F-****-PLOT	F**PL	Plotting targets and windows

Electrical
Building Information Layers

Long Format	Short Format	Layer Description
E-LITE	**ELI**	**Lighting**
E-LITE-SPCL	ELISP	Special lighting
E-LITE-EMER	ELIEM	Emergency lighting
E-LITE-EXIT	ELIEX	Exit lighting
E-LITE-CLNG	ELICL	Ceiling-mounted lighting
E-LITE-WALL	ELIWA	Wall-mounted lighting
E-LITE-FLOR	ELIFL	Floor-mounted lighting
E-LITE-OTLN	ELIOT	Lighting outline for background (optional)
E-LITE-NUMB	ELINU	Lighting circuit numbers
E-LITE-ROOF	ELIRO	Roof lighting
E-LITE-SITE	ELISI	Site lighting (see also civil group)
E-LITE-SWCH	ELISW	Lighting switches
E-LITE-CIRC	ELICI	Lighting circuits
E-LITE-IDEN	ELIID	Luminaire identification and text

Electrical
Building Information Layers

Long Format	Short Format	Layer Description
E-POWR	**EPO**	**Power**
E-POWR-WALL	EPOWA	Power wall-outlets and receptacles
E-POWR-CLNG	EPOCL	Power ceiling receptacles and devices
E-POWR-PANL	EPOPA	Power panels
E-POWR-EQPM	EPOEQ	Power equipment
E-POWR-SWBD	EPOSW	Power switchboards
E-POWR-CIRC	EPOCI	Power circuits
E-POWR-URAC	EPOUR	Under floor raceways
E-POWR-UCPT	EPOUC	Under carpet wiring
E-POWR-CABL	EPOCA	Cable trays
E-POWR-FEED	EPOFE	Feeders
E-POWR-BUSW	EPOBU	Busways
E-POWR-NUMB	EPONU	Power circuit numbers
E-POWR-IDEN	EPOID	Power identification and text
E-POWR-SITE	EPOSI	Site power (see also civil group)
E-POWR-ROOF	EPORO	Roof power
E-POWR-OTLN	EPOOT	Power outline for backgrounds
E-CTRL	**ECT**	**Electrical contol systems**
E-CTRL-DEVC	ECTDE	Control system devices
E-CTRL-WIRE	ECTWI	Control system wiring
E-GRND	**EGR**	**Ground system**
E-GRND-CIRC	EGRCI	Ground system circuits
E-GRND-REFR	EGRRE	Reference ground system
E-GRND-EQUI	EGREQ	Equipotential ground system
E-GRND-DIAG	EGRDI	Ground system diagram
E-ELEV	**EEL**	**Elevations**
E-ELEV-OTLN	EELOT	Building outlines
E-ELEV-PATT	EELPA	Textures and hatch patterns
E-ELEV-IDEN	EELID	Identification numbers

Electrical
Building Information Layers

Long Format	Short Format	Layer Description
E-SECT	**ESE**	**Sections**
E-SECT-MCUT	ESEMC	Material cut by section
E-SECT-MBND	ESEMB	Material beyond section
E-SECT-PATT	ESEPA	Textures and hatch patterns
E-SECT-IDEN	ESEID	Identification numbers
E-DETL	**EDE**	**Details**
E-DETL-MCUT	EDEMC	Material cut by section
E-DETL-MBND	EDEMB	Material beyond section
E-DETL-PATT	EDEPA	Textures and hatch patterns
E-DETL-IDEN	EDEID	Identification numbers

Electrical Auxiliary Systems
Major and Minor Groups

Long Format	Short Format	Layer Description
E-AUXL	**EAU**	**Auxiliary systems**
E-LTNG	ELT	Lightning protection system
E-FIRE	EFI	Fire alarm and fire extinguishers
E-COMM	ECO	Telephone and communication outlets
E-DATA	EDA	Data outlets
E-SOUN	ESO	Sound or PA system
E-TVAN	ETV	TV antenna system
E-CCTV	ECC	Closed-circuit TV
E-NURS	ENU	Nurse-call system
E-SERT	ESE	Security
E-PGNG	EPG	Paging system
E-DICT	EDI	Central dictation system
E-BELL	EBE	Bell system
E-CLOK	ECL	Clock system
E-ALRM	EAL	Miscellaneous alarm system
E-INTC	EIN	Intercom system

Electrical Auxiliary Systems
Modifiers

Long Format	Short Format	Layer Description
E-****-CIRC	E**CI	Circuit information
E-****-IDEN	E**ID	Identification text
E-****-EQPM	E**EQ	Equipment layout
E-****-DEVC	E**DE	Utilization device layout
E-****-WALL	E**WA	Wall-mounted device layout
E-****-CLNG	E**CL	Ceiling-mounted device layout
E-****-FLOR	E**FL	Floor-mounted device layout
E-****-DGRM	E**DG	Interconnection diagram
E-****-WIRE	E**WI	Wiring line work and information
E-****-NUMB	E**NU	Numbers for systems (zones, etc.)

Electrical
Drawing Information Layers

Long Format	Short Format	Layer Description
E-SHBD	ESH	Sheet border and title block line work
E-SHBD-TTLB	ESHTT	Project title block and project name
E-SHBD-LOGO	ESHLO	Project or office logo
E-PLIT	EPL	Lighting plan
E-PPOW	EPP	Power plan
E-PCOM	EPC	Communication systems plan
E-PAUX	EPA	Auxiliary systems plan
E-PROF	EPR	Electrical roof plan
E-P***	EP*	Other electrical plans
E-LEGN	ELE	Legend of symbols
E-1LIN	E1L	One-line diagrams
E-RISR	ERI	Riser diagram
E-ELEV	EEL	Elevations
E-SECT	ESE	Sections
E-DETL	EDE	Details
E-SCHD	ESC	Schedules and title block sheets
E-****-NOTE	E**NO	Notes, callouts, and key notes

Electrical
Drawing Information Layers

Long Format	Short Format	Layer Description
E-****-TEXT	E**TE	General notes and specifications
E-****-SYMB	E**SY	Symbols, bubbles, and targets
E-****-DIMS	E**DI	Dimensions
E-****-PATT	E**PA	Cross-hatching and poche
E-****-TTLB	E**TT	Sheet name and number
E-****-NPLT	E***NP	Nonplot information and construction lines
E-****-PLOT	E**PL	Plotting targets and windows

Civil Engineering and Site Work
Building Information Layers

Long Format	Short Format	Layer Description
C-PROP	**CPR**	**Property lines and survey benchmarks**
C-PROP-ESMT	CPRES	Easements, right-of-ways, and setback lines
C-PROP-BRNG	CPRBR	Bearings and distance labels
C-PROP-CONS	CPRCO	Construction controls
C-TOPO	**CTO**	**Proposed contour lines and elevations**
C-TOPO-EXST	CTOEX	Existing contour lines and elevations to remain
C-TOPO-DEMO	CTODE	Existing contour lines and elevations to be changed
C-TOPO-SPOT	CTOSP	Spot elevations
C-TOPO-BORE	CTOBO	Test borings
C-TOPO-RTWL	CTORT	Retaining wall
C-BLDG	**CBL**	**Proposed building footprints**
C-BLDG-EXST	CBLEX	Footprints of existing buildings to remain
C-BLDG-DEMO	CBLDE	Footprints of existing buildings to be demolished

Civil Engineering and Site Work
Building Information Layers

Long Format	Short Format	Layer Description
C-PKNG	**CPK**	**Parking lots**
C-PKNG-STRP	CPKST	Parking lot striping and handicapped symbol
C-PKNG-CARS	CPKCA	Graphic illustration of cars
C-PKNG-ISLD	CPKIS	Parking islands
C-PKNG-EXST	CPKEX	Existing parking lots to remain
C-PKNG-DEMO	CPKDE	Existing parking lots to be demolished
C-PKNG-DRAN	CPKDR	Parking lot drainage slope indications
C-ROAD	**CRO**	**Roads**
C-ROAD-CNTR	CROCN	Center lines
C-ROAD-CURB	CROCU	Curbs
C-ROAD-EXST	CROEX	Existing parking road to remain
C-ROAD-DEMO	CRODE	Existing parking road to be demolished
C-STRM	**CST**	**Storm drainage catch basins and manholes**
C-STRM-UNDR	CSTUN	Storm drainage pipe (underground)
C-ECTR	**CEC**	**Site electrical substations and poles**
C-ECTR-LITE	CECLI	Site lighting
C-ECTR-UNDR	CECUN	Underground electrical lines
C-ECTR-POLE	CECPO	Electric poles
C-ECTR-OVHD	CECOV	Overhead lines
C-COMM	**CCO**	**Site communication (telephone poles, boxes, towers)**
C-COMM-UNDR	CCOUN	Underground communication lines
C-COMM-OVHD	CCOOV	Overhead communication lines
C-WATR	**CWA**	**Domestic water (manholes, pumping stations, storage tanks)**
C-WATR-UNDR	CWAUN	Domestic water (underground lines)

Civil Engineering and Site Work
Building Information Layers

Long Format	Short Format	Layer Description
C-FIRE	**CFI**	**Fire protection hydrants and connections**
C-FIRE-UNDR	CFIUN	Fire protection (underground lines)
C-NGAS	**CNG**	**Natural gas manholes, meters, and storage tanks**
C-NGAS-UNDR	CNGUN	Natural gas (underground lines)
C-SSWR	**CSS**	**Sanitary sewer (manholes, pumping stations)**
C-SSWR-UNDR	CSSUN	Sanitary sewer (underground lines)
C-ELEV	**CEL**	**Elevations**
C-ELEV-OTLN	CELOT	Building outlines
C-ELEV-PATT	CELPA	Textures and hatch patterns
C-ELEV-IDEN	CELID	Identification numbers
C-SECT	**CSE**	**Sections**
C-SECT-MCUT	CSEMC	Material cut by section
C-SECT-MBND	CSEMB	Material beyond section
C-SECT-PATT	CSEPA	Textures and hatch patterns
C-SECT-IDEN	CSEID	Identification numbers
C-DETL	**CDE**	**Details**
C-DETL-MCUT	CDEMC	Material cut by section
C-DETL-MBND	CDEMB	Material beyond section
C-DETL-PATT	CDEPA	Textures and hatch patterns
C-DETL-IDEN	CDEID	Identification numbers

Civil Engineering and Site Work
Drawing Information Layers

Long Format	Short Format	Layer Description
C-SHBD	CSH	Sheet border and title block line work
C-SHBD-TTLB	CSHTT	Project title block and project name
C-SHBD-LOGO	CSHLO	Project or office logo
C-PSIT	CPS	Site plan
C-PELC	CPE	Site electrical systems plan
C-PUTL	CPU	Site utility plan
C-PGRD	CPG	Grading plan
C-PPAV	CPP	Paving plan
C-P***	CP*	Other site, landscape or civil plans
C-ELEV	CEL	Elevations
C-SECT	CSE	Sections
C-DETL	CDE	Details
C-SCHD	CSC	Schedules and title block sheets
C-****-NOTE	C**NO	Notes, callouts, and key notes
C-****-TEXT	C**TE	General notes and specifications
C-****-SYMB	C**SY	Symbols, bubbles, and targets
C-****-DIMS	C**DI	Dimensions
C-****-PATT	C**PA	Cross-hatching and poche
C-****-TTLB	C**TT	Sheet name and number
C-****-NPLT	C***NP	Nonplot information and construction lines
C-****-PLOT	C**PL	Plotting targets and windows

Landscape Architecture
Building Information Layers

Long Format	Short Format	Layer Description
L-PLNT	**LPL**	**Plant and landscape materials**
L-PLNT-TREE	LPLTR	New trees
L-PLNT-TXST	LPLTX	Existing trees to remain
L-PLNT-TDMO	LPLTD	Existing trees to be removed

Landscape Architecture
Building Information Layers

Long Format	Short Format	Layer Description
L-PLNT-GRND	LPLGR	Ground covers and vines
L-PLNT-BEDS	LPLBE	Rock, bark, and other landscaping beds
L-PLNT-TURF	LPLTU	Lawn areas
L-PLNT-PLAN	LPLPL	Schematic planting plans
L-IRRG	**LIR**	**Irrigation system**
L-IRRG-SPKL	LIRSP	Irrigation sprinklers
L-IRRG-PIPE	LIRPI	Irrigation piping
L-IRRG-EQPT	LIREQ	Irrigation equipment
L-IRRG-COVR	LIRCO	Irrigation coverage
L-WALK	**LWA**	**Walks and steps**
L-WALK-PATT	LWKPA	Walks and steps cross-hatch patterns
L-SITE	**LSI**	**Site improvements**
L-SITE-FENC	LSIFE	Fencing
L-SITE-WALL	LSIWA	Walls
L-SITE-STEP	LSIST	Steps
L-SITE-DECK	LSIDE	Decks
L-SITE-BRDG	LSIBR	Bridges
L-SITE-POOL	LSIPO	Pools and spas
L-SITE-SPRT	LSISP	Sports fields
L-SITE-PLAY	LSIPL	Play structures
L-SITE-FURN	LSIFU	Site furnishings
L-ELEV	**LEL**	**Elevation**
L-ELEV-OTLN	LELOT	Building outlines
L-ELEV-PATT	LELPA	Textures and hatch patterns
L-ELEV-IDEN	LELID	Identification numbers
L-SECT	**LSE**	**Sections**
L-SECT-MCUT	LSEMC	Material cut by section

Landscape Architecture
Building Information Layers

Long Format	Short Format	Layer Description
L-SECT-MBND	LSEMB	Material beyond section
L-SECT-PATT	LSEPA	Textures and hatch patterns
L-SECT-IDEN	LSEID	Identification numbers
L-DETL	**LDE**	**Details**
L-DETL-MCUT	LDEMC	Material cut by section
L-DETL-MBND	LDEMB	Material beyond section
L-DETL-PATT	LDEPA	Textures and hatch patterns
L-DETL-IDEN	LDEID	Identification numbers

Landscape Architecture
Drawing Information Layers

Long Format	Short Format	Layer Description
L-SHBD	LSH	Sheet border and title block line work
L-SHBD-TTLB	LSHTT	Project titleblock and project name
L-SHBD-LOGO	LSHLO	Project or office logo
L-PSIT	LPS	Site plan
L-PPLA	LPL	Planting drawing
L-PIRR	LPI	Irrigation drawing
L-PWLK	LPW	Walks and paving plan
L-P***	LP*	Other landscape plan drawings
L-ELEV	LEL	Elevations
L-SECT	LSE	Sections
L-DETL	LDE	Details
L-SCHD	LSC	Schedules and title block sheets
L-****-NOTE	L**NO	Notes, callouts, and key notes
L-****-TEXT	L**TE	General notes and specifications
L-****-SYMB	L**SY	Symbols, bubbles, and targets
L-****-DIMS	L**DI	Dimensions
L-****-PATT	L**PA	Cross-hatching and poche
L-****-TTLB	L**TT	Sheet name and number

Landscape Architecture
Drawing Information Layers

Long Format	Short Format	Layer Description
L-****-NPLT	L***NP	Nonplot information and construction lines
L-****-PLOT	L**PL	Plotting targets and windows

16-Division CAD Layering Protocols

The 16-Division CAD Layering Protocols use a five-digit layer number based on the Construction Specifications Institute (CSI) 16-division MasterSpec system. The following are the sixteen divisions:

1 Specific
2 Civil/Landscape
3 Concrete
4 Masonry
5 Metals
6 Wood & plastics
7 Thermal & moisture protection
8 Doors & windows
9 Finishes
10 Specialties
11 Equipment
12 Furnishings and CAD oddities
13 Special construction
14 Conveying systems
15 Mechanical
16 Electrical

In most divisions, the last digit is used as a modifier:

00001 Existing to remain
00002 Existing to be removed
00003 New
00004 Text
00005 Dimensions
00006 Hatch patterns
00007 User-defined
00008 User-defined
00009 User-defined

Layer 05125, for example, would contain structural steel framing dimensions. Layer 07802 would contain existing skylights to be removed. The entire 16-Division CAD Layering Protocols follow.

DIVISION 1: SPECIFIC

Layer Name	Layer Description
01010	Column grids, bubbles and text
01020	Building footprint
01030	North arrow
01040	Location symbol
01050	Graphic scale
01060	Section lines, etc.
01070	Match lines, etc.
01080	Detail title
01090	Exp joint
01110	Generic dimensions, arrows, etc.
01120	Key notes
01130	User definable
01140	User definable
01150	Room numbers/boxes
01160	Room names
01170	User definable
01180	User definable
01190	User definable
01210	Title block — X-fine pen – 0.25mm
01220	Title block — fine pen – 0.35mm
01230	Title block — med pen – 0.50mm
01240	Title block — bold pen – 0.70mm
01250	Licensure
01260	Logos – a/e
01270	Logos – client
01280	Logos – project
01510	1 hr fire rating symbol

16DIV Layer Protocols, Version 3.0, Copyright 1990, by Facilities Data Management

DIVISION 1: SPECIFIC

Layer Name	Layer Description
01520	2 hr fire rating symbol
01530	3 hr fire rating symbol
01540	4 hr fire rating symbol
01610	Site area calculations
01620	Bldg area calculations
01630	Dept area calculations
01640	Zone area calculations
01710	Site volume calculations
01720	Bldg volume calculations
01730	Dept volume calculations
01740	Zone volume calculations

DIVISION 2: CIVIL/LANDSCAPE

Layer Name	Layer Description
02010	Boring locations
02020	Property lines
02050	Buildings/structures
02210	Grading (contour lines)
02220	Excavation lines (limits)
02300	Tunnels (utility or pedestrian)
02450	Railroad trackage
02480	Marine work (sea walls, etc.)
02520	Roads
02527	Vehicles
02530	Curbs
02560	Airfield paving
02580	Pavement marking
02610	Manholes
02640	Hydrants
02660	Water distribution
02667	Domestic water (potable)

DIVISION 2: CIVIL/LANDSCAPE

Layer Name	Layer Description
02668	Fire water
02669	Heating water
02670	Water wells
02680	Fuel distribution
02687	Natural gas
02688	Oil
02689	Steam
02710	Drainage piping
02720	Storm sewer
02730	Sanitary sewer
02740	Septic systems
02770	Ponds and reservoirs
02780	Electric power distribution
02790	Communications distribution
02810	Landscape irrigation
02820	Fountains
02830	Fences and gates
02840	Walkways
02860	Playfields
02870	Hardscape
02890	Footbridges
02910	Trees
02920	Shrubs
02930	Boulders
02940	Groundcover
02950	Planting plan
02960	Landscape schedule

DIVISION 3: CONCRETE

Layer Name	Layer Description
03200	Concrete reinforcement
03300	Concrete (cast-in-place)
03340	Concrete edge
03400	Precast concrete

DIVISION 4: MASONRY

Layer Name	Layer Description
04210	Brick
04220	CMU
04250	Masonry veneer
04270	Glass unit masonry
04290	Adobe masonry
04400	Stone masonry
04550	Refractories

DIVISION 5: METALS

Layer Name	Layer Description
05120	Structural steel framing
05160	Geodesic dome systems
05170	Metal space frames
05210	Steel joists
05310	Metal deck
05410	Load-bearing metal stud system
05500	Mtl fabrications (unistrut, etc)
05510	Metal stairs and ladders
05520	Handrails/guardrails

DIVISION 6: WOOD & PLASTICS

Layer Name	Layer Description
06100	Rough carpentry
06130	Heavy timber construction
06150	Wood chord metal joists
06180	Glu-Lam construction
06190	Prefab wood trusses
06200	Millwork
06410	Custom casework
06430	Stairs and handrails
06450	Trim
06470	Screens and shutters
06610	Fiberglass fabrications
06630	Historic plastic reproductions

DIVISION 7: THERMAL AND MOISTURE PROTECTION

Layer Name	Layer Description
07100	Waterproofing membranes
07210	Building insulation
07220	Roof/deck insulation
07240	Exterior cementitious insulation
07250	Fireproofing
07310	Roofing shingles
07320	Roofing tiles
07330	Roof overhang
07400	Preformed roofing
07600	Flashing and sheetmetal
07720	Roof accessories
07800	Skylights

DIVISION 8: DOORS & WINDOWS

Layer Name	Layer Description
08100	HM doors
08110	HM frames
08120	Aluminum doors and frames
08210	Wood doors
08310	Sliding doors
08320	Security/cold storage doors
08330	Coiling doors
08350	Prefab accordian doors
08370	Aircraft hanger doors
08410	Aluminum entrances/storefronts
08470	Revolving doors
08510	Steel windows
08520	Aluminum windows
08610	Wood windows (incl plastic clad)
08650	Special windows
08810	Glass and glazing
08910	Glazed steel curtainwalls
08920	Glazed aluminum curtainwalls
08950	Translucent wall/skylite systems

DIVISION 9: FINISHES

Layer Name	Layer Description
09120	Ceiling suspension systems
09200	Lath and plaster partitions *
09250	Gypsum board partitions *
09520	Plaster ceiling assemblies
09550	Wood flooring
09600	Stone/masonry flooring

= metal or wood stud independent

DIVISION 10: SPECIALTIES

Layer Name	Layer Description
10100	Chalk/tack/marker boards
10150	Toilet compartments/cubicles
10200	Wall louver assemblies
02500	Service wall systems
10270	Access floor systems
10300	Manufactured fireplaces/stoves
10350	Flagpoles
10400	Identifying devices
10450	Pedestrian control devices
10500	Lockers/basket racks
10520	Fire protection specialties
10550	Postal facility specialties
10610	Prefab partition systems
10650	Operable partition systems
10670	Storage shelving/closet systems
10750	Telephone specialties
10800	Toilet accessories

DIVISION 11: EQUIPMENT

Layer Name	Layer Description
11010	Maintenance
11020	Security/vault
11030	Teller and banking
11040	Ecclesiastical
11050	Library
11060	Theater and stage
11070	Musical instrument
11100	Mercantile
11110	Laundry/dry cleaning
11120	Vending
11130	Audio-visual

DIVISION 11: EQUIPMENT

Layer Name	Layer Description
11140	Service station
11150	Parking control
11160	Loading dock
11170	Solid waste handling
11190	Detention
11400	Food service
11450	Residential appliances
11460	Unit kitchens
11470	Darkroom
11480	Athletic/gymnasium
11600	Laboratory
11650	Planetarium
11710	Medical sterilizing
11720	Exam/treatment
11730	Patient care
11740	Dental
11750	Optical
11780	Mortuary

DIVISION 12: FURNISHINGS and CAD ODDITIES

Layer Name	Layer Description
12200	CAD symbols for people
12300	Manufactured casework
12400	CAD symbols for office equipment
12610	Open-office systems
12620	Furniture
12700	Multiple seating systems
12760	Telescoping bleachers
12770	Pews and benches
12800	Interior plants and planters

DIVISION 13: SPECIAL CONSTRUCTION

Layer Name	Layer Description
13010	Air supported structures
13030	Prefab special purpose rooms
13120	Pre-engineered structures
13150	Swimming pools
13170	Animal shelters/enclosures
13600	Solar energy systems
13700	Wind energy systems

DIVISION 14: CONVEYING SYSTEMS

Layer Name	Layer Description
14100	Dumbwaiters
14200	Elevators
14300	Escalators
14320	Moving walkways
14500	Material handling systems
14520	Hospital transport systems
14550	Conveyors/conveyor belts
14560	Chutes

DIVISION 15: MECHANICAL

Layer Name	Layer Description
15310	Wet pipe sprinkler
15320	Dry pipe sprinkler
15410	HW piping
15420	CW piping
15430	Waste/vent piping
15440	Plumbing fixtures
15450	Plumbing equipment
15470	Plumbing special systems
15480	Medical gases
15487	Medical air

DIVISION 15: MECHANICAL

Layer Name	Layer Description
15488	Medical NO^2
15489	Medical O^2
15490	Medical gases, cont.
15497	Medical vacuum
15498	Medical deionized water
15499	Medical distilled water
15510	Steam piping
15520	Condensate piping
15530	Refrigerant piping
15550	Boilers
15610	Furnaces
15650	Compressors
15670	Condensers
15680	Chillers
15710	Cooling towers
15750	Heat exchangers
15780	Packaged air conditioners
15830	Heating terminal units
15850	Air handlers
15860	Supply ducts
15870	Return ducts
15880	Supply diffusers
15900	Return air grills/registers

DIVISION 16: ELECTRICAL

Layer Name	Layer Description
16110	Raceways
16120	Wiring (circuiting)
16130	Devices
16160	Cabinets
16210	Generators
16310	Substations

DIVISION 16: ELECTRICAL

Layer Name	Layer Description
16320	Transformers
16420	Switchgear
16430	Meters
16510	Lighting fixtures
16530	Emergency fixtures
16630	Battery power systems
16720	Alarm/detection systems
16730	Data cable systems
16740	Telephone systems
16750	Nurse-call systems
16760	Intercom systems
16770	Public address systems
16780	Television systems
16850	Electrical resist. heating

A CAD Manager
Resource Guide

Most CAD managers and users have trouble keeping up with the continually changing CAD industry; this resource guide should help make the job easier. Wherever possible, a contact address and phone number are provided so that you can get more information on these valuable resources.

Selected Books

Look for these books at a bookstore or public library near you.

Building Local Area Networks
Patrick H. Corrigan and Aisling Guy
M&T Publishing, Inc. ©1989

An excellent book on choosing and installing Novell NetWare networks by recognized NetWare experts.

Customizing AutoCAD, Second Edition
J. Smith and R. Gesner
New Riders Publishing ©1989

The definitive guide to complete AutoCAD customization. Includes many examples and exercises.

Fundamentals of Interactive Computer Graphics
James D. Foley and Andries Van Dam
Addison-Wesley Publishing Co. ©1982

A popular textbook on the basics of CAD graphics.

High Output Management
Andrew S. Grove
Random House ©1983

Philosophies of management by the president of Intel Corp.

Inside AutoLISP, First Edition
J. Smith and R. Gesner
New Riders Publishing ©1989

The de facto reference and tutorial on the AutoLISP programming language.

Local Area Networks
Donne Florence, CAL Industries
John Wiley & Sons, Inc. ©1989

A good product-independent primer on networking concepts and technology.

Networking Personal Computers
Michael Durr and Mark Gibbs
Que Corp. ©1989

An excellent guide to network selection and current technologies by former Novell employees.

Sketchpad: A Man-Machine Graphical Communication System
Ivan Sutherland
Garland Publishing, Inc. ©1980

The historical and technical account of Sketchpad by Ivan Sutherland in his master's degree thesis.

The Situational Leader
Dr. Paul Hersey
Warner Books ©1984

The complete exposition of Dr. Hersey's leadership behavior model.

UNIX Administrator's Guide for System V
Rebecca Thomas and Rik Farrow
Prentice Hall ©1989

A complete guide to UNIX system administration.

Using Novell NetWare
Bill Lawrence
Que Corp. ©1990

An in-depth guide to NetWare usage, configuration, and optimization.

Magazines

The following magazines can help you stay up to date on many topics. They also can help you find hardware and software vendors for your AutoCAD and networking needs.

Architectural & Engineering Systems
12 issues: U.S.–$40, Canada–$60, elsewhere–$80
Mediacom, Inc.
769 Whalers Way, Suite 100-A
Fort Collins, CO 80525
(303) 229-0029

Reviews and features on microcomputer and minicomputer CAD use for architects and engineers.

CADalyst
Professional Management of AutoCAD Systems
12 issues: U.S.–$39; Canada–$47; elsewhere–$90
314 E. Holly Street #106
Bellingham, WA 98225-9904
(604) 737-1088

An excellent source of information on AutoCAD usage primarily focused on the A/E/C trades.

CADENCE
Using AutoCAD in the Professional Environment
12 issues: $34.95
Ariel Communications, Inc.
P.O. Box 203550
Austin, TX 78720-3550
(512) 250-1700

The first magazine dedicated to AutoCAD, covering a broad array of professional topics.

CAD User
12 issues: £34 in Europe, Scandinavia, and UK; £39 elsewhere
24 High Street
Beckenham
Kent
BR3 1AY
081-663-3818

The complete and only European guide to AutoCAD.

Computer Graphics Review
12 issues: U.S.–$48; elsewhere–$84
Free to qualified subscribers
Intertec Publishing Corp.
P.O. Box 12950
Overland Park, KS 66215
(913) 541-6678

Computer Graphics Review reports on the leading-edge of computer graphics on all popular platforms.

Computer Graphics World
12 issues: $42
PennWell Publishing Company
P.O. Box 122
Tulsa, OK 74101-9966
(800) 331-4463 Ext. 400
(918) 831-9497 (FAX)

The organizational publication of the National Computer Graphics Association on computer graphics technology and trends.

Design Management
12 issues: $35
Communication Channels, Inc.
P.O. Box 1145
Skokie, IL 60076-9736
(312) 647-7124

Design Management reports on the application of workstation and PC-based CAD to real world A/E/C design projects.

InfoWorld
Weekly: $110; free to qualified subscribers
P.O. Box 3014
Northbrook, IL 60065
(708) 564-0694

Almost everything that happens in the computer industry appears first in InfoWorld.

LAN
The Local Area Networking Magazine
12 issues: $19.97
Miller Freeman Publications
P.O. Box 41094
Nashville, TN 37204
(800) 933-3321

News, features, reviews, tutorials, and interviews on local area networking.

LAN Technology
The Technical Resource for Network Integrators
12 issues: $29.97
M&T Publishing
P.O. Box 52315
Boulder, CO 80321-2315
(800) 456-1654

A useful guide to the more technical aspects of network installation and management primarily targeted at NetWare users, but also encompassing other popular systems.

LAN Times
McGraw-Hill's Information Source for Network Managers
Semimonthly: free to qualified U.S. subscribers; Canada $39.95 to $49; elsewhere $60 to $120
McGraw-Hill
P.O. Box 652
Hightstown, NJ 08520
(609) 426-7070

Product reviews, test results, late-breaking news, and product developments in the local area networking industry with a heavy emphasis on Novell NetWare.

Macintosh-Aided Design
12 issues: $39.95
Auerbach Publishers
210 South Street
Boston, MA 02111
(800) 950-1217

An objective journal of all the CAD software available for the Macintosh.

Mechanical Engineering Systems
6 issues: $125
Auerbach Publishers
210 South Street
Boston, MA 02111
(800) 950-1216

A very technical look at software-independent CAD theories and practice for machine design engineers.

MicroCAD News
Integrated Solutions for Design and
Engineering
12 issues: $34.95
Ariel Communications, Inc.
P.O. Box 203550
Austin, TX 78720-3550
(512) 250-1700

*The vendor-independent guide to PC
CAD trends, technologies, and news.*

Network Computing
Computing in a Network Environment
12 issues: free to qualified subscribers
for a limited time
P.O. Box 4751
Manhasset, NY 11030-4751
(516) 562-5071
(516) 562-5474 (FAX)

*A young but capable guide to corporate
multi-vendor networking.*

Network World
The Newsweekly of User Networking
Strategies
Weekly: free to qualified subscribers
P.O. Box 1021
Southeastern, PA 19398-9979
(508) 875-6400

*An independent news magazine
dedicated to enterprise-wide
networking and communications.*

Articles and Reports

The following documents offer detailed, expert advice on specific CAD or networking
issues. Most of these documents are available from the contacts listed here. Some
articles may be available from magazine back issues at your public library.

*1990 PSMJ CADD Application and
User Survey*
$145
Practice Management Associates, Ltd.
Ten Midland Ave.
Newton, MA 02158
(617) 965-0055

*The third annual report summarizing
the usage and costs of CAD, compiled
from a survey of 442 design firms
totalling 46,000 employees.*

*A Theory of Productivity in the Creative
Process*
James T. Brady, IBM General
Products Division
IEEE CG&A May 1986

*An article on cognitive research applied
to computer graphics productivity
within IBM.*

Datapro Manufacturing Automation Series
CAD/CAM/CAE Systems 1 year: $412
Management and Planning 1 year: $412
Datapro Research
600 Delran Parkway
Delran, NJ 08075
(800) 328-2776

A huge volume of information on CAD hardware and software of all types, and objective reports on management and technologies, updated monthly.

Distributed Application Processing in the NetWare Environment
Part No. 452-760076-001
Novell Inc.
122 East 1700 South
Provo, UT 84606
(800) LANSWER

A fairly objective overview of distributed computing and Novell's product approach.

Managing Personal Computers in the Large Organization
Nolan, Norton & Co.
Send $2.00 and a self-addressed, stamped envelope to:
Nolan, Norton & Co.
The Nolan, Norton Institute
One Cranberry Hill
Lexington, MA 02173
(617) 862-8820

An executive-level report prepared for and with Lotus Development Corp. on economic and end-user management methods.

NetWare Buyer's Guide
Part No. 482-000020-003
Novell Inc.
122 East 1700 South
Provo, UT 84606
(800) LANSWER

A nearly 400-page guide to Novell NetWare products.

Network Backup
Part No. 479-000063-001
Novell Inc.
122 East 1700 South
Provo, UT 84606
(800) LANSWER

A complete essay on network backup basics, hardware technology, software technology, and data protection methodologies from Novell Research.

Selecting Personnel to Work on the Interactive Graphics System
UCRL-83663
Frederick J. Norton
Lawrence Livermore Laboratory
©1979

A condensed version of Mr. Norton's thesis on human behavioral patterns, benefits, and social and educational problems as a result of implementing CAD.

System Reliability Report
Part No. 479-000018-001
Novell Inc.
122 East 1700 South
Provo, UT 84606
(800) LANSWER

An in-depth look at network system reliability and risk analysis with general countermeasure guidelines, and a description of SFT NetWare with benchmarks.

The Cost of LAN Downtime
$295 (executive summary free)
Infonetics
3235 Kifer Road, Suite 100
Santa Clara, CA 95051
(408) 746-2500
(408) 746-2418 (FAX)

An independent study of the effects of LAN downtime on 100 Fortune 1000 companies.

When Faced With the Office Wiring Decision, "Let the Buyer Beware"
Belden Wire and Cable
P.O. Box 1980
Richmond, IN 47375-1980
(800) BELDEN-4

The pros and cons of shielded versus unshielded twisted pair wiring for network cabling, from a major cable manufacturer.

Newsletters

The following newsletters provide expert opinions on CAD and networking technology.

CE Computing Review
ASCE's Newsletter on Computing in Civil Engineering
12 issues: $96 for members; $120 for nonmembers
American Society of Civil Engineers
345 E. 47th St.
New York, NY 10017
(800) 548-ASCE

News and reviews of CAD topics relating to civil engineering.

Design Systems Strategies Newsletter
The Management Report on Automation and Productivity for A/E Design Professionals
12 issues: $149
Design & Systems Research Publishing Co., Inc.
P.O. Box 500

Chamisal, NM 87521
(505) 587-1010
(505) 587-1015 (FAX)

Informative articles on A/E/C CAD systems management by industry leaders.

Layer 1700
Facilities Data Management
P.O. Box 675
Gig Harbor, WA 98335
(206) 857-2185
(206) 857-2186 (FAX)

News about the 16-division layer protocols and CAD management tips from the protocols' author and chief proponent. Contact the publisher for subscription information.

The Anderson Report
12 issues: $247
4525 E. Industrial Street, Suite 4L
Simi Valley, CA 93063
(805) 581-1184
(805) 581-1239 (FAX)

An executive management report on high-end workstation CAD trends and news.

The Clarke Burton News Analysis
An Analysis of Significant News
Events in the Network Computing
Industry
17 issues: $595
Clarke Burton Corp.
Attn: Sales Manager
215 South State St.
Salt Lake City, UT 84111
(800) 657-6340
(801) 595-8705 (FAX)

This periodical shines a critical light on developments in the local area networking industry as they happen.

The Clarke Burton Report
The Authority in Network Computing
12 issues: $995
Clarke Burton Corp.
Attn: Sales Manager
215 South State St.
Salt Lake City, UT 84111
(800) 657-6340
(801) 595-8705 (FAX)

This periodical provides independent, strategic analysis of network technologies and vendors for the networking executive. From a founder and former executive vice president of Novell and a former Novell author.

Trade Shows and Seminars

At each of the following events, CAD managers can get hands-on experience and see demonstrations of new CAD and networking products, hear expert advice on a variety of topics, and find instruction at all levels of expertise.

AEC Expo
Held annually at various sites
Expoconsul International, Inc.
c/o Compusystems, Inc.
P.O. Box 6430
2535 25th Ave.
Broadview, IL 60153-6430
(800) 766-EXPO

One of the leading conferences for A/E/C professionals. The expo offers tracks and workshops on management, networking, construction, and many other topics.

A/E/C Systems/AutoCAD Expo/
Advanced CAD Management Forum
Held annually at various sites
A/E/C Systems
P.O. Box 310316
Newington, CT 06131-0316

The largest show for A/E/C CAD managers and users.

AutoFACT
Held annually at various sites
Society of Manufacturing Engineers
One SME Drive
P.O. Box 930
Dearborn, MI 48121
(800) 733-ASME

The automotive industry's primary CAD/CAM/CIM and robotics expo.

Effective CADD Production Management Workshop
Philip M. Bennett
Program Director
Department of Engineering
Professional Development
University of Wisconsin at Madison
432 North Lake Street
Madison, WI 53706
(608) 263-4705

An annual program developed for the present and future CAD manager to increase the knowledge base necessary for effective decision making and creative management.

Techniques, Applications, and Control Systems for Quality Working Drawing Production
Philip M. Bennett
Program Director
Department of Engineering
Professional Development
University of Wisconsin at Madison
432 North Lake Street
Madison, WI 53706
(608) 263-4705

An annual program focusing on how to achieve high quality working drawings/graphic communications using state-of-the-art automation systems—from CAD to systems drafting applications.

Advanced CAD Production Management Workshop
Techniques, Applications and Control Systems for Quality Working Drawing Production
Philip M. Bennett
Program Director
Department of Engineering
Professional Development
University of Wisconsin at Madison
432 North Lake Street
Madison, WI 53706
(608) 263-4705

An annual workshop structured for the more experienced CAD manager to explore and evaluate successful management techniques.

NCGA Conference and Exposition
Held annually at various sites
2722 Merrilee Drive
Suite 200
Fairfax, VA 22031
(800) 225-NCGA

An annual conference and exposition, sponsored by the National Computer Graphics Association, and dedicated to computer graphics applications in architecture, engineering, graphic design and publishing, manufacturing/ operations, marketing, sales and finance, MIS/IRM, and research and development.

National Design Engineering Show and Conference
P.O. Box 7005
North Suburban, IL 60199-7005
(203) 964-0000

A comprehensive show for machine design engineers including short courses on design sponsored by the American Society of Mechanical Engineers, the Autodesk CAD/CAM Showplace, numerous CAD/CAM/ CAE/CIM and manufacturing products displays, and special pavilions.

Networld
Held semi-annually at various sites
Bruno Blenheim, Inc.
Trade Show Management
385 Sylvan Ave.
Englewood Cliffs, NJ 07632
(800) 444-EXPO Ext. 143
(201) 569-1153 (FAX)

The premiere local area networking showplace.

Professional Associations

The following associations give the CAD manager a national support network of like-minded professionals, providing on-going career development and industry promotion.

National Computer Graphics Association
2722 Merrilee Drive, Suite 200
Fairfax, VA 22031
(800) 225-NCGA
(703) 698-9600
(703) 560-2752 (FAX)

The leading association for the advancement of computer graphics at all levels and in all industries.

National Association of CAD/CAM Operators
NACO
10801 Hammerly, Suite 220
Houston, TX 77043
(713) 932-6352
(713) 932-8473 (FAX)

$50 membership fee; testing fees additional

NACO is a nonprofit professional organization founded solely for the recognition, advancement, and promotion of CAD operators.

American Management Association
Attn: Director of Membership
The American Management Association Building
135 West 50th Street
New York, NY 10124-0019
(212) 903-8270

$150 annual dues per individual

An international membership-based, not-for-profit educational organization dedicated to broadening the management knowledge and skills of people, and by doing so, strengthening their organizations.

The CADD Management Institute
Strategic Systems Group
1431 Brassie Ave.
Chicago, IL 60422
(708) 799-0729
or
1313 Fifth St. S.E.
Minneapolis, MN 55414
(612) 379-3807

Computer-related information management association for the design and construction industry. Maintains a professional contact network, publishes a quarterly journal, performs funded research, provides discounts on CAD products and services, and hosts an annual management conference concurrent with the A/E/C Systems show.

AutoCAD User Groups

Your local AutoCAD user group is one of the best places to find help with AutoCAD problems and to get involved in all kinds of activities in your area. Check the following list for the group nearest you. If the information for your group is out of date (user groups move often), check with your local AutoCAD dealer.

Special thanks to *CADalyst* magazine for making its listing available.

Alaska AutoCAD Users Group
560 E. 34th Avenue
Anchorage, AK 99503
(907) 561-1666

CAD Users of Birmingham
P.O. Box 43462
Birmingham, AL 35243
(205) 969-1984

AutoCAD Users Group
P.O. Drawer 580
Eufaula, AL 36027
(205) 687-3543

AutoCAD Users Group
2130 Automation Drive
Leeds, AL 35094
(205) 640-7058

Arkansas MicroCAD Users Group
2801 S. University Avenue
Little Rock, AR 72204
(501) 569-8222

Western Area User Groups
4100 East Broadway
Suite 150
Phoenix, AZ 85040-8810
(602) 437-0405

Phoenix Chapter AutoCAD Users Group
4220 W. Northern
Suite 119
Phoenix, AZ 85051
(602) 266-7883

Tucson Area AutoCAD Users Group
6701 S. Midvale Park Road
Tucson, AZ 85746

AutoCAD Users Group
13717 Artesia Boulevard
Cerritos, CA 90701
(213) 926-1511

AutoCAD User Group
300 West Pontiac Way
Clovis, CA 93613
(209) 275-5561

AutoCAD Users Group
5055 Santa Teresa Boulevard
Gilroy, CA 95020
(707) 847-1400

CAD Group International
13198 Green Horn Road
Grass Valley, CA 95945
(916) 273-9647

Healdsburg AutoCAD User Group
6329 West Dry Creek Road
Healdsburg, CA 95448
(707) 433-8954

Valley AutoCAD User Group
4 North Main Street
Lodi, CA 95240
(209) 334-2332

Los Angeles Area AutoCAD User Group
5301 Laurel Canyon Boulevard
#108
North Hollywood, CA
91607-2736
(818) 762-9966

Los Angeles AEC User Group
6425 Hollywood Boulevard
#349
Los Angeles, CA 90028
(213) 856-9275

Oakland Area AutoCAD Users Group
3317 Brundell Drive
Oakland, CA 94602
(415) 530-8870

Orange County AutoCAD Users
2011 West Chapman
Suite 100
Orange, CA 92668
(714) 385-1132

Coachella Valley AutoCAD Users Group
66780 E. 4th Street
Suite A
Desert Hot Springs, CA 92240
(619) 329-0055

Silicon Valley AutoCAD Users Group
777 California Avenue
Suite 100
Palo Alto, CA 94304
(415) 326-8686

AutoCAD Users Group
6695 Owens Drive
Pleasanton, CA 94566
(415) 463-0431

AUGIE (AutoCAD Users Group
Inland Empire)
900 E. Washington Street
Suite 160
Colton, CA 92324
(714) 370-3600

Sacramento AutoCAD Users Group
P.O. Box 0840
Folsom, CA 95630-0840
(916) 666-3187

AutoCAD Users Group of San Diego
122 Nardo Avenue
Solana Beach, CA 92075-2021
(619) 755-0854

San Francisco AutoCAD User Group
662 Bay Street
San Francisco, CA 94133
(415) 923-9228

San Francisco/Marin AutoCAD Users
Group
85 Federal Street
San Francisco, CA 94107
(415) 777-4025

AutoCAD Users Group of Santa Cruz
221 20th Avenue
Santa Cruz, CA 95062
(408) 462-0448

California Central Coast AutoCAD
Users
3839 Constellation Road
Lompoc, CA 93436
(805) 928-2794

Sonoma County AutoCAD User Group
503 Squirrel Court
Santa Rosa, CA 95401
(707) 538-0643

Redwood Empire AutoCAD Users'
2320 Marinship Way
Sausalito, CA 94965
(707) 762-5772

Colorado Springs AutoCAD User Group
1303 E. Platte Avenue
Colorado Springs, CO 80909
(303) 603-7066

Professional AutoCAD Users Group
P.O. Box 527
Broomfield, CO 80020-0527
(303) 433-8393

Front Range AutoCAD User's Group
10110 Depew Street
Westminster, CO 80020
(303) 465-0413

Northern Colorado AutoCAD Users
Group
P.O. Box 682
Fort Collins, CO 80522
(303) 352-6000

AutoCAD Users Group
P.O. Box 1081
West Hartford, CT 06107
(203) 236-2365

Greater Hartford AutoCAD Users Group
100 Allyn Street, 4th Floor
Hartford, CT 06103·
(203) 525-8651

Orange Research Inc
140 Cascade Boulevard
Milford, CT 06460
(203) 877-5657

KishinSujan Peabody Engineering
39 Maple Tree Avenue
Stamford, CT 06906
(203) 327-7000

Brandywine Area AutoCAD User Group
c/o Gore & Assoc.,
750 Otts Chapel Road
Newark, DE 19714
(302) 368-2575

Broward County AutoCAD Users Group
5601 North Powerline Road
Suite 303
Fort Lauderdale, FL 33309
(305) 791-2900

*NW Florida AutoCAD Professionals
Association*
242 Vicki Leigh Road
Fort Walton Beach, FL 32548-1314
(904) 862-3330

Pompano/South Florida Users Group
2003 Cypress Creek Road
Fort Lauderdale, FL 33309
(305) 772-7300

Club CADD
6318 Holly Bay Drive
Jacksonville, FL 32211
(904) 396-5583

Electro Design Engineering, Inc.
P.O. Box 3270
Brandon, FL 34299
(813) 646-5481

AutoFab with AutoCAD
4730 N.W. 128th Street
Miami, FL 33054
(305) 685-7978

Odessa/Tampa AutoCAD Users Group
2150 Byrd Drive
Odessa, FL 33556
(813) 920-7434

Central Florida AutoCAD Users Group
P.O. Box 1340
Orlando, FL 32802
(407) 646-4824

AutoCAD Users of Palm Beaches
P.O. Box 15318
West Palm Beach, FL 33416-5318
(305) 793-3030

Pensacola AutoCAD User Group
1412 Croquet Drive
Cantonment, FL 32533
(904) 476-1082

Pensacola CAD User Group
P.O. Drawer 12526
Pensacola, FL 32573-2526
(904) 433-5601

Tampa Bay AutoCAD Users Group
P.O. Box 12248
Petersburgh, FL 33733
(813) 381-2000

Southern Electric Users Group
Bldg. 64A
Perimeter Center East, Bin 202
Atlanta, GA 30345
(404) 668-2756

Middle Georgia CAD Group
P.O. Box 110
Macon, GA 31202-0110
(912) 745-4945

Savannah Area AutoCAD User Group
(SAUG)
P.O. Box 23192
Savannah, GA 31403
(912) 233-9003

Hawaii AutoCAD Users Group (HAUG)
c/o CADTECH
1188 Bishop Street
#2206
Honolulu, HI 96813-3309
(808) 526-2886

Mid Iowa AutoCAD Users Group
1015 Tuttle Street
Des Moines, IA 50309
(515) 244-6000

ComputerLand
101 North Court
Ottumwa, IA 52501
(515) 682-5468

Idaho AutoCAD User's Group
P.O. Box 1059
Caldwell, ID 83606
(208) 454-4572

Chicago Computer Society
AutoCAD SIG
P.O. Box 8681
Chicago, IL 60680
(312) 942-0705

AutoCAD Users Group
1600 1st Avenue E.
Milan, IL 61264
(309) 787-1761

Central Illinois AutoCAD Users
2200 East Eldorado Street
Decatur, IL 62525
(217) 421-2265

Greater Chicago AutoCAD Users Group
Inc.
1412 West Hood
Chicago, IL 60660
(312) 648-1155

Central Illinois AutoCAD Users Group
110 East Main Street
Suite 209
Ottawa, IL 61350
(815) 433-5865

Dedicated Registered AutoCAD
Workers
701 E. South Street
Albion, IN 46701
(219) 636-2028

Indy AutoCAD Users Group
122 W. Carmel Drive
Carmel, IN 46032
(317) 575-9606

AutoCAD Users and Abusers Group
1108 S. High Street
P.O. Box 7013
South Bend, IN 46618-1096
(219) 232-3900

Association of Central Indiana Users Group
1231 Cumberland Avenue, #A
West Lafayette, IN 47906
(317) 497-1550

SW Kansas CAD User's Group
1007 Eaman Road
Garden City, KS 67846
(316) 275-0144

AutoCAD Users Group
KC-CAD 1250 N. Winchester
Suite D
Olathe, KS 66061
(913) 764-2203

Mid Kansas ACAD User Group
P.O. Box 17
Salina, KS 67402
(913) 825-1611

Western Kentucky AutoCAD Users Group
909 Happy Valley Road
Glasgow, KY 42141
(502) 651-8891

Bluegrass Area AutoCAD Users Group
237 Moloney Building
Cooper Drive
Lexington, KY 40506
(606) 257-3650

Kentuckiana AutoCAD Users Group (KAUG)
435 South Third Street
Louisville, KY 40202
(502) 569-3600

Baton Rouge AutoCAD Users Group
9969 Professional Boulevard
Baton Rouge, LA 70809
(504) 387-0303

Lafayette AutoCAD User Group
P.O. Box 51408
Lafayette, LA 70505
(318) 264-4313

CAD Com
3200 Ridgelake Drive
#211
Metairie, LA 70002
(504) 835-4984

The Boston Computer Society
One Center Plaza
Boston, MA 02108
(617) 367-8088

Cape Cod AutoCAD Users Group
P.O. Box 1430
Buzzards Bay, MA 02532-1430
(508) 888-3841

Greater Boston AutoCAD Users Group
P.O. Box 119
Lowell, MA 01853
(617) 666-2006

Baltimore Area AutoCAD Users Group
836 Ritchie Highway
Severna Park, MD 21146
(301) 647-8686

Baltimore AutoCAD User's Dialog
(BAUD)
800 S. Rolling Road
Baltimore MD 21228
(301) 455-4110

CAD/CAM Special Interest Group
15 Orchard Way, North
Rockville, MD 20854
(301) 279-7593

Central Maine AutoCAD Users Group
c/o Platz Assoc.
2 Great Falls Plaza
Auburn, ME 04210
(207) 784-2941

Eastern Maine ACAD Users Group
354 Hogan Road
Bangor, ME 04401
(207) 941-4619

AutoCAD Users Group
Dyer Street
North Berwick, ME 03906
(207) 676-2271

Southern Maine CADD Users Group
P.O. Box 4772
Portland, ME 04112
(207) 775-1059

AAAUG: Ann Arbor Area AutoCAD
Users Group
P.O. Box 7937
Ann Arbor, MI 48107
(313) 485-0305

West Michigan AutoCAD Users Group
3310 Eagle Park Drive NE
Grand Rapids, MI 49505
(616) 456-4274

Iron Mountain AutoCAD Users Group
P.O. Box 686
Iron Mountain, MI 49801
(906) 774-8000

Mid-Michigan AutoCAD User Group
123 W. Ottawa Street
4th Floor
Lansing, MI 48901
(517) 371-6090

Saginaw Valley AutoCAD Users Group
213 E. Larkin
Midland, MI 48740
(517) 631-4917

Northeastern Ontario AutoCAD User
Group
P.O. Box 834
Sault Ste. Marie, MI 49783
(705) 945-3010

Main. Mnu
22255 Greenfield
Suite 500
Southfield, MI 48075
(313) 275-5226

MAIN.MNU Group
AutoCAD Users Group
28425 West Eight Mile Road
Livonia, MI 48152
(313) 476-6620

Toledo AutoCAD Users Group
126 East Church Street
Adrian, MI 49221
(517) 263-5217

AutoCAD User Group
13201 Stevens
Warren, MI 48085
(313) 754-5100

AutoCAD.EXE User Group
416 South 5th Street
Brainerd, MN 56401
(218) 765-3440

CADRE
40 West Highland Park
Hutchinson, MN 55350
(612) 587-3797

AutoCAD.EXE
P.O. Box 141075
Minneapolis, MN 55414
(612) 379-7543

AutoCAD Users Group
Building 235 – 3F04
St. Paul, MN 55144
(612) 736-2099

Missouri Southern State College
Joplin, MO 64801-1595
(417) 625-9327

AutoCAD Users Group
1107 S. 291 Highway
Lee Summit, MO 64063
(816) 524-5580

Ozark AutoCAD User Group
P.O. Box 3499 G.S.
Springfield, MO 65808
(417) 869-7350

Forest Park AutoCAD User Group
5600 Oakland
St. Louis, MO 63110
(314) 644-9291

Charlotte Area AutoCAD User Group
7851 Rainbow Drive
Charlotte, NC 28212
(704) 394-8341

Piedmont AutoCAD Users' Group
P.O. Box 16341
Greensboro, NC 27406
(919) 674-5372

Triangle AutoCAD users Group (TAG)
P.O. Box 52144
Durham, NC 27717
(919) 490-8977

Willmington AutoCAD Users Group
243 North Front Street
Willmington, NC 28401
(919) 343-1048

Mid-Con AutoCad Users Group
Box 44
Fargo, ND 58107
(701) 232-3271

AutoCAD Users of Nebraska
3721 Chapin Circle
Lincoln, NE 68506
(402) 478-4257

Omaha AutoCAD Users Group
37th and Ames
Omaha, NE 68111
(402) 554-6500

State of New Hampshire AutoCAD U.G.
100 Saranac Drive (Morse Associates)
Nashua, NH 03062
(603) 880-4980

State of NH AutoCAD User Group
220 Center Street
Sullivan, NH 03445
(603) 847-3373

Southern New Jersey AutoCAD User
Group
P.O. Box 106
Bordentown, NJ 08505
(609) 298-7449

AutoCAD Users Group
c/o Olympia & York, 395 Lantana
Avenue
Englewood, NJ 07631
(201) 494-9708

Princeton Area AutoCAD User Group
210 Carnegie Center Suite 201
Princeton, NJ 08540
(609) 951-9001

Northeast AutoCAD Users Group
(NAUG)
12 Howland Circle
West Caldwell, NJ 07006
(201) 228-3869

Northeast AutoCAD Users Group
(NAUG)
983 Madison Avenue
Plainfield, NJ 07060
(201) 757-9573

Albuqerque AutoCAD Users Group
P.O. Box 80376
Albuqerque, NM 87108
(505) 247-3705

AULA (AutoCAD Users of Los Alamos)
P.O. Box 1663, M/S D-410
Los Alamos, NM 87545
(505) 667-2485

Las Vegas AutoCAD Users Group
P.O. Box 27140
Las Vegas, NV 89126-1140
(702) 878-7974

Albany AutoCAD Users Group
40 Colvin Avenue
Albany, NY 12206
(518) 438-6844

Buffalo AutoCAD Users' Group
703 Washington Street
Buffalo, NY 14203
(716) 684-0002

Long Island AutoCAD Users Group
27 Pine Ridge Drive
Smithtown, NY 11787
(516) 543-7777

Metro NY AutoCAD Users
20 West 20th Street
New York, NY 10011
(212) 691-4722

Rochester Area AutoCAD Users Group
c/o Olin Corporation
P.O. Box 205
Rochester, NY 14601
(716) 436-3030

Niagara Frontier AutoCAD Users Group
2400 Buffalo Avenue
Niagara Falls, NY 14303
(716) 278-6428

Akron Area AutoCAD Users Group
710 N. Hawkins Avenue
Akron, OH 44313
(216) 376-2242

Greater Cincinnati AutoCAD User's Group
2220 Victory Parkway
Cincinnati, OH 45206-2822
(513) 556-5311

CADUS
1501 Spring Garden Avenue
Lakewood, OH 44107
(216) 228-9777

North Coast AutoCAD Users Group (NORCAD)
37527 Park Avenue
Willoughby, OH 44094
(216) 951-8070

Northeast Ohio AutoCAD Users Group
4555 Emery Industrial Parkway, #102
Cleveland, OH 44128-5767
(216) 765-1133

Columbus Computer Society
CAD/CAM SIG.
1484 Morse Road
Columbus, OH 43229
(614) 457-8111

Dayton Area AutoCAD Users Group (DACAD)
1660 Kettering Tower
Dayton, OH 45423
(513) 228-4007

Licking County Professional CAD Users
P.O. Box 515 "D" Bldg.
Granville, OH 43023
(614) 587-4301

NW Ohio AutoCAD User Group Caller
#10,000
Oregon Road
Toledo, OH 43699
(419) 666-0580

Tri-County AutoCAD User Group
P.O. Box 385
North Benton, OH 44449
(216) 584-7651

Southern Oklahoma AutoCAD User
Group
P.O. Box 197
Asher, OK 74826
(405) 784-2411

Oklahoma City Metro User's Group
(OKMUG)
P.O. Box 20400
Oklahoma City, OK 73156-0400
(405) 478-5353

AutoCAD ACE Users Group
P.O. Box 32797
Oklahoma City, OK 73123
(405) 949-1442

Compugraph Professional CAD User
Group
P.O. Box 3346
Tulsa, OK 74101-3346
(918) 582-4545

AutoCAD Users Group
3103 N. Hemlock Circle
Suite 110A
Tulsa, OK 74101
(918) 251-4470

Eugene AutoCAD Users Group
50 Oakway Center
Suite A
Eugene, OR 97401

Central Oregon AutoCAD Users Group
Central Oregon Community College
Bend, OR 97701
(503) 389-2584

AutoCAD Users Group
P.O. Box 1084
Corvallis, OR 97339
(503) 371-1032

Wilbanks Engineering Support Group
P.O. Box 1209
Hillsboro, OR 97124
(503) 648-3183

ACADemy User Group
1025 E. Powell
Suite 202
Gresham, OR 97030
(503) 666-5564

AutoCAD Users' Group of Portland
8339 SW 41st Avenue
Portland, OR 97219
(503) 222-5840

Corps of Engineers
20846 SW Martinazzi
Tualatin, OR 97062
(503) 221-3841

---

*Philadelphia AutoCAD Users Group
(PAUG)*
161 Jefferson Court
Norristown, PA 19401
(215) 275-9866

_____

AutoCAD Users Group
P.O. Box 453
Clarks Summit, PA 18411
(717) 586-1488

_____

*KEYstone ACADemy AutoCAD Users
Group*
Box 149
LaPlume, PA 18440
(717) 945-3232

_____

Presque Isle AutoCAD Users Group
2950 Mechanic Street
Lake City, PA 16423
(814) 774-2631

_____

*SE Pennsylvania AutoCAD Users'
Group*
Route 2, Box 158
East Earl, PA 17519
(717) 445-6701

_____

*Greater Pittsburgh AutoCAD Users
Group*
104 Julrich Drive
Pittsburgh, PA 15317
(412) 941-7853

_____

Pittsburgh Area AutoCAD Users Group
105 Pine Street
Imperial, PA 15126
(412) 695-3413

_____

*Susquehanna Valley AutoCAD Users
Group*
One College Avenue
Williamsport, PA 17701-5799
(717) 327-4775

_____

OceanCAD Users Group
2364 Post Road
Warwick, RI 02886
(401) 732-1123

_____

AutoCAD S.I.G.
Palmetto P.C. Club
P.O. Box 2046
1331 Elmwood Avenue
Columbia, SC 29202
(803) 254-6382

_____

Greenville AutoCAD User's Group
P.O. Box 25563
Greenville, SC 29616
(803) 297-9281

_____

*Piedmont AutoCAD User Group Drawer
4386*
Spartanburg, SC 29305-4386
(803) 591-3674

_____

Sumter AutoCAD Users Group
P.O. Box 1734
Sumter, SC 29151
(803) 481-6351

_____

Sioux Falls Area AutoCAD Users Group
600 West Avenue N.
Sioux Falls, SD 57104
(605) 336-3722

_____

Dyersburg Area AutoCAD Users Group
P.O. Box 648
Dyersburg, TN 38025
(901) 285-6910

Jackson Area AutoCAD Users Group
P.O. Box 2468
Jackson, TN 38302-2468
(901) 668-8600

Smokey Mountain AutoCAD User Group
114 Antioch Drive
Oak Ridge, TN 37830
(615) 482-4916

AutoCAD Users Group: Memphis Chapter
P.O. BOX 241938
Memphis, TN 38124
(901) 685-0230

Nashville AutoCAD Users' Group (NAUG)
30 Burton Hills Boulevard
Suite 230
Nashville, TN 37215
(615) 353-3462

Northwest Tennessee ACAD
User Group
P.O. Box 550
Paris, TN 38242-0550
(901) 642-4251

Austin AutoCAD Users Group
3636 Executive Center Drive
Suite 150
Austin, TX 78731
(512) 346-8399

Brazos Valley
Rt. 3, P.O. Box 297
College Station, TX 77840
(409) 776-8820

AutoCAD User's Group
Dallas Chapter
P.O. Box 878
Commerce, TX 75428
(214) 886-7673

Dallas-Ft. Worth AutoCAD
Users Group
Box 112 HK
Route 3
Farmersville, TX 75031
(214) 782-6660

El Paso AutoCAD Users Group
11501 James Watt Drive
El Paso, TX 79936
(915) 591-5600

HAL P.C. ACAD S.I.G.
430 Merriweather
Webster, TX 77598
(713) 480-4606

Southeast Harris County AutoCAD User's
P.O. Box 34311
Houston, TX 77234
(713) 943-5301

PRO-CAD Users Group
12601 High Star
Houston, TX 77072
(713) 463-0196

Northwest Houston AutoCAD User Group
P.O. Box 40308
Houston, TX 77240-0308
(713) 890-3300

Lufkin AutoCAD User Group
P.O. Box 1768
Lufkin, TX 75901
(409) 639-1301

AutoCAD Users Group
City of Odessa
411 West Eighth Street
P.O. Box 4398
Odessa, TX 79761
(915) 337-7381

Tyler Area ACAD User's Group
P.O. Box 9020
Tyler, TX 75701
(214) 531-2351

ACADUSR
9160 South 300 West
#22
Sandy, UT 84070
(801) 561-0525

Tidewater Area AutoCAD Users Group
c/o Glenn & Assoc.
P.O. Box 12154
Norfolk, VA 23502
(804) 461-9130

Central Virginia AutoCAD Users Group
P.O. Box 29599
Richmond, VA 23229
(804) 756-7743

Northern Virginia AutoCAD Users Group
7929 Westpark Drive
McLean, VA 22102
(703) 556-0700

Bellingham User Group (BUG)
Technology Department, Western Wash. U.
Bellingham, WA 98225
(206) 676-2976

Battelle Boulevard
Richland, WA 99352
(509) 375-3930

Seattle Area AutoCAD Users Group
P.O. Box 6371
Lynnwood, WA 98036
(206) 771-5334

Architects Engineers Planners Users Grp 2102
North 52nd Street
Seattle, WA 98103
(206) 634-0849

AutoCAD Users Group
West 1720 Fourth Avenue
Spokane, WA 99204
(509) 838-6466

Tacoma AutoCAD Users Group (S.I.G.)
1509 N. Juniper
Tacoma, WA 98406
(206) 752-0145

Fox Valley AutoCAD User Group
P.O. Box 249
Waupaca, WI 54981
(715) 258-8511

Chippewa Valley AutoCAD Users
Group
c/o Envirosystems
1030 Regis Court
Eau Claire, WI 54701
(715) 833-2393

Kohler AutoCAD Users Group
444 Highland Drive
Kohler, WI 53044
(414) 457-4441

Coulee Region AutoCAD User Group
P.O. Box 3206
La Crosse, WI 54602-3206
(608) 788-8451

Greater Madison Area AutoCAD User
Group
3822 Mineral Point Road
Madison, WI 53705
(608) 238-6761

Wisconsin Local AutoCAD Users Group
P.O. Box 12365
3879 North Richards Street
Milwaukee, WI 53212
(414) 542-6060

NorthStar AutoCAD Users Group
600 N. Twenty-first Street
Superior, WI 54880
(715) 394-6677

Central Wisconsin AutoCAD User's
Group
1000 Campus Drive
Wausau, WI 54401
(715) 675-3331

Greater Tri-State AutoCAD Users
Group
200 Ken Lake
Winfield, WV 25213
(304) 755-9677

AutoCAD Users Group
Lavalle 482 – 8th "A"
Buenos Aires, Argentina
4047 Argentina
(54) 322-6912

Newcastle AutoCAD User Group
26 Palmer Street
Mulbring 2323
Australia
(049) 380194

Northern Territory AutoCAD User's
Group
G.P.O. Box 4032
Darwin NT 0801
Australia
(089) 81 6885

AutoCAD Users Group
1 Colo Place
Pendle Hill
New South Wales 2145
Australia
(02) 818-8245

AutoCAD Users Group
99 Nicholson Street
St Leonards
New South Wales 2065
Australia
(02) 929-0400

Queensland AutoCAD Users Group
1677 Mt Cotton Road
Burbank QNSLD 4156
Australia
(07)390-3677

*AutoCAD User Group of
South Australia*
Woodford Road
Elizabeth South Australia 5112
Australia
(08)255-2044

AutoCAD Users Group of SA
P.O. Box 116 Kensington Park
South Australia 5068
Australia
(08) 277-1711

AutoCAD Users Group
P.O. Box 396
Valley Road
Devonport Tasmania 7310
Australia
(004) 24-4211

Tasmanian AutoCAD Users' Group
P.O. Box 88
Moonah Tasmania 7009
Australia
(002) 78 4512

Victorian AutoCAD User Group
202 Little Page Street
Middle Park
Victoria 3206
Australia
(03) 690-7494

AutoCAD Users Group
2 Havelock Street
West Perth
West Australia 6005
Australia
(09) 222-5555

Vienna AutoCAD Users Group
Neubaugasse 76
Vienna A-1070
Austria
(011)4352663630

Belgium AutoCAD Users Group (UAB)
Rumoldusstraat 66A Dilbeek
B1750
Belgium
(02) 569-4924

Brazilian AutoCAD Users Group
Av. Paulista, 1754
Conj. 108
Sao Paulo SP 01310
Brazil
(011) 287-0764

Calgary AutoCAD Users Group
210, 8181 Flint Rd. SE
Calgary
AB T2H 2B8
Canada
(403) 255-5511

Northern Alberta PC Users Group
10436–82 Avenue
Edmonton
AB T6E 2A2
Canada
(403) 431-0237

Vancouver AutoCAD Users Society
Box 727-810 West Broadway
Vancouver BC V57 4C9
Canada
(604) 684-9311

Kalamalka Computer Users Group
7000 College Way
Vernon BC V1T 6Y5
Canada
(604) 545-7291

Ministry of Transportation
and Highways
940 Blanchard Street
Victoria
BC V8W 3E6
Canada
(604) 387-7754

New Brunswick Area AutoCAD Users
Group
102 Queen Street
Fredericton
NB E3B 1A5
Canada
(506) 459-6080

Nova Scotia AutoCAD User Group
5251 Duke Street
Suite 1112
Halifax
NS B3J 1P3
Canada
(902) 420-0207

Great Slave AutoCAD Users Group
P.O. Box 1777
Yellowknife
NWTX1A 2P4
Canada
(403) 920-2842

SCALE
1 Georgian Drive
Barrie ON L4M 3X9
Canada
(705) 728-1951

Northern College AutoCAD Users Group
140 Government Road
East Kirkland Lake
ON P2N 3L8
Canada
(705) 567-9291

AutoCAD Users Group
39 Glen Manor Drive
Nepean ON K2G 3E9
Canada
(613) 225-4854

AutoSAR
118 North Victoria Street
Sarnia ON N7T 5W9
Canada
(519) 332-4400

*Northern Ontario AutoCAD Users
Group*
107 Cumberland Street
North Thunderbay
ON P7A 4M3
Canada
(807) 345-6375

*Toronto Region AutoCAD Exchange
(TRACE)*
1400 Petrie Way
Mississauga
ON L5J 1G5
Canada
(416) 792-8999

Windsor AutoCAD User Group
U.of Windsor Phys. Plant
401 Sunset Boulevard
Windsor ON N9B 3P4
Canada
(519) 253-4232

*City of Saskatoon Planning
Department*
City Hall
Saskatoon
SK S7K 0J5
Canada
(306) 975-2684

AutoCAD Users Group
P.O. Box 46
Limassol
Cyprus
(357) 9-515324

Cyprus Association of CAD Users
14 Kefallinias Street, Acropolis
Nicosia Cyprus
(357) 2-427597

Midlands AutoCAD User Group
26 Dam Street
Lichfield, Staffs
WS13 6AA
England
(054) 325-1511

AutoCAD Users Group
United Kingdom
36 Avenue Road
London N6 5DW
England
(81) 348-3040

AUG 53 Derngate
Northampton
NN12ET
England
(06) 042-0093

AutoCAD Users Group
Fitzherbert Road
Farlington, Portsmouth
O6 1RR
England
(070) 537-0961

AutoCAD User Group UK
Pelham House
25 Pelham Square Brighton
East Sussex BN1 4ET
England
(02) 73-600411

Club Utilisateur AutoCAD
115, Rue de Musselburg
Champigny/Marne 94500
France
(1) 49 83 01 83

"ATHENS1" AutoCAD Users Group
Vriaxidos 18 Athens 116 35
Greece
(01) 777-1292

*EAMC (New Delhi AutoCAD Users
Group)*
50, Kailash Hills
East of Kailash
New Delhi 110024 India
(91) 11-684-5184

Bhubaneswar AutoCAD User Group
P.B. No. 82
Bhubaneswar
Orissa
751012 India
0674-53038

Israel AutoCAD User Group
P.O. Box 39079
Tel-Aviv 61390
Israel
(972) 3-5464054

Japan AutoCAD User Group
Unosawa Tokyu
Bldg 4F, 1-19-15
Ebisu Shibuya-Ku, Tokyo
150 Japan
(03) 473-9511

Japan AutoCAD Users Group
4-6-13-701 Kudan Minami
Chiyoda-kuTokyo
102 Japan
(03) 262-4255

Jordan AutoCAD User Group
P.O. Box 925740
Amman
Jordan
962 6 818360

Lebanese AutoCAD User Group
P.O. Box 16-5182
Beirut
Lebanon
(961) 1-324122

Mexico City AutoCAD Users Group
50 Munich 142
Vialle Dorado
Mexico
54020
Mexico
391-20-22

Autocad gebruikers groep VCA
Geestbrugweg 42 Rijswijk
2281 CM
Netherlands
(070) 95-4243

CIADPO
Box 74
Zoetermeer
2700 AB
Netherlands
(31) 79-2193-24

Auckland AutoCAD Users' Group
P.O. Box 76-128
Manukau City
New Zealand
(09) 267-7531

Canterbury AutoCAD User Group
Christchurch Polytechnic
P.O. Box 22095
Christchurch
New Zealand
(03) 798 150

AutoCAD Peru Apartado 18-0934
Lima
Peru 18
Peru
(51-14) 45-2394

Scotland AutoCAD User Group
117 Renfrew Street
Glasgow, Scotland
(041) 332-9797

Johannesburg AutoCAD Users Group
17 Basil Street Ferndale
Randburg 2194
South Africa
(011) 793-5698

AutoCAD Users Group
Asicom, SAc/ Aragon, 264 Barcelona
Barcelona 08007
Spain
(343) 215-9000

Club de Usuarios de AutoCAD, Editisa Alda.
Recalde 64Bis, EPTA
Bilbao 48010
Spain
(34) 4-4435365

Abu Dhabi AutoCAD Users Group
P.O. Box 26562
Abu Dhabi
U.A.E.9712660543

AutoCAD User Group
Meza 24
Dravograd Slovenia 62 370
Yugoslavia
(602) 83 413

Index

B

T

Add to Your New Riders Library Today
with the Best Books for the Best Software

Yes, please send me the productivity-boosting material I have checked below. Make check payable to New Riders Publishing.

☐ **Check enclosed**

Charge to my credit card:

☐ **VISA**   ☐ **Master Card**

Card # _____

Expiration date: _____

Signature: _____

Name: _____

Company: _____

Address: _____

City: _____

State: _____ ZIP: _____

Phone: _____

The easiest way to order is to pick up the phone and call 1-800-541-6789 between 9:00 a.m. and 5:00 p.m., EST. Please have your credit card available, and your order can be placed in a snap!

Quantity	Description of Item	Unit Cost	Total Cost
	Inside CorelDRAW!, 2nd Edition	$29.95	
	Managing and Networking AutoCAD*	$29.95	
	Maximizing Windows 3 (Book-and-Disk set)	$39.95	
	Inside AutoCAD, 6th Edition (for Release 10 and 11)*	$34.95	
	Maximizing AutoCAD: Volume I (Book-and-Disk set) Customizing Macros and Menus	$29.95	
	AutoCAD for Architects and Engineers*	$29.95	
	Inside Autodesk Animator*	$29.95	
	Maximizing AutoCAD: Volume II (Book-and-Disk set) Inside AutoLISP	$34.95	
	Stepping Into AutoCAD, 4th Edition*	$29.95	
	Inside AutoSketch, 2nd Edition*	$24.95	
	AutoCAD Reference Guide, 2nd Edition	$14.95	
	AutoCAD Reference Guide on Disk, 2nd Edition	$14.95	
	Inside Compuserve (Book-and-Disk set)	$29.95	
	Managing and Networking AutoCAD*	$29.95	
	Inside AutoCAD, Release 11, Metric Edition	$34.95	
	AutoCAD Sourcebook 1991	$27.95	
	Maximizing MS-DOS 5 (Book-and-Disk set)	$29.95	
	*Companion Disk available for these books	$14.95 ea.	

☐ **3 1/2" disk**

☐ **5 1/4" disk**

Shipping and Handling:	
See information below.	
TOTAL	

Shipping and Handling: $4.00 for the first book and $1.75 for each additional book. Floppy disk: add $1.75 for shipping and handling. If you need to have it NOW, we can ship product to you in 24 to 48 hours for an additional charge, and you will receive your item overnight or in two days. Add $20.00 per book and $8.00 for up to three disks overseas. Prices subject to change. Call for availability and pricing information on latest editions.

New Riders Publishing • 11711 N. College Avenue • P.O. Box 90 • Carmel, Indiana 46032

1-800-541-6789   1-800-4488-3804

Orders/Customer Service   **FAX**